THE POLITICS OF UNREASON

THE POLITICS OF UNREASON

Second Edition

RIGHT-WING EXTREMISM IN AMERICA, 1790–1977

Seymour Martin Lipset and Earl Raab

The University of Chicago Press
Chicago and London

Chapter 1 first appeared in the May 1970 issue of
The Anti-Defamation League Bulletin
in somewhat different form.

The University of Chicago Press, Chicago 60637
The University of Chicago Press, Ltd., London

ISBN 0-226-48457-2
LCN 77-92800

The Anti-Defamation League of B'nai B'rith wishes to record its appreciation to the Norman Tishman Memorial Fund and to Mrs. Norman Tishman for the generous support which helped make possible the research and publication of this study in the "Patterns of American Prejudice" series.

Contents

Tables

Preface

This particular analysis of right-wing extremism in America began to emerge in reaction to the McCarthyism of the early 1950's. Lipset's article attempting to place that phenomenon in a historical and sociological context was the first to apply the concept of the "radical right" to American social movements.[1] That article briefly surveyed some of the earlier movements from the Know-Nothings to the Ku Klux Klan, and pointed to ways in which American values made for a greater degree of political intolerance here than in other relatively stable democratic countries.

In 1959, the two of us addressed ourselves to another aspect of the problem, the social sources of prejudice against minority groups.[2] In this analysis, we developed the concept of the "Prejudiced Community," suggesting that analytically racism was more to be identified as discriminatory social situation than as prejudiced mind-set, however closely these two phenomena might become intertwined. We argued that as disadvantaged racial groups developed new and higher levels of aspiration, the commitments of the privileged to practices which sustained their special advantages would increasingly confront the American society with "an active social problem which would threaten . . . its functioning as an effective social order."[3]

The analysis of the sources and consequences of the "Prejudiced Community" was developed further in subsequent publications by Raab and Gertrude Selznick.[4] They argued that ethnic tension in America "has been created largely by the changing nature of American society."[5] And they described in brief the way in which the changing position of various minority populations, Catholics, Jews, and Negroes, have occasioned severe intergroup and political conflicts, as various minorities began to penetrate parts of American life from which they had been absent in the past. Raab contrived in various documents, to develop the view that political situations more often shape than are shaped by uses of bigotry.

Lipset included the analysis of right-wing extremism in his book *Political Man*, suggesting that a number of movements which have been classified as "fascist," because they sought to *preserve* certain special privileges or status by authoritarian means may be divided among "left," "center," and "right" fascisms. The movements shared in common strong particularistic (group self-interest) and nationalistic ideologies. They differed, however, as to whether they sought to protect the traditional position of old elites (right), to further the interests of the "middle-class" against threats from the state, large corporations, and unions (center), or appealed in populist fashion to the anti-elitist sentiments of the underprivileged (left).[6]

In another chapter in the same book, Lipset presented the concept of "working-class authoritarianism," or more accurately, the proposition, that the less sophisticated and more economically insecure a group is, the more likely its members are to accept the more simplistic ideology or political program offered to them. Consequently, the underprivileged frequently constitute the social base for authoritarian movements of the left and right. In that connection, Lipset also presented evidence to justify the analytic distinction between "economic" and "noneconomic" liberalism. Since support for economic liberalism correlates inversely with socio-economic class, while endorsement of noneconomic liberalism is associated with education and sophistication, it follows that movements which foster antielitism (economic liberalism) and intolerance of groups or ideas which are different (noneconomic illiberalism), should have a special appeal to the less privileged.[7]

However, Lipset pointed out that

it would be a mistake to conclude . . . that the authoritarian predispositions of the lower classes necessarily constitute a threat to a democratic social system; nor should similar conclusions be drawn about the antidemocratic aspects of conservatism. Whether or not a given class supports restrictions on freedom depends on a wide constellation of factors of which those discussed here are only a part. . . .

[For example, the] incorporation of the workers into the body politic in the industrialized Western world has reduced their authoritarian tendencies greatly, although in the United States . . . McCarthy demonstrated that an irresponsible demagogue who combines a nationalist and antielitist appeal can still secure considerable support from the less educated.[8]

In other words, the structural context, the special historical constellation of forces and pressures on different strata, will be crucial in affecting behavior. Following on our earlier analysis presented in *Prejudice and Society*, it was argued that involvement in particular institutional structures, e.g., unions, parties, regional cultures, religions, will be *most determinative* of specific political actions, a point often overlooked by some who have written in critical terms concerning this type of analysis.

In his next book, *The First New Nation*, Lipset returned to certain themes concerning the sources of extremist methods in American politics, first raised in "The Radical Right" essay. He suggested that the emphasis in non-aristocratic America on competing for success presses Americans to violate the conventional "rules of the game," in politics as in other areas of life. He also developed the theme that the "seemingly lesser respect for civil liberties and minority rights in . . . the United States" as compared to certain other Western democracies may be a function of the fact that elite status is not given generalized deference in this country.[9]

Both of us also stressed the continual efforts of the old "in-groups," particularly of white Protestant background, to protect their values and status, as a source of new social movements. "In almost every generation, 'old American' groups which saw themselves 'displaced,' relatively demoted in status or power by processes rooted in social change, have sought to reverse these processes through the activities of moralistic movements or political action groups."[10]

In tracing through some of our earlier published analyses of "right-wing extremism," we do not want to imply that our concern with this issue is purely "academic." We have tried in all our scholarly writings to be as objective as possible, a goal, which as Max Weber once argued, often requires scholars to lean over backwards to present and accept evidence which contradicts the propositions which their personal values or theoretical orientation would press them to prefer. But this endeavor is compatible with selecting topics for analysis which reflect strong political and social concerns. In this case, there can be little doubt that both of us are deeply committed opponents of extremist movements, both of the left and the right. We are both Jews of the generation of the holocaust. We were politically conscious during the period in which right-wing extremism, as practiced in Germany and other parts of Europe, murdered six million Jews. This is a fact, which must affect all that we write, say, and do about extremism. It is one which also helps determine our reaction to all forms of racism, no matter how understandable or benign they may appear at a given moment. Both of us have been active in different ways in politics, and in the struggle against political extremism. Raab has been a staff official of the Jewish Community Relations Council of the San Francisco area for many years, and has also been involved in many interracial civil rights and antipoverty activities in California. Lipset, as an academic, has taken part in various civil rights and civil liberties organizations and has lectured and written on behalf of such groups. We both have opposed a number of groups analyzed in this book, the Coughlinites, McCarthyism, the John Birch Society, and George Wallace's movement.

It is also relevant to note that both of us were active, when students at the City College of New York, in the Young People's Socialist League. We have remained dedicated opponents of all forms of communist totalitarianism. Our personal political sympathies remain with the democratic left or liberal movements, those which seek to effectively reduce inequalities and inequities, and sustain, at the same time, politically democratic tendencies. As we have grown older watching numberless efforts fail to achieve dramatic changes in the short run, we have become more cognizant of the stubborn ingrown nature of some of the social factors which help to sustain economic, status, and power stratification. We also have become somewhat hesitant about the value of efforts to eliminate "evil" simply by attacking and overthrowing societies which contain much that is very wrong. In our lifetime, we have witnessed many "successful" movements, which have overthrown social systems, often at great psychic and physical cost, only to create "new" societies which are at least as "bad" as those they overturned, and frequently worse. Consequently, we have developed another prejudice, relevant to this book. We tend to feel that in politics "true believers," deeply committed moralists, are too sure of what is right to be trusted with power in a complex world in which it is almost impossible to anticipate all the major consequences of social action.

We, therefore, have come to believe that continuous change, pushed to its limits, rather than instant transformation, is the only non-illusory and therefore quickest way to enlarge the democratic society, to provide for the maximum feasible participation of all. And though this book does not deal much with left-wing extremism, it should be clear that we regard such movements as regressive politically as those of the right. We have written and will continue to write both about, and against, these tendencies as well.

This particular book had its origins in two proposals which occurred in 1962. Daniel Bell, the editor of *The New American Right*, the volume containing essays analyzing McCarthyism, asked Lipset and the other authors in that book to write a new article reevaluating the earlier phenomenon and dealing with subsequent events, such as the rise of the Birch Society in the early sixties. About the same time, Oscar Cohen, the Program Director of the Anti-Defamation League, approached Charles Glock, then Director of the Survey Research Center at Berkeley, and

Lipset, with the suggestion that they direct a series of studies of anti-Semitic sentiments and activities in the United States, which would be financially supported by the ADL. Glock agreed to undertake the overall supervision of such an effort. Lipset expressed an interest to do a study of right-wing extremism since World War II, as a joint venture with Raab, with the understanding that such a work would not be primarily concerned with anti-Semitism, but rather with right-wing antidemocratic tendencies generally. Cohen agreed to this proposal, and we have been working on this book in one way or another ever since.

This work has involved our joint—and often interrupted—effort over a period of years during which our conception of the book has changed in several ways. Initially, it was planned as a detailed analysis of relatively recent movements, which would rely heavily on opinion data from a national sample of the American population conducted under the auspices of the Berkeley Survey Research Center, as well as earlier survey data collected by various opinion organizations. As an initial effort to this end, Lipset analyzed a number of previously gathered surveys which included questions dealing with three leaders and movements, Father Charles Coughlin in the 1930's, Senator Joseph McCarthy in the early 1950's, and the John Birch Society in the 1960's. This analysis was published in the revised version of the book edited by Bell.[11] The survey data pointed up the considerable differences in the backgrounds of the supporters of these three right-wing tendencies.

As a next stage in our work, we began to look into the record of right-wing, religiously, ethnically, and racially prejudiced extremist movements in American history. Our initial plan was to prepare a long "historical" chapter, i.e., one which discussed all the movements before the 1930's in fifty to seventy pages. As we began to study the record, however, we grew more interested in these earlier efforts. This work was particularly facilitated by a number of unpublished doctoral and master's dissertations and theses completed in universities around the country, which often went into considerable documentary and statistical detail. And though it was clear that there had not been organizational continuity on the far right, the evidence suggested that the various movements which arose over time were aware of their predecessors, drew on their theories, and often used and distributed the same books. Perhaps the most titillating example of such continuity has been the belief in the conspiracy of the Illuminati, a Bavarian-based Enlightenment affiliate of the Masons, which operated openly from 1776 to 1785. And though historians inform us that the only "real" group of Illuminati was dissolved in 1785, the belief that this organization has continued as an international conspiracy of intellectuals and others within the elite down to the present, has remained viable on the extreme right, particularly in the United States. The first major exposé of the Illuminati published in the United States, *Proofs of a Conspiracy Against All the Religions and Governments of Europe, carried on in the Secret Meetings of Free Masons, Illuminati and Reading Societies* by John Robison, a Scottish chemist, which came out in its first American edition in Boston in 1798, was republished in 1967 in Belmont, a suburb of Boston, by the publishing house of the John Birch Society, with a long introduction, describing some of the more recent nefarious activities of the Illuminati. A regular publication, *The Illuminator,* designed to maintain a continuous exposé of the secret order, now appears from New York, put out by a group which seems to be linked to the Minutemen and its "front" organization, the Patriotic Party. In the intervening century and three-quarters, information about the continuing conspiracy of the Illuminati has been spread by the Anti-Masonic party in the 1820's and 1830's, by the National Christian Association, and its offspring the American Party in the post-Civil War era, by *The Christian Science Monitor* in 1920, and by Gerald Winrod and Father Charles Coughlin, two leaders of the extreme right in the 1930's. Almost all the literature concerning the Illuminati has credited it with responsibility for various revolutionary movements both abroad, e.g., the various French Revolutions of the eighteenth and nineteenth centuries, and the Russian Revolution of 1917, and assorted domestic subversive movements from the Jeffersonian Clubs of the late 1790's to various Communist, leftist, and liberal movements of the present.

As our historical research developed other common threads, it became clear that our original intention to use this material for a background chapter had to be changed. No one had traced the connections and similarities (as well as major differences) among right-wing extremist tendencies in American history. There is an ideological link between the sermon voicing belief in the conspiracy of the Illuminati delivered by Jedidiah Morse in Boston in 1798, and the interview giving public expression of belief in the need to fight the same conspiracy by T. Coleman Andrews, the national chairman of the Wallacite American party, in Richmond in 1969. And as the reader can see, the result has been that a large part of this book deals with movements of the nineteenth and early twentieth centuries.

Our plans for the contents of the book were also changed by events. Originally, we anticipated ending our analyses of specific tendencies with the discussion of the John Birch Society. And in fact, our manuscript was largely completed in 1967. At this point, however, it seemed clear that George Wallace was planning to launch a major third party effort in 1968, one which would probably be the largest such venture on the far right, since at least the 1930's. Consequently, we decided to continue working on the book until the end of the 1968 campaign. The result of this decision may be seen in the two chapters dealing with the Wallace campaign, as well as in many other revisions and changes which this delay made possible. This rather extensive background story has been presented so that the reader might be able to better judge the intellectual background, values, and biases, which may have affected the book's contents. While we would like to stress our deep gratitude to the Anti-Defamation League and its Program Director, Oscar Cohen, for their financial support, we would also like to emphasize that we owe them an even deeper debt for their encouraging us to call the shots as we saw them, even though our conclusions might disagree with some of theirs. Thus, some of the research staff of the ADL who keep informed about anti-Semitic movements may believe that we have underestimated the role of anti-Semites among the followers of Senator Joseph McCarthy, or within the John Birch Society. In a real sense, we conclude that anti-Semitism has not been as important a *seminal* factor in extremist movements as some have traditionally believed. But neither Oscar Cohen nor anyone else connected with the ADL has ever pressed us to change any aspect of our research or conclusions. They have acted as all good sponsors of scholarly research should, to endow projects of interest to them, but to remove themselves from any interference with the research, once the money is given.

There are a number of students, research assistants, colleagues, and other friends, whose help we must gratefully acknowledge. A number of students worked with Lipset on theses and dissertations concerned with topics relevant to the concerns of this book. Much of what they found has been incorporated directly or indirectly into the relevant chapters or sections. Those former students and their theses are:

Immanuel Wallerstein, *McCarthyism and the Conservative* (M.A. Thesis, Department of Sociology, Columbia University, 1954).

Martin Trow, *Right-Wing Radicalism and Political Intolerance* (Ph.D. Thesis, Department of Sociology, Columbia University, 1957).

Gary Marx, *The Social Basis of the Support of a Depression Era Extremist: Father Charles E. Coughlin* (M.A. Thesis, Department of Sociology, University of California at Berkeley, 1962).

William Roy McPherson, *Parallels in Extremist Ideology* (Ph.D. Thesis, Department of Social Relations, Harvard University, 1967).

Edgar G. Engleman, *The Changing Appeals of the John Birch Society* (Honors Thesis, Department of Social Relations, Harvard University, 1967).

Wayne R. Anderson, *The Study of the John Birch Society* (Honors Thesis, Department of Government, Harvard University, 1967).

John Francis Beatty III, *Senator Joseph McCarthy: Sources of Support* (Honors Thesis, Department of Government, Harvard University, 1969).

Karl Boughan, *The Wallace Phenomenon: The Reemergence of Populism as an Electoral Force in American Politics* (Ph.D. Thesis, Department of Government, Harvard University, 1970).

Carl Sheingold, *Voting Against the Grain: A Sociological Analysis of the Wallace Vote* (Ph.D. Thesis, Department of Social Relations, Harvard University, 1971).

As will be obvious from a look at the footnote references, we have made extensive use of unpublished theses from many universities. Our debt to them is acknowledged in the footnotes in the same way as to regularly published sources.

Two of the authors of theses also worked as research assistants: Gary Marx, who helped analyze the survey data dealing with Coughlin's support, and Karl Boughan who did a similar job with respect to studies of Wallace's voters in the 1968 election. Natalie Gumas and Nancy Mendelsohn, then of the staff of the Survey Research Center of the University of California at Berkeley, handled the statistical work in the analyses of survey data bearing on support for Senator Joseph McCarthy. Metta Spencer and Ann Swidler were particularly helpful with respect to investigating the characteristics of Birch Society backers, as well as of the antidemocratic sentiments of the general public as revealed in national surveys. The statistical analyses contained in Chapter 11, which involved factor analyses of different issue publics or typologies of attitudes, were handled by Irvin C. Bupp, Jr. and Peter Natchez. We are particularly grateful to them for a document outlining the methodological problems involved in developing this typology, which we have used for the methodological appendix to this chapter. Karen Sapolsky of the staff of the Harvard Center for International Affairs has been generally responsible for coordinating the computer work involved. Gene Benardi of the Berkeley Survey Research Center was of considerable assistance in the historical research, while Lipset was at Berkeley.

Various people assisted by giving us access to relevant data which their organizations had collected. Mrs. Lucy Davidowicz of the American Jewish Committee provided free access to the files of that group dealing with extremism, as well as to the results of a secondary analysis of national opinion data made on the behalf of the AJC by Louis Harris Associates. Oscar Cohen supplied considerable materials gathered by the Anti-Defamation League. Irving Crespi of the Gallup Poll gave us early access to the IBM cards of a 1968 postelection survey, which inquired into patterns of shifting during the campaign, LeBaron Foster, of the Opinion Research

Corporation, assisted us in obtaining the cards from an ORC 1968 pre-election survey made on behalf of the Columbia Broadcasting Corporation, which contained a number of issue items. Daniel Yankelovich gave us the IBM cards containing the data collected from his 1968 national sample of college students, gathered for *Fortune* magazine, which included items on presidential choices. Philip Hastings, director of the Roper Public Opinion Research Center at Williams College, provided us with duplicate cards from a large number of surveys dealing with attitudes toward Father Coughlin, Senator Joseph McCarthy, and the John Birch Society, which had been collected since 1935 by different survey organizations. The relevant results of the secondary analyses of these studies are included in the appropriate chapters here. We are naturally extremely grateful to all of them, as well as to the sponsors of the studies we have used.

Many of our friends and colleagues helped us greatly through reading drafts of various chapters or the entire book, and suggesting ways we could improve them. Among these are Daniel Bell, Frank Freidel, Nathan Glazer, Paul Weaver, and James Q. Wilson of Harvard University, Charles Y. Glock, Gertrude Selznick, and Neil Smelser of the University of California at Berkeley, Morton Keller of Brandeis University, Richard Hofstadter of Columbia University, William Chambers of Washington University at St. Louis, and Everett Ladd of the University of Connecticut.

Last, but as we well know far from least, we must state our gratitude to our two aides who were really the most indispensable contributors to turning this into a publishable book. They are Margot Katz of San Francisco, and Mrs. Meena Vohra of Cambridge.

—SEYMOUR MARTIN LIPSET
EARL RAAB
Belmont, Massachusetts
San Francisco, California

Notes

1. S. M. Lipset, "The Radical Right," *British Journal of Sociology*, I (June 1955), pp. 176–209; also published in slightly revised form as "The Sources of the 'Radical Right,'" in Daniel Bell, ed., *The New American Right* (New York: Criterion Books, 1955), pp. 166–233. See also in the same book, Nathan Glazer and S. M. Lipset, "The Polls on Communism and Conformity," pp. 141–165.
2. Earl Raab and Seymour M. Lipset, *Prejudice and Society* (New York: Anti-Defamation League, 1959).
3. *Ibid.*, p. 9.
4. *Major Social Problems* (Evanston: Row, Peterson, 1959), pp. 173–236; *Major Social Problems* (New York: Harper & Row, 1964), pp. 173–234.

xxiv PREFACE

5. *Ibid.*, (1959), p. 209.
6. See S. M. Lipset, " 'Fascism'—Left, Right, and Center," in *Political Man* (New York: Doubleday, 1960), pp. 131–176.
7. *Ibid.*, "Working-Class Authoritarianism," pp. 97–130.
8. *Ibid.*, pp. 129–130.
9. S. M. Lipset, *The First New Nation* (New York: Basic Books, 1963), p. 270.
10. *Ibid.*, p. 339; see also Raab and Selznick, *op. cit.* (1964), pp. 470–471.
11. S. M. Lipset, "Three Decades of the Radical Right: Coughlinites, McCarthyites, and Birchers," in Daniel Bell, ed., *The Radical Right* (Garden City: Doubleday, 1963), pp. 313–377.

THE POLITICS OF UNREASON

CHAPTER

1

Political Extremism

Extremist movements designated "left" and "right" in America have frequently shared the same political technology, such as a working impatience with dissent. They have often moved in the same surface ideological directions, such as isolationism, or opposition to Wall Street banking. If there has been one constant, it has been the perception of extreme rightist movements as those which have risen primarily in reaction against the displacement of power and status accompanying change; while left-wing extremism has been seen as impelling social change; and, in that course, attempting to overthrow old power and status groups.

By that definition, extreme *rightist* movements have been more indigenous to America and have left more of a mark on its history. America's short life has been packed with a succession of social changes affecting or threatening displacement. There has been the shift of power from farms to cities, from agriculture to industry, from South to North and Midwest to East. There have been massive waves of immigration. There has been large-scale migration within the country. There has been the many-staged shift from slavery. The predominant positions of various regional, religious, economic, ethnic, and racial groups have continually been shaken and diminished.

Extremist politics is the politics of despair. The politics of despair in America has typically been the politics of backlash rather than that of thwarted progress. It is the politics of backlash, defined as right-wing extremism, which is the subject of this inquiry. This does not mean that left-wing extremism, as it is defined, does not require its own concern and treatment. Nor does it mean that the antipluralistic nub of political extremism is not very much the same for both left and right. Indeed, much of this inquiry has to do with what is probably that common nub. But, in this case, the specific context is the material, the history, and the constituency of backlash, right-wing extremism.

It should be noted that the term "extremism" is defined in a particular way for the purposes of this study. Common usage moves back and forth between two kinds of meaning: extremism as a generalized measure of deviance from the political norm; and extremism as a specific tendency to violate democratic procedures. The first is undoubtedly the more neutral and universally acceptable meaning. Political repression in a country whose traditional system includes political repression can, from that traditional vantage point, scarcely be called extremist. Conversely, in our "free enterprise" society, a socialist program might well be generally described as extremist. But in a more specific sense, any political program which is perceived as politically repressive, whether in the defense of socialism or of the free enterprise system, is also commonly called extremist. It is this sense of the term which gives "extremism" its special flavor in this political era and in those societies whose traditional vantage point is political liberty. And it is in this sense that "political extremism" is the focus of this study.

There will be an attempt, first of all, to define more clearly the phenomenon of extremism for purposes of the study and to suggest the elements of American society and history which have uniquely shaped that phenomenon. The major right-wing extremist movements in the country's history will then be examined in detail to explore some old and new hypotheses. Contemporary surveys of right-wing constituents will then be analyzed to test other hypotheses. From these examinations, some conclusions will be drawn about the genesis of right-wing extremism in America, its prognosis, and its relationship to such phenomena as ethnic, racial, and religious bigotry.

Extremism: A Definition

At its most general, extremism is a self-serving term. It may mean going to the limit, which can often be justified; or it may mean going beyond the limits, which by self-definition is never justified. But, the "limits," as defined by the basic institutions of society, have never been static. In terms of specific issues, extremism most simply means the tendency to go to the poles of the ideological scale. In its more pejorative sense—in the sense in which it is linked to such terms as "authoritarianism" and "totalitarianism"—as an absolute political evil, extremism is not so much a matter of issues as one of procedures. In this sense, extremism means going beyond the limits of the normative procedures which define the democratic political process. Many of these procedural norms are themselves constantly being redefined. For example, the boundaries of participation in self-governance have often been changed. Tax-paying requirements for voting rights went by the boards in the nineteenth century. Women were allowed to vote in the twentieth century. The age limit for voting will probably drop to eighteen before the end of the century. And now there are intensified attempts to find a more direct means than suffrage for citizens to participate in their own government. The legislatures and courts are continually relocating the boundaries of due process and free expression. But the unchanging heart of the democratic political process, as it is generally understood, is, T. V. Smith notes, a "state of mind"; and his collaborator, Eduard C. Lindeman, describes "proposition one" of that state of mind in these words: "Persons striving to adapt themselves to the democratic way of life are required to discipline themselves to one variety of unity, namely unity which is achieved through the creative use of diversity. A society which is by affirmation democratic is expected to provide and protect a wide range of diversities."[1] There have been numberless variations of this formulation, but, however expressed, such a pluralism remains commonly accepted as the fixed spiritual center of the democratic political process, around which the more mutable rules and mechanisms revolve.

At its most general, pluralism describes a society which tends to protect and nurture the independent coexistence of different political entities, ethnic groups, ideas. More specifically, pluralism describes the kind of societal structure which can sustain such a system of coexistence.

"Liberalism," writes Edward A. Shils, "is a system of pluralism. It is a system of many centers of powers, many areas of privacy and a strong internal impulse towards the mutual adaptation of the spheres rather than of the dominance or the submission of any one to the others."[2]

The kind of spheres to which Shils refers are the political, the economic, the religious, the kinship. Without an accommodating balance among them a society could become plutocratic, theocratic, or politically totalitarian. The mutual "separation of church and state' is one mark of a pluralistic society. But so is the mutual separation of business and state, family and state, university and state. These spheres all influence each other, have mutual responsibilities, and, at best, respect each other. But none of them takes over. This pluralistic principle can extend down through all the subspheres in society, such as the various major branches of government.

The concept of pluralism has another level. A pluralistic society is composed of a number of different interest groups and communities with which the individual can identify. This contrasts with the image of a society as a mass of individuals who connect directly somehow to the total society. Where there are many such groups and spheres, there are operative cross pressures among them which not only allow for more effective advocacy of private conflicting interests but also deter that total society from taking on a more extremist, nonaccommodating shape. And when an individual belongs to a number of different effective groups and spheres with cross interests, he is less likely to act out extremist non-accommodating attitudes.

This, of course, is a dynamic concept of pluralism, not just the description of a society in which there is static diversity. Lindeman's formulation suggests this when he refers to the fact that diversity is not only to be protected but to be *provided*; that is, a working pluralism foments change and *new* diversity. William Kornhauser thus differentiates among four kinds of societies: the Traditional, in which there are differentiated but fixed standards; the Populist, in which there are fluid but uniform standards; the Monistic, in which there are uniform and fixed standards; and the Pluralistic, in which there are differentiated and fluid standards.[3] Pluralism, then, embraces both diversity and change. The procedures which guarantee that condition are the normative democratic procedures whose breach constitutes extremism. The conceptual heart of those procedures is nothing less than the open market place of ideas.

By that token, extremism basically describes that impulse which is inimical to a pluralism of interests and groups, inimical to a system of many nonsubmissive centers of power and areas of privacy. Extremism *is* antipluralism or—to use an only slightly less awkward term—monism.[4] And the operational heart of extremism is the repression of difference and dissent, the closing down of the market place of ideas. More precisely, the operational essence of extremism, of monism, is the tendency to treat cleavage and ambivalence as *illegitimate*. This is a critical aspect of extremism because of certain premises that underlie the concept of "the open market place."

Thomas Jefferson stated these premises simply: "If there be any among us who would wish to dissolve this Union or change its republican form, let them stand undisturbed as monuments of the safety with which error of opinion may be tolerated where reason is left free to combat it."

It is an American article of faith that because of the ultimate efficacy of human reason, error is legitimate and tolerable. A direct attack on the popular properties of human reason has never been politically possible in America. This is one reason why mystical European fascism has not been adaptable to the United States. In America, Goebbels could not have said, as he did in Germany, that "the more freedom of opinion that is conceded to an individual, the more it can harm the interests of an entire people."

But there is more than one way to discount the legitimacy of error. What about those who are selling their wares on the market place under false pretenses? Is the human reason to be expected to cope with trickery as well as error? Theodosius said that if seditious words proceed from folly, they are to be pitied; if from malice, to be forgiven. This might be the modern extremist's version: if seditious words proceed from malice, they are to be forbidden; if they seem to proceed from folly, look for the malice. The market place was meant for honest, well-intentioned error which can then be sorted out; it was not meant for errors deliberately conceived with evil and hidden intent. Those who promulgate such errors destroy the innocent market place and do not deserve normal political rights or civil liberties.

It is not surprising that extensive theories of evil conspiracy have typically marked the history of procedural extremism in America—from Jedidiah Morse in the late eighteenth century to Robert Welch in the twentieth. But while procedural extremism is usually symptomized by conspiracy theory, it is, of course, more than that conceptually.

A Conceptual Model of Extremism

An initial model of the monistic impulse, as it is expressed and develops, can be constructed by examining the typical stylistic themes ribbing the ideology of extremism. Over a hundred of the staple books and pamphlets sold in the American Opinion book stores were reviewed. Although the American Opinion book stores are associated with the John Birch Society, they carry a representative cross section of contemporary right-wing literature. The authors cited are well known and widely read in extremist circles.

It has long been fashionable to note that such literature is typically distinguished by its recurrent and explicit advocacy of "simplism"; that is, the unambiguous ascription of single causes and remedies for multifactored phenomena.

Phyllis Schlafly makes the definitive statement when she denies that "present day problems are so complex that we must have sophisticated— not simple—solutions." To the contrary, she holds that "civilization progresses, freedom is won and problems are solved because we have wonderful people who think up simple solutions."[5] As examples, she offers the inventor of the sewing machine, who simply determined to put the eye of the needle into the point instead of in the other end; and the Wright Brothers, who confounded scholars and created heavier-than-air flight with two simple solutions: the curved wing and the propeller.

This emphasis, in one form or another, pervades the material. Elizabeth Linington writes: "I'd lay my money any day on the hick pharmacist in

Podunk Corner having a somewhat firmer grasp of the economic, social and moral facts of life than just about any one Congressman picked at random." Dean Manion writes: "In the field of political ideas . . . we have lost our touch for simplification and substitute complexity and contradiction."[6]

It is significant that 62 per cent of a right-wing letter-writers' sample, as against 28 per cent of the national population, hold that "the answers to our country's problems are much simpler than the experts would have us believe."[7]

But it is not just generic simplism which is found in the material but, most pertinently, a historical simplism. The ascription of simple and single causes to complex human events evokes the image of every historical moment as virginal. The relatedness of events and conditions to each other is dimmed. Manion writes: "American government is not the result of evolutionary processes with its origins and basic elements obscured in the dim and distant past. American government is the product of political architects who set out 178 years ago to fabricate a mechanism which would accomplish definite purposes."[8]

Henry Ford put it more succinctly: "History is bunk." History is a record of singular events, rather than a process in which events inexorably affect each other. Consequently, history is not constantly on the move, is not in continuous flow, but moves by fits and starts—and can stand still.

The substantive ideology of the right is classically liberal in its stress on individualism and libertarianism. Historical simplism tends to overlook the problems posed to classical liberalism by the modern industrial state. According to Verne Paul Kaub, "All present day issues, both domestic and international, are no more than mere aspects of the one paramount issue of collectivism vs. individualism. . . ."[9]

It is not simplistic to suggest that we are locked in a tension between individualism and collectivism, but it is simplistic to suggest that we must opt wholly and simply for one or the other, and this is the burden of much of the literature. Thus, the total elimination of the income tax is called for, as well as the elimination of social security, the elimination of any aid or management from the federal government.

The approach to civil rights is another example of simplism in the interpretation of domestic affairs. Robert Welch suggests that the "few" radical injustices which still exist could be remedied simply and that the civil rights disruption among the Negro people has been artificially inspired. He writes:

The only way to solve the problem at hand and to prevent the horror ahead is in our opinion the only way to deal with all the other aspects of the Communist conspiracy as a whole; and that is simply to bring about enough understanding on the part of enough people as to what the Communists are trying to do and how much progress they've already made.[10]

There is no reference to the various factors—of which, indeed, Communist stimulation may have been one—that have been involved in the disaffection of the Negro population in America in the past three decades. Allen Stang's book on the subject is entitled *It's Very Simple: The True Story of Civil Rights.*

In foreign affairs, as well, the emphasis is on "simpler" solutions. Schlafly recalls that when a traveling American citizen named Perdicaris was once captured by a Greek bandit named Raisuli, President Theodore Roosevelt had a "simple solution": he sent a cable reading, "Perdicaris alive or Raisuli dead." Perdicaris was released. Schlafly suggests that we use the same technique for American servicemen who are held as hostages by Red China. There is no reference to factors which may have developed in the last half-century to differentiate Greece then and China now, or the use of American power then and now.

"There is a very simple solution," she writes, "to what to do about the problem of world Communism: just stop helping the Communists. The Soviet empire would die of its own economic anemia if a Democratic administration didn't keep giving it massive blood transfusions such as the sending of 64 million bushels of American wheat."[11]

Dan Smoot has a short and simple plan for solving the problem of Berlin. The United States should announce that it is going to pull out of Europe in six months and expects the Russians to pull out of Germany at the same time. If they do not withdraw at the same time that we do, we would take the following measures: break off diplomatic relations with all Communist countries, refuse all Communist countries access to the United Nations, and exert "maximum pressures" to isolate all Communist countries economically and diplomatically from all non-Communist countries. "That," writes Dan Smoot, "is an American plan which would solve the German 'problem.' "[12]

Just as the theme of classic liberalism uncomplicated by time and history runs through the domestic ideology of this literature, so the theme of American power uncomplicated by time and history seems to run through its treatment of foreign affairs. But it is not just historical illiteracy, or, as Smoot's plan indicates, an abiding faith in America's insuperable military power, which undergirds this historical simplism. What is the constant factor which these writers find operating, unchanged, and omnipotent, throughout history?

Manion suggests that President Eisenhower could have made a revolutionary impact on world affairs if he had made a different speech before the tenth commemorative session of the United Nations in San Francisco, when Bulganin was in attendance. The President should have recited the Declaration of Independence. "By quoting our own revolutionary birth certificate," says Manion, "the President could have effectively hoisted Mr. Bulganin by his own petard."[13] Robert Welch, after five years of U.S. armed intervention in Vietnam, argues at the end of 1969 "the United States could end the war in three months by 'cutting the supply routes.' "[14]

There is, throughout the literature, a sense of the magical power of the word. But it is not the word vying in the market place of ideas. Rather, it is the recurrent implication that just *saying* the right thing, *believing* the right thing, is the substance of victory and remedy. Desire—at any given moment—becomes the chief and only important engine of history.

In short, historical moralism is revealed as the critical link to historical simplism. Historical moralism is defined, in this context, as the tendency to believe that human events are totally shaped by the supremacy of good intentions over bad at any given moment, or vice versa.

Throughout the literature, there is constant reference to the central role of deficient character, failure of good intention, as the fountainhead of social evil. Sidney L. DeLove writes that "character" is the best defense of the United States, not armaments.[15] Garet Garett refers to the "softness of American character."[16] John Beaty complains about "the suspension of the age of honor in 1933."[17] Senator Joseph McCarthy referred to the "manly American course,"[18] and John A. Stormer to the "noble American breed."[19] And Ezra Taft Benson quotes Lenin as saying that the best strategy in war is to wait for "the moral disintegration of the enemy."[20]

As general comments, most of these statements are as unexceptionable as they are undistinguished. But when such character deficiency is not seen as product as well as cause, when it is seen as total cause, when an act of character is in itself seen as total remedy—such as in the Smoot proposal for Berlin and the Manion proposal for Eisenhower—then they qualify as distinguishably moralistic.

The moralistic note is sounded as a central theme for the entire range of national life and as a central index of that life. Schlafly complains about the Presidential award to Edmund Wilson, and her first two items of exception are that he has had four wives and that he is the author of an immoral book.[21]

Smoot and others refer to the significance of rising crime rates. Benson talks about the need to protect America "from sin, from unrighteousness, immorality, from desecration of the Sabbath Day, from lawlessness, from parental and juvenile delinquency. We must protect it from dirty movies, filthy advertising, from salacious and suggestive TV programs, magazines and books."[22]

The moralistic note is regularly associated with Christianity. Beaty points out that Christianity was closely linked with the founding and growth of America and gave Americans their "conception of honor." It was because of the dereliction of church leaders "that public morality declined to its present state in America."[23] Stormer indicts a historian for allegedly writing that liberalism "dispensed with the absurd Christian myths of sin and damnation and believed what shortcomings men might have were to be redeemed, not by Jesus on the cross, but by the benevolent unfolding of history."[24] In referring to the Declaration of Independence, Manion says, "The indisputable fact of Almighty God is here made into the number one cornerstone of the Republic."[25] And Kaub makes the ultimate statement, "America will not be safe until America is Christian in truth and in fact, wholly, unreservedly Christian."[26]

Most of the material, however, is not *religious* in style or content; for the most part Christianity is used as the reference by which to identify the body of good intentions and good character in the world. The substantive body of Christian thought and theology is not typically discussed in this process. For example, Kaub first establishes the prime values of political good as free government and free enterprise and *then* validates them from a moralistic point of view by invoking Christianity as the ideology from which they sprang.

By the same token, Communism is often used as the broad, general reference by which to counteridentify the body of bad intentions and bad character in the world. Billy James Hargis writes that

in every generation, the adversary of Christ and His church has relentlessly fought God's dominion over the earth. . . . The strategy of the Evil One appears to change with the succeeding centuries, but its objective is always the same. . . . Today we find Satan incarnate in international Communism, and in its off-shoots in the United States, the "Far Left."[27]

Moralism is absolutistic by nature. Manion says that "the needed division is not between left and right but between *right* and *wrong*."[28] DeLove writes that citizenship education must be "built with the *concrete* of absolute truths and fixed human values."[29] The use of Christianity to validate the moralism also provides an apocalyptic framework within which the absolutism itself is validated. Welch writes about John Birch: "With his death and in his death the battle lines were drawn, in a struggle from which either Communism or Christian-style civilization must emerge with one completely triumphant and the other completely destroyed."[30]

Political Moralism and Monism

A critic of extremism, the political scientist John Bunzel uses the term "antipolitics" to describe political activity whose approach is basically moralistic.[31] Politics is the workings of a pluralistic society. It is the constant process of negotiation through which conflicting interests come to live with each other. It is not a body of knowledge or truth, but a regulated contest whose purpose, in Sheldon Wolin's words, is to construct agreements, "or, if this fails, to make it possible for competing forces to compromise in order to avoid harsher remedies."[32] For Bunzel, the distinction between politics and antipolitics is the distinction between democratic and totalitarian systems. "In one there is competition for power and disagreement over the uses to which it will be put; in the other there is just power, with those who hold and exercise it intent on implementing what they regard as fundamental truth."[33]

It has frequently been suggested that one of the prime sources of extremism is religious fundamentalism. David Danzig, for example, has traced the strength of political extremism to those states which once officially repudiated Darwinianism.[34] But, as Daniel Bell has pointed out, these are the states which have also been politically dispossessed, whose populations have a sense of having been deprived of power and status.[35] Their religious particularism presumably lends itself to political particularism. However, the application of any "fundamental"—that is, revealed—truth to the political scene, being undebatable, makes impossible the open market place of ideas and powers. If every political issue is a doctrinal struggle between good and evil for man's soul, and there is only one revealed path to salvation, the market place must be closed down. Bunzel refers to

those whose primary approach to politics has been to mistake its very nature by insisting that the political process in a democratic society make as its only order of business the implementation of ethical rules and moral principles. It is not that rules or principles are "wrong" or unnecessary. It is that . . . political activity which seeks to implement what is regarded as "fundamental truth" or to establish an ideal society may lead to tyranny.[36]

The road to tyranny is indeed paved with good intentions, as long as the political process is seen only as a struggle between good and bad intentions. Political moralism *is* such a view, the essence of antipolitics and anti-pluralism. John Silber, commenting on his experience with the campus extremists of the left, said that they were "indistinguishable from the far right. . . . They share a contempt for rational political discussion and constitutional legal solutions. Both want to be pure. They know nothing about the virtue of compromise. They know nothing about the horror of sainthood or the wickedness of saints."[37]

The general phenomenon of populism is another vantage point from which to see the relationship between political moralism, antipolitics, and monism. Edward Shils describes populism as proclaiming "that the will of the people as such is supreme over every other standard, over the standards of traditional institutions, over the autonomy of institutions and over the will of other strata. Populism identifies the will of the people with justice and morality."[38]

Monistic societies in the modern age typically parody democracy—and simultaneously frustrate it—by invoking populist themes. Nazi Germany effected its policies "in the name of the people" and justified them as "the will of the people." Communist societies have done the same and have gone by the name of "people's democracies" even at their most totalitarian. Populism is transformed from a thrust for more democratically distributed power to an antidemocratic hazard when it attempts to doctrinally sweep away the plural institutions which mediate between the people and their political leadership. Hitler drew a straight line between himself and the German people, and intervening centers of power or tradition were demolished. The specific populist movements in American history developed a contempt for laws or legal institutions, legislators, agencies, or politicians, all seeming to thwart the direct satisfaction of the people's will. The invocation of this corporate "will of the people" as the highest morality contains more than a touch of mysticism. It is not just public opinion on this issue or that; it is the soul of the people, the unfathomable—and unmeasured—sweep of their aspirations toward the good and the true. Conversely, it can be assumed that whatever is good and true *is* the people's will, even if the people are not aware of it at any given time. To return to a kaleidoscope of American Opinion book-store authors, John Beaty writes: "The patriotic people of America should not lose hope. They should proceed with boldness and joy in the outcome, for Right is on their side. Moreover, they are a great majority, and such a majority can make its will prevail any time it ceases to lick the boots of its captors."[39] Doctrinal populism thus becomes a seductive form of political moralism, inimical to pluralistic politics.

But while the monistic impulse is effectively created by political moralism, it most often comes to fruition with what might be considered the logical extension of that moralism: conspiracy theory. For if historical movement at every stage is almost exclusively a matter of good will or ill will, freely chosen, those who make a mistake are not just wrong; they are evil. And all our social and political pathologies are the result of deliberate evil-doing. Given the moralistic premise, how else could we account for them? Senator

Joseph McCarthy asked, "How can we account for our present situation unless we believe that men high in this government are concerting to deliver us to disaster?"[40]

This is the ultimate product of moralism rigorously applied, and the heart of the monistic impulse: error is arguable, evil intent is not; in the political process, error is admissible and legitimate, evil intent is inadmissible and illegitimate. Differences, cleavages, pluralism, ambiguity, based on evil intent are illegitimate.

The "conspiracy theory" as it has been used in extremist politics in America and elsewhere from the eighteenth century to the present has a distinctive conceptual model of its own. To begin with, conspiracy theory is *not* synonymous with every supposition that a conspiracy or collusion exists in a given case. Secret collusion and conspiracy is, in fact, a constant in political life. The first distinctive element of conspiracy theory is its *comprehensive* nature. The typical conspiracy theory extends in space: it is international in scope: it extends in time: it stretches back in history and promises to stretch ahead interminably. Richard Hofstadter calls this "the central preconception of the paranoid style—the existence of a vast, insidious, preternaturally effective international conspiratorial network designed to perpetrate acts of the most fiendish character."[41] The moralistic base of the conspiracy theory prescribes its comprehensive nature. William Guy Carr, a modern conspiracy theorist, writes: "History repeats itself because there has been perfect continuity of purpose in the struggle which has been going on since the beginning of time between the forces of Good and Evil to decide whether the Rule of Almighty God shall prevail, or whether the world shall literally go to the Devil. The issue is just as simple as that."[42] Although this apocalyptic vision must be concretized politically, these political forces of evil tend not to be localized, but are rather seen as global and historical. This explains the persistence of certain images which recur in conspiracy theories. The "Illuminati" are the prototype of such images, first mentioned in America as the central band of world conspirators at the end of the eighteenth century, and still being mentioned today, most notably by Robert Welch, the head of the Birch Society. William Guy Carr actually places the existence of the Illuminati as far back as the time of Christ, for whose execution they were responsible. "It was the Illuminati, and the false priests and elders in their pay, who hatched the plot by which Christ would be executed by the Roman soldiers. It was they who supplied the thirty pieces of silver used to bribe Judas. It was they who used their propagandists to misinform and mislead the mob."[43] And, according to Carr, it is the Illuminati who "use Communism today as their manual of action to further their secret plans for ultimate world domination."[44]

The conspiracy theory is comprehensive not only in time and space but, even more importantly, in *design*. It is an essential element of the conspiracy theory that such conspiracy is the *decisive* factor in turning history. This is again a consummate reflection of historical simplism and historical moralism. It is not just that there is political collusion but that this collusion is *the* explanatory factor in understanding history. Lyman Beecher, an eighteenth-century conspiracy theorist, put it this way in talking about *his* evil men of politics:

> No design! How does it happen that their duty and the analogy of their past policy and their profession in Europe and their predictions and exultations in this country and their deeds all well adapted to their end should come together accidentally with such admirable indications of design. If such complicated indications of design may exist without design, as well may the broader mechanism of the world be regarded as the offspring of chance.[45]

This element of the conspiracy theory not only permits a moralistic explanation of history but also permits a comprehensive conspiracy to be *inferred* from the distasteful turns which history actually takes. McCarthy said, "how can we account for our present situation unless" we accept the conspiracy theory. Carr indicates that when Christ was asked, "Who are the Illuminati?" He replied by saying "by their fruits ye shall know them."[46] Grand inference is built into conspiracy theories.

But comprehensiveness—of design and decisiveness, of time and space— is only one element in the model of the conspiracy theory. The second element, flowing indispensably from the same moralistic base, is *the manipulation of the many by the few*. At the most, the people are found to be highly manipulatable, especially by the powerful magic of the word, which is another aspect of the moralistic approach. But, finally, they must be misled by rather than be the engineers of evil—or else the entire structure would collapse. Moralism is predicated on the strong existence of free will—Kaub's definition of a free society is one in which men can exercise free will—and on the ultimately beneficent character of that will. John Rousselot refers to the "God-given upward reach in the heart of man."[47] There is constant reference throughout the literature to the "will of the people" which will eventually and rightfully assert itself.

In this era, and especially in the American setting, the people must be redeemable, cannot be the authors of the evil intentions which move history pathologically.

Thus the people are seen as soft and as seduced by the opiates of welfare and propaganda. John T. Flynn asks: "How could President Roosevelt and later Acheson and Marshall perform this appalling operation without a protest from the American people? The answer to that is that the

American people had to be drugged—drugged by propaganda. They had to be lied to."[48] DeLove talks about "a reshaping of the American mind, a passive shifting of American attitudes."[49] For him, this "quiet betrayal" was engineered chiefly by the educators. For others, bands of politicians and mass media operators have been instruments of seduction. The underlying hypotheses can range from the commonplace to the exotic. David Noebel suggests that the singing group, the Beatles, has been used as part of "an elaborate, calculating and scientific technique directed at rendering a generation of American youth useless through nerve-jamming, mental deterioration and retardation."[50] Conde McGinley, for years one of America's most prolific publishers of extremist material, wrote: "The rear occiput of the left lobe of the brain contains brain tissue which is responsible for the individual's power to resist domination. Sodium fluoride narcotizes this area and makes the person in question submissive to the will of those who want to govern him."[51] But whatever the underlying physiological or psychological theories, the fact is that if the moralistic approach is to stand up, some small group of evil intenders must be identified.

The nature of this small group of manipulators has changed, of course, with historical circumstance. But certain characteristics remain fairly constant. For example, the manipulators are usually seen as "intellectuals." This property explains their ability to manipulate the minds of the mass. It also marks them off from the mass and helps to characterize them as both *secret* and *alien,* dealing as they do in arcane subjects. These are also constant properties of the manipulators, by definition. They would not be able to manipulate the mass if they were not doing so secretly, nor would their secret purposes be so antithetical to the common population if they were not somehow alien to that population.

But these very qualities create a constant problem for conspiracy theories. It is necessary for the conspirators to be secret, but it is also necessary for them to be somehow identifiable. For the *personification* of evil in history is another essential element of conspiracy theory. The secrecy which characterizes the manipulators tends to make them abstract; the personification becomes difficult unless they are made more concrete. As politically effective weapons, many conspiracy theories have floundered on this contradiction. The image of the Illuminati has generally proved too abstract, by itself, to serve the purposes of personification. The Protocols of the Elders of Zion has proved more effective through the years because it is associated with a visible body of people, the Jews. The conspiracy theories surrounding the Vatican have also been associated with a visible body of people, while still possessing a secret, arcane center, the Vatican. The Kremlin has served the same kind of purpose. And the image of

"Wall Street Bankers" has also at times struck an effective balance between the abstract and the concrete.

The conspiracy theory is an extension of historical moralism, peculiarly designed to legitimate the closing down of the ideational market place—that is, providing a rationale for accomplishing the very thing the conspiracy theory is presumably directed against: the manipulation of the many by the few. It is a central property of extremism, of monism, but it is not the exclusive property of right-wing extremism. Left-wing extremism has habitually invoked the conspiracy theory out of its own political needs and its own historical moralism. And there is another quality of the conspiracy theory which both extremist poles typically share: an underlying belief in the perfectibility of man. This brings us back full circle to the moralistic base of the conspiracy theory. If there is only one "right" way, if people are capable of it, then if they stray from it, the cause must be evil dereliction of some kind on somebody's part. Norman Cohn described this quality in his analysis of the medieval millennial sects of Europe who erected their own religious variants of the political conspiracy: "the refusal to accept the ineluctable limitations and imperfections of human existence, such as transience, dissension, conflict, fallibility, whether intellectual or moral. . . ."[52] Karl Popper put it this way: "The adoption of the conspiracy theory can hardly be avoided by those who think that they know how to make heaven on earth."[53]

The conspiracy theory caps the model of monism and legitimates the forceful suppression of pluralism and pluralistic process. The breach of due process, the use of violence which is implicit and explicit in monistic political movements, flow from—and inspire—the construction of such a conceptual model.

"The Left"

The same model can be constructed from the body of "left-wing" literature, with somewhat different language and superstructure. For example, William McPherson examined about five thousand statements on civil rights and Vietnam in extreme left and moderate left publications, as well as several thousand similar statements in extreme right and moderate right publications.[54] He defined extremism as "value-oriented movements which refuse to participate fully in democratic politics or make cynical use of politics as means to other goals."[55] In short, he was defining monism: procedural extremism, the intolerance of cleavage. It was on the strength of apparent monistic impulse that the Maoist Progressive Labor party (*Challenge*) was designated for purposes of the study as "extreme" and the Socialist party (*New America*) and the Americans for Democratic Action (*ADA*

World) as "moderate" on the left. It was on the strength of apparent monistic impulse that the Birch Society (*Bulletin*) was designated as "extreme" and William Buckley's periodical (*National Review*) and Americans for Constitutional Action (*Human Events*) as "moderate" on the right.

On both left and right the more monistic publications are more likely to moralistically "simplify issues and reduce them to an emotional choice between two alternatives." The *Worker* (Communist party) suggested that one must line up simply on one or the other side of "peace or war, democracy or fascism, civil rights or Jim Crow,"[56] while *American Opinion* (Birch Society) described the choices as being "between good and evil . . . freedom and slavery . . . Sin and Virtue."[57]

This kind of polarization and attribution of evil motives was designated as "absolutism" in the McPherson study. The ostensible expression of such sentiments was measured quantitatively in the various publications, right and left, extreme and moderate. While measurement of this kind is necessarily impressionistic, and comparisons between left-wing and right-wing publications on this basis may be particularly unreliable because of essential differences in rhetoric and issue salience, the differences that emerged within each end of the political spectrum at least were significant. On civil rights issues, about 63 per cent of the *Challenge* statements were coded as absolutistic, as against 24 per cent of those in *New America* and 13 per cent in the *ADA World*. On the right, 43 per cent of the Birch *Bulletin* statements were coded absolutistic, as against 32 per cent of those in the *National Review* and 29 per cent in *Human Events*.[58] On Vietnam issues, the percentage of absolutistic statements were, on the left: 56 per cent for the *Challenge*, 40 per cent for *New America*, and 12 per cent for the *ADA World*; and on the right: 60 per cent for the Birch *Bulletin*, 35 per cent for the *National Review*, and 27 per cent for *Human Events*.[59]

The statements in these publications were coded also for conspiracy emphasis. On civil rights issues, 20 per cent of the *Challenge* statements struck this note, as against 2 per cent in *New America* and none in the *ADA World*; 41 per cent in the Birch *Bulletin*, as against 6 per cent in the *National Review* and 11 per cent in *Human Events*.[60] On Vietnam issues, the figures were 28 per cent for the *Challenge*, 5 per cent for *New America*, and 3 per cent for the *ADA World*; 40 per cent for the Birch *Bulletin*, 14 per cent for the *National Review*, and 19 per cent for *Human Events*.[61]

Significantly, both extremes end up by attacking the same government establishment as a prime source of conspiratorial evil. Left and right both present themselves as the disestablished.

Thus, the elements of moralistic simplism and conspiracy are the common core of monism, of that procedural extremism which illegitimates cleavage and legitimates violations of democratic procedure—whether by direct assaults on due process of law, on freedom of speech and assembly, or by informal techniques of suppressing dissent through smear or disruption. Monism is clearly not one pole of the left-right or liberal-conservative axis Monism-pluralism is an independent gradient.

This does not mean, of course, that the circumstances, rhetoric, and effects of left-wing extremist movements are identical to those of right-wing movements. Right wing has been defined basically in terms of *preservatism*; left wing in terms of *innovation*. More particularly, the preservatism of the right wing has to do with maintaining or narrowing lines of power and privilege; the innovation of the left wing has to do with broadening lines of power and privilege. Thus, in the 1960's, both the Goldwater Republicans in America and the Kremlin-oriented politicians in Czechoslovakia found themselves on the right-wing pole of the preservatist axis. Historically, of course, the right wing has also been associated with a certain *ideological* direction, and the left wing with another. This ideological axis in modern history has become individualistic or antistatist at one pole and statist at the other. This is generally seen in modern practice as the "conservative-liberal" axis. Conservatism, so defined, then describes a rather particular ideological direction, while preservatism describes a condition of power and privilege. The generic meanings of the words "conservatism" and "preservatism" are of course the same, and the words are interchangeable. However, because of specific political history the word "conservative" has taken on a secondary meaning, which sometimes engulfs its primary meaning. There are identifiable "conservative" political programs which exceed the general meaning of the term conservatism. The political program of conservatism at any given time, while presumably stemming from a conservative or preservatist thrust, is not coterminous with that thrust, and may indeed change adaptively from time to time. The term "preservatism" avoids that confusion because it is not encumbered with the same particularistic political history.

G. B. Rush, after examining right-wing literature and a number of definitions, proposes this one: "The extreme right (specifically that set of attitudes which may be called extreme rightism) is a political expression of the principle of individualism which expression is articulated in opposition to collectivist tendencies in government . . . international relations, social organization and modern social philosophy."[62] It is true that in America, the right-wing preservatist impulse has generally been built around such a "conservative" (antistatist) ideology, because our history has fallen out that way. In fact, however, this has not invariably been the case even in America. The Coughlinite movement in the 1930's, for example, had strong collectivist proclivities, yet is universally thought of as a "right-wing" movement. It is the axis of preservatism which most essentially and invariably distinguishes "Left Wing" from "Right Wing." The poles on the axis of statism may often coincide, but are not defining. And the poles on neither axis automatically define extremism or monism as we have defined it. Of course, it is obvious that "extreme" positions on any axis are conducive to procedural extremism, that is, monism. Being on the tip of any axis means, by definition, being separated from the normative center of power and ideology and would raise the risk of frustration which presumably is conducive to the monistic impulse.

Further, contradiction and ambiguity belong on the statism–individualism axis. The absence of *any* social security and welfare programs, *any* civil rights laws, *any* management of economy and population would clearly flout modern needs and aspirations. On the other hand, the proliferation of these activities just as clearly creates even greater bureaucratic controls and at least the hazard that these controls can become politically oppressive. There is a necessary tension between these two directions. In moving toward the poles, there is the risk of unspringing that tension, of eliminating the natural ambiguities, and therefore a greater risk that the monistic complex will set in. Or conversely, the monistic impulse will increase the probability of movement toward the ideological poles. But while the ideological poles and the monistic impulse are likely to intersect, they do not always do so, and—most important—they are not the same quality. On the other hand, while the model of monism would apply to either the left or the right, the Liberal or the Conservative, it is right-wing extremism which is under examination here; and certain distinctive historical circumstances have been associated with the development of right-wing extremism in America.

American Values and Extremist Movements

How do American life and political history articulate with these hypothetical models of monism and extremism? The genius of the American society is that it has legitimized ambiguity. The American ideology embraces contradictory values; the Constitution is a hot house of ambivalence; the political parties are amalgams of inconsistency. But these are not strains on America as much as they are the strains that have made America American.

Many observers have noted the paradoxes with which this society is replete: deep veins of materialism and of idealism; high rates of crime committing (among developed countries) and of church attending; parallel emphasis on majority rule and minority rights, conformity and individualism, lawfulness and rebellion, federalism and centralism. These paradoxes reflect the universal condition of human impulses and are not peculiar to the American people. But the American society and ideology as shaped by history have peculiarly encapsulated and even sanctified these paradoxes. Here lies a clue to America's traditional rejection of extremist political parties, which specialize in utopian attacks on ambiguity.

All efforts to create radical "third" parties, whether of the left or right, have failed miserably. America is one of the few countries in the free world without any socialist party which has parliamentary representation. On the other hand, while it has been difficult to build stable "third" parties, there have been a variety of social "movements" which have had considerable support. Many of these have taken on an extremist character. These include the nativist movements and parties preceding the Civil War, which secured the support of more than one-quarter of the electorate in the 1850's. The abolitionist movement imposed many of its views on both parties, particularly the more middle-class-based Whigs and Republicans. The prohibition movement, like the abolitionists, failed to build a new party, but succeeded in obtaining its objectives through the actions of major party representatives. Perhaps the largest extremist movement, the Ku Klux Klan, has been credited with a membership of from 3,000,000 to 6,000,000 in the early 1920's and clearly had considerable influence in electing candidates to major offices in both northern and southern states. During the 1930's opinion polls indicated that as many as 25 per cent of those polled approved the policies of Father Charles Coughlin, a populist, profascist, and anti-Semitic agitator. Yet when Coughlin backed third-party candidate Representative William Lemke running for President on the Union party ticket in 1936, Lemke received less than 2 per cent of the vote. During the 1950's, Senator Joseph McCarthy secured massive backing in the opinion polls for his crusade against treason in high places, his investigations of Communist subversion in government. Candidates backed by McCarthy seemingly had success in defeating opponents in party primaries, and important leaders of both parties shied away from resisting his activities. Yet McCarthyism, which began in 1950, was dead by 1954 and left no organizational residues. Over two-fifths of the American population expressed approval of George Wallace's activities in 1968, but only a small proportion of them voted for him as Presidential candidate.

Thus, it may be noted that while it is difficult to build a new *party* in the United States, largely because of the electoral system which has pressed electors to choose between two major candidates for the Presidency and local executive offices, it has been relatively easy to create new *movements*. The politics of social movements as distinct from that of party creates a sharply divergent image of the degree of stability and instability. If we contrast the American polity and those of a number of stable European nations (for example, Great Britain and Scandinavia) with respect to the frequency of the formation of major movements, the United States is clearly less stable; that is, it gives rise to more movements, much as it sustains more new religions. Conversely, the United States ranks lower on a scale of formation of electorally viable parties.

The implications of this distinction between movement and party may be pointed up by a brief comparative look at Canada and the United States. Since World War I, Canadian politics has witnessed the growth of many "third parties." There were the Progressives in the 1920's, who became the second largest party and controlled the government of a number of provinces; New Democracy, the Cooperative Commonwealth Federation (renamed the New Democratic Party in the '60's), and Social Credit during the 1930's, the latter two continuing down to the present, and a host of French Canadian parties which have had transient success in Quebec. The proverbial man from Mars, looking at the statistics of Canadian federal and provincial election results since 1920, would conclude that it has been one of the most unstable and tension-ridden polities in the world, clearly more unstable than the apparently unchanging United States. This country, with the lone exception of the LaFollette Progressive campaign of the 1920's, had largely witnessed shifts between Republican and Democratic ranks between 1913 and 1968. But evaluating political stability primarily in terms of the rise and fall of ideological parties to the left or right of the two major centrist ones would clearly be an error.

Canada has not been more unstable than the United States. The difference which gives rise to party in Canada and movement in the United States is a product largely of two highly disparate electoral systems. A parliamentary system with single-member districts in which voters do not vote for a central executive, but solely for a local representative, permits new movements with ecologically distinct sources of strength—that is, in occupational, ethnic, religious, or regional groupings—to elect candidates to office. Furthermore, the British parliamentary system stresses party discipline in the House of Commons in order to avoid the election which must follow government defeat on a given issue. This means that groups or factions within a party must secede if they disagree with the line of their traditional party on some issue of crucial importance to the group. The American system allows dissident groups to express and vote their opposition in Congress while continuing in the broad electoral coalitions which are essentially the meaning of the term "party" in the United States. Within these coalitions, diverse minorities seek to get their policies adopted by other formal means, such as the primaries—and by the development of new pressures where their formal means are unsuccessful. Many American political movements have begun with this impetus. And many American social movements which have begun with aspirations toward becoming third parties have ended up instead as streams within one or another existing party coalition. But they were nevertheless streams of significant dissidence, and within the content of the American system, they have left strong marks on our history.

In Neil J. Smelser's definitive effort to lay out the theoretical basis for the development of political movements in general, he posed at least three initial requisites:

1. The existence of a social strain of ambiguous proportions which creates widespread anxiety.

2. The designation of a specific cause for that strain. Without such a designation, there would be no movement, only hysteria.

3. The designation of a specific solution. Without such a specific designation there would be no movement, only a kind of wish-fulfillment.[63]

The nature of the strains which have given rise to political movements, and the kinds of causes and solutions which have been embodied in those movements, have been different, of course, for right-wing and left-wing movements. With respect to the strain, the nature of the ambiguity changes with the historical situation. But the nature of the anxiety, as it touches on the development of political movements in this country, has typically been related to a sense of power and status deprivation. There are groups which feel that they have never gained their proper share of power and status. And there are groups which feel that they are losing their power and status. There are, among the deprived, the "never-hads" and the "once-hads."

In the first instance, the discontent becomes sharpest when relatively low but stabilized expectations are disrupted (as in the case of the working class during an economic depression) or when depressed expectations are swiftly rising (as in the case of the Negro population after World War II). On the other hand, certain groups still among the more socially and economically privileged may feel that prevailing trends in society threaten them with loss of status or power, as in the case of doctors who feel the weight of growing government controls, or working-class whites who feel the pressure of Negro demands on their schools and neighborhoods.

It is not that never-hads and once-hads are necessarily extremists, but that extremism typically draws its strength and substance from these two types of deprivation. The first type tends to be manifest as economic deprivation and to result in demands for state action to achieve economic reforms. The chief purchase on power held by these groups is, after all, the public government on which they have some claim. The second type of deprivation tends to be manifest as sheer loss of status and influence; it cannot be assuaged directly by government action, and indeed an increment of government power typically means, for these groups, a diminution of their traditional power. Consequently, these two types of deprivation tend to be, respectively, "liberal" and "conservative" on the ideological axis of statism. And, of course, they tend to be "left-wing" and "right-wing" on the axis of preservatism.

The fluidity of the American social structure—the fact that no group has enjoyed a status tenure in the style of European social classes—has meant that the problem of status displacement has been an enduring characteristic of American life. New areas, new industries, new migrant groups, new ethnic groups, have continually encroached upon the old as important and influential. On these occasions, various formerly entrenched American groups have felt disinherited. These situations have in America been the typical wellsprings of right-wing movements and, indeed, of right-wing extremism.

Right-Wing Values in America

Meanwhile, there have been distinctive elements of American history and society which have circumscribed the nature of right-wing politics and political appeals in this country. These elements have comprised an inter-related web of stresses on individualism, egalitarianism, antielitism, and moralism. Egalitarianism and antielitism are ideological reflections of the fluidity of the American social structure, the source of right-wing discontent and presumably a left-wing approach—but right-wing politics have been forced to operate within that context in America. They have been able to do so chiefly, not just by preempting the slogans, but by turning the peculiar American stress on individualism, which is one base of egalitarianism and antielitism, to their own uses. This individualism does lend itself to the ideological bent of the right wing in American history, antistatism; but, more than that, it lends itself to the kind of moralistic approach which the right wing had to substitute for economic class appeal in America. And this moralistic approach, already built into the American version of individualism, has always been conducive to the development of the conceptual model of political monism.

The United States is the bourgeois society par excellence. Feudal aristocratic, premodern orientations are at a minimum in this country as a result of its having developed as a new society without a feudal past, in which the dominant religious tradition has been Protestant "nonconformist" with a congregational (autonomous) rather than episcopalian system of church organization. The American Revolution not only overthrew monarchical institutions; it led to a withdrawal from the United States of many of the leading elements who favored elitist deferential class relationships, and it established as the legitimate political tradition the values of equality and democracy. Though the United States in 1789 lacked many of the attributes of a political democracy, the liberal reformers from that day on could appeal to the values enunciated in the Declaration of Independence as the superordinate justification of their reforms, of their seeking to widen the suffrage and the basis of opportunity.

The settlement of numerous "new societies" as the nation moved westward gave increased sustenance to the egalitarian and democratic doctrines. The preservatists, in the form of the Federalist and the Whig parties, were in an almost permanent minority. It soon became evident that the only way such groups could hope to win elections was by themselves adopting an egalitarian antielitist posture, by nominating candidates who seemingly symbolized log-cabin roots. Whether Whig or Democrat, Americans saw themselves as progressives.

The democratic tradition was tied up with a strong emphasis on achievement, personal success, self-orientation. These notions were inherent both in the political doctrines and in the religious ethos which increasingly became Arminian; that is, stressed the need for the personal attainment of grace. These approaches may be contrasted to the European aristocratic and Catholic-Anglican-Lutheran emphases, which on the political side stressed the *noblesse oblige* role of the state to intervene to keep society in balance and to help the poor, and on the religious side involved state-supported birthright churches in which the individual basically related to God through his membership in the church. Arminian Christianity in the form of Methodism basically assumed in practice, if not in theology, the perfectibility of man, or rather his obligation to avoid sin.

The American, therefore, as political and religious man set forth an ideal of the good society. He was and is a utopian moralist. And almost from the beginning of American history, one finds a plethora of "do-good" reform organizations seeking to foster peace, protect the Sabbath, reduce or eliminate the evils of alcoholic beverages, end slavery, eliminate corruption, extend the educational system, and so on. These groups have tended to draw their support from middle-class evangelical Protestants.

The value system not only fostered efforts at more uplift; it also pressed men to work hard to succeed. Each American could and should hope to attain a good position in life. Social background was not supposed to be a qualitative obstacle. And consequently, if a man failed, it was his own fault. The assumptions of meritocracy could be much more punitive for the unsuccessful than those of an ascriptive society, in which it is accepted that men basically remain in the spot where they started. As Robert Merton noted, America is

a society which places a high premium on economic affluence and social ascent for all its members. . . . This patterned expectation is regarded as appropriate for everyone, irrespective of his initial lot or station in life. . . . This leads naturally to the subsidiary theme that success or failure are results wholly of personal qualities, that he who fails has only himself to blame, for the corollary to the concept of the self-made man is the self-made man. To the extent that this cultural definition is assimilated by those who have not made their mark, failure represents a double defeat: the manifest defeat of remaining far behind in the race for success and the implicit defeat of not having the capacity and moral stamina needed for success. . . . It is in this cultural setting that, in a significant proportion of cases, the threat of defeat motivates men to the use of those tactics, beyond the law or the mores, which promise "success."

The moral mandate to achieve success thus exerts pressure to succeed, by fair means if possible and by foul means if necessary.[64]

The strong emphasis on egalitarian achievement, on getting ahead, has been linked by many analysts of American society with making it an "ends-oriented" as distinct from a "means-oriented" culture. In the former, winning is what counts, not how one wins. Conversely, in a more ascriptive aristocratic social system, the norms stress conforming to the proper code of behavior; that is, to the means. The statement by Leo Durocher that "nice guys finish last" may be countered with the Olympic motto that "it matters not who wins the game, it matters how you played." The latter, of course, is the code of aristocracy, of a ruling class which "won" some generations back and which, in effect, tells the "outs" not to press them too hard. But the difference between an achievement-oriented culture's stress on ends as contrasted with an ascriptive one's focus on means is real and affects many aspects of life.

Politically, it implies that there should be fewer inhibitions against using unscrupulous tactics, against violations of rules of the game, in an achievement-oriented culture. The campaign methods and oratory of both major parties throughout American history reflect this stress on ends, on winning, rather than on means. Leaders on each side have been denounced in the most violent language for having been guilty of the most heinous crimes, including even treason. The charges by Joseph McCarthy and recent radical rightists that Democrats and liberals were conscious or unconscious agents of Communists may be paralleled by Franklin Roosevelt's denunciation of some of his opponents as "copperheads" (the Civil War term for northern supporters of secession). Some Republicans after the Civil War charged that the Democrats were agents of an alien church seeking to control America; that is, the Catholics. For much of the nineteenth century, the conservative parties were willing to appeal to religious and anti-immigrant prejudice to defeat the Democrats. The latter, in turn, were not loath to appeal to anti-Negro prejudice in fighting the Republicans. Hence, those who resort to extreme tactics have support on one level of the American ethos.

The emphasis on attaining ends, on success, is linked also to the strong belief in individualism as distinct from community orientation. European society, descendent from feudalism, Catholicism, and aristocracy, retains values which assume the propriety of community or *noblesse oblige* responsibility for inferior orders. The traditional collectivity orientation of socialism and the welfare state is linked to that *noblesse oblige* concept of the leadership role or responsibility of aristocracy. The community, aristocrats, the church, the state, are responsible for helping the less fortunate, for the maintenance of welfare institutions. Such welfare objectives were not designed to facilitate upward social mobility, to break down class barriers. Thus various conservatives such as Bismarck and Disraeli could approve of socialist objectives. The objection of Kaiser Wilhelm to the German Social Democrats before World War I was much more to their internationalism, their lack of patriotism, and their challenge to the leadership role of the old elite than to their economic doctrines. Disraeli could argue that the Tories could realistically hope to win the approval of the masses in a suffrage democracy, because they, rather than the bourgeois Liberals, sought to better the condition of the poor, were genuinely interested in them. The doctrines of laissez faire, of opposition to state intervention, were those of Manchester liberalism, of the manufacturers and businessmen, not the traditional conservative aristocracy. And, basically, the values of the old dominant classes were preserved and facilitated the transition to the welfare and social democratic state.

The preservation of the historic collectivity traditions helped to sustain in Europe an establishment conception of upper-class and elite status. Egalitarianism, the assumption that every man by virtue of his human status has a right to be respected by others, was never completely legitimated as a key aspect of any European society the way that it was in America.

The antistatist individualist emphasis which defined nineteenth-century American liberalism has remained important in the United States. While the European conservatives have often accepted enhanced state power either in the form of benevolent Tory welfare state, or even in some form of authoritarianism, American conservatives, so called, have stressed local rights, laissez faire, almost to the extent of being libertarian. A conservative magazine like William Buckley's *National Review* is proud to describe its ideology as libertarian. The leading big-business opposition to the Roosevelt New Deal in the 1930's took the form of the Liberty League, which encouraged complete laissez faire; many of its doctrines were revived in the Goldwater campaign in 1964. Thus American conservatives, as contrasted with British, Scandinavian, or even Canadian, find the growth of the welfare state much more antithetical to their values, to their sense of moral rectitude.

Conversely, although American liberals and leftists now support a welfare state, a collectivity-oriented set of political doctrines, they retain a counter-commitment to traditional individualism as well. The concern with bettering education, with eliminating cultural deprivation, as means of encouraging the poor to enter the race for success, reflects this. The War on Poverty initiated by President Johnson was premised on the assumption that people are poor because they lack the attributes to succeed, such as education, skills, and motivation. This position is not very different from that of the conservative Republicans who also traditionally have believed that the poor are poor because they are lazy or stupid. The great concern with extending state support of education which has characterized the United States from the early nineteenth century on is a reflection of this effort to foster individual success. Europeans have invested state resources heavily in welfare measures like unemployment insurance, old age pensions, state-supported medical care, while Americans have invested community funds in schools and universities. These varying patterns have been exported to the colonies. The two former American colonies, the Philippines and Puerto Rico, were for some decades second and third in the world in proportions of age cohorts attending university; the former British, French, Belgian, and Dutch colonies had sent a veritable handful to universities before independence.

The abiding concern for individualism in the American tradition may be seen most recently in the conjoint criticism of programs of urban planning and renewal by the ideologists of the American left and right. The left has defended the values and social organization of the slum dweller against the bureaucratic planner who is only concerned with good new housing. Leftists point to the fact that the destruction of neighborhoods to facilitate renewal undermines local autonomy and culture. The conservatives also attack urban renewal, in part because they would deny increased power to the state, in part because, like the left, they urge that it be handled locally. In recent years in both Boston and Berkeley, the left and the right have united against urban renewal. In Boston, the new left organization, Students for a Democratic Society, and the John Birch Society campaigned a few years ago in a white working-class area—North Harvard Street—against efforts to tear down working-class housing and replace it by apartments. Birch members of the police department actually contributed to the bail bond funds of SDS members arrested in civil disobedience campaigns in the area. In Berkeley, the various new left and old left groups strongly opposed efforts at urban renewal in an area south of the Berkeley campus, which was fostered by the liberal Democrats on the city council and opposed by the conservative Republicans. Under pressure from both ends of the spectrum, the plan finally was dropped.

There is similar congruence in emphasis on the left and the right—as against "standard" liberal positions—on substituting self-help programs for increased welfare payments or social services. The individualistic position thus reasserts itself; and indeed it is especially in America that so-called liberalism is so often at odds with itself because, as Hans Morgenthau has pointed out, "it has been unable to reconcile its original libertarian assumptions and postulates with its latter-day philosophy of the administrative and welfare state."[65]

The American utopia has been one of equality and achievement, of an individualistic race for success, in which the state is only supposed to enter to guarantee to the offspring of the less privileged each generation a fair chance in the race. Hereditary inequality is regarded as a violation of the ethos. But to complete the circle, in this emphasis on equality and rugged individualism also inheres resistance to any generalized deference to elite groups, whether of intellect, wealth, or political power.

The lack of respect for any generalized elite inhibited efforts to create an equivalent of an upper-class establishment. There has emerged no single leadership class, automatically dominant in the church, military, politics, intellect, and civil service. Decentralization and autonomy have contributed to a pattern of differentiated elites somewhat in competition with one another. The absence of respect for an elite establishment has meant that the type of respect for law and order, for legitimate authority, which emerged in Britain and other parts of northern Europe, did not develop to the same degree in the United States. The old elites were thrown out by the 1830's; the intellectual elite which dominated in the Revolution and early days of the republic lost out in favor of populistic leadership. Various elites of business, of intellect, of professions, of politics, have repeatedly felt themselves to be unloved. This has meant among other things the absence of any kind of social establishment which commanded deference from the mass of the population.

The quality of antielitism has made many with a claim to high status much more insecure about their status than would be true for their equivalents in many European countries. Many of the American elite are status-anxious, feel threatened and insecure, and react politically to this sense of being under attack, to lacking legitimacy. They feel weak and rejected by the majority—a feeling which makes some of them antimajoritarian.

Thus, what has been called backlash politics has characterized certain segments of the American right wing for much of American history. Backlash politics may be defined as the reaction by groups which are declining in a felt sense of importance, influence, and power, as a result of secular endemic change in the society, to seek to reverse or stem the direction of change through political means. Since their political concern has been activated by decline, by repeated defeats and failures, backlash politics is often extremist. The first such set of events involved New England Federalists, Congregationalists and merchants, who reacted to their decline by discovering foreign-based conspiracies and emphasizing religion and moralism. They later threatened to secede from the Union at the Hartford Convention in 1814. The repeated alliances with anti-Catholic nativism by the Federalists and Whigs illustrate the willingness of elites to sustain extremism in their efforts to hold or retain power. Among the masses, burgeoning movements like the Know-Nothings in the 1850's, the American Protective Association in the 90's, or the Klan in the 1920's were responses of evangelical Protestants to a sense of change which was eroding their moral values or social position. In recent years, backlash politics seems to characterize the declining evangelical Protestants whose cultural-ethnic values are now weaker than ever; members of the small and moderate-size business class which still believe in laissez faire, low taxes, and weak unions and find history against them; and those who feel a stake in white domination, who find the success of the civil rights movement threatening. The more extremist radical right has been attractive to these types. But right-wing groups typically have to appeal to the populace within the framework of values which are themselves a source of right-wing discontent in the first place: antielitism, individualism, and egalitarianism. These remain the supreme American political values. Commitment to these values *is* the American ideology, there being no more concrete political philosophy or dogma. Indeed, the nature of these values is such that the American commitment tends to be more moralistic than ideological. This moralistic commitment has been the constant strength of our democratic life. But the same values and the same moralistic commitment provide the substance of extremist threats to that democratic life. They have shaped the kinds of anxieties and discontents on which extremist movements in America have been based; they have lent themselves readily to the kind of moralistic personification and conspiracy theory which is the indispensable ingredient of the monistic impulse; they have given strength to the ends-oriented breach-of-rules approach which is the final resting place of procedural extremism. The democratic, pluralistic impulse and the undemocratic, monistic impulse, drawing from the same sources in America, have existed side by side. It is perhaps the ultimate paradox that extremist movements in this country have been powerfully spawned by the same American characteristics that finally rejected them.

The following two chapters are predominantly historical in nature, sketching the development of right-wing political movements in nineteenth-century America. The surface issues changed from one period to another, but the essential nature of right-wing extremism did not change; and certain essential aspects of national social and political life which shaped political extremism in the nineteenth century continue to shape it today.

Notes

1. T. V. Smith and Eduard C. Lindeman, *The Democratic Way of Life* (New York: Mentor, 1951), p. 91.
2. Edward A. Shils, *The Torment of Secrecy* (Glencoe: The Free Press, 1956), p. 154.
3. William Kornhauser, *The Politics of Mass Society* (New York: The Free Press, 1959), pp. 102–107.
4. The term "monism" has, of course, been used before in a political context. For example, Hans J. Morgenthau refers to "the monistic assumption of a monopoly of political truth vested in a minority . . ." in *The Restoration of American Politics* (Chicago: University of Chicago Press, 1962), p. 74; and William Kornhauser develops a typology of political societies using the term *op. cit.*, p. 105.
5. Phyllis Schlafly, *A Choice Not an Echo* (Alton, Ill.: Pere Marquette Press, 1964), p. 90.
6. Elizabeth Linington, *Come to Think of It* (Boston: Western Islands, 1965), p. 78.
   Dean Clarence Manion, *Let's Face It* (South Bend, Ind.: Manion Forum, 1956), p. 8.
7. This is a sample of 400 people who, in 1963, wrote letters to a U.S. Senator protesting a speech in which he attacked right-wing "extremism." A more detailed description of this sample is presented in Chapter 11.
8. Manion, *op. cit.*, p. 3.
9. Verne Paul Kaub, *Collectivism Challenges Christianity* (Madison, Wisc.: American Council of Christian Laymen, 1961), p. XV.
10. Robert Welch, "With Two Revolutions at Once," *American Opinion* (October 1965), p. 21.
11. Schlafly, *op. cit.*, p. 93.
12. Dan Smoot, *The Invisible Government* (Boston: Western Islands, 1962), p. 135.
13. Manion, *op. cit.*, p. 20.
14. "90% of Students Are Backed by Welch," *New York Times*, December 7, 1969, p. 44.
15. Sidney L. DeLove, *The Quiet Betrayal* (Chicago: Independence Hall of Chicago, 1960), p. 33.
16. Garet Garett, *The People's Pottage* (Boston: Western Islands, 1965), p. 65.
17. John Beaty, *The Iron Curtain over America* (Barboursville, W. Va.: Chestnut Mountain Books, 1962), p. 157.
18. Joseph R. McCarthy, *America's Retreat from Victory* (Boston: Western Islands, 1965), p. 135.
19. John A. Stormer, *None Dare Call It Treason* (Florissant, Mo.: Liberty Bell Press, 1964), p. 93.
20. Ezra Taft Benson, *A Nation Asleep* (Salt Lake City: Bookcraft, 1963), p. 13.

21. Schlafly, *op. cit.*, p. 17.
22. Benson, *op. cit.*, p. 11.
23. Beaty, *op. cit.*, p. 191.
24. Stormer, *op. cit.*, p. 92.
25. Manion, *op. cit.*, p. 4.
26. Kaub, *op. cit.*, p. 229.
27. Billy James Hargis, *The Real Extremists—The Far Left* (Tulsa: Christian Crusade, 1964), p. 16.
28. Manion, *op. cit.*, p. 142.
29. DeLove, *op. cit.*, p. 87.
30. Robert Welch, *A Brief Introduction to the John Birch Society* (Belmont: John Birch Society, 1962), p. 7.
31. John H. Bunzel, *Anti-Politics in America* (New York: Knopf, 1967).
32. Cited in *ibid.*, p. 8.
33. *Ibid.*, p. 9.
34. David Danzig, "The Radical Right and the Rise of the Fundamentalist Minority," *Commentary*, XXXIII (April 1962), 291–298.
35. Daniel Bell, "The Dispossessed—1962," in Daniel Bell, ed., *The Radical Right* (New York: Doubleday, 1963), p. 21.
36. Bunzel, *op. cit.*, p. 22.
37. John R. Silber, as quoted in Nan Robertson, "The Student Scene: Angry Militants," *New York Times,* November 20, 1967, p. 30.
38. Shils, *op. cit.*, p. 98.
39. Beaty, *op. cit.*, p. 229.
40. McCarthy, *op. cit.*, pp. 135–136.
41. Richard Hofstadter, *The Paranoid Style in American Politics* (New York: Knopf, 1965), p. 14.
42. William Guy Carr, *Pawns in the Game* (Toronto: National Federation of Christian Laymen, 1956), p. 1.
43. *Ibid.*, p. 12.
44. *Ibid.*, p. 13.
45. Lyman Beecher, *A Plea for the West* (Cincinnati: Truman and Smith, 1835), p. 93.
46. William Guy Carr, *News Behind the News*, II (July–August 1958), 2.
47. John H. Rousselot, *Congressional Record*, Tuesday, June 12, 1962.
48. John T. Flynn, *While You Slept* (Boston: Western Islands, 1965), p. 33.
49. DeLove, *op. cit.*, p. 91.
50. David A. Noebel, *Communism, Hypnotism and the Beatles* (Tulsa: Christian Crusade Publications, 1965), p. 1.
51. Conde McGinley, *Common Sense*, XIII (October 1, 1958), 3.
52. Norman Cohn, *The Pursuit of the Millennium* (London: Secker and Warburg, 1957), pp. 309–310.
53. Karl Popper, "Critiques of Classical Theories of History," in Patrick Gardiner, ed., *Theories of History* (Glencoe: The Free Press, 1959), p. 282.
54. William Roy McPherson, *Parallels in Extremist Ideology* (Ph.D. Thesis, Department of Social Relations, Harvard University, 1967).
55. *Ibid.*, p. 16.
56. *Ibid.*, p. 129.
57. *Loc cit.*
58. *Ibid.*, p. 124.

59. *Ibid.*, p. 137.
60. *Ibid.*, p. 85.
61. *Ibid.*, p. 96.
62. G. B. Rush, Speech at Annual Meeting of the Pacific Sociological Association, Portland, Oregon, April 25, 1963. Rush's analysis and concepts are laid out in considerable detail in his *Status Crystallization and Right-Wing Extremist Attitudes* (Ph.D. Thesis, Department of Sociology, University of Oregon, 1965), pp. 38–65.
63. Neil J. Smelser, *The Theory of Collective Behavior* (New York: The Free Press, 1963).
64. Robert K. Merton, *Social Theory and Social Structure* (Glencoe: The Free Press, 1957), pp. 167–169.
65. Morgenthau, *Op. cit.*, p. 29.

2

Before the Civil War

The strains giving rise to new political movements in America have typically been characterized by the emergence of new groups and the displacement of others, with some pattern of these cleavages: economic interest, regional or urban-rural residence, ethnic-racial origin, or ideological-religious commitment. These sets of politicizing differences have often been intrinsically related to one another.

The earliest years of the American nation saw the development of such patterns of ascendancy and displacement, with attendant political movements and monistic tendencies. Before the turn of the eighteenth century the mercantile interests, centered in New England and the seaboard cities, began to feel the displacing pressure of the farmers, expanding into the new frontier. Associated with the threatened lapse in power of the old New England elite was that of the Congregational church, disestablished by the Revolution and now being challenged by deviationists and worse.

"The revolution of 1800," as Jefferson called it, was the first thrust of the new, the agricultural populists and the religious irregulars. The Federalists found themselves in a position which was to recur again and again for conservative parties in American history. They could not win elections by appealing to narrow class interest, nor by too openly assailing the more egalitarian line of their opponents.

The camp of displacement and preservatism, threatened with distasteful social change and political impotence, responded with the basic model of monistic logic which was also to be repeated often in similar circumstances throughout American history: the cause of the distress was a group of evil and conspiratorial—therefore politically illegitimate—men; the remedy was to repress such men by any means, as a matter of high morality.

Remarkably, the continuity of this design down through the years is dramatized by the fact that the first full-fledged conspiracy theory introduced in the 1790's, that of the Illuminati, kept replaying the American scene, most recently in the 1960's. An organization called the Illuminati had indeed been formed in Bavaria in 1776 by Adam Weishaupt, a professor of law, as a secret Masonic society which opposed the Jesuits and advocated its own version of anticlerical Enlightenment doctrines. It never had more than a few thousand members and was suppressed by the Elector of Bavaria in 1785.[1]

The Augsburg Jesuits advanced the theory that the Illuminati were behind the effort to spread the French Revolution. This plot theory was in turn taken up by a Scottish scientist, John Robison, in a book published in 1797, *Proofs of a Conspiracy Against All the Religions and Governments of Europe, carried on in the Secret Meetings of Free Masons, Illuminati and Reading Societies*. This work was reprinted in New York in the following year. At about the same time, a Jesuit, the Abbé Barruel, published a four-volume tract, *Mémoires pour servir à l'histoire du Jacobinisme*. Translated into English and published in England and the United States, this work also argued that "there was a 'triple conspiracy' of anti-Christians, Freemasons, and Illuminati to destroy religion and order."[2]

The Barruel version of the conspiracy argued that it dated back to the Middle Ages with the conversion of the Order of the Templars into a secret society after their suppression in 1314. The purpose of the society was supposedly to overthrow monarchies and the papacy, to preach total liberty, and to create a world republic which it would dominate. The Freemasons were captured by the secret society in the eighteenth century. In France, men like Voltaire, Turgot, Condorcet, and the Abbé Sieyès supposedly worked with it and helped to create a revolutionary organization which was to make the Great French Revolution. The controlling center of the conspiracy, however, was the Bavarian Illuminati led by Adam Weishaupt.[3]

The Robison work, which was to have the most important influence in the United States, argued that the Illuminati were both the tools of the Jesuits and of the opponents of irreligion. It sought to defend Protestantism against all possible enemies, religious and political. "Illuminatism presented the threat of both 'popery' and 'atheism'; politically it could lead to the return of absolutism, or equally bad, the rise of radical democracy. The Jesuit, the atheist, and the political revolutionary had in common the demand on the individual for absolute loyalty. . . ."[4] The Illuminati image therefore provided all the basic elements of a perfect conspiracy theory:

it was based on a seed of truth, the one-time existence of a secret society of that name; it posited a comprehensive conspiracy, with world-wide network and immodest goals; because it was so secret and vague, it was flexible enough to serve any given purpose; it had been associated at one time with a core of "intellectuals"; it carried with it some arcane literature that could be brought into "hard" evidence.

The Illuminati plot theory was introduced into the United States by a prominent Boston Congregationalist minister, Jedidiah Morse, who secured a prepublication copy of Robison's book and delivered two sermons on it in May 1798.[5]

He solemnly announced that the world was in the grip of a secret revolutionary conspiracy, engineered by the Order of the Illuminati—that Genêt's clubs of five years before had been surface manifestations of this underground plot, and that the Republicans in America . . . were the dupes and accomplices of this same pernicious organization, which labored everywhere, at all times, patiently, implacably, and behind the scenes, to overthrow all government and all religion.[6]

Timothy Dwight, the president of Yale, delivered a Fourth of July speech, two months after Morse's sermons, in which he asked dramatically: "Shall our sons become the disciples of Voltaire, and the dragoons of Marat; or our daughters the concubines of the Illuminati?"[7] The notion of a great conspiracy of the Illuminati was now taken up by the New England clergy. One received the impression that "the country was swarming with them."[8]

The plot was given direct partisan connotations. One Federalist wrote that Dwight's speech had convinced him that Jefferson

". . . is the *real Jacobin*, the very child of *modern illumination*, the foe of man, and the enemy of his country." Another argued that the zeal of the Democrats for office was to be treated as a part of the scheme of Illuminatism in America "to worm its votaries into all offices of trust, and importance, that the weapon of government, upon signal given, may be turned against itself." Still another contended that the one concern of the Democrats of Connecticut was to dispense "to the people of this state the *precious doctrines* of the Illuminati."[9]

In 1799, Morse, who had introduced the Illuminati to America, reported that he could prove what had long been suspected: "that secret societies, under the influence and direction of France, holding principles subversive of our religion and government, existed somewhere in this country." And in words prescient of a junior Senator from Wisconsin a century and a half in the future, he announced:

I have now in my possession complete and indubitable proof that such societies do exist, and have for many years existed, in the United States. I have, my brethren, an official, authenticated list of the names, ages, places of nativity, professions, etc. of the officers and members of a Society of *Illuminati* . . . consisting of *one hundred* members, instituted in Virginia, by the *Grand Orient* of FRANCE. . . . How many of equal rank they have established among us that I am not informed.

You will perceive, my brethren . . . that we have in truth secret enemies . . . whose professed design is to subvert and overturn our holy religion and our free and excellent government. . . . Among these fruits [of their endeavors] may be reckoned our unhappy and threatening political divisions; the increasing abuse of our wise and faithful rulers; the virulent opposition to some of the laws of our country; and the measures of the Supreme Executive; the Pennsylvania insurrection . . . the industrious circulation of baneful and corrupting books, and the consequent wonderful spread of infidelity, impiety, and immorality; . . . and lastly, the apparently systematic endeavor made to destroy, not only the influence and support, but the official existence of the Clergy.[10]

The invocation of general immorality, including the distribution of "corrupting books," has always been an essential part of conspiracy theories, pinning down the evil quality of the conspirators which is the ultimate basis for considering them politically illegitimate in the normative political market place. The belief that a conspiracy emanating from France threatened the American republic had been voiced by George Washington and John Adams before Jedidiah Morse had concretized it in the Masonic Order of the Illuminati. It is not surprising, therefore, that many Federalists seized on the supposed evidence of the existence of the Illuminati plot as a means of reducing the legitimacy of their opponents. If much of the opposition was linked to an evil foreign-controlled conspiracy, government would be justified in taking strong measures against them.

This logic led to the passage of the Alien and Sedition Acts designed to protect the country against both foreign and domestic supporters of Jacobinism. The language of the Alien Enemies Act was explicit in its concern with conspiratorial activities, giving the President authority to deport all aliens "he shall judge dangerous to the peace and safety of the United States, or shall have reasonable grounds to suspect are concerned in any treasonable or *secret machinations* against the government."[11]

However, the agitation concerning the Illuminati gradually disappeared as it became clear that the advocates of the existence of the conspiracy could not locate any hard evidence concerning its activities in America. They found it impossible to produce any facts to meet the demand of the Jeffersonians that they submit materials which could lead to prosecutions of the plotters.

Thus, the dilemma of conspiracy theories was revealed early in American history. On the one hand, the purported conspiracies are necessarily shadowy affairs, conducted by hidden figures in secret parlors. On the other hand, it is difficult to sustain a popular concern with a conspiracy unless there is some fleshly referent to its existence. A political conspiracy theory, after all, is a matter of personifying the causes of some social strain. Apparently this personification cannot remain very abstract and be persuasive. It is not usually enough to corporealize a plot theory by identifying a vague group of elite intellectuals as the prime manipulators. It is helpful to have a more concretely identifiable group that can be seen as associated with the prime manipulators, as their natural reservoir of support, their fellow travelers, their particular witting or unwitting instruments.

The other side of that coin is that a plot theory will presumably gain popular support only when there is some salient social strain which that theory will serve the purpose of "explaining"; and the plot theory is most cogent when the social strain can itself be personified through that theory.

So it is that through most of America's history, ethnic groups have served as a key link between extremist groups, the social strains they have addressed themselves to, and the plot theories with which they explained these strains. These ethnic groups have often been used to flesh out both the strain and the conspiracy.

The early Illuminati furor did not have such a corporeal target. And it is significant that the vague and hidden Illuminati began to be replaced as a target by the flesh-and-blood Society of United Irishmen, which had been founded in the United States in August 1797. Federalist spokesmen charged that it was a copy of the Jacobins in France. When Irish rebels, aided by France, rose in revolt in the summer of 1798, this seemed to prove the link between the Irish in Ireland and America and the French revolutionaries. The Federalist *Gazette of the United States* argued that this revolt proved the existence of plots stimulated by the "*secret spirit of the Illuminati*" and suggested that the Irish who had failed at home were now conspiring in alliance with the French Jacobins in America.[12] John Fenno, the editor of the paper, wrote that the United Irishmen were a group of assassins and asked other editors to keep an eye on the activities of the Irish.

The Federalists, as a declining party after 1800, also initiated the pattern of the more preservatist party seeking to appeal to popular prejudices against immigrants as a means of winning the mass support which their conservative ideology prevented them from gaining. Considerable prejudice had developed against Irish immigrants, on grounds similar to those which would be evoked all through American history against "those whose ways were different . . . intensified by the glaring inferiorities in the standards of living among the newcomers. Not only were they different in race, religion, and political tradition, but uncouth, uncleanly, ignorant, unskilled, and frequently immoral."[13] On Christmas Day, 1806, a bloody riot developed in New York City between mobs of nativists and Irishmen, in which many were hurt and a number of houses were looted.

The Federalists, who were now out of power in New York and found that the immigrant vote was going to their Jeffersonian opponents, turned to overt nativism as an electoral tactic. A leading party paper described the party slate in New York in 1807 as the "American ticket."

The name was taken up with great enthusiasm; it announced that nativism was accepted as the leading issue and it was used as the party designation for several years. "I observe that your ticket in New York is called the American ticket," wrote Colonel Troup to [Rufus] King. "Would not this be a favorable occasion of our party to assume a popular and significant name, free from the hobgoblins attached by many to Federalism?"[14]

Similar tactics designed to make the party "more reputable with the scorned, but now all powerful 'average men' " were followed in Massachusetts and Pennsylvania as well. The Hartford Convention called by the New England Federalists to oppose the War of 1812 proposed that the Federal Constitution be amended to bar naturalized citizens from holding any public office.[15] Meanwhile the surge of Irish immigrants to this country was visibly on the increase.

The Anti-Masonic Movement

The time was ripe, then, for adding larger quantities of the "missing element," the ethnic element, to the plot formula, when the traditionalists and the camp of displacement faced an even more serious crisis in the late 1820's. A conservative member of the Adams family was again in the White House, but clearly was in political difficulty. This time, the Jacksonians and the common man stood ready to take over the government, with the skeptic and the new urban workingman in the wings. As the first major history of the Anti-Masonic party put it:

The first thing that strikes our attention upon closer inspection is that this agitation occurred in the remarkable period of the Jacksonian Democracy, an era in America of the Renaissance of the Rights of Man, and of renewed Jeffersonianism. It was a period, too, of the extension of the franchise, of humanitarian movements such as temperance, abolition of capital punishment, and of imprisonment for debt, of the struggle for workingmen's rights, of educational reforms, of Owenism, of Fanny Wrightism, of the beginnings of the Abolition agitation, and of many other equally radical movements. In religion also it was an age of free thought discussion, struggles over dogma, and with it a strong reactionary spirit which was almost fanatical in its hatred of the new French ideas and of Unitarianism and free thought in general. . . . Europe was occupied with the French and Polish revolutions which especially excited American sympathies.[16]

The Anti-Masonic movement represented perhaps the first example in the United States of a preservatist antielitist mass movement based on the more provincial and traditional elements in the society; it was a sociological precursor of movements like the Ku Klux Klan and McCarthyism. Its enemy was the Order of the Masons, a group which presumably consisted of the "select class in the community."[17] The combination of antielitism and preservatism found in Anti-Masonry may be understood by reference to the fears not only of the declining elitist opponents of Andrew Jackson but of the embattled devotees of orthodox religion.

Organized traditional evangelical religion had been under attack from liberals and deists. Many of the Democratic-Republican leaders tended to look upon much of organized religion and the evangelical theologies as outmoded beliefs which would dwindle away. As in the case of the European Enlightenment thinkers, they saw the modern world of the early nineteenth century as growing beyond the superstitions which were regarded as hangovers from medieval and monarchical society. Many argued explicitly that the United States was not a Christian nation in any sense. This opposition to any link with religion led in 1810 to the passage by Congress of a law which provided that the mail should be delivered seven days a week.[18] The evangelical denominations sought to resist these trends and formed various organizations to support the sanctity of the Lord's Day. In spite of such efforts, Congress in 1825 extended the requirements that the federal government provide public services on Sunday.[19] In 1829, a committee of the United States Senate stated explicitly that religion and irreligion had equal rights in the United States. The Senate report went on to say that to declare Sunday a day of rest, or to curtail government services on Sunday, would constitute an injustice against irreligious people or non-Christians.

This position was fostered by the Jacksonians in Congress. It was reiterated in another congressional report in 1830.[20] The author of both reports, Richard M. Johnson, was a prominent spokesman of the Jacksonian democracy and was subsequently nominated and elected Vice-President in 1836. A contemporary account stated that he achieved his great popularity among the Democrats for his stand on religion and that the "Report has made Richard M. Johnson Vice-President of the United States."[21] The struggle of the religiously orthodox to resist these liberal doctrines almost inevitably involved an attack on Masonry, which had been associated by conservatives "with the secret, infidel orders of Revolutionary France: with deism, radicalism, and terrorism."[22] During the early 1820's, a number of religious bodies insisted that one could not be a member of their church and also belong to the Masons.[23]

Increasingly, the religiously orthodox felt at odds with the spirit of the times. A number of religious books were published in 1826 attacking Masonry. The event which sparked the Anti-Masonic movement was the disappearance and presumed murder of an unemployed bricklayer, William Morgan. Morgan, who had belonged to the Masons, was writing an exposé of Masonry. The Masons made various efforts to prevent the book from being published, including burning a press which was setting up the book. The final drastic effort to stop publication involved kidnaping Morgan from jail at Canandaigua, New York, where he was being held on a charge of having stolen a shirt and tie. The warrant had been secured by the master of the Canandaigua Masonic lodge. Morgan was never seen again, and there is some evidence that he was murdered by his Masonic kidnapers.[24]

The Anti-Masonic movement first took the form of committees seeking to learn the truth about Morgan's disappearance. Many books and articles appeared outlining the heinous crimes of the Masons. The first convention of Anti-Masons held in Leroy, New York, in March 1828 took steps to further the work of exposure and destruction of Masonry. The convention charged the "entire subjugation [of the press] throughout the Union to the control of Free Masonry" and proposed "the establishment of free presses," which would expose the hidden conspiracy.[25] Many newspapers were soon started. By 1830, the Anti-Masons claimed that they had begun 124 papers, mainly in rural areas, dedicated to educating the public about Masonry.

Convinced that most public officeholders were Masons, the Anti-Masons also decided that they must enter politics as a separate party. By 1828, a functioning party which elected six state senators and 17 assemblymen was operating in New York State. On September 11, 1830, the party held a national convention in Philadelphia, the first such convention in American political history. On the level of state politics, it attained considerable strength, electing governors in Vermont and Pennsylvania. In Massachusetts, 150 of the 490 elected to the lower house in 1831 were Anti-Masons, and the successful National Republican candidate for governor declared himself in favor of the abolition of Masonry. In Rhode Island, an Anti-Mason became speaker of the house in 1831.[26] In New York, the state in which it was born, the party's candidate for governor secured close to half of the vote in 1830.[27]

Basically, the Masons were seen as a conspiratorial order of evil, immoral men who sought to control politics and community life. Church groups passed resolutions denouncing the order as not only anti-Christian but also engaged in profanity and sinful revelry.[28] "Masonry . . . [was] portrayed as a secret, sinister monster with powerful tentacles which reached everywhere and threatened everybody."[29] As concern over Morgan's disappearance died down, many of the Anti-Masonic papers published accounts of other "Masonic Murders," charging that the Masons had killed a number of their opponents.[30] The editors of the Anti-Masonic almanacs which were distributed widely to the rural population "called forth the passions: fear—terror of Masonic conspiracy, whether designed against Justice, Religion, the Constitution or against the Virtue of one's wife or daughter."[31]

There was clearly much in this Anti-Masonic movement reminiscent of the earlier conspiracy theories about the Illuminati. Given the fact that this second attack on Masonry occurred but a quarter of a century after the first, and that it had somewhat similar roots, it is highly probable that men who had believed in the first conspiracy were active in promoting the idea of the second one. And "indeed, the works of writers like Robison and Barruel were often cited again as evidence of the sinister character of Masonry."[32] The state convention of the Massachusetts Anti-Masonic party in 1828 appointed a committee to look into the matter of the Illuminati. The committee reported its conviction that there was a direct connection between the Illuminati and the Masons. The convention of 1830 passed a resolution: "Resolved, on the report of the committee appointed to inquire how far Free Masonry and French Illuminism are connected. That *there is evidence* of an intimate connection between the high orders of Free Masonry and French Illuminism."[33] The Vermont party convention in the same year also received a report from an investigatory committee which suggested that a conspiracy had existed to quell the knowledge contained in the various exposés of the Illuminati by Robison, Barruel, Morse, and Payson.[34]

It is not surprising, therefore, that a comparative analysis of the attacks of the late 1790's with those of Anti-Masonry concludes that "there was a tradition of Anti-Masonry carried from the earlier generation to the later one, that the rhetoric of Anti-Masonry was almost identical in each period."[35]

However, there were several significant differences between the first and second wave. By the 1820's, America's democratic values had become more explicit and more unassailable. The Anti-Masons of the 1820's viewed American democracy in positive terms and identified the Masonic elite as plotters against the millennial reform mission of America. "In both . . . stages of Antimasonry, Masonry had been made to stand for all evil in the world. In both stages Masonry was a symbol of potential conspiracy against America. In 1827 this appeal was made to a country self-conscious of the mission it was thought destined to perform."[36] In political terms, this meant that the Anti-Masonic movement was designed to appeal directly to the larger populace. In the same vein, the second wave differed from the first in not being directly linked to the preservation of the rights of a single established church, the Congregationalists, as was the early anti-Illuminati agitation. Rather, the second movement was concerned with defending evangelical religion generally against "the last great effort on the part of the forces of darkness to destroy religion."[37] The Masons were attacked as "an 'infidel society' at war with true Christianity."[38] It was argued that "Whatever was not for Christ was against Him; and Free-masonry was not for Christ since it admitted the fellowship of Jews, Mohammedans and deists."[39]

Thus, the Anti-Masonic movement of the 1820's and 1830's was able to identify the Masons with various other foes of evangelical Protestantism, and an ethnic corporealization of the conspiracy theory was introduced somewhat more strongly through the door of religious identification. While the liberal religions, Unitarianism and Universalism, were also anathema to Anti-Masons,[40] the Catholics and even the Jews received heavy emphasis as the personae of the plot.

Masonry, Roman Catholic Faith, Monks, and the Inquisition were put in the same class. "Popery and Free-Masonry" were considered as "schemes equally inconsistent with republicanism," and any victory over the "horrid oath-binding systems" was an "emancipation from the very fangs of despotism."[41]

Bitterly resenting Masonic claims to ancient tradition and Christian sanction, anti-Masons charged that the Order was of recent origin, that it was shaped by Jews, Jesuits, and French atheists as an engine for spreading infidelity, and that it was employed by kings and aristocrats to undermine republican institutions. Their charge was often repeated that higher degrees of Freemasonry were created by the "school of Voltaire" and "introduced to America by Jewish immigrants."[42]

This emphasis merged with more direct strands of nativism, of antagonism to foreign immigrants as expressed by some Anti-Masonic leaders. Benjamin Hallett, the editor of the party's Boston organ, the *Free Press*, proposed to the delegates of the Massachusetts state convention of 1834 that they "address 'a memorial to Congress, praying for an alteration in the laws relating to the naturalization of foreigners, so as to increase the pre-requisite qualifications, before the exercise of the rights citizenship, and re-quiring a renunciation of all oaths of allegiance or service to secret societies.' . . ."[43]

The Anti-Masonic movement, with its broader appeal, effected the first *mariage de convenance* between a displaced elite and an unstable mass. The instability of the mass seems to depend on two kinds of factors: (1) Some discontent, related to economic or symbolic disprivilege; (2) A low level of education, which is presumably related to bigotry and a lack of commitment to the values of pluralistic democracy;[44] (3) A condition of "political disorganization" characterized by traditional political loyalties and alignments breaking down or being in high flux. Political disorganization was certainly characteristic of the new nation in the early years of the nineteenth century. No strong and coherent national political parties in the modern sense had developed. After the decline of the Federalists in 1820, the only "party" holding the field was the Democratic Republicans. But in 1828, when Jackson defeated the conservative John Quincy Adams, his conservative opposition coalesced in a formal political configuration. This was the National Republicans, basically Federalist in tradition and economically conservative in thrust. At that point economic conservatives—businessmen—were interested in government assistance, as were a sector of farmers who also supported the National Republican party. There were a set of cultural issues which also separated them from the Jacksonian Democrats, reminiscent of the earlier preservatist temper of the Federalists. The National Republican party was interested in preserving the religious and moral verities: old-time religion, the Sunday laws, and so forth.

But another political party sprang up in preservatist opposition to the more "liberal" less evangelical Democrats. This was the Anti-Masonic party, whose social base was much lower on the economic scale and whose main political program had to do with cultural, not economic, preservatism. Their political activity was conducted mainly on a state level. While their program was essentially antielitist in nature, they and the elitist National Republicans found various alliances politically convenient, until by the mid 30's they had effectively coalesced into the Whig party in all states except Pennsylvania and Vermont. The coalescence was typical of what was to follow in American history. The Whig party did not endorse the more extreme doctrines of Anti-Masonry, but was essentially the more conservative party, and fostered a program of cultural preservatism.

In America, such a *mariage de convenance* between tendencies appealing to a segment of the masses as well as to the economically affluent is obviously critical to the life of any conservatively oriented movement. This is the political background against which the Anti-Masonic movement of this period must be seen.

It is true that "Antimasonry was essentially a New England movement." Most of its leaders came from there. Areas in other states that had been settled by New Englanders tended to constitute its principal electoral centers of strength.[45]

But the movement's other key social characteristic was its appeal to the less privileged, less educated, more ecologically isolated rural population, with its already growing sense of conflict with the urban centers of affluence, culture, change, and immigration. An analysis of the party support in western New York, its main center of strength in that state, reported that it lay in the regions "removed from the cosmopolitan life of the Erie canal towns."[46]

Its strongest state was Vermont, the state with the smallest urban population, which was also furthest removed from major metropolitan centers. In Massachusetts and Pennsylvania, the party's strength lay almost entirely in rural areas, which resembled those of western New York. The two counties carried by the Anti-Masons in the former state "were made up mainly of agricultural communities with no cities or towns of any considerable size."[47]

The party's weakness in urban areas, including even relatively small towns, may be due to the influence of the Masons, who often included most of the influential elite, but also undoubtedly stemmed from its overt hostility to urban life. In Pennsylvania, the party was identified with "hatred of Philadelphia." The address of its 1829 convention stated: "The country has generally looked upon the city as overweening, arrogant and dictatorial."[48] In New York State, "the movement may justly be described as an early evidence of rural jealousy toward urban superiority. . . ."[49]

There is some limited impressionistic evidence that the support of Anti-Masonry came from the less educated and less well-to-do groups. Thus, Thurlow Weed, one of the prominent leaders of Anti-Masonry in western New York, wrote in his *Autobiography* that "While Anti-Masonic sentiment was strong among the farmers, it was weak in the villages, especially among the wealthy and influential classes."[50]

The *New York Whig*, edited by an Anti-Mason, wrote in 1832, "It has been a reproach to our [Anti-Masonic] cause that it takes first among the lower classes."[51] John Quincy Adams, one of the few prominent politicians to lend some support to Anti-Masonry, wrote in 1834 that the movement "came from the . . . less educated and most numerous class of the population."[52] A Report of the National Corresponding Committee of the Anti-Masonic party explicitly pointed up their appeal to the less educated, while engaging in a variety of anti-intellectualism in its attack on the Masons.

> Wherever anti-masons go, they promulgate their opinions, and the facts they rest on. . . . It is due to the "blessed spirit"—the spirit of anti-masonry—to declare, that it makes eloquent the tongue of its humblest possessor; insomuch that the unsophisticated but intelligent yeoman, imbued with it, proves himself . . . an overmatch for the learned defenders of the secret order.[53]

The appeal of Anti-Masonry to the unattached, the uninvolved, less privileged elements is also suggested by an examination of the effect of Anti-Masonic participation in elections. Studies of electoral participation in recent times agree, in a number of countries under varying conditions, that the nonvoters tend to be composed largely of the less privileged and less educated, who are also uninvolved in the normal political communications system. Whenever there is a sharp increase in turnout, it tends to come, therefore, from this stratum. Data from Vermont and Massachusetts indicate that the entry of the Anti-Masons in the race brought a sharp increase in the numbers voting, presumably from elements such as described above. Thus, in Massachusetts, between 1825 and 1829, no election brought as many as 30 per cent to the polls. However, "the Antimasons did succeed in bringing to the polls men to whom the major parties had little appeal. Voter participation rose markedly after 1830."[54]

The same thing happened in Vermont. The proportion voting increased from less than 30 per cent, before the entry of the new party, to over 50. "The Antimasons undoubtedly attracted the major portion of those 'new' voters."[55]

The appeal of the anti-Jacksonian and antielitist, conservative, religious Anti-Masons to important sectors of the rural population gave to preservatist politicians an opportunity to recruit a mass base from groups which, on the basis of their economic position, might have been expected to back Andrew Jackson.

The Antimasonic movement, in view of the parlous situation in which the conservatives found themselves, must have appeared to men like Weed and Granger as being in the nature of a heaven-sent opportunity. Here was a cause . . . with such a potent appeal to democratic instincts in general that, skilfully used, it might prove the salvation of the conservative interests.[56]

The Anti-Masonic movement illustrated another pattern which was to characterize many extremist movements in America: the pattern of success-in-failure. The Anti-Masonic movement failed to become a cogent political party, partly because it was absorbed by a main-stream party. But some of the emphases of the Anti-Masonic movement were absorbed as well and thus came to political fruition.

In order to create a viable electoral opponent to the Jacksonian Democrats, the National Republicans needed an alliance with the Anti-Masons. Such a realignment was difficult to create in various states, but ultimately it came about through the conscious efforts of a number of politicians. The alliance ultimately culminated in the Whig party. Anti-Masonry came to an end with this merger. The crusade against Masonry had seemingly triumphed, since membership in the Order dropped tremendously during the Anti-Masonic crusade. The Northern Whig party accepted many of the moral strictures which concerned the Anti-Masons with respect to Sunday blue laws, temperance, and antislavery. This alliance and subsequent merger between the relatively uneducated believers in hidden conspiracies and the privileged, well-educated Whig conservatives, many of whom were or had been Masons, was to be the first of a number of occasions in which extremist bigotry was to find its political home in the conservative Whig or Republican parties. And the fact that the latter could derive considerable support from the less well-to-do more bigoted elements by showing some receptivity to their concerns has confounded those who look for a clear-cut class division between the two parties. The conservative party has been able at different times to unite the more affluent economic conservatives with those less privileged, less educated, and more susceptible to the monistic impulse.

Later Movements: The Native Americans and Know-Nothings

The creation of a successful monistic movement, combining an elite leadership and a mass base, apparently depends to some extent on the ability to corporealize both the social strains felt by the unstable mass and the conspiracy theory which purports to explain that strain. Ethnically identifiable population groups have served that purpose well in America. The heavy immigration by ethnic groups who have introduced "un-Protestant" and "un-American" values and modes of behavior into this society has often been blamed by displaced strata as the main source of the threat to their values or position. Economic unrest has engendered mass anti-immigrant and anti-Catholic movements among the less privileged classes, since "alien" competition for jobs has been perceived as the cause of unemployment. And loss of elections, the growth of urban machine politics, and changes in general state of social morality commonly have been interpreted by groups losing their economic, social, political, or religious dominance as the fault of foreign and non-Protestant groups who, by their presence or activities, have undermined the traditional structure of status and authority. Arising out of common circumstances, many of these nativist movements have been closely interlinked with the other organized expressions of Protestant morality. And because nativism has so openly identified religious and ethnic group appeals, it has been of primary importance in structuring and maintaining the correlations between membership in specific religious and ethnic groups and party choice.

The early Anti-Masonic movements had begun to invoke this ethnic dimension, largely as antagonism to Catholicism which blurred with opposition to the Irish who gave dramatic and visible body to the presence of Catholicism in this country. This line was advanced considerably in the 1830's and 1840's, following on the rapid increase of the Irish Catholic population, with the organization of various nativist Protestant parties and associations known as Native Americans.[57]

Protestant antagonism to Catholic immigration not only stemmed from religious feeling but was undoubtedly related to the fact that Catholic immigrants, as the most recent newcomers, lived in the worst urban slums. The typical characteristics of slum dwellers of the period were stereotyped as Catholic, just as today they are often identified with Negroes, Puerto Ricans, or Mexicans. Much of the negative feeling about Catholics, then, was the reaction of the clean middle class to the poorest, least educated, dirtiest, most criminal section of the urban population. As early as the 1830's, the

disproportionately large number of foreign-born in almshouses was repeatedly emphasized by writers who made a conscious effort to depict them as lazy and indolent, content either to accept public charity or beg upon the streets but unwilling to do the necessary hard work which the country required. . . . Nativists . . . [pointed to] the large number of criminals among the aliens and the increase in crime since their coming in the same way.[58]

In 1850, more than half of those convicted of criminal offenses were foreign-born, though those from abroad represented only 11 per cent of the national population. Proportionately, ten times as many foreign as native-born were receiving public support as paupers.[59]

A New York State census in 1855 revealed that half of the Irish in New York City were either unskilled workers or domestic servants, while in Boston almost two-thirds were in such jobs.[60] Such facts were often gathered and publicized by nativist groups as evidence of the inherent inferiority and propensity to immoral behavior of those of non British-Protestant origin.

In addition, strong antipapist sentiments still existed among various Protestant denominations, particularly those with "dissenting" and Puritanical traditions. Before the Civil War there were many political and religious charlatans who were prepared to manufacture all sorts of horror stories about what went on in convents, monasteries, and other Catholic institutions. These atrocity stories had a great vogue. Former Catholics, some of whom claimed to have been priests, nuns, or monks, toured lecture circuits with speeches "exposing" these "foreign institutions."

Some religious conservatives, fearing a growing threat to their way of life in Catholic immigration, began to see signs of a plot by the hated Papists, by the Jesuit Order. The traditions of the nation were being undermined by hidden plotters. The very growth of the country, the increase in immigration which permitted many natives to move up, the publicity given urban symbols of status by the media, created insecurity as well as opportunities. Much of the insecurity was not experienced as economic, particularly among those who were intensely religious. They felt that their values, their concept of the good life and the good society were being undermined by the open society. As the historian David Brian Davis has well put it:

The exposure of subversion was a means of promoting unity but it also served to clarify national values and provide the individual ego with . . . [moral] righteousness. Nativists identified themselves repeatedly with a strange incoherent tradition in which images of Pilgrims, Minute Men, Founding Fathers, and true Christians appeared in a confusing montage. Opposed to this heritage of stability and perfect integrity, to this society founded on the highest principles of divine and natural law, were organizations formed by the grossest frauds and impostures, and based on the wickedest impulses of human nature. . . .

Moreover, the finest values of an enlightened nation stood out in bold relief when contrasted with the corrupting tendencies of subversive groups. Perversion of the sexual instinct seemed inevitably to accompany religious error. Deprived of the tender affections of normal married love, shut off from the elevating sentiments of fatherhood, Catholic priests looked on women only as insensitive objects for the gratification of their frustrated desires. . . .

In his image of an evil group conspiring against the nation's welfare, and in his vision of a glorious millennium that was to dawn after the enemy's defeat, the nativist found satisfaction for many desires. His own interests became legitimate and dignified by fusion with the national interest, and various opponents became loosely associated with the un-American conspiracy. . . .

In a rootless environment shaken by bewildering social change the nativist found unity and meaning by conspiring against imaginary conspiracies.[61]

The Catholics—somewhat like the Jews in the next century—provided a great foil for extremist purposes, because this visible body of ethnic immigrants was connected to images of secret, exotic, and conspiratorial institutions.

Again, the marriage of convenience between an embattled conservative elite and a mass base of the less privileged but bigoted was in order. Again it was reflected by a flirtation between the respectable preservatist party and the extremist movement. This time, however, there was a new partner to the marriage: the native Protestant workingman of the city.

The Anti-Masonic movement, as we have seen, drew most of its support from the religious rural population, generally among those somewhat removed from any urban influence. It had little or no support in the large cities and, in fact, evidenced hostility to the cities as centers of irreligiosity. Although antielitist in its attack on Freemasonry, it united ultimately with the conservatives of the National Republican party to form the Whigs. By so doing, it gave the Whigs a rural base among the relatively underprivileged which countered the appeal of the Jacksonians to other segments of the rural population. The nativist political movements which arose first in the 1840's, coalescing as the American Republican party, and then hitting a crescendo of power in the Know-Nothing American party of the 1850's, were to fulfill a similar function for the Whigs and Republicans in urban areas.

The nativists seemingly appealed to two sources of discontent among Protestants in addition to reflecting the traditional hostility and fear of the Catholic church: the first was the threat of the immigrant as a competitor for jobs; the second was the political power of the immigrants which seemingly reinforced the strength of the Democrats. The decision to turn the Native American associations into a third party was linked to the fact that the Whigs, although more sympathetic to nativism than the Democrats, refused to pass legislation favored by the anti-immigrant groups.[62] In New York, the state Whig party under the leadership of Governor William Seward sought to break the Catholic immigrant population from their Democratic allegiance by proposing to share state support for education, then going exclusively to the Protestant-oriented Public School Society, with Catholic parochial schools. Discouraged with both parties, the Native Americans in New York in 1843 established the American Republican party, which spread out to other cities in the state and along the coast. The party secured 23 per cent of the New York City vote in the election of that year, a fact which strongly impressed the Whigs. In 1844, the Whigs made a tacit alliance with the nativists, supporting their local and congressional candidates, in return for American Republican backing for the Presidential Whig ticket of Henry Clay and Theodore Frelinghuysen and for Millard Fillmore for governor of New York. The nativists were triumphant, electing six congressmen in New York City and Philadelphia and winning the mayoralty contests in New York and Boston. Clay and Fillmore, however, failed to carry New York State because 15,000 voters cast their ballots for the Liberty party abolitionist candidate. The alliance between the Whigs and the American Republicans was facilitated by the fact that Frelinghuysen, the Vice-Presidential candidate, was a prominent nativist. Millard Fillmore, the Whig gubernatorial nominee, and Vice-President and President from 1849 to 1853, was to appear on the national scene in 1856 as the Know-Nothing Presidential aspirant.

Since much of the Catholic immigration settled in the cities, the overt hostility to them was largely an urban phenomenon. Studies of the support of the American Republican party in New York and Boston, where it had won mayoralty contests in 1844, indicate that much of its base was working-class.

In Boston, an analysis of the backgrounds of the men participating in the movement, drawn from names listed in the party's newspaper, the *Eagle*, who were then located in the *Boston Directory* of 1845, revealed that they were "small shopkeepers, laborers and mechanics, with a sprinkling of professional men." The occupations listed as characteristic of party activists were "shipwrights, provision dealers, coachmen, mechanics, painters, glassblowers, a few physicians, etc." The newspaper files indicated that "no Bostonian, of any importance, was associated with the party."[63]

In New York, "a large majority of its adherents apparently were urban, native Protestants of skilled worker, mechanic, or lower middle class socioeconomic status, who resented competition and contact with immigrants of 'strange' cultures, faiths and languages."[64] Much of their vote in local elections came, of course, from traditional Whig voters, fulfilling their part of the bargain in the electoral alliances. It is noteworthy, however, that in the first election carried by the nativists in 1843, two of their strongest wards had almost always been among the top Democratic wards in preceding city elections. These were predominantly Protestant working-class districts. The wards which remained with the Democrats before and after the new party entered the elections "contained higher numbers of immigrants."[65]

An analysis of the backgrounds of 60 of the leaders of the party indicated that few "were ever really prominent in public affairs."[66] Twelve of them could not even be located in city directories. Of the remaining 48, 11 were "artisans," 3 were employed in the building trades, 10 were professionals, 10 were shopkeepers and dealers, 4 were financiers, while the rest were in varying white-collar and self-employed categories. Some, in fact, were quite wealthy, but the group as a whole "were chosen from what contemporaries called the 'respectable' element of society (with very little representation from the unskilled working class). . . ."[67]

As in Boston, the New York nativists increasingly sought to appeal to the skilled workers. One of their newspapers, the *Native Eagle and American Advocate*, concentrated on calling for "protection to American labor, by protecting the American laborer" and demanded restrictions on immigration.[68] This same view was expressed by many of the other papers which sprang into existence in a number of cities to capitalize on the success of the American Republican party. "The constant propaganda which they voiced against immigrants and Catholics proved effective particularly among the lower classes."[69] The Massachusetts party increasingly took on an explicit class character: "the party became more and more the laboring man's party until, by 1847, it was his active champion."

The *Boston Eagle* complained that the workingman was not only forced to compete with cheap labor but was also the victim of capitalistic legislation. The ten-hour day would never be accepted as long as there were foreign laborers who would work longer. . . . We can see no reason why the laborer has not the same right to protection on his capital (labor) that the rich man has on his which is money distinct from labor.[70]

More important perhaps than the direct effects of ongoing immigration, per se, in creating working-class support for nativism was the way in which the combination of technological innovation and mass immigration was undermining the status of the skilled workers. It was not poverty, nor even direct economic deprivation, that was disturbing these workingmen as much as a sense of status deprivation.

Skilled workers mourned that the influx of aliens was breaking down the system of apprenticeship. For generations native artisans and tradesmen had been accustomed to the division of labor by which apprentices learned to become journeymen. . . . This occupational differentiation had bred a keen spirit of exclusiveness in each craft. Technological improvements, however, weakened the skilled worker's monopoly of the labor supply, and new techniques of production led to the employment of unskilled or poorly trained hands. Moreover, the arrival in the Empire City of untrained Europeans aroused charges that a mechanic's reputation no longer guaranteed him a job. House painting ceased to be a monopoly of the painters. . . . In other trades employers fired skilled workers. . . . By 1845 apprenticing in the shoemaking trade had largely disappeared. . . . As skilled workers saw the futility of apprenticeship under these conditions they banded together in protest meetings in New York, Brooklyn, Poughkeepsie, and other nearby towns to demand the restriction of immigration. . . . Economic nativism was, therefore, an expression of the American craftsman's desire to preserve his monopoly from the determined attempts of the foreign born to gain a foothold.[71]

Although the American Republicans sought to maintain their integrity against the Whigs in local elections after their successes in 1844, they were unable to do so and disappeared from the ballot in a few years. Again, it proved too difficult for a third party to survive against the lure of a major national party which nodded in the direction of its principles. In 1847, the Native Americans "nominated as their own Presidential candidate General Zachary Taylor, the Whig's standard-bearer," who was to be successful.[72] In 1852, the Whig Presidential candidate was Winfield Scott, who "had expressed sympathy with the nativists' stand in the early 1840's."[73]

The largest nativist party to appear on the national scene was the American party founded by the secret nativist Order of the Star-Spangled Banner in 1854. Again, the troubles of the Whig party were to pave the way for the growth of nativist politics. The Whigs had suffered a disastrous defeat in 1852, which many of them blamed on the supposed fact that the Catholic and immigrant vote had been cast overwhelmingly for the Democratic candidate, Franklin Pierce. "When Pierce named a Catholic postmaster general and appointed several foreign-born Democrats to diplomatic posts, nativists and Whigs were convinced that he was paying an election debt and that immigrant voters controlled the United States."[74]

Party lines had begun to break down during this period as a result of the slavery issue. The Free Soil party had entered as a major third-party force. The Whigs, linked to evangelical Protestants, now collapsed under pressure from northern abolitionists to take an antislavery stance, while their southern supporters demanded that they back slavery in the territories and new states.

The American party essentially stepped into this vacuum left by the disrupted and defeated Whig party. By focusing on anti-Catholicism and nativism, it temporarily found a means of uniting much of the moralistic Protestant community behind a religiously inspired cause, which could by-pass the slavery issue. And in 1854 and 1855, the party seemingly was able to sweep through to victory in many states in both the North and the South. Like the American Republicans before them, the new American party—the "Know-Nothings"—depended heavily on working-class support.

This working-class support for the Know-Nothings cannot be linked to unemployment and depression conditions. The depression had ended in the late forties; the great gold rush of 1849 had resulted in an inflation which both sent prices up and brought labor into short supply. This economic change also served to refurbish working-class nativism, since wages did not rise as rapidly as prices, and the discrepancy was blamed on the availability of cheap foreign labor.[75] As important, generally, were the social strains introduced by rapid urbanization, industrialization, and mass immigration, particularly in port cities such as Boston, New York, Baltimore, and New Orleans. The banner state of Know-Nothingism was Massachusetts. Between 1820 and 1850, the manufacturing population of the state had jumped sixfold. This was far greater proportionately than in any nonfrontier state. Only New York exceeded it in the absolute number employed in industry. Although Massachusetts was the most densely populated state in the Union in 1840, its population increase in the next decade was also greater than that in any other of the older states. At the same time, it was sending a large part of its home-bred population to settle the western states.[76]

Similar developments were occurring in the other rapidly growing eastern cities. The year 1854, in which the Know-Nothings entered politics, witnessed the entry of 427,833 immigrants, over five times the number that had entered in 1844 and more than the number which would arrive in any future year up to 1873. The larger cities not only had to absorb a considerable proportion of this immigration but also continued to attract many native-born from smaller communities and rural areas.

The strains faced by skilled native workmen following on these changes had given rise to a number of working-class-based secret nativist and anti-Catholic societies even before the American party was formed in 1854. The Order of United Americans, formed both as a benevolent society and to expose competition from immigrants, limited its membership to American-born workers. By the mid-1850's it had 50,000 members in sixteen states. "Many features of this organization were taken over bodily by the

Know-Nothing party when it came into being."[77] The Order of United American Mechanics, also dedicated to reforming naturalization laws and restricting immigration, rose up about this time.

The alliance between the more conservative elite and the more bigoted workingmen was often an uneasy one. In reading the description of the politics of the period, we gain the impression that most of the middle- and upper-class Whig Protestants, who sympathized with the anti-Catholic and nativist cause, either never joined or quickly dropped out of the ranks of the more explicitly bigoted organizations. The violent language and occasional violent action, as well as class-conscious rhetoric, presumably did not appeal to them. The Philadelphia riots of 1844 which saw a Catholic church burned, thirteen people killed, and the militia called out to restore order hurt the nativist cause, since

respectable citizens throughout the country shrank from a party which sanctioned mob rule. . . . [They] deeply shocked . . . [those] whose natural conservatism led them to view any attack on private property with suspicion. Particularly alarmed were the sober, church-going citizens who had been attracted to the anti-Catholic cause by the New York school controversy and who now shrank from a continued alliance with such a lawless group as the nativists had demonstrated themselves to be.[78]

This pattern of withdrawal by middle-class bigots from the violent consequences of moralistic rhetoric was to recur a century later as a reaction to the activities of the Ku Klux Klan.

Neither the extremist language and violent actions of the nativists nor their attacks on capital, however, prevented the Whigs from forming covert coalitions with the American party, or later from seeking to absorb their support through advocacy of nativist doctrines. Seemingly Whig sympathies for nativism contributed to their maintaining and enlarging their Protestant working-class base, and the flirtation continued, varying from state to state. In New York State, where the Whig party had been divided between radical abolitionists led by former Governor Seward and conservatives who were willing to tolerate slavery to maintain the Union, the conservative faction known as the Silver Grays saw in the growing nativist movement a method of regaining political power for conservatives after the demise of the Whig party.[79] Thus many of the Silver Gray faction joined the Know-Nothings in 1853 and helped to provide a cadre of professional political leadership.[80]

In Massachusetts, on the other hand, Whig political leadership tended to stay out of the new party. On a lower level, however, the American party recruited strongly among abolitionist supporters, including those who had backed the Free Soil party. It soon added antislavery to its advocacy of nativist doctrines.[81] In Connecticut also the party failed to get support from leading Whigs, but recruited heavily among party activists on the secondary level and eventually became a strongly antislavery party.[82] In the southern states, the American party was largely the Whig party reassembled under another label. Sympathetic to slavery, like the Whigs, it was also strongly pro-union and favorable to the Missouri Compromise.

Although a number of prominent Whigs vigorously opposed the nativist doctrines of the American party as un-American and sought to maintain their old party, or joined in forming the new Republican party, also founded in 1854, electoral analysis indicates that the bulk of the ballot support of the Americans came from former Whigs. "The [Pearson] coefficient of correlation between the Know Nothing vote in 1855 and the Whig vote in 1850 is +.9 in Utica; +.7 in Rochester; +.6 in New York and Syracuse."[83] Former Whig support, however, cannot account for the major electoral victories of the Know-Nothings in the various local and state elections in 1854 and 1855. In many parts of the East and South, particularly in the cities and towns, the new party did much better than the Whigs had ever done.

The available evidence would suggest that much of this additional backing came from Protestant workers who had formerly voted Democratic. In Massachusetts, the strongest Know-Nothing state in the nation, analyses of the backgrounds of American party legislators and of the membership list of chapters of the Know-Nothing Order point to the movement's reaching into the working class for leadership and support, in a way that no other major non-Democratic political tendency had ever done before. The legislature of 1854, which was almost entirely composed of Know-Nothings, contained few men who had ever served previously. As compared to the preceding session, the number of farmers and lawyers dropped off greatly. This was balanced by a gain in the ranks from the building trades and shop industries and also Protestant ministers. "In no other profession was the increased representation so marked as in the clergy. Twenty-four clergymen were members, four times as many as in 1854. . . . But for lawyers, the Know-Nothings had little use; like the Populists of today [1896], they seemed to hold them in distrust."[84]

The conclusions concerning working-class involvement drawn from the analysis of the social background of Know-Nothing legislators in Massachusetts were iterated by the studies of the membership of the Order in Boston and Worcester. The records of the Boston Wigwam No. 5 contained a list of 806 members, of whom 504 could be located in the *Boston Directory* for the years 1853–1855. These showed that

the great majority of the Boston Know-Nothings were "mechanics"; some worked at the same shop or wharf with fellow members of the Wigwam. The most common occupations were wheelwrights, carpenters, clerks and machinists:

of the five hundred-four Wigwam members under consideration, 12.3 per cent or sixty-two members were wheelwrights; 7.6 per cent or thirty-eight men were housewrights or carpenters; 5.6 per cent or twenty-eight members were clerks; and 4.0 per cent or twenty men were machinists.[85]

The proportion of skilled and semiskilled workers belonging to the Boston Wigwam was considerably higher than the percentage which these occupations constituted of the Suffolk County and Boston labor force. Thirty per cent were "mechanics" of some kind. On the other hand, although "twenty per cent of the County was of the 'merchant class' [they contributed] . . . less than two per cent of the Wigwam's membership." There was likewise a small number of professional men associated with the party; only 0.8 per cent of the membership could be so classified.

Another study of the movement in Massachusetts which located the documents of the East Boston Wigwam reports that the constitution of the lodge "bore signatures and addresses of 806 East Boston Know-Nothings, many of whom found the task of spelling street names correctly almost as formidable as that of safeguarding American institutions."[86] Edward Everett, former Senator from Massachusetts, who lived in Boston, wrote that "the rank and file of the Know-Nothing order is 'almost wholly . . . made up of the laboring classes.' "[87]

The Boston findings and Everett's impressions correspond to conclusions reached in an investigation of the Order's support in Worcester, which were derived from an analysis of the "list of autograph signatures of members of Council 23 of the American Party."[88] Two different lists of members, one of 1,120 in 1854, and the other of 414 in 1856, were used as the basis for specifying the social background of the membership.

It will be noticed that the vast majority of these members were from Worcester's shops and stores. This point deserves emphasis, for the comradeship, the somewhat exclusive guild feeling, of men who day by day work at the same bench or behind the same counter goes far toward explaining the phenomenal growth of this order. . . . It is impossible to trace those names in the directory without being struck by the large proportion—one in four, if not one in three—of those who are put down not as householders but as boarders. . . . Another peculiarity about these lists, not without its significance, is the individuality which the signers show in matters of orthography. . . . Of these signers, 189 have shown a decided preference for their own spelling of street names instead of that adopted by the city's signboards. Hiland, heighland (Highland), Orringe (Orange), Orchod (Orchard), sumar (Summer), Washanton, Washntn, Worshington (Washington), may serve as typos.

. . . The names of 324 of these Know-Nothings of 1856 have been found upon the assessor's books. . . . Six paid a tax on real estate exceeding $100. Including these, the average for the 324 is $13.73. Excluding these six, the average of the remainder is $6.47. The average tax on personal property was

$4.95; excluding the three who paid personal property tax exceeding $100, the average tax for the remaining 321 becomes $2.53. One hundred and fifteen paid a tax on real estate, 89 on personal property, while 156 of the 329 were payers of a poll tax only.

These figures are not complete; but they are sufficient for illustrative purposes. Had the assessor's and registrar's lists been in such condition as to make a full canvass of the names possible . . . the completed figures would have materially cut down the averages, rather than have raised them: for the men whose names are hard to find on assessor's lists from year to year are not the names of men of wealth. . . . But what these statistics do show clearly, I believe, is that Worcester wealth felt but slight apprehension of danger from foreigners, and that the bulk of this organization was made up of poll-tax payers or very small property holders,—that it was made up very largely of the "unattached," the "boarding" class, which feels few responsibilities and little conservatism.[89]

An analysis of the occupational backgrounds of the two lists, the 1,120 of 1854 and the 414 of 1856, also points to the relatively low status of the Know-Nothings. In both years, 69 per cent were employed in the factories of the city. Another 3 per cent in each year were classified as "laborers," while 3 per cent in the first year and 4 per cent in the second were employed in "Express, Hack, and Trucking." Thus three-quarters of the membership came from manual pursuits. Conversely, 10 per cent in 1854 and 11 per cent in 1856 were in "mercantile" jobs, including "clerks" who presumably made up the bulk of this group. Only 5 out of the 1,120 in the former year were in "banking, insurance and real estate," a figure which rose to 9 out of the 414 in the second. Professionals varied from 1 to 2 per cent, and farmers contributed 3 per cent in the former and 4 per cent in the latter.[90]

These data which point to the working-class base of Know-Nothingism are even more impressive when we note that one-quarter of Worcester's population at the time were of foreign birth. Eighty per cent of these came from Ireland and were employed almost entirely in manual occupations. Consequently the working-class membership of the Know-Nothing lodges was drawn from a native-born population which was disproportionately middle class.

A further indication of Know-Nothing appeal to the more socially deprived segment of the community may be found in the fact that like the Anti-Masons before them, they seemingly appealed to groups which ordinarily did not vote. "Everywhere the success of the party rested upon thousands of new men drawn into politics by nativism."[91] Characteristically, the Know-Nothing movement, like other bigoted tendencies, helped bring the ignorant into the electorate.

Voting patterns in Baltimore, a city which was dominated by the movement for many years, point in the same direction as the data from Massachusetts. In Maryland, in general, as in other parts of the country, the American party secured the bulk of its votes from the Whig opponents of the Democrats, since it served as the sole major electoral alternative.

In Baltimore City . . . [however] the Know Nothings received great accessions from the Democrats. The most marked change was in the Eighteenth Ward. This ward had been one of the Democratic strongholds, and it now became the *banner ward* of the Know Nothings. This ward, adjacent to the Baltimore and Ohio Railroad shops, was inhabited mainly by mechanics and workingmen, and gives a clue as to the social status of a great number of the Know Nothing party.[92]

A similar pattern of support occurred in the other great seaport city of the slave states, New Orleans. There, too, the American party was able to dominate local politics completely through securing the backing of the old Whig partisans who had been tied to important elements in the business community, plus the Protestant section of the working class. This new coalition organized around nativism wrested power from the Democrats who, based on the Creole Catholics, had controlled the city. The two strata, however, did not remain unified after the demise of the national American party. The "monied element" withdrew from the party in 1858.

It was now in the hands of the ward clubs, located in neighborhoods inhabited by workingmen who had moved to New Orleans in the last ten or fifteen years. . . . This element did not hesitate to use violence to achieve political success. It was probably they who dressed as Indians, paraded through the streets intimidating Democratic voters, and made the American party the party of thugs. Increasingly, the Know Nothings depended upon and courted this element.[93]

As a predominantly working-class-based party, the Know-Nothings remained in control of New Orleans until the Civil War. The last two prewar mayors elected by the American party were skilled workers, one a stevedore, John Monroe, who "had long been a labor leader," and the other Gerald Stith, a printer. They belonged to "the only two trades which had formed strong local unions."[94] In elections, the Americans repeatedly charged their opponents "with having the wealth, but not the quality of the city in their ranks."[95]

The working-class composition of the Know-Nothing organization in a number of cities clearly does not mean that the American party was a labor-based movement which challenged the power of the well-to-do, as occurred during its final years in New Orleans. As the largest or second largest party in many states in the East and South, it necessarily had considerable strength among the rural population. As the successor party to the Whigs, it absorbed the vote of the more well-to-do areas which had backed that party. Various studies of Whig strength in New York and New England indicate that the "conservative" party tended to draw its votes from native-born Protestants and from the more affluent. Given the fact that most eastern Whigs temporarily moved over to back the American party in the interregnum between the collapse of their party and the rise of the Republicans, it is not surprising that the correlations between various social factors and the Know-Nothing vote were similar to those with the Whigs earlier and with the Republicans later on. All three parties drew disproportionately from middle-class Protestants of native Anglo-Saxon background. The Democrats, in turn, held the support of the Catholic and recent immigrant voters, usually among the poorest groups, from the less religious Protestants, and from among the less well-to-do Protestants.[96] Seemingly what converted the minority Whig position into a majority American and later Republican vote was the shift to the Know-Nothings of many workers who were attracted to nativist doctrines.

Success-in-Failure

The pre-Civil War extremist movements failed, as extremist movements would throughout American history, in the sense that they did not become durable political movements or create viable national political parties. They failed because their single-minded and bigoted emphasis did not equip them for the kind of coalition politics needed by a national party in America. They failed because the Whigs and their Republican successors were so well equipped for coalition politics that they could fit sizable amounts of conflicting single-mindedness and bigotry in their commodious national packages. But they succeeded in changing the shape of American politics through their impact, most directly on the conservative party. Their goals were partly taken over by a regular party; and in that sense they were deterred from becoming an independent party.

The American party's demise was also associated with another factor which was obviously to play a role in the fate of some other extremist movements in America's future: a sharp change in historical circumstances, the development of a new configuration of social strains to which the movement was not adapted. In this case it was the slavery issue. Once the party began to face up to the need for a national policy for the impending elections of 1856, the slavery issue proved to be as disastrous for them as it had been for their Whig predecessors. When the National Council adopted a proslavery platform in June 1855, the northern sections withdrew. From then on, the national party was essentially a southern movement. In the election of 1856, over four-fifths of its vote came from slave states, largely from former Whigs. In the north, it was largely absorbed into the new

Republican party, which, like the Whigs before them, was willing to make important concessions for nativist support.

Indeed, like their predecessors, the Anti-Masons and American Republicans, the Know-Nothings' most important political effect would seem to have been to pave the way for new sources of support for the major Protestant-based, middle-class-oriented party from less privileged Protestant Democrats. In spite of their extensive series of victories in municipal and state elections in 1854 and 1855, the vast majority of northern Know-Nothings who were strongly antislavery left the party to support the Republicans in the election of 1856. The new party, formed out of a coalition of northern Whigs and those involved in the antislavery third parties, made a conscious, seemingly successful effort to win the backing of the nativists.

Statistical analysis of the relationship between Know-Nothing support and subsequent Republican strength have been completed for various cities in New York State. The American party had received 34 per cent of the vote in the state elections of 1855, but there was a heavy drop-off in the Presidential election of the following year, followed by the almost total extinction of the party in later state contests.

Correlating the Know Nothing vote of 1855 and the Republican vote of 1857, we find in New York City a correlation of +.71. A correlation of the 1855 Know Nothing vote and the Republican vote of 1856 is +.70 for the 1858 Republican vote, the correlation is +.65. In Utica much the same situation holds true. Correlating the Know Nothing vote of 1855 and the Republican vote of 1856 we find a correlation of +.94; for the Republican vote of 1857 and Know Nothing vote of 1855 +.87 and the Republican vote of 1858 and the Know Nothing vote of 1856 a coefficient of correlation of +.83. In Syracuse the same situation, though not as drastic, prevails. . . . In Rochester, much the same relationship is found.[97]

Outside of New York, the dominant factions in the American party in the various New England and Middle Atlantic states endorsed Frémont and the Republican Presidential ticket in 1856. In most of these states, there was a formal agreement between the two parties to present a joint slate of electors. In Pennsylvania, the Republican and American parties cooperated closely in the election of 1856 on the state level. The Republicans officially endorsed a plan for a joint ticket of Presidential electors for the two parties.[98] In 1858, the two parties created a "people's party to elect a Know Nothing as Governor."[99] In Massachusetts, where the Know-Nothings had been stronger than anywhere else in the North, they formed a *de facto* coalition with the rising Republican party.

[In 1856] the latter [Republicans] nominated no candidate to oppose Gardner [the incumbent Know-Nothing] for the governorship, and most Know-Nothings voted for Frémont. Thereafter the Know-Nothings in the state were absorbed in the tremendous growth of the new party. . . .

Produced by the same reform impulse that fathered Know-Nothingism, the Republican party continued to express animosity toward the Irish, "their declared and uncompromising foe." The defeat of Frémont in 1856 was laid at the door of the Irish-Catholics, and confirmed the party's hostility to them. In retaliation, it helped pass an amendment in 1857 making ability to read the state constitution in English and to write, prerequisites to the right to vote; and in 1859, another, preventing foreigners from voting for two years after naturalization.[100]

The Know-Nothing movement in most of the northwestern states had never attempted to clash with the Republican party. From the start of the latter in 1854, the Know-Nothings "cast their lot with the Republicans rather than nominate candidates of their own. Under their influence the Republican party in many northwestern states took on a decided nativistic tint."[101] In Wisconsin, for example, "the abolition of the . . . immigration agencies by the Republicans in 1855, just after the party had won a major election with Know-Nothing aid, looked suspiciously like the carrying out of a campaign promise."[102]

In 1860, the Democrats, who had fought the Know-Nothings when they were powerful, continued to attack nativism. The platform of the northern Democratic party "repeated their 1856 opposition to Know Nothing principles. There was no word of anti-nativism in the Democratic platform."[103] Their candidate for President, Stephen Douglas, was married to a Catholic. He had a record of active opposition to the Know-Nothings. Lincoln, though he had privately expressed opposition to Know-Nothing principles, had never made an issue of this and had, in fact, occasionally cooperated with Know-Nothings in Illinois politics. Given these differences between the two parties, it is not surprising that much of the immigrant and Catholic vote continued to go to the Democrats, while the Republicans picked up further Know-Nothing support.

The Republican victory in the election of 1860 was a result of the Republican vote in six salient states—in Illinois, Indiana and Pennsylvania primarily, and in Iowa, New York and Chicago secondarily. In the election of 1856, the Know-Nothings had held the balance of power in most of these states. Most of the Know-Nothing vote of 1856 was Republican in 1860. Republican gains and Know-Nothing losses show remarkable similarities. The 1860 election returns in the counties where Know-Nothings were strong in 1856 demonstrate this indisputably.[104]

The Moralistic Dimension

This early American history suggests a series of propositions with respect to the development of a mass, monistic appeal movement in America:

Such a movement requires a coalition between some elite groups and some plebian groups, both of which are in some state of preservatist backlash against different forms of displacement or status deprivation in a period of sharp change. Identifiable ethnic groups put flesh on the strain felt by the lower-class group, susceptible to bigotry. But it is not bigotry as much as a conspiracy theory which provides the ideological bridge between the elite and the nonelite and provides as well the central drive for a political movement. This purported conspiracy is necessarily thought to be conducted by some secret band of "intellectuals," but is also fleshed out most convincingly for the mass base of the movement if it can be connected also to the ethnic group or groups already in question. The result is a master monistic design, antipluralistic with respect to population groups, antipluralistic with respect to the democratic process itself. However, it is a complicated design, requiring much gap-jumping, much passionate and antipolitical evasion of reality. According to the model of monism, it is a shared moralism and moralistic approach to politics which would provide the glue for this design. It is such a moralistic approach that can fully evoke the measures of evil required for a full-fledged theory of political conspiracy and can at the same time bind into the design the deviant behavior of an appropriate ethnic group.

During the first half of the nineteenth century, the strong existence of just such a pervasive moralism was evident in the movements already described and thickly evident in the general climate, a special brand of Protestant moralism that fitted the politics of American displacement. Perhaps the first example was the temperance movement which developed in the early years of the nineteenth century. To a considerable extent this movement was dominated by members of the failing Federalist upper class and the disestablished Congregationalist ministers. Requiring some explanation for this social discontinuity, they found it in the low cultural level of the "common man," his drunkenness and lack of education. The drive against alcohol became part of a "Puritan Counter-Reformation" designed to rebuild its influence over the "common man."[105] "The early temperance advocates of New England, for example, were so strongly Federalist in their political affiliations that Federalism and temperance became entangled in public thinking."[106]

But perhaps the most important issue in American history in which moralistic and even extremist politics linked to religious belief were strengthened by the support of once powerful groups which were being "downgraded" was abolitionism. Abolitionism was largely a product of New England leadership which had become increasingly frustrated over the fact that it had lost its influence on the country.

Numerous New Englanders developed a political self-consciousness born of frustration; it manifested itself in a particular type of tactics well adopted to the Protestant attitude. This peculiar political behavior was dominated by ways of thought inherited directly from the Puritans. The unhappiness and frustration from which New England suffered must be due to sin, and, urged on by conscience, the dissatisfied soon found that the sin was the sin of slavery.[107]

The same processes were at work in New York State also.

Antislavery . . . [and other religious linked movements were] strongest in those counties which had once been economically dominant but which by the 1830's, though still prosperous, had relatively fallen behind their more advantageously situated neighbors.[108]

In analyzing the support for the antislavery struggle, it is necessary to differentiate between the initiators and leaders of the abolitionist fight and the subsequent large rank-and-file base. The social background of the leaders most clearly reflects the strains produced by social discontinuities, although once the movement became part of the larger political struggle, it drew support from those who were predisposed for religious and other reasons to oppose slavery, but were not as deeply affected by the same displacement factors.

The leadership, which came almost entirely out of New England, may be divided into two groups: one, the largely Transcendentalist intellectuals, mainly of old-family, often Unitarian, background, who provided the arguments; and second, the actual leaders of the cause. For the most part the Transcendentalists were not active in abolitionist movements as such, but in their writings and sermons, they gave a major impetus to the growth of such activities. Characteristically, a young Transcendentalist (they were, for the most part, very young) has been described as "a young man of talent, learning and sensibility with ties to an earlier era—either of family or simply of local tradition—[who] was just not attracted to those careers in the way he might once have been. . . . In *this* sense such a group as the Transcendentalists could quite properly be called a 'displaced elite.' "[109] The second group, the actual leaders of abolitionist organizations, was drawn from substantial upper middle-class old and distinguished Federalist families, predominantly Congregational-Presbyterian and Quaker, though they also included many Methodists.[110] Few of them were born in large cities; almost all came from small communities. "Throughout the crusade many of the anti-slavery leaders seemed to feel an instinctive antipathy toward the city."[111] As in the case of the temperance crusades, their enthusiasm for abolition reflected their situation as "an elite without function, a *displaced class* in American society."[112]

Descended from old and socially dominant Northeastern families, reared in a faith of aggressive piety and moral endeavor, educated for conservative leadership, these young men and women who reached maturity in the 1830's faced a strange and hostile world. . . . Too distinguished a family, too gentle an education, too nice a morality were handicaps in a bustling world of business. Expecting to lead, these young people found no followers. . . .

In these plebeian days they could not be successful in politics; family tradition and education prohibited idleness; and agitation allowed the only chance for personal and social self-fulfillment. . . .

With all its dangers and all its sacrifices, membership in a movement like abolitionism offered these young people a chance for reassertion of their traditional values, an opportunity for association with others of their kind, and a possibility of achieving that self-fulfillment which should traditionally have been theirs as social leaders. Reform gave meaning to the lives of this displaced social elite.[113]

In a real sense, then, abolitionism, like the temperance movement of a generation earlier, reflected the combination of Protestant moral emphases acting on a socially displaced elite, some of whose members sought an outlet in moral political action against the "immorality" of the society which rejected them. Almost all of them strongly opposed Jacksonian democracy which, together with money-grabbing businessmen, represented the crassness of the expanding society. But it should be noted that it was not simply the combination of social change and old distinguished family origins which affected their reactions; many Episcopalians also came from similar backgrounds, but an Episcopalian upbringing apparently did not provide men with the moral outlook which justified participation in the abolitionist crusade.

The extreme moral fervor poured into the abolitionist movement cannot be attributed solely, or even primarily, to the "backlash" reaction of displaced groups. The moralistic concerns were stimulated by the direct link to evangelical Protestantism and its commitment to oppose sinful behavior. Once men are led to define certain aspects of the society as evil, their religious background presses them to work actively to eliminate it. This aspect of American politics was exacerbated by the shift in American Protestantism from the Calvinist emphasis on predestination to the Arminian doctrine of free will. The Methodists, who were the largest Protestant group, comprising fully 40 per cent of the total, "had proclaimed free will and free grace from the beginning."[114] The second largest denomination, the Baptists, which included 25 per cent of all Protestants, had mainly rejected orthodox Calvinism and were "almost Arminian on matters of election and free will and leaned as well toward 'new measures' and interfaith fellowship," a point of view which also described the beliefs of most Congregationalists and New School Presbyterians.[115] In large measure, the extensive revivalist activities which had swept the country for decades before the Civil War, regardless of denomination, had emphasized individual responsibility for salvation, the achievement of grace, and the casting out of sin—beliefs which enhanced the conviction that good Protestants must act against flagrant examples of immorality, such as liquor, slavery, and Catholicism.

A number of studies have associated the mass growth of the antislavery movement in the North with these denominations.[116] Conversely, membership in the Lutheran, Episcopalian, and Catholic churches seems to have been unrelated to active concern for the abolitionist cause. Abolition had particular strength in areas which had been subject to successful revivalist campaigns.[117] The clue to understanding these reactions lies in the attitudes toward sin which had emerged among the deeply religious evangelical American Protestants:

> The most significant characteristic of the Protestant attitude was a consciousness of the evil nature of sin. Protestant expounders made a simple and clear-cut distinction between right and wrong. Man was either saved or damned. Righteousness would be rewarded, sin punished. Sin must be fought. . . .
>
> This sense of duty, this sensitiveness to the promptings of conscience, had been the main precept in the education of a large proportion of those who in the [eighteen] fifties were at years of maturity. . . .
>
> This cancer of society [slavery] should be cut out, and stern duty called upon foes of sin to remove it. . . . These intense foes of the South were going to do everything possible to destroy slavery. They found their duty all the more compelling as the sin was largely in the body politics of the South, and attack upon it must weaken those who held power.[118]

But though the more evangelical denominations fostered abolitionist sentiment in the North, it is significant to note that membership in the very same churches was related to support for slavery in the South. Thus the three groups which split into the northern and southern wings and remained divided down to the recent present have been the Presbyterians, the Baptists, and the Methodists. The Presbyterians suffered their first division in 1837–1838. "Although the split of New School and Old School was ostensibly along theological lines, in fact the South remained with the Old School and the alliance of abolitionism and revivalism shaped the New School General Assembly."[119]

The latter two also separated in 1844–1845, long before the Civil War, as a result of "contrasting attitudes on the part of the two sections of the church on a moral question, slavery."[120] And though most southern leaders tried to deny that the Civil War was over the issue of slavery, a wartime Assembly of the Southern Presbyterian Church affirmed "that it is the peculiar mission of the Southern church to conserve the institution of slavery. . . ."[121] Just as evangelical Protestantism helped to make the conflict "irrepressible" by bolstering the moral fiber of abolitionism, it served the same role south of the Mason and Dixon line by defining the sectional conflict as one of God versus Satan as well:

> The South, men said and did not doubt, was peculiarly Christian; probably, indeed, it was the last great bulwark of Christianity. . . . From pulpit and hustings ran the dark suggestion that the God of the Yankee was not God at all but Antichrist loosed at last from the pit. The coming war would be no mere secular contest but Armageddon, with the South standing in the role of the defender of the ark, its people as the Chosen people. . . .
> Every man was in his place because He had set him there. Everything was as it was because He had ordained it so. Hence, slavery, and indeed, everything that was, was His responsibility, not the South's. So far from being evil, it was the very essence of Right. Wrong would consist only in rebellion against it.[122]

Roy Nichols has pointed up the specific denominational sources of the support of slavery:

> The bitter resentment welling up in the South was intensified by the fact that its people shared the prevailing Protestantism. . . . The Methodists, Baptists, and Presbyterians particularly set much store by preaching, and they stressed the Protestant tenets earlier described, emphasizing morals, conscience, and the hatred of sin. Stung to anger by attacks upon their institutions and by slurs upon their moral integrity, their pulpits became rostrums of defense. . . . Southern divines became increasingly satisfied that slavery was ordained of God and justified in the Bible. God would condemn those who bore false witness against the South—the northern hypocrites who attacked the South as morally delinquent.[123]

The Lutheran, Episcopalian, and Catholic churches, each of which had come out of a tradition of having been state and total society churches, do not see their mission as prescribing behavior, in the same way that the sects or denominations with sectarian origins do. Hence, these could tolerate a wide variety of attitudes on the issues of slavery and the Negro. The sects, however, had to be moral and consequently were inclined to support abolitionism or to defend slavery as a matter of religious ethos. "Thus southern clergymen fought northern ministers in the same Protestant vocabulary. . . ."[124]

In a real sense, it may be argued that the fact that evangelical moralism characterized American religion was causally related to the fact that we required a Civil War to eliminate slavery. As Stanley Elkins has put it:

> The simple and harsh moral purity of our own anti-slavery movement, from the 1830's on, gave it a [special] quality. . . . Every phase of the movement combined to produce in our abolitionists that peculiar quality of abstraction

which was, and has remained, uniquely American. For them, the question was *all* moral; it must be contemplated in terms untouched by expediency, . . . uncorrupted even by society itself. It was a problem of conscience which by mid-century would fasten itself in one form or another, and in varying degrees, upon men's feelings everywhere.[125]

The strong moral fervor of evangelical Protestantism exhibited in the antislavery and temperance movements—designed to eliminate those aspects of American life which contravened their sense of rectitude—frightened those Americans who did not belong. The Jews, although presumably sensitized by their history and values to sympathize with the cause of Negro freedom, abstained from any strong identification with the abolitionist cause. Many, like Isaac Mayer Wise, a leading rabbi, "distrusted the religious fanaticism that inspired the anti-slavery extremists, and feared that its next victim after the South had been crushed would be the Jews."[126] The Catholic attitude resembled that of the Jews. Although Catholic councils issued statements in support of gradual emancipation, few Catholics were active in the abolitionist movement. "One factor in this widespread Catholic attitude was a tendency to associate the anti-slavery forces with anti-Catholicism. It was noted that many Protestant abolitionists were extremely antagonistic toward the Roman Catholic Church."[127] These non-Protestant instincts were correct and had already been informed by the events of the preceding half-century. It was this brand of Protestant moralism which helped bind together the elites and masses, helped charge the conspiracy theories and bigotries, all of which shaped the monistic impulse in America for the next three-quarters of a century.

Notes

1. Robert R. Palmer, *The Age of the Democratic Revolution: The Struggle* (Princeton: Princeton University Press, 1964), pp. 429–430, 453; Anonymous, "The Illuminati," *Horizon*, VI (Spring 1947), 16–38.
2. Richard Hofstadter, *The Paranoid Style in American Politics* (New York: Knopf, 1965), p. 12, see pp. 10–15; Jacques Droz, "La légende du complot illuministe et les origines du romantisme politique en Allemagne," *Révue Historique*, CCXXVI (1961), 313–338; Norman Cohn, *Warrant for Genocide* (New York: Harper & Row, 1967), pp. 25–31.
3. *Ibid.*, pp. 25–26.
4. Lorman A. Ratner, *Antimasonry in New York State: A Study in Pre-Civil War Reform* (M.A. Thesis, Cornell University, 1958), p. 13.
5. James K. Morse, *Jedidiah Morse, a Champion of New England Orthodoxy* (New York: Columbia University Press, 1939), pp. 55–58.
6. Palmer, *op. cit.*, pp. 542–543.
7. Hofstadter, *op. cit.*, p. 13.
8. *Ibid.*

9. Vernon Stauffer, *New England and the Bavarian Illuminati* (New York: Columbia University Press, 1918), p. 283. Emphases in the original.

10. *Ibid.*, pp. 200–293. Emphasis in the original.

11. J. Wendell Knox, *Conspiracy in American Politics, 1787–1815* (Ph.D. Thesis, Department of History, University of North Carolina, 1965), p. 115. Emphasis supplied.

12. *Ibid.*, p. 124. Emphasis in the original.

13. Dixon Ryan Fox, *The Decline of Aristocracy in the Politics of New York 1801–1840* (New York: Harper Torchbooks, 1965), p. 78.

14. *Ibid.*, p. 80.

15. Ray Allen Billington, *The Protestant Crusade 1800–1860* (New York: Rinehart, 1938), p. 24.

16. Charles McCarthy, "The Antimasonic Party: A Study of Political Anti-Masonry in the United States, 1827–1840," *Annual Report of the American Historical Association for the Year 1902* (Washington: Government Printing Office, 1903), I, 537–538.

17. *Ibid.*, p. 539.

18. John R. Bodo, *The Protestant Clergy and Public Issues 1812–1848* (Princeton: Princeton University Press, 1954), pp. 39–43.

19. Anson Phelps Stokes, *Church and State in the United States* (New York: Harper, 1950), II, pp. 12–20.

20. *Ibid.*, p. 18.

21. An American Gentleman [Calvin Colton], *A Voice from America to England* (London: Henry Colburn, 1839), p. 286.

22. Whitney R. Cross, *The Burned-over District* (Ithaca: Cornell University Press, 1950), p. 123.

23. Leland M. Griffin, *The Anti-Masonic Persuasion: A Study of Public Address in the American Anti-Masonic Movement, 1826–1838* (Ph.D. Thesis, Department of Speech, Cornell University, 1950), pp. 46–47.

24. *Ibid.*, pp. 66–83.

25. *Ibid.*, p. 229.

26. *Ibid.*, pp. 269–272.

27. Lee Benson, *The Concept of Jeffersonian Democracy: New York A Test Case* (Princeton: Princeton University Press, 1961), p. 42.

28. Griffin, *op. cit.*, pp. 205–208.

29. Benson, *op. cit.*, p. 55.

30. Griffin, *op. cit.*, pp. 610–621.

31. *Ibid.*, p. 695.

32. Hofstadter, *op. cit.*, p. 14.

33. Stauffer, *op. cit.*, p. 345.

34. *Ibid.*

35. Ratner, *op. cit.*, p. 46.

36. *Ibid.*, p. 52.

37. *Ibid.*, p. 47.

38. Benson, *op. cit.*, p. 193.

39. Griffin, *op. cit.*, p. 345.

40. Stokes, *op. cit.*, I, 673.

41. Michael Williams, *The Shadow of the Pope* (New York: McGraw-Hill, 1932), p. 59; see also Benson, *op. cit.*, pp. 544, 475.

42. David Brian Davis, "Some Themes of Counter-Subversion: An Analysis of Anti-Masonic, Anti-Catholic and Anti-Mormon Literature," *Mississippi Valley Historical Review*, XLVII (1960), 215.
43. Griffin, *op. cit.*, p. 410.
44. This hypothesis is explored in later chapters.
45. McCarthy, *op. cit.*, p. 547.
46. *Ibid.*, p. 47.
47. George M. Blakeslee, *The History of the Anti-Masonic Party* (Ph.D. Thesis, Department of History, Harvard University, 1903), Chapter VII, p. 31; for Pennsylvania, see Philip S. Klein, *Pennsylvania Politics, 1817–1832* (Philadelphia: Historical Society of Pennsylvania, 1940), pp. 279–286.
48. *Ibid.*, p. 281.
49. Cross, *op. cit.*, p. 117.
50. Benson, *op. cit.*, pp. 24–25, footnote 13.
51. *Ibid.*, p. 24.
52. Blakeslee, *op. cit.*, Chapter XI, p. 18.
53. Cited in Griffin, *op. cit.*, p. 274.
54. Richard P. McCormick, *The Second American Party System* (Chapel Hill: University of North Carolina Press, 1966), pp. 47–49.
55. *Ibid.*, p. 75. For a summary of the evidence dealing with the social bases of Anti-Masonry, see Edward Pessen, *Jacksonian America* (Homewood, Ill.: Dorsey, 1969), pp. 279–280.
56. Glyndon Van Deusen, *Thurlow Weed, Wizard of the Lobby* (Boston: Little, Brown, 1947), p. 45.
57. Carl F. Siracusa, *Political Nativism in New York City 1843–1848* (M.A. Thesis: Department of History, Columbia University, 1965).
58. Billington, *op. cit.*, pp. 194–195.
59. *Ibid.*, p. 324.
60. Maldwyn Jones, *American Immigration* (Chicago: University of Chicago Press, 1960), p. 130.
61. Davis, *op. cit.*, pp. 215–216, 223–224.
62. Billington, *op. cit.*, p. 200.
63. William G. Bean, *Party Transformation in Massachusetts with Special Reference to the Antecedents of Republicanism 1848–1860* (Ph.D. Thesis, Department of History, Harvard University, 1922), pp. 232–233.
64. Benson, *op. cit.*, p. 214.
65. Syracusa, *op. cit.*, pp. 102–103.
66. *Ibid.*, p. 90.
67. *Ibid.*, p. 92.
68. Billington, *op. cit.*, p. 210.
69. *Ibid.*, pp. 210–211.
70. Bean, *op. cit.*, pp. 233–234.
71. Robert Ernst, "Economic Nativism in New York City during the 1840's," *New York History*, XXIX (1948), 175–176.
72. Peter H. Odegard, *Religion and Politics* (New York: Oceana Publications, 1960), p. 24.
73. Billington, *op. cit.*, p. 397, in footnote 7.
74. *Ibid.*, p. 326.

75. George Haynes, "A Chapter from the Local History of Know-Nothingism," *New England Magazine*, New Series 15 (September 1896), p. 83; Ernst, *op. cit.*, p. 183; Billington, *op. cit.*, p. 335.

76. George H. Haynes, "The Causes of Know-Nothing Success in Massachusetts," *American Historical Review*, III (October 1897), 70–72.

77. Billington, *op. cit.*, p. 337.

78. *Ibid.*, pp. 233–234.

79. Thomas Joseph Curran, *The Know Nothings of New York* (Ph.D. Thesis, Department of History, Columbia University, 1963), p. 80.

80. *Ibid.*, pp. 103–104.

81. John Raymond Mulkern, *The Know-Nothing Party in Massachusetts* (Ph.D. Thesis, Department of History, Boston University, 1963), pp. 82–93.

82. *Ibid.*, p. 106.

83. Curran, *op. cit.*, p. 306.

84. George H. Haynes, "A Know Nothing Legislature," *Annual Report of the American Historical Association for the Year 1896* (Washington: Government Printing Office, 1897), I, 179. There were 46 lawyers in 1854, but only 11 in 1855 (p. 179).

85. Gerald P. Daly, *Manifestations of Nativism in Massachusetts with Special Reference to the Know-Nothing Movement* (Honors Thesis, Department of History, Harvard University, 1963), pp. 82–83.

86. Mulkern, *op. cit.*, pp. 63–64.

87. *Ibid.*, p. 83.

88. Haynes, "A Chapter . . . ," *op. cit.*, p. 84.

89. *Ibid.*, pp. 87–88.

90. *Ibid.*, p. 96.

91. Oscar Handlin, *Boston's Immigrants* (Cambridge: Harvard University Press, 1959), p. 201.

92. Lawrence F. Schmeckebier, *History of the Know Nothing Party in Maryland* (Baltimore: Johns Hopkins Press, 1899), p. 67.

93. Leon C. Soule, *The Know-Nothing Party in New Orleans: A Reappraisal* (Ph.D. Thesis, Department of History, Tulane University, 1960), pp. 126–127.

94. *Ibid.*, pp. 128, 152, 165.

95. *Ibid.*, pp. 128–129.

96. Billington, *op. cit.*, p. 326.

97. Curran, *op. cit.*, p. 307.

98. Henry R. Mueller, *The Whig Party in Pennsylvania* (New York: Columbia University Press, 1922), pp. 233–234.

99. Charles G. Hamilton, *Lincoln and the Know Nothing Movement* (Washington: Public Affairs Press, 1954), p. 8.

100. Handlin, *op. cit.*, p. 204.

101. Billington, *op. cit.*, p. 395.

102. *Ibid.*, p. 399, in footnote 32; see also Kenneth Stampp, *Indiana Politics during the Civil War* (Indianapolis: Indiana Historical Bureau, 1949), p. 5.

103. Hamilton, *op. cit.*, pp. 11–12.

104. *Ibid.*, p. 20.

105. David M. Ludlum, *Social Ferment in Vermont, 1791–1850* (New York: Columbia University Press, 1939), p. 65; Joseph Gusfield, "Status Con-

flicts and the Changing Ideologies of the American Temperance Movement," in David Pittman and Charles R. Snyder, eds., *Society, Culture and Drinking Practices* (New York: John Wiley, 1962), pp. 105–106; Joseph Gusfield, *Symbolic Crusade, Status Politics and the American Temperance Movement* (Urbana: University of Illinois Press, 1963), pp. 36–44.

106. Alice Tyler, *Freedom's Ferment* (Minneapolis: University of Minnesota Press, 1944), p. 317.

107. Roy F. Nichols, *The Disruption of American Democracy* (New York: Collier Books, 1962), p. 43.

108. David Donald, *Lincoln Reconsidered* (New York: Vintage, 1961), p. 28.

109. Stanley M. Elkins, *Slavery: A Problem in American Institutional and Intellectual Life* (Chicago: University of Chicago Press, 1962), p. 167.

110. Donald, *op. cit.*, pp. 27–29.

111. *Ibid.*, p. 29.

112. *Ibid.*, p. 33. Emphasis supplied.

113. *Ibid.*, p. 33–35; see also Avery Craven, *The Coming of the Civil War* (New York: Scribner, 1942), pp. 125–131.

114. Timothy Smith, *Revivalism and Social Reform in Mid-Nineteenth Century America* (New York: Abingdon, 1957), p. 33.

115. Timothy Smith divides mid-nineteenth century Protestantism into four categories: *Traditionalism*—High Church Episcopal and Old Lutheran; *Orthodox Calvinism*—a "dying dogma" composed of Old School Presbyterians, Antimission Baptists, and a few others: *Revivalistic Calvinism*—"almost Arminian on the matters of election and free will and leaned as well toward 'new measures' and interfaith fellowship," which comprised the vast majority affiliated to denominations of Calvinist origin, such as New School Presbyterians, most Congregationalists, Regular Baptists, and many others; and *Evangelical Arminianism*—which included the Methodists, the Quakers, many new Lutherans, and some Presbyterians and Baptists. *Ibid.*, pp. 32–33.

116. See Donald, *op. cit.*, p. 29; Franklin Hamlin Littell, *From State Church to Pluralism* (Garden City: Doubleday-Anchor, 1962), p. 57; Tyler, *op. cit.*, p. 505; Benson, *op. cit.*, p. 212.

117. Gilbert Barnes, *The Anti-Slavery Impulse, 1830–1844* (Glouster: Peter Smith, 1957), p. 107; Littell, *op. cit.*, p. 64.

118. Nichols, *op. cit.*, pp. 35, 43.

119. Littell, *op. cit.*, p. 64.

120. H. Richard Niebuhr, *The Social Sources of Denominationalism* (New York; Meridian, 1957), p. 194.

121. Cited in *ibid.*, p. 198.

122. W. J. Cash, *The Mind of the South* (Garden City: Doubleday-Anchor, 1954), pp. 91–93; see also Kenneth Stampp, *The Peculiar Institution* (New York: Knopf, 1956), pp. 158–162.

123. Nichols, *op. cit.*, p. 48; see also Elkins, *op. cit.*, p. 36.

124. Nichols, *op. cit.*, p. 48.

125. Elkins, *op. cit.*, pp. 27–28. Emphasis supplied.

126. Jones, *op. cit.*, p. 166.

127. Charles L. Sewrey, *The Alleged "Un-Americanism" of the Church as a Factor in Anti-Catholicism in the United States, 1860–1914* (Ph.D. Thesis, University of Minnesota, 1955), pp. 155–156.

3

The Protestant Crusades from the Civil War
to World War I

If the United States had a Golden Age, it was the half-century following the Civil War. At least, it was during this period that the uniquely American drama was unfolding and that the peculiarly American heroes of this drama were being created for future fable: the omnivorous industrialists and financiers, the hard-driving immigrants, the brawling frontiersmen and cowboys of the West.

Between the end of the Civil War and the turn of the century, the number of manufacturing establishments in the nation more than doubled, and manufacturing production increased more than fourfold. The great new industries and finance houses were booming. At the end of the Civil War there were more farm workers than nonfarm workers in the nation; by the turn of the century there were almost twice as many nonfarm workers as farm workers. There were great aggregations of wealth in the cities, along with great waves of immigrant population. About 25 million immigrants came to America between the end of the Civil War and the beginning of World War I. In dramatic numbers, they entered the laboring class, came to the cities, and were heavily Catholic.

Against this background, and in reaction to specific political and historical events, the monistic impulse quickened in America, under the banner of Protestant nativism. This nativism often served the purpose of wedding conservative political interests with an appeal to the Protestant common man.

The Republican Party and Anti-Catholicism

The political situation in the post-Civil War period remained quite similar to the antebellum one outside of the new one-party South. In spite of being the party which had won the war and saved the Union, the Republicans found that the Democrats retained considerable support in the North. Control over Congress was almost evenly divided between the two parties until the 1890's. The Democrats were extremely powerful in many cities and states, where they retained the support of the immigrant and Catholic sectors of the electorate. To win elections, the Republicans relied in part on waving the "bloody shirt," appealing to the large army of Union veterans as the party which kept the country united, while denouncing the Democrats as the party of secession. At the same time, many Republicans engaged in a "religious version of the 'bloody shirt' political technique," arguing that the largely Democratic Catholics had supported slavery and opposed the Union during the war.[1] *Harper's Weekly,* which polemicized against Catholicism for more than a decade after the war, wrote in 1872: "The unpatriotic conduct of the Romanish population in our chief cities during the late rebellion is well known. They formed a constant menace and terror to the loyal citizens; they thronged the peace meetings, they strove to divide the Union; and when the war was over they placed in office their corrupt leaders and plundered the impoverished community."[2] Although these allegations were denied by Army authorities, they continued to circulate. There was some degree of validity in the attacks, since, as compared to the various Protestant groups, the Catholic clergy had not supported abolition, but rather favored gradual emancipation. Most Catholic papers opposed fighting a war to preserve the Union.[3]

The efforts to link the northern Catholics with treason reached their height in the contention that the assassination of Lincoln had been a Catholic plot. A number of books published after the war argued this thesis.[4] A former Catholic priest, Charles Chiniquy, who had known Lincoln personally, circulated widely the story that Lincoln himself had believed "that Catholics were plotting against the republic."[5]

More important in the long run than arguments over the Catholic role in the war were the debates concerning Catholic political power, particularly as it affected the school system. In many states, Republicans raised the issue of keeping public schools free from ecclesiastical influence and advocated longer residence by immigrants before admitting them to citizenship and voting rights. This controversy was in large part linked to continued Catholic efforts to secure public funds for parochial schools. On this issue, "often the local and state Democratic parties became allied with the Catholic point of view or at least were not hostile," while the Republicans took "the opposite stand."[6]

In New York City, Tammany Hall, under the leadership of William M. ("Boss") Tweed, strongly supported the city's granting large sums of money to church institutions, particularly schools, of which the bulk went to Catholic ones during the late sixties and early seventies. "Republican newspapers consequently used the religious issues against the Democrats."[7] *Harper's Weekly* denounced Francis Kernan, the Democratic nominee for governor of New York in 1872, on the grounds that "he is a Roman Catholic and will obey the orders of the Church."[8]

In Indiana (in 1875) the Republican convention resolved that it was "incompatible with American citizenship to pay allegiance to any foreign power, civil or ecclesiastical," thus, in effect, denying that Catholics had a right to citizenship and impugning their loyalty to American institutions. During the campaign of 1875 in Wisconsin the Republicans attempted to arouse the religious prejudices of the German population by comparing the school controversy with the struggles of Luther and Bismarck with the papacy.[9]

"Running for governor of Ohio in 1875, Rutherford B. Hayes worked fiercely to smear the Democrats as subservient to Catholic designs."[10] He pointed to the alleged Democratic-Catholic alliance and "asserted that sectarian military organizations equipped by the Democratic controlled State existed in Ohio."[11] President Ulysses S. Grant, who had a record of public and private anti-Semitic views, who had briefly belonged to the Know-Nothing Order before the Civil War, and whose two Vice-Presidents had both been active Know-Nothings, in addressing a veterans' reunion in the fall of 1875 openly proclaimed the possibility of a new civil war based on religious differences. He stated: "If we are to have another contest in the near future of our national existence, I predict that the dividing line will not be Mason and Dixon's; but between [Protestant] patriotism and intelligence on one side, and [Catholic] superstition, ambition and ignorance on the other. . . . Keep the Church and the State forever separate."[12]

In 1876, the Republicans nominated Rutherford B. Hayes, who had used anti-Catholicism effectively in the Ohio gubernatorial election of the preceding year, as their Presidential candidate. Attacks on the church were to be a feature of the Presidential election as well. The Republican Congressional Campaign Committee openly issued a number of anti-Catholic documents.

The most important was *Vaticanism in Germany and the United States.* Published in both English and German, this pamphlet asserted that the Church compelled her communicants to support the Democrats in order to defeat Hayes, and so prepare for a change in our form of government. Calling on all citizens, whether of native or foreign birth, to vote the Republican ticket, the pamphlet alleged that "our country" would be in danger "if the Ultramontane element of the Church, through the success of the Democracy, should obtain control of our national affairs."[13]

The religious issues also divided the parties in Congress. In 1876, James G. Blaine, the Republican leader in the House of Representatives, introduced a Constitutional Amendment which specified that no governmental authority could allow any public property, revenues, or loans to be used for the support of any school or other institution under the control of any religious sect. Though seeking to outlaw support for private religious schools, the Amendment explicitly permitted the "reading of the Bible in any school or institution," a clause which "revealed the Protestant inspiration of the resolution," since Catholics had opposed Bible reading, which almost invariably meant use of a Protestant version.[14] The Blaine proposal "failed to secure the necessary two-thirds majority in a strictly party vote, the Republicans voting for it and the Democrats against it."[15] President Hayes appointed an anti-Catholic publicist, Richard Wiggington Thompson, the author of *The Papacy and the Civil Power,* as Secretary of the Navy. Thompson contended that "there was an irreconcilable conflict between papal theory and popular government." The Republican party clearly had the "reputation of champion of the public schools and anti-Catholicism, a position to which it continued to give lip service, at least, in succeeding party platforms for years."[16]

From 1876 on, it was a rare Presidential election in which the Catholic question was not raised in one way or another. Republican leaders were frequently accused [by Catholic publications] of deliberately fostering anti-Catholic prejudice for political ends. During the 1880 campaign, Republicans campaigning for Garfield in New York State asserted that the common schools would be in danger if the Democrats won.[17]

The Republican election platform in 1880 continued to call for the passage of the Constitutional Amendment proposed by Blaine. More significantly, perhaps, in 1884, James G. Blaine was nominated for President. On the local level, anti-Catholicism continued to be a major weapon in the Republican arsenal. In 1880, in opposing William Grace, the Democratic nominee for mayor of New York, the first Catholic nominated for this post, the Republicans "stressed Grace's religion as a major obstacle to his election, Elihu Root asserting that his nomination meant that it was proposed to deliver control of the municipal government 'to one sect to the exclusion of all others. . . .' "[18] Similar tactics were used in Boston and other parts of Massachusetts.

There has been considerable controversy among historians concerning the impact of the religious issue on the Presidential election of 1884, in which the Republicans suffered their first defeat since the Civil War. Many credited the defeat on an unfortunate remark made in the last week of the campaign by a Protestant minister who in an address welcoming James Blaine, the Republican candidate, to a meeting of ministers, referred to the Democratic party as one "whose antecedents have been Rum, Romanism and Rebellion." Recent evidence based on electoral research challenges the assumption that these remarks harmed Blaine greatly, since his vote in 1884 was quite similar to the vote secured by the Republican ticket four years earlier.[19] In fact, the slight decrease in the Republican vote between 1880 and 1884 which accounts for their loss of key electoral votes seems to be associated much more with an increase in the support of the Prohibition party, a movement which, of course, largely appealed to Protestants.

The conclusion that "Rum, Romanism and Rebellion" did not cost Blaine the election should not be surprising in view of the historical record. As has been noted, Blaine himself, as Republican leader in the House, vigorously opposed Catholic school policies. In addition, it is clear that the remark of the Reverend Mr. Burchard in 1884 was but one of a large number of such comments which had been made by Protestant ministers and Republican politicians all through the preceding history of the party. One might guess, therefore, that this comment simply gave Democratic Catholics one more good reason for sticking to their party.[20]

Extremist Movements and the American Protective Association

It has been noted that the antebellum Know-Nothings had achieved a classic victory in defeat: they disappeared as a political party because they became a successful political force in the main-stream Republican party. The strong reliance by the Republican party on anti-Catholicism during these years after the Civil War was an index of this victory. There seemed to be no great "need," under these circumstances, for the existence of independent extremist groups to match social discontents with conspiracies and corporealize them both with anti-Catholicism. But, as always, "fringe" extremist groups persisted even during this period, which have largely escaped historical attention. A number of nativist and anti-Catholic societies, founded before the war, continued to exist into the postbellum era with memberships fluctuating from 50,000 to 150,000.[21] The most important of these were the Order of United American Mechanics, the Junior Order of United American Mechanics, and the Patriotic Order of the Sons of America.

Composed largely of workmen and members of the lower middle class, these organizations reflected the nationalistic and religious animosities of many of the native-born Protestants of these groups. . . .

In order to diminish the influence of the foreign born, they favored the restriction of the numbers of immigrants who could enter the country and advocated a longer period of residence before naturalization. Opposing the election of Romanists and foreigners to public office, they made the doctrine that "Americans should rule America" their fundamental principle.[22]

During the seventies, new anti-Catholic secret societies were formed in the cities. In 1876, the various organizations joined to create the American Alliance, to cooperate politically. They opposed Roman Catholic political groups and "urged all citizens to vote only for the native-born for public office."[23] In general, as might be expected, these groups strongly supported Republican candidates. The American Alliance endorsed Hayes for President in 1876, and its president received a letter from Hayes's secretary who wrote that Hayes was "deeply gratified" by the endorsement.[24]

It should be noted that these various streams of right-wing nativism included efforts to revive antebellum Anti-Masonry. In May 1868, a national convention of "Christians opposed to secret societies" met in Pittsburgh to revive the Anti-Masonic movement. This attempt was clearly linked to concerns over growing secularism and the loss of status of evangelical Protestantism. Spokesmen for the new movement called attention to the revival of Masonry, charging that Masons had protected each other, both north and south, during the Civil War. They also resurrected the charges that Masons held the majority of public offices in the country and prevented fellow Masons from being convicted of crimes. The reason that Masonry had revived was that it represented the ongoing activities of Satan and his human agents.[25] As in the case of the earlier movement the new effort involved attacks on liberal Protestants, foreigners, Catholics, and Mormons as well.[26] The new movement set up a permanent organization, the National Christian Association, which has continued to the present. In 1874, it sought to revive political Anti-Masonry by creating the American (Anti-Masonic) party.[27] The president of the organization declared at its 1875 convention: "Freemasonry must be destroyed if the country is to be saved. That fellowshipping Freemasonry is disintegrating the church. That voting for adhering Masons is voting for men who in practice deny the first principles of Republican government."[28]

The *Christian Cynosure,* the monthly magazine of the movement, reprinted and repeated almost every ancient charge against the Masons, including the story of the conspiracy of the Illuminati.[29] An exposé of the Masonic conspiracy, published in 1870, argued that the then contemporary Masonry, Mormonism, and Kukluxism were expressions of the movement started by Adam Weishaupt in Bavaria, a movement "calculated and designed to overturn the Christian system and all Christian governments."[30]

Although the revived movement never attained significant proportions, it helped keep the various stories of Masonic Satanic plots in circulation in the United States, until they reemerged on a major scale again during and following the Depression of the 1930's. One indication that the subsequent concern with the continuing activities of the Illuminati has links with the post-Civil War Anti-Masonry is that the bête noire of the National Christian Association, General Albert Pike, the Grand Commander of the Southern Masons from 1859 to his death in 1891, has entered the demonology of the Illuminati conspiracy. Pike was repeatedly denounced as the master Masonic plotter by the National Christian Association in the nineteenth century. In the 1950's, a book circulating among the radical right outlining the relations between the Illuminati and the Communist movement reported that Pike had given instructions in 1871 to unite various revolutionary organizations in Europe to destroy "the powers of the Tsars, and . . . subjugate the Russian people in order that the Illuminati could turn the Russian Empire into the stronghold of Atheistic Communism."[31] Stemming from the attacks on him while he was alive, Pike remains, in the contemporary literature exposing the Illuminati, as the head of the organization during the 1870's, as the man who "revised and modernized the ritual of the Black Mass celebrated to emphasize the Luciferian and Satanic victory achieved in the Garden of Eden. . . ."[32]

The 1876 national platform of the American (Anti-Masonic) party clearly points to fundamentalist roots similar to those of Anti-Masonry of the 1820's and 1830's. Thus not only did it demand that "the charters of all secret lodges granted by our Federal and State Legislatures should be withdrawn, and their oaths, prohibited by law," but it went on to state a full moralistic Protestant creed, including advocacy of total prohibition of the sale of intoxicating drinks. The program declared in its first two planks:

1. That ours is a Christian nation and not a heathen nation, and that the God of the Christian Scriptures is the author of civil government.
2. That God requires and man needs a Sabbath.[33]

The Anti-Masonic American party received 2,508 officially counted votes in the Presidential election of 1876 and 1,045 in 1880.[34] The party apparently reorganized shortly thereafter, since much of its program, including the demand that the charters of the secret lodges be withdrawn and their oaths prohibited by law, reappeared in the platform of the American Prohibition National party in 1884. This group also insisted that the Protestant Bible be used as the basis of scientific and cultural education in the schools, that Mormon polygamy "be immediately suppressed by law," and that the immigration of "contract labor from foreign countries . . . which creates competition with free labor to benefit manufacturers, corporations, and speculators" be stopped.[35]

American Protective Association

The largest anti-Catholic and nonsouthern extremist organization of the late nineteenth century, the American Protective Association (APA), was organized in 1887. The movement, which was to claim 2,500,000 supporters in the mid-nineties, was founded in the small city of Clinton, Iowa, as a result of what appeared to be a local situation. A municipal slate of labor-union (Knights of Labor) candidates had been elected in 1886. It was then defeated one year later, "owing, it asserted, to the voters of the fourth ward, the majority of whom were Irish, or of Irish descent."[36] A small group of seven men, some of whom were lawyers, and others members of the Knights of Labor, decided to form the American Protective Association to fight the power of the Catholic church in politics.[37]

Like the Know-Nothings before them and the Ku Klux Klan afterward, the APA was a secret organization, which engaged in elaborate rituals and fancy costumes in its private meetings. The major issues of the APA, as officially stated in its formal program drawn up early in 1894, were "simply to defend 'true Americanism' against the 'subjects of an un-American ecclesiastical institution' by fighting for a free public school system, for immigration restriction, and for a slower, more rigid system of naturalization."[38] The predominant issue of the APA was, of course, anti-Catholicism. "Every recruit took an oath never to vote for a Catholic, never to employ one when a Protestant was available, and never to go out on strike with Catholics."[39] The conspiracy theory, anti-Catholic variety, was also used by the APA to link popular nativist bigotry with conservative political issues, specifically antagonism to trade-unions and a strong nationalist and jingoistic focus. The Pope and the Catholic church were repeatedly denounced for trying to subvert American institutions on behalf of a "foreign power."[40] During the 1890's, the papacy was placed "alongside Chile, Italy, and Great Britain as one of the powers against which an inflamed populace prepared to do battle."[41]

Although the emphasis on religious prejudice, on boycotts of Catholic merchants, on discrimination against Catholic labor, may be sufficient to place the APA in the category of monistic organizations, its procedural emphases in other respects bolster this categorization. Analysts of the movement agree that slander and libel were characteristic of the group. It relied on forged documents purportedly proving Catholic plots and sponsored lectures by bogus ex-nuns and former priests who had allegedly escaped from captivity in monasteries.[42]

The most famous forged document distributed by the APA, described as the bogus encyclical, was published as a document "addressed to American Catholics by Pope Leo XIII. It absolved them from any oaths of loyalty to the United States and instructed them 'to exterminate all heretics.' "[43] To legitimate its own potential use of extralegal forces, the APA contended that hundreds of thousands of "papal soldiers" were ready to spring into action. Catholic priests were accused of "lecherous" activities inside of convents.[44] In criticizing and exposing the supposed power, crimes, and sins of Catholics, the tone was moralistic to the point of paranoia.

The APA posited a conscious plot, concocted by a conclave of Catholic prelates in 1851, "to concentrate Catholic immigration from Europe in large American cities and by its vote to seize them for the Catholic Church."[45] The APA claimed that "although only one-eighth of the population of the United States was Catholic . . . one half of all the public office-holders were Catholics . . . that Catholics were favored in Civil Service examinations, and that all civil servants were forced to contribute to Catholic charities."[46]

The hysteria which seized many Protestants reached its height in the summer of 1893 with the widespread acceptance of the belief that the Pope had written a letter ordering Catholics to "exterminate all heretics found within the jurisdiction of the United States of America."[47] Although there are reports that members of the Order sought to arm themselves in protection against this Catholic plot in various parts of the country, the efforts to constrain Catholic assassins through purchase of arms reached a peak in Ohio.[48]

In Toledo, the mayor had the National Guard on duty for a week in September to protect Protestants against this monstrous Catholic mass murder plot. "The *Toledo Blade* stated that thousands of people had believed in the authenticity of the papal letter and had expected an attempt to exterminate all heretics to begin on September 5."[49] In Columbus, seventeen leading citizens, including the president of Ohio State University, several professors, and a number of Protestant ministers, felt it necessary to issue a circular to quiet the hysterical fears of many Protestants. The statement said that its signers had learned of "a state of anxiety amounting almost to a panic in many of the communities of this region over an apprehended uprising of the Roman Catholics to ravage the land."[50]

When the outbreak predicted by the APA did not occur, this did not upset those who had distributed the forged papal letter. "It was now described as an example of Jesuit trickery to get Protestants off guard so that an attack at a later time could be more successful."[51]

The Roots of the APA

In the context of its own unique historical circumstances, the growth of the APA reflected those elements which have always been typical to the development of right-wing extremist movements in America: status strains at higher levels of society; social discontent at lower levels; a common corporeal target—all against the background of shifting political loyalties.

The APA arose in the late 1880's following a period of rapid growth which had encouraged the rise of an extremely wealthy *nouveau riche* class, the development of a visible Catholic middle class, and the growth of Catholic political power in urban Democratic party machines which began to win many municipal elections. Humphrey Desmond, the first historian of the APA writing in 1911, explicitly suggested that much of its growth could be explained by the status concerns of established members of the Protestant middle class who resented these developments. He argued that the emergence of the APA in 1887, like that of some of the earlier social movements, was a reflection of status concerns brought about by shifts in the economic structure:

Latter day Know-Nothingism (A.P.A.ism) in the west, was perhaps due as well to envy of the growing social and industrial strength of Catholic Americans.

In the second generation, American Catholics began to attain higher industrial positions and better occupations. All through the west, they were taking their place in the professional and business world. They were among the doctors and the lawyers, the editors and teachers of the community. Sometimes they were the leading merchants as well as the leading politicians of their locality.[52]

While the APA itself appealed to the disenfranchised of the middle class rather than of the upper class, it was part of the design of response to the status strains of the period. Those descended from the old wealthy of the pre-Civil War era found their claims to superior status threatened by the newly wealthy, many of whom were often of non-Anglo-Saxon background. The newly wealthy, in turn, discovered that wealth alone was not sufficient to earn them admission to high-status groups. As John Higham describes the situation:

At every level so many successful people clamored for admission to more prestigious circles that social climbing ceased to be a simple and modest expectation. . . . A hectic social competition resulted from the greater penalties of being left behind and the greater opportunities for getting ahead. In order to protect recently acquired gains from later comers, social climbers had to strive constantly to sharpen the loose, indistinct lines of status. With a defensiveness born of insecurity, they grasped at distinctions that were more than pecuniary, through an elaborate formalization of etiquette, the compilation of social registers, the acquisition of aristocratic European culture, and the cult of genealogy.[53]

A possible link between the urban lower middle-class-based APA and the status concerns of the more well-to-do old family American Protestants is indicated by the fact that the publisher of the APA's anti-Catholic books was also the publisher of *The Social Register*. This work was first put out in 1887, the year in which the APA was founded, and was designed to protect the status of old families from the threat engendered by the many new millionaires of the era.

Societies concerned with emphasizing ancestral origins followed hard on each other during this period. The Sons of the Revolution was founded in 1883, the Colonial Dames in 1890, the Daughters of the American Revolution in 1890, the Aryan Order of St. George or the Holy Roman Empire in the Colonies of America (for those descended in a male line from families ennobled or decorated by royalty) in 1892, the Military Society of the War of 1812 in 1892, the Society of Colonial Wars in 1893, the Colonial Order of the Acorn (for those descended in a direct male line from colonial families) in 1894, the Society of Mayflower Descendants in 1894, the Daughters of Cincinnati (Revolutionary officers) in 1894, the Order of Founders and Patriots (for those descended from families which were in the colonies before 1657 and whose ancestors fought in the Revolution) in 1896.[54]

Except for a few prominent individuals, there is little evidence that those active in the ancestral organizations backed the APA. The latter appealed to lower middle- and working-class Protestants. The hereditary groups attracted the well-to-do and better educated. A study of their membership indicates that they drew support from professionals and prosperous businessmen.[55] And while they eschewed cooperation with the more vulgar APA, those active in the hereditary societies also saw in increased immigration the source of the growing radicalism and corruption which were eroding the traditional verities of the American society.

Below the social level of the hereditary societies appeared a large number of patriotic societies, which like them stressed patriotic and national themes. Many of these societies rallied to the support of the American Protective Association, and, as the latter grew, in

most instances lost their identity in the latter. The best known of these are the Order of the Native Americans, Order of the American Union, "The Crescents," Templars of Liberty, Patriotic League of the Revolution, Order of American Freemen, National Order of Videttes, American Patriotic League, Loyal Men of American Liberty, and Order of the Little Red School House.[56]

In December 1895, at Washington, D.C., the APA was able to dominate a convention or council of the lower-status patriotic organizations, including representatives

> from the Orangemen, the Junior Order of United American Mechanics, the Society for the Protection of American Institutions, and "similar organizations" which represented "more than 3,000,000 members. . . ." [A] platform was adopted and notice given members of both houses of Congress as well as the representatives of the great political parties, that restricted immigration and legislation against alleged tendencies of the Roman Catholic Church were regarded as essential to the welfare of the United States. . . .[57]

The interlocking character of the concern of APA members for identification with patriotic symbols may be seen in the background of W. J. H. Traynor, the second president of the organization. A Canadian by birth, he "joined the Independent Order of Good Templars when a boy and the Loyal Orange Institution at the age of seventeen. . . . Among the later crop of American patriotic orders, in addition to the 'A.P.A.,' he is or was connected with the Order of the American Union, the Crescents . . . [and] the American Patriotic League."[58]

The APA and the Working Class

Working-class nativism had been stimulated during the period by the industrial depression of 1883–1886. A number of organizations were forced to limit immigration. Pennsylvania coal miners demanded an end to the importation of contract labor. "About 1887 a poll of 869 Wisconsin workers in varied occupations showed approximately half of them convinced that immigration was injuring their trade."[59]

Although the APA had considerable working-class support from the start, it grew slowly during the prosperous years from 1887 to 1893 with its strength located largely in midwestern cities characterized by strong Catholic political influence. Its period of rapid growth began in the depression year 1893, when it recruited hundreds of thousands of new members in cities all through the country, with the exception of the South. This growth clearly seems to have been a response to the severe economic conditions. APA spokesmen throughout the country blamed the occurrence on Catholics. The collapse of many banks was attributed to a Catholic conspiracy designed to pave the way for a seizure of power. The unemployed were told that their jobs had been taken by Catholic immigrants.

> According to the A.P.A., the Catholics, sometimes in the person of T. V. Powderley, [head of the Knights of Labor], were fomenting strikes and labor problems as part of a larger plot to overthrow American institutions. Protes-

tants were warned to avoid all unions dominated by papists, to discard the strike as . . . useless . . . and to place no confidence in free silver.[60]

The growth of labor unions and strikes was explained by the APA as derivative from the presumed fact that "the Irish were already in control of the great American cities."[61]

The only available reports by historians which deal with the social base of the movement refer to its extensive working-class backing, even in the early period. Like the Native Americans of the 1840's and the Know-Nothings of the 1850's, it had considerable support among workers, including many active in trade-unions. John Higham states, "Much of this early support came from disaffected union members, especially from the Knights of Labor. . . ."[62] Earlier studies indicate that the APA from the start secured a very large "following among railroad workers."[63] In fact, "so many trainmen, switchmen and clerks joined the A.P.A. that it was at first popularly regarded as a railroad organization."[64] Railroad union leaders, like Eugene V. Debs, were so troubled by the APA's influence among workers that they devoted a great deal of energy to attacking it.[65] Alvin Stauffer, in his detailed reports on the growth of the APA in various midwest industrial towns and cities, locates the appeal of the Order among workers who resented Catholic inroads into their occupations, particularly in view of the growth in unemployment from 1890 on.[66] Coal miners in Pennsylvania and Illinois were also a strong source of APA support.[67] In Pennsylvania, Protestant workers in the iron and steel mills, as well as in the coal mines, exhibited strong hostility to Catholics and immigrants who "were willing to work for extremely low wages. . . ."[68]

The APA-aligned Junior Order of American Mechanics, which was aggressively nativist, gained greatly in the late 1880's and early 1890's in Pennsylvania, recruiting tens of thousands of workers.[69] Even foreign-born Protestant coal and steel workers from Scotland and Wales, who were barred from membership in the nativist organization, joined the anti-Catholic Orange Order and the British-American Association.[70]

The Junior Order also "expanded rapidly in 1890 and 1891 [in Maryland and West Virginia], establishing numerous councils in the coal-mining regions of these states. . . ."[71] In Toledo, Ohio, the APA triumphed in the 1892 municipal elections, supposedly as a result of the fact that its "large native American working class enthusiastically supported the A.P.A. candidate."[72]

APA support among workers increased sharply with the onslaught of the severe depression of 1893. Under the influence of "hard times" and APA propaganda, religious antagonism steadily increased among workmen. In fact, they seem to have formed a large majority of the APA councils then springing up all over the Middle West. Mrs. A. P. Stevens, writing in the *Chicago Vanguard,* declared that nine out of ten members of the anti-Catholic societies belonged to the working class. If this estimate is too high, there can be no doubt that in industrial districts wage earners formed the backbone of the movement. In many places labor organizations were almost destroyed by bitter dissensions between their APA and Catholic members.[73]

The APA also grew rapidly among railroad workers and miners in the mountain states during the depression. It elected its tickets in a number of Colorado mining communities.[74] The considerable Montana strength of the APA also lay largely in mining centers. Other areas of strength among miners and railroad workers were Nevada, Idaho, Wyoming, and Utah.[75]

Perhaps the most continuous history of nativist activities designed to limit competition with American workers in the late nineteenth century occurred in California. The most noteworthy group in the state was the Workingman's party of California, formed in 1877, which was strongly dedicated to ending Chinese immigration. The party, which had its main base among San Francisco workers, grew strong enough to win a majority of the delegates to a Constitutional Convention elected in 1878. The Constitution adopted at this convention contained a section which

forbids all corporations to employ any Chinese, debars them from suffrage, forbids their employment on any public works, annuls all contracts for "coolie labor," directs the legislature to provide for the punishment of any company which shall import Chinese to impose conditions on the residence of Chinese, and to cause their removal if they fail to observe these conditions.[76]

The Workingman's party was followed in 1886 by the formation of a new California-based movement, the American party, which had national aspirations. This party was primarily concerned with immigration from Europe, signaling out the Irish for special abuse.[77] The party secured considerable strength in San Francisco and Oakland, although it failed to elect any candidates. It "found recruits chiefly among young men of a lower middle-or-working-class background."[78] Efforts to form a national party to contest the elections of 1888 failed miserably, and the party declined rapidly, disappearing after 1891.

The APA, which entered California in 1893, was much more successful than the American party. Working at first largely through the Republican party, it succeeded in electing many supporters in local, legislative, and congressional contests.[79] Although the APA had its share of supporters and members from the business strata (it published a directory of those who were pledged to its principle), its leading journalistic opponent, the

Catholic *Monitor,* which ran frequent exposés of APA members, argued that its base was largely composed of "laborers." And a student of the California movement concluded that if "the order had its quota of bums, as it very probably did in a city like San Francisco, it was not entirely composed of 'sewer rats' as the *Monitor* charged."[80]

That the APA did have a large working-class base was reflected in the operation of its subsidiary, the American Labor Bureau, which had branches in San Francisco and Oakland. The Bureau offered to "furnish at short notice: Agents, Bench Hands, Book Keepers, Blacksmiths, Brass Melters, Butchers, Cabinet Makers, Cooks, Carpenters, Clerks, Conductors, Coachmen, Collectors, Draughtsmen, Electricians, Engineers, Janitors, Laborers, Machinists, Metal Roofers, Nurses, Porters, Planing Mill Hands, Painters, Paper Hangers, Photographers . . . etc."[81] One historian concluded that the movement had gained "relatively more strength in labor circles than among other social groups, that it had introduced discord and mistrust into trade unions and made the task of organizing wage-earners extremely difficult."[82]

The studies of the APA do not include any statistical analysis of the social characteristics of its membership or of the supporters of the APA-endorsed candidates in various municipal elections in different parts of the country. Some basis for such analysis does exist in the form of membership lists of the Order published by newspapers for Minneapolis and a number of northern California cities and in a table giving the state membership of the APA and affiliated patriotic organizations for the entire country, derived from official APA reports. We do not know how reliable these reports are, but these data do give us some basis for further description. Presumably, though the membership reports may be exaggerated, the bias should be consistent.

The analysis of the occupations of the members of the APA in the different cities is reported in Tables 1–4. The results are plainly inadequate with respect to any conclusion concerning a special working-class base for the organization. It is clear that the APA secured considerable working-class backing; but on the other hand, in Minneapolis, Oakland, San Francisco, and San Jose, over 40 per cent of its members whose occupations could be identified were in middle-class jobs. Since the group presumably recruited largely from native-born Protestants, who, as a stratum, were more well-to-do than the foreign-born and the Catholics, it may be argued that on the whole it drew somewhat more heavily from the working class than from the middle class within the native-born Protestant population. It should also be noted in evaluating these data that many studies of the membership of voluntary organizations, including those which are political action groups, indicate that lower-status, less educated people are much less likely

Table 1. OCCUPATIONS OF MEMBERS OF THE MINNEAPOLIS APA, 1894,
COMPARED WITH THE CENSUS REPORTS, 1900

	APA Members (1894)	All Minneapolis Males	Native-Born		Foreign-Born Whites
			Native Parents	Foreign Parents	
Manual	41.0 %	65 %	47 %	65 %	77 %
Policemen	6.5	1	1	1	1
Firemen	6.5	1			
Total manual and service	54.0	66	48	66	78
Nonmanual	46.0	33	52	34	22
Number	(199)	(65,450)	(18,334)	(16,562)	(28,892)
Unlocatable in Directory	29.0 %				
Number	(282)				

SOURCES: Names and addresses of APA members were taken from the Minneapolis news-paper. *Town Talk*, I (September 1, 1894), 2. The occupations were secured from *Davison's Minneapolis Directory, 1894* and *1895* (Minneapolis: 1894 and 1895). The data for the occupations of different groups in the Minneapolis labor force are from *Special Reports, Occupations at the Twelfth Census: 1900* (Washington: Government Printing Office, 1904), pp. 614–617.

Table 2. OCCUPATIONS OF MEMBERS OF THE APA IN
THREE SMALL CALIFORNIA CITIES, 1894

	Sacramento	San Jose	Los Gatos	Total Three
Manual	60 %	29 %	67 %	53.0 %
Police	8	7	—	5.0
Total manual and police	68	36	67	58.0
Nonmanual	32	64	21	39.5
Farm	—		12	2.5
Number	(89)	(58)	(52)	(199)

SOURCES: Table computed from lists of names and occupations of APA members in the three cities as reported in the *Monitor* (San Francisco) (November 3, 1894), Supplement (September 22, 1894), p. 12, (September 29, 1894), p. 12; presented in Priscilla F. Knuth, *Nativism in California, 1886–1897* (M.A. Thesis, Department of History, University of California, Berkeley, 1947), Appendix C, pp. 225–227.

to join organizations than the better educated strata. It is also likely that those whose names could not be located in city directories were in more lowly pursuits.

There are no reliable reports on the membership of the APA. At its high point around 1895, it officially claimed a membership of about 2,500,000. This figure, however, included members of the APA itself and affiliated patriotic societies. Donald Kinzer, the foremost historian of the movement, estimates that there were "perhaps one hundred thousand" dues-paying adherents of the APA lodges themselves. Some rough estimates of the relative geographic sources of APA membership may be derived from a

Table 3. OCCUPATIONS OF MEMBERS OF THE APA IN OAKLAND, CALIFORNIA, 1897, COMPARED WITH THE CENSUS REPORTS, 1900

Occupations	APA Members	All Oakland Males	Native-Born Native Parents	Native-Born Foreign Parents	Foreign-Born Whites
Manual	42.1 %	50.7 %	38.0 %	44.1 %	51.1 %
Police	3.6	1.0	1.1	1.4	.9
Total manual and police	45.7	51.7	39.1	45.5	52.0
Nonmanual	54.3	48.3	60.9	54.5	48.0
Number	(84)	(20,870)	(6,921)	(5,490)	(7,110)
Unlocatable in Directory	31.0 %				
Number	(122)				

SOURCES: See under Table 4.

Table 4. OCCUPATIONS OF MEMBERS OF THE APA IN SAN FRANCISCO, 1894, COMPARED WITH THE CENSUS REPORTS, 1900

Occupations	APA Members	All San Francisco Males	Native-Born Native Parents	Native-Born Foreign Parents	Foreign-Born Whites
Manual	51.9 %	55.7 %	44.8 %	51.5 %	58.3 %
Nonmanual	48.1	44.3	55.2	48.5	41.7
Number	(77)	(131,315)	(26,460)	(40,037)	(53,327)
Unlocatable in Directory	50.6 %				
Number	(156)				

SOURCES: The names of the members of the San Francisco APA are taken from the *Monitor*, October 6, 1894, p. 1, and October 13, 1894, p. 8. The Oakland names are from the *Monitor* of February 27, 1897, pp. 6–7, and March 6, 1897, pp. 6–7, 13, as reported in Priscilla F. Knuth, *Nativism in California, 1886–1897* (M.A. Thesis, Department of History, University of California, Berkeley, 1947), pp. 227–228, 236–237. The names were checked for occupations in various city directories. The data for the occupations of the different groups in the labor forces of Oakland and San Francisco, California, are from *Special Reports: Occupations at the Twelfth Census, 1900* (Washington: Government Printing Office, 1904), pp. 660–661 and 720, respectively. For purposes of computing the percentage of manual workers in both cities, agricultural workers were excluded.

report broken down by states of the membership of the APA federation (including the patriotic societies).[83] The original source of this list suggests that although estimates of state membership may be inexact, the report "has the virtue of demonstrating relative strength by states for the federation."[84]

More striking than the variations in the class base of the APA is the indication in the state membership data that the APA's greatest appeal was to residents of the western states which had been most recently settled and were growing most rapidly. The breakdown by region is given in Table 5.

Table 5.   REGIONAL DISTRIBUTION OF MEMBERSHIP OF APA
AND AFFILIATED PATRIOTIC SOCIETIES

	Membership	Percentage of Population
East	514,550	2.7
Border	201,250	3.2
South	219,360	1.3
East Central	489,350	3.8
West Central	422,140	4.8
Mountain	169,800	12.4
Pacific	377,195	17.7

SOURCE: Computed from table presented in Albert C. Stevens, *The Cyclopedia of Fra-ternities* (New York: Hamilton Printing and Publishing Company, 1899), p. 114, as repro-duced in Donald L. Kinzer, *An Episode in Anti-Catholicism: The American Protective Association* (Seattle: University of Washington Press, 1964), pp. 178–179.

It is difficult to explain why the APA and affiliated patriotic societies should have their greatest membership in the Mountain states and the Far West. It is true that the most successful effort to link nativism to third-party politics in the late nineteenth century occurred in California.

The correlations between the ratio of membership in the APA and allied organizations to adult males in each state and various political and social characteristics of the states presented in Table 6 both reinforce and contra-dict certain generalizations by various historians of the movement. Unex-pectedly, there seems to be no relationship between APA strength and urban-ism or presence of Catholics in the population. On the other hand, there is a low correlation with proportion of native whites in the different states. This finding suggests that the APA appealed as a nativist organization to native-born Protestants, rather than to all Protestants. Most interesting of all is the fact that the largest correlation is between rate of population increase and APA membership. This relationship is not simply another way of saying that the APA was strong in the West. When the states were divided into three regional groups—southern states, states west of the Mississippi, and those east of the river—the relationship with population growth held up in the two nonsouthern regions; that is, in the East and West. (The APA had very little strength in the South.) Thus these data, plus the regional breakdowns, indicate that the APA like other movements had its greatest appeal in regions in which a larger portion of the population were relative newcomers. As a membership organization, which gave its adherents a sense of identity and status, it seemingly may have attracted those enduring the strains of migration. Or, conversely, the relationship may reflect the fact that the most rapidly growing areas suffered from the greatest social tensions flowing from the difficulties of absorbing large numbers of new-comers.

Here is a clue to the nature of nativist bigotry which develops more clearly in later American history. During the period of pristine Protestant nativism in America, it is easy to make an automatic relationship between political anti-Catholicism and the fundamental Protestant religious biases of the anti-Catholics. This has been refined to include the postulate of an automatic relationship between political animus against culturally offensive immigrants and the cultural stance of natives. A relationship there is, surely, but the pattern of causality becomes more complicated as the stereotypes become less convenient. The suggestion is here, strongly supported later, that Protestantism, fundamentalism, manners, and morals are often less the motivation than the excuse for nativist bigotry—its "cultural baggage" rather than its engine. This does not mean that the nature of this cultural baggage did not lend much ferocity to the extremist movements. It is important to note the strong evangelical tone of late nineteenth-century anti-Catholicism. One contemporary (1894) account of the causes of the "social paranoia" afflicting the country in the form of the APA blamed it in part on "bad theology." The "bad theology" referred to "was the hell fire and total depravity doctrines that were then being preached with con-siderable gusto. . . ." The extreme forms of anti-Romanism were reported to have been almost entirely confined to orthodox Protestantism. "Members of more liberal groups were not greatly alarmed. 'And the more orthodox they are,' Hubbard concluded, 'the fuller of fight they seem.' "[85]

The relationship between APA strength and voting patterns reinforces the evidence that the Democrats opposed the APA and that where the Democrats were strong the APA was weak. Most of the analyses of APA politics, however, point up the links between the organization and sections of the Republican party. This relationship is borne out by our statistical analysis when we only consider the relative proportion of the two major party votes received by the Republicans. The early 1890's, however, witnessed a three-party race in much of the country. The Popu-list or People's party sought to build a new movement directed against the banks and monopolies. And the state-wide statistics indicate that the APA tended to be strong in states in which the Populists received a high vote. This correlation, though statistically significant, does not necessarily mean that the same people adhered to both movements. It is possible that both were strong in states more subject to social and economic difficulties, but that they recruited from different strata in the same areas. The only direct links pointing to some degree of overlap come from a study of the California APA, which reported that a number of Populist leaders were members of the APA. This study, however, mentions many more Republi-can candidates for office who were APA members than Populists.[86]

The APA's greatest political power was evidenced in local elections. APA tickets were elected in many cities throughout the Midwest, as well as to a lesser degree in all other sections of the country with the exception

Table 6.   CORRELATION (PEARSON r) BETWEEN PROPORTION OF APA MEMBERS OF
ADULT MALE POPULATION (OVER TWENTY-ONE)
WITH VARIOUS STATE STATISTICS

Percent Catholic, 1890	—.046
Percent Native White, 1890	.329
Percent Urban, 1890	.168
Percent Population Increase, 1880–1890	.561
Percent Democratic of total Presidential vote, 1892	—.525
Percent Republican of total Presidential vote, 1892	.179
Percent Populist of total Presidential vote, 1892	.457
Percent Democratic of two major party vote, 1892	—.352
Percent Republican of two major party vote, 1892	.352
Percent Democratic of total vote in three party congressional races, 1894	—.472
Percent Republican of total vote in three party congressional races, 1894	.228
Percent Populist of total vote in three party congressional races, 1894	.345
Percent Democratic of two major party congressional vote, 1894	—.414
Percent Republican of two major party congressional vote, 1894	.415

SOURCES: The proportion of APA members of adult (over twenty-one) male population
is from Donald L. Kinzer, *An Episode in Anti-Catholicism: The American Protective Asso-
ciation* (Seattle: University of Washington Press, 1964), pp. 178–179, and the *Eleventh
Census of the United States: 1890*, Report on Population of the United States, Part I
(Washington: Government Printing Office, 1895), p. 751. Per cent Catholic, 1890, is from
H. K. Carroll, *The Religious Forces of the United States* (New York: Christian Literature
Company, 1893), pp. 76–77, and the *Eleventh Census, op. cit.*, p. 2. Per cent native white,
1890, is from the *Eleventh Census, op. cit.*, p. 681. Per cent urban, 1890, is from the
Fifteenth Census of the United States: 1930, Report on Population of the United States
(Washington: Government Printing Office, 1933), II, 14–15. Per cent population increase
1880–1890 is from the *Eleventh Census, op. cit.*, I, 4. The Presidential vote of 1892 is from
W. Dean Burnham, *Presidential Ballots 1836–1892* (Baltimore: Johns Hopkins Press, 1955),
pp. 246–257, and Svend Petersen, *A Statistical History of the American Presidential Elections* (New York: Frederick Ungar, 1963), pp. 57–58. The congressional vote of 1894 is
from "Election Returns—Votes for Representatives in Congress, 1894," *World Almanac
and Encyclopedia, 1896* (New York: Press Publishing Company, 1896), pp. 415–465.

of the South.[87] These municipal campaigns were usually fought on issues
revolving around Catholic influence in the local school situation, or domination over municipal patronage. The Order largely operated within the
Republican party, and its electoral influence was taken seriously by many
prominent Republican politicians.[88] Democrats generally condemned the
organization in strong terms.

Thus it must be noted again that as in the case of the Anti-Masons with
the National Republicans in 1832, of the Native Americans with the Whigs
in 1844, of the Know-Nothings with the Republicans in 1856 and thereafter, and of the American Alliance with the Republicans in 1876, in many
areas, GOP politicians entered into both overt and tacit alliances with the
APA. A renewed effort to identify the Democratic party with low-wage
Catholic immigrant labor and with a Catholic political conspiracy seemingly
could only resound to the advantage of the Republican party, and many of
its leaders knew this. On the other hand, their surprisingly large depression-
based victory, particularly in the East, in the congressional election of 1894

suggested that too close a link with the APA might mean the loss of a possible opportunity to make inroads among the rapidly growing immigrant population of the large cities. Many analysts, then and since, concluded that the Republicans finally had broken through the Democratic monopoly of the immigrant and Catholic vote. Consequently, William McKinley, Republican Presidential nominee in 1896, and his advisers rejected the APA as an ally. Thus, instead of increased influence within the GOP as a result of what it thought was its major contribution to the 1894 victory, the Order found itself on the outside. Men who had been elected with its support repudiated it. This political rejection by the party of Protestantism with which it identified seems to have contributed to its rapid decline thereafter.

In 1896, the Order divided over the Presidential election, and many members, including presumably the Populists among them, turned to the support of William Jennings Bryan, the evangelical Protestant nominee of the Democratic and Populist parties. Statistical analysis of the 1896 Presidential returns indicates no significant relationship between APA strength and Presidential vote.

Enter Anti-Semitism

In the latter part of the nineteenth century, anti-Semitism began to make a serious if still minor appearance on the extremist scene. Like the Catholics, the Jews began to offer a substantial visibility in the cities, with massive waves of immigration from eastern Europe. And like the Catholics, the Jews came equipped with an arcane presence that lent itself to conspiracy theory. They had no Pope and no Vatican, but a special aura of secrecy and intrigue deeply imbedded in the folklore of Christian civilization. In addition, the occupational bias of the Jews as merchant and middleman, at once an image of the civilization's folklore and a reality imposed by that civilization, lent itself especially to the discontents and conspiracy theories of the economic era that was developing. Sections of the Democratic party, and various agrarian-based organizations like the Granger movement and the Greenback party, attacked the economic policies of the Republicans as banker-dominated and injurious to the farmers. "From valid—if exaggerated and misguided—complaints about the failure of the [banking] system to provide cheap farm credit, there is an ever-growing allusion to 'usurers,' 'money-lenders,' and the 'money-power.' "[89] And with the concentration on Wall Street, the banks, and the money monopoly as the sources of the farmers' financial difficulties came the image of the Jewish banker.

For the American Agrarian [of the 1870's] there was a special reason for suspicion of the Jews. They were aliens, outside the charmed circle of the "producing classes." "Brick" Pomeroy, who for all his years in New York and Chicago was perfectly attuned to the rural mind, attacked the Jews as men who "do not pay much attention to farming or to raising hogs for market, but who for their peculiarities are skimmers, gleaners, gatherers who can scent a dollar as far as a Yankee politician can a carpet bag." The Jew was a non-producer, one of the detested middle-men. More immediately, for the greenbacker he was a "capitalist"; a money lender and a banker. . . . [The agrarians] learned from the Greenback leaders of the great international banking houses of the Seligmans, Speyer, and Belmont, and above all Belmont's backers, the Rothschilds. The Jew came to represent the money power of "Wall Street," itself the personification of sinister forces. "Wall Street Jews" became a common epithet of the soft money men, and even the national banks were held to be dominated by "the same corporate Jew class."[90]

Anti-Semitism was not prevalent in the 1870's among farmers. Yet its appearance in this form is extremely important, for the monetary reformers of this period introduced a theme which was to recur time and again: the concern with bankers and those who controlled the credit system sliding over to an image of a Jewish international conspiracy. Not surprisingly, the status anxieties of the late nineteenth century resulted in the emergence of anti-Semitic episodes. Wealthy Jews, who had taken part in upper-class social clubs in many cities during much of the century, suddenly found themselves excluded, sometimes from clubs that had once had Jewish officers.

Almost without exception, every [elite] club in America now developed a caste-like policy toward the Jews. They were excluded, as a people or race, regardless of personal qualities such as education, taste or manners. It is important, moreover, to stress the fact that this caste line was only drawn at the end of the nineteenth century, when, as we have seen, the members of the upper class were setting themselves apart in other ways.[91]

Many, at different levels in the social structure, pointed to the growing position of wealthy Jews in the society as an explanation for the different ills that they found present in the expanding plutocratic society of the late nineteenth century. Some agrarian Populists identified the Jews with international finance capitalism, while in the urban slums, anti-Semitism spread among various recent immigrant groups, who were involved "in intimate competition for living space, livelihood, and status."[92]

A number of publications and political statements issued during the nineties suggested the existence of various Jewish conspiracies, both economic and political. The prominence of Jews among the international banking fraternity indicated to some that there was an "invisible empire."[93]

Henry and Brooks Adams were among the many Brahmins who identified the Jews as the source of materialistic corruption. Writing to Henry in 1896, Brooks described the Jews as "a vast syndicate, and by controlling London, they control the world."[94] A number of writings which came out of the free silver and monetary reform movements, strong among the agrarians of the day, also alluded to Jewish international conspiracies.[95]

Although the Populist party itself was clearly not anti-Semitic, it believed in a conspiracy theory as related at least to financial crises. The party platform of 1892 proclaimed: "A vast conspiracy against mankind has been organized on two continents, and it is rapidly taking possession of the world. If not met and overthrown at once, it forbodes terrible social convulsions, the destruction of civilization, or the establishment of an absolute despotism."[96] In 1896 it went on to say: "The influence of European money-changers has been more potent in shaping legislation than the voice of the American people. . . . We demand the establishment of an economic and financial system which shall make us masters of our own affairs and independent of European control. . . ."[97] In 1900, the pro-Bryan wing of the party denounced the monetary act passed by Congress in that year "as the culmination of a long series of conspiracies" and pledged the party "never to cease the agitation until this great financial conspiracy is blotted from the statute books."[98]

The Democratic party, when nominating William Jennings Bryan and entering into coalition with the Populists in 1896, though using less violent rhetoric, indicated that it, too, believed in conspiracies. Its 1896 platform took up the charge frequently voiced by monetary reformers that the depression of 1873 had been caused by the influence of the international moneylenders (often identified with the Rothschilds) on the American government. It asserted: "We declare that the Act of 1873 demonitizing silver *without the knowledge* or approval of the American people has resulted in the appreciation of gold and a corresponding fall in the process of commodities produced by the people [in] . . . the enrichment of the money-lending class at home and abroad."[99]

One student of the election of 1896 has argued that the Populist and Free Silver elements who supported William Jennings Bryan had a strong streak of anti-Semitism. He points to the fact that they frequently associated Jews with international banking, that those who were sensitive to the role of banking as a source of economic difficulties often also mentioned Jewish names in this connection.[100] Anti-Semitism in this form tended to be linked with Anglophobia, in the belief that the London money market exploited the United States. Some of this literature, as we have noted, identified English Jewish bankers as the heart of an international conspiracy which had brought about the depression of 1873 in an effort to maintain the gold standard. An Associated Press dispatch from St. Louis at the time that both the Free Silver and Populist conventions of 1896 were meeting there reported serious levels of anti-Semitism: "One of the striking things about the Populist Convention, or rather the two conventions here and those attending them, is the extraordinary hatred of the Jewish race. It is not possible to go into any hotel in the city without hearing the most bitter denunciation of the Jews as a class and of the particular Jews who happen to have prospered in the world."[101]

It is difficult to estimate exactly how important anti-Semitism was as a political force. Two historians who have carefully examined the record of Populist state conventions in local newspapers indicate that they found relatively few anti-Semitic statements or references, that anti-Semitism was limited to a few prominent individuals.[102] Yet, at the same time, even those studies suggest a heightened awareness of the role of Jews among the international banking fraternity, so disliked by the midwestern and southern agrarians.

Examination of American Jewish publications of the day indicates that they were concerned about the presence of anti-Semitism in Populism and in the Bryan 1896 campaign. There were a number of references to reports in the secular Jewish press of anti-Semitic speeches, particularly in Michigan, Ohio, and Indiana by Populist-Democratic leaders. Mary Lease, a prominent Populist, toured the country speaking for Bryan in a manifest anti-Semitic vein.[103] After the election, Jewish Democrats who had supported Bryan complained that he had lost thousands of Jewish votes because of Populist orators who attacked the Jews.[104]

But if the emerging signs of antagonistic sensitivity to Jews during the 1890's indicated a potential for political anti-Semitism, it is important to note that it was only a potential, that none of the major political and social movements of the day used anti-Semitism as a political tactic. Anti-Catholicism was the anti-Semitism of the Protestant nineteenth century. The social processes which were to lead to the massive virulent anti-Semitism of the Ku Klux Klan in the 1920's and Father Coughlin in the 1930's were obviously in motion, but at the end of the nineteenth century, the Catholics still constituted the main scapegoat of the politically uneasy bigots.

Bigotry in the Beginning of the Twentieth Century

The decline of the APA to near extinction, following on bitter internecine warfare over its role in the 1896 election campaign, did not eliminate extremist bigotry in the pre-World War I period. Perhaps the most important such organization from the late nineties to the war was the old Junior

Order of the United American Mechanics. This group is reputed to have grown from 15,000 members in 1885 to 60,000 in 1889. Supplanted by the APA, it declined sharply after this, but it gained after the decline of the APA. In the decade from 1904 on, it jumped from 147,000 members to 224,000 in 1914. Clearly this was not an unimportant organization.[105]

In many ways, the Order resembled the APA in its policies. It also was concerned with resisting the influence of Catholics and the foreign-born. It sought to protect native-born Americans from the competition of immigrants; that is, to see that only native-born were employed and that the businesses of "Americans" were patronized in preference to those of foreigners.[106] Both monopolies and Catholic-controlled unions were enemies. The country was "suffering from the selfishness of plutocratic capitalists and striking workers. . . ."[107]

The attacks on immigration were directed both at the increase in the number of Catholics and more strikingly at " 'Anarchists and all that class of heartless and revolutionary agitators' who come 'to terrorize the community and exalt the red flag of the commune above the Stars and Stripes'."[108] At the same time the leaders of the organization felt it to be "their duty to watch . . . the Church of Rome and frustrate the designs of the Pope."[109]

Most indicative of the growing mass appeal of anti-Catholicism in the decade before World War I was the growing influence of a weekly, the *Menace,* published in a small Ozark town. This paper, founded in 1911, had a circulation of over one million within three years. Its sole stock in trade was anti-Catholicism, arguing that the Vatican was trying to take over the country through immigration.[110]

The prewar anti-Catholic movement differed from its predecessors in two significant ways. First, it was allied to an antielitist, even leftist tradition. The *Menace* attacked the Catholic church as being for big business and hostile to trade-unions. The paper "showed a vague, guarded sympathy with the Socialists."[111]

To understand the shifting base of support of anti-Catholic nativism, it is necessary to look at the broad context of the political changes of the nineties and the years before World War I. The various movements were a continued expression of a succession of movements which had much of their roots among evangelical Protestants. Different sections of this broad stratum sought to retain their power and status on one hand against the incursion of non-Anglo-Saxon Protestant immigrant groups, and on the other against the newly powerful class of urban capitalists and monopolists. The nativist movements, the various temperance and prohibitionist organizations, and the Populists and Progressives all involved efforts to protect different groups from challenges to their values and influence stemming from the large-scale monopolies and trusts and the horde of immigrants. Both the monopolies and the immigrants were centered in the growing metropolitan areas, and the rising tide of resentment focused against evils seen as a consequence of one or both of these trends.[112]

During the nineties, the Populist party, whose strength lay almost exclusively in the Midwest and in southern rural Bible Belt areas, while showing some nativist and even anti-Semitic aspects, concentrated on seeking to regain the conditions which would sustain a stable agrarian society and focused the fire of its attack on urban-controlled banks, railroads, and monopolies. It was essentially an economic reform party appealing to those who sought direct economic help from the government. Although the party must have included many who were sympathetic to the diverse strands inherent in Protestant moralism, these tendencies were repressed or negated in the Populists' efforts to win support for economic reform. Since the principal strength of the Populists lay in traditional Republican midwestern areas, the party in a number of states became the major opponent of the dominant Republicans. It sought to secure the votes of the Democratic minority, many of whom were foreign-born, through direct appeals, coalition, or fusion. Consequently, the Populists in Kansas, the movement's strongest state, did not support prohibition and passed a resolution at the party convention of 1894 condemning the APA as "un-American" for seeking to divide people on the basis of creed.[113] In the Middle West, the APA, as we have noted, was pro-Republican and thus anti-Populist.[114]

There was some difference between the attitudes and behavior of Populists in rural and urban areas. "Within the People's party the rural (Farmer's Alliance) element was not so aggressively nativistic and insistent upon immigration restriction and exclusion as the urban (Citizen's Alliance) membership . . . especially . . . [the latter's] political leaders. . . ."[115] A study of the APA in California reports that a number of Populist candidates in two northern cities in 1894 were members. These included the San Jose candidates for Sheriff and County Recorder, Sacramento candidates for Sheriff, Clerk of the Supreme Court, District Attorney, Public Administrator, and two assembly seats.[116]

Perhaps the foremost link between the Populists of the 1890's and the repressive nativism, racism, and religious bigotry which were to reach their height in the powerful Ku Klux Klan of the 1920's was Tom Watson, the most important southern leader of the People's party. He had strongly opposed anti-Negro and anti-Catholic activities in the nineties and refused to join in the coalition with the "old-line" Democrats which occurred around the nomination of William Jennings Bryan in 1896. He ran for President on the remnant Populist ticket in 1904 and 1908. Yet, by the second decade of the new century, Watson had become a flaming bigot. *Watson's Magazine* strongly attacked Negroes, Catholics, and Jews, although he continued also to support revolutionary causes abroad and treated Wall Street as a symbol of evil at home.[117] In 1910, he attacked the Catholic hierarchy as "the deadliest menace to our liberties and our civilization."[118] The anti-Catholic crusade continued unabated for seven years until the suppression of his paper for opposing the war in 1917.

In 1914, Watson launched a campaign designed to convict Leo Frank, a wealthy Georgian Jew, accused of murdering a fourteen-year-old girl. Watson charged that Frank was supported by a "gigantic conspiracy of Big money."[119] He proclaimed: "Frank belonged to the Jewish aristocracy, and it was determined by the rich Jews that no aristocrat of their race should die for the death of a working-class Gentile."[120] When Frank's death sentence was commuted, Watson recalled the role of lynch law and of vigilante committees. And when Frank was lynched in 1915, Watson strongly defended the action.[121] Watson rewrote all the hoary attacks on the Catholic church drawn from Samuel Morse, the Know-Nothings, and the APA. He wrote a book, *Maria Monk and Her Revelation of Convent Crimes,* arguing that her three-quarter-century-old charges about sex and infant murders in convents were true. And he raised again the APA charges of a Catholic armed conspiracy. *"The Pope's secretly organized traitors, the Knights of Columbus, are armed to the teeth with the best of modern rifles."*[122]

Watson continued his vitriolic anti-Semitic campaign for years after Frank was lynched. He revived the medieval charges that Jews engage in ritual murder of Christians. *Watson's Magazine* adopted for its own the Russian Czarist government's charges that a Jew, Mendel Beiliss, had killed a small boy near Kiev. When Beiliss was acquitted in 1913, Watson concluded that "the same mighty engine of agitation and suppression that had worked for Dreyfus was put in motion for Beiliss."[123] The power of the Jews was identified as synonymous with that of capitalists and bankers. Even the Hearst papers were denounced as "Jew owned" because of their stand on the Frank case. And bringing his two religious antipathies together, Watson concluded: "There is no longer any doubt that the Roman priests and the opulent Jews are allies."[124]

The outpouring of hate against Catholics, Jews, and Negroes contained in Watson's papers, which had a national circulation before America's entry into World War I, was to take institutionalized form in the mass movement of the Ku Klux Klan of the 1920's. There is no evidence that Watson himself played any direct role in the formation of the Klan. Yet it should be noted that Leo Frank was lynched on August 16, 1915. Shortly thereafter Watson wrote in his paper, *The Jeffersonian,* that it may be necessary to organize "another Ku Klux Klan."[125] The second Ku Klux Klan, to be discussed in detail in the following chapter, was founded on a mountaintop outside Atlanta on Thanksgiving Eve, 1915.[126]

The timing of the formation of the Klan with the culmination of the Leo Frank case was not a coincidence. Colonel William Simmons, the founder of the revived Klan, had long dreamed of reforming the post-Civil War order. And the thirty-three men who gathered with him to bring the modern Klan into existence were all members of the Knights of Mary Phagen, an organization formed under Tom Watson's sponsorship to make certain Leo Frank died for Mary Phagen's murder.[127] As Vann Woodward has aptly commented: "If Watson had any hand in launching the new organization, no record has been found that reveals it. Yet if any mortal man may be credited (as no one man may rightly be) with releasing the forces of human malice and ignorance and prejudice, which the Klan merely mobilized, that man was Thomas E. Watson."[128] There can be little doubt that Watson in his latter bigoted days continued to appeal to many of the same forces that he did when he was one of the group of Populist leaders. In 1917, he opposed America's participation in the war as subservience to "our Blood-gorged Capitalists." He strongly defended Eugene V. Debs, the Socialist leader, in his opposition to the war. Running successfully for Senator in 1920, he held up the "Catholic menace" as an alternative to the Red menace. As a Senator, he attacked the oil companies and the United States Steel Corporation and demanded the recognition of the Soviet Union. Watson died in 1922.

Eugene Debs, recently released from the penitentiary, wrote in a letter to Mrs. Watson: "He was a great man, a heroic soul who fought the power of evil his whole life long in the interest of the common people, and they loved and honored him."

. . . Most conspicuous among the floral tributes [at his funeral] was a cross of roses eight feet high, sent by the Ku Klux Klan.[129]

It must be remembered that Watson's excursions into bigotry were not made under the aegis of the Populist party and cannot be identified with that party. It is just that his bigotry grew out of the same soil of discontent as did that party, with which he had been identified. The turn of the century was a culminating period of large-scale displacement in American society. The Populist party was an expression of reaction to the displacement of agrarian America. The Progressive movement, which arose after the turn of the century within the Republican party, reflected not only that displacement, but also the displacement which was taking place *within* the cities.

The Progressive movement blamed the decline of traditional American values on the corrupt urban Democratic machines based on the largely

Catholic immigrants and the monopolies and trusts dominated by ruthless *nouveau riche* elements. The Progressives secured considerable support in the rural and small-town Midwest, but unlike the Populists, they also found both leaders and followers inside the city itself, essentially from elements who were migrants from, or socially in comparable positions to, the Protestant middle class or nonurban America.

One of the keys to the American mind at the end of the old century and the beginning of the new was that American cities were filling up in every considerable part with small-town or rural people. The whole cast of American thinking in this period was deeply affected by the experience of the rural mind confronted with the phenomenon of urban life, its crowding, poverty, crime, corruption, impersonality, and ethnic chaos. To the rural immigrant, raised in respectable quietude and the high-toned moral imperatives of evangelical Protestantism, the city seemed not merely a new social form or way of life but a strange threat to civilization itself. . . .

In many great cities the Yankee found himself outnumbered and overwhelmed. . . . Often the Yankee felt himself pushed into his own ghetto, marked off perhaps by its superior grooming but also by the political powerlessness of its inhabitants.[130]

The leadership of the movement, particularly when it took the form of an independent political party, the Progressives, which split off from the Republicans, was largely in the hands of urban upper middle-class men. In many ways they resembled the abolitionist leaders.

They, too, were a "displaced elite." As Frank Carlton pointed out, writing of the social sources of humanitarian leadership in the heyday of the Progressive movement (1906): "Business men and the children of business men who have been pushed to the wall by the 'trustification' of industry furnish the raw material out of which the new humanitarian movement is being created."[131] They were native-born Protestants almost to a man. And Alfred Chandler, who studied the backgrounds of 260 of them, documented this: "Though they lived in the city, they were in no way typical men of the city. With very rare exceptions, all these men had been and continued to be their own bosses. . . . As individuals, unacquainted with institutional discipline or control, the Progressive leaders represented, in spite of their thoroughly urban backgrounds, the ideas of the older, more rural America."[132]

It would be a mistake, however, to conclude that the massive Progressive movement of the first decade of the century, and the Progressive party which formed behind Theodore Roosevelt in 1912, securing 27.4 per cent of the presidential vote, could be fitted neatly into a simple single-factor analytic framework. When turning to the few studies of the movement and party on a local level, we find disparate results. In a study of California leaders, George Mowry essentially reports a comparable pattern to that indicated by Chandler.[133]

Other quantitative evidence of the link between the Progressive movement and the previous patterns of Protestant reform in terms of both backgrounds and motivations may be found also in a study by Richard Ravitch dealing with the New York Progressive party:

> It would be wrong to assume that the Progressives were anti-Catholic, but it was unusual for a political party in New York to have only one Catholic in its midst. Several Bull Moose Progressives had belonged to the Guardians of Liberty, an organization which attacked the Church; but they withdrew to avoid the political repercussions. Certainly it can be said that the overwhelming religious affiliation was that of the Conservative Protestant sects.
>
> They were men conspicuous for their lack of association with the two groups which were slowly becoming the dominant forces in American life—the industrialist and the union leader. They were part of an older group which was losing the high status and prestige once held in American society. The Progressives represented the middle-class of the nineteenth century with all its emphasis on individualism and a set of values that was basically provincial. Resenting the encroachment on "his" America by the corporations and urban masses, the formation of the Progressive Party may be considered his way of protesting what was now his defensive position in the bewildering "drift" which characterized 20th century society.[134]

Studies of Progressive leaders in Iowa and Washington, however, could not establish clear-cut differences between those involved in the reform efforts and these active at the summits of the more conservative wings of the Republican party. And as a reform party which advocated many "welfare-state" measures, the Progressives were able to secure more support from manual workers and non-Democratic relatively recent immigrant groups than from the conservative stalwarts in places as different as Burlington, Iowa, and the East-side Jewish districts of New York City.[135]

Although the Populist and Progressive movements did foster antitrust legislation, the other reforms associated with the Protestant middle-class crusades between the Civil War and World War I did not succeed in the legislative arena. The prohibition movement could not outlaw the sale of liquor, and the various efforts to limit the immigration of foreigners also were unsuccessful. Seemingly, the efforts of the evangelical middle class to enforce their moral and economic values had failed. Until the war stopped immigration, millions of immigrants from central and eastern Europe and Ireland continued to pour through the portals of America, thus reducing the proportions committed to Protestant values. The large cities, which were centers of opposition to the morality and senses of status and power of the small town and rural middle class, also increased rapidly. In spite of the passage of antimonopoly legislation, big business firms continued to occupy a larger share of the economic structure, thus further reducing the relative importance of the moderate-size family corporations which had dominated the business life in the nineteenth century.

The failure of the various political, moralistic, and nativist movements to hold back the changes centered in the growing cities were seemingly most bitterly felt in the rural areas which had been the center of Populism. And the more frustrated farmers who had resisted the appeals of religious bigotry and racism in favor of class political action now seemingly were turning to such doctrines in their desperation, as evidenced by the rural location of centers of nativism before World War I.

This inverted the structure of former anti-Catholic movements and marked a historic transition in the character of Protestant nativism. During the nineteenth century the tradition drew its main strength from the larger towns and cities where Catholics were actually settling. Even in the 1890's, when the excitement invaded the midwestern countryside in a grotesquely jingoistic form, anti-Catholic xenophobia remained primarily an urban movement. But in the twentieth century it re-emerged most actively in rural America, where adherents of the hated faith were relatively few. . . .

[The farmers,] at least, had never abandoned the old-time religion. In fact they were beginning in the years after 1910 to pass over to the offensive against the diluted doctrines and moral laxity of their urban brethren. The rise of a militant rural fundamentalism coincided with the upsurge of rural nativism. Perhaps the two came partly from a common need, aggressive fundamentalism ministering to the same unfulfilled urges that sent rural Protestants crusading against popery. At any rate the reassertion of the straight Gospel truth undoubtedly quickened the rural war on Rome. In large parts of the South, Catholics were so uncommon that nativists found popular sentiment harder to rouse than in the Midwest, but in both areas the movement was definitely taking hold. In both, barnstorming evangelists lent an apocalyptic fury to the assault; and the devout could often be seen going to church with the Bible in one hand and *The Menace* in the other.[136]

The relative weakness of anti-Catholicism in urban areas does not mean, of course, that the various sources of urban bigotry had disappeared. The Guardians of Liberty, a strongly anti-Catholic and anti-immigrant secret society, was formed in 1911 by retired military officers, various upstate New York civic leaders, and—curiously for such company—Tom Watson. The Chief Guardian was General Nelson A. Miles, former Chief of Staff of the United States Army. Miles toured the country before the war, attacking the Catholic menace. As noted earlier, a number of the New York State leaders of the 1912 Progressive party had been members of the Guardians. Here again was a direct linkage between the resentments against the trusts and monopolies of sections of the privileged strata and hostility to the growing influence of Catholics and other immigrants.[137]

The growing anti-Semitism, discussed earlier, was perhaps the more significant form of urban bigotry in this period. It rarely took a manifest political form on the part of conservative elements, except in parts of the South, possibly because the large Jewish populations of the big cities were viewed as potential allies for the Republican and Progressive opponents of the Catholic-based Democratic machines. Considerable tensions existed between the Jews and other working-class immigrant groups, most of whom were Catholic, and these tensions were reflected in politics.

The Jews of New York had voted strongly against Tammany in the mayoralty election of 1901.[138] The strong tensions between the Jews and the Irish resulted in open violence in 1902, when a Jewish funeral procession passed through an Irish industrial district and was pelted with iron nuts and bolts. The largely Irish police force intervened against the Jews, using abusive language, arresting many, and injuring two hundred through use of clubs.[139] Although many Jews voiced their antagonism to the Irish politicians by voting Socialist, still others backed the Republicans. In 1912, three of the four New York City districts which gave Roosevelt a majority on the Progressive ticket were inhabited by east European Jews.[140] While the conflicts between the Jews and other impoverished immigrant groups inhibited any tendencies toward a blanket anti-immigrant policy among the Protestant urban elite, they also pointed up the potential for a working-class-based anti-Semitic movement such as was to arise in the form of the urban part of the Ku Klux Klan in the twenties and of Coughlinism in the thirties.

American participation in World War I both heightened the process of change, making the country more urban and more industrial, and by moving large populations around in the military and war industry brought home to many the dramatic revisions in behavior and values associated with urbanization. The war also legitimated the position of those who sought to identify an American moral way of life which should be protected against foreign influences. It encouraged attacks on "un-American" elements, particularly radicals and the foreign-born. The Irish, the Germans, and the Jews, the three most visible immigrant groups, had been opposed to the Allied cause because of antagonism to Britain among the Irish, antipathy to Czarist Russia among the Jews, and loyalty to ancestral ties among the Germans. The struggle over entry into the war was to some extent a fight between those of Anglo-Saxon ancestry and those of Continental and Irish backgrounds, thus exacerbating the bases for a cultural religious cleavage between those whose status and values were identified with the American ethnic and religious past and those who were seeking to change America and were linked with the foreign enemies. The stage was set for the repressive actions and bigoted movements of the 1920's.

Notes

1. Charles L. Sewrey, *The Alleged "Un-Americanism" of the Church as a Factor in Anti-Catholicism in the United States, 1860–1914* (Ph.D. Thesis, University of Minnesota, 1955), p. 152.
2. Cited in *ibid.*, p. 153, from *Harper's Weekly*, XVI (1872), 717.
3. *Ibid.*, p. 156.
4. *Ibid.*, p. 162.
5. *Ibid.*, p. 163.
6. R. Freeman Butts, *The American Tradition in Religion and Education* (Boston: Beacon, 1950), p. 142.
7. Alvin P. Stauffer, *Anti-Catholicism in American Politics, 1865–1900* (Ph.D. Thesis, Department of History, Harvard University, 1933), p. 44.
8. Cited in *ibid.*, p. 44.
9. *Ibid.*, pp. 65–66.
10. John Higham, *Strangers in the Land* (New Brunswick: Rutgers University Press, 1955), p. 28.
11. Stauffer, *op. cit.*, p. 67.
12. *Ibid.*, pp. 68–69.
13. *Ibid.*, pp. 76–77.
14. Butts, *op. cit.*, p. 143.
15. Anson Phelps Stokes, *Church and State in the United States* (New York: Harper, 1950), II, 68.
16. Donald L. Kinzer, *An Episode in Anti-Catholicism* (Seattle: University of Washington Press, 1964), p. 10.
17. Sewrey, *op. cit.*, pp. 313–314.
18. Stauffer, *op. cit.*, p. 93.
19. See Lee Benson, "Research Problems in American Political Historiography," in Mirra Komarovsky, ed., *Common Frontiers in the Social Sciences* (Glencoe: The Free Press, 1957), pp. 143–146.
20. For a discussion of the issues involved, see David G. Farrelly, "Rum, Romanism and Rebellion Resurrected," *Western Political Quarterly*, VII (1955), 262–270.
21. Stauffer, *op. cit.*, p. 2.
22. *Ibid.*, p. 3.
23. *Ibid.*, p. 61.
24. *Ibid.*, p. 80.
25. "The Speech of Rev. J. R. Baird," in *Minutes of the National Christian Convention Opposed to Secret Societies* (Chicago: Ezra A. Cook, 1868), pp. 44–45.
26. See various statements in the *Minutes, ibid.*, pp. 65–69, 80–81.
27. J. Blanchard, *Freemasonry a Fourfold Conspiracy* (Chicago: Ezra A. Cook, 1898), p. 4.
28. *Ibid.*, p. 16.
29. See quotations from the *Christian Cynosure* in John Levington, *Origin*

of *Masonic Conspiracy* (Dayton: United Brethren Publishing House, 1870), pp. 304–305.

30. *Ibid.*, pp. 300–302.

31. William Guy Carr, *The Red Fog over America* (Toronto: National Federation of Christian Laymen, 1957), p. 225.

32. *Ibid.*, pp. 233–234.

33. Thomas H. McKee, ed., *The National Platform of All Political Parties* (Washington: Statistical Publishing Co., 1892), p. 103. See also D. W. Wilder, *The Annals of Kansas* (Topeka: T. Dwight Thacher, Kansas Publishing House, 1886), pp. 714–715; James C. Malin, *A Concern about Humanity* (Lawrence, Kans.: privately printed, 1964), p. 22.

34. Svend Petersen, *A Statistical History of the American Presidential Elections* (New York: Frederick Ungar, 1963), pp. 45–49.

35. "American Prohibition National Platform of 1884," in Kirk H. Porter and Donald B. Johnson, eds., *National Party Platforms 1840–1956* (Urbana: University of Illinois Press, 1956), p. 63.

36. Mary C. Hynes, *The History of the American Protective Association in Minnesota* (M.A. Thesis, Department of History, Catholic University, 1939), pp. 1–2.

37. *Ibid.*, pp. 2–3; Ruth Knox Stough, *The American Protective Association* (M.A. Thesis, Department of History, University of Nebraska, 1931), pp. 1–5.

38. Higham, *op. cit.*, p. 83. See also W. J. H. Traynor, "Policy and Power of the A.P.A.," *North American Review*, CLXII (1896), 659; Albert C. Stevens, *The Cyclopedia of Fraternities* (New York: E. B. Treat, 1907), pp. 295, 297; Gustavus Myers, *History of Bigotry in the United States* (New York: Capricorn, 1960), pp. 171, 172; Malcolm Townsend, *Handbook of United States Political History* (Boston: Lothrop, Lee and Shepard, 1905), pp. 152–153; and Humphrey J. Desmond, *The A.P.A. Movement* (Washington: New Century Press, 1912), pp. 38–43.

39. Higham, *op. cit.*, p. 62; Desmond, *op. cit.*, pp. 35–38; and Thomas J. Jenkins, "The A.P.A. Conspirators," *Catholic World*, LVII (1893), 690–691.

40. Fritief Ander, "The Swedish American Press and the American Protective Association," *Church History*, VI (1937), 168; John Higham, "The Mind of a Nativist, Henry F. Bowers and the A.P.A.," *American Quarterly*, IV (1952), 21.

41. Higham, *Strangers . . . , op. cit.*, p. 84.

42. Desmond, *op. cit.*, pp. 52–54; Myers, *op. cit.*, pp. 183–184.

43. Higham, *Strangers . . .* , p. 85. For further details of the contents of forged documents and slanderous leaflets, see Myers, *op. cit.*, pp. 164, 167, 169–185; Stevens, *op. cit.*, p. 298; Jenkins, *op. cit.*, pp. 691–692; Ander, *op. cit.*, pp. 165, 166, 172, 173.

44. Ross S. Johnson, *The A.P.A. in Ohio* (M.A. Thesis, Department of History, Ohio State University, 1948), p. 25; Myers, *op. cit.*, p. 183.

45. *Ibid.*, p. 174. This plot was previously discussed by Samuel F. B. Morse and the Know-Nothings before the Civil War.

46. Ander, *op. cit.*, p. 166; see also Stevens, *op. cit.*, p. 294.

47. Johnson, *op. cit.*, p. 25; Desmond, *op. cit.*, pp. 19–20; Stough, *op. cit.*, pp. 46–48.

48. *Ibid.*, pp. 47–48; Mary E. Murphy, *The History of the American Protective Association in Ohio* (M.A. Thesis, Department of History, Catholic University, 1939), pp. 66–68.
49. Johnson, *op. cit.*, pp. 27–28.
50. In *ibid.*, p. 26.
51. *Ibid.*, p. 29.
52. Desmond, *op. cit.*, pp. 9–10; Higham, *Strangers . . .* , p. 80; Michael Williams, *The Shadow of the Pope* (New York: McGraw-Hill, 1932), p. 97.
53. John Higham, "Social Discrimination against Jews in America, 1830–1930," *American Jewish Historical Society*, XLVII (1957), 10; John Higham, "Anti-Semitism in the Gilded Age: A Reinterpretation," *Mississippi Valley Historical Review*, XLIII (1957), 566.
54. William E. Davies, *Patriotism on Parade* (Cambridge: Harvard University Press, 1955), pp. 54–73.
55. *Ibid.*, pp. 79–80.
56. Stevens, *op. cit.*, p. 294.
57. *Ibid.*, pp. 297, 308; Kinzer, *op. cit.*, pp. 123–124.
58. Stevens, *op. cit.*, pp. 295, 296.
59. Higham, *Strangers . . .* , *op. cit.*, p. 46.
60. *Ibid.*, p. 82; see also Kinzer, *op. cit.*, p. 30.
61. Ander, *op. cit.*, p. 166.
62. Higham, *Strangers . . .* , *op. cit.*, p. 62.
63. Stauffer, *op. cit.*, p. 186; Stough, *op. cit.*, pp. 34–35.
64. *Ibid.*, p. 187.
65. Higham, *Strangers . . .* , *op. cit.*, p. 82; Kinzer, *op. cit.*, p. 85; Stough, *op. cit.*, p. 35.
66. Stauffer, *op. cit.*, pp. 203–223.
67. Higham, *Strangers . . .* , *op. cit.*, p. 82.
68. Stauffer, *op. cit.*, p. 274.
69. *Ibid.*, p. 284.
70. *Ibid.*, p. 285.
71. *Ibid.*, p. 288.
72. *Ibid.*, p. 322.
73. *Ibid.*, p. 329; see also Higham, *Strangers . . .* , *op. cit.*, p. 82.
74. Stauffer, *op. cit.*, p. 348.
75. *Ibid.*, p. 349.
76. James Bryce, *The American Commonwealth* (Toronto: Copp, Clarke, 1891), II, 399.
77. John Higham, "The American Party, 1886–1891," *Pacific Historical Review*, XIX (1950), 40.
78. *Ibid.*
79. Priscilla F. Knuth, *Nativism in California, 1886–1897* (M.A. Thesis, Department of History, University of California, Berkeley, 1947), pp. 138–140, 167–170.
80. *Ibid.*, p. 210.
81. *Ibid.*, p. 141.
82. Stauffer, *op. cit.*, p. 374.
83. Albert C. Stevens, *The Cyclopedia of Fraternities* (New York: Hamilton

Printing and Publishing Company, 1899), p. 114, cited in Kinzer, *op. cit.*, p. 179.

84. Kinzer, *op. cit.*, p. 177.
85. Cited in Sewrey, *op. cit.*, pp. 300–301.
86. Knuth, *op. cit.*, pp. 225–226.
87. Desmond, *op. cit.*, pp. 63, 69; Higham, *Strangers* . . . , *op. cit.*, pp. 80–81.
88. Desmond, *op. cit.*, pp. 33–34; Kinzer, *op. cit.*, pp. 140–141; Walter Nugent, *The Tolerant Populists* (Chicago: University of Chicago Press, 1963), pp. 154–155; Murphy, *op. cit.*, pp. 31–36; Johnson, *op. cit.*, pp. 6–7, 32–34.
89. Irwin Unger, *The Greenback Era. A Social and Political History of American Finance* (Princeton: Princeton University Press, 1964), p. 209.
90. *Ibid.*, pp. 211–212.
91. E. Digby Baltzell, *The Protestant Establishment* (New York: Random House, 1964), p. 138; Higham, "Anti-Semitism . . . ," *op. cit.*, p. 567.
92. *Ibid.*, p. 575; Oscar Handlin, "American Views of the Jew at the Opening of the Twentieth Century," *American Jewish Historical Society*, XL (1951), 323–344.
93. *Ibid.*, p. 333.
94. Frederic Cople Jaher, *Doubters and Dissenters: A Study of Cataclysmic Thought in America, 1885–1918* (Ph.D. Thesis, History of Civilization Program, Harvard University, 1961), p. 390.
95. Ignatius Donnelly, *Caesar's Column* (Chicago: F. J. Schulte, 1891); William H. Harvey, *A Tale of Two Nations* (Chicago: Coin Publishing Co., 1894); William H. Harvey, *Coin's Financial School* (Chicago: Coin Publishing Co., 1894); S. E. V. Emery, *Seven Financial Conspiracies Which Have Enslaved the American People* (Lansing: D. A. Reynolds, 1887); Gordon Clark, *Shylock as Banker, Bondholder, Corruptionist and Conspirator* (Washington: No publisher listed, 1894); Mary E. Hobart, *The Secret of the Rothschilds* (Chicago: Charles H. Kerr, 1898); Ebenezer Wakely, *The Gentile Ass and the Judean Monetary Establishment* (Chicago: Mighty Quotient Series, 1895). For a discussion of some of this literature, see Richard Hofstadter, "Free Silver and the Mind of 'Coin' Harvey," in his *The Paranoid Style in American Politics* (New York: Knopf, 1965), pp. 238–315.
96. "People's Platform of 1892," in Porter and Johnson, *op. cit.*, p. 90.
97. "People's Platform of 1896," in *ibid.*, p. 104.
98. "People's (Fusion Faction) Platform of 1900," in *ibid.*, p. 116.
99. "Platform of 1896," in *ibid.*, p. 98.
100. Edward Flower, *Anti-Semitism in the Free Silver and Populist Movements and the Election of 1896* (M.A. Thesis, Department of History, Columbia University, 1952).
101. New York *Sun*, July 23, 1896, p. 2, as reported in Flower, *op. cit.*, p. 27. For a later newspaper account in the same vein, see p. 28.
102. Norman Pollack, "The Myth of Populist Anti-Semitism," *American Historical Review*, LXVIII (1962), 76–80; Norman Pollack, "Hofstadter on Populism: A Critique of the Age of Reform," *Journal of Southern History*, XXVI (1960), 478–500; and Nugent, *op. cit.*, pp. 14–16, 20–21, 109–115, 120–121.
103. Flower, *op. cit.*, pp. 25–37, 45–50.

104. *Ibid.*, p. 53.
105. Higham, *Strangers* . . . , *op. cit.*, pp. 57, 173, 174.
106. Stevens, *op. cit.*, p. 313.
107. Higham, *Strangers* . . . , p. 58.
108. *Ibid.*
109. Arthur Preuss, *A Dictionary of Secret and Other Societies* (St. Louis: B. Herder, 1924), p. 208.
110. Williams, *op. cit.*, p. 117; Higham, *Strangers* . . . , p. 180.
111. *Ibid.*
112. See Richard Hofstadter, *The Age of Reform* (New York: Vintage, 1960).
113. Nugent, *op. cit.*, p. 163.
114. *Ibid.*, p. 155; Kinzer, *op. cit.*, p. 141.
115. Malin, *op. cit.*, p. 13.
116. Knuth, *op. cit.*, pp. 225–226.
117. C. Vann Woodward, *Tom Watson: Agrarian Rebel* (New York: Oxford University Press, 1963), pp. 379–380, 385, 418–425; Myers, *op. cit.*, pp. 192–216.
118. Woodward, *op. cit.*, p. 419; Myers, *op. cit.*, p. 195.
119. Woodward, *op. cit.*, p. 438.
120. *Ibid.*; Myers, *op. cit.*, p. 208.
121. Woodward, *op. cit.*, pp. 438–445.
122. Cited in Myers, *op. cit.*, p. 198. Emphasis in the original in *Watson's Magazine* (December 1913).
123. Myers, *op. cit.*, p. 207.
124. Cited in *ibid.*, p. 208.
125. Woodward, *op. cit.*, p. 446.
126. David Mark Chalmers, *Hooded Americanism. The First Century of the Ku Klux Klan: 1865 to the Present* (Garden City: Doubleday, 1965), p. 30.
127. Leonard Dinnerstein, *The Leo Frank Case* (New York: Columbia University Press, 1968), pp. 149–150.
128. Woodward, *op. cit.*, p. 450.
129. *Ibid.*, p. 486.
130. Hofstadter, *op. cit.*, pp. 176–178.
131. Frank T. Carlton, "Humanitarianism, Past and Present," *International Journal of Ethics*, XVII (October 1906), 54.
132. See Alfred D. Chandler, Jr., "The Origins of Progressive Leadership," in Elting Morison, ed., *The Letters of Theodore Roosevelt* (Cambridge: Harvard University Press, 1954), III, 1462–1465.
133. George Mowry, *The California Progressives* (Berkeley: University of California Press, 1950), pp. 88–89.
134. Richard Ravitch, "The Genteel Revolt against Politics—A Study of the New York State Progressive Party in 1912" (unpublished paper, Department of History, Columbia University, 1954).
135. See the references in Samuel P. Hays, "Political Parties and the Community-Society Continuum," in William N. Chambers and Walter D. Burnham, eds., *The American Party Systems* (New York: Oxford University Press, 1967), pp. 163–164, and Higham, *Strangers* . . . , *op. cit.*, p. 190.
136. Higham, *Strangers* . . . , *op. cit.*, pp. 181–182.

137. Woodward, *op. cit.*, pp. 422–423; Higham, *Strangers* . . . , *op. cit.*, p. 182; Williams, *op. cit.*, pp. 114–115.
138. Higham, "Anti-Semitism . . . ," *op. cit.*, p. 578.
139. *Ibid.*
140. Higham, *Strangers* . . . , *op. cit.*, p. 190.

CHAPTER

4

The Bigoted Twenties

The decade following the end of World War I seemingly witnessed the triumph of the moralistic Protestant crusades of the previous century. In fact, it was a backlash triumph in a backlash decade, the last desperate protest of a nineteenth-century Protestantism in the course of eclipse. And it was during this period that the pattern of right-wing extremism took on some of its particular twentieth-century characteristics, partly as a result of America's new involvement in the world and the changing nature of that world.

The quickening of the monistic impulse during the 1920's was made manifest by the general climate of repression. In 1921 an immigration law was passed which not only put a drastic ceiling on total immigration but imposed an even more drastic national-origins quota system excluding all but a trickle of immigrants from other than the Protestant countries of northern Europe. Legislation to outlaw the teaching of evolution in the public schools was introduced into the legislatures of half the country and was actually enacted into law in a few. The Prohibition Amendment was passed by Congress and ratified by forty-six states. On federal, state, and local levels, strong official actions were taken to limit the rights of political dissenters through explicit legislation, threatening investigations, and administrative fiat. Official action was matched by repressive private action, which included tarring and feathering and, in some instances, lynching political offenders.

As John P. Roche put it, one gets

a sense of the twenties which is terrifying: as an age of hate, disaster, and repression totally lacking in omens of impending succor. . . . In 1926, the *Annual Report* of the American Civil Liberties Union noted morosely that only 20 meetings had been broken up by mobs as compared with 40 in 1925 and 225 in 1922. This decline brought no joy to the A.C.L.U. since it appeared to them not to reflect a growth in libertarian sentiment, but an unwillingness on the part of dissenters to hold meetings which might provoke disruption.[1]

This age of repression took its most dramatically organized shape in the Ku Klux Klan, which had between 3,000,000 and 6,000,000 members. In those terms, restricted as it was to the adult native-born Protestant male, active KKK membership blanketed about 15 to 20 per cent of the total adult male population and 25 to 30 per cent of the Protestant population. It dominated "for a time the seven states of Oregon, Oklahoma, Texas, Arkansas, Indiana, Ohio, and California."[2] It also had considerable strength in the rest of the South, other states in the Midwest, and Maine.

A curious footnote of the monistic twenties was the short-lived campaign to nominate Henry Ford for President in the 1924 elections. This was a period in which Ford's virulent anti-Semitic and even antidemocratic views were extremely well known, certainly among the politically involved. His *Dearborn Independent* had a circulation of over 600,000. His opinions were widely circulated in the mass media. Years after he had closed down the *Dearborn Independent* and issued statements denouncing anti-Semitism, most Americans knew about his views. "A poll conducted for Ford in 1940 by Maxon, Inc., one of the company's advertising agencies, revealed that an astonishing 80.3 per cent of the American male public had heard that Ford was anti-Semitic."[3] A second survey two years later produced comparable results.

Yet, during 1923, *Collier's* magazine reported that Ford led all other possible candidates in its national Presidential preference poll. Of the 259,553 persons who were polled by *Collier's* agents, 34 per cent were for Ford, 20 per cent backed the incumbent Republican President, Warren Harding, and 8 per cent supported Senator William McAdoo, the leader among Democrats mentioned. Although the survey was clearly not a representative sample, *Collier's* reported that it believed that the poll was a "genuine cross-section of American political opinion, with the one exception of the farmers, whom our agents were not able to call upon in large numbers in the short time at their disposal."[4] Other straw votes in the Midwest also reported that Ford led all candidates.[5]

William Randolph Hearst, then the publisher of the largest newspaper chain in the country, announced in May that he was prepared to back Ford for President on a third-party ticket.

Social Strains

Economic Preservatism

In 1920, Senator Warren Harding told a group of Boston businessmen that the country needed "not nostrums but normalcy; not revolution but restoration." And indeed it was the spirit of restoration which imbued the "back to normalcy" politics of the 1920's. America's classic economic conservatism—the absence of government interference with business—had been seriously breached in the previous decades. A hated income tax had been imposed. Minimum-wage and maximum-hour laws had made their federal appearance. So had other labor-protective measures and federal appropriations for various rudimentary programs in education, rehabilitation, public health. Against that wave the forces of economic preservatism began to fight a historically losing battle. Harding, Coolidge, and Hoover were presumably restoration Presidents, but while economic conservatives found conditions much more to their taste, it became clear that there was to be no return to the age of McKinley. In the language of a later era, "rising expectations" and the nature of the American political process not only made such a return impossible but suggested the necessity of a constant rearguard action against further encroachment on the unfettered activities of business and the economic market. That encroachment had a double column. On the one hand, there was government regulation; the "welfare state" began to peek out of the wings and, by one name or another, became a staple target for twentieth-century right-wing preservatist politics. On the other hand, there was the growing encroachment of organized labor, which reached a peak of about 5,000,000 members in 1920.

The 1920's represented an attempt to return America to normalcy in the matter of its foreign affairs as well. The previous decade had seen this nation's total embroilment in world affairs and its clear emergence as a major world power; but, more significantly, American foreign policy had been brought to the brink of "internationalism." Entanglement in supranational ventures such as the League of Nations was opposed by economic conservatives who feared limitations on domestic affairs at home and economic thrusts abroad. They were joined by those ethnic populations, heavily concentrated in the rural Midwest and among the Irish and Jews in the cities, who did not care for the English-French bias of America's intervention, and by many who were generally caught up in the postwar disillusionment. Harding's election presumably marked the restoration of a traditional isolationist policy. But, again, American foreign policy could never be the same, nor the debate about it.

Despite the vigor of the new isolationist coalition, the friends of international organization were more numerous, more vocal, and more potent in the 1920s than they had ever been in the quiet years before the holocaust. . . . The isolationists were trying to hold back the integrating forces of the twentieth century. Once the United States had been initiated into the wiles of power politics, there was no turning back, for the lessons of the war had been too encompassing. At home and abroad horizons were steadily widening. Provincialism was lessened by trips in Model T Fords, by movies filmed in Hong Kong or Timbuktu, and by radio broadcasts tuned in through crystal sets from the capitals of the world. Foreign correspondents, books, and magazines all stressed European and Asiatic affairs. Although soldiers brought back stout prejudices, they also returned with a more cosmopolitan outlook. Isolationism now had to be defended, something quite unnecessary when the policy reflected genuine salt-water insulation.[6]

"Internationalism," by whatever name, became a symbol of evil for twentieth-century reactionary ultra-rightist politics. But the term had taken on a new meaning for the conservatives, since the missionary quality of the Russian Revolution had raised the threat of socialism and the "welfare state" to a higher order.

Fundamentalism: The General Protestant Backlash

Religious fundamentalism as the linchpin in preservatist ideology came to a climax in the 1920's, perhaps on July 10, 1925, when a schoolteacher was brought to trial in Dayton, Tennessee, for teaching the theory of evolution in his classroom. A newsman wrote:

A few years ago we couldn't have imagined the United States eagerly awaiting the news from some church convention. . . . The break came suddenly, about two years ago. . . . the country waited eagerly while the Presbyterians, assembled in Columbus, Ohio, actually took a ballot on the Virgin Birth. A little later the Associated Press and all the other news agencies of the nation were covering in World Series, play-by-play fashion an argument in a Tennessee courtroom on the all-important problem of where Cain's wife came from and whether God could have worked by the day before he invented the sun.[7]

On its face, the antipluralistic particularism of highly conservative religion seems consonant with the monistic excesses of right-wing extremism. But virulent fundamentalist backlash was revealed again in the 1920's as an instrument of status preservatism, rather than an engine of generalized right-wing tendencies. As one Protestant historian of Protestantism put it:

On closer inspection, it becomes clear that the conservative is by no means primarily interested in taking the Bible as the literal, infallible word of God.

His primary interest is in the preservation of orthodox Christianity, and he has chosen to make the doctrine of the errorless scripture his first line of defense. Paul Tillich has pointed out that whenever a movement is under attack, it tends to narrow itself. It retires within what it hopes to be an impenetrable forest and battles, not only the invader from without, but also the subversive within.[8]

But, if biblical literalness was just a line of defense, so was orthodox Christianity, and so was Protestant morality. It was a way of life that was at stake, that was losing its dominance; more particularly, the people who embodied that way of life were losing their social supremacy.

The sudden increase in the political power of those who sought to enforce fundamentalist Protestant orthodoxy by law may be seen as a "backlash" reaction to the basic loss of evangelical strength in the nation, resulting from broad demographic and ecological changes which had occurred between 1890 and 1920—changes due to the increase of large-scale industry, the concomitant rapid urban growth, and the influx of millions of European Catholic and Jewish immigrants. Traditional Protestantism was well on the way to being a minority culture from having been the majority one. The ideal typical Republican, Protestant, God-fearing, deeply religious, moralistic, middle-class American, living in a stable nonurban community, was losing control of the society which his father had dominated and which he had expected to inherit as his birthright.

American society was becoming cosmopolitan, secular, and metropolitan, with consequent negative consequences for evangelical Protestantism. The census of 1920 reported that for the first time in American history urban dwellers were in the majority. The city had never been the center of the previously predominant evangelical Protestant culture. The two major evangelical and moralistic denominations, the Methodists and the Baptists, had formed a majority of American Protestantism since early in the nineteenth century, but both groups had always been rooted in small towns and rural areas. On the other hand, the Episcopalians, the Catholics, the Unitarians, the Presbyterians, the Congregationalists, and the Jews have had disproportionate support in the cities. In 1890, when about one-quarter of the total population lived in cities with more than 25,000, less than 8 per cent of the Methodists and Baptists did. Conversely, close to half of the Episcopalians and Unitarians were urban dwellers, as were two-fifths of the Catholics and most of the Jews. The varying distribution of the different Protestant denominations among communities of different sizes in 1890 is recorded in Table 7.

Symbolically, metropolitan areas had become the center of Jewish and Catholic influence, with white Protestants a numerical minority.[9] And not only were white Protestants a minority in the large cities, but as compared with Catholics and Jews, the majority of those who lived in metropolitan

Table 7. PROTESTANT COMMUNICANTS ACCORDING TO SIZE OF COMMUNITY, UNITED STATES, 1890

	Cities 500,000 and over	Cities 100,000–500,000	Cities 25,000–100,000	Smaller Towns and Rural Areas	Total
Baptist	12.6 %	15.7 %	18.2 %	27.9 %	26.1 %
Congregational	4.7	4.9	7.7	3.2	3.6
Episcopal	17.6	10.5	9.1	2.3	3.7
Lutheran	14.7	13.9	8.9	8.0	8.6
Methodist	17.8	20.9	26.7	34.0	32.2
Presbyterian	18.4	12.9	10.6	8.2	9.0
Other[a]	14.1	21.1	19.0	16.6	16.8
	99.9 %	99.9 %	100.2 %	100.2 %	100.0 %
Number	(525,797)	(804,214)	(869,376)	(12,057,007)	(14,256,394)

SOURCE: United States Census of Religious Denominations, 1890, reported in H. K. Carroll, *The Religious Forces of the United States* (New York: Christian Literature Co., 1893), pp. 394–397, 406–407, 414–415, 430–435.

[a] "Other" communicants do not include Catholics and Jews, but do include non-Protestant bodies, the largest of which are the Russian Orthodox (13,504 members) and the Greek Catholics or Uniates (10,850 members). The category is, however, almost entirely Protestant.

areas had not been reared in such communities. A study made in the twenties concluded: "The Protestant Church in American cities is largely the property and product of rural immigrants. . . . Counts made of those attending city churches indicate they are largely made up of rural immigrants; seventy-five per cent of those present are frequently found to have been born in the country."[10] Hiram Evans, head of the KKK, cried out plaintively that the "Nordic American today is a stranger in a large part of the land his fathers gave him."[11]

The changes in moral behavior which became manifest during and after World War I had served in large measure to arouse the violent antipathies of the evangelical Protestants. One historian summed up the changes and reactions:

> The 1920's meant "modernism." And "modernism" among other things meant the waning of church influence, particularly over younger people, the breaking down of parental control, the discarding of the old-fashioned moral code in favor of a freer or "looser" personal one, which manifested itself in such activities as purchasing and drinking contraband liquor, participating in ultra-frank conversations between the sexes, wearing skirts close to the knees, engaging in various extreme forms of dancing in smokefilled road houses, and petting in parked cars. A host of Americans were unwilling, or unable, to adapt themselves to this post-war culture. In the Klan they saw a bulwark against the hated "modernism," an opportunity to salvage some of the customs and traditions of the old religio-moralistic order.[12]

The Second Ku Klux Klan

The first Ku Klux Klan had been created by Confederate veterans in 1866 as a kind of resistance movement to the newly won status of their former slave population, especially where they feared domination by that Negro population. Thousands of Negroes and some northern carpetbaggers were beaten, tortured, or lynched during the ensuing decade. The fury of this first KKK was dimmed partly by action of federal military forces and by the fact that, as political power became stabilized again in white southern hands, local laws and patterns were established to ensure the subordination of the Negro population. The second Ku Klux Klan was created in Georgia in 1915, but, unlike the first, was not restricted to the southern states or to an immediate issue of white supremacy. This interpretation is supported by a detailed study of the Klan in the four southwestern states, Texas, Oklahoma, Arkansas, and Louisiana. Charles Alexander reports "a strikingly small amount of hostility toward Negroes."[13] He concludes that in the Southwest, morality concerns were dominant.

Judging from the evidence at hand, the Klan's growth in the Southwest stemmed mainly from a desire to protect and defend the native American's own conception of what was right and wrong—not so much from "alien" influences, as from such home grown evils as the rise of the city, the advent of the bootlegger, and a general postwar letdown in private and public morals. . . .

The rural-mindedness which lay at the bottom of the Klan movement throughout the nation featured not an isolated provincialism, but a sharp conflict between rural values and the changing mores of a society undergoing rapid industrialization and concentration.[14]

This evangelical attack on modern immorality was not only present in the efforts of the Klan to punish drunks, adulterers, and other violators of the traditional moral code. Henry Ford, who was of rural Methodist origins and remained rural-minded and anticosmopolitan all his life (he refused to allow his son Edsel to go to college and told his biographer that he did not like to read books, "they muss up my mind"), gave expression to these values in his widely read *Dearborn Independent*. "He attributed the difficulties of youth to the influence of modern music. He advanced the notion that contemporary jazz, like the excesses of alcohol and finance capital, were the means by which international Jewry hoped to destroy mankind."[15] "It is interesting to note that the founding 'Emperor' of the Klan, William J. Simmons also complained bitterly about jazz. Our music has been lost amid the barbaric meaningless medley of sounds called 'jazz' suggestive of the low and the lewd."[16]

A study of the Klan at its height in 1924 by sociologist John Mecklin clearly pointed up the fact that its central "ideological" buttress was a traditional Protestant moralism:

[I]t is well to remember that men joined the Klan because it appealed to their patriotism and their moral idealism more than to their hates and prejudices. . . . [Often] the Klan secures a foothold in the community and makes itself felt, . . . in the role of moral reformer, unearthing the bootlegger or chastising criminals and disreputable characters that have escaped the law. . . . In almost every instance where the Klan is defied it is because of its efforts at local reform. . . .[17]

However, it is again necessary to point out that the congruence of Protestant fundamentalism and moralism with right-wing extremism is in one sense a historical accident. Moralism does not create right-wing extremism. Desperately preservatist or restorative movements—that is, backlash movements—require an aggressively moralistic stance and will find it somewhere. There needs to be invoked some system of good and evil which transcends the political or social process and freezes it. Efforts to preserve economic advantage invoke such a system because there is no public recourse in America to privileged class interest. Status backlash, particularly low-status backlash, must invoke such a system because, finally, the moral superiority of one group over another is all that can be invoked. This kind of group self-perception may be pervasive enough at all times, but becomes raised to an ideological and politically active level when group status is threatened. It is true that the Protestant branch of moralism is ideally suited for this purpose, but modern history suggests that other brands can be as effectively developed and applied. In this case, however, it was American Protestants who were involved.

Similarly, religious fundamentalism does not create right-wing extremism, although it is tempting to believe so because of the particularistic nature of both. Again, people or groups who are the objects rather than the beneficiaries of change tend to seek a general "fundamentalism" in order, as Paul Tillich put it, "to have a principle which transcends their whole disintegrated existence in individual and social life."[18] But that kind of generic fundamentalism, which would also have to be found if it did not exist, does not have to take the form of religious, much less Protestant, conservatism. Rather, the backlash of the 1920's demonstrated again the simple phenomenon of status substitution, whereby the public arena features not the status and status prerogatives of a group, but the status of their unique cultural and ideological baggage. The decline of a "way of life" is most disturbing to people attached to that way of life when it signals a decline of their status, of their social weight. Protestant moralism and fundamentalism, although eminently suitable, became the currency of the backlash of the 1920's because it happened to be the prime cultural property of those being displaced.

Being displaced were: traditional American Protestantism in general; the small-town centers of traditional Protestantism; those who remained in those centers; and many of those who were forced to migrate from them to the larger cities.

The rapid economic growth involved in rapid industrialization and urbanization which characterized most of the twentieth century up to the Great Depression resulted in considerable geographical and upward social mobility. While many improved their economic position and social status, most did not. Those who remained in the small town could see themselves falling behind the emerging elite of the large cities. Most of those who migrated to the more metropolitan areas lacked the education, skills, and capital to succeed. And Mecklin argued that the very openness of American society,

the stress and strain of social competition . . . made . . . the average man of native American stock . . . realize his essential mediocrity. Yet according to traditional democratic doctrine he is born free and the equal of his fellow who is outdistancing him in the race. Here is a large and powerful organization offering to solace his sense of defeat by dubbing him a knight of the Invisible Empire. . . . He becomes the chosen conservator of American ideals, the keeper of the morals of the community. . . . This flatters the pride of the man suffering from the sense of mediocrity and defeat.[19]

A more recent analysis of the Klan by a historian concludes that during its height in the twenties, the Klan secured most of its backing "in the states of the western reaches of the lower Mississippi Valley, the Pacific Coast, and the Middle West. . . . The secret fraternity drew its millions primarily from the villages and small towns which had been left rather undisturbed by the immigration, industrialization, and liberal thought of modern America."[20]

Yet it would be a major mistake to accept the frequently voiced conclusions that the Klan was largely a movement of the small-town and rural Protestant lower middle class. Perhaps the earliest observer to note that the Klan had considerable urban backing was the Swedish sociologist Gunnar Myrdal, who noted in his classic study of the Negro in America: "The Ku Klux Klan and similar secret societies thrive . . . in industrial communities."[21] Even in the South, the Klan of the 1920's was particularly weak in the rural black belt states such as Mississippi, Alabama, and South Carolina.[22] As Myrdal pointed out, in "the plantation areas where the social and political subordination of Negroes is solidified, there is not much need for special organizations of vigilantes to effect the extra-legal sanctions."[23]

Although the Klan had considerable strength in many of the small towns of the South, its strongest chapters were in the growing cities of the region, such as Atlanta, Memphis, Knoxville, Chattanooga, Nashville, Richmond, Birmingham, Mobile.[24] The list of cities in the Southwest in which the Klan was powerful and dominated local politics is almost coterminous with citation of the urban centers of the area. Among those in which the Klan was able to win election were Little Rock, Oklahoma City, Tulsa, Dallas, Fort Worth, Houston, Austin, El Paso, Beaumont, Shreveport, and many others.[25] Even in cosmopolitan New Orleans, with its heavy Catholic population, a strong chapter existed.[26]

A similar pattern of urban strength occurred outside of the South as well. In Ohio, the Klan had over 50,000 members in Akron and had other centers of urban strength in the Dayton-Springfield area, Youngstown, and Marietta.[27] The Klan won local elections in Toledo, Akron, Columbus, Youngstown, and other Ohio cities in 1923 and to a lesser extent in 1925.[28]

A study of the Indiana Klan locates its principal strength in urban areas. It dominated Indianapolis.[29] In Wisconsin, Milwaukee and Madison were centers of Klan membership. It was able to win elections also in Kenosha,

Racine, and other cities.[30] In Michigan, the Klan was extremely powerful in Detroit, and in Flint it succeeded in electing a Klan candidate as mayor.[31] In Iowa, the Klan was much stronger in Des Moines, the state's largest city, where it elected three members of the school board in 1925, than in the rural areas.[32] Other centers of Klan strength in the Midwest were Dubuque in Iowa; Grand Forks in North Dakota; Wichita, Emporia, and Kansas City in Kansas; and Denver in Colorado.[33] Even in Chicago, the nation's second largest city, the Klan had eighteen chapters and held initiation rallies in 1922 which drew tens of thousands.[34]

On the West Coast, the Klan was powerful in Oregon, where it dominated state politics for a brief period. It had considerable support in Portland, as well as in Eugene, Salem, and other urban centers.[35] In California, the Klan was particularly strong in and around Los Angeles.[36] The largest klaverns in the state of Washington were in Seattle, Spokane, Walla Walla, and Tacoma.[37] Although the Klan was weakest politically in the eastern and New England states with their heavy Catholic and Jewish population, it secured considerable urban support there as well. In Pennsylvania, it had over 260,000 members in 1924 concentrated in the "coal and steel towns," in cities such as Pittsburgh, Homestead, Johnstown, and Altoona in the western part of the state, and in Philadelphia, which had 35,000 members, and various mining areas in the east.[38] In Maine, the strongest center of Klan support in New England, the organization was extremely powerful in the state's largest city, Portland, and was able to influence or control elections in many of the other cities as well.[39]

In New Jersey, Klan "strength centered . . . in the urban and industrial belt which girdled the center of the state."[40] In New York State, the Klan had important support in suburban Long Island, in Binghamton, Buffalo, and other upstate cities.[41]

Given this enumeration of major urban centers of Klan strength, it is difficult not to agree with Charles Alexander that the many "historians [who] have assumed that the Klan thrived in the small towns throughout the country but not usually in the cities" have been in serious error. As he concludes, this "assumption is not valid for Klan history in any part of the country except the northeastern United States."[42]

It is interesting to speculate why so many observers, both journalists and historians, have missed noting the fact that the Klan was at least as much an urban as a small-town movement. Perhaps the most plausible explanation is that the most dramatic activities of the Klan, its violence against immoral persons, did not occur in the city. As Kenneth Harrell has pointed out in his discussion of the Louisiana Klan:

The Old Hickory [New Orleans] unit was an important chapter in the Louisiana Realm until the mid 1920's when Klan influence waned, yet there is no evidence linking it with the night riding activities. . . . It is quite apparent that indulgence in clandestine operations outside the law was closely related to the size of Louisiana towns or cities in which the Klan was active. Large metropolitan centers simply did not lend themselves to kidnappings, whippings, or posted warnings for which the Klan was notorious. City residents either did not know who was drinking and wenching, or did not care. The city was impersonal, the small town intensely interested in the doings of its citizens.[43]

Protestant Migrants

Although Mecklin stressed the appeal of the Klan to Protestants in small towns, he noted that many big cities contained large numbers reared in small towns. He quoted a "close observer of the Klan from Texas," who pointed out that "Dallas and Fort Worth (where the Klan is especially strong) [are] being largely populated by men and women reared in obscure towns and country places. . . ."[44]

In a more recent effort to analyze sources of urban Klan backing in the Southwest, Charles Alexander reported "a correlation between the rapid growth of southwestern cities and the presence of prosperous Klan chapters. . . ." The Klan support came from relatively recent migrants to the city who, "living in an urban environment but seeking to preserve the values of their rural upbringing, saw in the Klan a method to bring 'law and order' to the cities."[45] In Virginia, the greatest strength of the Klan "lay in a series of growing, industrializing cities, most notably Norfolk, Newport News, Portsmouth, Lynchburg, Danville, and Roanoke." David Chalmers' explanation of the sources of socially deprived support for the Klan also traces it to dislocation strains felt by migrants to the large city:

Into the factories and slums of the rapidly growing, unplanned cities moved the rural folk—white and Negro—of Virginia. These Virginians were simple, proud, direct people, unused to the tempos of the world of industry and the impersonal life of the raw manufacturing town. . . . Although [the white worker] competed only at the level of unskilled labor, it was important that the Negro be kept in his place. . . . For the relocated rural folk living in belts around the industrial cities, the membership in the Klan became second only to the church as a source of both social and ethnic expression.[46]

Similar interpretations have been suggested for western and northern urban Klan support. The Detroit workers who backed Klan candidates largely were migrants from small towns and rural areas, often from the South.[47] Akron, a rapidly growing industrial city in the 1920's and the strongest Klan center in Ohio, also drew its labor force from "southerners [who] had flocked from the hills to the rubber factories and industrial plants until they constituted more than half the city's population."[48]

The Los Angeles Klan seemingly recruited from the large migrant population from the small towns and rural areas. In Indiana, "evidence seems to indicate that in communities . . . where the transplanted, agrarian-born, Hoosier saw changes taking place that he could not accept, where he had little status, and where he might be threatened by competition or Negro, the Knights of the Ku Klux Klan provided an opportunity for association of like-minded Americans with similar needs."[49]

In Maine, the one New England state in which the Klan was very strong, its chief bastion was in the largest city in the state, Portland, but "this support . . . was concentrated in the Deering section of the city, a relatively new section of the city *which was heavily populated by those who had only recently moved from small towns and farms.*"[50]

The fact that many of the Protestants living in cities after World War I were migrants—some estimates run as high as 75 per cent—helps to explain why so many were ready to join up. The rootless individual, everywhere, is receptive to the appeal of groups with a high sense of social solidarity. He has what psychologists have described as a great "need for affiliation." As David Chalmers pictured the process with respect to the Klan:

The internal migrant brought his heartland values and his defensiveness with him to the metropolis. . . . Poorly educated and unsure of himself, he was a likely recruit for the Klan. . . .

The nature of the psychic value which the Klan offered went far beyond night riding, reform, economic gain, or political advantage. It provided recreation and a sense of belonging. Probably the greatest strength of the Invisible Empire lay not in its creed but in its excitement and its in-group fraternalism. As Mecklin so well grasped, merely belonging to the Invisible Empire solved many of the Klansman's problems. . . .

The Klan offered a degree of mystery and a thrill of power greater than that of any other fraternal order. . . .[51]

It should be noted, however, that one detailed analysis of the community backgrounds of Klan members, those who belonged to the Knoxville chapter, does not agree with these other findings. "On the contrary . . . one-third of the members were lifelong residents and the remainder had lived in the community for an average of more than nine years."[52]

The reports of the various studies of the Klan in specific cities are iterated by a correlation analysis of the relative membership strength of the Klan in sixty-eight cities, as reported by Jackson, and various census characteristics. As the results of this analysis presented in Table 8 indicate, the urban Klan was strongest in cities characterized by a large proportion of native-born whites and nonwhites, while it was weakest in cities with a heavy immigrant population. To a considerable extent this is another way of documenting the greater support of the Klan in the urban South, or that where the white population included a large contingent of immigrants or the children of immigrants, the Klan was relatively weak. These relations are hardly startling. Perhaps our most significant statistic is the one which indicates that Klan strength correlated with rate of population increase. This finding tends, of course, to validate the assumptions of the various students of the organization who have suggested that it appealed to recent migrants or that its strength reflected the social strains imposed by rapid community growth.

Table 8.   CORRELATIONS (PEARSON r) BETWEEN KLAN MEMBERSHIP AS A PERCENTAGE
OF THE WHITE POPULATION AND SELECTED CENSUS STATISTICS
FOR SIXTY-EIGHT CITIES

Per cent population increase, 1920–1930	.462[a]
Per cent native white, native parents, 1930	.544
Per cent native white, alien parents, 1930	—.572
Per cent foreign-born white, 1930	—.527
Per cent nonwhite, 1930	.376

SOURCES: Data for Klan membership as a percentage of the white population in cities are from Kenneth Terry Jackson, *The Ku Klux Klan in the City, 1915–1930* (New York: Oxford University Press, 1967), p. 239, and the *Fifteenth Census of the United States: 1930* (Washington: Government Printing Office, 1933), II 67–73. The population characteristics are from the *Statistical Abstract of the United States: 1940*, Sixty-second number (Washington: Government Printing Office, 1941), pp. 22–26.

[a] Jackson reports that he "used the Spearman rank correlation coefficient to measure the association between the percentage growth of a city between 1910 and 1930, and the percentage of white natives who joined the Klan. Eighteen cities were ranked according to the two criteria, and the resulting correlation between city growth and Klan size was .627." *op. cit.*, footnote 7, p. 289.

The Klan As Low-Status Backlash

Few of the studies have attempted to relate the characteristics of individual members such as their occupational or class traits, although lists of members exist for some areas. In Buffalo, for example, a police agent produced the names of some 4,000 members. The only report on them states that they "included school teachers, ministers, directors of insurance companies, city officeholders, café owners, mechanics, laborers, and farmers."[53] Yet some consensus does appear among the assorted reports on Klan activities in different parts of the country.

There is general agreement that the Protestant clergy were disproportionately represented in the membership and leadership of the Klan. The moralism, religious fervor, fundamentalism, and anti-Catholicism espoused by the hooded order appealed to many who were occupationally committed to these values and were themselves embodied symbols of displacement.

A report by the National Catholic Bureau of Information stated that twenty-six of the thirty-nine national Klan lecturers were Protestant ministers.[54]

Such support varied, of course, by denomination among clergy and laymen. "On the whole the Presbyterian, Episcopal, Lutheran, Universalist, and Congregationalist ministry was unfavorably disposed toward the Klan. Most of the support from the cloth was offered by Baptists, Methodists, and Disciples of Christ."[55] The one detailed analysis of the background of Klan members drawn from an actual file of membership applications, that for Knoxville, Tennessee, reports that of the 296 members, 71.2 per cent belonged to Baptist churches and 24.4 per cent adhered to Methodist ones. The remaining other denominations had a total of 4.3 per cent among them.[56]

Curiously, the one particular occupation, other than that of minister, which appears frequently in the reports on the characteristics of Klansmen is that of policeman. The Klan leaders "took particular pride in emphasizing the large number of law enforcement officers and ministers that had joined their order."[57] Seemingly, the police, like sections of the clergy, were attracted to an organization which was dedicated to uphold the moral order and to punish evil-doers. Typical of Klan propaganda in this area was the plank in the program of the Chicago Klan which called for "Supporting officials in all phases of law enforcement,"[58] a slogan to be revived four decades later by the John Birch Society. Membership lists seized in different parts of California indicated that "roughly 10 per cent of the . . . policemen in practically every California city," including the chiefs of police of Los Angeles and Bakersfield and the sheriff of Los Angeles County, belonged to the Klan.[59]

In Atlanta, the home base of the Klan, "a very high percentage" of the police belonged to the secret order.[60] A study of the Dallas Klan reports the organization dominated the police force of that city as well.[61] Considerable police support for the Klan was reported in Portland, Oregon,[62] in Tulsa,[63] in Madison,[64] in Memphis,[65] and various other places.

There seems general agreement that the Klan attracted considerable support in the days of its early rapid growth (1921–1923) from some of the leading citizens and businessmen of the various communities in which it had strength. Such support undoubtedly reflected the insecurities of these men with the rapid changes occurring after the war. Their support also may have been related to the Klan's emphasis on morality, control of crime, and opposition to radicalism and trade-unions. The initial strength of the Klan in the middle-class community was not simply a response by segments of this group to the program of the Klan. Klan organizers made a conscious effort to recruit first among the most prestigious. Moreover, it has been argued that "it was just another lodge for many respectable businessmen who joined the organization. In fact, the Kleagles commonly began their solicitations in a town by calling on the local Masonic lodge. In 1923 the Klan claimed that 500,000 Masons were citizens of the Invisible Empire."[66] In Wisconsin, the first group invited to form a Klan in the fall of 1920 "were all members of Milwaukee's business and professional classes."[67] In Portland, Oregon, "many prominent businessmen, quite a number of public utility officials, and several hotelkeepers were Klansmen. It was said, too, that local business interests were well represented in Klan membership."[68] In Kansas, one of the principal Klan leaders was "the attorney for the Associate Industries, which was composed of such major corporations as the packers and the railroads."[69]

In many places in the Southwest, the prominence of Klan members meant that "membership in the Klan became quite a status symbol."[70] In New Orleans, the Klan "included a number of prominent New Orleanians—lawyers, politicians, and an unusually large number of doctors."[71]

But if the Klan was able to appeal successfully to many of the leading citizens of the communities in which it had strength, the evidence would also suggest that these were among the first to defect. While the Klan undoubtedly retained large numbers of middle-class supporters until its ultimate decline, the available evidence suggests that these were largely among the socially marginal and status-deprived elements in the stratum, particularly outside of the South. In Ohio, "members were recruited most often from the less successful members of the white collar class, the clerks and the shopkeepers, or from those who moved on the fringes of the professions."[72] Mecklin, writing as a contemporary observer, also noted that the Klan did not recruit from the successful members of the business or professional community, but rather from the "mediocre."[73]

To a considerable degree, the Klan's propensity to engage in vigilante activities, its blatant appeals to ethnic and racial bigotry, seemingly affronted the better educated and higher-status elements of the community. As the Klan grew, it attracted its preponderant support from the poorer and less educated strata. Its leaders spoke the language of the underdog Protestant. And as newspapers and public officials exposed the crimes of the Klan, it became increasingly difficult for the order to retain backing from the upper middle class. As a simplistic moralistic bigoted movement, the Klan increasingly became a movement of the less educated and less privileged strata who adhered to the more fundamentalist denominations. A description by the Lynds of the changes in the Klan in Middletown (Muncie, Indiana) would probably hold true for many communities:

> Brought to town originally, it is said, by a few of the city's leading business-men as a vigilance committee to hold an invisible whip over the corrupt Demo-cratic political administration and generally "to clean up the town," its ranks

were quickly thrown open under a professional organizer, and by 1923 some 3,500 of the local citizens are said to have joined. [The population was about 35,000.] As the organization developed, the businessmen withdrew, and the Klan became largely a working class movement. Thus relieved of the issue that prompted its original entry into Middletown, the Klan, lacking a local issue, took over from the larger national organization a militant Protestantism with which it set about dividing the city; the racial issue, though secondary, was hardly less ardently proclaimed. . . . Tales against the Catholics ran like wildfire through the city. . . . To this Catholic hatred was added Negro and Jewish hatred fed by stories that the Negroes have a powder which they put on their arms which turns their bodies white, and that the Jews have all the money. . . .[74]

Writing in 1924, the sociologist John Mecklin reported, on the basis of hundreds of questionnaire returns and personal studies of the Klan in various communities, that many of the economic and professional elite "who at first identified with the Klan . . . afterwards resigned."[75] (It should be noted that Mecklin believed that the large majority of such groups was opposed to the Klan from the start.) Describing events in Louisiana, Kenneth Harrell also pointed to the fact that "the so-called 'better element' was the first to desert the secret order," leaving the lower socioeconomic groups behind.[76] In the southwestern states, thousands of solid middle-class citizens who joined "to promote observance of the law and moral uplift" left when they discovered that it "attracted all kinds of native white Protestants. . . ."[77] And a historian studying "the decline of the Ku Klux Klan" stated generally that "the more respectable members of the Protestant community had begun to resign quietly or cease paying dues to the secret order as early as 1922. Scarcely missed in the burgeoning membership rolls in 1923 and 1924, responsible citizenry was sorely lacking when the Order came under increasing attack in later years."[78]

Another close student of the activities and views of the national leadership of the Klan concluded that they were consciously aware of appealing to the lower-status, less educated segments of the population. The great period of Klan growth occurred after two professional public relations experts, Edward Young Clarke, Jr., and Mrs. Elizabeth Tyler, were explicitly given a contract in June 1920 by William Simmons, the founder and first head of the Klan, to sell the organization.

The secret of the two publicists' success in propagating the Klan cause was simple. They knew what segment of the American public would buy, and they seemingly had a realistic appraisal of those factors within the Klan complex which made the strongest appeal. Simmons was always fond of professing that his Klansmen were the "best people of the community." This was not the case, and it is difficult to conceive that even the often unrealistic Emperor believed it. Some men of prominence and civic leaders were attracted to the order, of course, but the main body of the Klan was always the common, less-educated whites, industrial and rural. . . . Clarke and Mrs. Tyler obviously knew the same. Their propaganda was never intellectual in tone but always aimed at the emotions.

They were . . . aware of the value of ritualism and vigilantism as an appeal to the "plain people." Clarke actively used the former as a means of attraction, and at least tolerated the latter for the same reasons.[79]

The various reports that the membership of the Klan was largely drawn from the socially deprived, once it had shown its true colors as a lawless organization, are attested to by Hiram Evans, the Grand Wizard of the Order. Writing in 1926, he stated:

We are a movement of the plain people, very weak in the matter of culture, intellectual support, and trained leadership. We are demanding, and we expect to win, a return of power into the hands of the everyday, not highly cultured, not overly intellectualized, but unspoiled and not de-Americanized, average citizen of the old stock. . . .

This is undoubtedly a weakness. It lays us open to the charge of being "hicks" and "rubes" and "drivers of second-hand Fords." We admit it.[80]

And in 1933 he reiterated that the Klan's "membership is mostly composed of poor people."[81] These reports of Evans jibe with a picturesque indicator of the status of the Klan members given in accounts of Klan parades in Indiana. One local observer commented: "You think the influential men belong [to the Klan] here? . . . Then look at their shoes when they march in a parade. The sheet doesn't cover their shoes."[82] And a description of another Indiana Klan parade reported: "In the great mass of marchers there was not any eye, face or a hand in sight, nothing to read but a broken ripple of old shoes—square toed, cracked, run over at the heels. . . ."[83]

Various reports mainly related to 1923 and later agree that Klan support in the cities, like that of earlier nativist groups, came largely from the working-class and marginal middle-class groups. William Allen White, writing after his defeat as an anti-Klan candidate for governor of Kansas in 1924, commented: "Here was a funny thing: labor in the Middle West is shot through with the Ku-Klux Klan. . . . It will be a decade before labor recovers what it has lost by flirting with the Ku-Klux Klan."[84] "It was because the Klan had planned a full dress parade to intimidate strike breakers in Arkansas City that Governor Henry J. Allen brought suit against the Klan to expel them from Kansas" in 1922.[85]

Klan organizers from Oklahoma infiltrated over the Kansas border during a crippling railway strike in that state and became very active in its rail centers along the Oklahoma border such as Arkansas City, Coffeeville, and Pittsburgh. As the railways had, in many cases, employed Negroes as strike breakers the Klansmen made an effective recruiting drive amongst laboring ranks with the war cry that "white supremacy" was in danger. It seems ludicrous that the Klan should have been successful in enlisting many union members in a state where they had circulated that "Ti-Bo-Tim" postcard which gave one of the Klan's purposes as "preventing unwanted strikes by foreign labor agitators."[86]

The growing strength of the Klan among Oklahoma workers led the *Oklahoma Federationist,* the organ of the state AFL, to editorialize in 1922, "It is one of the greatest menaces that we have ever had to deal with. . . . The intolerance as taught by a certain organization based upon religious, racial and national prejudice is slowly creeping into the labor movement."[87] Klan support in the labor movement reached out to Indianapolis, the city which was then the national headquarters of a large number of labor unions.

A resolution condemning the Klan passed the Central Labor Union Council by only four votes after heated debate in the summer of 1923. A number of locals, including the carpenters, sheet-metal workers, typographers, and painters, withdrew from the council after the passage of this resolution.[88] The Klan also had considerable support among trade-union coal miners in other parts of Indiana, as well as in Pennsylvania. In Louisiana, the most important city dominated by the Klan was Shreveport. The membership there was "composed largely of Standard Oil Refinery workers. . . ."[89]

An analysis of the occupations of lists of Klan members in Chicago published by opposition groups indicates that they were "lower echelon white-collar workers, small businessmen, and semi-skilled laborers, many of whom resented the economic, social, and political pressure of the city's Catholics and second-generation immigrants, and were equally alarmed by the rapid influx of Negroes into an ever-expanding ghetto."[90] An examination of the addresses of Klan members in Chicago revealed that they were strongest on the south side, the part of the city which faced the large Negro migration.

Electoral data from various cities point up the working-class base of the Klan. In Milwaukee, its main backing came from working-class supporters of the dominant local Socialist party, who were strongly anti-Catholic.[91] In Detroit, a Klan candidate was almost elected running as a *write-in* candidate for mayor in 1924. In Protestant sections, his opponent ran ahead only "in the most 'respectable' districts of the city."[92]

An analysis of the 1925 Detroit mayoralty election, in which the Klan candidate ran again, indicates that his opponent did "particularly well in the silk stocking districts in the North End and northwest sections of the city."[93] A report on the membership of the Detroit Klan states that it "appealed to those persons who were of an economic level a little higher than the Negroes. . . ."[94]

In the school board elections in 1926 in Des Moines, a strong Klan center, "the results tended to show the divisions along which Klan and anti-Klan sentiment split. In the parts of the city east of the gilded renaissance dome of the capitol building, where Swedish, Negro, and Italian settlements were encroaching on the homes of factory and office workers, the Klan did well. The upper-income, still-fashionable West Side of the city voted against it."[95]

In Emporia, Kansas, "an identifiable labor vote" helped give the Klan electoral victories.[96] In Chattanooga, Tennessee, where the Klan's candidates received just under 50 per cent of the vote, their strength was concentrated among "the men who worked in the foundries, furniture plants, and textile mills south of the railroad tracks and in East Chattanooga."[97]

The most recent and comprehensive study of the Klan's urban support, which is based on chapter records and membership lists of Klan groups in six cities and the precinct returns of local elections in seven areas "where the Ku Klux Klan was a dominant issue," reinforces the conclusions concerning the Klan's social base reached by the various earlier studies summarized above:

Few men of wealth, education, or professional position affiliated with the Invisible Empire. . . . White-collar workers in general provided a substantial minority of Klan membership and included primarily struggling independent businessmen, advertising dentists, lawyers, and chiropractors, ambitious and unprincipled politicians and salesmen, and poorly paid clerks. The greatest source of Klan support came from rank and file non-union, blue collar employees of large businesses and factories. Miserably paid, they rarely boasted of as much as a high school education and more commonly possessed only a grammar or "free school" background. The religious loyalty was to conservative, non-ritualistic Protestant denominations such as the Baptist, Methodist, or Christian churches.[98]

It is possible to add a seemingly more precise estimate of the sources of Klan strength through a correlation analysis of the relationship between relative Klan strength in different states and various demographic and political characteristics of the states. We write "seemingly more precise" because we have no judgment as to the reliability of the published figures concerning Klan membership by state given at different times. We can only hope that inaccuracies in reporting are fairly constant, an assumption which, unfortunately, is unlikely to be warranted. For the purpose of this analysis, we have used the estimate reached by Kenneth Jackson, author of the most recent historical study of the Klan, who reports on the total number of persons who ever belonged to the Klan up to the 1940's. This figure, however, totaled almost 2,500,000, which is much less than reported by various other surveys. The correlations between estimates of state Klan membership and the other factors are presented in Table 9. They are given separately for the southern states and the rest of the country, since the Klan's strength was disproportionately southern, and the internal patterns varied somewhat between the regions.

Table 9. CORRELATION (PEARSON r) BETWEEN ESTIMATES OF TOTAL KLAN MEMBERSHIP (1915–1944) AS A PERCENTAGE OF THE WHITE PROTESTANTS AND VARIOUS CHARACTERISTICS OF THE STATES

	Non-South	South
Percent urban, 1930	.125	.508
Percent population increase, 1920–1930	.016	.470
Percent population increase, 1910–1920	−.028	.370
Percent Protestant, 1926	.260	−.636
Percent Catholic, 1926	−.251	.694
Percent Jewish, 1926	−.037	.053
Percent Negro, 1930	.152	−.062
Percent Democratic vote, 1924	.230	−.012
Percent Republican vote, 1924	.106	−.057
Percent Progressive vote, 1924	−.257	.152
Percent Democratic vote, 1928	−.263	−.075
Percent Republican vote, 1928	.247	.063
Percent change, Democratic vote, 1920–1928	−.397	−.099
Percent change, Republican vote, 1920–1928	.435	−.044

SOURCES: Klan Membership as a percentage of the white Protestant population, 1926, are from estimates of Klan membership by states as reported in Kenneth T. Jackson, *The Ku Klux Klan in the City 1915–1930* (Ph.D. Thesis, Department of History, University of Chicago, 1966), p. 343; the *Fifteenth Census of the United States: 1930*, Report on Population of the United States, Vol. III, Part I (Washington: Government Printing Office, 1933), p. 24; and *Religious Bodies: 1926*, Vol. II, Separate Denominations (Washington: Government Printing Office, 1929), pp. 647, 1256. Per cent urban, 1930, is from the *Fifteenth Census, op. cit.*, I, 8. Per cent population increase, 1920–1930 and 1910–1920, are from the *Fifteenth Census, op. cit.*, I, 24, 12. Per cent Protestant, Catholic, and Jewish, 1926, are from the *Fifteenth Census, op. cit.*, Vol. III, Part I, p. 24, and *Religious Bodies: 1926, op. cit.*, pp. 647, 1256. Per cent Negro, 1930, is from the *Fifteenth Census, op. cit.*, II, 37. The votes for 1924 and 1928, as well as the per cent change in vote from 1920 to 1928, are from Svend Petersen, *A Statistical History of the American Presidential Elections* (New York: Frederick Ungar, 1963), pp. 83–90.

There are some differences between the pattern indicated for Klan support in the South, as contrasted with that for the rest of the country. The southern part of the movement was seemingly strongest in states characterized by being more urban, growing more rapidly, and containing more Catholics, than those in which the Klan was relatively weak. Curiously, there is little relationship between Klan support and party voting, even in 1928, when Al Smith's presence at the head of the Democratic ticket, led a number of southern states to vote Republican for the first time since Reconstruction. In the northern states, on the other hand, Klan strength does not correlate much with demographic factors, with the possible exception of religion. It was strongest in the more heavily Protestant states. It is, however, associated with shift away from Democratic party voting in 1928. Students of the 1928 election have suggested that the principal variable affecting presidential voting in that year in the South, was proportion of Negroes. In heavily black areas, the whites who were the only ones who voted, opted for Al Smith, to preserve the one-party system in their area. Protestants, elsewhere, in the South shifted away. Presumably this concern overrode the impact of past Klan influence. Conversely, in the North, Klan membership was probably a good indicator of the weight of religious prejudice in an area, and, therefore, correlated with shifting away from the Democrats when they nominated a Catholic. These statistics also serve to confirm the argument that the Klan was not a predominantly rural, nonurban group. In general, however, these findings are not very exciting. But given our doubts that the original membership data are reliable, and the gross character of the state as a basic unit, these results are probably as much as can be expected.

Anti-Radicalism, Bigotry, and Conspiracy

The 1920's represent a classic chapter in the history of backlash movements in America just because the standard elements of such movements were so starkly revealed during that period.

1. *Social Strains.* In preservatist terms, these strains are created by deprivation or threatened deprivation of once-held power and/or status. As we have seen, preservatist movements are effective to the extent that they can somehow combine the apparently contradictory strains of power deprivation at some elite level with status deprivation at some mass level. In the 1920's, the struggle for the restoration of unfettered power by the business elite was explicit; only slightly less explicit was the attempt to preserve a failing social dominance by the general Protestant populace, especially those residing in or migrant from the dwindling rural areas.

2. *Ideological Projection.* The projection of a social strain in other than its pragmatic terms is scarcely unique to, but is always characteristic of, the left wing. For reasons indicated, the public grounds for preservatism are invariably moralistic. The projection is, in Smelser's terms, the part of the generalized belief that restructures an ambiguous situation by explaining what is happening in a way that is satisfactory to those to whom it is happening. In other terms, it is status substitution: the cultural trappings of a group stand in for the group and become invested with special significance, at once the measure and battleground of waning dominance. So it was with traditional Protestant forms in the 1920's.

3. *Backlash Targetry.* Finally, a backlash movement is incomplete

without a population group target of some kind. If the ideological projection defines, in negotiable terms, that which is to be preserved, the targetry defines those from whom it has to be preserved. In Smelser's terms, it is part of the generalized belief which diagnoses the forces and agents causing the strain. But this diagnosis is overtly addressed to the projection of the strain, rather than to the strain itself. History is too frustrating to deal with when the grievances are immediate and urgent. The Luddites, a preservatist force, attacked the industrial machines in what might finally have been an expressive action, along the lines of ghetto rioters burning down their own buildings. But if the targets are to be instrumental—and this is the only basis on which political mobilization can take place—they must become the cause, not just the symbol, of the ailment, of the projected strain. And if the double strain—that of the power elite and that of the mass—is to combine effectively in a political movement, a single target must be the catalyst.

Again, the 1920's provided a textbook illustration. Radicalism was the ideological projection of the social strain under which the preservatist power elite were suffering. It was their fundamentalism, the sharp line to which they withdrew to prevent the incursion of any substantial change. The relatively mobile America has never had a significant revolutionary movement. But what radicalism there was had the immigrant stamp. Even in the Socialist party, which was more a resting place for many disparate kinds of reformers than a revolutionary movement, 33,000 of the 80,000 members in 1917 were enlisted by way of foreign language affiliations.[99] And the Communist party (that is, the Workers party which was the American affiliate of the Communist Internationale) averaged about 15,000 members in the 1920's, only about 15 per cent of whom were English-speaking.[100] The links between revolutionary activity and ethnic immigrant groups were ready-made (even though the extent of that activity and of the total immigrant involvement in it had to be exaggerated).

But, at least to the eye, these were the same ethnic immigrant groups who were emerging, taking control of the cities, changing the mores of the country. These immigrants were the dramatic spearhead of the changes which were displacing the traditional Protestant population. It was around this situation—along with traditional Protestant anti-Catholicism—that the bigotry of the 1920's flourished. And the nature of bigotry itself is one of the phenomena that an examination of this period further clarifies. There is no doubt that bigotry tends to build on an already existing storehouse of historical animosities toward, and images of, certain groups. But that storehouse is not itself bigotry nor coterminous with it. In the course of American history, status backlash, especially low-status backlash, has been the chief determinant and constituent of bigotry. It is true that the groups at the base of the Klan had a special historical storehouse of anti-Catholic bias which had been refreshed again and again during backlash periods in America. The Klan population also drew its strength from the less educated who are the least constrained by cross pressures against bigotry and the most vulnerable to bigotry. But it was finally status backlash which distinguished the groups identified with the bigotry of the 1920's. Bigotry in that period, as in so many others, can most accurately and operationally be defined as backlash targetry.

Bigotry so defined was the magical link between the apparently contradictory strains of power elite and those of the status-deprived mass. The immigrants represented radicalism on the one level and modernist change on the other; political immorality on one level and personal immorality on the other. The levels of image merged into one common complex of targets.

This brand of targetry, as we have seen, was not new to America, but now had a new force and dimension. There was an explicit international agency abroad, cloistered in the distant Kremlin. International Communism not only espoused radicalism and the ultimate modernist alteration of mores but sponsored secret revolutionary activities on their behalf. The conspiracy theory, without departing from its traditional lines, was given new flesh—always through the immigrant groups whom the uses of bigotry lent en masse to the plot.

So it was that the right-wing monism of the 1920's was a mélange of antiradicalism, bigotry, and conspiracy theory. Frederick Lewis Allen described the temper of the times:

Politicians were quoting the suggestion of Guy Empey that the proper implement for dealing with the Reds could be "found in any hardware store," or proclaiming, "My motto for the Reds is S.O.S.—ship or shoot. I believe we should place them all on a ship of stone, with sails of lead, and that their first stopping-place should be hell." College graduates were calling for the dismissal of professors suspected of radicalism; school teachers were being made to sign oaths of allegiance; business men with unorthodox political or economic ideas were learning to hold their tongues if they wanted to hold their jobs.[101]

Institutions and strata which were perceived as being opposed to the traditional *status quo,* such as trade-unions or the intellectuals, were under fire for links to radicalism. The Attorney-General accused various unions of being Communist-controlled and explained various strikes as Communist-inspired.[102] The General Intelligence Division of the Attorney-General's office, established to investigate radical activities, "received many complaints regarding prominent teachers and writers. . . ."[103]

That Division "gathered and indexed the histories of over sixty thousand persons" within three and a half months after it was created. "Before long two hundred thousand names were in the suspect indexes."[104] All this activity was without the benefit of supporting legislation. Attorney-General A. Mitchell Palmer "appeared before a Congressional committee to advocate legislation for the suppression of sedition in time of peace. Seventy bills were pending in Congress five months later." Although none of these measures was passed, "the agents of the Department of Justice in a series of dramatic raids [in November 1919] took more than five thousand persons into custody. . . ."[105]

In describing the raids of January 2 and 6, 1920, on the Communist and Communist Labor party organizations, William Preston suggests that many injustices were committed:

> The net was so wide and bureau detectives were so careless that some ten thousand persons were arrested including many citizens and many individuals not members of either party. Abuse of due process characterized the early stages of the drive. This ill-treatment proceeded from the official decision to protect undercover informers. Indiscriminate arrests of the innocent with the guilty, unlawful searches and seizures by federal detectives, intimidating preliminary interrogation of aliens held incommunicado, high-handed levying of excessive bail, and denial of counsel were the government's response to stiffening alien radical resistance to deportation.[106]

A detailed description of the illegal practices of the federal government was presented in an analysis by Dean Roscoe Pound of the Harvard Law School and eleven other leading lawyers and law professors. This document, which is called a *Report on the Illegal Practices of the United States Department of Justice*, contains confidential documents issued by the Department to its regional staffs in which they are, among other things, instructed to engage in illegal search and seizure, if they can get away with it.[107]

The Lusk Committee of the New York State Legislature, established to investigate radical activities, also engaged in frequent raids on suspected premises, using search warrants, permitting confiscation of all property in the hands of "John Doe, Richard Roe, Thomas Poe, and Mary Roe, the said names being fictitious."[108]

Local prosecutors pressed for the conviction of radicals on charges of conspiracy, sedition, and the like. The Attorney-General of the State of Washington, meeting with county prosecutors to discuss the trials of radicals, advised them "to try defendants en masse in order to save public funds, and to insure the greatest number of convictions. He also advised the local prosecutors to keep close watch on jury panels so that only 'courageous and patriotic' jurors would hear the cases."[109]

The efforts to repress dissent were not limited, of course, to government actions or to radicals. Vigilante activity in support of antiradical endeavors, or to enforce prohibition, were widespread. The Klan engaged in such activities on a broad scale, in both the North and the South. One of the Klan's crusades was to eliminate the Bolshevik agents who were perceived as largely based among the urban immigrants—a crusade which the latter-day Klans have continued. During the 1940's, one post-World War II leader of the Klan, Dr. Samuel J. Green, was wont to iterate that it was his order which first "discovered Communism in the United States and which first assailed it. . . ."[110]

The current bigotry and conspiracy theory merged with the antiradical activity. Even the old specter of the Illuminati, dating back to the 1790's in America, was resurrected. On June 19, 1920, the staid *Christian Science Monitor* printed a lead editorial, "The Jewish Peril," in which it discussed the ideas contained in *The Protocols of the Elders of Zion,* and argued that they are coincident with the doctrines of Adam Weishaupt of the Illuminati, as outlined in John Robison's old book. (The *Monitor* editor reported that the Illuminati had reappeared in the beginning of the twentieth century, headed by Leopold Engels.) The editorial suggested that the Illuminati concern for power, regardless of ends used to attain it, may explain much of the troubles of the world. There is a "conspiracy of evil against humanity. . . . Whether it constitutes a 'Jewish peril,' is a question for consideration itself, but that it exists, as a peril, is entirely undeniable."[111]

On the same day that the *Monitor* editorial appeared, the *Chicago Tribune* also published a major article which argued that Bolshevism was only "a tool" for the establishment of Jewish control of the world. The Jewish plot involved the use of a variety of methods and ideologies, not just Communism. And, contended the *Tribune,* the Jewish-dominated conspiracy was "primarily anti-Anglo-Saxon."[112]

Henry Ford launched a campaign against the malevolent influence of international bankers, Bolsheviks, and Jews. His newspaper, the *Dearborn Independent,* reprinted large portions of the *Protocols of the Elders of Zion* and for seven years, 1920 to 1927, hammered away at the theme of an international Jewish conspiracy. The first series of eighty articles in the paper which appeared from May 1920 to January 1922 were reprinted in book form in *The International Jew: The World's Most Foremost Problem.* Over 500,000 copies of this book, which argued that most Bolshevik leaders, including Lenin, were Jewish, were distributed throughout the United States. In 1922, the *Dearborn Independent* published a new series of articles on money "which charged the Jews with controlling the money markets of the world."[113] In 1924–1925, the paper ran articles claiming "that there was a Jewish plot to grab control of American wheat farming."[114] The *Independent* warned American farmers of a major conspiracy against them: "This whole Kahn-Baruch-Lasker-Rosenwald-Sapiro program is carefully planned to turn over to an organized international interest the entire agricultural interest of the Republic. . . . Between the lines one reads the story of the Jewish Communist movement in America, which seeks to make the United States what it has already made of Russia."[115]

In its discussions of the Jewish problem, the *Dearborn Independent* also took notice of the conspiracy theory which identified the Masons and the Illuminati as the source of revolutionary disturbances from the French Revolution down to the Russian. The twentieth-century exponents of the plot differed among themselves as to whether the Jews were behind the conspiracy, or whether the Illuminati sought to conceal knowledge about their own role by stimulating anti-Semitism. Ford's newspaper came down decisively on the side of the anti-Semitic version of the conspiracy; that is, it argued that the Jews were actually behind the conspiracies which had been blamed on the Illuminati and the Masons both in the 1790's and the 1820's and 1830's in the United States, and in more recent times.

Twice in the history of the United States, the people have been aroused by a sense of strange influences operating in their affairs [in the late 1790's and during the days of the Anti-Masonic Party in the 1820's and 1830's], and each time the real power behind the influences was able to divert suspicion to the Freemasons. . . . Books were written, sermons preached, newspapers took up the search, but none of the observers saw the Jewish influence there.

. . . A pseudo-Masonry, of French origin, given to atheistic and revolutionary purposes, strongly patronized by Jews, was the disturbing element, but all that the public was able to see was the Masonic similitude and not the Jewish hand. . . .

This is to serve notice on the leaders of American Jewry that this time they will not be permitted to hide behind the name of Masonry, nor will they be permitted to hold up the name of Masonry as a shield to blunt the darts or as an ally to share the shafts aimed at their subversive purposes. That game has succeeded twice in the United States; it will never succeed again.[116]

It would be impossible to give the full sense of the aggressive anti-Semitism of Ford's articles in the *Dearborn Independent*. Some of the flavor of the articles may be seen from the titles: "Jewish Gamblers Corrupt American Baseball," "Jewish Jazz Becomes Our National Music," "How the Jewish Song Trust Makes you Sing," "Jew Wires Direct Tammany's Gentile Puppets," "The Scope of Jewish Dictatorship in America," "Rule of the Jewish Kehilla Grips New York," "How Jews Gained American Liquor Control," "The Jewish Associates of Benedict Arnold," and so forth.

Among the many anti-Jewish campaigns waged by the paper was one which resulted in America's Dreyfus case—a case which was prominently featured in the press for a number of years. A Jewish army captain, Robert Rosenbluth, was charged with the murder of his superior officer, Major Alexander Cronkhite. Cronkhite, then ill with influenza, was killed by a self-inflicted accidental wound, while out on maneuvers in the state of Washington, on October 25, 1918. The *Dearborn Independent,* however, sustained a campaign for more than three years charging that Rosenbluth had murdered Cronkhite. Although a number of federal and local investigations made from 1920 to 1922 concluded that the original report on the death was correct, the Attorney-General of the United States, under considerable public political pressure, largely inspired by Ford's paper, ordered Rosenbluth indicted on October 13, 1922. The *New York Times* reported:

The trial proved an utter fiasco. . . . Rosenbluth was discharged . . . not a suggestion being made that there was the slightest evidence which justified his indictment, thus virtually admitting that his bitter and determined prosecution was without probable cause, just as the Prosecuting Attorney of Pierce County, Mr. Selden, had three years before publicly and officially declared. Yet for three long years Rosenbluth was relentlessly subjected to the torments of hell, but when the day of reckoning came the infamous charge vanished like the mists of the morning.

And the *Times,* in commenting on the trial, placed the blame for Rosenbluth's persecution directly on Henry Ford. "Ford's columns were filled with cunningly contrived appeals to passion and prejudice. . . . Will Ford now make a retraction? Will he do anything to rehabilitate the victim of his savage and baseless attacks?"[117] The *Dearborn Independent* did not apologize; rather it pointed to Rosenbluth's acquittal as "illustrative of the length to which an alien type of mind will go to neutralize the safeguards which have been set up for the people in our laws and courts."[118]

To American Jews in the 1920's, Henry Ford was the enemy, the epitome of all evil. Louis Marshall, the President of the American Jewish Committee, reacted strongly to the *Dearborn Independent*'s continued post-trial attacks on Rosenbluth and his supporters: "Ford, the intellectual brother of the Ku Klux Klan, the inspirer of Hitler and Ludendorf, whose textbook is 'The International Jew,' which is distributed throughout the world by this irresponsible disseminator of libels, instead of making reparations, persists as one would expect a man of his low mentality to do, in his crusade against him upon whom he has inflicted so terrible a wrong."[119]

Years later Ford was to repudiate the articles on "The International Jew." He claimed that the attacks on the Jews in his weekly paper had occurred without his knowledge. Some indication of his personal views, however, may be found in a lengthy interview published by *Collier's* after its 1923 opinion survey had revealed Ford to be in the lead among prospective candidates for the Presidency. In it, he made clear his antipathy to the Jews. International financiers were synonymous with Jews. He commented, "Jew financiers are not building anything."[120] He went on to link two of his hates, Jews and trade-unions:

> You probably think the labor unions were organized by labor, but they weren't. They were organized by these Jew financiers. The labor union is a great scheme to interrupt work. It speeds up loafing. It's a great thing for the Jew to have on hand when he comes around to get his clutches on an industry.[121]

In this interview, given during the height of the campaign to nominate him for President, Ford also indicated his contempt for the democratic process and his willingness to serve as President only under extralegal conditions.

> The industrialist had to find out what the people want and get it to them. The politician can still content himself with finding out what they *think* they want and promising it. . . . Shouldn't wonder if industry would eventually absorb the political government. But not yet awhile. These things take time. . . .
> I can't imagine myself today accepting any nomination. Of course I can't say what I will do tomorrow. There might be a war or some crisis of the sort, in which legalism and constitutionalism and all that wouldn't figure, and the nation wanted some person who could do things and do them quickly.[122]

Henry Ford's activities dramatized the full entry of political anti-Semitism into the American extremist rhetoric during this period. The Jews were eminently adaptable to the new turn in conspiracy theories. They were quite visible in radical circles, although their numbers were wildly exaggerated. And they were central in the contemporary conspiracy theories which had been spawned for political purposes in Germany and Czarist Russia. The Catholics, on the other hand, tended to represent the older rather than the newer immigrants and were not adaptable to conspiracy theories centering around world revolution. But while the decline of anti-Catholicism as the bigotry of America was being signaled, Catholics, who were now in full control of the political machines of many big cities, remained a prime target for groups whose language was that of Protestant fundamentalism.

The *Searchlight,* the national organ of the Klan, raised anew the old fear of the APA that a secret Catholic army proposed to take over the country by force. On different occasions it asked: "What are nearly a million Knights of Columbus arming for?" and, "Do the K.C.'s intend to shoot religion into the heretics?"[123] Other Klan publications raised the specter that Irish Catholic policemen were being prepared to shoot Protestants as heretics. They projected a plot in which the six Catholic churches near the Capitol, together with Georgetown and Catholic Universities, would be used as bases for capturing Washington and placing the Pope in power.[124] Klan spokesmen reiterated charges of the APA that Catholic conspirators had been behind every assassination of an American President from that of Lincoln on. A description of a Klan organizer at work reports him haranguing a crowd in the following terms: "Who killed Garfield? A Catholic. Who assassinated President McKinley? A Catholic. Who had recently bought a huge tract of land opposite West Point and another overlooking Washington? The Pope. . . . The Pope was about to seize the government. To the rescue, Klansmen!"[125] Klan editors raised the charge that President Harding, who died in San Francisco in 1923 from a "coronary embolism," had been assassinated. They pointed to the suspicious fact that there had been no autopsy. One Klan paper suggested that Harding had been killed by "hypnotic telepathic thought waves generated in the brains of Jesuit adepts."[126]

But Klan orators and publications were also replete with elaborate Jewish conspiracies. The most prominent northern leader of the organization, D. C. Stephenson, former Socialist party organizer, argued that Jewish international bankers were responsible for starting World War I and that they had a systematic plan designed to limit economic opportunities for Christians. Others stated categorically that the Jews had organized the Bolshevik revolution and were behind Communism everywhere. Klan publications frequently reprinted parts of *The Protocols of the Elders of Zion* which they took from Henry Ford's *Dearborn Independent*. Some Klan leaders combined the Catholic and Jewish conspiratorial themes and suggested that Jews and Catholics were united in a plan to control the nation's press, economy, and political life. They pointed to New York as the example of an evil city controlled by Jews and Catholics.[127]

The focus of the Klan attack varied with locality. A *Weekly Newsletter* published in Atlanta, which was sent out to all the kleagles (paid organizers), suggested varying targets:

Catholic office holders in New England, Catholic power in the Middle West, Jewish predominance in the large cities, "white supremacy" in the South, the I.W.W. in the Northwest, the "yellow peril" in California, dislike of Mexicans (most of whom also were Roman Catholics) in Arizona and Texas; and anywhere and everywhere, employers' dislike of union labor, . . . farmers' distaste for city folk and vice versa, the prohibitionists' prejudice against brewers and bootleggers, the desire to suppress crime and vice and the latest local scandal.[128]

But whatever the target, it had to be integrated into the conspiracy theory. As Emerson Loucks indicated:

The belief in the minds of the nativists that there was a serious plot against American ideals and institutions, the success of which only immediate organization and united action could prevent, was as important for the growth of the Ku Klux Klan as the belief in the Devil and his angels was for the growth of the medieval Christian Church. It was the sine qua non of its existence.[129]

Another theme was struck by the conspiracy rhetoric of the 1920's, which was in keeping with American extremist tradition, but was to have special significance in later years. From the start, it included a note of anti-intellectualism. Conspiracy theories, as we have seen, need to feature an imagined high-powered intellectual core, capable of devious manipulation of the national mind. Intellectuals were also identified as proponents of change, and blurred with "liberals." As one Klan leader put it:

> In a nation toleration becomes a vice when fundamentals are in danger. . . . The American liberals . . . have extended their liberality til they are willing to help the aliens tear at the foundations of the nation. They have become one of the chief menaces of the country, instead of the sane intellectual leaders they should be. . . . They give an almost joyous welcome to alien criticism of everything American. The unopposed attack on the Puritan conscience is only one illustration; our liberals today seem ashamed of having any conscience at all. . . . Tolerance is more prized by them than conviction.[130]

A leader of the American Defense Society declared that "Professors Felix Frankfurter and Zacharia Chafee [sic] of Harvard and Frederick Wells Williams and Max Solomon Mandell of Yale were 'too wise not to know that their words, publicly uttered and even used in classrooms, are, to put it conservatively, decidedly encouraging to the Communists.' "[131]

This note carried with it another component: antielitism. The intellectuals were, after all (when they were not Jews), the elite, the college graduates—and even the Ivy College rather than the midwestern land grant college graduates—as distinct from the common man.

Although the Klan attacked immigrants and Negroes, who were economically deprived, it did not see itself as seeking to maintain the privileges of the traditional elite groups. Rather its most successful spokesmen found that the best way to appeal to prospective followers was by casting "the native white Protestant—not as belonging to the predominant and controlling group . . . but as the oppressed poor, oppressed sufferer, plundered by foreigners, tricked by 'Jesuits' and robbed of his birthright by scheming descendants of Abraham." Ironically, they appealed to "the sympathy generally shown by the mass of Americans to the underdog, the fellow who they feel hasn't had a fair chance."[132] Thus the Klan, like its predecessors from the Anti-Masons on, linked itself to the antielitist and equalitarian tradition of America while fostering bigotry.

A curious footnote on the seductive accommodation possible between antielitism and bigotry was provided by Henry Ford's candidacy for the Presidency. It was generally agreed that the most probable ticket for Ford would be the Farmer-Labor or Progressive party; that is, a "left" nomination. Senator Robert La Follette, who actually did run as a third-party Progressive-Socialist candidate in 1924, declared in the summer of 1923 that "Ford had great strength among the Progressives."[133] Later that year, "a group of Progressives, Farmer-Laborites, Independents, and Liberals from fifteen states met in Omaha on November 21 at the request of Roy M. Harrop, national temporary chairman of the Progressive Party. They passed a resolution endorsing Ford for President on a ticket to be known as the People's Progressive Party. . . ."[134] Seemingly the image of Henry Ford as an opponent of international bankers, Wall Street, and monopolies carried more weight with many Progressive leaders than his anti-Semitism and anti-labor views. Their willingness to ignore these as well as his opposition to democratic procedures suggests parallels to the attitudes and behavior of many Populist spokesmen in the 1890's, who tolerated anti-Semites and APA members among their leaders.

The interest in Ford's candidacy shown by the Progressive leaders apparently did not result in a transference of Ford's support to the actual third-party Progressive candidacy of Senator Robert La Follette in the 1924 election. An analysis (Table 10) of the correlations between Ford's support in different states in 1923 and various characteristics of these states, including their voting record in 1924, shows no significant relationship between support for Ford in the *Collier's* poll and La Follette's strength. The analysis does indicate, however, that Ford did pull heavily in nonurban states, which were relatively slow in population growth, were disproportionately Protestant, and were also centers of Ku Klux Klan strength.

The "Marriage"

The "marriage" of the antielitist preservatists and the elite preservatists in the 1920's was not organic. As we have seen, the more respectable elements soon defected from organizations like the Klan. From one camp came the main thrust of bigotry; from the other, the main thrust of anti-radicalism. But neither could have effectively dominated the scene without the other, and the functional symbiosis between the two was more than abstract.

In a campaign speech in 1920, Warren G. Harding, in advocating immigration restriction, spoke of the dangers to America inherent in "racial differences" and recommended that the United States admit in the future only those immigrants who could be assimilated and whose background

Table 10.   CORRELATIONS (PEARSON r) BETWEEN FORD STRENGTH IN COLLIER'S POLL
AND SELECTED CHARACTERISTICS OF DIFFERENT STATES

Percent urban, 1930	−.348
Percent population increase, 1920–1930	−.226
Percent Protestant, 1926	.361
Percent Catholic, 1926	−.320
Percent Jewish, 1926	−.467
Percent Negro, 1930	.087
Percent Progressive vote, 1924	−.049
Percent Democratic vote, 1924	.086
Percent Republican vote, 1924	.081
Percent KKK membership of white Protestant population, 1925	.351

SOURCES: Ford Vote is taken from "Ford First in Final Returns," *Collier's*, LXXII (July 14, 1923), 5. The estimate of Ku Klux Klan membership is taken from a report in the total estimated membership of the Klan from 1920 to 1925 in the *Washington Post*, November 2, 1930, p. 14, as presented in Lawrence M. Moores, Jr., *The History of the Ku Klux Klan in Maine, 1922–1931* (M.A. Thesis, Department of History and Government, University of Maine, 1950), pp. 25–26.
Per cent urban, 1930, is from the *Fifteenth Census of the United States: 1930*, Report on Population of the United States (Washington: Government Printing Office, 1931), I, 8. Per cent population increase, 1920–1930, is from the *Fifteenth Census, op. cit.*, Vol. III, Part I, p. 24. Per cent Protestant, Catholic, and Jewish, 1926, are from *ibid.*, and from *Religious Bodies: 1926*, Vol. II, Separate Denominations (Washington: Government Printing Office, 1929), pp. 647, 1256. Per cent Negro, 1930, is from the *Fifteenth Census, op. cit.*, II, 37. The election figures for 1924 are from Svend Petersen, *A Statistical History of the American Presidential Elections* (New York: Frederick Ungar, 1963), pp. 86–88.
KKK membership of white Protestant population, 1925, is from estimates of Klan membership by states as reproduced in Moores, *op. cit.*, pp. 25–26; the *Fifteenth Census, op. cit.*, Vol. III, Part I, p. 24; and *Religious Bodies, op. cit.*, pp. 647, 1256.

indicated that they could develop "a full consecration to American practices and ideas."[135]

Writing in *Good Housekeeping* magazine in 1921, Calvin Coolidge, then Vice-President-elect, argued that "biological laws show us that Nordics deteriorate when mixed with other races."[136] James J. Davis, Secretary of Labor under both Harding and Coolidge, went even further to argue that the older Nordic "immigrants to America were the beaver type that built up America, whereas the newer immigrants were rat-men trying to tear it down; and obviously rat-men could never become beavers."[137]

The third of the trio of Republican Presidents of the twenties, Herbert Hoover, also joined in the criticism of the new immigrants. As Secretary of Commerce, he declared in a speech to the Poles of Buffalo that "immigrants now lived in the United States on suffrance . . . and would be tolerated only if they behaved."[138]

Respectable magazines like the *Atlantic Monthly* carried a number of articles elaborating on these themes. A series in the *Saturday Evening Post* by Kenneth Roberts, the novelist, dealt in detail with the sources of immigration to the United States and argued that most of those who might come in the future were unfit to be American citizens. He attacked the idea that the melting pot was a good thing and concluded that America had been "founded and developed by the Nordic race, but if a few more million members of the Alpine, Mediterranean and Semitic races are poured among us, the result must inevitably be a hybrid race of people as worthless and futile as the good-for-nothing mongrels of Central America and South-eastern Europe."[139] Many of the leading novelists of the 1920's fostered anti-Semitic images of the Jew in their fiction.[140]

In June 1922, President A. Lawrence Lowell of Harvard openly advocated, in his graduation address, quotas designed to limit the number of Jewish students. Although the Overseers of Harvard turned down this proposal, many other universities were following such policies at the time.[141]

In a real sense, important sections of the privileged and intellectual strata of America publicly indicated that they were concerned over the inroads on the American cultural and status system of the children of non-Nordic, non-Protestant immigrants who were beginning to claim their place in American university, literary, business, and political life. Most expressions of such feeling were made in much more polite and sociological language than the fulminations of Klansmen or the *Dearborn Independent,* but they were made.

The Decline of Extremist Movements

The question of why an organization such as the Klan should have declined when it clearly appealed to a widespread and deeply felt set of needs, and when it held a great deal of political power, is difficult to answer. A kind of Gresham's law has been seen to operate in American organizations whose stock in trade has been overt bigotry. "Bad" leaders constantly drive out the more respectable, who find a remote partnership and a less gross approach more tolerable. The resultant poverty and inferior brand of leadership often has its own deteriorative consequences.

For example, the Klan leaders themselves contributed to the growth of moral revulsion among their members. The short history of the organization as a mass movement was characterized by bitter public fights and resignations among the leadership, on both a national and a regional level. In attacking each other, the different leaders often leveled charges of sexual and financial immorality.

As the residue of extreme passions generated by the war and subsequent Red Scare began to recede, the membership could take a more sober look at their "Klan crusade." Many must have found what they saw disquieting. In 1922 and

1923 they were presented with the sensational leadership fight [between Simmons and Evans, the first and second heads of the organization]. It was a good deal easier to overlook and discount charges of corruption which came from the outside than those generated within the order. Who, in fact, was the corrupter of Klancraft? Harry Terrell said it was Clarke. Clarke said it was Evans. Simmons aligned himself with Clarke. Evans threw the blame on Simmons. David Rittenhouse, leader of the 1923 Pennsylvania insurgents, claimed that both Simmons and Evans were guilty. The only thing that seemed clear, and no one had denied, was that there had been a degree of perversion in the nobility of the order. Under these circumstances how could the average Klansman have real confidence in any of the leaders.[142]

The suspicion of Klan leaders generated by these exposés was culminated by the arrest and subsequent conviction of D. C. Stephenson, the head of the massive Indiana Klan, for a particularly repulsive rape murder. All efforts to prove that this charge was a frame-up by anti-Klan elements failed, since the major evidence against Stephenson was a deathbed statement by his victim. Clearly, the Puritanical conscience of the evangelical Protestant Klansmen could not long abide the revelations that their organization itself was led by men who were morally corrupt.

However, another possible answer to the decline of the repressive character of the 1920's, and of the Klan which epitomized that character, may be found in the principle of "defeat in victory," which characterized earlier monistic movements. The issues which concerned the Klan, and evangelical Protestants generally, seemed to have been settled in their favor or to have lost saliency. The passage of the immigration-restriction and quota legislation of 1924 represented the final triumph of the Protestant nativist crusade; in various southern states, legislation outlawing the teaching of evolution meant victory for the fundamentalists; prohibition was firmly in the saddle, enforced by federal agents; the fears that Negro war veterans would upset the *status quo* vanished; the effort to take the United States into the League of Nations and the World Court opposed by the provincial nationalists had failed; and as World War I receded into memory, the emphasis on 100 per cent Americanism and alien plots declined. Both major parties had nominated conservative Protestants for President in 1924. And the victorious candidate, Calvin Coolidge, was an outspoken nativist in his statements concerning foreign immigration. He was also the epitome in his behavior, personality, and values of all that Protestant small-town and rural America held dear. Thus, for a brief moment, the white Protestant provincial American could believe himself back in control of his country.

The Klan was to be the last major purely Protestant nativist movement, and the election of 1928 was perhaps the final occasion in which aggressive evangelical Protestantism, in rejecting Al Smith's bid for the Presidency, could defeat a symbol of the urban non-Puritanical groups which were taking over the country. Moreover, the Klan formed a bridge between the traditional forms of nativist protest and those which were to come on the extreme right. Not only was it anti-immigrant and jingoistic, it also was anti-radical and specifically anti-Communist.

Notes

1. John P. Roche, *The Quest for the Dream* (New York: Macmillan, 1963), pp. 103–104. Emphasis in the original.
2. Frederick Lewis Allen, *Only Yesterday* (New York: Harper, 1931), p. 66.
3. *Ibid.*, p. 311.
4. "Ford First in Final Returns," *Collier's*, LXXII (July 14, 1923), 5.
5. Allen, *op. cit.*, p. 283.
6. Selig Adler, *The Isolationist Impulse* (New York: Collier Books, 1961), pp. 112–113.
7. Charles E. Wood, "Religion Becomes News," *Nation*, XII (August 19, 1925), 204.
8. William Hordern, *A Layman's Guide to Protestant Theology* (New York: Macmillan, 1955), p. 66.
9. The only detailed investigation of religion made by the United States Census based on a large sample survey in 1957 reported that 58 per cent of all Americans, fourteen or older, were white Protestants, while Negro Protestants were 9 per cent. In metropolitan areas, however, 250,000 in population or more, white Protestants were in a definite minority, 38 per cent, while Catholics constituted 38 per cent, Negro Protestants 11 per cent, and Jews 8 per cent. See U.S. Bureau of the Census, *Current Population Reports: Population Characteristics*, Series P–20, No. 79, February 2, 1958, p. 1. See also Michael Argyle, *Religious Behavior* (Glencoe: The Free Press, 1958), p. 136, for comparable data from sample surveys.
10. From *World Survey of the Interchurch Movement*, American Volume, p. 226; cited in Peter H. Odegard, *Religion and Politics* (New York: Oceana Publications, 1960), pp. 29–30.
11. Charles O. Jackson, *The Ku Klux Klan 1915–1924: A Study in Leadership* (M.A. Thesis, Emory University, 1962), p. 86.
12. Arnold Rice, *The Ku Klux Klan in American Politics* (Washington: Public Affairs Press, 1962), p. 16.
13. Charles C. Alexander, *The Ku Klux Klan in the Southwest* (Lexington: University of Kentucky Press, 1965), p. 23.
14. *Ibid.*, pp. 26–27.
15. Keith Sward, *The Legend of Henry Ford* (New York: Rinehart, 1948), p. 113.
16. Charles O. Jackson, *op. cit.*, p. 17.
17. John M. Mecklin, *The Ku Klux Klan: A Study of the American Mind* (New York: Harcourt, Brace, 1924), pp. 13, 28.
18. Paul Tillich, *The Protestant Era* (Chicago: University of Chicago Press, 1957), p. 227.
19. Mecklin, *op. cit.*, pp. 107–108.

20. Rice, *op. cit.*, pp. 13–14; see also William E. Leuchtenburg, *The Perils of Prosperity, 1914–1932* (Chicago: University of Chicago Press, 1958), p. 209.
21. Gunnar Myrdal, *An American Dilemma: The Negro Problem and Modern Democracy* (New York: Harper, 1944), I, p. 560.
22. Kenneth T. Jackson, *The Ku Klux Klan in the City, 1915–1930* (New York: Oxford University Press, 1967), p. 26.
23. Myrdal, *op. cit.*, I, p. 33.
24. Kenneth Jackson, *op. cit.*, p. 27 and *passim*.
25. Alexander, *op. cit.*, p. 28.
26. Kenneth E. Harrell, *The Ku Klux Klan in Louisiana, 1920–1930* (Ph.D. Thesis, Department of History, Louisiana State University, 1966), pp. 118–122.
27. Embrey B. Howson, *The Ku Klux Klan in Ohio after World War I* (M.A. Thesis, Ohio State University, 1951), pp. 31–32.
28. *Ibid.*, pp. 71, 82.
29. John A. Davis, *The Ku Klux Klan in Indiana, 1920–1930* (Ph.D. Thesis, Department of History, Northwestern University, 1966), pp. 50–51.
30. Norman F. Weaver, *The Knights of the Ku Klux Klan in Wisconsin, Indiana, Ohio, and Michigan* (Ph.D. Thesis, Department of History, University of Wisconsin, 1954), pp. 285 ff.
31. Kenneth T. Jackson, *The Decline of the Ku Klux Klan, 1924–1932* (M.A. Thesis, Department of History, University of Chicago, 1963), p. 22.
32. Don Stuart Kirschner, *Conflict in the Corn Belt: Rural Responses to Urbanization, 1919–1929* (Ph.D. Thesis, Department of History, State University of Iowa, 1964), p. 171.
33. David Mark Chalmers, *Hooded Americanism: The History of the Ku Klux Klan* (New York: Doubleday, 1965), pp. 138, 140, 142, 145, 127.
34. *Ibid.*, p. 183.
35. Eckard V. Toy, Jr., *The Ku Klux Klan in Oregon: Its Character and Program* (M.A. Thesis, Department of History, University of Oregon, 1959), pp. 56–71; Lawrence J. Saalfeld, *Forces of Prejudice in Oregon, 1920–1925* (M.A. Thesis, Department of History, Catholic University, 1950), pp. 43–44.
36. Chalmers, *op. cit.*, p. 119.
37. *Ibid.*, p. 216.
38. Emerson Loucks, *The Ku Klux Klan in Pennsylvania* (Harrisburg: Telegraph Press, 1936).
39. Lawrence M. Moores, Jr., *The History of the Ku Klux Klan in Maine, 1922–1931* (M.A. Thesis, Department of History and Government, University of Maine, 1950), pp. 52–55.
40. Chalmers, *op. cit.*, p. 243.
41. *Ibid.*, pp. 257–258.
42. Alexander, *op. cit.*, p. 29 in footnote 18.
43. Harrell, *op. cit.*, pp. 119–120.
44. Mecklin, *op. cit.*, p. 107.
45. Alexander, *op. cit.*, p. 29.
46. Chalmers, *op. cit.*, p. 231.
47. Weaver, *op. cit.*, p. 285.
48. *Ibid.*, p. 177.

49. Davis, *op. cit.*, p. 331.
50. Edward B. Whitney, *The Ku Klux Klan in Maine, 1922–1928* (Honors Thesis, Department of History, Harvard University, 1966), p. 16. Emphasis in the original.
51. Chalmers, *op. cit.*, pp. 114–115.
52. Kenneth Jackson, *The Ku Klux Klan in the City* . . . , *op. cit.*, p. 241.
53. Chalmers, *op. cit.*, p. 258.
54. Robert R. Hull, "Regarding Klan Agitators," Appendix III in Michael Williams, *The Shadow of the Pope* (New York: McGraw-Hill, 1932), p. 317.
55. Chalmers, *op. cit.*, p. 293; Hull, *op. cit.*, pp. 318–319; Alexander, *op. cit.*, p. 87; Howson, *op. cit.*, pp. 23–24; Toy, *op. cit.*, pp. 137–139.
56. Kenneth Jackson, *The Ku Klux Klan in the City* . . . , *op. cit.*, p. 63.
57. Howson, *op. cit.*, p. 23.
58. Kenneth Jackson, *The Ku Klux Klan in the City* . . . , *op. cit.*, p. 121.
59. *Ibid.*, p. 190; see also Chalmers, *op. cit.*, p. 118.
60. Soloman Sutker, *The Jews of Atlanta: Their Social Structure and Leadership Patterns* (Ph.D. Thesis, Department of Sociology, University of North Carolina, 1950), p. 17.
61. Lois E. Torrence, *The Ku Klux Klan in Dallas, 1915–1928* (M.A. Thesis, Department of History, Southern Methodist University, 1948), pp. 66–67.
62. Chalmers, *op. cit.*, p. 52.
63. Weaver, *op. cit.*, p. 8.
64. Chalmers, *op. cit.*, p. 118.
65. Kenneth Jackson, *op. cit.*, p. 51.
66. Alexander, *op. cit.*, p. 94.
67. Weaver, *op. cit.*, p. 51.
68. Saalfeld, *op. cit.*, p. 43.
69. Chalmers, *op. cit.*, p. 145.
70. Alexander, *op. cit.*, p. 95.
71. Harrell, *op. cit.*, pp. 120, 296–297.
72. Howson, *op. cit.*, p. 23.
73. Mecklin, *op. cit.*, pp. 155–156, 107–108.
74. Robert S. and Helen M. Lynd, *Middletown* (New York: Harcourt, Brace, 1929), pp. 481–483.
75. Mecklin, *op. cit.*, pp. 93–94.
76. Harrell, *op. cit.*, p. 295.
77. Alexander, *op. cit.*, p. 246.
78. Kenneth Jackson, *The Decline of the Ku Klux Klan* . . . , *op. cit.*, p. 27.
79. Charles O. Jackson, *op. cit.*, pp. 45–46. Emphasis in the original.
80. From an article by Evans in *The North American Review* cited in William Pierce Randel, *The Ku Klux Klan* (Philadelphia: Chilton, 1965), pp. 201–202.
81. Hiram W. Evans, "We Need Pastors," *The Kourrier*, IX (February 1933), 2.
82. Allen, *op. cit.*, p. 67.
83. Morton Harrison, "Gentleman from Indiana," *Atlantic Monthly*, CXLI (1928), 680, cited in Earlene T. Barker, *The Ku Klux Klan of the 20's* (M.A. Thesis, Department of History, Memphis State University, 1960), p. 24.
84. Leuchtenburg, *op. cit.*, p. 127.

85. Nina A. Steers, *The Ku Klux Klan in Oklahoma in the 1920's* (M.A. Thesis, Department of History, Columbia University, 1965), p. 134.
86. *Ibid.*, p. 133.
87. *Ibid.*, p. 134.
88. Davis, *op. cit.*, pp. 50–51.
89. Harrell, *op. cit.*, p. 128.
90. Kenneth Jackson, *The Ku Klux Klan in the City* . . . , *op. cit.*, p. 126.
91. Weaver, *op. cit.*, pp. 74–75.
92. Kenneth Jackson, *The Ku Klux Klan in the City* . . . , *op. cit.*, p. 136.
93. Chalmers, *op. cit.*, p. 197.
94. Weaver, *op. cit.*, p. 285.
95. Chalmers, *op. cit.*, p. 140.
96. *Ibid.*, p. 145.
97. *Ibid.*, p. 152.
98. Kenneth Jackson, *The Ku Klux Klan in the City* . . . , *op. cit.*, pp. 240–241.
99. Nathan Glazer, *The Social Basis of American Communism* (New York: Harcourt, Brace, 1961), p. 24.
100. *Ibid.*, pp. 42, 46.
101. Allen, *op. cit.*, p. 58.
102. Homer Cummings and Carl McFarland, *Federal Justice* (New York: Macmillan, 1937), pp. 455, 456.
103. *Ibid.*, p. 429.
104. *Ibid.*
105. *Ibid.*
106. William Preston, Jr., *Aliens and Dissenters: Federal Suppression of Radicals, 1903–1933* (Cambridge: Harvard University Press, 1963), p. 221.
107. For other descriptions of this period, see also Constantine M. Panuzio, *The Deportation Cases of 1919–1920* (New York: Federal Council of Churches of Christ in America, 1921); Louis F. Post, *The Deportation Delirium of Nineteen-Twenty* (Chicago: Charles H. Kerr, 1923); Milton R. Konwitz, *Civil Rights in Immigration* (Ithaca: Cornell University Press, 1953); Preston S. Slosson, *The Great Crusade and After* (New York: Macmillan, 1930); William S. Bernard, "Arms and the Alien: Post War Hysteria and the Americanization Crusade," *Rocky Mountain Law Review*, XI (1938–1939), pp. 171–185; Roger Burlingame, *The Sixth Column* (New York: Lippincott, 1962).
108. Lawrence H. Chamberlain, *Loyalty and Legislative Action: A Survey of Activity by the New York State Legislature, 1919–1949* (Ithaca: Cornell University Press, 1951), pp. 20–21.
109. Robert L. Tyler, "Violence at Centralia, 1919," *Pacific Northwest Quarterly*, XLV (October 1959), 117–118.
110. Rice, *op. cit.*, p. 10.
111. "The Jewish Peril," *Christian Science Monitor*, June 19, 1920, p. 16.
112. Norman Cohn, *Warrant for Genocide* (New York: Harper & Row, 1967), pp. 156–157.
113. Gordon W. Davidson, *Henry Ford: The Formation and Course of a Public Figure* (Ph.D. Thesis, Department of History, Columbia University, 1966), p. 261.
114. *Ibid.*, pp. 263–264.

115. Gustavus Myers, *History of Bigotry in the United States* (New York: Capricorn, 1960), p. 301.
116. *Jewish Activities in the United States*, Vol. II of *The International Jew: The World's Foremost Problem* (Dearborn, Michigan: Dearborn Publishing Co., 1921), pp. 186–187. Emphasis in the original.
117. See the article summing up the history of the case in *The New York Times*, October 17, 1924, as reprinted in Harry Schneiderman, ed., *The American Jewish Yearbook 5686* (Philadelphia: Jewish Publication Society of America, 1925), XXVII, 451–456.
118. Cited in *ibid.*, p. 457.
119. Reported in *ibid.*, p. 458.
120. "If I Were President," *Collier's*, August 24, 1923, p. 27.
121. *Ibid.*
122. *Ibid.*, pp. 27, 29.
123. Kenneth Jackson, *The Ku Klux Klan in the City . . .* , *op. cit.*, p. 33.
124. Benjamin H. Avin, *The Ku Klux Klan: 1915–1925: A Study of Religious Intolerance* (Ph.D. Thesis, Department of History, Georgetown University, 1952), pp. 154–156.
125. Barker, *op. cit.*, pp. 28–29.
126. Avin, *op. cit.*, p. 166.
127. *Ibid.*, pp. 186–192.
128. *Ibid.*, p. 85; Barker, *op. cit.*, pp. 14–15; Charles O. Jackson, *op. cit.*, pp. 43–44.
129. Loucks, *op. cit.*, p. 38.
130. *Ibid.*, p. 36.
131. Allen, *op. cit.*, p. 60.
132. Loucks, *op. cit.*, p. 35.
133. Davidson, *op. cit.*, p. 283.
134. *Ibid.*, p. 286.
135. Thomas F. Gossett, *Race, the History of an Idea in America* (Dallas: Southern Methodist University Press, 1963), p. 405.
136. Calvin Coolidge, "Whose Country Is This?" *Good Housekeeping*, LXXII (February 1921), 14, cited in *ibid.*, p. 405.
137. *Ibid.*
138. Oscar Handlin, *Boston's Immigrants* (Cambridge: Harvard University Press, 1959), p. 149.
139. Kenneth L. Roberts, *Why Europe Leaves Home* (Indianapolis: Bobbs-Merrill, 1922), pp. 230–231. This is a collection of articles which Roberts published in the *Saturday Evening Post*. See Gossett, *op. cit.*, p. 403.
140. Milton Hindus, "F. Scott Fitzgerald and the Literary Anti-Semitism," *Commentary*, III (June 1947), 508–516; Handlin, *op. cit.*, p. 149; Carey McWilliams, *A Mask For Privilege: Anti-Semitism in America* (Boston: Little, Brown, 1948), pp. 181–182.
141. Cited in Handlin, *op. cit.*, p. 38–39.
142. Charles O. Jackson, *op. cit.*, pp. 126–127.

CHAPTER

5

The 1930's: Extremism of the Depression

The 1930's were an eccentric decade of right-wing extremism in America. The very differences of the period underline the possible variations in the monistic potential of the country.

The distinctive social strains of this decade were occasioned, of course, by the Great Depression. The gross national product, in constant dollars, plummeted by one-third between 1929 and 1933, as did disposable personal income. The squeeze was not only on the working force generally, 3 per cent of whom were unemployed in 1929 and 26 per cent of whom were out of work in 1933. The value of stocks on the New York Stock Exchange had dropped by over 80 per cent in that period, representing a face loss to stockholders of about 75 billion dollars. About five thousand American banks failed. Many large financiers and industrialists were in difficulty, but the middle class was in greater personal trouble. Middle-class savings were wiped out, and small business shared with the working class the immediate personal disaster of a lost purchasing power. In one formerly prosperous farm county in Iowa, it was reported that 25 per cent of the mortgaged farm real estate was foreclosed in 1931–1932.[1] White-collar and middle-class distress was dramatically separate from that of the equally distressed blue-collar class. In 1932, the *New York Times* reported the organization of an Association of Unemployed College Alumni, estimated at more than 10,000 in New York City alone. Among colleges represented at the organizing meeting were Harvard, Vassar, Columbia, Swarthmore, Columbia Law School, and New York Dental School. "In a statement prepared at the meeting the group pointed out that since June, 1929, it had been increasingly difficult for university graduates to obtain positions. Distress consequent upon employment was more acute among college-trained men and women, according to the announcement, because of their relatively high standards of living and education. . . ."[2]

There were no emerging population groups during this period and no burgeoning ethnic groups of any kind. Immigration had been substantially cut off by the new immigration law and dried up further as a result of the depression. In the period 1926–1930 about a million more aliens had come to this country than had departed, about half the number of the previous five years. But in 1931–1935, about a quarter of a millon more aliens departed than arrived.

In general, the Great Depression of the 1930's was clearly conducive to the growth of interest and class politics. The election of 1932, held during the depths of the depression, resulted in a considerable increase in the Socialist and Communist vote, from about 300,000 in 1928 to close to one million. In a number of states, left-wing factions operating in Democratic or Republican primaries, or as third parties, succeeded in gaining considerable support. Thus in California the perennial Socialist author and candidate Upton Sinclair captured the Democratic nomination for governor running on a socialist program and polled over 800,000 votes in the general election. In Oregon and Washington, a near-socialist group, the Cooperative Commonwealth Federation, was very successful in the Democratic primaries and succeeded in electing a number of candidates in the northernmost state. In Minnesota, the Farmer-Labor party, which advocated a cooperative commonwealth and government ownership, held the governor's chair for a number of elections and also was successful in senatorial and congressional races. In nearby Wisconsin, the Progressive party, established by the La Follettes with the subsequent cooperation of the Socialists, also had considerable electoral success as a left-wing state-wide third party. In other Great Plains states, the left-wing Non-Partisan League, operating as a faction within the Republican party, was able to elect state-wide officials and to secure congressional representation, particularly in North Dakota. In more industrial states such as Michigan, the Democratic party moved toward the left in its economic policy and established close relations with the trade-union movement. Many former members of the Socialist party who were trade-union leaders joined the Democrats in different states and secured considerable influence. There is no need to repeat here the story of the rise of the CIO as a trade-union movement and the support given to unions by Democratic state and national administrations. And, of course, the biggest political story of the thirties was the Roosevelt New Deal administration which, based on the economically deprived and the ethnic and racial minorities, enacted a host of welfare state laws, drastically changing the role of the state in the economy.

But if the leftist social movements and the New Deal reforms constitute the main stream of social change in the 1930's, right-wing extremist movements had considerable success as well. There have been various estimates that from 100 to 800 movements of the extremist right arose during the Depression. The House Committee on Un-American Activities referred to "at least 200" of them.[3] Such groups varied, of course, from the ones which were mere letterheads or clubs in single communities to mass movements. All the groups called "right wing extremist" during this period were heavily shaped by the particular strains imposed by the Depression, and they variously shared certain characteristics. But there were several different kinds of major impulses in evidence among them:

1. *The Nativist Impulse.* There were a large number of small nativist organizations which resembled the Klan and other Protestant-based groups of earlier decades in their ideology and base of support.

2. *The "Fascist" Impulse.* The two most widely publicized and massive right-wing extremist movements during this period, though quite different in many ways, were both based on an attack on big business interests, and both broke from the more traditional patterns of American nativism. One was Huey Long's Share-Our-Wealth movement, which had considerable strength in 1934 and 1935 until the assassination of its leader in the latter year. The other was the National Union for Social Justice, founded by Father Charles Coughlin, which began, like Huey Long's, with a primary expressed concern for the economic ills of the time. Huey Long's movement was described by various observers as having fascist potential; toward the late middle of the 1930's, Father Coughlin's movement became overtly profascist as well as racist.

3. *The "Conservative" Impulse.* The American Liberty League was formed in 1934 by a number of prominent businessmen to halt the spread of radicalism and of government intervention in the economy. This organization was essentially antifascist, neither traditionally nativist nor monist in its appeal, and generally ineffective. However, it pointed to certain future developments in right-wing extremism, just as the Protestant nativist groups pointed to the extremist past.

These three models of the 1930's raise some new questions about the nature of right-wing extremism itself.

Most of the previous right-wing extremist movements in America had their genesis and often their greatest strength during periods of economic growth and prosperity. The status displacement approach to the emergence of social movement implies that strata or groups which have been relatively privileged or powerful have reacted negatively to the rise of new social groups which have tended to supplant them in position, or to weaken their moral or power position within their area or in the country at large. In the class marriages that, in one form or another, had made so many previous extremist movements viable, the preservatist thrust of the privileged economic groups was often class-based, but the preservative thrust of the lower-income groups was primarily status-based. It was this low-status backlash which had been the *sine qua non* of right-wing extremist movements.

But, on the whole, periods of depression have typically witnessed the emergence of interest and/or economic class-related politics during which diverse strata, including the lower, have sought, above all, economic remedies for their distress. As Joseph Gusfield has pointed out, class movements tend to be instrumental in their objectives, while status ones are more disposed to be expressive, since they are primarily concerned with the relative degree of prestige.[4]

Presumably, since the right-wing movements of the thirties were appealing to the victims of depression, they could not simply invoke the moral virtues of the past; they needed a program for the future. As Morris Janowitz has indicated, the earlier movements had attacked

particular religious and ethnic groups . . . but the leaders of these movements did not pretend to criticize or attempt to modify the basis of the American economic or political system. Nor did they reject the social system as such, except with respect to the toleration of particular religious and ethnic groups. However, during the Great Depression, such organized intolerance movements as the Black Legion began to assume a new character. They began to agitate against the existing political and economic *system* as such, and sought an alternative system, albeit not a clearly defined one.[5]

But why are these called "right-wing" movements at all? It is not consequential whether any given movement can be neatly classified as right or left, and some obviously cannot be; but it would be analytically important to identify the right or left aspects of any given movement, if only to help distinguish certain common characteristics, as well as a common terminology.

"Right-wing" has been equated so far with preservatist or restorative tendencies which somehow limit new access to power and status. "Left-wing" correspondingly would refer to innovative or revolutionary tendencies which somehow broaden access to power and status. These terms have been differentiated from the monism-pluralism poles on the axis of political democracy because both right-wing and left-wing movements have sat on either pole at various times. As many observers have pointed out, the leveling of status can be concomitant with, and is sometimes conducive in its own way to, the development of a politically repressive state and society.[6]

Kornhauser has identified traditionalism with differentiated but fixed standards; pluralism with differentiated and fluid standards; populism with uniform but fluid standards; and monism with uniform and fixed standards. The uniform standards of populism become monistic when they are institutionally fixed by a state which has accrued power in the name of that populism. That is one aspect of the monistic potential of left-wing extremism. Right-wing extremism, on the other hand, is identified with repressive backlash, desperate preservatism in the face of imminent change. But neither preservatism nor innovation is automatically related to political monism; that is, extremism.

A third axis has been differentiated: that of group bigotry and tolerance. While bigotry is obviously one variant aspect of monism, and some characteristic relationships between right-wing tendencies and bigotry have already been demonstrated, these are not automatic nor monopolistic relationships. It has also been demonstrated that populist movements have on occasion had their own functional relationship with bigotry. A broadening status base can, of course, still be particularistic and exclusive.

A fourth axis has to do with economic statism on the one hand and laissez faire on the other. The left wing, with its egalitarian bias in the face of private power, tends to be identified with economic statism. In America, antistatism has been known as economic conservatism. During the 1920's, the right-wing preservatist movements were conservative. This is one riddle of the Long and Coughlin movements, which were statist and yet called rightist.

A fifth axis has been suggested which would embrace that riddle. It would measure right-left tendencies by social base. The left pole is formed by "blue collar" workers and the rural poor; the right pole by large industrialists, farmers, and the managerial class generally, usually backed by independent professionals. But there is also a distinctive "center" on this axis, formed by what is sometimes known as the lower middle class, the petite bourgeoisie, the small businessmen and white-collar workers.

The point has been made that each of these class positions has a corresponding ideology with respect to the economy. The "left" on the axis is statist (socialist). The "right" is antistatist (conservative). The center normally resembles the right in being antistatist and laissez faire—opposed to socialism and strong trade-unions, but resembling the left in being opposed to big business and traditional elitism. However, the center is volatile and moves toward the left or right, depending on its historical circumstances.

During the development of Western industrial democracies, the center was typically the "liberal" center, not only because it was antistatist both economically and politically but because it allied itself with power-broadening and status-broadening movements, essentially left-wing and innovative in nature. However, in certain periods of latter-day stress, the center moved precipitately toward the right wing. In its economic despair, the center became statist, in a kind of restorative backlash against big business, and at the same time sought some political means of rigidifying the social structure against the power-leveling, status-leveling movements of the left.[7]

This describes classic fascism, the fascism of Nazi Germany, the extremism of the social base of the center. Nazism has been called revolutionary fascism because it was statist on the ideological axis, because it was anti-elitist and antitraditional (centrist on the social-base axis) and had a corresponding populist flavor; *but it was right-wing* on our basic axis of definition, because its essential impulse was power and status preservatism in the face of broadening change. The adoption of *this* axial characteristic to commonly identify certain movements as "right-wing"—even though they have many dissimilarities because of differences in social base and in economic ideology—will finally enable us to pinpoint the historically useful distinctions between right-wing and left-wing extremism and to establish the common thread in American extremism.

In 1942, Talcott Parsons justified the use of the term "radicalism of the right" to describe fascism in these words:

In the first place Fascism is not "old conservatism" of the sort especially familiar before 1914, although elements which were once conservative in that sense have often been drawn into the Fascist movements. . . . Perhaps the most important reason why we are justified in speaking of [Fascism as] "radicalism" lies in the existence of a popular mass movement in which large masses of the "common people" have become imbued with a highly emotional, indeed often fanatical, zeal for a cause. These mass movements, which are in an important sense revolutionary movements, are above all what distinguishes Fascism from ordinary conservatism. They are movements, which, though their primary orientation is political, have many features in common with great religious movements in history. . . . A second important feature is the role played by privileged elite groups, groups with a "vested interest" in their position. While from some points of view the combination of these two elements in the same movement is paradoxical . . . it is of the very essence of the phenomenon and perhaps more than anything else throws light on the social forces at work.[8]

This "paradoxical" marriage of different classes characterizes, in one form or another, not only fascism but, as has been indicated, all successful right-wing extremist movements in America. But the apparent paradox melts away with the understanding that in such movements the disparate classes share a common core of preservatism. In so doing, they are defined as right-wing and can comprise a single right-wing movement, although the unique centers of their separate preservatist goals are quite different. Furthermore, while the preservatism of the upper class and often of the middle class may be both class-directed and status-directed, the preservatism of the lower economic class must chiefly be status-directed. Therefore, the common core of effective right-wing extremist movements is symbolic rather than instrumental in nature. This does not mean that such movements do not also have instrumental goals, but it is the symbolic core which distinguishes them and gives them their particular aspect of similarity to religious movements.

The common core of status preservatism that had characterized American right-wing extremism through the nineteenth century and had come to a climax in the 1920's was some variation of Protestant nativism. The status deprivation of the involved lower class was corporealized by the variously emerging ethnic groups in America. This foreign stock also embodied for the privileged classes the threat of social change, epitomized by the alien radicalism of the 1920's. And those same immigrant groups provided some visible referent for the conspiracy theories at the heart of the extremist reactions. This common core of status backlash also constituted the phenomenon known as nativist bigotry.

But, of course, the failing status of lower-class groups was more often and increasingly dramatized by, rather than caused by, the emergence of new ethnic groups. And in the 1930's even this dramatic association became less feasible. In some cases, such groups lost their power to bestow status prestige because of their declining power in the society; conversely, many individuals were without a sense of status because they no longer had strong identification with a status-bearing group. This is the condition variously associated with advanced urbanization, social disorganization, anomie, social atomization, mass society. Kornhauser described mass society as a

situation in which an aggregate of individuals are related to one another only by way of their relation to a common authority, especially the state. That is, individuals are not directly related to one another in a variety of independent groups. A population in this condition is not insulated in any way from the ruling group. . . . For insulation requires a multiplicity of independent and often conflicting forms of association, each of which is strong enough to ward off threats to the autonomy of the individual. . . . Social atomization engenders strong feelings of alienation and anxiety, and therefore the disposition to engage in extreme behavior to escape from these tensions. In a mass society there is a heightened readiness to form hyper-attachments to symbols and leaders.[9]

And Parsons refers to

the need for sufficiently concrete and stable system of symbols around which the sentiments of the individual can crystalize . . . An increase in anomie may be a consequence of almost any change in the social situation which upsets previously established definitions of the situation, or routines of life, or symbolic associations.[10]

Anomie can thus be seen as an inverted form of status deprivation, through an attenuation of symbolic group associations. The result may be, paradoxically enough, the energizing of preservatist and restorative impulses directed toward substitute symbolic associations. Protestant nativism served this preservatist impulse in earlier America, but was no longer so cogent or relevant by the 1930's. Virulent nationalism, "Americanism," and an abstract kind of racism began to replace old-fashioned nativism as the preservatist common core of right-wing extremism. Linton's definition of nativism as "any conscious, organized attempt on the part of a society's members to revive or perpetuate selected aspects of its culture"[11] emphasizes the continuity among these different phenomena and their preservatist nature.

It was through this kind of attachment to status goals that lower-class segments became engaged in expressive cross-class right-wing movements. The 1930's prove a rich laboratory in which to trace these post-Protestant-nativist developments.

The Nativist Successor Organizations

The movement which had most direct ties with the 1920's was the Black Legion. It was formed by former Klansmen in the industrial cities in Indiana, Ohio, and Michigan, in which the Klan had been strong. According to one account, it modeled its activities quite closely on the Klan with the exception that it dyed its robes black. Members of the Order took an oath to keep "the secrets of the order to support God, the United States Constitution, and the Black Legion in its holy war against Catholics, Jews, Communists, Negroes, and aliens."[12] The Legion retained an evangelistic, moralistic fervor. "Religious symbolism pervaded the organization, as well as did a sense of mission to correct degenerate morals in the community."[13]

Operating coincidentally with the rise of fascist and Nazi parties in Europe, the Legion imitated them to some extent. The Legion "was organized along military, authoritarian and hierarchical lines . . . [with] constituent cells, each of which remained relatively isolated from the others."[14] It featured military rather than fraternal titles and trained its members to use guns and rifles.

However, the similarities were superficial. Insofar as the Legion had economic beliefs addressed to the distress of the times, they were traditionally conservative: that is, rugged individualism and self-help. The organization opposed government regulation of industry, relief, and trade-unions. The Black Legion declaration of principles indicated its commitment to the capitalist system.

We believe in the creation of wealth through initiative, labor, and industry, and wealth must be distributed to the people through wages.

We believe that every American businessman, if qualified, will make a success of his efforts. Wholesale and retail prices of necessities must be governed solely by supply and demand and not by government commissions, business combinations, trusts and monopolies.[15]

There is no evidence that the Legion had any grandiose plan for taking over the country or any program of major revolutionary social change. Rather it sought to maintain its version of established institutions and morality. Although its national commander, Virgil Effinger, once described it as "a guerilla army designed to fight the Republican and Democratic parties," it was opposed to third-party efforts.[16]

Furthermore, there is no evidence that the Legion established links with the other protofascist groups of the 1930's. Some leaders carried on discussions with William Pelley, the leader of the Silver Shirts, but decided not to cooperate with him. The Legion's main base in Michigan overlapped that of Father Charles Coughlin, but the Legion viewed Coughlin as an enemy because of his religion. Some members even plotted to assassinate Coughlin, and newspapers charged that the Legion had been behind the burning of Coughlin's Shrine of the Little Flower in 1936.[17]

A number of its members were convicted of two murders, one of a WPA worker, Charles Poole, who was a Catholic and was supposedly punished for beating his pregnant wife; the other was of a Negro hod carrier, Silas Coleman, who was shot.[18] There were a number of other murders in Michigan which were attributed to the Black Legion. Two Hudson Motor Company workers who were found murdered had been accused by Black Legion members of supposed Communist party membership. More than fifty members of the Black Legion in Michigan were convicted of various crimes, including arson, kidnaping, flogging, and plotting to kill different individuals.[19] Many acts of arson occurred against the homes of supposed Communists, or places at which Communists met.

There is no reliable information as to the membership of the Legion at its high point in 1936. Its Oakland County regiment, which was investigated by a grand jury, was reported to have had between 2,200 and 4,500 members. Estimates of total membership ranged around 40,000. Most of the membership was clearly in Michigan. The membership of the Order was largely unskilled and semiskilled workers who had migrated to the industrial areas from the hill sections of the South.

They brought with them to the industrial environment of the Detroit area a predilection for organization which promised dedication to the principles of their forebearers. The closeness of their community facilitated recruitment. Unused to the urban environment, the insecurity and monotony of the working situation made them more eager than the average person to seek membership in an organization which promised power and adventure.[20]

Here was the classic image of the displaced, status-stripped, small-town migrant, as well as of the low-status backlash which is known as nativist bigotry. Michigan authorities conducted several hundred interviews with Black Legion members, from which a prototype description of the typical adherent could be drawn:

He came from a small farm in the South. He had gone through grammar school, though he had not received a high school diploma. Married, the father of two children, working on construction or as unskilled labor in a steel plant or auto assembly line, he had never come to reconcile himself to city life or industrial work. His greatest concern was obtaining and holding a job for his family's sake. To the general insecurity of the times was added the fear that alien labor might displace him. Detroit had a large immigrant labor population, and this offered further justification for the traditional nativist dislike of alien groups. . . .[21]

In this manner were the workingmen of the Black Legion able to cross class lines to form a right-wing movement. The common preservatist core in this case was the symbolism of Americanist antiradicalism as embodied in the flesh by aliens. The labor unions became part of this symbolic network. At the upper economic levels, the National Association of Manufacturers was making references to the alien nature of the unions, calling them "un-American . . . anti-America . . . [and contrary to] the freedom for which the Anglo-Saxon has been struggling and fighting for centuries."[22] And the workers of the Black Legion took the same line. There is no evidence of active collusion. Charges that the Black Legion was supported by Detroit industrialists as a means of fighting trade-unions were carefully investigated by the Michigan Federation of Labor. The Federation reported that it could find no evidence to sustain the allegations.[23]

Although the Black Legion was officially nonpartisan and condemned the leadership of both parties, most of its activity seems to have been directed toward the Republican party. There is some evidence that a number of local officials in different parts of Michigan belonged to the order. "The Oakland County Grand Jury report published the names of eighty-six public officials who had been members of the Black Legion, including a state representative, the county prosecuting attorney, the city treasurer, and the chief of police in Pontiac, the county seat."[24]

A second important Protestant nativist movement of the 1930's was led by Reverend Gerald B. Winrod, of Kansas. Winrod, the son of a small-town evangelist, had started a fundamentalist magazine in 1925. After Franklin Roosevelt became President in 1933, Winrod concentrated on political attacks on Roosevelt as an agent of Communism and the Jews. He formed an organization, the Defenders of the Christian Faith. After a trip to Nazi Germany in 1933, he became overtly pro-Nazi.

In that sense, the Winrod operation was more explicitly fascist than was the Black Legion. The Defenders of the Christian Faith was overlaid with a mimicry of Hitlerian anti-Semitism that differed in kind and emphasis from traditional nativist patterns of bigotry. But the similarity was again superficial. The main tone was still that of moralistic fundamentalism, and no cogent plan was offered for the reorganization of the economy or society. Winrod argued that German Nazism had been a justified response to the Jews' role "as contaminators in the moral realm as well as despoilers in the business field."[25] Indicative of the concern for traditional morality were the repeated discussions by Winrod of all sorts of sexual vice in pre-Hitler Germany. The charges were reminiscent of the earlier attacks by the Klan and others on Jewish corruption in Hollywood and American big cities. Thus a typical comment by him reflects this emphasis:

One of the first things that disgusted Hitler was that he discovered that centers of vice, nudist colonies, the filthy screen and stage as well as the poison literature, to be *under control and direction of an organization of Jews*, who, for money, were willing to tear down the Gentile morals of the nation. The women saw the tide of mass immorality sweeping their country and organized to give defiant opposition to every form of unbridled lust about the time Adolf Hitler appeared on the scene making a dynamic appeal to popular imagination. By degrees he won the confidence of the women and succeeded in enlisting their support behind his movement. They came to him like an avalanche because his political philosophy provided for the upbuilding of the moral standards of the nation.[26]

Winrod, from 1933 on, became an ardent exponent of the idea of an international Jewish conspiracy as outlined in *The Protocols of the Elders of Zion*. He argued that three hundred men, largely Jews, "had planned and caused the social chaos of the thirties."[27] Liberalism was a political tool which would pave the way for socialism, communism, and fascism. The Roosevelt administration was denounced as "Jewish-controlled."

Although Winrod concentrated the focus of his attack on Jewish plots, international finance capitalism, and Communism, he was also strongly anti-Negro and anti-Catholic.[28] *The Defender* described Catholic plots to take over the country, called the Jesuits "the secret service department of the Pope," and charged that the Catholics were in alliance with the Jews in the Roosevelt administration. Winrod attacked Coughlin a number of times.[29]

Most fascinating of all the conspiracy theories advanced by Winrod was his reactivation of the old plot of the Illuminati, which had swept through New England in the late 1790's and had had a partial revival in the form of Anti-Masonry in the 1820's and 1830's. Winrod linked the anticlerical Illuminati to the Jesuits and the Jews. According to his mythology, Ignatius Loyola, the founder of the Jesuits, was a Jew. Adam Weishaupt, the founder of the Illuminati, in turn, is alleged to have been an active Jesuit. The Jesuits had cooperated with the Jews ever since the Reformation to destroy the Protestant "heretics." The Illuminati was an organization led by Jesuits and Jews. Weishaupt, although probably not a Jew himself, "was in the center of a Jewish circle."

> Winrod, in his book, *Adam Weishaupt, A Human Devil*, showed how he [Weishaupt] gained control of all masonic lodge rooms in Europe and changed them into secret societies of revolutionary planning. *"A study of the Illuminati,"* Winrod emphasized, *"will show where all the modern ideas of Bolshevism originated."* The French and Russian revolutions were brought on by this agency. Yes, he concluded, *"Modern Communism and old Jewish Illuminism are* one and the same thing."[30]

Much of Winrod's writings about the Illuminati is taken from Robison's book published in 1798. His information concerning the connection between the Jews and the Jesuits comes from various European books written about *The Protocols of the Elders of Zion*. In March 1934 he referred to a "Protocol of 1849" and to information which he had received about Jesuit-Jewish meetings from other books.[31] Contemporary Communism is a direct offspring of this Jesuit-Jewish conspiracy, which still existed. Thus Jews, Jesuits, and Communists were allied to destroy fundamentalist Protestantism. Huey Long's assassination was blamed on the Jewish-Catholic conspiracy, as evidenced by the fact that his killer had been a Catholic of German Jewish origins.[32]

The conspirators had strength within Protestantism, itself, since the "Modernists" in the Federal Council of Churches and the National Conference of Christians and Jews had Jewish views. They were, in effect, judaized Protestants.[33] The liberal Protestant churches, therefore, were also attacked as fronts for Jewish Communists.

The best estimate of Winrod's following comes from data available on the circulation of his magazine, *The Defender*. It seemingly rose steadily from about 20,000 in the early thirties to 100,000 from 1936 until the war.[34] A detailed study of its content over the years concludes that the level of articles and types of advertisements in it "argue for appeal to readers of lower educational levels. . . . In addition, the subscription price of fifty cents . . . seems to indicate that Winrod, too, judged his readers to be a low income group."[35] Ralph Roy also reports that *The Defender* circulated "among lower economic groups."[36] Gustavus Myers describes Winrod's supporters as "mainly the hidebound folk vegetating in small towns and rural sections . . . in many States."[37] This conclusion is iterated

by the rarity of Winrod's speeches in large cities. Occasionally he has talked in Kansas City, but apparently in no other large city. Indicative reports describe him as speaking at Manhattan, Kansas, before a group of "earnest souls from the Nazarene and Free Methodist Churches" or at Peoria, Illinois, under the auspices of the Peoria Tabernacle, an evangelistic organization, or at Peabody, Kansas, under the auspices of the local American Legion Post.[38]

His only direct venture into politics was to run for the Republican nomination for Senator in Kansas in 1938. The primary results gave him 53,140 votes, or 22 per cent of the total.[39]

Winrod's followers essentially resembled the rural and small-town part of the Klan which had flourished in the same midwestern plains area a decade earlier. The depression had given a new urgency to their discontent, and they now seemingly focused on Communism as symbolic of the threat to the evangelical Protestant way of life.

Communism is thought of in Fundamentalist terms as something that can be foretold and exposed though a proper understanding of Biblical prophecy. . . . They hold to an individualistic economic philosophy. They are firmly convinced that their moral standards should be accepted by the entire American people. Cities—with their polyglot and "alien" populations of Jews and recent Catholic immigrants from Southern Europe, with their multiplicity of moral philosophies —represent . . . the centers where their "fundamental Americanism" is threatened by "Communism"—as they conceive of Communism.[40]

A third well-publicized movement with apparent links with the nativism of the twenties was the Silver Shirts, organized in 1933. It included a large number of former Klansmen among its members and leaders.[41] As its name suggests, the Silver Shirts was an avowedly fascist organization. William Dudley Pelley, leader of the organization, openly advocated a fascist dictatorship, the use of violence, and the suppression of trade-unions, calling on industrialists to back him in his struggle for power.

The Silver Shirts, indeed, was a kind of hybrid, between the traditional nativist movements and the new mode of revolutionary fascism. A clue to its hybrid nature lay in the fact that Pelley did propose a scheme for drastically reorganizing the American economy along populist lines—but he called this scheme the *Christian* Commonwealth. Also, Pelley broke with traditional Protestant nativism in not attacking Catholics. However, this break was not without a struggle.

Pelley himself came from a fundamentalist Protestant background. His father had been an itinerant Methodist preacher. In an autobiographical report, he commented that "Orthodox Protestant theology, as it was forty years ago, was far more plentiful in my father's household than bread, butter, clothes, and fuel."[42] During the 1920's he became involved in spiritualist activities, from which he turned to fascism. Pelley wrote in an early issue of his paper, *Liberation*, of the need to build up "a Native-son, Protestant-Christian political machine."[43]

However, a detailed analysis of his literature by Portzline revealed that anti-Catholic statements were very infrequent, and Pelley once boasted to the House Un-American Activities Committee that approximately "50 per cent of my membership are prime young Catholics."[44] While there may have been some Catholics in the organization, the available evidence indicates that its membership was almost exclusively Protestant. In its early years, there was apparently considerable discussion among the leaders as to whether or not they should attack Catholics and bar them from membership. Paul von Lilenfeld Toal, the "Foreign Adjutant" of the Silver Shirts, once proposed that they "lay down a definite rule for admitting Catholics into the S.S. ranks. My advice is this: Let them sign . . . a paper that they, forthwith, renounce allegiance to His Holiness, the Pope, and swear allegiance to the Silver Legion and our Beloved Chief."[45] However, this traditional Protestant nativist strain did not prevail, and Pelley applauded Father Coughlin's *Social Justice* as "one of the outstanding weekly papers in the United States."[46] Instead, the Silver Shirts became even more concentratedly anti-Semitic than Winrod, blaming the Jews and their world-wide conspiracies for all the ills of society, the depression, Communism, and the spread of immorality.[47]

Although the organization claimed members in forty states and held well-publicized meetings in a number of eastern and midwestern cities, there seems little doubt that its basic strength was on the West Coast. A check by the House Committee on Un-American Activities of express shipments of its literature revealed that in 1937 "Pelley made 12 express shipments to points south of the Mason and Dixon line and 57 to points North of it, but 1,022 to the West Coast; and that in the first seven months of 1938 he made 14 such shipments to the East Coast, but 1,154 to the West Coast."[48]

The Los Angeles post is reported to have been the largest in the country, with five to six hundred people attending its meetings. Los Angeles had been growing rapidly, drawing in many migrants from rural and small-town areas.

Strong, in his analysis of the Silver Shirts, reports the presence of many professional people in the group. It is doubtful whether these members were typical, since the organization apparently sought to give the impression of strength among the middle class by publicizing the names of such members and referring to members as thirty-second-degree Masons. A somewhat different impression is given from a report of a lawyer who sampled Pelley's correspondence of several hundred thousand letters, while they were under subpoena in 1934. He reported:

> They were uneducated (judging from the grammatical errors); poor (many had suffered recent economic reverses); few professional people; a high proportion of neurotics (to judge from the language they employed); practically all elderly; a high proportion were female; they were seldom prominent in their community. . . . They came from small communities in general, mostly from the Middle West and the West Coast. Very little interest was manifested in the South.[49]

These conclusions are reinforced by the testimony of an observer in a small Washington town in 1938 who stated, "I have taken the auto license numbers of many who attend [Silver Shirt meetings], but I have not found one prominent person among them in the community."[50]

Pelley proposed an economic program for these economically distressed people, which was summarized by him in a book called *No More Hunger*.[51] The United States would be formed into one huge corporation, each citizen receiving a share in that corporation at birth. The government would grade the various occupations, and the citizens would be paid according to their contributions to the corporation. But, while this was as statist a version of the economy as could be conceived, it was differentiated sharply from socialism and Communism. Christian economics, Pelley said, does not make "the gigantic error of assuming that all men are truly born free and equal or are entitled to equal privileges and possessions merely because each has a head, two arms and two feet."[52] He classified the Negroes, Indians, and aliens into distinct castes and proposed that these "improvident and shiftless" people be made wards of the government.[53] Thus, Pelley set up a model of depression right-wing extremism by offering a revolutionary program, but spiking it with a dramatic preservatist core, which finally provided the distinctive emphasis of the movement. As a result, the working-class base of the movement was able to engage in cross-class alliances, at least on an ideological level. However, as compared with such pure remnants of the 1920's as the Black Legion, the symbolic baggage of the Silver Shirts was shifting from Protestant fundamentalism to a more universal substance.

At this bridge point to modern American extremism, the progression from the particular to the less particular on several different levels is noteworthy.

The movement from corporate status preservatism to disjunctive or anomic status preservatism has already been noted. In one case the operational emphasis is that the group has lost its former status, and the individual seeks to restore that group status which embraces him. In the other case, the operational emphasis is that the individual has lost his identification with the group—perhaps because the status of the group has effectively collapsed—and is attempting to preserve his residual, now more individualized, sense of special status through some other symbolic identification. This progression takes into account the deepening urbanization of the Protestant small-town migrant.

The further tendency is for the nature of the identifying cultural baggage to change from the more concrete to the more abstract; from fundamentalist Protestantism to fundamentalist Christianity; from a special quality of ethnicity to a special quality of nationalism. Or to put it more basically, in the context of Linton's definition, the character of the nativism has moved from the more concrete to the more abstract. And necessarily, the nature of the population target which defines the status line has moved from the more concrete to the more abstract.

This is one of the significances of the movement from anti-Catholicism to anti-Semitism, and to a special kind of political anti-Semitism at that. The traditional nativists had defined themselves against identifiable and emerging ethnic groups. Now, in the 1930's there were no emerging ethnic groups: neither the Catholics, the Irish, the southern Europeans, nor even the Jews. The earlier nativist conspiracies had often posited a Catholic conspiracy, and sometimes a Jewish conspiracy, which had featured *the* (abstract) Catholic, *the* (abstract) Jew, and *the* (abstract) alien as distinct from concrete Catholics, Jews, and aliens. But this had been coupled with and made easier by the tension-producing existence of real Catholic and real Jewish immigrants. The backlash was generated out of a *parallel* concrete ethnic identity. With the status of that ethnic identity disappearing, with real Catholics and Jews diminishing as specific status threats, the pattern of nativism changed. The status identification was not old-fashioned Protestantism with its select membership, but old-fashioned Americanism with its select membership. The parallel out-groups now were those who did not share in being American. The leveling threat was still represented by real people, radicals, unionists, aliens; but the identity of that group, which indeed seemed to be emerging, had blurred. Nativism had become more generalized; ethnicity itself had become more undefined and had even begun to take on an ideological cast.

Such a shift from the particular to the general, from the concrete to the abstract, has been suggested in other terms as a characteristic of "mass behavior." In analyzing "available nonelites" as those who have lost group attachments, Kornhauser notes that

people are available for mass behavior when they lack attachments to proximate objects. When people are divorced from their community and work, they are free to reunite in new ways. Furthermore, those who do not possess a variety of relations with their fellows are disposed to seek new and often remote sources of attachment and allegiance. . . . Unlike pluralist society, mass society does not keep men's sentiments from fastening on remote objects, precisely because it fails to absorb enough of the interest and emotions of its members into a variety of proximate concerns.[54]

The shift from corporate status preservatism to anomic status preservatism emerged fully in the 1930's as an American phenomenon affecting extremist movements. It is in that framework that the alteration in the nature of American status backlash, shaping American nativism, took place.

The distinction between more concrete and more abstract nativism is precisely the distinction that has been made in other terms by Eva Reichmann between "objective" and "subjective" anti-Semitism. She pointed out that the Nazis' use of subjective anti-Semitism did not spring from the actual tensions that existed between German and recent Jewish immigrants.[55] And drawing on her distinction, Dennis Wrong pointed out that "if the Nazis' ideological anti-Semitism and its echoes in this country represent the extreme of subjective anti-Semitism, social discrimination against Jewish *nouveaux riches* . . . represents the most clear-cut form of objective anti-Semitism. . . ."[56]

There emerged in the 1930's, for the reasons indicated, a more "subjective" (abstract) nativism in general, which became epitomized as political anti-Semitism in particular. The special vulnerability of the Jews to abstract nativism will be discussed later. But the span between the Black Legion and the Silver Shirts represented in miniature the initial break between old and new right-wing extremism in America, between old and new modes of status preservatism, between old and new modes of nativism.

However, while the Silver Shirts began to foreshadow some of the characteristics of the new right wing, its links with the past were still strong. Its economic program was rudimentary. Its tolerance for Catholicism was marginal; it was still basically grounded in fundamentalist moralism. By and large, these movements failed to capitalize seriously on the discontents of the Great Depression. They also suffered from the traditional leadership failures of fragmented extremist movements in America.

Janowitz suggests that a major reason for their organizational ineptness was that the type of men who became leaders of such groups reflected disturbed psychological traits—paranoia, megalomania, aggression, and personal disorganization—which made it difficult for them to cooperate with each other.[57] A study of sixty nativist leaders suggests this conclusion.

The social careers of nativist leaders present interesting uniformities, since many of the group were born on farms or in small towns and during late adolescence drifted into large urban centers. . . . In America the agitator who seeks to address and unite the urban middle-class and the working-class seems to be either of small town origin or an alien in the metropolitan center in which he chooses to propagandize. He comes to hate the city and to dedicate his life to preaching against what he believes to be its evils.

These leaders are mainly lower-middle-class in social origin, their fathers small businessmen, preachers, or, occasionally, professional men. Over half of the group were first reported to have undertaken active propaganda-work during the depths of the depression. Their lives were marked by constant occupational difficulties—they were always losing their jobs and never getting ahead—and by constant financial difficulties. Criminal records arising out of financial fraud appear among the group.[58]

The Oakland County Grand Jury decided that it could not label the Black Legion as a fascist conspiracy, since "the men who are listed as officers of the Black Legion . . . are not possessed of even average intelligence. . . . They are not leaders, not even worthy followers."[59] Indeed, the Black Legion was finally destroyed by the exposure that it was involved in murders in 1936, accompanied by the arrest and conviction of many of those involved.

Portzline remarks that "the personal animosities and internal dissensions that marked the short history of the Silver Shirts also tend to substantiate Janowitz's thesis."[60] Pelley himself was characterized by a congressional committee as a "racketeer engaged in mulcting thousands of dollars annually from his fanatical and misled followers."[61]

The Coughlin Movement

The right-wing movement of the 1930's which broke most sharply from the old nativist tradition was, of course, that of Father Charles E. Coughlin. His was America's most distinctively "fascist" movement in the sense that it espoused a genuinely revolutionary program built around a strongly preservatist core. But it differed from the centrist European fascism of the time in the nature of its social base.

Coughlin had been broadcasting regularly since October 1926, mainly on religious matters. Beginning in 1930, when he secured a national network, he began to talk about politics. His early discourses combined a strong emphasis on anti-Communism with a powerful indictment of the behavior of American capitalists. He urged government intervention to protect workers from exploitation. He also spent much of his time denouncing the evils caused by prohibition. His antibusiness tirades took the form of frequent denunciations of "international bankers," whom he held responsible for the Depression. Coughlin criticized President Hoover for his refusal to take over responsibility for unemployment relief on a federal level. His denunciations of wealth led him to be attacked by conservatives in the church such as William Cardinal O'Connor of Boston. Such criticisms from within the church, then and later, had little effect on the activities of the radio priest, since he was strongly backed by his hierarchical superior, Bishop Michael Gallagher of Detroit.[62]

Thus, before the 1932 election, Father Coughlin had a regular audience for his Sunday program which ran into the millions. The hundreds of thousands of letters which poured into his offices testified to the appeal of his magnificent oratory and attacks on the bankers and Communists. Following Roosevelt's inauguration, Coughlin continued his attacks on the banking system. His proposed solution to the crisis was a revaluation of the dollar, which would put more money in circulation and presumably create increased purchasing power. Through the first year of the Roosevelt administration, Coughlin supported the President, although he was publicly critical of many specific measures. He became increasingly militant in his criticisms of the business system.

He urged American capitalists to forego their usual 6 per cent profit for a year and concentrate on putting the unemployed back to work, but he saw little possibility of American capitalism reforming itself: "Capitalism is doomed and not worth trying to save." The radio priest called for a new economy based on the Sermon on the Mount. In more specific terms, Coughlin advocated some form of "socialized" or "state capitalism" to solve the distribution problem. He argued that since modern capitalism had refused to reform itself there was no alternative but for the government to control credit: "Call this credit by what name you will—a bonus, a check, or an unemployment insurance. But call it what you will, credits must be issued to all." Without outlining a specific plan, the priest insisted that all Americans who were willing to work should be guaranteed an annual wage sufficient to enjoy their share of the material abundance produced by United States industry and agriculture.[63]

In the fall of 1934, Father Coughlin proclaimed the formation of the National Union for Social Justice. The organization was established to press for the economic changes favored by Coughlin. His listeners were told to join up by sending in post cards. Increasingly the program advocated for the National Union became more radical in terms of advocacy of government ownership and control of the banks in order to guarantee full employment at reasonable wages.[64] However, though it approved of trade-unions, it opposed strikes and lockouts as "absolutely unnecessary."

By the end of the year, Coughlin was proclaiming that he saw no hope for modern capitalism or modern democracy in this country. America's only solution was a new system called social justice. However, the content of this system in economic or political terms was left undefined. Many early liberal and leftist critics saw in this vague position an embryonic fascist policy.

The year 1935 witnessed a complete break with Roosevelt and the New Deal. Early in the year, Coughlin organized a vigorous campaign against the President's proposal that the United States join the World Court. His radio broadcasts seemingly produced considerable pressure on the Senate through telegrams and letters, and many gave him the major credit for the defeat of the treaty. Following this victory, Coughlin began denouncing the domestic achievements of the administration, charging that it had accomplished little and had strengthened the position of the bankers.

Much of Coughlin's speeches in this period were couched in populist terms. He denounced rich and well-educated easterners, "the luxury of Park Avenue and Westchester County" against "widows, orphans and inarticulate farmers," or "Wall Street attorneys, the erudition of Harvard, of Yale, of Princeton, of Columbia," directed against servant girls, laborers, farmers.[65]

In foreign policy terms, he showed a consistent attachment to a strong, highly nationalistic, and isolationist position. During the Italo-Ethiopian war, he supported fascist Italy against Ethiopia, denouncing the latter as "a camouflaging Marauder."[66] He strongly opposed the League of Nations and sanctions against Italy. Anti-Communism was the third consistent and constant theme in Coughlin's ideological repertoire. Communism was evil because it was antireligious, internationalist, and a false solution to the economic problems posed by materialistic capitalism.[67]

In 1936, Coughlin and the National Union entered partisan politics. In March, he started his own weekly newspaper, *Social Justice*. The first issue denounced the two-party system as a "sham-battle." But the first electoral efforts of the new movement involved endorsing candidates for Congress in various primaries.

It is difficult to estimate Coughlin's actual influence in this period. In Pennsylvania, the National Union endorsed twenty-four congressional candidates, and twelve of them won a nomination. In Ohio, thirteen of the candidates who had accepted an endorsement of the National Union, and committed themselves to cooperating with it, were nominated.

On June 19, Coughlin announced that he was supporting Representative William Lemke of North Dakota as a candidate for President on a Union party ticket. The new party's program was similar to that of the National Union. Soon after it was formed, Gerald L. K. Smith, now the head of the Share-Our-Wealth movement, founded by Huey Long, and Dr. Francis Townsend, the head of the Townsend Old Age movement, endorsed Lemke. With these three movements united behind the third party, it could expect a massive vote. Further primary elections seemed to confirm this impression. Louis Ward, Coughlin's Washington lobbyist, came within 3,800 votes of winning the Democratic nomination for Senator in Michigan in September. In Massachusetts, the Union Party's Vice-Presidential candidate received 37,000 write-in votes in the Democratic senatorial primary in that state.

Coughlin clearly expected a considerable vote. He claimed 5,000,000 members in the National Union. A June 1936 Gallup poll suggested that 7 per cent of the electorate would vote for a candidate advanced by Coughlin. The same survey indicated that 10 per cent would be behind a candidate endorsed by Dr. Townsend. Gerald L. K. Smith stated that his Share-Our-Wealth movement had 3,000,000 supporters.[68] In line with such impressive backing, Father Coughlin publicly announced that if Lemke did not receive at least 9,000,000 votes, he would stop his radio broadcasts. The November elections gave the Union party candidates less than 900,000 votes, and on November 7, Father Coughlin told his radio audience that he was leaving the air.

Coughlin's absence from the airways was short-lived. He returned to a regular weekly broadcast on January 24, 1937. From then on, his politics took on an increasingly aggressive and more overt fascist-like posture. Early that year he denounced Governor Frank Murphy of Michigan for not using state troops to crush a strike at General Motors, and he launched what was to be a fairly continual attack on John L. Lewis and the CIO for their linkages with Communism. In midyear he announced the formation of Social Justice Councils, from which all non-Christians (Jews) were to be excluded. He announced that his great mistake in 1936 had been to think that democracy could work. He attacked the majority of American politicians for being pro-Communist. In March 1938, he proposed a Corporate State for America in which congressmen would no longer be elected by districts, but by functional groups such as auto workers, farmers, capitalists, and so on. He openly advocated the abolition of political parties. The President would be elected by the House of Representatives rather than by the people. Later that year, he created the Christian Front which would not be "afraid of the word 'fascist.' . . ."[69]

As the decade drew to a close, Coughlin showed increasing willingness to advocate a profascist position. The May 23, 1938, issue of *Social Justice* listed Mussolini as its "Man of the Week." In September, articles in the magazine justified Hitler's demands for the Sudetenland, enthusiastically endorsed Chamberlain's actions at Munich, and bitterly attacked Churchill and Eden. In July of the same year, *Social Justice* reprinted *The Protocols of the Elders of Zion* and began to publish various articles linking Jews with Communism. In 1939, the magazine defended the persecution of the Jews by Fascists and Nazis. Following the outbreak of the war in Europe, Coughlin strongly attacked any efforts to aid the Allies, while at the same time he blamed the war and efforts to get the United States into it on the Jews. Hitler was repeatedly praised. Even after the United States entered the war, *Social Justice* continued to hold the Jews responsible for the conflict.

The Coughlin movement finally met its demise through wartime suppression. The larger radio stations on which he had been broadcasting refused to renew his contracts, and he was forced to cancel his 1940–1941 series. In the spring of 1942, the Postmaster-General banned *Social Justice* from the mails as seditious. To avoid a sedition trial against the radio priest, Archbishop Mooney of Detroit was asked indirectly by the Attorney-General to silence him and agreed to do so. On May 1, 1942, the Archbishop told Coughlin to "cease all public pronouncements for the duration of the war under penalty of defrockment."[70] Father Coughlin acquiesced, and his political career was over.

Social Base

The key to the Coughlin movement as an idiosyncratic expression of right-wing extremism lies in the nature of his popular support. This is the first movement under discussion for which there are reliable data concerning that support. Various public opinion agencies asked questions concerning Coughlin during the late 1930's and the early 1940's. These opinion poll data suggest that as many as one-quarter of the population had favorable opinions of him at different points in his career. In April 1938, 27 per cent of a national sample interviewed by Gallup stated they approved of Coughlin, 32 per cent disapproved, and 41 per cent had no opinion. A second poll in December reported 23 per cent approving and 30 per cent opposing.[71]

A survey conducted by Gallup in July of 1939 indicated that his support had declined during that year. Only 15 per cent stated that they agreed with his ideas, while 38 per cent indicated disagreement.[72]

His support remained at this level during the first year of the war. In April 1940, in response to the question: "In general do you approve or disapprove of what he [Father Coughlin] says?" 17 per cent told Opinion Research Corporation interviewers that they approved, while 29 per cent disagreed, and 54 per cent voiced no opinion.[73]

Through use of surveys, it is possible to describe their characteristics.

This secondary analysis is based on two surveys conducted by the Gallup organization in April and Dècember 1938. Although conducted seven months apart, they show no significant differences with respect to the social characteristics of those indicating approval of Coughlin. Approximately 25 per cent of each sample stated they supported the radio priest.

The most important correlate of support for Father Coughlin in 1938 was religion. Although many Catholic priests and bishops openly opposed him and attacked many of his views as being in conflict with Catholic doctrine, there can be little question that Catholics were much more in favor of him than were Protestants.

As the data in Table 11 suggest, over two-fifths of the Catholics supported him and one-quarter opposed him in December 1938.[74] Among Protestants, less than one-fifth favored Coughlin, while almost one-third expressed disapproval. Coughlin was better known among Catholics than among Protestants; 33 per cent of the former had no opinion of him, as contrasted with over 50 per cent of the latter.

As might be expected, Protestants varied according to denomination in their opinions. Baptists showed the highest excess of disapproval over approval; Methodists and Presbyterians occupied a middle position, somewhat more opposed than favorable; Lutherans were the one Protestant group in which supporters outnumbered opponents (Table 12).[75]

The opposition to Coughlin of Episcopalians and Congregationalists may reflect their position as the churches of high-status, old-stock Americans. The Coughlin support among Lutherans may be due to the fact that Lutherans were often of recent German origin and hence likely to be isolationists in the years preceding World War II.

The conclusion drawn from the opinion surveys that Coughlin's primary appeal was to his coreligionists is sustained by an ecological analysis of the vote for Lemke on the Union party ticket in 1936. Nick Masters reports that the "correlation between the Roman Catholic areas and the Union Party vote has a coefficient of .78. This coefficient shows .that approxi-

Table 11.   RELATION OF RELIGIOUS AFFILIATION TO ATTITUDES
TOWARD COUGHLIN, DECEMBER 1938 (GALLUP)

Attitude Toward Coughlin	Religious Affiliation			No Religious Choice
	Catholics	Protestants	Jews	
Approve	42 %	19 %	10 %	19 %
Disapprove	25	31	63	28
No opinion	33	50	27	53
	(380)	(1,047)	(67)	(560)

Table 12. ATTITUDES TOWARD COUGHLIN AMONG DIFFERENT PROTESTANT GROUPS,
DECEMBER 1938 (GALLUP)

Attitude Toward Coughlin	Baptist	Meth- odist	Lu- theran	Presby- terian	Episco- palian	Congre- gation- alists	Other Protes- tants
Approve	16 %	20 %	29 %	20 %	21 %	21 %	12 %
Disapprove	30	29	21	27	45	43	33
No opinion	54	51	50	53	33	36	55
Number	(147)	(293)	(125)	(164)	(84)	(47)	(190)
Excess of approval over disapproval	−14 %	−9 %	+8 %	−7 %	−24 %	−22 %	−21 %

mately 60% of the Union vote is associated with the Catholic population."[76]

The second major factor that differentiated supporters of Coughlin from opponents was economic status. Among both Catholics and Protestants, the lower the economic level, the greater the proportion of supporters to opponents (see Table 13). Among Catholics of above average means, the proportion approving was only slightly more (4 per cent) than those disapproving, while among poor Catholics, many more (19 per cent) favored Coughlin than opposed him. The same relationship with economic status held among Protestants. Protestants of above average economic level indicated great disapproval, while the proportion approving and disapproving was about the same among poorer Protestants. Occupational varia-tions (not presented here) showed about the same pattern. Manual workers, those on government public works (WPA), and the unemployed were most likely to be Coughlin supporters among both Catholics and Protes-tants, while in both religious groups, professionals and those in business revealed the least approval and the most opposition.

For some reason, the relative position of white-collar workers differed according to religion. Catholic white-collar employees were among the high-support groups, as high as or higher than the manual workers. Among Protestants, white-collar occupations resembled the professionals and busi-nessmen, giving little support to Coughlin. Farmers, both Catholic and Protestant, tended to be high on the Coughlin side. Although the number of cases in each analytic cell becomes small, the pattern holds when three variables—religion, occupation, and income—are held constant: within a given religious and occupational group, approval of Coughlin increased as economic status decreased.

The combination of socioeconomic position and religion explains much of the difference between supporters and opponents, but other factors, of course, played a role. Age was important as a source of differentiation;

Table 13. RELATIONSHIP OF RELIGION AND SOCIOECONOMIC STATUS TO ATTITUDES TOWARD COUGHLIN, DECEMBER 1938 (GALLUP)

| | Attitudes toward Coughlin (Per Cent) | | | | | | | | | |
| | Catholics | | | | | Protestants and No Religious Choice | | | | |
Socioeconomic Status	Approve	Disapprove	No opinion	Difference[a]	Number	Approve	Disapprove	No opinion	Difference	Number
Above average	38	34	28	+ 4	(40)	13	48	39	−35	(264)
Average	41	28	31	+13	(121)	17	33	51	−16	(609)
Poor +	46	25	29	+21	(43)	21	29	50	− 8	(209)
Poor	42	23	35	+19	(77)	19	18	63	+ 1	(277)
On relief	41	20	39	+21	(98)	24	24	52	0	(245)

[a] Per cent difference between approval and disapproval.

older people were more likely to back Coughlin than others, holding both religion and income constant. Also, men seem to have been slightly more favorable to Coughlin than women were.

Rural areas and small towns have traditionally been identified as centers of conservatism, populism, and anti-Semitism in the United States and other countries. This pattern held true regarding attitudes toward Coughlin. The ratio between support and opposition was most favorable for Coughlin in rural areas and small towns. Only 6 per cent of Catholics living on farms disapproved of Coughlin, as compared with 28 per cent opposed among those living in urban areas. Regionally, Coughlin's support followed the pattern one might expect from a spokesman in the populist and social-credit tradition. His greatest support came from the west central region of the country (Wisconsin, Minnesota, Iowa, Missouri, South Dakota, Nebraska, and Kansas). New England, with its high concentration of Irish Catholics, was second highest. The areas of least Coughlin support were the West Coast and the South.

The appeal of Coughlin to these areas may have reflected the fact that he "was in some respects in the Populist tradition. . . . His advocacy of silver coinage and inflationary measures, his denunciations of Wall Street and international bankers, and his 'Bryanesque rhetoric spoken with an Irish brogue' won Coughlin an ardent following among farmers in the old Populist areas of the midwest."[77]

Although public opinion surveys did not secure information on ethnic background during the 1930's, and hence it is impossible to relate these findings to ethnicity, other sources suggest that the regional support for Coughlin may have reflected his specific ethnic appeal to German and Irish Catholics. An ecological analysis of the 1936 vote for Coughlin's Presidential candidate, Lemke, indicates that it was concentrated in areas that were disproportionately Irish and German Catholic.

Outside of North Dakota [his home state] Lemke got more than 10 per cent of the vote in thirty-nine counties. Twenty-one of these counties are more than 50 per cent Catholic. In twenty-eight of these thirty-nine counties, the predominant nationality element is German. The only four cities where Lemke got more than 5 per cent of the vote are also heavily German and Irish Catholic.[78]

The analysis of the demographic background factors suggests clearly that Coughlin was strongest among Catholics and Lutherans, in contrast to other Protestants, and to Jews; among the less well-to-do; among farmers and those living in small communities; among older people, as compared with young ones; and among those living in the Midwest and New England, as contrasted with the Far West and the South.

Coughlin's weakness in the South and the Far West may have reflected the strength of anti-Catholicism in these areas, particularly in the former. It was also a product of a decision on his part not to spread his resources thin in these regions. His radio network rarely extended into these two sections. The regional center of his organized support seems to have changed over time. The National Union for Social Justice had its main strength before the 1936 elections in the Midwest and the East. The Christian Front, which was a much smaller group, had its principal membership in 1939 and 1940 in large eastern cities which were centers of Catholic population. "Unlike the National Union for Social Justice, there were no Front units organized in rural, farm areas."[79]

There is some indication that his class base may have also shifted. During the 1933–1935 period, Coughlin drew considerable adherents from the middle classes, but these dropped away as he moved first into third-party, and later fascist, politics. The New Deal had become attractive to much of the middle class as a moderate solution. An examination of letters received at the White House from Coughlin supporters in the first period indicates that "a surprisingly large number of the letters were written by fairly well-educated people, small entrepreneurs or professional men. Since most of the writers also identified themselves as Roman Catholic, it is strongly suggested that the most active Coughlinites were of old immigrant, Roman Catholic, lower middle-class origins."[80] An analysis of letters written to Monseigneur John Ryan, a sharp critic of Coughlin's, in October 1936, during the final weeks of the Union party campaign, found that almost all were Irish or German Catholics, who had a strong sense of identity with the poor and oppressed against the wealthy. These letters contained frequent mistakes in grammar or spelling, suggesting that their writers were of much lower status than those who had written to the White House before 1935. "The tone of many of the letters is that of people whose distress is too urgent to permit them to have any sympathy for experiments or half-measures."[81]

Reports on the membership of the Christian Front in the latter years of Coughlin's activity also suggest that it was "predominantly Irish Catholic of the low and moderate [income] groups."[82] The first meeting of any group calling itself the Christian Front in New York City took place in a Paulist church in July 1938. "Fifty men, most of them workers and union members, met on July 14 to hear lectures on Communism and tirades against the Jews."[83] Subsequent reports on meetings of the Front indicate that "unemployed longshoremen attended street meetings, and the Bronx Coughlinites who supported Joe McWilliams were by and large of the working class. Those who attended a September, 1939 meeting in Brooklyn included longshoremen and truck drivers as well as white collar workers, policemen and, at the other end of the occupational spectrum, a former college professor."[84] One occupational group which seems to have been attracted to the Front was policemen. An official investigation of the New York force revealed that 407 of New York's finest belonged to the Christian Front.[85]

The leadership of the Coughlinites, however, was quite different from this rank-and-file base. Many priests played an active role in the Christian Front, as did lawyers and politicians. These three occupations, of course, provided most of the leadership of the Irish American community generally.[86]

The surveys permit some limited specification of the attitudes of Coughlin's supporters. The best available measure of opinion on foreign policy at the time is the posture toward the protagonists in the Spanish Civil War. Religious affiliation played a major role in affecting the opinions of both supporters and opponents of Coughlin. Catholics as a group favored the Rebels (40 per cent for Franco, 20 per cent for the Loyalists): Protestants backed the Loyalists (40 per cent to 10 per cent). Among both Catholics and Protestants at each economic level, Coughlin supporters were more disposed to favor Franco than were those who disapproved of the radio priest. However, in spite of Coughlin's repeated concentration on the Spanish Civil War issue, only 43 per cent of his Catholic supporters and a mere 8 per cent of his Protestant followers espoused his position regarding Franco. Seemingly, concern with the Communist issue in the Spanish Civil War was not a major source of Father Coughlin's popular appeal.

Analysis of attitudes toward domestic issues suggests that, religious identification apart, Coughlin's support was due in large part to economic dissatisfaction. Coughlin backers at every economic level were much more discontented with their lot, with the economic state of the country, and with prospects for the future than were his opponents. For example, two-thirds of his supporters felt that their personal economic situation had been declining, while among those opposed to Coughlin slightly less than one-half felt that their situation had worsened.

The antagonism expressed by Coughlin to the existing business system, to exorbitant profits, to bankers (Jewish and others), and the fact that his support came largely from the lower class would lead one to expect that Coughlinites would express greater antipathy to Republicans and conservatism than to Democrats and liberalism. The data do not bear out this assumption. Those who approved of Coughlin in 1938 were more likely to support the GOP than the Democratic party, and conservatism rather than liberalism. Supporters of Coughlin were only slightly more favorable to a third party than his opponents (11 per cent, as compared to 8 per cent). The party preferences of Coughlin supporters may be inferred from responses to a question posed in the April 1938 survey: "If you were voting for a Congressman today, would you be most likely to vote for the Republican, the Democrat, or a third party candidate?" Among Coughlin supporters who expressed a partisan choice, 40 per cent preferred the Democrats, while 55 per cent of Coughlin's opponents backed the Democrats. These differences are evident in each economic category as well (see Table 14).

Preservatism, Nativism and Conspiracy

The data concerning the social characteristics of Coughlin's followers challenge the generalizations expressed by some that Coughlinism as a form of fascism appealed primarily to the middle class. Arthur Schlesinger, Jr., for example, wrote that the

followers of the demagogues [Coughlin, Townsend, and Long] mostly came from the old lower-middle classes, now in an unprecedented stage of frustration and fear, menaced by humiliation, dispossession and poverty. . . . They came, in the main, from the ranks of the self-employed, who, as farmers or shopkeepers or artisans, felt threatened by organized economic power, whether from above, as in banks and large corporations, or from below, as in trade unions.[87]

A contemporary account of Coughlin described him as having a program which "appeals simultaneously to agriculture, the middle class and the big employer."[88] But, as contrasted with European fascist movements, which recruited disproportionately from the middle strata (small-business and white-collar elements), Coughlin, religious appeal apart, drew his support from manual workers and the unemployed. The one common link between the class base of the Coughlin movement and that of the European fascists was the farmers. Populist antagonism toward the bankers, together with general antielitist and anticosmopolitan attitudes, may have accounted for this support. If Coughlin's movement was a fascist movement, it represented a version of "proletarian" fascism more comparable to that of Perón in Argentina than to that of Hitler.[89]

The Perónist movement was, of course, built around the preservatist spine of the military, and clergymen provided a similar spine for the Coughlin movement. However, it was clear that Coughlin's movement, like Perón's and unlike Hitler's, was heavily based on the working and under class, and its right-wing characteristics derived more exclusively from some preservatist impulse of that class. In the case of Coughlin's movement, that impulse was to be found in his primary social base: the Irish Catholics.

Although Father Coughlin had admirers in many sections of the country and among diverse elements in the population, the Irish in the cities were the hard

Table 14. RELATIONSHIP BETWEEN ATTITUDE TOWARD COUGHLIN AND VOTE INTENTION, APRIL 1938 (GALLUP)

	Attitude toward Coughlin (Per Cent)							
	Approve of Coughlin 1939 Vote Intention				Disapprove of Coughlin 1939 Vote Intention			
Income Level	Republicans	Democrats	Third Party	Number	Republicans	Democrats	Third Party	Number
Above average	66	25	9	(69)	57	37	6	(128)
Average	58	34	8	(203)	39	52	9	(285)
Poor +	46	45	9	(111)	36	57	7	(132)
Poor	47	40	13	(124)	24	67	9	(115)
On relief	24	61	15	(85)	15	72	13	(69)
Total	49	40	11	(592)	37	55	8	(729)

core of his following. The cities in the East and Middle West that carried his program were those with large Irish populations. Later, when he organized his pressure group, the Union for Social Justice, more than half the members of the Board of Trustees had conspicuously Irish names. . . . The Irish listened to Father Coughlin and believed in him because he was a priest. With other institutions crumbling and other symbols tarnished, the Church was a tower of certitude.[90]

The Church was, by then, for the urban Irish a symbol of their own special ethnic status, their own special wellspring of honor and privilege. It was a symbol of the Irish establishment in the cities. Moynihan wrote:

New York used to be an Irish city. Or so it seemed. There were sixty or seventy years when the Irish were everywhere. *They* felt it was their town. It is no longer and they know it. That is one of the things bothering them.[91]

It began to bother them substantially in the 1930's. In 1932, in the wake of Al Smith's defeat,

when the chance came to redress this wrong, the Democrats, instead of renominating Smith, turned instead to a Hudson Valley aristocrat with a Harvard accent who had established his reputation by blocking Murphy's nomination of "Blue-eyed Billy" Sheehan for the U.S. Senate, and was soon to enhance it by getting rid of Jimmy Walker. . . . A distinctive quality of the anti-New Deal Irish during the 1930's is that they tended to identify the subversive influences in the nation with the old Protestant establishment.[92]

The phenomenon was nativism, turned on its head, but nativism nonetheless, and the American Irish Catholic's first experiment with saving the status he had just achieved. This was the core of preservatism in the Coughlin movement. Coughlin himself wrote: "What we strive for is not revolution, but restoration of principles. . . ."[93]

While Coughlin's movement was, in this sense, based on a kind of corporate rather than anomic nativism, it could never be so explicitly. It therefore took on the abstract quality of the right-wing extremism of the 1930's. To be protected was the quality of Americanism. The group to be protected against were not aliens, but people with alien ideas. Because of the abstract nature of the status and the abstract nature of the enemy, nativism and conspiracy theory merged into a single focus for Coughlin, as it had for Hitler. "Subjective anti-Semitism" came into its own. The abstract Jew embodied the abstract alien in America's midst.

Although Coughlin did not openly present his beliefs in the existence of a Jewish international conspiracy allied with bankers and Communists until the late thirties, the available evidence suggests that he had been a covert believer in conspiracy theories much earlier. Thus a number of writers report that he had one of the most extensive libraries of anti-Semitic conspiracy literature and had close friends who were committed anti-Semites, even before he began discussing politics in his broadcasts.[94] Most intriguing of all is the indication that Coughlin was aware of, and believed in, the conspiracy of the Illuminati, the secret high-placed Masonic order, which had first appeared in American political life in the 1790's, and which also constituted a major element in Gerald Winrod's paranoid image of the world. Coughlin referred to Adam Weishaupt, the founder of the Illuminati, as the inspirer of Karl Marx and the founder of Communism. Coughlin never openly talked about the conspiracy of the Illuminati, but these references to Weishaupt's supposed influence on Communism point up his belief in it. Thus, as early as 1931 he spoke as follows:

> What is this thing called Communism? According to its founder, Adam Weishaupt, from whom Karl Marx drew his inspiration, Communism is necessarily identified with atheism. . . . Following his master, Karl Marx emphasized the fact that *"religion is the opium of the people."* This accounts for the fact that every form of religion has been practically banned in Russia.[95]

Adam Weishaupt appears in other Coughlinite works. An early official biography by his Washington lobbyist and close friend Louis Ward reports on conversations with Father Coughlin in which he outlined the course of history. Weishaupt is described as the first to assail "the new theory of capitalism with the weapons of radicalism."[96] Perhaps the most explicit restatement of the role of Weishaupt and the Illuminati appears in a work by Gertrude Coogan which was "a basic book in Coughlinite literature."[97] Immediately after reporting that Edouard de Rothschild, of Paris, had "discouraged as useless all opposition to the strong current of State Socialism," she wrote:

> There is a historical background for Socialism which has been purposefully concealed. All of the theories and practices advanced by the present-day Socialists are copied directly from the organization known as the Illuminati—"enlightened men."
>
> The order of the Illuminati was founded in 1776 by Dr. Adam Weishaupt of Bavaria. Weishaupt spent five years in collaboration with other conspirators and outlined a method for destroying the economic and social order of any country. He aimed at nothing less than World Revolution. His order, and the dupes whom he succeeded in getting to carry out his vicious schemes, advocated abolition of the laws which protected private property; advocated sensual pleasures; abjured Christianity, and called patriotism and loyalty narrow-minded prejudices. They intended to root out all religion and ordinary morality, and break down the bonds of domestic life.[98]

Coughlin himself did not openly mention the conspiracy of the Illuminati in his radio talks. The closest he came to doing so was in a radio speech delivered in 1936 opposing sanctions against Fascist Italy for its invasion of Ethiopia. In this talk, Father Coughlin revealed his belief in the continued existence of international conspiracies involving the Masons.

I shall not weaken in my fight against the political force which in this country is seeking to drag America with the tow lines of English banking capitalism or Russian communism against the Italy of Benito Mussolini in order to increase the sanctions, which are so much the more iniquous and ignoble because they have undertaken to damage a great and civilized nation. They are the results of a plot which has been slowly woven with the active support of international Masonry, the exponents of high finance and international Communism, all allied at Geneva to defeat Fascism. Now since Masonry, high finance, and Communism are also our enemies as Americans and Catholics we shall not abandon the struggle until the conspiracy has been completely frustrated.[99]

Although Coughlin must have known of the literature which linked the Illuminati, the Masons, and the Russian Revolution with the conspiracy outlined in the *Protocols of the Elders of Zion*, he repressed any overt references to the latter until 1938. Seemingly, although a believer in these plot theories, he was aware during the first stages of his political career that an emphasis on conspiratorial theories would be unpolitic. He told intimates that anti-Semitism would not succeed in the United States. On the other hand, he may have been trying to signal those in the country who, like himself, believed in these conspiracies that he was aware of them. The mentions of Adam Weishaupt and the frequent citing of Jewish names were, in effect, his means of recruiting those who believed in the conspiracies of the Illuminati and the Elders of Zion. Presumably, Coughlin did not share Winrod's view that Adam Weishaupt was a Jesuit and that the Jesuits and Jews working together used the organization to dominate the Masons. He did accept the theory that the Jews were powerful among the Masons and that the origins of contemporary Communism may be traced to a series of events which began with the Jewish role in the Masons and the French Revolution. An article in *Social Justice* in 1939 stated that "Jews simply as Jews are not responsible for subversion, but rather . . . *Jews as Oriental Freemasons are the powers behind the throne of darkness.*"[100]

Looking through Coughlin's speeches in the early period (1930–1936), one can find frequent implicit anti-Semitic references. Thus in 1931, in discussing Communist leaders, he referred to "Trotsky from New York, Lenin from Germany, Bela Kun from Hungary" and to "the atheism and the treachery preached by the German Hebrew Karl Marx."[101] His attacks on "international bankers" were personified as in "the Rothschilds and Lazarre Freres, . . . the Morgans, the Kuhns and Loebs."[102] "Mentioning Alexander Hamilton, he would casually add, 'whose original name was Alexander Levine.' "[103]

In one of his most important and best-publicized speeches in March 1935, answering General Hugh Johnson's attack on him and Huey Long, Father Coughlin spent a large part of his speech attacking Bernard Baruch, insisting that Johnson was the mouthpiece of Baruch, the leader of the international bankers and Wall Street. He "suggested that it was more than mere coincidence that Baruch's middle name was Manasses, the same name as that of the ancient prince who had Isaiah killed for criticizing him."[104] (His middle name actually was Mannes.) He went on to link his attack on Baruch, the "prince of high finance," to the same names he used on other occasions, "the Rothschilds in Europe, the Lazarre Freres in France, the Warburgs, the Kuhn-Loebs, the Morgans and the rest of that wrecking crew of internationalists whose god is gold and whose emblem is the red shield of exploitation—these men I shall oppose to my dying days."[105]

It is perhaps beside the point here to explore why the "abstract Jew" has been such an ideal instrument for abstract nativism and concomitant conspiracy theory in the modern Western world. Yehezkel Kaufman has suggested the unique background that has helped to create this singular pattern:

> Its grounds are general, but their composition and combination have made Jew-hatred ("anti-Semitism") a unique historical complex. Religious fanaticism, national rivalry, hatred of aliens, economic and social competition—all these are general phenomena. But in Jew-hatred all these have been joined in permanent (and hence intensified) combination and have become historically fixed. . . . Wherever there is contact between [different] religious, ethnic and economic groups there necessarily develop irritations and quarrels that breed enmity. Through the dispersion [of the Jews] the areas of contact between Israel and other peoples grew immeasurably. It was contact with a society differing in religious and racial stock, alien in the land, and beyond any hope of being merged in a common union. The irritants of hostility towards this society were intensified by continuous contact with it, by the multiplicity of areas of contact with it, and by the multiple grounds of difference. It was not a local but a universal hatred, encompassing almost all the nations, for Jews came in contact with everyone. These intensified irritants of hostility converged on a single object, were borne by one people, and accumulated around them generation by generation. Through the continuity of its object, this hatred became a sort of idea, a conception, a system.[106]

It is true that there was always a backlog of traditional anti-Semitism in America, culturally transmitted from all corners of the Western world. But backlog is not yet backlash. When nativism was concrete in America, because of the concrete identities of the nativist groups as well as of their targets, the Jews were just one of the objects of active bigotry, and not the first among them. But when nativism became more abstract, because of the

less explicit identity of the nativists, then the accumulated backlog of anti-
Semitism as "a sort of idea, a conception, a system" became pertinent and
prime.

Of course, the advantage of this kind of abstract anti-Semitism for
fascist movements is that it is ambidextrous. It can go to the left and to the
right simultaneously.

For Coughlin's revolutionary thrust, the conspiratorial Jew was the International Banker, retarding the growth of power and status among the
lower class. This has been a populist and left-wing image on occasion. For
Coughlin's preservative thrust, the abstract Jew was the alien Communist,
propounding the leveling of all status and values. And there was enough
real Jewish presence on the American scene to give *post hoc* flesh to this
abstract image.

The Principle of Selective Support

It has often been noted that the tight ideological structure enunciated
by the leaders does not reflect itself neatly in the ranks of their social
movement. This disparity is presumably even greater when a leader's
"audience" is distinguished from his formal "membership." The Coughlin
movement was both. Coughlin's potential strength was most often measured,
not by the formal membership of the National Union for Social Justice,
but by his apparent "following" throughout the nation. The polls indicated
that about a quarter of the American people "approved" of him. But, to
begin with, approval of Coughlin may have meant sharply different things to
those of differing economic position. Though at every level Coughlin
backers were more often for the Republicans than were those who opposed
him, the percentage of those who preferred the Democratic party and also
endorsed Coughlin increased with lower income. The same pattern occurred
with respect to attitude toward President Roosevelt; that is, most of the
poor and those on relief who approved of Coughlin supported Roosevelt.

The data on party support and opinion of Roosevelt presented in
Table 15 suggest that many poor people who backed Coughlin did so in
spite of, or without knowledge of, his attitude toward Roosevelt. It is
likely that among the less educated and the underprivileged both Coughlin
and Roosevelt were viewed in similar lights. Those who felt friendly to
Father Coughlin were clearly not of one political persuasion, and he failed
to get more than a small minority of them to back his third-party candidate.
It seems evident that his well-to-do supporters were a different group
ideologically than his lower-strata backers. The former may have found
him to their liking because of his antagonism to Roosevelt and the New
Deal, his opposition to the rise of the CIO unions, and his advocacy of

Table 15. RELATIONSHIP BETWEEN ATTITUDES TOWARD COUGHLIN AND ROOSEVELT,
APRIL 1938 (GALLUP)

Income Level	Proportion Opposed to Roosevelt			
	Attitudes toward Coughlin			
	Approve		Disapprove	
	%	Number	%	Number
Above average	74	(79)	58	(157)
Average	62	(246)	37	(341)
Poor +	52	(142)	30	(155)
Poor	42	(157)	20	(135)
On relief	25	(99)	18	(82)

militant action to block the rise of Communist forces at home and abroad.
For his lower-class supporters, Coughlin's attacks on capitalism, the banks,
Jewish financiers, and inept government handling of the depression may
have been crucial. Though he failed to build his own party or movement,
he did reach a large audience every Sunday on the radio and was regarded
favorably by a considerable section of the populace, many of whom were
traditional Catholic and working-class Democrats. One might speculate,
therefore, as to whether the issues raised by Coughlin may have contributed
to the drop-off in Democratic support, particularly among Catholics, in
1938 and 1940. Coughlin may have been instrumental in transferring support from the Democratic to the Republican party.

Evidence tending to confirm this hypothesis may be found in comparisons
between the 1936 Presidential vote and 1938 opinion on parties and candidates. In the latter year, Coughlin supporters who had voted for Roosevelt
in 1936 were more likely to have changed their opinion concerning the
President than were Roosevelt voters who disapproved of the radio priest.

The same relationship holds in a comparison of the 1936 vote with the
party choice of voters in the 1938 congressional elections. Among those
who voted for Roosevelt in 1936 and approved of Coughlin in 1938, only
50 per cent said they would vote Democratic, while among Roosevelt
voters who disapproved of Coughlin, 64 per cent remained faithful to the
Democrats (Table 16).

It is also clear that while Coughlin served as a kind of prototype of
American fascism, the 15 or 25 per cent of the population who in 1938
and 1939 supported him did not actually believe in fascism. There is a
question as to whether most of Coughlin's supporters agreed with his anti-
Semitism. Although Coughlin turned overtly and continually anti-Semitic
in July of 1938, had been openly supportive of Francisco Franco from the
beginning of the Spanish Civil War, and had been sharply attacked by

Table 16. RELATIONSHIP BETWEEN 1936 PRESIDENTIAL VOTE AND 1938 CONGRESSIONAL VOTE, APRIL 1938 (GALLUP)

Attitude Toward Coughlin	1936 Presidential Vote (Per Cent)											
	Roosevelt 1938 Party Choice					Landon					
	Republicans	Democrats	Third Party	No opinion	Number		Republicans	Democrats	Third Party	No opinion	Number
Approve	21	50	9	20	(342)		78	5	4	14	(256)
Disapprove	9	64	9	19	(509)		73	11	2	11	(323)
No opinion	13	64	4	19	(477)		84	2	3	14	(231)

liberal critics for being profascist and sympathetic to anti-Semitism as early as 1935, some Jews and half of the Negroes interviewed approved of him in the December 1938 survey. Many who spoke approvingly of Coughlin to interviewers were also quite positive about Franklin Roosevelt, and some of them were supporters of Loyalist Spain.

Unfortunately, none of the surveys inquiring about attitudes toward Coughlin solicited opinions about the Jews. Other surveys made during this period did, however, contain questions on anti-Semitism, and these permit some estimate of the relationship of Coughlin support to expressed prejudice, since it is possible to examine the beliefs of Union party voters. As expected, most of those who reported in 1938 that they had voted for Lemke in the previous Presidential election indicated approval of Coughlin. Lemke voters were more likely to indicate anti-Semitic beliefs than the rest of the population, but the difference was not large. The data from two 1939 Gallup surveys that asked whether respondents would support "a campaign against Jews" indicate that 21 per cent of 1936 Lemke voters, 12 per cent of Roosevelt supporters, and 8 per cent of Landon voters were overtly anti-Semitic. Further, in national surveys both before and after Coughlin began his anti-Semitic attacks, the same proportion (12 per cent) reported that they would support a campaign against Jews. While these findings suggest that Coughlin's backers were probably more anti-Semitic than the population in general, it is well to keep in mind that the large majority of his Union party supporters did not give anti-Semitic responses to the survey questions.

It seems clear also that many anti-Semites were also anti-Catholic and thus may have been anti-Coughlin. A Gallup survey conducted in November 1938 asked a national sample whether they approved of the Nazis' treatment of Jews in Germany and similarly whether they approved of the treatment of Catholics. Among non-Catholics who approved of the persecution of the Jews, almost half, 43 per cent, also favored the Nazis' attacks on Catholics, 45 per cent opposed them, and 12 per cent had no opinion. This finding suggests that about half the extreme anti-Semites were also anti-Catholic.

Such contradictions between the views of leaders and followers are not unusual. They have been reported for almost every major figure and political party since opinion surveying began. In most European countries, a significant minority of Socialist voters are opposed to nationalization of most industries, while 10 to 15 per cent of those who back conservative parties favor public ownership. Many observers of the German scene before 1933 have reported that the Nazis were supported by many who were not anti-Semitic. An analysis of opinion data in 1940, however, reports that the majority of Coughlin's supporters in 1940 tended to agree with his *central* ideas.[107]

The Coughlin pattern suggests that the principle of selective support operates on two levels. It may mean selecting the occasions on which such a movement will be supported. And it may mean selecting certain aspects of the movement for support. Thus a social movement, particularly its element of "audience following," can serve as a purely expressive outlet on some occasions for citizens who wish to flex their preservatist or revolutionary impulses, but will, on critical occasions otherwise, vote the practical balance of their instrumental and symbolic needs. This is one explanation of the disparity between the Coughlin support and the Lemke vote.

The lack of a marked differential of anti-Semitism among Coughlin sympathizers may have another aspect. Nativism has, of course, two dimensions: the coveting of preferential status on some group-culture grounds; and the identification of cultural out-groups who are seen as threatening that status. It has been suggested that in the nativism of the 1930's, the former was becoming more generalized and the latter more abstract. As the identity of these out-groups became more abstract, their perception by the spectrum of nativists becomes less uniform. The targetry (bigotry) becomes the more cognitive and the less effective dimension of nativism for many of the followers—not, of course, for either the ideologues or the intellectuals of the movement.

This inference that anti-Semitism is often an ideological satellite rather than the effective center of abstract nativism could be inferred in another way. There was apparently a substantial historical backlog of objective anti-Semitism among Americans in general. In the late 1930's, according to the surveys, about one-third of all Americans thought Jews were less patriotic than other Americans; almost half of all Americans felt there was good reason for anti-Jewish feeling; about half thought Jewish businessmen were less honest than others; and almost two-thirds found Jews to have some objectionable qualities.[108]

However, indices of salience for political action were uniformly much lower. About 10 to 15 per cent of the respondents in each case thought that Hitler was justified in taking Jewish property, or felt that Jews were actually a menace to the United States, or said they would support a campaign against Jews or would support an anti-Semitic candidate.[109] Undoubtedly a number of hard-core, high-salience anti-Semites among these supported Coughlin *because* of his anti-Semitism, but they were of such a relatively small number that they did not effect a significant differential in anti-Semitic measurement between sympathizers and non-sympathizers. In the main, it would be suggested, political anti-Semitism was not at the center of Coughlin's differential appeal, but his sympathizers were willing to embrace it as an ideological satellite. Such tolerance could be the consequence of either the general level of objective through low-salient anti-Semitism or a general lack of commitment to countervailing values of democratic life; and probably it is a consequence of both kinds of phenomena, which have in many analyses been shown to be closely connected and concomitantly associated with lower educational and socio-economic levels. In 1940, one survey found that while only 14 per cent of the American people indicated that they would be influenced to vote for a congressional candidate because he declared himself to be against the Jews, 29 per cent said it would not make any difference, and 12 per cent said, "Don't know."[110]

Whether the supporters of an anti-Semitic political movement are rabid anti-Semites or satellite anti-Semites has little consequence for the nativist effect of the movement—or for the Jews. It has been indicated that a similar pattern of anti-Semitism was operative for Hitler's movement. Of course, a principle of self-fulfilling commitment could proceed to raise the levels of salient anti-Semitism among increasingly involved members of a movement, but Coughlin's movement was cut down summarily by international developments before any traces of this could develop.

Huey Long

In a few short years, Huey Long, governor of Louisiana in 1928 and United States Senator from 1932 until his death in 1935, built a mass movement of the poor whose ideological quality differed significantly from that of Coughlin. Coughlin appealed to the revolutionary class interest of his audience, as well as to its symbolic preservatist impulses. Huey Long appealed almost exclusively to the class interest of his mass following.

Long himself was the son of a poor Baptist farmer, born and reared in one of the poorest areas, Winn, in northern Louisiana—an area which had strong left-wing Populist traditions. The parish had given the Socialists a majority in 1908. Entering politics in 1918, he ran for a position on the Railway Commission "on an anti-corporationist program."[111] In office, he successfully pressed for reductions in telephone, gas, streetcar, and intrastate railway rates. These activities were to set a model for much of his career. Essentially from the time he entered politics to his assassination in 1935, he espoused some version of the "share-our-wealth" ideology, of taking from the rich and giving to the poor. As governor, he removed the poll tax, provided considerable extra facilities to the public school system, and increased taxes to pay for the new schools and farm roads. He was the first poor white to hold the governor's office. His principal attacks were on "the corporations and urbanites, the 'better elements' and the professional politicians."[112] He insisted that he would make the millionaires of the country contribute to the support of the poor.[113] He proposed to provide a minimum wage of $2,500 a year, to limit hours of work, to end unemployment, to give every family a gift from the confiscation of millionaire wealth of $4,000 each, and to provide that every boy of college-level abilities should attend college at federal government expense.[114]

The new movement's ideology was clearly in the populist tradition. Its slogan, "Every Man a King," was taken directly from a speech of William Jennings Bryan.[115] Long and his paper, *American Progress*, attacked the power of Wall Street, its alleged control of the press, J. P. Morgan's ill-gotten gains, the spending by the wealthy on yachts; it even discussed plots by Standard Oil to kill Huey Long. The enemies of the movement were described as "High-brow Brain Trusters, brutish . . . low-brow eastern politicians, top-hatted . . . cigar-smoking Wall-Streeters," who were allied in various plots to cheat the common man.[116]

As a consequence, on a state-wide level, Huey Long clearly had the support of the less privileged portions of the population and was opposed by the majority of the middle and well-educated strata. Sindler identified Huey Long's victory in the gubernatorial race in 1928 "as the culmination of the class struggle in Louisiana. . . . His criticisms and promises merged in an emotional appeal to the masses to overthrow the 'old gang' and the corporations, in an invitation to lower-class whites to displace the ruling alliance and grasp political power for themselves."[117] His continued public opposition to the large corporations, and their attacks on him, in particular the effort supported by Standard Oil lobbyists to impeach him as governor, presumably should have reinforced his appeal to the less privileged.

The detailed evidence drawn from ecological studies of state voting patterns confirms this impression. In rural areas, Huey Long's greatest strength came first from the poorer hill regions and other centers of small farming in north central and western Louisiana. Later he found support in the small farming regions of the southern part of the state.[118]

"In 1929 a fairly close relation prevailed between the distribution of Long's popular strength and that of the Populist candidate for Governor in 1896."[119] Long, like the Populists, was originally weak in urban areas, but by 1932 he had secured considerable backing among city workers. The general hostility of the more well-to-do precincts was presumably a reaction to his populist and antielitist demagogy, his dictatorial methods, and the use of naked force to secure contributions.

On a national level, Long began as an enthusiastic supporter of Franklin Roosevelt in 1932. He quickly broke with him, however, charging that the President was actually an enemy of the poor. In January 1934, Huey Long formed a national organization, the Share-Our-Wealth movement, and started a regular weekly national radio program. He talked of either capturing the Democratic convention in 1936 or starting a third party. He appealed to the deprived as a man of quick action, who by confiscating the wealth of the rich would end unemployment and give to everyone a home, automobile, and high income.

It is difficult to estimate how much backing Huey Long had on a national level before his assassination in September 1935. His "files of February 1, 1935, showed a total of 27,431 clubs, while his staff claim to have the names and addresses of 7,682,768 members on file, the number having more than doubled since November, 1934."[120] One report states that there was at least one club in every state, but that "membership in 1935 was concentrated in the South and the far North-central states."[121] Another indicates that outside of Louisiana, the states with the largest number of Long clubs were "Arkansas, Mississippi, California (the 'joiner' state), New York (the state with the largest population) and Minnesota (backlog of the Farmer-Labor movement)."[122]

Perhaps the best estimate of Huey Long's following is contained in a "secret" public opinion poll conducted for the Democratic national committee in 1935 which sought to find out his potential strength as a third-party Presidential candidate. It indicated that he would get somewhere between 3,000,000 and 4,000,000 votes, or somewhere between 7 and 9 per cent of the national turnout. James Farley, who commissioned the poll, commented on it:

> His probable support was not confined to Louisiana and near-by states. On the contrary, he had about as much following in the North as in the South, and he had as strong an appeal in the industrial centers as he did in the rural areas. . . . It was easy to conceive a situation whereby Long, by polling more than 3,000,000 votes, might have the balance of power in the 1936 election. For example, the poll indicated that he would command upward of 100,000 votes in New York State, a pivotal state in any national election. . . .[123]

The records of this survey, which was conducted for Emil Hurja, the statistician of the Democratic national committee, are available in the Roosevelt Library in Hyde Park. Our analysis of them points to various significant aspects of Long's appeal. First, it was clearly class-linked. Although the survey did not inquire as to the occupation or socioeconomic status of respondents, questionnaires were divided between those completed by voters receiving government assistance through various programs, and those filled in by others, that is, those still employed in cities, or who had an adequate income as farmers. In the 30 states for which such differentiated data exist, Long received 16 per cent of the 11,578 ballots cast by the less privileged voters, as compared with 8 per cent among the 15,439 questionnaires submitted by the economically better off. As might be expected from these results, the large majority of those opting for Long had voted for Roosevelt in 1932. The Share-Our-Wealth appeal was strongest among the less privileged Democrats. An effort to correlate the Long support, state by state, with the actual vote received by previous protest candidates—Eugene Debs in 1912, Senator Robert La Follette in 1924, and Norman Thomas in 1932—permitted some limited estimate of the relationship of the Long appeal to that of earlier leftist third-party Presidential candidates. Two sets of correlations were calculated: one for all states, and a second eliminating Louisiana, Mississippi, Arkansas, and Texas (Long's home state and its three neighbors), since Long's personal influence gave him much more support in this area than in other parts of the country. The results of these analyses are presented in Table 17.

Table 17.   CORRELATIONS (PEARSON r) BETWEEN LONG'S SUPPORT IN AN
AUGUST 1935 POLL WITH SUPPORT FOR OTHER CANDIDATES
AND SOCIAL CHARACTERISTICS BY STATE

Percentage of Electorate or Population	All States		With Four States Removed	
	Employed	On Assistance	Employed	On Assistance
Debs (1912)	.296	.354	.418	.642
La Follette (1924)	.147	.055	.485	.596
Thomas (1932)	.257	−.068	.381	.245
Lemke (1936)	.132	.225	.141	.245
Urban, 1930	−.063	−.226	.055	.080
Protestant, 1936	.081	.286	.235	.090

SOURCES: Long data secured in files of Roosevelt Library at Hyde Park. Debs, La Follette, Thomas, and Lemke figures are from Svend Petersen, *A Statistical History of the American Presidential Elections* (New York: Frederick Ungar, 1963), pp. 79, 88, 93, 95. Per cent urban is from the *Fifteenth Census of the United States: 1930*, Report on Population of the United States (Washington: Government Printing Office, 1931), I, 8. Per cent Protestant is from the *Fifteenth Census, op. cit.*, Vol. III, Part I, p. 24, and *Religious Bodies: 1936* (Washington: Government Printing Office, 1941), pp. 758, 1531.

The results of this analysis help to confirm the assumption that Huey Long appealed basically to those sectors of the population predisposed to the left. As in elections in his home state, Huey Long's antielitist attacks found a receptive audience in the same states which had been attracted to Eugene Debs in 1912, when he received 6 per cent of the national vote, and to Senator La Follette in 1924, when he secured 16.6 per cent.

The correlation analysis also suggests that Long's support did not differentiate between the more or less urbanized states. Seemingly, his appeal to the less privileged extended to both the rural and the urban sectors. This finding through correlation analysis is sustained by the questionnaire data. The 1935 Democratic national committee study separated the ballots filled out by residents of a number of large cities from others in the states in which these cities were located. Among the ballots of the nonrelief recipients, 7.03 per cent of those in the large cities were for Long, as contrasted to 7.41 per cent of the others. A larger difference occurred among those on government assistance: 16 per cent of those outside of metropolitan areas were for Long, as compared with 13 per cent of those in the big cities. It should be noted that the indicators of urbanization in our correlation analysis and the survey are quite different. The first relied on the census definition, which is communities with more than 2,500 population, while the second dealt with metropolitan areas.

The survey study also permitted a specification of Long's regional strength. As was indicated above, Long's greatest following was in his home state of Louisiana and its three neighbors. Surprisingly for a native southerner, he was relatively quite weak in the rest of the South. He also lacked strength in New England and the Middle Atlantic states. Although the sectional differences are small, it would appear that his greatest appeal lay in the old centers of Populist protest, the Midwest and the Mountain states, as well as on the Pacific Coast (Table 18).

Table 18. LONG'S 1935 POLL STRENGTH IN DIFFERENT REGIONS

	Employed		On Government Assistance	
	Per Cent	Number	Per Cent	Number
Four personal influence states	13.9	(1,100)	29.8	(951)
Other South	5.4	(1,085)	10.6	(1,005)
Border States	7.9	(1,888)	13.5	(1,114)
New England	5.0	(1,532)	16.8	(500)
Middle Atlantic	5.5	(4,437)	12.4	(2,335)
East North Central	8.8	(5,382)	18.5	(3,090)
West North Central	9.3	(1,901)	13.7	(285)
Mountain	10.0	(540)	22.2	(239)
Pacific	9.0	(2,004)	18.1	(1,059)

Unfortunately, there do not seem to be any other reports of opinion surveys dealing with Huey Long which describe the character of his support in more detail. Some further indication that it came largely from the poorer strata may be found in an analysis of letters written to him by his supporters. Studies of letter writers to congressmen or the President indicate that they are largely from middle-class people who are accustomed to writing. However, in 1934 "90 per cent of Long's mail consisted of letters written in pencil on rough note paper. Less than 5 per cent was typewritten on printed or engraved letterheads."[124] Later in the year, as the movement spread, "the percentage of typewritten letters jumped to 27 per cent. . . . A large percentage of Long's better-class mail now comes from lawyers, architects, engineers, and school teachers."[125]

Right or Left?

Under these circumstances, why was Huey Long so commonly assigned to the category "right wing"? Partly, it was out of a confusion by observers between right-wing tendencies and monistic tendencies—which are not the exclusive preserve of the right wing.

Long's reputation as an authoritarian and a cryptofascist comes in large part from his actions as the dominant figure in Louisiana politics from 1928 to 1935. During that period, he and his minions in the legislature violated due process and sought successfully to intimidate and repress opposition. Many observers have described the state as being under a dictatorship. The State Supreme Court, which Long controlled, legitimated all his actions. These included taking over the prosecutor's office in any area where the prosecutor was not cooperative and maintaining the largest military establishment of any state, which together with the state police "were used frequently during elections and at other times to seize registrar voting lists, to raid vice and gambling, to arrest dangerous opponents, to break opposition movements such as the Square Dealers, to destroy local self-government, and above all, for dramatic display."[126] He changed the law so that all election commissioners, supervisors, and watchers were appointed by the governor, or those he had appointed.[127] He gained control over business and banking by means of "four coercive whips." These were "stern inspection, executive power to raise or lower severance and manu-facturing taxes, to raise or lower assessments, and sudden capital levies. . . ."[128]

He also attempted to interfere with the freedom of the press by placing "a 2 per cent tax on advertising in papers having a circulation of over twenty thousand."[129] This tax would have crippled the New Orleans dailies, all of which were against him. This law, however, was declared uncon-stitutional by the United States Supreme Court.[130]

Long made clear his dictatorial propensities on a nation-wide scale after he started his national Share-Our-Wealth movement.

Huey frankly predicted that his [radio] listeners would see an end to both the Democratic and Republican parties under his regime [as President]. He told

New York newspapermen that in place of the parties would arise a new, single organization, his organization. . . .

To Forrest Davis he made the assertion that he would remain as President for four terms. His theory of democracy was this: "A leader gets up a program and then he goes out and explains it, patiently and more patiently, until they get it. He asks for a mandate, and if they give it to him, he goes ahead with the program in spite of hell and high water. He don't tolerate no opposition from the old-gang politicians, the legislatures, the courts, the corporations or anybody."[131]

Huey, in effect, believed in a theory of the general will, a policy in which the leader appealed directly to the people for support. Parties were divisive and the expression of selfish interest groups. Many of his views were reminiscent of those expressed by Tom Watson at the turn of the century and of various French Revolutionary theorists. Direct democracy with initiative, referendum, and plebiscite, rather than party, was the ideal system.[132]

Actions such as those reported above, of course, do not make Huey Long an incipient fascist; rather the attacks on business might put him in the category of a leftist or populist authoritarian. There is, however, considerable evidence from his public record in Louisiana of actions inconsistent with the populist image conveyed by his dramatic public works and pronounced over-all objectives. These suggest that he resembled Mussolini in fostering leftist demagogy, while basically maintaining the existing system of privilege. Thus, one contemporary report comments:

[After] seven years of Huey's control Louisiana still lacks minimum wage and child labor laws, unemployment insurance and old age pensions, although other states possess these intermediate measures of social justice. . . . There is also some uneasiness at the Kingfish's quiet efforts to convince Wall Street that he is far less radical than Roosevelt and so deserves the support of Big Business. . . . These undeniable facts cast a bar sinister across the Long Movement and go far to justify the label of "Fascist" which is applied to it.[133]

Several analyses conclude that Huey Long was antirelief and antilabor. Kane stated:

During his lifetime, the state did little to share in the support of the unemployed. . . . Louisiana, under Huey, declined to adopt the Federal Child Labor Amendment, while children worked day in and day out in the strawberry fields, in cotton areas, in the factories of New Orleans and the shrimp-packing plants of South Louisiana, sometimes at wages as low as six cents an hour. State payments also went down to ten cents, in line with Huey's declaration that the prevailing wage was a wage as low as a person could be prevailed to take. When the NRA set minimum scales of forty cents an hour, the Louisiana Highway Commission by law paid thirty.[134]

Beals is of the opinion that the taxing of large corporations was offset by his reduction of assessments on their properties. He quotes from a Baton Rouge paper, *Freedom*:

In East Baton Rouge Parish in 1928 the assessed valuation of the Standard Oil Company was $44,662,150. In 1932 this was reduced to $36,931,000 and in 1933, by a further reduction, to $34,191,000. In other words, a reduction of about $10,000,000 from 1928 to 1933 in East Baton Rouge alone. The total reduction to all property valued in the entire parish between these years amounts to less than the reduction of Standard Oil property alone. But the average man's property was raised in value.[135]

Huey Long also did not oppose antilabor forces in the state.

Locally, he largely owed his political start to W. K. Henderson, the bitter anti-labor iron-monger of Shreveport, who has placarded his factory NO UNION LABOR EMPLOYED HERE and toured the country, giving open-shop talks. At the same time he bitterly fought Greer, the head of the state A.F. of L. . . . Jules Fisher, the shrimp king of Barataria, known as the worst exploiter of labor, in his canning factories, of any man in the state, was an associate of Steinberg in monopolizing with Huey's aid, 60 per cent of the fur lands of the state. He put over with Huey's consent, a vicious trespassing law which made it possible to wipe out the independent trapper, and he also killed the 8-hour day for women in 1932 . . . with Huey's consent.[136]

Concerning the sincerity of Long's anticorporation protestations and of his belief in Share-Our-Wealth principles, the most damning accusation

is that of Elmer Irey, who labeled Long, on the basis of his information as head of Internal Revenue, as the "greatest confidence man in the century." . . . Irey made no mention of the source of Huey's money, but two of Huey's brothers publicly charged him with selling out to the business interests he attacked from the stump. Brother Earl alleged that Huey personally had accepted a $10,000 bribe from a utilities executive in late 1927. Brother Julius testified at the Overton hearings, "as a candidate for Governor for the first time, Huey Long received his principal financial support from the Southwestern Gas and Electric Company and their allied interests. . . ."[137]

Indeed, there is abundant evidence that major sections of the most powerful business forces in the state collaborated with him, once he was in power. As Michie and Rynlick report:

Huey had at his command the purses of the Big Businesses he attacked on the stump. . . . As the Kingfish's political powers grew, oil, sulphur, railroad, banking, and utility interests hastened to purchase his good will with heavy contributions. Harvey Couch, Wall Street's satrap in the South and a utility and railroad magnate in his own right, was on very friendly terms with Huey. The New Orleans Cotton Exchange, the Vasarro fruit and steamship interests, the monopolistic fur companies, and almost everyone who wanted to do business in Louisiana, took pains to get behind the Long machine. DuPont built three large chemical plants in the state during Huey's reign, and the Mellons cooperated closely with him.[138]

Absence of Nativism

Although Huey Long came out of an evangelical Protestant background and reflected it in his Bible-quoting campaign style, he worked closely with Catholics and Jews in Louisiana. As a matter of fact, he made special efforts to gain the support of Catholics, an important bloc in that state. Following the passage of a textbook law, which gave free books to parochial as well as public schools, the Catholic farmers of southern Louisiana joined with the Protestant ones of the north in backing him.[139] While Long straddled the Klan issue when he first ran for governor in 1924, Negroes regarded him as relatively friendly. There is no record of his using the race question in his campaigns.

Not only was the Long movement without nativism; it was without a conspiracy theory worth the name. His rhetoric had it that big business was exercising its power cruelly and against popular will. But it was projected as a naked exercise of power for profits, not as a secret comprehensive plot to control America's soul. Nor, although moralistic in tone, did Long invoke the kind of apocalyptic moralism which is at the heart of conspiracy theories. Not in the tradition of moralistic Protestantism, he was antiprohibition and Frank Costello claimed Long had invited him into Louisiana to set up slot machines.[140] And he did not substitute as a moral cornerstone of his movement the latter-day diabolism of anti-Communism. He was an ardent nationalist, and as a United States Senator played a major role in helping to defeat American participation in the World Court. But this sentiment seemed to lie in an isolationism based on class rather than symbolic interests.

He stated that Wall Street had taken us into World War I for its own profits and against the opposition of 90 per cent of the people.[141] In short, Huey Long's monism smacked more of Tammany Hall than of Berchtesgaden and the Kremlin. Nor was he, in any striking sense, either left-wing or right-wing. He spoke revolution, but offered only some grandstand reforms. He was probably preservatist in intent, but he made no significant appeals to the preservatist impulses of the poorer class that followed him. Whereas Coughlin was at least in the fascist style, Long was pure species demagogue. In his own bailiwick he was a populist political boss, dramatically successful, but not all that unique on the local American scene. But he was cut off by a personally inspired assassination before he could demonstrate whether a pure demagoguery which was neither here nor there could create a significant national political movement. The opinion poll results were undoubtedly subject, as were Coughlin's, to the principle of selective support. Despite the tendency to consider him an embryonic fascist, it was generally assumed that when people expressed sympathy for Long, they were expressing the left-oriented aspect of their depression discontent. Raymond Moley and Frederick Lewis Allen concluded that one of the major forces pressing Roosevelt to move to the left ideologically was his fear of the Long movement.[142]

Raymond Moley, then one of Roosevelt's closest advisers, reports that the President was so concerned about Long's appeal that he began to discuss ways of wooing some of his support by stealing "Long's thunder" through making a "counteroffer" to the voters.[143] And in 1935 Roosevelt proposed to Congress the wealth-tax act, "a proposal to increase the taxes upon the rich—to levy a big toll upon inheritance and large incomes and a graduated tax upon corporation incomes," all very reminiscent of Huey Long's Share-Our-Wealth program.[144]

It can be suspected, however, that put to the test of time and power, Long's demagoguery would have had to move into more definitive channels in order to be successful. And it can be further suspected, given Long's proclivities and connections, that these channels would have been right-wing in quality, with all the traditional appurtenances thereof. These suspicions are given some support by the character of the man whom Long selected as the national organizer of the Share-Our-Wealth movement. Gerald L. K. Smith, the minister of the fundamentalist King's Highway Church in Shreveport, Louisiana, was hired in 1934 to act as Long's political alter ego on the national circuit, to make speeches which the Senator did not have time to make. Smith was a third-generation minister in his church. Early in his career, in the 1920's, while serving as a minister in Indianapolis, he became well known as a leading member of the Indiana Ku Klux Klan. With the outbreak of the depression, he took to the air in Shreveport and attacked public utilities, corporations, and sweatshops. During this period he was forced out of the church for political activity. He then turned to work with Pelley's Silver Shirts and gave lectures on topics such as "Why I Left the Conventional Pulpit to Join the Christian Militia of the Silver Shirts." Huey Long hired him to help lead the Share-Our-Wealth movement, while he was involved with the overtly fascist Silver Shirt movement. Although Smith did not engage in racist political activities while Huey Long was alive, he was reported to make anti-Semitic statements in private.[145]

In the autumn of 1935, in discussing the prospects for the Share-Our-Wealth movement, he argued that they might be able to sweep the nation quickly and thus "duplicate the feat of Adolf Hitler in Germany."[146] Apparently nothing in Smith's background or views gave Long any qualms about making him second-in-command of the national movement. He proudly declared on one occasion: "Next to me, Gerald L. K. Smith is the greatest rabble rouser in the country."[147]

After Long's death, Smith's attempt to take over the movement failed dismally. It failed partly because Huey Long was still mainly a Louisiana political boss. His political collaborators in Louisiana were not interested in Smith. Long's shadowy national movement collapsed with his death, and Smith's failure to resurrect it was aggravated by his abandonment of Long's class theory.

The Conservative Impulse in the 1930's

During the 1930's, many contemporary writers raised the specter of fascism as a major threat to American democracy. For those on the left, including many liberals, the principal source of this danger came from big business or great wealth. Many assumed that fascist dictatorship in Germany and Italy involved an effort by capitalism to save itself against the possibility of being overthrown by leftist forces, or to suppress various mass-based organizations such as trade-unions and left-wing parties in order to prop up the profit system by reducing the wages and working conditions of the working class. This image of fascism resulted in a search by many political analysts for evidence that the American upper class was engaged in efforts to create a fascist movement.

An examination of the historical record does indicate that large numbers of the wealthy actively engaged in hard-line conservative politics, particularly in the form of the American Liberty League. There is, however, little evidence of upper-class efforts to create a right-wing dictatorship. One student of fascist movements of the thirties concludes that with the exception of one unsuccessful effort, involving a few people, "there appears to be no evidence that any native Fascist organizations received large sums of money from prominent and wealthy businessmen."[148] The incident in question was a report by Major General Smedley Butler (retired) of the Marine Corps that he had been approached in 1934 by Gerald McGuire, a Wall Street bond salesman, to lead a new veterans organization, modeled on fascist veteran groups of Europe, which would take over the government. McGuire claimed to represent various prominent businessmen. The story of the plot was investigated by the McCormack-Dickstein Congressional Special Committee to Investigate Nazi Activities in the United States. The story was denied by the various businessmen mentioned as concerned with the plot. The press, in general, "ridiculed the Butler story off the stage."[149]

Some of the organizations discussed earlier are reputed to have been financially backed by large business. Gerald L. K. Smith seemingly had some backing from Harry Bennett, of the Ford Motor Company, while Smith was engaged in some antilabor activities in Michigan in the late 1930's. Huey Long is supposed to have had discussions with Wall Street figures. Coughlin secured financial aid from a number of wealthy Catholics. In general, however, the record of corporate wealth's sponsorship of overtly or covertly fascist movements is rather meager. Big business clearly was politically concerned during the 1930's, resented Roosevelt's New Deal, and fought the rise of trade-unionism; but the ideology which it fostered was sharply antagonistic to centralized state power, including the power of fascist states.

The major explicit effort by American wealth to influence the political process was through the activities of the American Liberty League. The League was formed on August 23, 1934, by a number of prominent businessmen to halt the spread of radicalism and government intervention in the economy.[150] Most of the men who assembled to form the Liberty League had worked closely together in the Association Against the Prohibition Amendment (AAPA). From 1926 to repeal in 1933, this group had been dominated by a number of millionaires, mainly connected with the DuPont and General Motors companies. They had poured great sums of money into the cause of repeal. "Money was only one form of power which these men were able to wield. They had great influence, also, through newspapers and other widely read publications. For sheer power and professional efficiency the propaganda machine of the AAPA surpassed anything the country had ever seen."[151]

Following repeal, the AAPA officially dissolved in December 1933. Within a few months, however, its millionaire leaders, who had learned to work together for political ends and had a sense of being able to accomplish things as evidenced by the repeal effort, had decided to form a new organization, the American Liberty League. The ideas behind forming the new group were expressed in a letter by R. R. M. Carpenter, a retired DuPont vice-president, written in March 1934 to John Raskob proposing that "the DuPont and General Motors groups, followed by other big industries . . . [should] definitely organize to protect society from the sufferings which it is bound to endure if we allow communistic elements to lead the people to believe all businessmen are crooks."[152]

The leaders of the new organization thought that the tactics which had produced spectacular results in the fight against prohibition would also work in defeating the new liberal administration. They raised large sums of money to hire a big public relations staff to turn out pamphlets, press releases, radio speeches, canned stories for newspapers. Jouett Rouse, who had moved from the presidency of the AAPA to that of the Liberty League, announced in August 1934 that he expected to recruit 4,000,000 members.[153] The organization also announced that it expected to set up functional divisions of farmers, workers, and other groups.

By all criteria, except success in enlisting millionaires and raising money, the Liberty League was a dismal failure. Its maximum membership in the summer of 1936 was 124,856. Membership, however, only involved sending in one's name and address to be put on the mailing list.[154] In March 1936 the League filed a list of "contributing members" with the House of Representatives, which only contained 22,433 names.[155] The only functional groups which it formed were one for college students, which reputedly had 345 campus chapters and over 10,000 members in April 1936, and a Lawyer's Division, which issued reports on the constitutionality of various New Deal legislation.[156] A subsidiary, the Farmer's Independent Council, failed to enroll any real farmers.[157]

Although the leaders spoke of becoming a mass organization and recruiting support from all strata, in fact the League never made any real efforts to do so beyond its general propaganda. Its speakers were sent out to bar associations and business and civic clubs; that is, groups predisposed to be conservative. "Thus, Liberty League speakers sought to appeal to audiences which were largely composed of college educated people, business men, and professional people. At no time did any League speaker ever address a local audience which consisted primarily of working class people."[158]

The only real success of the League was its ability to get its stories into newspapers. Between August 1934 and November 1936, the League made the front-pages of the *New York Times* thirty-five times.[159] Perhaps the best testimony to the consequences of the Liberty League's activities is the fact that in 1936, the Republicans regarded support of the Liberty League as a liability, while the Democrats viewed its opposition as one of their principal assets.[160]

The Administration was delighted with the possibilities of branding the Liberty League the tool of organized wealth to further the political interests of the rich regardless of what happened to others. Here was the "gaping hole in the battlelines of the opposition" of which Farley spoke. "Wishing to take advantage of that," the National Chairman wrote later, "the Democratic National Committee's first 'battle-order' was to ignore the Republican Party and to concentrate fire on the Liberty League."[161]

Alfred Landon, the Republican Presidential nominee, described the League's support as a "kiss of death." Arthur Krock wrote in the *New York Times* that John Hamilton, Republican party chairman, "would have walked a mile out of his way rather than be seen in the company of a leaguer."[162]

The Liberty League was clearly a failure. Most of its public activities ceased after the 1936 election, and the organization dissolved in 1940. The League was never a political movement, its activities being confined largely to single-issue propaganda and pressure group tactics. It could scarcely qualify as an "extremist" group, since, at worst, it only gingerly embraced the pattern of monism. It did not call for the serious alteration of the democratic process; it evinced no nativism; it only hinted at conspiracy. The League was, of course, anti-Communist and anti-internationalist. In the course of its polemic, it was not averse to calling the New Deal a Marxist conspiracy. But the term was used as a vague epithet rather than as an explanatory theory. Statism itself, rather than the conspiracy of statism, was at the center of the League's concern. Many Liberty Leaguers, especially in its earlier years, denounced the New Deal as fascist, as imitating the policies of Mussolini.

The Liberty League was the first of a series of efforts by American right-wing conservatives, largely drawn from the ranks of businessmen and self-employed professionals, to resist the growth of what has come to be known as the "welfare state." Since 1933, those groups which identify with nineteenth-century economic values of laissez faire, rugged individualism, social Darwinism, have attempted in various ways to reverse the dominant trends. As George Wolfskill put it, the new situation which dates from 1933 has meant that the "group who had long been on the side protested against; now . . . [was] in the unaccustomed role of protester."[163]

The League was, of course, preservatist, but its weakness was that it appealed only to the preservatism of the economically privileged. It made no appeal to the class interests of the less privileged—a difficult task for conservatism at any time, but especially during a depression. And it made no alternative appeal to the preservatist impulses among the less privileged. Conservative movements of the future were to try somewhat harder on that score.

In all, the essential dynamics of right-wing extremism had not altered during the 1930's, depression or not; but some of the appurtenances had changed. The burden of its thematic baggage had shifted from Protestant nativism to a more abstract nativism; in its most abstract, just a kind of nationalistic antiradicalism. It was this thread that Senator Joseph McCarthy picked up and tested in the first major preservatist movement of the postwar period.

Notes

1. Ramley J. Glass, "Gentlemen, the Corn Belt!" *Harper's*, CLXVII (July 1933), 200.
2. *New York Times*, July 27, 1932, as reported in David A. Shannon, *The Great Depression* (Englewood Cliffs, N.J.: Prentice-Hall, 1960), p. 91.

3. Morris Schonbach, *Native Fascism during the 1930's and 1940's: A Study of Its Roots, Its Growth, and Its Decline* (Ph.D. Thesis, Department of History, University of California at Los Angeles, 1958), p. 8.

4. Joseph R. Gusfield, *Symbolic Crusade, Status Politics and the American Temperance Movement* (Urbana: University of Illinois Press, 1963), pp. 20–21.

5. Morris Janowitz, "Black Legions on the March," in Daniel Aaron, ed., *America in Crisis* (New York: Knopf, 1951), pp. 309–310. Emphasis in the original.

6. William Kornhauser, *The Politics of Mass Society* (New York: The Free Press, 1959), pp. 25–30.

7. See Seymour Martin Lipset, "Fascism, Left, Right and Center," *Political Man* (New York: Doubleday, 1960), pp. 131–175.

8. Talcott Parsons, *Essays in Sociological Theory* (Glencoe: The Free Press, 1954), p. 125.

9. Kornhauser, *op. cit.*, p. 32.

10. Parsons, *op. cit.*, pp. 126–127.

11. Ralph Linton, "Nativistic Movements," in R. H. Turner and L. M. Killian, eds., *Collective Behavior* (Englewood Cliffs, N.J.: Prentice-Hall, 1957), p. 388.

12. Lynn Dolgin, "The Black Legion: A Study of American Nativism during the 1930's" (unpublished paper written for a graduate seminar conducted by Professor John Higham, Department of History, University of Michigan, March 1967), p. 16.

13. Janowitz, *op. cit.*, p. 308.

14. *Ibid.*, p. 306.

15. *Report of Black Legion Activities in Oakland County*, George B. Hartrick, Circuit Court Judge presiding (Detroit: Interstate Brief and Record Co., September 1, 1936), cited in Dolgin, *op. cit.*, p. 26.

16. Cited in Janowitz, *op. cit.*, p. 306.

17. Dolgin, *op. cit.*, pp. 35–36.

18. *Ibid.*, pp. 20–21.

19. *Ibid.*, pp. 9–10.

20. *Ibid.*, p. 24.

21. *Ibid.*, pp. 24–25; see also David Mark Chalmers, *Hooded Americanism: The History of the Ku Klux Klan* (New York: Doubleday, 1965), p. 309, and Janowitz, *op. cit.*, p. 307.

22. Cited in Donnel Byerly Portzline, *William Dudley Pelley and the Silver Shirt Legion of America* (Ph.D. Thesis, Department of Education, Ball State University, 1965), p. 178.

23. Dolgin, *op. cit.*, pp. 27–28.

24. *Ibid.*, pp. 8–9.

25. Gustavus Myers, *History of Bigotry in the United States* (New York: Capricorn, 1960), p. 366.

26. *The Defender*, March 15, 1935, as quoted in *ibid.*, p. 367.

27. Ann Marie Buitrage, *A Study of the Political Ideas and Activities of Gerald B. Winrod, 1926–1938* (M.A. Thesis, Department of Political Science, University of Kansas, 1955), p. 56.

28. Ralph Roy, *Apostles of Discord* (Boston: Beacon, 1953), p. 28.

29. Buitrage, *op. cit.*, p. 83.
30. *Ibid.*, pp. 83–85. Emphasis in the original.
31. *Ibid.*, p. 177, footnote 69.
32. *Ibid.*, p. 85.
33. Roy, *op. cit.*, p. 28; see also Buitrage, *op. cit.*
34. Buitrage, *op. cit.*, pp. 163–164.
35. *Ibid.*, p. 13.
36. Roy, *op. cit.*, p. 27.
37. Myers, *op. cit.*, p. 369.
38. Donald S. Strong, *Organized Anti-Semitism in America* (Washington: American Council on Public Affairs, 1941), p. 76.
39. Buitrage, *op. cit.*, pp. 142–143.
40. Strong, *op. cit.*, p. 77.
41. *Ibid.*, p. 52.
42. Cited in *ibid.*, p. 41.
43. *Ibid.*, p. 52.
44. Portzline, *op. cit.*, p. 158.
45. *Ibid.*, p. 159.
46. *Ibid.*, p. 267.
47. Myers, *op. cit.*, pp. 349–352.
48. Strong, *op. cit.*, p. 51.
49. *Ibid.*, p. 54.
50. *Ibid.*, p. 55.
51. William D. Pelley, *No More Hunger* (Asheville, N.C.: Pelley Publishers, 1939).
52. *Ibid.*, p. 57.
53. Portzline, *op. cit.*, p. 75.
54. Kornhauser, *op. cit.*, pp. 60, 64.
55. Eva G. Reichmann, *Hostages of Civilization* (Boston: Beacon, 1951), pp. 37–39.
56. Dennis Wrong, "The Psychology and the Future of Anti-Semitism in America," in Charles Herbert Stember *et al.*, *Jews in the Mind of America* (New York: Basic Books, 1966), p. 330.
57. Janowitz, *op. cit.*, pp. 317–318.
58. *Ibid.*, pp. 318–319.
59. Dolgin, *op. cit.*, p. 38.
60. Portzline, *op. cit.*, p. 268.
61. *Ibid.*, p. 109.
62. Eleanor Paperno, *Father Coughlin: A Study in Domination* (M.A. Thesis, Department of Sociology, Wayne State University, 1939), pp. 8–35.
63. Charles J. Tull, *Father Coughlin and the New Deal* (Syracuse: Syracuse University Press, 1965), pp. 52–53.
64. *Ibid.*, p. 66.
65. David Harry Bennett, *The Demogogues' Appeal in the Depression: The Origins and Activities of the Union Party: 1932–1936* (Ph.D. Thesis, Department of History, University of Chicago, 1963), p. 37.
66. *Ibid.*, p. 77; see also Myles M. Platt, *Father Charles E. Coughlin and the National Union for Social Justice* (M.A. Thesis, Department of Government, Wayne State University, 1951), p. 65.
67. Nick Arthur Masters, *Father Coughlin and Social Justice* (Ph.D. Thesis,

Department of Political Science, University of Michigan, 1955), pp. 62–71.

68. Tull, *op. cit.*, pp. 164–165.

69. *Ibid.*, p. 190; Edward C. McCarthy, *The Christian Front Movement in New York City, 1938–1940* (M.A. Thesis, Department of History, Columbia University, 1965), pp. 7–8.

70. Tull, *op. cit.*, p. 335.

71. From secondary analysis of the data from Gallup surveys obtained from the Roper Public Opinion Library.

72. Hadley Cantril, *Public Opinion, 1935–1946* (Princeton: Princeton University Press, 1951), p. 148.

73. Stember *et al., op. cit.*, p. 113.

74. The April 1938 study did not inquire as to the respondent's religion.

75. In reading these tables it should be noted that the important measure of support or opposition is the difference in per cent between those opposing and those supporting. The presence of a large and varying group with "No opinion" makes reliance on the portion supporting alone misleading.

76. Masters, *op. cit.*, p. 302.

77. McCarthy, *op. cit.*, p. 93.

78. Samuel Lubell, *The Future of American Politics* (New York: Doubleday-Anchor, 1956), p. 152.

79. Masters, *op. cit.*, p. 243.

80. James P. Shenton, "The Coughlin Movement and the New Deal," *Political Science Quarterly*, LXXIII (1958), 360.

81. *Ibid.*, pp. 366–370.

82. Strong, *op. cit.*, p. 67.

83. McCarthy, *op. cit.*, p. 11.

84. *Ibid.*, p. 98.

85. Strong, *op. cit.*, p. 68.

86. McCarthy, *op. cit.*, pp. 95, 99.

87. Arthur M. Schlesinger, Jr., *The Politics of Upheaval* (Boston: Houghton Mifflin, 1960), p. 68.

88. Raymond G. Swing, *Forerunners of American Fascism* (New York: Julian Messner, 1935), p. 51.

89. Lipset, *op. cit.*, pp. 170–173.

90. William V. Shannon, *The American Irish*, rev. ed. (New York: Macmillan, 1966), p. 303.

91. Nathan Glazer and Daniel Patrick Moynihan, *Beyond the Melting Pot* (Cambridge: M.I.T. Press, 1963), p. 217. Moynihan wrote the chapter on the Irish, while Glazer was primarily responsible for the rest of the book.

92. *Ibid.*, pp. 265–266.

93. Cited in Shannon, *op. cit.*, p. 512.

94. Bennett, *op. cit.*, p. 51.

95. Charles Coughlin, *By the Sweat of Thy Brow* (Royal Oak, Mich.: Radio League of the Little Flower, 1931), p. 45. Emphasis in the original.

96. Louis Ward, *Father Charles E. Coughlin, an Authorized Biography* (Detroit: Tower Publications, 1953), p. 35.

97. Victor C. Ferkiss, *The Political and Economic Philosophy of American*

Fascism (Ph.D. Thesis, Department of Political Science, University of Chicago, 1954), p. 229 in footnote 2.

98. Gertrude Coogan, *Money Creators* (Chicago: Sound Money Press, 1955), pp. 280–281. The apparent source of Miss Coogan's information is the same book by John Robison which upset New England in 1798. See her discussion on page 206.

99. Platt, *op. cit.*, p. 65.

100. Ben Marcin in *Social Justice*, IV (September 25, 1939), 13, as reported in Ferkiss, *op. cit.*, p. 229. Marcin was a pseudonym which has been attributed to Coughlin himself. Emphasis in the original.

101. Coughlin, *op. cit.*, p. 46.

102. Charles E. Coughlin, *The New Deal in Money* (Royal Oak, Mich.: Radio League of the Little Flower, 1933), p. 109; see also pp. 27, 43.

103. Schlesinger, *op. cit.*, pp. 16–23.

104. Tull, *op. cit.*, p. 84.

105. Charles E. Coughlin, *A Series of Lectures on Social Justice* (Detroit: Radio League of the Little Flower, 1935), p. 225.

106. Cited by Ben Halpern, "Anti-Semitism in the Perspective of Jewish History," in Stember *et al.*, *op. cit.*, p. 277.

107. Stember *et al.*, *op. cit.*, p. 113.

108. *Ibid.*, pp. 116, 82, 69, 54.

109. *Ibid.*, pp. 140, 128, 131, 134.

110. *Ibid.*, p. 134.

111. Alan P. Sindler, *Huey Long's Louisiana: State Politics, 1920–1952* (Baltimore: Johns Hopkins Press, 1956), pp. 46–47. T. Harry Williams, *Huey Long* (New York: Knopf, 1969), p. 90.

112. Sindler, *op. cit.*, p. 112.

113. See Huey Long, *My First Days in the White House* (Harrisburg: Telegraph Press, 1935), pp. 75–77, for a list of millionaires who would be required to give up their wealth.

114. Sindler, *op. cit.*, p. 84; Williams, *op. cit.*, pp. 692–697.

115. Bennett, *op. cit.*, p. 160.

116. *American Progress*, January 4, February 1, and May 4, 1935, as cited in *ibid.*, p. 161.

117. Sindler, *op. cit.*, pp. 308–309.

118. Perry H. Howard, *Political Tendencies in Louisiana, 1812–1952* (Baton Rouge: Louisiana State University Press, 1957), pp. 155–156, 189–190; Sindler, *op. cit.*, pp. 57–58.

119. V. O. Key, Jr., *Southern Politics in State and Nation* (New York: Knopf, 1949), pp. 161–162.

120. Unofficial Observer, *American Messiahs* (New York: Simon and Schuster, 1935), pp. 20–30. See also Hartnett T. Kane, *Louisiana Hayride: The American Rehearsal for Dictatorship* (New York: William Morrow, 1941), p. 120, and Thomas O. Harris, *The Kingfish* (New Orleans: Pelican, 1938), p. 133.

121. Sindler, *op. cit.*, p. 85.

122. Unofficial Observer, *op. cit.*, p. 24; Williams, *op. cit.*, pp. 700–701.

123. James A. Farley, *Behind the Ballots* (New York: Harcourt, Brace, 1938), p. 250; Bennett, *op. cit.*, p. 167.

124. Unofficial Observer, *op. cit.*, p. 1.
125. *Ibid.*, p. 21.
126. Carleton Beals, *The Story of Huey Long* (Philadelphia: Lippincott, 1935), p. 370.
127. Raymond Moley, *27 Masters of Politics* (New York: Funk and Wagnalls, 1949), pp. 226–227; Allan Michie and Frank Rynlick, *Dixie Demogogues* (New York: Vanguard, 1939), p. 112; Kane, *op. cit.*, p. 124; Sindler, *op. cit.*, pp. 90–91.
128. Beals, *op. cit.*, pp. 370, 377; Carter, *op. cit.*, p. 446.
129. Beals, *op. cit.*, p. 377.
130. Carter, *op. cit.*, p. 442.
131. Kane, *op. cit.*, p. 124.
132. Ferkiss, *op. cit.*, p. 161; Williams, *op. cit.*, p. 762.
133. Unofficial Observer, *op. cit.*, pp. 30–31.
134. Kane, *op. cit.*, p. 142.
135. Beals, *op. cit.*, p. 355.
136. *Ibid.*, p. 336.
137. Sindler, *op. cit.*, p. 106.
138. Michie and Rynlick, *op. cit.*, pp. 666–667.
139. Sindler, *op. cit.*, p. 59; Carter, *op. cit.*, p. 439.
140. Williams, *op. cit.*, pp. 824–825; Sindler, *op. cit.*, p. 105.
141. Ferkiss, *op. cit.*, p. 161.
142. Dixon Wecter, *The Age of the Great Depression, 1939–1941* (New York: Macmillan, 1948), p. 206; Frederick Lewis Allen, *Since Yesterday* (New York: Harper, 1940), p. 191.
143. Raymond Moley, *After Seven Years* (New York: Harper, 1959), p. 305.
144. Allen, *op. cit.*, p. 191.
145. Bennett, *op. cit.*, pp. 144–149, 174.
146. *Ibid.*, p. 164.
147. *Ibid.*, p. 162.
148. Schonbach, *op. cit.*, p. 236.
149. George Wolfskill, *The Revolt of the Conservatives: A History of the American Liberty League, 1934–1940* (Boston: Houghton Mifflin, 1962), p. 97; Schonbach, *op. cit.*, pp. 233–236.
150. See Frederick Rudolf, "The American Liberty League, 1934–1940," *American Historical Review*, LVI (October 1950), 19–33; Wolfskill, *op. cit.*; Morton Keller, *In Defence of Yesterday, James M. Peck and the Politics of Conservatism* (New York: Coward-McCann, 1958), pp. 257–262; Linda K. Gerber, *Antidemocratic Movements in the United States since World War I* (Ph.D. Thesis, Department of Political Science, University of Pennsylvania, 1934), pp. 97–116; George W. Ziegelmueller, *A Study of the Speaking of Conservatives in Opposition to the New Deal* (Ph.D. Thesis, Department of Speech, Northwestern University, 1962), pp. 44–118.
151. Wolfskill, *op. cit.*, p. 40.
152. Rudolf, *op. cit.*, p. 19.
153. *Ibid.*, p. 25.
154. Wolfskill, *op. cit.*, p. 62.
155. Ziegelmueller, *op. cit.*, p. 50.
156. Wolfskill, *op. cit.*, pp. 68–74.

157. Ziegelmueller, *op. cit.*, p. 54.
158. *Ibid.*, p. 64.
159. *Ibid.*, pp. 56–57.
160. *Ibid.*, p. 59; Wolfskill, *op. cit.*, pp. 214–215.
161. *Ibid.*, p. 210.
162. *Ibid.*, p. 214–215.
163. *Ibid.*, p. 139.

CHAPTER

6

The 1950's: McCarthyism

In the 1950's McCarthyism became a synonym for procedural extremism throughout the world. In the more than three years during which he exercised a reign of terror over the public sector of America, Senator Joseph McCarthy was compared constantly to the archmonist who had just been bloodily excised from the world, Adolf Hitler. Finally, however, McCarthy was not a totalitarian leader, but a politician who stumbled almost accidentally into the new darkening corners of America's mind. McCarthyism was not a monistic movement as much as a political umbrella under which the various streams of the monistic tendency in America temporarily came together and demonstrated their awesome potential.

The postwar period was one of unparalleled prosperity in the United States. Nor was it just a period in which a relatively few men amassed great wealth. More notably it was a period in which the wartime economic gains of the working class were consolidated and grew. America had crossed an economic threshold, and, barring a cataclysm, the advance was apparently irreversible. National income had tripled in the previous decade, and so had the median income of the American worker. This amounted to more than a 25 per cent increase in average purchasing power. Furthermore, this increase in real income was shared disproportionately by the lower economic groups. The economic pyramid was flattening out. In the fifteen years since mid-depression, still within troubled memory, the lowest economic fifth had improved its average real income by about 70 per cent, as against about 40 per cent by the highest fifth.

Significantly, it was the second and third lowest fifths which had each improved their real income by about 80 per cent.[1] The members of America's underclass had not yet been "discovered" beneath these statistics. But even their living conditions improved somewhat during this period, spurring their own self-discovery, and the general sense of real and spiraling affluence was pervasive. But beneath that dazzling prosperity there existed some deep social strains and nagging doubts.

New Wealth, New Insecurities

First of all, the spread of new wealth led to a rise of status insecurity on various levels. The most obvious example was the *nouveau très riche,* whose numbers had indeed multiplied from 1940 to 1950. The man who amasses wealth himself feels more insecure about keeping it than do people who possess inherited wealth. He also feels more aggrieved about social reform measures which involve redistribution of the wealth, as compared with individuals, still wealthy, who have grown up in an old traditionalist background, with the values of tolerance associated with upper-class aristocratic conservatism. The new millionaires and near millionaires exhibited the same uneasy symptoms of having just arrived that such groups had exhibited a half-century earlier in America.

While the most important significance of the newly wealthy lies in the power which their money can bring, rather than in their numbers, there is a mass counterpart for them in the general population, the small independent businessmen. Statistical data on social mobility in the United States indicate a great turnover in the ranks of these groups. A large proportion, if not a majority of them, come from other social strata: the small storekeepers and businessmen often are of working-class origin; the small manufacturer often comes out of the ranks of executive, white-collar, or government workers.

These small businessmen, perhaps more than any other group, feel constrained by progressive social legislation and the rise of labor unions. They are squeezed harder than large business, since their competitive position does not allow them to pay increases in wages as readily as can big firms. Governmental measures such as social security, business taxes, or various regulations which require filling out forms all tend to complicate the operation of small business. In general, these people are oriented upward, wishing to become larger businessmen and take on the values or imagined values of those who are more successful.

But Edward Shils was referring to yet another level of wealth and an even larger group of new possessors when he commented that the increased prosperity, elevating people into new standards of living and into the perception of new possibilities, also led some of them to become more anxious about the future, to be troubled about a depression and about the precariousness of their possessions. The novelty of their new style of life made them more sensitive to the impingement of remote events; it made them more sensitive to questions of status; it increased their ideological receptivity.[2]

Since 1940 the labor force had increased by about 13 per cent, but the number of workers classified as "white collar" had increased by about 34 per cent. Also the status of the blue-collar working class had changed dramatically. Labor-union membership had almost doubled in ten years. There was not only increasing wealth but increasing stability and dignity.

With the possession of status comes the fear of dispossession, in the face of threatening change. The new mass elite and mobiles of the working class found themselves in a world where the pressure of "change" was already an ominous presence. The dislocating changes on the world scene were most dramatic, but some of the harbingers of domestic change were also beginning to be apparent. There was another immigrant wave to the cities, reminiscent in some ways of that which had troubled the working class a century before. The Negroes had been flowing into the industrial cities from the urban South. Between 1940 and 1950, the nonwhite population of New York City increased from 500,000 to 750,000; in Chicago from 250,000 to 500,000; in Detroit from 150,000 to 300,000; in Los Angeles from 100,000 to 200,000. The proportion of nonwhite males employed as skilled craftsmen doubled while the proportion of white males in that category was rising by about 25 per cent. But, as a century earlier, it was not the immediate economic competition of the immigrants that was threatening—as long as there was relatively full employment and room at the top for the older workers. However, by 1950, eight states had passed antidiscrimination laws with enforcement provisions, and every urban area was witnessing a growing fight behind the slogan of economic equality, mostly in the still rarefied political arena. And the tensions were building on a more purely symbolic front, as Negroes began to demand more status in general and even started moving into white residential areas, usually lower and middle-income in character. In 1951 an upward-bound Negro and his family tried to move into an apartment he had rented in a nonelite but all-white suburb of Chicago, and a three-day riot ensued which momentarily shook the country. Still bathed in the ideological glow with which World War II had been fought against a racist enemy, and still not threatened by organized Negro militancy, the nation did not yet openly face the "race question" which was to erupt a decade later. But the uneasy shadow of this change was already beginning to hang over the new status of the urban working class.

The New World

However, the longest shadow of change was cast by the postwar developments on the world scene. The United States had presumably emerged from World War II as the mightiest of all nations, economically and militarily. With that might, it had been the key figure in a terrible, exhausting struggle to crush the forces of aggression that had been abroad in the world. No sooner had it emerged, victorious and rich, to enjoy the fruits of an Armageddon well done, than it discovered in a swift series of shocks that there was another antagonistic, aggressive, and highly powerful force on earth. Russia's influence had been established swiftly across eastern Europe, where necessary by military coups and fabricated revolutions. The Chinese Communists had seized power in 1949. There had been Communist insurrections and *Putsches* in the Mediterranean, in southeast Asia, and in western Europe, where the Russians had just attempted to seize Berlin through a blockade. Most Americans saw themselves as involved helplessly in a series of expensive and extensive counterreactions to these activities, which became a massive commitment in 1950 when we found ourselves engaged in a formal, costly, and frustrating war with North Korea. The suspicion grew that the kind of economic and military might with which we had prevailed in World War II was no longer very relevant. For one thing, it was becoming apparent that the Communist phenomenon of widespread local insurgency was more difficult to deal with than a Nazi blitzkrieg. And the spread of nuclear power and deterrence had changed the rules of the game. In early 1950, a news magazine wrote: "Americans have long been comforted and invigorated by a belief that seemed as solid as the Rockies, and as ever renewable as the Mississippi: that, counting up its armor, its resources and its allies, the U.S. was as strong as any potential enemy. Last week, the U.S. could not feel so sure. Its supposed monopoly of A-bombs was gone."[3]

Against this background, the nation had witnessed a series of spectacular exposés of covert Communist activities in this country. There were Russian spies and American collaborators; and the biggest headlines of 1949 reported the testimony of former Communist Whittaker Chambers on the existence of Communist cells among government personnel, some of them highly placed.

The apparent decline of American power in the face of a pattern of world-wide Communist thrusts created a common anxiety in the nation. Notably, it catalyzed two disparate elements in the American population: the agrarian isolationists and a growing segment of urban Catholics. Samuel Lubell has suggested that "the hard core of isolationism in the United States has been ethnic and emotional, not geographic. By far the strongest common characteristic of the isolationist-voting counties is the residence there of ethnic groups with a pro-German or anti-British bias. Far from being indifferent to Europe's wars, the evidence argues that the *isolationists* are oversensitive to them."[4]

During two wars, the pro-German ethnic groups have been isolationists. In addition to the Germans, and some midwestern Scandinavian groups tied to them by religious and ecological ties, many Irish have also opposed support of Britain in two wars. Because German influence was concentrated in the Midwest, and in part because isolationist ideologies were part of the value system of agrarian radicalism, isolationism was centered in the Midwest. The former isolationist group, especially its German base, was under a need to justify its past and to a certain extent to gain revenge. The opportunity now to identify internationalist forces in American society with Communism would obviously have an appeal to this submerged current in American society.

This isolationist complex in America had changed character in the 1930's when interventionism was identified with the New Deal and social reform, turning the agrarian radical tendencies in a generally conservative direction. The mass midwestern base of agrarian radicalism had become even less rural as the farm population continued to decline, and even more small-town middle-class and conservative in nature.

The urban Catholic population was also vulnerable to the new anxieties of the world scene and not unaffected by the new anxieties at home. Some of the factors which had led to a disproportionate support of Coughlin by the Catholics were now intensified. As a rapidly rising group whose economic status was still generally low until World War II, Catholics might have been expected to be vulnerable to status-linked political appeals. In addition, Catholics as a religious group were more prone to support anti-Communist movements than any other sect, with the possible exception of the fundamentalist Protestant churches. This predisposition derives from the long history of Catholic opposition to socialism and Communism, an organized opposition which has been perhaps more formalized in theological church terms than in almost any other group. This opposition was magnified in postwar years by the fact that a number of the countries taken over by the Communists in eastern Europe were Catholic, and in Europe those countries which were most in danger of Communist penetration were, in fact, Catholic.

Traditionally, Catholics in the United States and other English-speaking countries had been prevalently allied with more "left-wing" parties. Even Coughlin's movement projected its preservatism bounded by economic liberalism. In Great Britain, Australia, and New Zealand, the Catholics tended to support the Labor party. In the United States, they backed the Democratic party, while in Canada they endorsed the Liberal party.

The identification of Catholicism with the left in the English-speaking countries, as compared with its linkages with the right in western Europe, is related to the fact that the Catholic church is a minority church in the English-speaking countries and has been the church of the minority ethnic immigrants who have been largely lower-class. As a lower-status group, Catholics have been successfully appealed to by the out-party, by the party of the lower class.

The rise of the Communist threat, however, and the identification of Communism with the left created a conflict for many Catholics. Historically, this ideological conflict developed just as the Catholic populations in most of these countries were producing sizable upper and middle classes of their own, which in economic terms were under pressure to abandon their traditional identification with the lower-class party.

The Shift to the Right

The anxieties of postwar America were thus sharply different from those of prewar America: new wealth as against pervasive poverty, Communism as against Fascism as an antagonist on the world scene. These differences induced a generally conservative mood and provided a radically different framework for the development of extremist political groups.

The period from 1930 to 1945 had seen the predominance of liberal sentiment in American politics. The depression emphasized the need for socioeconomic reforms and helped to undermine the legitimacy of conservative and business institutions. It was followed immediately by a war which was defined as a struggle against Fascism. Since Fascism was identified as a rightist movement, this fact tended to reinforce the political predominance of leftist liberal sentiments.

During this period the political dynamic in most democratic countries was in the hands of the left, and it used this strength to undermine the prestige of conservatism. In the United States, for example, several congressional committees conducted exposés of "undemocratic" activities of big business. In the thirties, the Nye Committee "exposed" the way in which Wall Street bankers had helped plunge the United States into World War I in order to maintain their investments, while the La Follette Committee revealed that large corporations employed labor spies and gangsters to prevent their employees from forming trade-unions. The famous Truman Committee often exposed big-business profiteering during World War II. All three committees helped to foster an antibusiness and anticonservative climate of opinion. It is quite true that the House Committee on Un-American Activities operated at the same time as the liberal committees, but though it secured considerable publicity, it was relatively unimportant compared with the role of antisubversive committees in the postwar years.

The period of liberal supremacy was also marked by a great growth in the influence of the Communist party. In the United States, the Communists were concerned with penetrating and manipulating liberal and moderate left groups, rather than with building an electoral party. The Communists, by concealing their real objectives, by acting positively for liberal causes, by being the best organizers of the left, were able to penetrate deeply into various liberal organizations and into the labor movement. An index of their success may be seen in the fact that close to a dozen congressmen, one state governor, members of the staffs of liberal congressmen and congressional committees, and a number of high-ranking civil servants showed by their long-term political behavior that they were close followers of the Communist party, that is, that they changed their policies on various issues in tandem with shifts in the C.P. line.

The postwar period, on the other hand, saw a resurgence of conservative and rightist forces. Where once we warred against Fascism, which is identified with the "right," we now warred against Communism, which identifies with the "left." And just as the Communists were able to secure considerable influence during the period of liberal ascendancy, right-wing extremists were able to make respectable headway during the conservative revival. The conservatives and the extreme right were now on the offensive. The "free enterprise" system which provided full employment was once more legitimate. Liberal groups felt in a weak position politically and now waged a defensive battle, seeking to preserve their conquests of the thirties, rather than to extend them. However, with all the conservative trends, the Republican party was unable to win the Presidential election in 1948. The various strains in American life were still not coalescing for political purposes. The backlash of the economic conservatism, urban and agrarian, against the social reforms of the New Deal did not mesh with the uneasiness of the general population which still had a fundamental stake in those social reforms.

It was Senator Joseph McCarthy who presumably put together a single package to attract these disparate elements in the population by personifying their fears in the name of anti-Communism.

Joseph McCarthy was born on a relatively poor farm in Wisconsin, worked his way through law school, became a Circuit Court Judge in 1939 and a United States Senator in 1946. In 1950, after some rather undistinguished years in the Senate during which he evinced only a vague interest in the subject of Communism, McCarthy precipitously became the voice of anti-Communism in America. On February 9 of that year, before a women's Republican club in Wheeling, West Virginia, he announced that he had in his possession the names of Communist party members who worked for the State Department, with the Department's knowledge. According to press reports he said:

> While I cannot take the time to name all of the men in the State Department who have been named as members of the Communist Party and members of a spy ring, I have here in my hand a list of two-hundred and five that were known to the Secretary of State as being members of the Communist Party and who nevertheless are still working and shaping the policy of the State Department.[5]

McCarthy was to juggle this figure of 205 several times and even to insist that he had just called them "security risks." But from then on, the press attention given him and his charges was national and explosive. Anti-Communism became Senator McCarthy's abiding passion. Covert Communists became for him the prime source of all social ills.

It is not that McCarthy invented this device. Under the historical circumstances, it was a natural direction for the ultraconservatives as they took the postwar offensive. Indeed, it is striking to observe the similarities in the rhetoric of the liberals and conservatives when on the offensive. In the thirties, conservatives, isolationists, business leaders, Republican Senators and congressmen were criticized by some liberals as being semi-fascist, or with being outright fascist. Now, many conservatives waged an attack on liberals, Democrats, and opponents of a vigorous anti-Russian foreign policy as pro-Communist, as "creeping Socialists." The sources of the violent attack on conservatism in the earlier period came in large measure from the Communists and their fellow travelers, although it was voiced by many liberals who had no connection with the Communist party and were unaware of the extent to which they had absorbed a Communist ideological position. In the postwar period, the extreme right wing of the American political spectrum became successful in setting the ideological tone of conservatism.

It is interesting to note the parallelism in the rhetoric employed by liberals when criticizing the State Department's policy toward the Loyalists in the Spanish Civil War of 1936–1939 and that used by many extreme rightists toward the policy of the same Department a few years later in the Chinese Civil War. The liberal left magazines portrayed an American foreign office staffed by men who were sympathetic to extreme conservatism if not outright fascism and who tricked President Roosevelt and Secretary of State Hull into pursuing policies which helped Franco. The postwar right-wing accusations that our Chinese policies were a result of Communist influence in government sounded like a rewritten version of the fascist conspiracy of the thirties. The State Department's refusal to aid Loyalist Spain was presented as convincing proof of the presence of fascist sympathizers in it. In the same way, the postwar extreme right refused to acknowledge that men may have made honest errors of judgment in their dealing with the Russians or the Chinese Communists.

Indeed, one may fittingly describe an extreme right doctrine of "Social Communism" comparable to the Communist term "Social Fascism" in the early thirties. The Communists, before 1934, argued that all non-Communist parties, including the Socialists, were "Social Fascists"; that is, they objectively were paving the way for fascism. The principal organ of the postwar ultraright, *The Freeman,* contended that all welfare states and planning measures were "objectively" steps toward the development of a totalitarian Communist state. The New Deal, Americans for Democratic Action, the CIO Political Action Committee, all were charged with "objective" totalitarianism. Both the Communists and writers for *The Freeman* argued that the "social" variety of fascism or Communism is more dangerous than the real thing, for the public is more easily deceived by a sugar-coated totalitarian program. The Communists in pre-Hitler Germany concentrated their fire not on the Nazis, but on the "Social Fascists," the socialists and liberals, and *The Freeman* and various sections of the radical right let loose their worst venom on the American liberals.

An example of the violent character of this ideology may be seen in a 1950 *Freeman* article which contended, "This new political machine, which . . . rules the old Democratic Party is an outgrowth of the CIO's Political Action Committee (PAC)." It further claimed that "every single element in the Browder [Communist Party] program was incorporated in the PAC program. It has been the policy of the Administration ever since." The labor movement organized around Truman because of the Taft-Hartley Act. Why, asked this *Freeman* writer, did labor unite against this act, which though it "injured the Communists . . . certainly did not injure the workers." The answer suggested was that the Communists executed another strategic retreat. They let go of their prominent offices in the CIO, but they still had control of the press and the policy-making and opinion-forming organs. Then they got their ideas into the opinion-forming agencies of the AFL, especially its League for Political Education.

How could the AFL be captured by the Communist policy-makers? It had a great tradition, but in the face of the CIO's "gains," its leaders thought they had to "do something." And the Communists were ready and waiting to tell them what to do—policies nicely hidden behind the cloak of higher wages, more benefits, but still fitting perfectly the symbols laid down to guide policy-makers by Earl Browder in 1944.

The article went on to ask,

What proof have we that the Politbureau in Moscow wanted the election of [Henry] Wallace? Wallace certainly did not poll the total Communist vote. For eight years they had worked on getting control of a major party. Why give up the Truman party? . . .

Practically every word of Truman's campaign came, again, from Browder's pattern of 1944, which is the policy of the PAC. Practically every word of his attack on the 80th Congress can be found earlier in the pages of the *Daily Worker* and the *People's Daily World*.

What then was the role of [Henry] Wallace and the third party? It was the old Communist dialectic. By setting up Wallace as the "left," the Communists could make Truman's platforms and speeches look like the "center."[6]

Thus, as the Communists saw a country controlled by a self-conscious plot of Wall Street magnates, of two "capitalist" parties competing just to fool the people, the extreme right saw a nightmarish world in which the Communists had two political parties in order to fool the people; in which Henry Wallace's million votes in 1948 only represented a presumably small part of total Communist strength.

Although such conspiratorial theories from the right were already floating around, it was McCarthy who was able to build an effective political tendency and draw together sizable and disparate sections of the population around them. In the first place, he had the personal capacity and the public position to dramatize them as no one else had. But, more than that, he was in the position to matchmake the classic *mariage de convenance* between the preservatist political elements and the less privileged mass base which any right-wing political movement in America requires. He was a United States Senator and a Republican of good standing. His practical political target was the Democratic party. Although McCarthy never formulated or espoused a comprehensive economic program or philosophy of any kind, he was supported financially by economic conservatives who were anxious to see the Democratic administration unseated. He was embraced, sometimes somewhat gingerly, by stalwarts of the Republican party like Taft who were clearly offended by his methods. But his anti-Communism apparently galvanized the populace and turned its animus toward politically fruitful targets. By ascribing conspiracy to the White House, McCarthy was hyperbolizing its failures and touching the raw nerve of the public:

The people, I am convinced, recognize the weakness with which the administration has replaced what was so recently our great strength. They are troubled by it. And they do not think it accidental. They do not believe that the decline in our strength from 1945 to 1951 just happened. They are coming to believe that it was brought about, step by step, by will and intention. They are beginning to believe that the surrender of China to Russia, the administration's indecently hasty desire to turn Formosa over to the enemy and arrive at a cease-fire in Korea instead of following the manly, American course prescribed by Mac-

Arthur, point to something more than ineptitude and folly. They witness the conviction of Hiss, which would not have happened had he not brought a private suit for damages against Whittaker Chambers; they follow the revelations in the Remington case, the Marzani case, and the others which have disclosed at the heart of Government active Soviet agents influencing policy and pilfering secrets; they note the policy of retreat before Soviet assertion from Yalta to this day, and they say: this is not because these men are incompetents, there is a deeper reason. How can we account for our present situation unless we believe that men high in this Government are concerting to deliver us to disaster? This must be the product of a great conspiracy, a conspiracy on a scale so immense as to dwarf any previous such venture in the history of man. Who constitutes the highest circles of this conspiracy? About that we cannot be sure. We are convinced that Dean Acheson, who steadfastly serves the interests of nations other than his own, who supported Alger Hiss in his hour of retribution, who contributed to his defense fund, must be high on the roster. The President? He is their captive. I have wondered, as have you, why he did not dispense with so great a liability as Acheson to his own and his party's interests. It is now clear to me. In the relationship of master and man, did you ever hear of man firing master? President Truman is a satisfactory front. He is only dimly aware of what is going on.[7]

The Democrats while in office could not ignore him and set up a subcommittee of the Foreign Relations Committee under Millard Tydings, of Maryland, to "conduct a full and complete study and investigation as to whether persons who are disloyal to the United States are or have been employed by the Department of State."[8] This committee investigated McCarthy's charges for six months and then absolved the State Department. Senator Tydings, however, was up for reelection in 1950 and was defeated, with McCarthy campaigning vigorously against him. Although it is debatable whether McCarthy played a major role in Tydings' loss, many in Congress and the press concluded that he did, a fact which gave him enormous influence during the next two years. The Republican leadership, seeking a way finally to defeat the Democrats, were now ready to approve of him. Senator Taft, though privately contemptuous of McCarthy's methods, stated publicly that "the pro-Communist policies of the State Department fully justified Joe McCarthy in his demand for an investigation."[9]

McCarthy remained a power in the Republican party through the 1952 election. He was lionized at the Presidential convention. After the election, Senator Taft, now majority leader of the Senate, placed McCarthy in charge of the Committee on Government Operations. McCarthy used this vantage point to make himself chairman of its Permanent Investigations Subcommittee, a position which enabled him to look into the activities of every agency of government. And for the next two years he pursued his drive against the hidden conspiracy in the Republican administration itself. It was not until he tried to take on the Army that a halt was finally called to his activities by the Senate.

McCarthyism

McCarthyism was not a political movement. It never had members, organized chapters, offered candidates, or formulated a platform. It was a tendency of the times, which McCarthy epitomized, to which he lent his name, but of which in a way he was finally an instrument rather than creator. He was, it is true, a particularly suitable and capable instrument.

As a Catholic, McCarthy was able to embody the traditional anti-Communism and the growing conservatism of that population, without the disability of Father Coughlin's collar. And as a Wisconsinite who followed a La Follette to the Senate, he was able to embrace the agrarian, isolationist, and ethnic sentiments of the Midwest. In fact, the states which were the backbone of agrarian radicalism before the New Deal gave McCarthy most of his support. A direct line has often been drawn between the La Follette Progressive populist tradition and McCarthy.[10] This line has been given different implications, however. There is little question but that McCarthy drew on the same anti-interventionist sentiment that La Follette had invoked. There is also a certain similarity between their tactics.

Both Wisconsin Senators conveyed a similar image of embattled insurgency. . . . McCarthy adopted the stance of continual attack that characterized the elder La Follette. McCarthy was a "fighter" for the people's interests, and the condemnation of respectable society only served to strengthen the image of McCarthy as "Battling Joe" just as it had worked for "Fighting Bob."[11]

But there is more implied in the comparison than tactics. In stating that "McCarthy is the heir of La Follette," Shils asks:

What was populism if not the distrust of the effete East and its agents in the urban Middle West? Was not populism the forerunner of "grass roots" democracy? Did it not seek to subject the government to the people's will, to tumble the mighty from their high seats, to turn legislators into registrants of the people's will? Was it not suspicious of the upper classes of the East? . . . Did not populism allege to protect the people and their government from conspiracies, from cells of conspirators, who, contrary to the people's will and through the complacency or collusion of their rulers, were enabled to gain control of society?[12]

Whether McCarthy personally "owed" these proclivities to the La Follette tradition is somewhat immaterial. McCarthyism did not, although the tendency prospered as a result of the consonance. Conspiracy theories in

America have always leaned heavily on the concept of direct democracy, as an antidote to the secret elite who allegedly were contravening the people's will. One of the intrinsic links between conspiracy theory and monism is the anticonstitutional bias of direct democracy. This is one of the rationales for by-passing the rules, as McCarthy and McCarthyism often did. When McCarthy's censure was being formally considered by the Senate, Herman Walker said "the ninety-six senators are not the judges. The 150,000,000 Americans are the judges of the trial of McCarthy."[13]

Likewise, conspiracy theories, by their nature, are anti-intellectual and invariably focus on some overeducated secret elite. In this case, the most singular link with midwestern populism was the identification of that elite with the eastern Brahmins. Even that identification coincided with the predispositions of other supporting populations: the Irish Catholics, the small businessmen, the new Texas millionaires.

As a matter of fact, McCarthy's was as abstract and "clean" an approach to conspiracy theory as any in American history and may have partly fallen of its own weight as a result. Since the first vague image of the Illuminati conspiracy in the eighteenth century, which also fell of its own weight, the effective conspiracy theories in America have involved two dimensions: a mysterious cabal and some less mysterious, more visible target group associated with the cabal. The offending Catholic immigrants in tandem with papist plots served this purpose; so did alien Jewish merchants in tandem with the Elders of Zion. Even nonethnic "eastern Bankers" could serve some purpose of group visibility for the agrarian mind. McCarthy invoked none of these. His traitors were pure: leaders who had sold out to a foreign power on an individual basis. There was the standard anti-intellectual, antielite appeal of denigrating the Ivy League character of many of the alleged conspirators—but finally there was no cogent group identity.

On first reading, McCarthy's plot theory seemed to be stated as vehemently and as explicitly as it had ever been stated. Our deplorable situation he ascribed to "an infamy so black and a conspiracy so immense as to dwarf any previous such venture in the history of man."[14] He seemed to accuse the President, General Marshall, many State Department officials and government leaders of being part of the plot; but after the fierce rhetoric, he invariably ended up accusing them of being failures rather than plotters. "We were not [ever before] misled and enfeebled by abstractions such as collective security and by the tortured twisted reasoning of men of little minds and less morals who for the first time in the history of this nation argue that we should not vigorously fight back when attacked."[15]

Of course, the Senator's stock in trade and his most effective tactic was promising to "name names." In his 1950 Wheeling, West Virginia, speech which abruptly launched his anti-Communist career he said, "I have here in my hand a list. . . ." He held many such lists in his hand during his public career. Not many names were ever actually revealed. But in any case they were only, finally, names of individuals who had presumably sold out to the foreign enemy.

For McCarthyism, the enemy was an ideology, Communism. True, there was a headquarters in Moscow, but the ideology was the enemy. When General MacArthur said in 1951 that the threat to America was not from the outside but "from the insidious forces working from within which have already so drastically altered the character of our free institutions, . . ."[16] the altered institutions themselves were his target, the "insidious forces" remaining abstract. When Senator William Jenner said that the "collectivist machine" operating in the White House, the State Department, and elsewhere "emanated from some control tower we cannot see,"[17] he illustrated the ambiguity of this approach to conspiracy. If the Kremlin was the control tower, the threat was, in one sense, external rather than internal and not really a conspiracy, but a kind of dirty war. But if the threat was that the American people were being seduced by collectivism and internationalism, thus permitting the traitors to more easily deliver us, the prime danger was in fact an ideology and not a band of conspiratorial handmaidens.

It was in this sense that McCarthy's enemy, and that of many of his cohorts, was Communism itself rather than any singular group of conspirators. McCarthy's approach to politics, in the monistic mode, was apolitical; that is, highly moralistic. But his moralism was in tune with the universalist religious framework of America and indeed with the new moral tempo of America. McCarthy was cited by friends as being "a good Catholic, but not the kiss-the-book light-the-candle Catholic."[18]

Richard Rovere noted that "where other politicians would seek to conceal a weakness for liquor or wenching or gambling, McCarthy tended to exploit, even to exaggerate, these wayward tastes. He was glad to have everyone believe that he was a drinker of heroic attainments, a passionate lover of horseflesh, a Clausewitz of the poker table, and a man to whom everything presentable in skirts was catnip."[19] But he could. accuse President Eisenhower of dealing with "the apostles of hell," of planning to make "territorial concessions to Red China."[20]

One biographer quotes McCarthy as saying in a home-town speech: "There are two fundamental truths of religion: there is a God who is eternal, and each and every one of you has a soul which is immortal." McCarthy then indicated that his anti-Communist crusade was not just political, and the biographer comments: "The implication was clear: the campaign was religious. God and Joe, with the voters' help, would emerge victorious."[21]

McCarthy himself stated it clearly: "The great difference between our western Christian world and the atheistic communist world is not political

. . . it is moral."[22] The thrust was to establish anti-Communism as the religion of America, with Communism as the antireligion. It cut across sectarian lines and blended with the secularized faith of America, although the fundamentalists could relate to it with their own more particularistic language.

Communism was being used as the broad general reference by which to identify the body of bad intentions and bad character in the world. It was not really that Communism was evil because it was atheistic, but rather that it was deemed "atheistic" because it was evil. The heart of the American religion was, simply, opposition to evil as it cohered in Communism, just as the heart of bedrock fundamentalism was opposition to evil as it cohered in Satan. Americanism was the set of values which embodied such an American religion.

In this sense, McCarthyist anti-Communism represented the ultimate movement to abstract and anomic nativism. The group identity was one of moral superiority. This had always been a characteristic of nativism, often as a kind of "cultural baggage" to strong and specific ethnic and regional ties. The appeal to ethnic and regional ties was still a subsurface nativist presence in many aspects of McCarthyism, but in general its nativism was more diffuse. On the other side of the nativist coin, it was not aliens but alien ideas which needed exorcising. Coughlin had moved toward such an abstract nativism; but in fusing his nativism with conspiracy theory, he had located a specific body of people as nativist backlash targets. In McCarthyism the same moral fervor and absolutism were present. The equating of Communism with anti-God was not new. But the relative absence of a singular cohesive body of plotters and fellow travelers was new to conspiracy theory.

Indeed, McCarthyism was more conspiracy style than conspiracy theory, more technique than theory of any kind. The technique, which bears his name, consisted of seeming to charge people with treason, without actually doing so. This involved "guilt by association," a phrase which resounded through the early 1950's in America; or innuendo, or the waving of undisclosed "lists." It spoke of conspiracy, but all it spelled out was treason and ideological defection. McCarthyism never succeeded in corporealizing the American conspiracy.

Smelser's step-by-step analysis of the development of a political movement suggests that without the designation of a specific cause for the social strain in question, there is no movement, only hysteria. He defines a hysterical belief as "a belief empowering an ambiguous element in the environment with a generalized power to threaten or destroy."[23] He cites certain institutionalized hysterical beliefs as superstitions, fears of witchcraft, demons, spirits, and the like. A corporealized conspiracy can provide specific cause. But McCarthy's Communism as an internal threat remained generalized, and McCarthyism remained more a hysteria than a political movement.

As a hysteria, however, it was potent; and even with a "faulted" conspiracy theory, it unlocked the monistic impulses of America. Partly, McCarthy and his associates were able to do this because there *were* traitors, there *were* spies, there *were* some significantly placed Communist cells in America. One of McCarthy's most severe journalistic critics affirmed that "a number, even if a relatively small number, of the shots called by McCarthy in his changing lists . . . of alleged loyalty, security and 'morals' risks were later proved to be on the target."[24] Some individuals in the clear service of a foreign power were exposed. The slavish devotion to Soviet foreign policy on the part of a few influential people was established. These people were security threats and it can be presumed that they created a great deal of mischief. But the accumulation of all their activities could not explain the plight of America, internally or on the world scene.

At that point, the hysteria took over. Throughout the country, there was a witch hunt, not so much for conspirators as for ideological defectors. The basic monistic formula was applied: Communism was evil, and those who trafficked in such evil were illegitimate and to be excluded from the market place of ideas—and even from the market place of jobs. Since ideological defection, as distinct from membership in any specific group, was a matter of varying judgment, it was pluralism which was under attack. In Washington, McCarthy conducted a lengthy and public investigation of the personnel of the Voice of America, which resulted in the discovery of no Communists, but the discharge or resignation of some thirty employees. "Black lists" of suspect personnel were established for the information of industry's hiring offices. Libraries around the country were under pressure, to which they did or did not give in, to remove arbitrarily suspect books and magazines from their shelves. For example, on one list of books, which the city manager of San Antonio said in 1953 should be burned, were "Einstein's *Theory of Relativity,* Thomas Mann's *Joseph in Egypt* and *The Magic Mountain,* . . . Norbert Wiener's *Cybernetics*; also various anthologies of poetry and folk songs, also books on sculpture, the mentally ill, alcoholics, child care, architecture and mystery novels."[25]

It was this kind of monistic attack which McCarthy symbolized and activated in America. Who supported him?

Social Base

A number of quantitative analyses of the sources of McCarthy's support indicate that it came disproportionately from Catholics, New Englanders, Republicans, the less educated, the lower class, manual workers, farmers, older people, and the Irish. Nelson Polsby, who in 1960 summarized the findings of many of these studies,[26] suggests that the evidence from these surveys and from an examination of the results of different election campaigns in which McCarthy or McCarthyism were issues indicates that most of McCarthy's support can be attributed to his identification as a Republican fighting Democrats. In other words, the vast bulk of his backing came from regular Republicans, while the large majority of Democrats opposed him.

Undoubtedly Polsby is correct in stressing the linkage between party identification and attitude toward McCarthy. Some earlier evidence making the same point was reported in a study of the 1954 election by the University of Michigan's Survey Research Center, which showed the positive relationship between degrees of party commitment and attitude toward McCarthy (Table 19).

Table 19.   RELATIONSHIP OF PARTY IDENTIFICATION TO ATTITUDE
TOWARD MCCARTHY, OCTOBER 1954

Attitude toward McCarthy	Party Commitment						
	Strong Demo-crat	Weak Demo-crat	Inde-pendent Demo-crat	Inde-pend-ent	Inde-pendent Repub-lican	Weak Repub-lican	Strong Repub-lican
Pro-McCarthy	10 %	9 %	8 %	12 %	12 %	12 %	25 %
Neutral	37	44	42	54	50	47	43
Anti-McCarthy	50	40	41	21	32	33	27
Other responses	3	7	9	13	6	8	5
	100 %	100 %	100 %	100 %	100 %	100 %	100 %
Excess of Antis over Pros	40 %	31 %	33 %	9 %	20 %	21 %	2 %
Number	(248)	(288)	(97)	(82)	(68)	(159)	(146)

SOURCE: Angus Campbell and Homer C. Cooper, *Group Differences in Attitudes and Votes* (Ann Arbor: Survey Research Center, University of Michigan, 1956), p. 92.
Based on replies to question: "If you knew that Senator McCarthy was supporting a candidate for Congress, would you be more likely to vote for that candidate, or less likely to vote for that candidate, or wouldn't it make any difference to you?"

The association between McCarthy support and Republicanism does not tell us, of course, how many former Democrats and Independents may have joined Republican ranks prior to 1954, because their social situation or personal values made them sympathetic to McCarthy's version of radical right ideology. As has been noted, a considerable section of Coughlin's 1938 backing came from individuals who had supported Roosevelt in 1936, but had later rejected him. There is no reliable means of demonstrating the extent to which McCarthy contributed to a move away from the Democrats, but the available evidence is at least compatible with the hypothesis that he was to some extent influential.[27] A 1954 study made available for secondary analysis by the International Research Associates (INRA) inquired as to the respondents' votes in 1948 and 1952. A comparison of the relationship between 1948 voting, attitude toward McCarthy, and 1952 Presidential vote indicates that over half of those who voted for Truman in 1948 and subsequently favored McCarthy voted for Eisenhower in 1952, while two-thirds of the anti-McCarthy Truman voters favored Stevenson (Table 20). A similar relationship between supporting McCarthy and shifting away from the Democrats is suggested in a study supplied to us for further analysis by the Roper public opinion organization.

Table 20.   RELATIONSHIP BETWEEN 1948 PRESIDENTIAL VOTE AND ATTITUDE
TOWARD MCCARTHY, 1952 (INRA)

| 1952 Vote | 1948 Vote | | | |
| | Truman | | Dewey | |
	Pro-McCarthy	Anti-McCarthy	Pro-McCarthy	Anti-McCarthy
Eisenhower	53 %	31 %	99 %	95 %
Stevenson	47	69	1	5
Number	(506)	(1,381)	(583)	(732)

A more detailed analysis of the sources of McCarthy's support conducted along the lines of the analysis of Coughlin's backing, however, belies the suggestion that party affiliation had more bearing on approval or disapproval of McCarthy than other explanatory variables. The 1952 Roper study and the 1954 INRA survey both suggest that the most important attribute associated with opinion of McCarthy was education, while a 1954 national study conducted by the University of Michigan's Survey Research Center indicated that religious affiliation was of greater significance than party. Table 21 shows the relationship between education, party identification, and attitude toward McCarthy.

The relationship between less education and support of McCarthy is consistent with what is known about the effect of education on political attitudes in general: higher education often makes for greater tolerance, greater regard for due process, and increased tolerance of ambiguity.

The findings from the surveys with respect to occupation are what might be anticipated, given the preceding results. Nonmanual occupations that require the highest education—that is, professional and executive or managerial positions—were the most anti-McCarthy (Table 22). Independent businessmen were the most favorable to McCarthy among middle-class or nonmanual occupations. Workers (including those engaged in personal service) were more favorable to McCarthy than were those in the middle-class occupations, with the exception of independent businessmen.

Table 21. SUPPORT FOR MCCARTHY BY EDUCATION AND
PARTY PREFERENCE, 1954 (INRA)
(Per Cent Difference between Approvers and Disapprovers)

Education	Party Identification		
	Democrat	Independent	Republican
Graduate school	—59	—44	—28
College	—44	—24	—19
Vocational	—41	—20	—19
High school	—27	— 8	— 5
Grammar school	—18	— 8	+ 6

NOTE: Cell entries refer to percentage differences between approval and disapproval of McCarthy. For example, among grammar-school Republicans, 24 per cent were pro-McCarthy and 18 per cent were anti-McCarthy; among Democrats with graduate education, 8 per cent were pro-McCarthy, and 67 per cent anti-McCarthy.

Table 22. RELATIONSHIP BETWEEN OCCUPATION AND ATTITUDES TOWARD MCCARTHY
(Per Cent Difference between Approvers and Disapprovers)

INRA 1954[a]			Roper 1952[b]		
	Per Cent	Number		Per Cent	Number
Professional	—35	(731)	Professional and		
Executive and managerial	—24	(511)	Executive	—17	(219)
White collar	—19	(1,144)	Small business	— 0	(123)
Industry and business	—14	(583)	Clerical and sales	—11	(387)
Supervisor and foreman	—16	(405)	Factory labor	— 3	(317)
Skilled	—14	(2,323)	Nonfactory labor	— 6	(235)
Unskilled	—14	(1,019)	Services	— 4	(178)
Personal service	—10	(677)	Farm owner/manager	— 6	(184)
Farmers	—21	(824)	Gallup—December 1954[c]		
Retired	— 3	(709)	Professional	—44	(163)
Students	—34	(59)	Executive	—24	(154)
Michigan 1954[c]			Clerical and sales	—23	(188)
Professional and business	—40	(246)	Skilled	—10	(237)
Clerical and sales	—44	(102)	Unskilled	8	(286)
Skilled	—30	(337)	Labor	7	(68)
Unskilled	—16	(144)	Service	—10	(103)
Farmers	—17	(104)	Farm owner	—9	(165)

NOTE: Cell entries represent difference between approval and disapproval of McCarthy. The more negative the entry, the greater the predominance of anti-McCarthy sentiment. See footnote 27 for source of data in this table.

[a] Occupation of respondent recorded as of chief wage earner if respondent is a housewife.
[b] Occupation of respondent recorded, housewives omitted from table.
[c] Occupation of head of household recorded.

Farmers were also a pro-McCarthy group, according to three of the four surveys we reanalyzed and the many studies summarized by Polsby. When viewed in occupational categories, McCarthy's main opponents were to be found among professional, managerial, and clerical personnel, while his support was disproportionately located among self-employed business-men, farmers, and manual workers.

In the INRA survey, it was possible to examine the attitudes of two groups not in the labor force: students and retired persons. Students were overwhelmingly opposed to McCarthy, while retired persons were among the groups least antagonistic to the Senator. These findings presumably re-flect the combined influences of age and education. The attitudes of the re-tired may have been colored by several factors associated with age, such as particular sensitivity to the rise of Communism and the decline of American prestige, greater political conservatism, and greater rigidity. Moreover, retired persons probably felt most acutely the effects of status deprivation because of both their decline in social importance and their disadvantageous economic position in a period of moderate inflation.

Thus far, the analysis suggests that McCarthy's support was in many ways similar to Father Coughlin's. Both men derived strength from the lower classes and the rural population. They differed only in the relatively greater appeal of the Senator to self-employed businessmen. These results would suggest that the differences in the ideologies of the two men are not paralleled by differences in the character of their support. However, when socioeconomic status rather than occupation is taken as an indicator of class, differing patterns of support emerge for the Senator and for Coughlin. The Coughlin analysis indicated a high correlation between socioeconomic status (a measure of the style of life of the respondent, largely reflecting income) and approval of the priest. Those of low status were much more likely to approve of him than those of high status. When the corresponding comparison is made for McCarthy, we find a much smaller, almost insignificant, association. Lower-status persons were slightly less likely to support McCarthy than the more privileged ones. This result is initially quite surprising, since both education and occupation, themselves highly correlated with socioeconomic status, were, as we have seen, related to attitudes toward McCarthy. The solution to this apparent puzzle lies in the finding that when either education or occupation is held constant—that is, when we compare those high or low on socioeconomic status within the same educational or occupational categories—the data show that *the higher the socioeconomic-status level, the greater the proportion of McCarthy supporters.* This finding holds true particularly among Republi-cans; in general, the socioeconomic-status level had little effect on attitude toward McCarthy among Democrats of a given occupational or educational level. Thus, while lower educational and occupational status were associated with support for the Wisconsin Senator, within either category *higher* socioeconomic status made for greater receptivity to his message among Republicans. Perhaps the higher-income people in lower occupational or educational strata were precisely those who were most drawn to an ideology that attacked as pro-Communist both liberal lower-class-based politics and moderate, conservative old upper-class-elitist groups.

It has been suggested that McCarthy's strength reflected the frustrations inherent in status discrepancies. In periods of full employment and widespread economic opportunity, some who rise economically do not secure the social status commensurate with their new economic position. Conversely, others, whose financial position has not improved at a corresponding rate (or has worsened), find their social status relatively higher than their economic position. Such status incongruities were presumed to have created sharp resentments about general social developments, which predisposed individuals to welcome McCarthy's attack on the elite and on the New Deal. Efforts to test these hypotheses with the data available for the most part proved unfruitful.

One study, however, did find some empirical support for these assumptions. Robert Sokol attempted to see whether the subjective perception of status discrepancy ("felt status inconsistency") was related to McCarthyism.[28] The analysis indicated that conscious concern with status inconsistency and McCarthyism were related: "The more strain, the greater will be the tendency to be a McCarthy supporter; with 62 per cent of the high-strain men being pro-McCarthy, in contrast with 47 per cent of those feeling a little strain and 39 per cent of those without any concern about the relative ranks of their statuses."[29] These findings held within different analytic subgroups. While much more work remains to be done to analyze the relationship between status strain and political protest and between objective discrepancy and subjective strains, Sokol's research suggests that the general assumptions about the relationship of the status strains of an open society and the type of political protest represented by McCarthy may have some validity.

Another hypothesis is that McCarthyism also reflected strains inherent in the varying statuses of different ethnic and religious groups in American society. It was assumed that Catholics and other recent immigrant groups with relatively low status, or with ethnic ties to neutral or Axis nations, were disposed to favor McCarthy, while those of high status or with ethnic links to Allied nations opposed the Senator. These generalizations also tend to be supported by survey data. It is clear, as has already been noted, that Catholics as a group were more pro-McCarthy than Protestants, who in turn were somewhat more favorable to him than were Jews. The strong relationship between religious affiliation and attitude toward McCarthy among supporters of the two parties may be seen in Table 23, taken from the University of Michigan study.

In the Protestant group, the ranking of the different denominations with respect to sentiment toward McCarthy corresponded on the whole to their socioeconomic status. As Table 24 shows, the higher the status of the members of a denomination, the more antagonistic the group was toward the Wisconsin Senator.

Methodists constitute an exception to this generalization; although a relatively low-status group, they were more anti-McCarthy than the Lutherans or Presbyterians. The rank order of denominations in terms of McCarthy

Table 23.   ATTITUDES TOWARD MCCARTHY ACCORDING TO RELIGION
AND PARTY IDENTIFICATION, 1954

Attitude toward McCarthy	Strong Demo- crat	Weak Demo- crat	Inde- pendent	Weak Repub- lican	Strong Repub- lican
			Protestants		
Pro	7 %	6 %	7 %	11 %	23 %
Anti	55	45	35	33	28
Excess of Anti over Pro	−48	−39	−28	−22	− 5
Number	(184)	(213)	(173)	(128)	(123)
			Catholics		
Pro	18 %	23 %	19 %	20 %	39 %
Anti	33	20	21	28	23
Excess of Anti over Pro	−15	+ 3	− 2	− 8	+16
Number	(51)	(58)	(55)	(25)	(18)

SOURCE: Angus Campbell and Homer C. Cooper, *Group Differences in Attitudes and Votes* (Ann Arbor: Survey Research Center, University of Michigan, 1956), p. 149.

Table 24.   PROTESTANT DENOMINATIONAL SUPPORT FOR MCCARTHY (ROPER)

Denomination	Attitude toward McCarthy—Per Cent					
	Per Cent of Group High in S E S	Agree	Dis- agree	Don't Know	Difference between Agrees and Disagrees	Number
Episcopalians	40	29	44	27	−15	(157)
Congregationalists	32	33	44	23	−11	(89)
Methodists	19	29	33	38	− 4	(509)
Presbyterians	27	37	36	27	+ 1	(208)
Lutherans	23	33	31	36	+ 2	(207)
Baptists	12	28	24	49	+ 4	(471)

support is, with the exception of the Baptists, identical with that reported earlier for Coughlin. Baptists ranked relatively high in opposition to Coughlin and in support for McCarthy. It is difficult to suggest any plausible explanation for this change in the position of the Baptists other than that they may have been particularly antagonistic to the Catholic church, and hence unwilling to approve the political activities of a priest, yet not deterred from supporting a Catholic Senator.

Both the INRA and Roper surveys contain information concerning the ethnic origins of respondents which permits an elaboration of the relationship between ethnic and religious identification and McCarthy support (see Table 25). Unfortunately, the two studies differed greatly in the wording of questions on ethnicity. Because INRA asked for the country of ancestors, while Roper asked for the country of the respondent's grandparents, the Roper survey reported many more Protestants as simply "American" in background. Among Catholics, too, the Roper survey reported a smaller proportion with German or British ancestry than did the INRA survey. On the other hand, INRA's request for country of ancestors produced a large "don't know" or "no answer" group. About 20 per cent of the whites did not reply to the question.

Differences in attitude among the ethnic groups were more pronounced among Catholics than Protestants in both the Roper and the INRA studies.

Table 25.   RELATIONSHIP BETWEEN RELIGION AND ETHNIC BACKGROUND
AND ATTITUDES TO MCCARTHY
(Per Cent Difference between Approvers and Disapprovers)

Roper—1952	Number		INRA—1954	Number	
Catholics			*Catholics*		
4th Generation, America	(198)	—11	No Answer	(252)	— 2
Ireland	(81)	+18	Ireland	(545)	+ 5
Italy	(61)	+16	Italy	(393)	+ 8
Germany	(54)	+13	Germany and Austria	(424)	— 6
Great Britain	(13)	*	Great Britain	(272)	+ 4
Poland	(36)	— 6	Poland	(246)	— 2
Protestants			*Protestants*		
4th Generation, America	(1,190)	— 2	No Answer	(1,037)	—22
Ireland	(29)	+ 7	Ireland	(487)	—21
Germany	(172)	+ 2	Germany and Austria	(1,266)	—19
Great Britain	(102)	— 8	Great Britain	(1,814)	— 5
Scandinavia	(68)	— 3	Scandinavia and Holland	(851)	—25
Negroes	(252)	— 7	Negroes	(438)	—13
Jews	(96)	— 6	*Jews*	(245)	—54

* Too few cases for stable estimates.

In the Roper survey, Irish Catholics were 18 per cent more favorable to the Senator than unfavorable, while "old American" Catholics were 11 per cent more negative than positive. Among Protestants, on the other hand, those of German origin were the most pro-McCarthy (2 per cent), while those of British ancestry were most opposed (−8 per cent).

Results from both surveys show that Irish and Italian Catholics were among the most pro-McCarthy groups. The Roper data indicate that Germans, both Catholic and Protestant, were disproportionately in favor of McCarthy, but the INRA materials do not confirm this finding. The explanation for this seeming inconsistency may lie in the differing formulation of the questions on ethnicity. It may be that McCarthy appealed successfully to the "Roper" Germans whose families had emigrated to the United States within the past three generations and consequently retained emotional ties to Germany that made them receptive to McCarthy's isolationist appeal. "INRA" Germans are likely to have included many old-stock Americans who, like other "old American" groups, were predisposed to disapprove of the Wisconsin Senator.

The most recent effort, by Michael Rogin, to analyze the social sources of McCarthyism reiterates Polsby's suggestion that some interpretations of the sources of McCarthy's support are more clever than they have to be. To the proposition that anti-Communism was only a pretext for the release of personal anxieties, whether induced by status or other problems, he counterproposed that Communism and the cold war were themselves the core of the anxiety which McCarthy dramatized.[30] "To many Americans, especially those in the lower classes who were not actively in touch with events in the political world, McCarthy was simply fighting Communism. Support for McCarthy meant opposition to Communism."[31]

Rogin's empirical findings, derived from ecological analyses of voting returns, however, basically agree with most of the earlier efforts to locate the social bases of McCarthyism based on analyses of opinion surveys. Thus he also concludes that it is a mistake to see McCarthyite strength as rooted in the status-stricken or among the midwestern agrarian populists, and argues that it is to be seen more simply as a conservative Republican movement feeding on these prevalent anxieties about Communism and the Cold War.[32] Rogin agrees with Nelson Polsby and the Michigan Survey Research Center in emphasizing Republican support of McCarthy and with Samuel Lubell concerning the strong relationship of McCarthyism to anxieties about Communism and the Cold War. He also finds evidence to sustain the objections raised by the results of the survey research to the ascription of a literally direct line between McCarthyism and agrarian radicals in the Midwest. McCarthy did not receive the electoral support of the La Follette stream in Wisconsin politics. He first defeated Senator Robert La Follette, Jr. in 1946, and continued to face the opposition of

La Follette's followers in succeeding years. McCarthy did not receive the electoral support of agrarian radicals as such. His support in the Midwest came from the economic conservatives.

The agrarian radicalism of the Populist era had shifted, of course, to a dominant conservatism in the Midwest because of a change in the economic character of the area. This development underlines the split in the Republican party, a coalition of a certain kind of Republican conservatism in the Midwest and of a certain kind of Republican liberalism in the East. McCarthy's main support was among the conservative Republicans, though after the shock of Truman's victory in 1950, many liberal Republicans by and large were willing to tolerate him for the usual political reasons. After Eisenhower's victory in 1952, the liberal Republicans were the first to pull away from him. It is true that much of the midwestern conservatism and ethnic isolationism which entered the stream of McCarthyism was in areas which had historically been Populist and Progressive areas. But, as has already been pointed out, it is not so much a matter of an identity between the backers of these earlier agrarian movements or their ideological descendants and the supporters of McCarthy. It is simply that insofar as this midwestern political tradition was laced with such tendencies as opposition to the effete eastern elite, and attraction to the concept of direct democracy, it affected the nature of McCarthyism.

But, more important, the distinction must be made between support for McCarthy and for McCarthyism. Electoral endorsement for McCarthy and poll support for McCarthyism, which Rogin properly differentiates, are discrete entities. McCarthyism cannot be measured on an electoral basis. It was never a political movement; it was a political tendency, unorganized, activating certain impulses in a sympathetic audience, which had certain effects in areas of public life. McCarthy as an electoral figure appealed to Republicans, to barely enough of them usually to enable his election. His support of other politicians was no more potent than his own electoral appeal. The impulses of McCarthyism, which McCarthy indeed activated, were much more widespread. McCarthy, as the symbol of McCarthyism, had more appeal, but this did not necessarily lead to direct political support. McCarthy as an electoral figure never served the classic right-wing extremist function of uniting elite and popular support. But, for a time, and in a limited fashion, McCarthyism did. It united different segments of the population for their own reasons. Republicanism was only one of those reasons, although it may have been the main reason for voting for McCarthy himself. Anti-Communism, as a real reaction to the Cold War, was also just one of those reasons. There is no reason to believe that there was substantially less uneasiness about global Communism among those who opposed McCarthyism than among those who embraced it. As one observer notes:

Communism was clearly more than an ideological and a symbolic issue to Americans in the post-war decade. Soviet Russia existed as a very real counterpoise to the extension of American power and values throughout the world, and presence of the Red Army in Europe and new communist states in Europe and Asia were undeniable. Yet it was the symbolic "Communism" . . . rather than the realities of international politics, that the McCarthyites chose to confront.[33]

The point is that it was not *realpolitik* anti-Communism which McCarthyism traded in, but a kind of religious hysteria which was called anti-Communism and embodied a whole set of preservatist impulses. The two obviously were not unconnected; but among American anti-Communists, those subject to the latter hysteria were the most likely to become McCarthyites.

From a different vantage point, support for McCarthyism carried with it another significance: a certain tolerance for monism. It is not just that McCarthy supporters backed McCarthy, they did not react against his techniques. There is some indication that those who ranked high on an Authoritarian Personality Scale were more likely to support McCarthyism (See Table 26). But the largest differences in response to McCarthy, as

Table 26. RELATIONSHIP BETWEEN ATTITUDES TOWARD THE MCCARTHY COMMITTEE AND SCORE ON AN "AUTHORITARIAN PERSONALITY" SCALE WITHIN EDUCATIONAL GROUPINGS, 1953 (NORC)

Education and Authoritarianism	Per Cent Difference between Approvers and Disapprovers	Attitude toward McCarthy Committee (Per Cent)			
		Approve	Disapprove	Don't Know	Number
Grammar School					
High authoritarian	42	56	14	30	(183)
Middle	43	57	14	29	(229)
Low	28	44	16	39	(57)
High School					
High	68	78	10	12	(139)
Middle	49	65	16	19	(252)
Low	37	61	24	15	(188)
College					
High	75	85	10	5	(20)
Middle	46	66	20	14	(84)
Low	10	49	39	11	(132)

NOTE: High equals an authoritarian response on at least four items; medium means an authoritarian score on two or three items; low indicates no or one authoritarian response out of the five items.

related to the authoritarian scale, occurred among the college-educated. As various studies have indicated, this scale serves best as a predictor of attitude predispositions among the well educated. Among the less educated, a high authoritarianism score reflects in some part attitudes common to the group. However, in the context of these variables, and in the general context of opposition to Communism, the data indicate that some combination of three kinds of population groups were most prone to support McCarthy: (1) the economic conservatives; (2) the status-volatile; (3) the uneducated. Insofar as they were different groups, McCarthyism was able to bind them together for a while under the banner of a moralistic, monistic, conspiracy-style anti-Communism, which had different significances for them.

McCarthyism's Failure

McCarthy's *mariage de convenance* failed to create a political movement, however, and finally proved to have had little substance. Several factors seem to have been involved: (1) the absence of a program to engage the "mass man"; (2) the absence of a corporealized target; (3) the withdrawal of conservative party support.

McCarthy ended his career bitterly attacking the Republican party and its President. But the Republican administration had already abandoned him. He had performed his best function for them in identifying Communism with the Democratic party. His continued inquiries into the loyalties of government and armed forces agencies and personnel began to be considerably less helpful to the Republican party after it had assumed the stewardship of the government. A number of Republicans, including President Eisenhower, had been only tolerant of McCarthy, embarrassed by his excesses, but this toleration had become less needful and more costly. And the economic conservatives made the belated discovery that McCarthy was not a conservative after all. When he voted, he was as likely as not to vote for more public housing, more social security, more federal subsidies. But the main point was that his single-issue usefulness, that of diverting popular votes to the Republican party in the name of anti-Communism, had been reduced.

In 1950, when McCarthy began his crusade, the Republicans were still suffering from their unexpected defeat by Truman in 1948, and the future looked grim for their party. In 1952 the party swept back into power with Eisenhower, but McCarthy did not change his antielitist course. He took on both Eisenhower's State Department and Army. Spurred by the treatment—or the lack of preferential treatment—of an aid, David Schine, who had been drafted, McCarthy escalated an investigation of the Army into a major and decisive boomerang. Beginning an investigation of security measures at Fort Monmouth, he proceeded to publicly "discover" that the promotion of an Army dentist was an index to Communist infiltration of the Armed Services. In pursuance of this discovery, he publicly humiliated a General and demeaned the Secretary of the Army. The midwestern branch of the Republican party was still with him, but the eastern "establishment" wing of the Grand Old Party was now quite ready to abandon him as surely as it had elevated him. Vice-President Nixon, as part of the Republican establishment, maneuvered a head-on confrontation between the Army, which charged that McCarthy had used his position to get preferential treatment for his aid, and McCarthy, who claimed that the Army was just trying to impede an investigation. The hearing ran for thirty-five days on television, and as many as 20,000,000 Americans watched it at any given time. At the end of that hearing, the Senate appointed a Select Committee to investigate McCarthy's behavior on several counts, and as a result of that investigation, the Senate voted 67 to 22 to "condemn" McCarthy.

The Republican Senators divided evenly in the vote, with almost all of those from eastern states plus Michigan voting against McCarthy, while most of the members from the Midwest and far western states voted for him. The cleavage, in part, reflected the isolationist and China-oriented section of the party on one side and the internationalist wing on the other. From another perspective, it located the Senators with the closest ties to big business against McCarthy, and those coming from areas in which the party was influenced by less powerful business groups on his side.

The establishment Republicans had clearly lined up against him. McCarthy's chief armament had always been the fear to oppose him, especially on the part of public officials. These officials had the sense that while McCarthy had no organized movement, he had a strong following in the populace—a feeling which the polls corroborated. They had no confidence that there was an effective defense against his arbitrary accusations. When Eisenhower was campaigning in Wisconsin in 1952, he deliberately omitted friendly references to his old chief General Marshall, whom McCarthy had been violently attacking, lest McCarthy be offended. But, in a modern version of the tale of the Emperor's Clothes, when the Army-McCarthy hearings and the subsequent Senate action revealed that McCarthy had finally been deliberately confronted and faced down by the establishment (he was even barred from White House social events), the magical fear evaporated. It evaporated the more surely because the fight seemed to go out of McCarthy as a person after this series of events. He died three years later at the age of forty-eight without much further political ado.

But the turnabout of the conservative political party which had used an extremist instrument in classic fashion could not account for such a swift collapse of McCarthyism. And the fact that McCarthy developed no organizational apparatus to carry on his crusade was more than a personal quirk. The indication is that McCarthy had less of a political hold on the populace than he was credited with. It is not that he did not have a vast influence on the public, or that he did not continue to have a large measure of their support. Even after the Senate condemnation, 40 per cent of those with opinions supported him in the polls.[34] But the principle of *selective support* applied, and in this case the nature of the selectivity was limited to a single issue. At a time in 1953 when about half the American people said they "supported" or "approved" McCarthy in the opinion polls, only 5 per cent indicated in a Roper poll that they would vote for him for President on a "third party" ticket against Eisenhower and Stevenson. In the spring of 1954, a poll taken by the *Boston Post* reported that 40.5 per cent of Maine voters backed McCarthy, while 41.4 per cent were against him. The same poll, however, found that only 10.6 per cent of those interviewed were in favor of Robert L. Jones, a strong supporter of McCarthy's, who was running in the Maine Republican primary against Senator Margaret Chase Smith, a bitter public opponent of the Wisconsin Senator. The vast majority, 85.5 per cent, were for Senator Smith, and she was an easy victor in the primary.[35] Clearly, many who approved the Senator for his anti-Communist activities were not prepared to back him or candidates he favored in elections.

The greatest support for McCarthy recorded by the polls occurred when questions were phrased in terms of whether the respondents believed that McCarthy's allegations about Communists in government were true, or whether they approved of his efforts to eliminate Communists. But questions implying a more direct evaluation of the Senator himself—for example, how McCarthy's endorsement of a candidate would affect one's vote—produced a very different pattern of response. When attitude toward the existence of Communists in government was not involved, somewhere between 10 and 20 per cent were favorable, while about 30 to 40 per cent were opposed to him. Once in existence as a concept, McCarthyism became a much more salient issue to the liberal enemies of the Senator than to his conservative or militantly anti-Communist friends. The Communist issue apart, many more people reacted negatively to the mention of his name than positively. Consequently it would appear that McCarthy's support for a candidate was likely to mobilize more opposition than backing for him. According to the electoral analyst Louis Bean, in "all states where McCarthy pinpointed his charges against Democratic Senatorial candidates the Democratic candidate ran ahead of the general ticket."[36]

McCarthy's inability to develop a committed following points up the limitations of anti-Communism as an issue. There has always been opposition to Communism on the part of the vast majority of American people. But, as Stouffer has pointed out, the opinion surveys on the question have almost invariably indicated that "the internal threat of Communism has not been a matter of salient concern" among most of these people.[37] For some, particularly the uneducated, Communism did not have to be especially salient in order to accept McCarthyism as a means of combating it. However, their acceptance of McCarthyism did not mean that they had a prime allegiance to him as a political leader.

Even in the New Deal period, survey data indicated that the bulk of the population supported the outlawing of the Communist party and approved of the original House Committee on Un-American Activities, led by Martin Dies. In November 1937, 54 per cent of a national Gallup sample favored a law permitting the police to "padlock places printing Communist literature"; only 35 per cent opposed such a measure. In June 1938, 53 per cent of a national sample indicated they were against allowing Communists to hold meetings in their community, while only 35 per cent were willing to give Communists this right. In November 1939, 68 per cent were opposed to allowing "leaders of the Communist Party [to] make speeches to student groups," and only 24 per cent approved. In June of 1942, at a time when the Soviet Union was a military ally of the United States, 50 per cent favored a law outlawing membership in the Communist party, while 36 per cent were against the proposed act. A number of surveys that inquired in 1938 and 1939 whether respondents approved of continuing the Dies Committee reported approximately three-quarters in favor.[38]

Popular awareness of the international Communist threat undoubtedly increased in the late 1940's and early 1950's, with the advent of the Berlin blockade in 1948, the fall of China in 1949, and the outbreak of the Korean War in 1950, but public acceptance of civil liberties for Communists neither increased nor decreased. However, this never meant that anti-Communism was the most salient political issue for the majority of the American people. They were just against Communism, and to the extent that their commitment to and understanding of pluralism was dim, they saw nothing wrong with repressing radicalism even beyond Constitutional limits.

McCarthy's anti-Communism, McCarthyism, became more pertinent than usual for a large number of people not just because of McCarthy's personal demagogic talents but because he struck a nerve that was more than anti-Communist. His anti-Communism was a banner around which various segments of the population could marshal their preservatist discontents and their generalized uneasiness.

There can be little doubt that American apprehension about the Communist threat was enhanced by political events, specifically the Korean War, which began in 1950 and ended in 1954, the span of McCarthyism.

But McCarthy rarely discussed the military threat posed by Communist expansionism. Rather he argued in 1952: "There is only one real issue for the farmer, the laborer, and the businessman—the issue of Communism in government." And he disparaged American intervention in Korea, saying in 1951, "So the administration which would not fight Communism at home undertook to prove to the American people that it was willing to fight Communism abroad."[39]

McCarthy's main targets were never the North Korean or Chinese or Russian Communists—not even seriously, Communist spies in America—but rather the American establishment. This was the general target which so many Americans savored. From all evidence in the opinion polls, a sizable minority of them would have continued to use him as a way to voice their various preservatist sentiments, even after the Korean War ended; but there is no indication that they would have gone out of the way to make him their over-all political leader. The single issue was not enough; he had no political program to offer the mass populace—either the urban workers or the farmers. Leroy Gore, a Wisconsin weekly newspaper editor who had been an avid McCarthy supporter, explained his weakness in his home state by saying: "Few Wisconsin farmers have ever seen a Communist. Joe's Commie search is purely academic. . . . The price of milk isn't academic."[40]

While it was chiefly a bread-and-butter political program that McCarthy lacked, from a technical point of view his conspiracy theory was also faulty. The enemy was an ideology; and the closest McCarthy came to personifying a group as that enemy in America was his attack on the elite. Thus, in his Wheeling speech he said:

The reason we find ourselves in a position of impotency is not because our only potential enemy has sent men to invade our shores, but rather because of the traitorous actions of those who have been treated so well by this nation. It is not the less fortunate, or members of minority groups who have been selling this nation out, but rather those who have had all the benefits the wealthiest nation on earth has had to offer—the finest homes, the finest college educations, and the finest jobs in the government that we can give. This is glaringly true in the State Department. There the bright young men who are born with silver spoons in their mouth are the ones who have been worst.[41]

The attack on the elite recurred frequently in the writings of the extreme right. *The Freeman* magazine wrote that "Asian coolies and Harvard professors are the people . . . most susceptible to Red propaganda."[42] In discussing McCarthy's enemies, *The Freeman* stated: "He possesses, it seems, a sort of animal, negative-pole magnetism which repels alumni of Harvard, Princeton, and Yale. And we think we know what it is: *This young man is constitutionally incapable of deference to social status.*"[43]

This was antielitism, which would have an obvious appeal to the midwesterners and to the eastern urbanites of non-Anglo-Saxon extraction. Here was a prosperity-born equivalent for the economic radicalism of depressions. For the resentment created by prosperity is basically not against the economic power of Wall Street bankers or Yankees, but against their status power. Peter Viereck called this "the revenge of the noses that for 20 years of fancy parties were pressed against the outside window pane."[44]

However, the "elite" in this case was a blurred population group. At times, the attack was just a form of anti-intellectualism. McCarthy referred to the "twisted thinking intellectual" who had taken over the State Department.[45] When the *Facts Form* attacked the "enemy," it referred to "the socially pedigreed, the culturally acceptable, the certified gentlemen and scholars of the day, *dripping with college degrees. . . .*"[46] And this antielitism was also a kind of Anglophobia, itself a variant of isolationist sentiment in America.

But while there was a heavy emphasis on the individuals, traitors, and defectors being drawn from the Ivy League elite, they were finally *individual* traitors and defectors. This experiment of building a conspiracy theory without an ethnically (or economically) identifiable group did not seem to be successful. A singular difference between McCarthy and earlier extreme right-wing anti-Communists was his lack of interest in investigating or publicizing the activities of men who belonged to minority ethnic groups. For several decades the monistic impulse in America had concentrated on Jews as the group target of anti-Communism. But McCarthy did not; to the contrary, he relied heavily and publicly on several Jewish advisers, such as Roy Cohn and David Schine. The evidence of surveys further indicates that McCarthy's supporters were not any more anti-Semitic than his opponents.

The INRA preelection study in 1954 asked respondents whether they would be more or less likely to vote for a congressional candidate if they knew he was Jewish. About 3 per cent said they would be more likely to vote for a Jewish candidate; 17 per cent gave an anti-Semitic response, saying that they would be more likely to oppose a Jewish candidate; while the remaining four-fifths of the sample said knowledge of Jewish background would not affect their vote decision. Comparing the relationship between sentiments toward Jewish congressional candidates and attitudes to candidates who were pro- or anti-McCarthy produced the startling result that the small group of philo-Semites—those who were favorable to Jewish candidates—were much more likely to be pro-McCarthy than those who were against Jewish congressional candidates. The latter were also much more likely to be anti-McCarthy than those who said their vote would not be influenced by the candidate's being Jewish (Table 27).

Table 27. RELATIONSHIP BETWEEN ATTITUDES TOWARD JEWISH CONGRESSIONAL
CANDIDATE AND TOWARD MCCARTHY, 1954 (INRA) (JEWS OMITTED)

Attitude toward McCarthy	Attitudes toward a Jewish Candidate		
	More Likely to Vote for a Jew	Immaterial whether Jew or Not	More Likely to Vote against a Jew
Pro	26 %	16 %	12 %
Anti	29	30	38
Difference between Pro and Anti	—3	—14	—26
Number	(234)	(7,557)	(1,640)

This outcome is so surprising as to suggest the existence of an intervening factor associated with one or the other attitude so as to produce a spurious result. To check on such a possibility, the relationship between McCarthyism and anti-Semitism was analyzed within education groups and party-identification groups. The finding, however, still occurred in all. Among the college-educated, as among the high-school- or grammar-school-educated, the same pattern held up: the small per cent of those who were philo-Jewish were more pro-McCarthy. Catholics were less anti-Semitic than Protestants, but in both religious groups McCarthy support and anti-Semitism were inversely related. The relationship was also sustained in the three political categories of Democrats, Republicans, and Independents.

The lack of a positive relationship between McCarthyism and anti-Semitism may have reflected a more general absence of any relationship between ethnic prejudice and McCarthy support. A 1954 Gallup survey inquired, "Would you object to having your children attend a school where the majority of pupils are Negro?" Over half of the sample (about 55 per cent) indicated they would object. When the sample was divided between followers and opponents of McCarthy within educational categories, there was no consistent relationship between the willingness to send one's children to a predominantly Negro school and attitude toward McCarthy. The followers of the Senator were no more and no less liberal on this issue than his opponents.

But if these surveys challenge the liberal intellectual's belief that McCarthyites were generally intolerant people, there is some evidence to suggest that at least one type of anti-Semitism may have contributed to a small part of McCarthy's support. Data from the 1953 National Opinion Research Center (NORC) survey suggest that individuals who believed that Jews were disproportionately apt to be Communists were somewhat more likely to approve of the McCarthy Committee than those who did not mention Jews. This survey, taken early in the Senator's career as chairman of the Senate investigating committee on government operations, found that a majority (60 per cent) approved of his committee. Of the 8 per cent in the sample who mentioned Jews as being disproportionately Communist, 69 per cent approved of the committee, while among respondents who did not list Jews, 59 per cent reacted favorably to McCarthy. While the results differ from those found in the other surveys, further specification of the relationship within social categories reduces their significance as indicators of greater anti-Semitic sentiments among McCarthyites. When elementary-school-, high-school-, and college-educated respondents are examined separately, the relationship holds among those who did not go beyond elementary school. Of this low-educated group, those who were pro-McCarthy more often mentioned Jews as being Communist than did those who were anti-McCarthy. Within the category of the high-school-educated, there was no relationship between propensity to identify Jews with Communists and attitudes toward the McCarthy Committee, while among the college-educated the relationship was reversed. In this stratum, presumably the best informed of the three, the anti-McCarthy group more often saw Jews as disproportionately Communist.

The four surveys are not directly comparable, of course, for many reasons. Cohn and Schine were not an issue when the 1953 NORC interviews were taken, but had become a major source of controversy by the time of the 1954 studies, at which period McCarthy had lost considerable support. More important perhaps is the fact that the studies were asking very different questions. The 1954 surveys were touching on general attitudes toward Jews, while the 1953 poll was tapping the reactions of the very small group who see Jews as more Communistically inclined than non-Jews. Most of the respondents felt that "only a few" Jews are Communists. In fact, studies of the social base of American Communism indicate that while the overwhelming majority of Jews have opposed Communism, Jews have contributed disproportionately to the support of the American Communist party.[47] Those, therefore, who mention Jews as Communists may be reflecting greater knowledge and concern about Communism rather than anti-Semitism as such.

Analysis of other data in the 1953 NORC survey tends to sustain the interpretation that the fact that McCarthy supporters were more likely to mention Jews as disproportionately Communist reflects concern with the Communist issue rather than anti-Semitism. Respondents were asked whether they had heard any criticism of Jews in the last six months. About one-fifth, 21 per cent, reported that they had heard such criticism. Those whose acquaintances included critics of Jews were proportionately *less* favorable to McCarthy than those who did not report hearing anti-Semitic remarks. The respondents mentioned the specific types of attacks they had heard. These break down into a variety of criticisms of Jews as having too much political or economic power, being unscrupulous in business, being socially clannish, and those involving charges that Jews are more likely than others to be Communists, or spies and traitors. Most of the anti-Jewish criticisms reported, however, did not concern Communism or spying. Individuals who mentioned hearing anti-Semitic comments not involving Communism were most likely of all to be anti-McCarthy, while the small group that mentioned having heard that Jews were Communists tended to show a larger than average support for the Wisconsin Senator. These results suggest that "normal anti-Semitic" stereotypes—that is, those concerning presumed negative Jewish economic or social traits—were more common in the social environment of people who were against the Senator than of those who were for him.

What we know about these anti-Semitic stereotypes is that they are more prevalent—an indeed still quite common—among the less educated. McCarthy never did *engage* the mass man with his single-issue Communism. He did not have a social program to engage him with. Nor did he move programmatically to engage and activate his prejudices.

Peter Viereck has suggested a phenomenon of "transtolerance," which deserves more attention than it has received.

> Transtolerance is ready to give all minorities their glorious democratic freedom —provided they accept McCarthyism or some other mob conformism of Right or Left. . . . "Right" and "Left" are mere fluctuating pretexts, mere fluid surfaces for the deeper anti-individualism (anti-aristocracy) of the mass man. . . .
> Transtolerance is also a sublimated Jim Crow: against "wrong" thinkers, not "wrong" races. . . . [I]t is the Irishman's version of Mick-baiting and a strictly kosher anti-Semitism. It very sincerely champions against anti-Semites "that American Dreyfus, Roy Cohn"; simultaneously it glows with the same mob emotions that in all previous or comparable movements have been anti-Semitic.[48]

In effect, Viereck is saying that the object of intolerance in America has never been as important as the style, the emotion, the antagonism, the envy toward some specified other who is seen as wealthier, more powerful, or particularly as a corrupter of basic values.

Thus "bigots" are able to overlook the traditional target characteristics of their bigotry, such as skin color or religion or ethnic identification, if those who bear these characteristics share important values with the bigots and are not the *real* sources of the bigots' discontent. This is, of course, another approach to stating the concept that bigotry is typically not the prime source of political behavior in the modern world, but more often its aftertrail, its baggage. Bigotry, as a politically active phenomenon, is backlash targetry. Whether McCarthy's supporters were more or less anti-Semitic in their traditional stereotypes was not so important; neither were Coughlin's; neither, insofar as we know, were Hitler's. What was important was that McCarthy did not invoke the Jews—or any other clear-cut population group—in his attempts to construct a conspiracy theory. If he had, as later discussion will suggest, he might well have drawn many of his supporters in accepting some version of political anti-Semitism, whatever their traditional attitudes toward Jews might have been.

He might have been able to do so, that is, if he had a solid mass of political supporters gathered around a salient and broadly gauged program. The indication is that, with his single issue, he did not have that kind of political program, support, or movement. In any case, he did not attempt to activate any traditional bigotries. It would not have been an opportune time for a national political figure to focus on ethnic bigotry so soon after World War II, which had embodied an American crusade against racism abroad, but there is no indication that McCarthy had any inclination toward such a focus.

After McCarthy's personal political collapse, there was evidence that some of McCarthyism's fringe forces would have liked to remedy this flaw in the conspiracy theory. A hastily organized committee calling itself Ten Million Americans Mobilizing for Justice rallied to McCarthy's defense and held a Madison Square Garden rally in November of 1954.

The more respectable elements of America's politically conservative community were absent. And James Rorty, reporting the presence at the meeting of such people as the dean of American anti-Semitism, Gerald L. K. Smith, also indicated that the conspiracy note began to sound more traditional, as Admiral Crommelein referred to "some hidden force or hidden power. . . ." And Rorty commented:

So far as the record shows, Admiral Crommelein has never exhibited anti-Semitic tendencies. [Actually he is a vitriolic anti-Semite.] The same can scarcely be said for General del Valle and other sponsors of Ten Million Americans, who in the past have been closely associated with Merwin K. Hart, Allen A. Zoll, Joseph P. Kamp, and other agitators for whom the Hidden Force is just an Aesopian euphemism for that myth of an international Jewish Communist conspiracy which is their theme.[49]

But these vestiges, which perhaps had once been imbedded as fragments in McCarthyism, were now isolated and could have no political effect. In both its failure as a durable political movement and in its considerable successes as a kind of hysteria, McCarthyism had demonstrated again, and under new circumstances, the kinds of ingredients that are necessary in America to create a viable extremist movement—and the serious potential for a monistic movement that still existed in this country if the proper ingredients were to combine.

Notes

1. U.S. Bureau of the Census, *Historical Statistics of the U.S. Colonial Times to 1957* (Washington: U.S. Government Printing Office, 1958), p. 166; U.S. Bureau of the Census, *Statistical Abstract of the United States, 1968* (Washington: U.S. Government Printing Office, 1968), pp. 312, 319.
2. Edward A. Shils, *The Torment of Secrecy* (Glencoe: The Free Press, 1956), p. 92.
3. *Time*, February 20, 1950, p. 13.
4. Samuel Lubell, *The Future of American Politics* (New York: Harper, 1952), p. 132.
5. Quoted in Richard Rovere, *Senator Joe McCarthy* (New York: Meridian, 1960), p. 125.
6. Edna Lonergan, "Anatomy of the PAC," *The Freeman*, I (November 27, 1950), 137–139.
7. Joseph R. McCarthy, *America's Retreat from Victory* (Boston: Western Islands, 1965), pp. 135–136. Originally published by Devin-Adair, New York, 1951.
8. Rovere, *op. cit.*, p. 145.
9. *Ibid.*, p. 179.
10. See Michael Paul Rogin, *The Intellectuals and McCarthy: The Radical Spectre* (Cambridge: M.I.T. Press, 1967); also Karl Ernest Meyer, *The Politics of Loyalty: From La Follette to McCarthy in Wisconsin, 1918–1952* (Ph.D. Thesis, Princeton University, 1956).
11. *Ibid.*, p. 184.
12. Shils, *op. cit.*, p. 99.
13. Quoted in Peter Viereck, *The Unadjusted Man* (Boston: Beacon, 1956), p. 132.
14. Joseph R. McCarthy, "America's Retreat from Victory," *Congressional Record*, Thursday, June 14, 1951, 9A Reprint, p. 1.
15. *Ibid.*, p. 3.
16. Quoted in Norman Graebner, *The New Isolationism* (New York: Ronald, 1956), p. 26.
17. William E. Jenner, "Let's Put America First," *Facts Forum News*, August 1955, p. 5.
18. *Time*, October 22, 1951, p. 22.
19. Rovere, *op. cit.*, p. 52.
20. Allen Drury, "Knowland Denies Any Peiping 'Deal,' " *New York Times*, August 2, 1955, pp. 4, 1.
21. Jack Anderson and Roland W. May, *McCarthy, the Man, the Senator, the Ism* (Boston: Beacon, 1952), p. 364.
22. *Congressional Record*, 81st Congress, 2nd Session (February 20, 1950), p. 1954.
23. Neil J. Smelser, *The Theory of Collective Behavior* (New York: The Free Press, 1963), p. 84.

24. James Rorty, "The Anti-Communism of Senator McCarthy," *Commentary*, XVI (August 1953), 124.

25. James Rorty, "The Attack on Our Libraries," *Commentary*, XIX (June 1955), 451.

26. Nelson W. Polsby, "Towards an Explanation of McCarthyism," *Political Studies*, VIII (October 1960), 250–271.

27. To answer this and other questions concerning McCarthy's support, we reanalyzed the data from four surveys and would like to acknowledge our gratitude to those who conducted these surveys for permission to use their data. These surveys are: a Roper study of 3,000 respondents made in May 1952; an eleven-state survey taken by International Research Associates (I.N.R.A.) in August–September 1954, three months before the Senate censured Senator McCarthy; the 1954 election survey of the University of Michigan's Survey Research Center, cited earlier; and a study conducted by the Gallup organization in December 1954, after McCarthy had been censured by the Senate, asking a national sample its opinion of the censure. The I.N.R.A. survey presented the analytical advantage of furnishing the largest sample, since it had been designed to report opinion in eleven states—California, Illinois, Ohio, Michigan, Minnesota, Massachusetts, Iowa, New Mexico, Oregon, Pennsylvania, and New Jersey. The total sample was 9,852. While this survey cannot be considered as representative of the national population, there seems no good reason to assume that subgroup variations (for example, religion, education, party, and so on) in these eleven states were not characteristic of reactions to McCarthy generally. One of its questions concerning reactions to McCarthy was identical with that of the University of Michigan's national study, and the distribution of replies was almost the same.

28. See Robert Sokol, *Rank Inconsistency and McCarthyism: An Empirical Test* (unpublished paper, Dartmouth College).

29. *Ibid.*

30. Rogin, *op. cit.*, p. 247.

31. *Ibid.*, p. 244.

32. Since Rogin devotes much of his book to an attack on Lipset and other contributors to Daniel Bell, ed., *The Radical Right* (Garden City: Doubleday-Anchor, 1964), for emphasizing McCarthy's direct links to populism, and underestimating his strength among conservatives, it would seem appropriate to quote from a summary of Lipset's empirical findings published in that work. "From a political standpoint, he [McCarthy] recruited more heavily from the conservative groups, from Republicans, backers of right-wing policies on domestic issues, isolationists, and those most concerned with the need for a 'tough' anti-Russian policy. . . . The studies analyzed here do not validate the assumption [concerning the impact of status strains] with respect to objective sources of status strain (high education and low economic position, for example). The evidence bearing on the belief that McCarthy appealed to the traditional 'populist' ideology, directed against organized labor and big business, also produces contradictory or ambiguous results." Lipset, "Three Decades of the Radical Right," in Bell, *op. cit.*, p. 420.

33. Les K. Adler, "The Red Menace Revisited," *Continuum*, VI (Autumn 1968), 313.

34. Rogin, *op. cit.*, p. 232.
35. See John Francis Beatty, III, *Senator Joseph McCarthy: Sources of Support* (undergraduate Honors Thesis, Department of Government, Harvard University, 1969), Chapter 4, p. 5.
36. Louis Bean, *Influences in the 1954 Mid-Term Elections* (Washington: Public Affairs Institute, 1954), p. 18; see also Polsby, *op. cit.*, p. 268.
37. Samuel A. Stouffer, *Communism, Conformity and Civil Liberties* (New York: John Wiley, 1966), p. 86.
38. Hadley Cantril, *Public Opinion, 1935–1946* (Princeton: Princeton University Press, 1951), pp. 130, 164, 244.
39. Rovere, *op. cit.*, p. 41.
40. Meyer, *op. cit.*, p. 235.
41. *Congressional Record*, 81st Congress, 2nd Session (February 20, 1950), p. 1954.
42. *The Freeman*, I (October 2, 1950), 13.
43. *The Freeman*, II (November 5, 1951), 72. Our emphasis.
44. Peter Viereck, "The Revolt against the Elite," in Bell, *op. cit.*, p. 162.
45. *Congressional Record*, 81st Congress, 2nd Session (February 26, 1950), p. 1958.
46. *Facts Forum*, Radio Program No. 57. Our emphasis.
47. Nathan Glazer, *The Social Basis of American Communism* (New York: Harcourt, Brace, 1961), pp. 130–168.
48. Viereck, "The Revolt . . . ," pp. 168–169.
49. James Rorty, "What Price McCarthy Now?" *Commentary*, XIX (January 1955), 33.

7

The Era of the John Birch Society

The John Birch Society, created in 1958 by Robert Welch, took the center of the right-wing stage in America for close to a decade. It combined two preservatist traditions: the economic class conservatism of the Liberty League and the symbolic "anti-Communism" of McCarthy.

The historical context was, on the one hand, the growing uneasiness of the American people in the face of gathering changes on the domestic front—the initial civil rights revolution was in full flower; and on the other hand, the fact that a Republican administration had been in power for six years without serving the serious preservatist interests of economic ultra-conservatives. It was the latter circumstance in which the Birch Society was most firmly anchored.

Antistatism

One of the twin centers of Birch ideology is antistatism. A Massachusetts businessman who retired to devote himself to his cause, Welch believes that government intervention in the affairs of man is bad: "Reduce all of the governments of all the nations of the world to one third of their present size . . . and you would immediately accomplish two things—you would reduce the likelihood and destructiveness of war by one ninth. The greatest enemy of man is, and always has been, government; and the larger, the more extensive that government, the greater the enemy."[1] The antagonism to government is pointed up in Welch's assumption that public authority, as contrasted with private institutions, is inherently corrupt. "For all governments with very rare exceptions indeed, are thoroughly dishonest."[2] In spite of this belief, however, Welch and other Birch Society publicists have attacked various politicians for immoral practices. The theme of corruption in government is a fairly constant one.

The Society emphasizes individualism and local government. In the ideal future, men "must be self-reliant. There are no grants from a Ford Foundation there, no government subsidies; . . . no civil rights."[3] "The history of liberty . . . is very much the history of local self-government; despotism can come only when local self-government is destroyed."[4] In general, the Society espouses a domestic program which would be familiar to any reader of ultraconservative publications. It strongly opposes the income tax and cooperates with the Liberty Amendment Committee, which seeks to get state legislatures to pass resolutions calling for a Constitutional Amendment to repeal the Income Tax Amendment. In 1966, the Society created a special front group for this purpose, the Organization for Repeal of the Federal Income Tax (ORFIT). Efforts to extend the welfare state such as "Medicare" are frequently targets for attack.

This aspect of Birch Society doctrine does not distinguish it, in substance, from other conservative groups. In the year of the Birch Society's birth, about 30 billion dollars were being spent by American governments for social welfare purposes. Whereas before the war there had been fewer than a million federal civilian employees, there were now well over two and a half million. Government taxes, bureaus, regulations, were maintained at a high level. And, most bitter to the hard-line conservatives, the accession of the Republicans to the White House did not result in any serious alteration of the welfare state.

In his 1954 message to Congress on the State of the Union, President Eisenhower said, "In a modern industrial society, banishment of destitution and cushioning the shock of personal disaster on the individual are proper concerns of all levels of government, including the federal government." The conservative backlash against the welfare state became more pronounced during these years with the failure of the Republican party to reverse the trend.

In the same year as the Birch Society was created, so was the Americans for Constitutional Action, designed for political education against "compulsory participation in Social Security, mandatory wage rates, compulsory membership in labor organizations, fixed rent controls, restrictions on choice of tenants and purchasers of one's property," and in favor of "progressive repeal of the socialistic laws now on our books."[5] And these years saw the development of the conservative periodical, *The National Review*, whose editor, William Buckley, wrote that the conservative mandate was "to maintain and wherever possible enhance the freedom of the individual to acquire property and dispose of that property in ways that he decides on."[6]

Conspiracy Theory

But while these conservative agencies, like the Liberty League before them, were vehemently anti-Communist and anti-internationalist and often hinted at skulduggery, they did not espouse a comprehensive conspiracy theory, the second ideological center of the Birch Society.

Welch recounts how he began to wonder why Eisenhower had helped destroy Senator McCarthy, made peace with the Communists in Korea, refused to support anti-Communist movements in Indochina, Berlin, Hungary, and other places, and extended the welfare statist policies introduced by left-wing Democratic regimes. Ultimately, he concluded that the only plausible explanation of such behavior was that Eisenhower was a Communist, or the dupe of the Communists.[7]

At first blush, Welch seems to have developed since then the very model of a conspiracy theory. His theory is, to begin with, grandly comprehensive in design; it stretches back in time and is global in nature. The conspiracy he projects is decisive for the important historical events and involves the secret manipulation of the pliant many by the evil few.

In the upper circles of this conspiracy, there is no slightest trace of noble purpose, or of the misguided idealism by which members of the lower echelons are sometimes deceived. There is only sordid self-interest of the most Faustian variety. For two centuries ruthlessly ambitious criminals, whom we shall call the *Insiders*, have been helping themselves, and each other to the prestige and wealth and power which were the only real objectives of their lives. They have been held together in all of these activities, however, and their efforts have been given coherence and direction, by their concerted dedication to the ultimate goal of world leadership for the *Insiders* of a later day. And that day is now almost upon us.

Already, by the time of Disraeli, he could safely boast a hundred years ago that the world was ruled by far different masters and means than were recognized by the masses. . . . In our task of exposing and opposing this gigantic and deep-rooted conspiracy, therefore, it is necessary to keep in mind just how diabolic, how far-reaching, and how all-inclusive are the tactics by which this strategy of world conquest is being carried out. Current examples include operations so diverse in scale and type and method as the following: (1) The cruel buildup of a third World War, controlled on both sides by the Communists; (2) the promotion of racial turmoil and riots in the United States; (3) the deliberate undermining of the American dollar; (4) the creation of the "hippie" mentality on our campuses; (5) the spread of pornographic filth throughout every cultural medium; (6) the encouragement of crime and protec-

tion of criminals by our Supreme Court; (7) the acceptance of known sexual
perverts as leaders of important organizations; (8) the claim of the government's right to lie to the public whenever it considers falsehood desirable; (9)
the pushing forward of the blasphemous theme that "God is dead"; (10) the
weakening of the family as a basic and dependable unit in the structure of
society; and (11), the open advocacy of foul means to obtain supposedly
desirable objectives.[8]

While the conspiracy is global, Welch concentrates on its American aspects,
on the underground conspiracy which supposedly dominates American life.

American Opinion, the Birch Society monthly organ, and its other publications have repeatedly carried stories which contend that both major
parties and various other national institutions such as large segments of
the Protestant churches, trade-unions, and universities are controlled by
Communist and other conspirators. The Birch Society periodically publishes
lists reporting on the strength of Communists around the world. Such lists
invariably place the United States as between 60 and 80 per cent under
Communist control. The Society sees all recent American Presidents as
having worked in the interests of the Communists and regards the American
government as honeycombed with Communist agents. Even the wars
against Communist forces in Korea and Vietnam are regarded as efforts
consciously designed to facilitate the growth of Communist power. The
Birch Society contends that in both cases, the United States has been
pursuing a "no win" policy; that is, that the American military forces have
been deliberately prevented from defeating the enemy. General Mac-
Arthur is one of the heroes in the Society's annals for having sought to
win in Korea. Presidents Truman and Eisenhower are charged with a
deliberate refusal to defeat Communism. Similarly, the Society argues that
Presidents Johnson and Nixon and their civilian colleagues have not wanted
to defeat the Viet Cong and the North Vietnamese. Rather they have been
engaged in a "phony war" against Communism designed to facilitate the
communization of the United States. Engagement in armed conflict serves
to justify the increased socialization of the United States as necessary for
the war effort. It has even been suggested that Vietnam has been primarily
used as a depot for transferring American supplies to Communist Asia.[9]

Identification of Conspirators

While the conspiracy theory of the Birch Society is more highly developed
than that of Senator Joseph McCarthy, it still faces the chief technical
problem of conspiracy theories: how to identify a corps of conspirators who
are esoteric and mysterious enough to make their comprehensive power
credible and yet concrete enough to make their existence visible to a mass

audience. In a way, the very enthusiasm and vastness of Welch's conspiracy theory compound this problem. Communism is sometimes used as another generic term for the total conspiracy; but as a specific phenomenon related to Moscow or Peking, it can only serve as a related subplot. The conspiracy, after all, predates Marx and Lenin and is larger than the boundaries of Marxist ideology.

Rather, Robert Welch accepts and propagates as official Birch Society doctrine the belief that the conspiracy of the Illuminati is the main source of the plot against American liberties. The Illuminati were seemingly first introduced to Welch and the Birch Society by Revilo Oliver, then a member of the Society's National Council and associate editor of *American Opinion*, in an article published in that journal in June 1962, in which he referred to the Weishaupt Illuminati. Welch took up the theme in a speech delivered in Chicago in June 1964, which was later published in part in *American Opinion*. In this talk, Welch described in detail the activities of the Illuminati in Europe in the late eighteenth century, quoting from the writings of Adam Weishaupt. He even repeated the charges, almost two centuries old, that Weishaupt had seduced the sister of another leader of the Illuminati and then had her murdered. He suggests that his "researches" point to the conclusion that Karl Marx wrote the Communist Manifesto as an agent employed by a branch of the Illuminati.

It could easily be that the League of Just Men [which supposedly employed Marx to write the Manifesto] was just a division of the Illuminati; that Karl Marx and, after him, Trotsky and Lenin and Stalin and Malenkov, and deGaulle and Castro and Nehru and Betancourt, and hundreds of other leftist leaders elsewhere throughout the world, and a dozen in this country whom we had better leave unnamed, have all been working for such an inner group, or in some cases, have been members of it.[10]

Welch returned to this theme in even greater detail in an article published in the November 1966 issue of *American Opinion*, which has since been reprinted as a separate pamphlet and widely distributed. He argues for the existence of a continuing conspiracy from 1776 to the present, whose aim "always has been, and still is, to impose the brutal tyranny of their rule over the whole human race."[11] In it Welch outlines the now familiar story of the Illuminati conspiracy which was involved in "planning and precipitating the holocaust known as the French Revolution." The works of Robison and Abbé Barruel, first brought to the attention of Americans by Jedidiah Morse at the end of the eighteenth century, are cited as sources for the activities of the Illuminati in this period.

In 1967, the Birch Society actually reprinted John Robison's *Proofs of a Conspiracy*, first published in 1797. The Introduction presents the book as one which accurately describes "the origin of history's most diabolical, long-range conspiracy."[12] This same conspiracy "now, has the world almost completely within its grasp."[13]

Welch indeed draws a straight line of Illuminati conspiracy between the fall of the Bastille in Paris in 1789 and the "Poor People's March" in Washington in 1968:

> Obviously we cannot go plunging all over the landscape, or delving into all the activities of the Society [the Illuminati], for revealing items of evidence. . . . We shall simply confine our argument to a comparative discussion of two events. One was the siege and fall of the Bastille in Paris in July, 1789. The other was the "Poor People's March" on Washington in 1968. . . . They were both planned by the same breed of conspirators, for almost identically the same purpose. . . .
>
> It took tremendous effort and expense, and a lot of cunning and planning, on the part of these Insiders, to foment the march of a huge mob on the Bastille, and make its capture look like the spontaneous action of an outraged people. . . .
>
> There is no doubt that the recent *Poor March* on Washington was originally planned to be as dramatic and useful an incident for their purposes as the siege and capture of the Bastille had been in 1789. Nor is there any doubt that the planning and organization behind this *Poor March* was tremendously more extensive and expensive than had been behind the attack on the Bastille.[14]

The Illuminati are credited with founding the Communist conspiracy in the nineteenth century and with being behind it ever since.

> But the Communist movement is only a tool of the total conspiracy. As secret as the Communist activities and organizations generally appear, they are part of an open book compared to the secrecy enveloping some higher degree of this diabolic force. The extrinsic evidence is strong and convincing that by the beginning of the *Twentieth* Century there had evolved an inner core of conspiratorial power, able to direct and control subversive activities which were worldwide in their reach, incredibly cunning and ruthless in their nature, and brilliantly farsighted and patient in their strategy.[15]

The Illuminati, referred to also as the Insiders, are credited with being responsible for all actions designed to "reduce the responsibilities and rights of individual citizens while steadily increasing the quantity, the reach, and the potential tyranny of governments."[16] They have been behind "everything in the way of 'security' legislation, from the first Workman's Compensation Acts under Bismarck to the latest Medicare monstrosity under Lyndon Johnson." Among their accomplishments in the United States "have been centralized banking, a graduated *personal income tax, and the direct election of Senators.*"[17]

In their struggle for power, the Illuminati have followed the strategy of divide and rule. Thus they have sought to divide mankind in conflicts along religious, racial, ethnic, and national lines and have often been on "both sides of all such bitter divisions among mankind." They are behind the racial conflicts going on today.[18] The Insiders are then credited with being responsible for both World Wars, for the Russian Revolution, for the expansion of Communism after World War II, for the breakup of the colonial empires, and for the formation of the United Nations.[19] In the United States today, the Insiders are destroying religious influence, indoctrinating the youth through their control over education and the communication and entertainment media "in a preference for 'welfare' and 'security' against responsibility and opportunity," constantly increasing government power, "destroying the power of the local police to preserve law and order," creating riots and revolutionary movements among Negroes, and "carrying on and steadily 'escalating' a completely phony foreign war in Vietnam (because the Communists are actually running both sides of it), as an excuse for gradually establishing more and tighter controls over every detail of our daily lives."[20]

The Insiders-Illuminati (a phrase which Welch uses) are also charged with a series of assassinations against their opponents. Since the Illuminati conspiracy is so secret, the Illuminati seek above all to prevent people from learning of their existence and power. Their methods run from ridicule to murder.

The controlling order, which we have dubbed THE INSIDERS, has given more attention and ruthless enforcement to keeping its very existence a secret than to any other objective in the whole *satanic* program. Anybody who even starts to point out the truth is mercilessly ridiculed as a believer in the "conspiratorial theory of history"; and anybody who approaches too close to an authoritative exposure of the higher levels of the conspiracy meets the fate of a *William Morgan*, a Dr. William Wirt, or a Joe McCarthy—a fate which is visibly intended for ourselves.[21]

The linkage of William Morgan, Dr. William Wirt, and Joe McCarthy, as three Americans who were killed for trying to expose the conspiracy, points up the continuity of the opposition with which Welch historically identifies. William Morgan, of course, was the member of the Masons who supposedly was about to publish a book in 1826 exposing the hidden activities of the Masonic Order, when he was kidnaped and presumably murdered by a band of Masons in upstate New York. His death led to the emergence of the Anti-Masonic party, a movement which Robert Welch presumably identifies as a predecessor of the John Birch Society (much as Henry Ford saw it as an early effort to resist the Elders of Zion). There are two men named William Wirt in American political history. The first was the Presidential candidate on the Anti-Masonic ticket in 1832. The one to whom Welch is referring, however, is probably a descendant, who went to Washington in the early days of the New Deal. Wirt once reported that he had been present at a dinner party of leading New Deal civil servants who spoke of Roosevelt as the American Kerenski and discussed their plans for an ultimate Communist takeover. He testified to this effect before a congressional committee and was denounced and ridiculed in the liberal press. There are frequent references in extreme right-wing journals to the supposed murders of Senator Joseph McCarthy and other conservatives and right-wingers. Welch himself wrote in 1959:

We don't know whether the peculiar cancer of which Bob Taft died was induced by a radium tube planted in the upholstery of his Senate seat, as has been so widely rumored. . . . We don't know whether John Peurifoy was actually so reckless a driver that he met his death as a result, on a little travelled road in Siam. We don't even *know* that James Forrestal did *not* commit suicide. But we do know something about the law of probability, when applied to so many unusual fatalities. We also know that there will be no proper investigation of even the most recent of these mysterious deaths, under the present [Eisenhower] Communist-infested administration.[22]

Efforts to link McCarthy's death with the Illuminati have been frequent in right-wing exposés of the secret Order. William Guy Carr, soon after McCarthy's death in 1957, suggested that he had been a victim of "the continuing Luciferian conspiracy," that he had been killed because he had discovered, as Welch suggests, that the Illuminati control Communism. Carr argued:

1. McCarthy was allowed to run "Hog Wild" just as long as he named those he accused of subversion as being Communists or pro-Communists. It was not until he had been informed that the Illuminati controlled international Communism AT THE TOP that he was forced into political eclipse.
2. Pressure was released when he appeared to accept defeat submissively. But when he explained to others, who took his place, how Weishaupt in 1776, and Pike in 1871, had laid down how Atheistic-Communism was to be used by the Illuminati to further THEIR secret plans and ambitions, then those who are "The Secret Power" behind the scenes of our elected governments, apparently decided it was time he was eliminated.[23]

But the Insiders-Illuminati being such a mysterious historical entity, and the Communists having been rendered of a vague metaphysical piece with them, who *are* the conspirators in America in fact and concrete image? Welch's specific identifications begin with political figures. The Insiders are able to have their way because they "now have working control over our government. . . ."[24] But Welch is again trapped by the grandness of his conspiratorial design. Almost no major leader of either party is spared implication in the conspiracy. President Roosevelt is accused of "deliberate treason" for supposedly consciously encouraging the Japanese attack on Pearl Harbor.[25] "George Marshall always conducted the American side of the war [World War II] for the benefit of the Kremlin. . . . Since sometime in the 1930's George C. Marshall has been a conscious, deliberate, dedicated agent of the Soviet conspiracy."[26] The Truman administration was "Communist dominated."[27] "Truman was passively *used* by the Communists, with his knowledge and acquiescence, as the price he consciously paid for their making him President."[28]

In the first private edition of *The Politician*, Robert Welch stated, "My firm belief that Dwight Eisenhower is a dedicated, conscious agent of the Communist conspiracy is based on an accumulation of detailed evidence so extensive and so palpable that it seems to me to put this conviction beyond any reasonable doubt."[29] This statement, together with others, was dropped from the public version published in 1963, but the latter still includes the statement that Eisenhower has been "consciously serving the Communist conspiracy, for all his adult life."[30] His brother Milton was described in the private version as his supervisor in the Communist movement and in the public one as his "superior and boss within the whole Leftwing Establishment."[31]

Welch reports his personal conviction that John Foster Dulles was "a Communist agent who has had one clearly defined role to play; namely, always to say the right things and always do the wrong ones."[32] Allen Dulles, in his capacity as head of the CIA, is described as "the most protected and untouchable supporter of Communism, next to Eisenhower, himself, in Washington."[33] Earl Warren is "at least an extreme left-wing socialist."[34] Articles in *American Opinion*, the main public organ of the Society, and in the Society's *Bulletin* have continued similar emphases with regard to high-ranking personnel in the Kennedy, Johnson and Nixon administrations. The three Presidents have been repeatedly attacked as being dupes of the Communists. The Bay of Pigs episode has been presented as a deliberate effort to protect Fidel Castro. As was noted earlier, American participation in the Vietnam War is viewed as being intended to facilitate the socialization of the United States, rather than defeating Communism. Following the Kennedy assassination, Revilo Oliver, then a member of the National Council of the Birch Society, wrote in *American Opinion* that Kennedy had been assassinated by the Communists because he was about to "turn American."[35]

Welch has posed a theory of "alternating strategy" used by the Insiders-Illuminati to explain the "Tweedledum-Tweedledee" characterization of Republican and Democratic leaders which he shares, of course, with left-wing conspiracy theorists.

During a long stretch under Roosevelt and Truman [the Insiders] used their influence to move us steadily and directly down the road to Communism. . . .

Then a growing awareness among the American people of what was really happening brought a rising revulsion against the whole Communist program. So the *Insiders* went through the proper motions, and put their reverse strategy to work.

For the next eight years, under Eisenhower, the movement into Communism was carried out more subtly, in the guise of opposing it. The Administration was constantly yielding to some part of some Communist-inspired demand, as the lesser of two evils. . . . In time the anti-Communist fervor of the American people . . . was dissipated . . . by this unceasing deception. . . . So the *Insiders* turned the switch again, and went back to their forward strategy. During the next eight years, under Kennedy and Johnson, we have seen measures that lead to total government. . . . But by the end of these eight years a new understanding, new revulsion and new determination were arising. . . . And it was time once more for the *Insiders* to go back to their strategy of reversal. . . .

In this next—and perhaps final—period of Armageddon, the *Insiders* wish above all to avoid precipitating too soon, in the United States, any open and determined revolt on the part of anti-Communists. . . . So the *Insiders* think they can accomplish far more for the Communist movement, *far more safely,* with an Eisenhower-type administration, this time under Richard Nixon, than they could with a Kennedy or a Humphrey as president.[36]

Antielitism

This broad-brushing of politicians, who emerge as puppet figures, leaves the identification of the Insiders still indistinct. Like the right-wing extremist movements that preceded it, and despite the fact that it is led by relatively wealthy heads of family-owned corporations (Welch was once a Board member of the National Association of Manufacturers), the Birch Society maintains a strong streak of antielitism. In words reminiscent of McCarthy's Wheeling, West Virginia, speech Welch writes:

> From the beginning Communism has been presented as a movement of the proletariat, as a rising of the supposedly shackled and downtrodden poor against the powerful, who were exploiting them. And this itself is one of the biggest lies in all history. For Communism has *always* been imposed from the top down by the very rich, the highly educated, and the politically powerful on the suffering masses.
>
> The ordinary happy and innocent American will frequently observe about some multimillionaire or some college president whose activities on behalf of the Communists are obvious: "But of course, he couldn't be a Communist himself. He's rich. . . ." To which the proper answer is: "Nuts! Where on earth do you think the leaders of Communism come from. . . . Almost invariably they have been from the wealthy or best educated classes. . . ."
>
> When you look at the Communist strength in America today, you don't find

it in the poor struggling beatniks who by and large comprise the small and insignificant officially presented Communist party. That Communist party exists primarily for propaganda needs in this very pretense. But the strength of the Communist conspiracy lies in the very top social, economic, educational, and political circles of our country. . . . I can find you a lot more Harvard accents in Communist circles in America today than you can find me overalls.[37]

In terms of conspiracy theory, this antielitism manifests itself in traditional style by isolating the "intellectuals" as a class. In the Introduction to the Birch Society edition of Robison's book on the Illuminati, its anonymous author presents the ongoing plot as one primarily of the intellectuals.

This was conspiracy conceived, organized, and activated by professionals and intellectuals, many of them brilliant but cunning and clever, who decided to put their minds in the service of total evil. . . .
It is obvious that this conspiracy, appealing to the conceit of half-baked intellectuals, would attract educators, writers, philosophers, publishers, and clergymen. Their counterparts who run America today—like the Galbraiths, the Rostows, the Kennans, the Bundy's, the Littells, the Lippmanns—have the same self-conceit, the same arrogance which seems to characterize the overly bright and overly sadistic in any age and any civilization. . . .
One tends to think of professors, philosophers, and writers as sitting in their ivory towers, perfectly harmless to the world. Robison and history prove otherwise. . . . From Woodrow Wilson—himself a professor—to Lyndon Johnson, we have had nothing but Presidents surrounded by professors and scholars. . . . All of which brings to mind Weishaupt's plan to surround the ruling authorities with members of his Order.[38]

The Introduction goes on to describe the anti-Illuminati agitation of the late 1790's and the activities of the Anti-Masonic party of the 1820's and 1830's. It argues, however, that Freemasonry is no longer a vehicle for Illuminati activities. "Their main habitat these days seems to be the great subsidized universities, tax-free foundations, mass media communication systems, government bureaus such as the State Department, and a myriad of private organizations such as the Council on Foreign Relations."[39] Thus it is now clear what is behind the menace to free institutions, "a conspiracy of intellectuals," which today as yesterday groups together "the cleverest and most diabolical minds."

Linked to the intellectual elite in this conspiracy are their tools in the business elite. These business elite are themselves often the product of the centers of intellectual conspiracy, the Ivy League colleges of the East. They are, at the same time, the heads of the eastern banking and corporate interests who represent the "liberal" center of the Republican party. Phyllis Schlafly, one of the chief ideological supporters of the Goldwater campaign in 1964, made explicit this division between liberal and conservative Republicans—which had, as we have seen, a role in the Mc-Carthy phenomenon. She argued that in the four previous Presidential elections, conservative Republican candidates such as Taft and Goldwater had been sabotaged by the eastern corporate and banking Republican interests. "It wasn't any accident, it was planned that way. In each of the losing presidential years, a small group of secret king makers, using hidden persuaders and psychological warfare techniques, manipulated the Republican national convention to nominate candidates who had sidestepped or suppressed the key issues."[40]

The image of the "Bilderbergers" is frequently raised by the Birch Society to support its conception that the heads of the great international corporations are part and parcel with the Communists in the tight world conspiracy. The Bilderbergers, according to one Birch Society organ, came to public attention in 1954 when a group of leaders of the Atlantic community nations met under the chairmanship of Prince Bernhard of the Netherlands at the Hotel de Bilderberg at Oosterberg in the Netherlands.[41] The Birch Society conception of the activities of this group indicates the ramifications of the conspiracy.

Many of those attending Bilderberger meetings have been executives of major oil companies, such as Standard Oil of New Jersey and Royal Dutch Shell. They are alleged to have been responsible for the liberation of Algeria and other oil-rich Arab states. The Algerian revolt began in 1954 six months after the Bilderberger meeting, a fact to which causal significance is attached. "As a result of the Communist anticolonialist crusade, which has been greatly aided by such organizations as the Council on Foreign Relations and the Royal Institute of International Affairs, all of these oil-rich territories in North Africa have become 'independent,' with Esso and Shell usually picking up the pieces."[42] De Gaulle was perceived as an agent of the Bilderberger-Communist conspiracy whose "betrayal" of French Algeria "fit in very well with Bilderberger plans." The Bilderberger clique now controls "the source of energy for the major industries of France and West Germany" and has been responsible for the "liberalization trend in Spain [which] began with the entry of the Bilderberg clique into that nation's economy."[43] The presumed goal of the Bilderbergers is to gain control of the economic life of the nations of western Europe and integrate them so as to facilitate world government. The American Bilderbergers are supposedly deeply involved in fostering economic ties between the United States and the Soviet Union. And the article on the Bilderbergers even suggests a remote link between the Bilderbergers and the Kennedy assassination.

Mr. John J. McCloy, a Director of Chase Manhattan (deeply involved in the Bilderbergers) and its former Chairman of the Board, had visited with

Khrushchev in 1961. . . . We shall never know what was discussed [between the two men] . . . ; however, it is indeed an interesting coincidence that only twenty days earlier, on July 8, 1961, Lee Harvey Oswald had made his first contact with the United States Embassy in Moscow to start the process of his return to the United States. And wouldn't you just know that John J. McCloy would become a member of the Warren Commission?[44]

Gary Allen, one of the contributing editors of *American Opinion*, in writing about the conspiratorial nature of the Council on Foreign Relations (CFR), has further explicated the motivations of the economic elite:

> Why would international bankers and financiers be interested in promoting a Socialist World Government? Clearly, socialism is only the bait to obtain the support of the political underworld and to create the structure necessary to maintain dictatorial control. What this small group of financiers and cartel-oriented businessmen are interested in is monopoly control over the world's natural resources, trade, transportation, and communications—something that despite their great wealth they could not achieve otherwise. Therefore, the super-capitalists become super-socialists, realizing that only a World Government under their control can give them the power necessary to achieve their goal. Only this could explain why these extremely wealthy men would be willing to support movements which seem to be aimed at their own destruction. The financiers and cartelists do not expect to be injured by the socialists so long as they can manipulate them, using them for their own purposes.[45]

However, even with its occasional name dropping, the "Bilderbergers" is finally just a theoretical extension of the abstract dimension of conspiracy theory. This dimension is dramatized by the very use of such terms as "Force X," the other name of the hidden conspiracy mentioned in the Birch Society *Review of the News*. Force X has been described in right-wing publications in terms highly reminiscent of the Illuminati. It is a "non-Communist group . . . [which] seems to use Communism, but not to be Communist. . . . The objective of this group is to achieve absolute power. . . . This force, which we can call 'X,' is closely coordinated. It is of one mind; it is in control of immense resources; it is convinced, passionate, efficient, and deadly. It fears only one thing—public opinion."[46]

However, the history of the use of conspiracy theory by extremist groups in America so far suggests that in addition to its abstract core, the theory needs to invoke some clearly defined group in order to catch mass imagination. The Birch Society conspiracy theory seems to be over-sophisticated for that purpose. To put it another way, extremist movements in America, in order to be effective on a national political level, have had to engage in some low-status backlash targetry. Abstract conspiracy theory has never been enough. In American history, the backlash targets have often fitted neatly into the nature of the conspiracy theories. Anti-Catholicism and anti-Semitism, in particular, have been able to provide both an identifiable group of people and a suggestion of arcane recesses. But right-wing extremist movements have always had to invoke some backlash targetry, whether or not it fits the ideologues' conspiracy theory, in order to engage a broad national audience. Welch's general appeal and his conspiracy theory have remained both abstract and class-based, involving no significant low-status backlash, or nativism. Even the very abstract nativist potential in McCarthyism, built around the alien ideology and thrust of world Communism, was no longer so viable in 1958. Communism was no longer sweeping the globe, as it seemed to be doing in the first years after World War II. The growing bitterness between China and the Soviet Union, the signs of restlessness in European satellites, the apparent domestication of the Soviet Union itself, all helped to reduce both the image of a monolithic world conspiracy and that of an alien threat.

Nativist Bigotry

Anti-Catholic nativism had not served a purpose for major right-wing movements since the 1920's, and certainly the Birch Society is not in that tradition. In fact, there is more evidence of links with prominent Catholics than with Protestant fundamentalists. Although there has never been any Protestant minister on the National Council of the Society, two Catholic priests have served in this capacity. Father Richard Ginder served as a member of the Council while he was also associate editor of *Our Sunday Visitor*, a national Catholic weekly which is the official publication for thirteen dioceses. Although he is no longer on the Council, he has been replaced by Father Francis E. Fenton, Pastor of the Blessed Sacrament Church in Bridgeport, Connecticut. Another important Catholic who has served on the Council for most of its history is Clarence Manion, former Dean of the Law School of Notre Dame University. Manion conducts a regular program on the radio, the "Manion Forum." He still speaks frequently under Catholic auspices. Father Fenton in a letter to the Jesuit magazine, *America*, answering an attack on the Society, went on to say: "There are a number of priest members of the John Birch Society, of which I am one. . . . There is a sizable percentage of Catholics in the John Birch Society."[47] An analysis of the role of Catholics in the right wing has argued that the Catholic priesthood had played a major role in recruiting laymen to the organization: "Catholics who are in the John Birch Society have placed great stress on the presence and support of priests in their first contacts with the Birch group."[48]

Although many members of the Catholic hierarchy have denounced the Birch Society, the Society has been able to point to support from some of them. Richard Cardinal Cushing of Boston stated on April 5, 1961, that Robert Welch should be supported as a dedicated foe of Communism.[49]

Cushing has since repudiated this and other tributes which he wrote about Welch. The Los Angeles archdiocese, which was headed until 1969 by the most extreme right-wing member of the American hierarchy, J. Francis Cardinal McIntyre, sent priests to meetings of right-wing forums, addressed by Robert Welch and other Birch leaders, in which the priest was listed as representing the Cardinal. *The Tidings*, the official paper of the archdiocese, recommended subscriptions to *American Opinion* and other Birch publications as a means of learning about Communism. Another "national Catholic weekly" which has cooperated with the Birch Society in exchanging recommendations, *The Wanderer*, published in St. Paul, Minnesota, carries on the first page of each issue a column by Archbishop William O. Brady of St. Paul.

There is, of course, no way of knowing how many members of the Catholic clergy support the Society. Robert Welch has claimed that 40 per cent of the membership is Catholic, a percentage considerably higher than in the adult American population. Fred W. Grupp's sample of the national membership indicates that about a quarter are Catholics.[50] Catholic critics of the Society have not denied the presence of a considerable body of Catholics in the group. Rather they have sought to explain the phenomenon and to criticize those who are involved.

The liberal Catholic magazine *Commonweal* has editorialized in sharp terms about the propensity of their coreligionists to back the extreme right, including the Birch Society.

It is inescapable that American Catholics bear a special responsibility for the rise and support of at least some of these groups. Without Catholic supporters, many of them would be trifling irritations only. Many would not even exist. Almost all, to a greater or lesser degree, depend upon the aid of Catholics: for approval, manpower, money and publicity. While it is difficult to get any kind of statistics on such support, what is known is sufficient—or ought to be—to show a highly disturbing and unflattering picture.[51]

The large majority of the Catholic hierarchy may have been clearly disturbed by this behavior. As early as 1961, the annual meeting of Catholic bishops attacked reckless radical-right charges. The liberal pronouncements of Pope John and the various reforms in the church enacted at the Vatican Councils have legitimated the position of liberal clergy and Catholic intellectuals. They have attacked Catholic rightists for taking positions which are incompatible with Catholic teachings. Such efforts, however, have not prevented Catholics from continuing to participate in extreme rightist activities which are, like the Birch Society, not in the Protestant nativist tradition.

The appeal of the preservatist movements for many modern Catholics has been discussed in connection with the Coughlin and McCarthy movements. One Catholic priest, editor of the *Catholic Star Herald* in New Jersey, made this interpretation of his observation that the Birch "groups in our area (South Jersey) are dominated by Catholics":

Throughout all this I have often asked myself why the John Birch Society has such an attraction for some Catholics. I believe it is the residue of the Coughlin-McCarthy eras. . . . Deeper than anything else, however, is the popular mystique that inspires some Catholics—to hate Communism is to love God.

They reason that since Communism promotes militant atheism, what nobler cause could there be than to fight those who deny God? And, since Communist atheists hate America and plot its destruction, what more patriotic cause is there than to thwart those who would wreck this nation? For such Catholics, the Birch Society provides an opportunity to combine piety and patriotism in a single endeavor.[52]

But, in addition, one preservatist factor which may have affected Catholics during the Coughlin and McCarthy periods was stronger than ever. The winds of change threatening to disturb the now solidly established Catholic institutions in America were blowing not just from the left, but from within. In the wake of the Vatican reforms, many Catholics, like fundamentalist Protestants before them, found their own church dropping many of the practices and beliefs in which they had been reared. Some formed their own organization, the Cardinal Mindszenty Foundation, which, like the Protestant fundamentalist organizations, built into its general preservatism the specific cultural baggage of Catholic traditionalism. This group, named after the Hungarian Cardinal who played a major role in the Hungarian Revolution of 1956, was founded in 1958, the year of the Birch Society's birth, by the Very Reverend C. Stephen Dunker, a Vincentian missionary, who had served for twenty years in China. Many in the clergy who have served as missionaries in countries now dominated by Communists are active in the leadership of the Foundation. Like the Birch Society, it runs study groups and seminars around the country. The Foundation claims that there are four thousand such groups. It also has a regular fifteen-minute weekly radio program heard on stations in every section of the country. Aside from the religious neutralism of the Birch Society, the Foundation resembles the Birch Society in outlook, as well as in its activities. A number of priests and laymen apparently belong to both organizations.

The evidence strongly suggests that the Birch Society is not in the anti-Catholic tradition of Protestant nativist movements because it is *not* Protestant fundamentalist in any sense and that the Birch Society syndrome is not related to Protestant fundamentalism. There is, in fact, not only no fundamentalist appeal in the Birch Society material or approach; there is no particularistic religious appeal of any kind. In the McCarthyite tradition, the religious references are flattened to the dimension of a secularized "American religion," and anti-Communism becomes the moral equivalent of old-time religion. Thus, in calling for "religious neutralism," Robert Welch describes "the deeply religious nature of most earnest anti-Communists" as consisting of their understanding that "underlying the struggle in which we are now engaged, there is the ages-old conflict between the forces of good and evil."[53]

The lack of concern with traditional religious matters by the Birch Society may also be seen in the fact that during 1964–1967 not a single religious leader appeared on the front cover of *American Opinion*. "Moreover, a religious interest was hardly a prerequisite for those who actually appeared on the covers. Of the words and phrases used to describe such 'great Americans' only 4% made reference to religion. . . ."[54] A content analysis of the *Bulletin* and *American Opinion* also points in the same direction. In spite of the Society's criticisms of the liberal clergy, actual attacks on them were quite rare.[55]

Robert Welch's personal theology is further in point. He attends the Unitarian Church in Belmont, Massachusetts, even though the minister has delivered sermons against the Society while he was present. He has reported this to his members in *The Bulletin* in telling about a particularly unhappy week in his life.

> Sunday turned out to be the blackest day in this whole dark continuum. . . . As you know . . . I am a Unitarian. And I'll be darned if our minister did not pick this particular Sunday to make his whole sermon an attack on, or maybe I should say an exposition of, the John Birch Society. I got the impression that a lot of other Unitarian ministers are doing the same thing these days, all within a stretch of two or three weeks although I do not know how or by whom any such concerted action was arranged.[56]

A Unitarian minister, Brooks R. Walker, who has written a book about Christian right-wingers, has summed up Welch's theology "as liberal, and . . . universalistic."[57] His intellectual hero is Ralph Waldo Emerson, who shaped much of Unitarian thought in the nineteenth century. Welch believes there are common values in all religions, that as man becomes more rational and science learns more, our religious conceptions become more profound, that the Bible represents a relatively primitive and egocentric stage of human loyalty and morality, which both the religious rationalists and fundamentalists can share.[58]

Welch's best friend in the clergy is James W. Fifield, Jr., retired minister of the First Congregational Church of Los Angeles, who "is probably one of the most theologically liberal and at the same time politically conservative ministers in the continuing Congregational movement."[59]

Anti-Semitism

More to be expected than anti-Catholicism in the Birch Society ideology would be the kind of abstract, "subjective," anti-Semitic nativism which began to develop in the 1920's and came to flower in Coughlin. Indeed, there is evidence of an impulse to incorporate this element in the Birch Society conspiracy theory. Thus, Revilo Oliver wrote in an *American Opinion* article:

> Since it was clear that there was a conspiracy inside the outer (Marxist) shell, it was only natural that attempts should be made to identify it. Various sincere and thoughtful writers have positively identified the inner conspiracy as composed of one of the following: "Force X," Illuminati, Satanists, "Bilderbergers," Zionists, Pharisees, Khazars, Fabian Socialists, International Bankers, Rockefellers, Rothschilds, or a gang of otherwise unidentified "messianic materialists."[60]

This impulse has been counter to the explicit ideology of the Birch Society. Not only has Robert Welch consistently expressed opposition to anti-Semitism, but also there can be little doubt that he and the majority of the Executive Council of the Society regard overt anti-Semitism as harming the work of the organization. *The Bulletin* sent out to all members has argued repeatedly that "Jewish-Gentile antipathy is valuable grist to the Communist mill."[61] In 1963, Welch published a pamphlet, *The Neutralizers*, which devoted considerable space to proving that Communism is not a Jewish conspiracy.[62] In it, Welch argued that those who engage in anti-Semitism "neutralize" the efficacy of the Society. A number of people who became identified as overt anti-Semites were pointedly dropped from the Birch Society. Thus, in 1963, the membership of Robert De Pugh, the head of the Minutemen, was revoked. In 1965, the Society expelled James Oviett, active in Los Angeles, after the Anti-Defamation League (ADL) had publicized the fact that he was a major distributor of anti-Semitic literature, including *The Protocols of the Elders of Zion*.[63] Westbrook Pegler, a frequent contributor to *American Opinion*, was dropped by the magazine in the same year for including anti-Semitic comments in his articles. This action also followed an ADL exposé of the content of Pegler's writings. Welch, at the time, wrote to the ADL stating: "We were already becoming unhappy ourselves with some of the attitudes in Mr. Pegler's writings."[64]

As an example of what made Welch unhappy, Pegler wrote two years before Welch decided to drop him: "Lehman is the prophet of a sect of pushcart sophists who wouldn't be judges if they did not share his bigotries and morals. Honor and conscience are no more thinkable in such pettifoggers than in the dregs which are found in the tank of a county jail on a Monday morning."[65]

Perhaps the most aggressive anti-Semite active in the Society has been Revilo Oliver. Oliver, discussed earlier as the man who introduced the Illuminati to the pages of Birch publications, was one of the founding members of the Society in 1958 and served on its Executive Council and as associate editor of *American Opinion*. His frequent articles in *American Opinion* referred constantly to a variety of hidden conspiracies and occasionally contained references to the involvements of Jews, Khazars, Zionists, and Rothschilds in the Illuminati or Communist plots. These and other anti-Semitic activities of Oliver did not affect his membership or leading role. He was, however, finally expelled in August 1966 after making a widely reported speech at the New England Rally for God, Family, and Country in Boston on July 2, 1966. In it he described a Jewish conspiracy which was responsible for moral decay, and went on to say, as reported in the *New York Times*: "If only by some miracle all the Bolsheviks or all the Illuminati or all the Jews were vaporized at dawn tomorrow, we should have nothing more to worry about."[66]

The necessity for the Birch Society to engage continually in such defensive actions underlines the attraction of the Society for anti-Semites and the strength of the impulse to "close the gap" of the conspiracy theory with a related, if abstract, nativism. There have been persistent reports of anti-Semitism at some local Birch Society meetings and of the fact that many of the local *American Opinion* book stores have carried a variety of books and pamphlets written by notorious anti-Semites.[67]

Robert Welch offered his own reasons for constantly acting as a brake on the marked anti-Semitic impulses in his organization: "We could not [be anti-Semitic] by our very nature in the first place; and in the second place, we were too well aware of what had happened to people like Conde McGinley—who otherwise would have become and remained a tremendous force in the fight against Communism."[68]

Conde McGinley was a notoriously explicit anti-Semite of the time, whose publication, *Common Sense*, became devoted almost entirely to anti-Jewish diatribe. He had no movement of any kind and was generally considered beyond the fringe of political responsibility. In referring to "what had happened" to him, Welch was presumably referring to the fact that McGinley's diversionary preoccupation with anti-Semitism had deflected him from the main fight against Communism. But he also may have been referring to McGinley's loss of respectability, and therefore of effectiveness, as a result of this preoccupation. But whatever the nature of Welch's convictions or strategic assumptions on this score, and whatever the validity of these assumptions, the fact remains that while the Birch Society may be a vessel of some anti-Semitism, it has not become an organizational vehicle for anti-Semitism.

The Birch Society and the Negro

The record of the Birch Society with respect to anti-Negro sentiments is somewhat different from that regarding anti-Semitism. Officially, it opposes race prejudice as much as religious antagonism. Robert Welch stresses that it has a thousand Negro members. Not one of the 650 Birch Society members who filled out an anonymous questionnaire acknowledged being black.[69] Yet the Society claims that of the forty-nine persons listed in the national roster of the American Opinion Speakers Bureau, six are Negroes. One-quarter of all speeches sponsored by the Society's Speakers Bureau in January 1966 were by Negroes.[70] Yet Negroes are clearly in a different category than Jews. One of the principal bêtes noires of the organization is the civil rights movement, and political activities designed to end segregation or to benefit the Negro's economic and social position are strongly opposed.

The civil rights movement and civil rights legislation are frequently attacked for seeking to extend federal power and for refusing to recognize that the Negro can improve his situation only through individual initiative. "The Negro should be encouraged to make full use of the educational facilities already available . . . by the do-it-yourself spirit. Other minority groups have achieved this sense of advancement without endangering the nation."[71] But while the overt reason for such opposition is a generalized antagonism to government intervention into the private affairs of men, of resistance to increases in federal power, many of the statements made clearly manifest strong racist sentiments. Riots in the ghettos were described in the following terms: "The indigenous animals began to riot, loot, bomb, and burn."[72]

The civil rights movement is frequently referred to as controlled by Communists or the Illuminati-Insiders. The "Negro Revolution" has developed "exactly as planned and plotted [by the Communists] ever since 1928." Writing in *The Bulletin* in March 1970, Welch states that the "Black Panthers . . . are being *used* by agents of the *Insiders* far above them, to beat their breasts and make loud noises, like the gorillas whom they so much resemble. . . ."[73] Prominent Negro leaders are denounced as immoral men, engaging in "sexual perversion" and lewd activities.[74] Foreign aid is pictured as involving distributing American wealth to "spear-toting Bantu, [and] three-toed Caribs with thumbs on their feet."[75] Resistance to admitting Negroes into white neighborhoods is defended on the grounds that many of them "are the kind of people who have made slums of [good] neighborhoods. . . . Slums are made by slum-people not vice versa."[76]

The ambiguity of the Birch Society on this issue is seen, for example, in the fact that it has featured Negro speakers on its Speakers Bureau and has established a scholarship fund for deserving Negro students; and on the other hand, within hours after the Watts race riots in 1965, a directive was sent to Birch chapters in the Los Angeles area to mobilize for an anti-civil rights propaganda drive "to exploit the white reaction. . . ."[77]

The reemergence of objective nativism on the American scene is suggested, this time related to American Negroes. The application of the term "nativism" to the anti-Negro patterns in this country at this time is a commentary both on the nature of nativism and on the changing state of the American Negro. Although the term "racism" has become bastardized in the heat of modern controversy, the term has a biological connotation. Racism is an ideology in itself which says that some physically distinguishable group is genetically superior or inferior. Thus, Hitler, in extolling "Aryan blood," legislated the biological inferiority of *all* Jews for ancestral, presumably Mendelian, reasons. In shoring up the slavery system in the South, after the invention of the cotton gin, Americans similarly established a racism which included *all* Negroes on a genetic basis. On the other hand, the objective nativism of America had been essentially cultural rather than biological in its ideology. It had tended to be issue-oriented rather than people-oriented. Samuel F. B. Morse said of the Irish Catholics that they "in an especial manner clanned together, and kept alive their foreign feelings, associations, habits and manners."[78] Sometimes these associations and habits were seen as subversive, sometimes as immoral, sometimes as just disgusting and unaesthetic. But it was theoretically possible for an individual to escape them by a kind of cultural conversion.

The Birch Society line on the Negroes foreshadowed the fact that anti-Negro sentiment was tending to become more issue-oriented and less people-oriented. The overt controversy was centering more and more around the issues of integration, of housing, of "violence in the streets"—around habits and manners rather than genetic characteristics per se. The focus of resistance increasingly was the *lower-class* Negro. But, in whatever form, this development marked the reemergence of low- and middle-status backlash of traditional nativist proportions. The ambiguity of the Birch Society line on the Negro and civil rights reflects this metamorphosis in American life, although perhaps dimly perceived by the Birch Society itself. Indeed, it would be an error to overcomplicate the motivations and perceptions of the "official" Birch Society, which is substantially run by one man. Robert Welch's, and therefore the Birch Society's, official line on civil rights may well have stemmed primarily from his overwhelming preoccupation with antistatism on every level. But the Society also served as an unofficial vessel for many points of view which had a common denominator, but many disparate elements. Several of the prime organizational goals outlined by Welch in *The Blue Book* had to do with the establishment of reading rooms and libraries for the dissemination of all kinds of antistatist and anti-Communist books and the stimulation of audiences for the spectrum of periodicals and radio commentators who held those broad points of view.

The fact is, however, that while the emergent nativism directed against Negroes may have been reflected by many of the people drawn to the Birch Society, and by many of the articles and publications disseminated by the Birch Society, the Society itself did not consciously attempt to build a mass appeal around the issues.

Changing Appeals

Indeed, the Society never seriously attempted to build a mass appeal of any kind. This is in keeping with Welch's concept of the Birch Society as not a political party, but a striking force, in the image of the Communist party, establishing *ad hoc* front organizations, writing letters, and bringing specific pressures to bear, particularly in the Republican party. Welch's failure to soften his antistatist posture, even to accommodate to the basic pocketbook concerns of the working class, is another index to his lack of interest in creating a mass base. The Society's main concern has consistently been with other conservatives. However, the Society has been interested in broadening its base within at least that population and has attempted to adapt its program accordingly. The main problem has been the "uneducated" appeal of Welch's abstract Illuminati-type conspiracy theories to educated segments of the conservative population. It raised the problem of respectability which had led many conservatives to abandon earlier right-wing movements marked by grossly unenlightened conduct or theories of history.

Attacks on the Society by liberals and leftists do not bother the Society much; those by conservatives do. And the Society has been under heavy fire from various Republican leaders as well as the spokesmen of intellectual conservatism. The *National Review*, edited by William Buckley, has devoted many articles, and one special issue, to the problem of the Birch Society.[79] The writers for the *Review* have argued generally that the conspiracy theories of Robert Welch are prima facie ridiculous, charging that Eisenhower and the Dulleses are Communists; that they clearly make no rational sense and are repudiated by almost all Americans. The Society's activities are a handicap to the Republican party and the conservative cause. They enable liberals to embarrass conservative candidates with charges that they are supported by the Birch Society. James Burnham, an associate editor of the *National Review*, concludes that "any American who seriously wants to contribute to his country's security and well-being and to oppose Communism will have to stay clear of the John Birch Society."[80]

Other leaders of the conservative wing of the GOP, such as Senators John Tower of Texas and Barry Goldwater of Arizona, have joined in the attack against Robert Welch. Both of them have commended the *National Review* for its campaign, and Goldwater called on those members of the Society who seek to aid the Republican party to "resign from the Society. . . ."[81] The period of greatest growth and increase in popular support for the Society occurred between the end of 1963 and the middle of 1965. Epstein and Forster estimate that "its membership . . . almost doubled" and "its cash income more than quadrupled."[82] A questionnaire survey of a scholarly selected random sample of 650 Birch Society members sent out from the national office of the Society in July of 1965 indicates that one out of three of those who replied had joined during the preceding twelve months.[83] The number of full-time coordinators employed by the Society was doubled during this time with the hiring of an additional thirty-five. Since it costs the Society about $15,000 to hire a new coordinator (salary and equipment), those added at this time "represented an investment by the Birch organization of roughly half-a-million dollars."[84]

The source of this growth in support during 1964–1965 seems fairly clear: the Goldwater campaign. Birch members threw themselves into the preconvention drive and continued to be active after the convention. Their participation seemingly helped to legitimate their role and also extended their contacts with other activist right-wing Republicans.

Birchers and other such extremists were active, welcomed, defended and, to a certain extent, triumphant. At the Republican convention, the Birch Society covered itself with a kind of respectability, Birchers misused the campaign as a vehicle to spread their own political propaganda and to recruit new members. Many Americans were swept into the Birch ranks on the emotional tide of the campaign period. Many others joined after Election Day, when the frustration of defeat made them ripe for recruitment and when the Birch Society's post-election appeal to this group was summed up in the simple slogan: "*Now* Will You Join The John Birch Society?"[85]

The questionnaire study of Birch Society members found that those recruited in this period differed significantly in a number of ways from those who had joined earlier. They were "much more apt to have learned of the Society through the mass media (replacing friends as the most frequently cited introductory agent)"; "they were much less likely to have relatives in the Society"; they were "less committed ideologically to the Society's programs"; and they were much more committed to the Republican party. Fred Grupp, the author of this study, concluded, "The evidence indicates that the great majority of these recent additions were Goldwater supporters for whom the greatest attraction was his 'hard line' foreign policy."[86]

Growth and access to previously unavailable sectors of the population affected the Society in ways comparable to other radical organizations. It sought to gain "respectability," to reduce emphases on themes which might be unacceptable to those not already committed to its complex ideology. Or as Edgar Engleman has put it, summing up the results of his content analysis of the Society's publications, it tried to "become more legitimate in terms of issues and arguments."[87]

Two content analyses of its literature both suggest similar shifts. The first, by Frances Dahlberg, reports that between 1960 and 1965 "the number of mentions of Communism in *American Opinion* . . . decreases."[88] There is also "a significant shift of focus from foreign countries to the United States as the scene of immediate problems. No longer do Russia and China hold the spot light: attention has shifted to the United States and even to the immediate communities of the members."[89]

The declining emphasis on discussions of the Communist conspiracy, particularly abroad, has been replaced by a greater stress on the activities and role of the John Birch Society itself in waging various specific issue campaigns at home. "The original goal of fighting Communism has been displaced by the means which include maintaining and expanding the Society. Campaigns against the Communists have been displaced by more positive campaigns concerned with issues at home."[90] In 1965, three campaigns had become most important. These were "Impeach Earl Warren," "Support Your Local Police," including contributions to a Police Award Reserve Fund "to aid the families of policemen killed in the line of duty," and the "Civil Rights Campaign" generally. The latter was stressed most often. In a sense, the first two are derivative parts of the concern with the civil rights issue and Negro violence and crime. The "Get the US out of the UN" issue and the efforts to win support for the Liberty Amendment to repeal the Income Tax Amendment, which were important issues in 1960, continued to be mentioned as significant action issues in 1965.[91]

Communists, of course, are still the source of much of the difficulties, both foreign and domestic, but the emphasis has changed from simply exposing and attacking the Communist conspiracy to dealing with particular issues through pressing politicians and building the Society. The actual number of times in which Communism is mentioned, however, has consistently gone down.[92]

The second study, completed in 1967 by Edgar Engleman, which used somewhat different techniques from Dahlberg's, reports consistent results. It sought to compare trends in *American Opinion*, which is designed for general readership, with the *Bulletin*, published for circulation among members only.

The data reveals that "Communist Conspiracy" has declined as a domestic item in both *American Opinion* and the *Bulletin*. It is clear that in all years examined [1960–1966], this item is far more dominant in the *Bulletin* than it is in *American Opinion*. But the decline is of similar proportions in both publications. That this decline appears to be accelerating is evidenced by the fact that the proportionate yearly drop in item-frequency is greater during the period 1964–1966 than during the period 1960–1964. . . .

What is most remarkable about the decline of "Communist Conspiracy" is its consistency. It is consistent over time; it is consistent at every level of observation (topic, item, theme); and it is evident in both publications.[93]

Engelman also found in both magazines a "decline in foreign topics [which] is matched by a parallel increase in the frequency of domestic topics."[94] In *American Opinion*, the percentage of pages devoted to domestic issues jumped from 23.4 in 1960 to 59.3 in 1966, while those given to foreign matters dropped from 63.3 in 1960 to 30.6 in 1966.[95] Civil rights, which was not even mentioned once in the *Bulletin* or *American Opinion* in 1960, jumped to 8.5 per cent of the pages of the latter in 1964 and to 11.8 per cent in 1966. Economic issues, mentioned on 3.5 per cent of *American Opinion*'s pages in 1960, rose to 10.6 per cent in 1964 and to 12.3 in 1966.

There seems to be some evidence that most recently the Society has been placing greater stress on "Nationalist" themes. Vietnam did not appear in the pages of *American Opinion* in 1960 and 1964. Up to the summer of 1966, Welch took the position in speeches and pamphlets that American participation in the war was part of the Communist conspiracy designed to weaken us as a nation, to facilitate greater collectivism at home, and to divert our attention from elsewhere. This position clearly put it in conflict with almost every other extreme conservative or radical rightist group. In the summer of 1966, however, the Society shifted its position, and since then *American Opinion* has supported "a quick victory in Vietnam" position.

Robert Welch, however, still gives voice to his belief that the decision to enter the Vietnam War was part of a conscious plot to increase federal power, to put government controls, such as national price and wage controls and food rationing, into effect. In 1969, he argued that we have a deliberate policy "to enable our Communist enemies in Asia to uphold their side of the war, to escalate it, and to keep it going. . . ."[96] Thus Welch remains consistent in his analysis of the war; what has changed is that the Society now both presses for a more vigorous American military strategy, while urging that we get out if we do not fight to win. The change in the direction of support for increased military action has been paralleled by growing evidence of admiration for military leaders. In 1964 and 1965, only two of the men pictured on the front cover of *American Opinion* were military leaders; this figure rose to five in 1966,[97] and continues high. Increased nationalism may also be reflected in the fact that the space devoted to anti-UN items also increased.

As the Birch Society grew in membership and public attention, it turned from esoteric themes which could be of relevance to only a small minority of committed members to issues which were presumably of relevance to at least a somewhat larger public. But while its appeal may have become more broadly preservatist, its basic appeal remained immutably antistatist and economically preservatist.

Side by side with the newly flourishing Birch Society, there continued to exist two other traditional strains of American right-wing extremism: a vestigial movement based on Protestant fundamentalism, and the explicit nativist bigotry of the KKK and associated organizations.

Protestant Nativism

The most important of the traditional Protestant nativist groups is Billy James Hargis' Christian Crusade, which publishes a magazine, *Christian Crusade*, with a claimed circulation of well over 100,000, and has regular broadcasts on over 400 radio stations.[98] Hargis combines advocacy of conservative political principles and fundamentalist Protestantism with a strong attack on the Communist conspiracy, which is seen as behind every major crisis and problem in the United States.[99] Although Hargis has never indicated any knowledge of or concern with the theory of a Satanic Illuminati conspiracy behind Communism, he does identify Communism with Satan and the anti-Christ.[100] The real threat, however, perceived by Hargis is the Liberals—both secular ones and those who control the National Council of Churches.

"A giant gangster conspiracy threatens to take away our freedoms and enslave us all," he says, a conspiracy of evil that is universal in scope and unbelievably complex in nature; it is both domestic and external. But the greatest threat "is not so much from the outside as it is from the inside"; and even there, "our greatest threat is not internal communism per se . . . the greatest threat to freedom . . . is the powerfully entrenched Liberal Establishment."

What is the nature of this establishment? "The Liberal Establishment," says Hargis, "is a sinister brotherhood that reaches into the fields of education, politics, religion, labor and management—dedicated men determined to abolish the free enterprise system and bring about a world government of socialist nations." They are, he continues, men "who distrust democracy because they feel the people are not capable of governing themselves. . . . With this hatred of the less educated masses . . . the Liberal Establishment works fever-ishly to enslave us all."

"Left-wing liberals," we are told, are under "a satanic influence." As a matter of fact. "The entire left-wing movement is of the devil." Communism and liberalism are cut from the same cloth.[101]

Much of Hargis' secular ideology is close to that of the Birch Society. Hargis also sees the United States as on the verge of being completely controlled by the Communists. He and Welch differ in the relative weight of their emphasis on domestic versus foreign Communism. Hargis sees the domestic menace as the main problem and pays little attention to other countries. But the basic distinction between Welch and Hargis is derived from the fact that the latter is a fundamentalist Protestant minister who sees his politics as directly derivative from the Gospel and believes that the United States has been and should be a Christian Protestant nation. He writes:

In every generation the adversary of Christ and His church has relent-lessly fought God's dominion over the earth. The father of liars, Satan's occupation is warfare; and faithful to that pursuit, he battles ceaselessly against the Church of Jesus Christ. . . . Today we find Satan incarnate in inter-national Communism and in its offshoots in the United States, the "Far Left." These American adherents of socialism in one form or another . . . consider the "orthodox" Church of Jesus Christ to be the only international force that is capable of blocking the growth of world Communism and socialism.[102]

This is, of course, a pole apart from the language of Unitarian Robert Welch, who calls for religious neutralism and appeals to the common-denominator "religious" impulses of Protestants, Catholics, and Jews alike.

Hargis is also distinct from Welch in his tendency toward a more explicit nativism, which he places in a religious framework. Redekop points out the Hargis notion that "a modern Israel must constantly be alert to the wiles and infiltrations of a modern Philistia, and aliens and the colored race threaten the concept of national-racial peculiarity. Presumably God's call to America and Americans did not extend to the Negro slaves or to their descendants."[103]

As Billy Hargis and his Christian Crusade have grown in strength and national publicity, he has sought to refrain from points of view and asso-ciations which might enable critics to label him a racial bigot. Thus, Hargis no longer advocates racial segregation, which he once espoused in an early book. However, like the Birch Society, he attacks the civil rights movement as being Communist-controlled, and he opposes government action against segregation. He also now abstains from direct connections with well known anti-Semites. This also was not true in the past. Writing in the October 1959 issue of his magazine, *Christian Crusade*, Hargis mentioned his obligation to Gerald Winrod, the leader of the pro-Nazi, virulently anti-Semitic movement of the 1930's, which was revived after World War II and continued until his death in the mid 50's. Hargis stated that Winrod had counseled him on how to organize a radio-based movement. Hargis also wrote on a number of occasions for Winrod's anti-Semitic magazine, *The Defender*, during the early 1950's and sent a letter to the Federal Communications Commission stating his appreciation of Winrod's broadcasts. Hargis promoted subscriptions to *The American Mercury* in 1956 at a time when it had become a blatantly anti-Semitic magazine.[104] During the 1960's, however, Hargis has avoided such associations.

Hargis has adapted his fundamentalist Protestantism to modern reality in one respect: he has refrained from anti-Catholic activities and, in fact, includes a number of Catholics on his advisory board. The same cannot be said of the second major figure on the fundamentalist radical right, the Reverend Carl McIntire, who was expelled from the Presbyterian church for opposing liberalizing trends in 1936, and now has his own denomination, the Bible Presbyterian Church. More important, however, is the American Council of Christian Churches, which he formed in 1941 to unite a number of fundamentalist groups. Hargis has been active in this group, as well. The Council claims to have 300,000 members in fourteen affiliated denominations.[105] McIntire's most important work, however, has been to publish a weekly paper, *The Christian Beacon*, and to conduct a five-day-a-week radio program which is heard on close to 600 radio stations, called The Twentieth Century Reformation Hour.[106]

McIntire's ideology and theology are close to those espoused by Billy James Hargis, with the addition of a strong element of anti-Catholicism. Some indication of his doctrines may be seen in one of his regular letters to his listeners sent out in 1963:

> Gus Hall, the leading Communist spokesman in the United States, presents his praise of Pope John XXIII's encyclical in the Communist *Worker* . . .; also, Khrushchev's praise, and President Kennedy's approval. Things are shaping up rapidly. The Communists want us to trust them and the Pope says disarmament must rest on "mutual trust alone." President Kennedy also has learned from the Pope.[107]

Both McIntire and Hargis preach the "old-time" religious philosophy that one must accept the Bible as literal truth and believe in the return of Christ; that there is an enduring conflict between God and Satan, in which Satan is engaged in conspiracies with men to destroy the true faith and the social institutions linked to it, such as capitalism.

Robert Welch's disagreement with fundamentalist theology has led to attacks on him from adherents to such doctrines. One spokesman of religious traditionalism, Lester DeKoster, wrote a pamphlet in which he contended that a careful examination of the teachings enunciated in *The Blue Book* were incompatible with those of the Bible:

> The Blue Book of the John Birch Society proclaims a doctrine of God which the Christian is bound to reject. It teaches a doctrine of man which the Christian must deny. It professes an interpretation of history which the Christian cannot accept. It makes declarations concerning the State which run counter to the clear teaching of the Scriptures. In short, it advocates a "theology" which the Christian can only call heresy, and which is a far cry from the "Gospel" which Captain John Birch, on whose name the Society trades, intended to give his life to preach.[108]

The Klan—and White Citizens Councils

Although, as we have seen, the Klan declined greatly during the late 1920's and played a relatively insignificant role during the 1930's, organizations which call themselves the Ku Klux Klan have continued down to the present. Students of these groups indicate that at the end of the sixties they had close to 60,000 members, as many as the John Birch Society. And though these Klans are relatively unimportant on the national political scene, they retain considerable support in the South. Two national opinion surveys, one in 1946 and the other in 1965, conducted by the Gallup poll, report that as many as 6 per cent nationally, over 10,000,000 Americans, approve of the work of the Klan.

The organizational continuity of the second Klan, which had been revived in 1915, was broken in 1944 when the United States Bureau of Internal Revenue filed a lien for back taxes of over $685,000. The Klan was forced to sell all its assets and go out of business.[109] Various new Klans were formed immediately after the war, of which the Association of Georgia Klans, under Dr. Samuel Green, was the most prominent. This group, which claimed strength in many states, engaged in night raids, floggings, and parades in hooded uniforms. It was, however, subject to severe police scrutiny and denunciations by the press and the ministry all over the South. This effort at a Klan revival, although gaining 20,000 members, was broken up after Green's death in 1949.

Following the Supreme Court desegregation decision in 1954, the Klan experienced a major revival and undertook campaigns of violence and terror in many southern communities. A report on racial violence in the first four years after the decision specified 530 cases of overt violence, including 6 Negroes killed, 29 persons shot and wounded, 44 individuals beaten, 30 homes bombed, 15 homes hit by gunfire, 7 Jewish temples and buildings bombed, and 17 towns and cities threatened by mob action.[110]

A detailed investigation of the so-called "Third Klan" by the House Committee on Un-American Activities in 1965 found that there were over a dozen different Klans with a membership of about 50,000. Although most of the local klaverns were in the South, units existed in many northern states.[111]

One reason for the relative weakness of the "third" Klan has been the considerable strength of the White Citizens Councils. The "respectable" southerners who resisted integration sought to emphasize that they were law-abiding. They stressed their differences with the more militant Klan. The Councils were founded in the Mississippi Delta in 1954 immediately after the Supreme Court's school desegregation decision. Their concern with respectability has been almost obsessive. Their propaganda has stressed that their leadership is drawn from among "the best people," that they include "the most prominent, well-educated and conservative businessmen in each community."[112]

There are no reliable estimates of Council membership, but a report by the American Jewish Committee judged it to be around 1,000,000 before the 1964 election campaign.[113] Although the Councils concentrated on opposition to integration, their literature generally took on a right-wing cast with respect to economic and other issues, strongly opposing liberal legislation and the welfare state. The civil rights movement was described as Communist-controlled, and Council papers attacked the Jews for supporting desegregation.

The overwhelming support of the Councils at their height was in "the heavily Negro-populated Black Belt regions of the Deep South."[114] In these areas, which had heavily supported the states rights campaign of Strom Thurmond for President in 1948, Council chapters were "typically composed of white small farmers, sharecroppers, planters, and those closely related to the plantation economy (e.g., ginners, managers, etc.) as well as from the town, the mayor, the chief of police, the bankers, the lawyers, and most of the merchants."[115] The principal strength of the Councils was in the small Deep South communities.

The Councils attempted to secure strength in other areas, including non-southern ones. They claimed units in twenty-nine states, outside of the small towns of the Deep South. These have been small, however, and tended to resemble units of the Klan. These Councils were "primarily an urban phenomenon, generally small in membership, and usually composed of individuals from workingclass and lower middle class stations."[119]

The failure to block some measure of formal integration has resulted in a considerable decline in Council membership. As in the case of the Klan in the early twenties, this decline has been greatest among the middle-class "respectable" elements. Thus, as the Councils have grown weaker, they have come to resemble the Klan. Their papers and activities have become increasingly extremist.

Perhaps the best example of the growing similarity between the Citizens Councils and the Klan after 1964 may be found in the biweekly newspaper, the *Councilor*. This paper is published in Shreveport, the city which was the strongest base of the 1920's Klan. It began life as the organ of the Louisiana White Citizens Council, a group which in ideology and support bore closer resemblance to the Klans than to the larger Councils of the Black Belt states. The *Councilor* gradually has taken over the function of serving as the organ of the anti-Negro right wing, the country over. During 1965, the paper changed its identity from a local organ to a national newspaper serving "the movement" generally. It claims a readership of well over 200,000 in all the fifty states and boasts that it is the most widely read right-wing publication in the United States. It tends to report on speeches and statements by right-wing leaders adhering to different organizations such as Gerald L. K. Smith, Robert Welch, the head of the Birch Society, and Robert Shelton, the leader of the largest and most effective Klan organization. Indicative, perhaps, of its importance in the larger movement is the fact that Westbrook Pegler chose it as the principal outlet for his views beginning in 1965. Its issues are replete with constant attacks on Negroes, stressing the notion that Negroes are biologically inferior and that they desire sexual relations with whites, both legitimate and illegitimate. The paper is also strongly anti-Semitic. It seeks to connect Jews with Communism and with control of the civil rights movement. Fidel Castro is described as the scion of an old Jewish family, which has had connections with the Rothschilds.[117] The Rothschilds, in turn, are reported as controlling "most of the world's gold supply and most of the political parties in the major countries."[118] The National Council of Churches is described as "working closely with communist front groups in fomenting racial discord."[119]

The *Councilor* has frequently reported on a vast variety of Communist plots stemming from Cuba and the Soviet Union designed to foster integration. One of its favorite themes is the Kennedy assassination. It is as convinced as the various left-wing critics of the Warren Commission Report that the Commission covered up the true story. Oswald is pictured as having been part of a vast Communist conspiracy which included his killer, Jack Ruby, always identified in the paper as Rubenstein. But though President Kennedy was a victim of a Communist plot, his brother Robert was linked with another Communist "murder," that of Marilyn Monroe, identified in the *Councilor* as "Mortenson." Thus the paper inquired, "Did the communists kill Norma Jean Mortenson? Was she talking too much about her close friendship with Bobby Kennedy?"[120]

The *Councilor* clearly sees itself as part of a continuing and larger right-wing movement. It has described Charles Lindbergh as a man persecuted for his efforts to preserve American independence before World War II. Father Charles Coughlin appears on its pages as a major figure of the thirties who warned America against Communism. And in December 1964, Coughlin was quoted in a current warning against a plot "to strip America of firearms, as outlined in State Department document 7277."[121]

The story of this document is a favorite theme of many extreme rightists who contend that in it the State Department has urged that the United States yield control over its defenses to the United Nations. Coughlin's old theme that the United States has given over control of its monies to the bankers, and that such control must be regained, is also repeated in this right-wing organ.[122]

Various themes which were raised by Senator McCarthy in the early fifties are also dealt with in the *Councilor*. Thus its issues contain many stories concerning Communist influence in television, motion pictures, the press, the churches, and various agencies of government. The charges found in many right-wing publications that the liberals and radicals in government are using psychiatrists to imprison right-wingers in mental institutions are also frequently reported.[123] Sexual immorality in high places disturbs the editors of the *Councilor*. Homosexuality, in particular, is supposedly common in high government circles.

Perhaps the most fascinating aspect in the modern propaganda of this paper is its identification with long past history. In July 1965, it reported the formation of "The Know-Nothing Society" designed to counterbalance left-wing secret societies such as the ADL and the Illuminati. The new Know-Nothings are concerned with infiltrating leftist groups, exposing left-wing politicians, preventing integration through use of harassing tactics, forcing merchants to stop selling goods from Communist countries, and the like. "The Know-Nothings are instructed not to reveal their identity in order to maintain maximum effectiveness. Many of them have infiltrated leftwing organizations. . . . In some instances, entire existing organizations are becoming affiliated with the Know-Nothings and work through one contact man in the organization."[124]

The concern of the modern Know-Nothings in combating secret societies, including the Illuminati, points to what is perhaps the most continuous conspiratorial belief of rightist extremists: the conviction that the Illuminati have continued to exist over the centuries and that they are behind various Jewish, Communist, and other evil plots. The *Councilor* has published a number of articles and many advertisements dealing with reports of their past and present activities. Thus the assassinations of Lincoln, Kennedy, and others are credited to the Illuminati.

The *Councilor* claims that it has clues pointing "to the existence in New Orleans of a secret society organized nearly 200 years ago in Bavaria. This society uses political assassination as a method of controlling world money markets. . . ."[125] The Illuminati are linked by the *Councilor* with causing the Mexican War, with "starting the U.S. Civil War, . . . the death of American Presidents from Lincoln forward. . . . U.S. money policy and favoritism in such matters as military procurement and federal contracts . . . Jacobinism, Bolshevism, and Communism."[126]

Judah P. Benjamin, the Jewish Secretary of State of the Confederacy, is held to have been an Illuminati who, together with his law partner, John Slidell, and in cooperation with northern Jews, the Seligman brothers, August Schoenberg, Meyer Lehman, and the Rothschilds in Europe, helped start the Civil War and later organized the assassination of Lincoln. The full conspiracy, as outlined by the *Councilor* and the Klan organ, *The Fiery Cross*, and repeated in various issues, needs little interpretation:

1. There is an international "conspiracy" which seeks to pervert and control the governments of men.

2. This conspiracy aims to erect a world despotism, ruled by anti-Christians.

3. Adam Weishaupt is really the father of Bolshevism—not Karl Marx—and the principles of Leopold Engels were a direct outgrowth of the principles of Weishaupt.

4. The *Jacobins* of the French Revolution were controlled by the Bavarian Illuminati.

. . . The "Conspiracy" to-day controls communism. Earlier it used the destructive forces of "Bolshevism" and "Jacobinism." The first two forms were controlled from Frankfort-on-Main by the Bavarian Illuminati. The latter forms, "communism" and related types of social revolt, are controlled from New York, London, Moscow, and Biro Bidjan. Historians can trace the same revolution or dialectic materialism back through medieval Rabbinism to the oriental centers of the Khazars. The philosophies are almost identical to the teachings of the Pharisaic seminary at Babylon after the Diaspora which was allegedly based on the unwritten "tradition" of the Pharisees who prospered prior to the birth of Christ.[127]

Readers of the *Councilor* are often offered books which detail the Illuminati conspiracy. A frequently repeated advertisement links the Illuminati and Communism to the continued existence of the Satanic "Black Mass."

Advanced students of "communism" are usually surprised to learn about the "Black Mass" ritual which is indulged by many of the leaders of international conspiracy. These leaders are not necessarily "communists" but they own and control communism. . . .

Subsequent investigations indicated that the Illuminati was involved. The Black Mass is a sordid ritual which is purposely anti-Christian. You will be surprised to learn the role of occultism and depravity in high places—often involving persons high in government.[128]

There is, of course, no way to discover how many supporters of the Klan and the more extremist wing of the Citizens Councils believe in the complex ideology and assorted conspiracies presented in the *Councilor* and the various books which are advertised in it and other right-wing organs. The fact, however, that it has outdistanced its journalistic competitors on the right, particularly in the openly racist segments, does suggest that there are many who welcome detailed conspiratorial theories of the reasons for the changes in American life which they so dislike.

The fantastic world of Jewish international financiers and Communist and Illuminati conspirators which bedevils the life of the readers of the mass circulation *Councilor* and the more rabid Klansmen, Minutemen, and Citizens Council members reaches out to many others on the extreme right. Perhaps the most energetic distributor of such plots within the right in recent decades has been William Guy Carr, an Englishman who lived in Canada from 1920 to his death in 1959. Carr published seven books in the post-World War II era elaborating on the conspiracy of the Illuminati.[129] His two most widely circulated works were *Pawns in the Game*[130] and *The Red Fog over America*.[131] He also published a periodical, *News Behind the News*, which circulated among right-wing groups.[132] Other right-wing pamphleteers circulated versions of the conspiracy taken either from Carr or from Nesta Webster, an Englishwoman who wrote two anti-Semitic books dealing with the Illuminati in the early nineteen-twenties.[133] (She served on the Headquarters Committee of the British Fascists.)

These modern versions of the great conspiracy theory have even identified the struggle between good and evil as dating back to ancient times and seemingly involving the battle between God and Satan. The Jews are generally perceived as involved in the conspiracy, being either the founders and controllers of the Illuminati or its dupes. *The Protocols of the Elders of Zion* is frequently linked to the activities of the Illuminati. Essentially Carr perceived "a continuing revolutionary movement that may be traced ultimately to the Heavenly revolution of Lucifer against God."[134] He argued that "the same conspiracy Christ exposed and condemned is going on today."[135] Carr even quotes Jesus as attacking the Illuminati by name.[136] The Illuminati are linked, of course, to every revolutionary movement from the French Revolution on. They use the Masons and the Jews to achieve their ends of controlling the world. Among their many collaborators and tools are internationalists, World Federalists, international bankers, Communists, Zionists, and integrationists.

Many other writers and right-wing publications have focused directly on the Jew as the anti-Christ and the source of the conspiracy which is undermining America and Christian civilization. The plot of the Elders of Zion is taken literally, and Communism is described as a totally Jewish-controlled movement.

Particular emphasis is placed on desegregation by these writers, since they feel that mongrelization of the white race is now taking place. The conspiracy theorists stress that integration and mongrelization (the latter always follows the former) are old Jewish tricks. The Jew, they argue, was able to destroy the Roman Empire by this method. The Jew realizes that racial purity, Christian morality and patriotism are synonymous, and deceitfully preaches equality so that the races will be thrown together.[137]

Similar positions are taken by Gerald L. K. Smith in his monthly magazine, *The Cross and The Flag*, and by the National States Rights party, formed in the spring of 1958, as a union of a number of splinter extremist parties. Anti-Semitism has been "the most constant theme" in Smith's propaganda.[138] He also sees the country as the victim of complex conspiracies. "The twins of the anti-Christ, Zionism and Communism, are seeking to destroy not only the foreground of our tradition, but the background of our tradition."[139] *The Thunderbolt*, the organ of the States Rights party, has argued that the FBI is a major part of the conspiracy: "The FBI stands for the 'civil rights' of a nigger to rape your wife, daughter or sister. To be effective, a conspiracy must camouflage itself and its true purpose and pretend to be the opposite of what it really is. That is the method of J. Edgar Hoover, the Master of Deceit, and the Communist-Jewish Conspiracy which placed him at the head of the FBI."[140]

These different organizational strains of right-wing extremism—the economic ultraconservatism of the Birch Society, the Protestant fundamentalism of Hargis and McIntire, and the overt racism of the KKK—reflected, as might be expected, different kinds of constituencies. All, however, were to come together in George Wallace's campaign for the Presidency in 1968.

Notes

1. Robert Welch, *The Blue Book* (Belmont: Robert Welch, Inc., 1961), p. 108.
2. Robert Welch, *The New Americanism* (Boston: Western Islands, 1966), p. 4.
3. E. Merrill Root, "Our Frontier," *American Opinion*, XI (October 1968), 31.

4. Robert H. Montgomery, "From the North," *American Opinion*, IX (April 1966), p. 61.

5. Arnold Forster and Benjamin R. Epstein, *Danger on the Right* (New York: Random House, 1965), p. 188.

6. Quoted in *ibid.*, p. 255.

7. For the most detailed version of Robert Welch's beliefs, see his manuscript *The Politician* (Belmont: Robert Welch, Inc., 1963).

8. Birch Society *Bulletin* (July 1968), p. 4.

9. See Medford Evans, *The Usurpers* (Belmont, Mass.: Western Islands, 1968), pp. 180–182.

10. Welch, *The New Americanism*, *op. cit.*, p. 136; see pp. 125–137 for the full discussion of the Illuminati.

11. Robert Welch, *The Truth in Time* (Belmont: American Opinion, 1967), p. 1.

12. John Robison, *Proof of a Conspiracy* (Boston: Western Islands, 1967), Publisher's "Introduction," first page (the "Introduction" has no numbered pagination). See also *Seventeen Eighty-Nine. An unfinished manuscript which explores the early history of the Communist conspiracy* (Belmont: American Opinion, 1968).

13. Robison, *op. cit.*, Introduction, sixth unnumbered page.

14. Birch Society *Bulletin* (August 1968), pp. 9–11. For a reiteration of the Robison and Barruel exposés as applying to the present and more on the link between the attack on the Bastille and the Poor People's march, see *Ibid.* (January 1970), pp. 1–8.

15. Welch, *Truth in Time*, *op. cit.*, p. 3.

16. *Ibid.*, p. 5.

17. *Ibid.*, pp. 5–6.

18. *Ibid.*, p. 8. Emphasis in the original.

19. *Ibid.*, pp. 8–15.

20. *Ibid.*, pp. 22–23.

21. *Ibid.*, p. 22. Emphases ours.

22. In John Birch Society, *Bulletin for November* (October 31, 1959), p. 1, cited in Eckard V. Toy, Jr., *Ideology and Conflict in American Conservatism, 1945–1960* (Ph.D. Thesis, Department of History, University of Oregon, 1965), p. 249.

23. William Guy Carr, *The Red Fog over America* (Toronto: National Federation of Christian Laymen, 1957), pp. 258–259. The Pike referred to above is "General Albert Pike," supposed "Sovereign Pontiff of Universal Freemasonry and head of the Illuminati" around the 1870's. *Ibid.*, pp. 224–225. See also The Cardinal of Chile (Maria Cardenal Caro Y Rodriguez), *The Mystery of Freemasonry Unveiled* (no publisher listed, no date of publication). The first edition of this book was apparently published in Santiago, Chile, in 1925. It is currently available in English in the United States; see pp. 175–181 and *passim*. This book also expounds the theory that the Illuminati and Masonry generally are engaged in a Satanic plot to destroy religion and dominate the world.

24. Welch, *Truth in Time*, *op. cit.*, pp. 21–22.

25. Welch, *The Politician*, *op. cit.*, p. 13.

26. *Ibid.*, p. 15.

27. *Ibid.*, p. 259.

28. *Ibid.*, p. 279.
29. Cited in J. Allen Broyles, *The John Birch Society: Anatomy of a Protest* (Boston: Beacon, 1966), p. 7.
30. Welch, *The Politician, op. cit.*, p. 278.
31. *Ibid.*, p. 222.
32. *Ibid.*, p. 223.
33. *Ibid.*, p. 227.
34. *Ibid.*, p. 236.
35. Revilo P. Oliver, "Marxmanship in Dallas," *American Opinion*, VII (February 1964), 18.
36. Birch Society Letter, "To Some Very Patient and Patriotic People," dated September 30, 1968. See also *Bulletin* (January 1969), p. 8.
37. Welch, *The New Americanism, op. cit.*, pp. 78–79. Emphasis in the original. See *Bulletin* (March 1969), p. 11.
38. Introduction to Robison, *op. cit.*, sixth and seventh unnumbered pages.
39. *Ibid.*, eighth unnumbered page.
40. Phyllis Schlafly, *A Choice Not an Echo* (Alton, Ill.: Pere Marquette Press, 1964), p. 25.
41. See "The Bilderberger Queen," in *Review of the News*, September 21, 1966, pp. 17–24. This is a Birch Society publication.
42. *Ibid.*, pp. 19–20.
43. *Ibid.*, p. 21.
44. *Ibid.*, p. 24.
45. Gary Allen, "The C.F.R., Conspiracy to Rule the World," *American Opinion*, XII (April 1969), 56.
46. See "Organization," leaflet distributed by the *Midnight Cry* (July 1966). This is a fundamentalist magazine.
47. *America*, CVI (January 20, 1962), 510–511.
48. Edward T. Gargan, "Radical Catholics of the Right," *Social Order* (November 1961).
49. "Senator Cautions Birch Unit Foes," *New York Times*, April 6, 1961, p. 16.
50. Frederick W. Grupp, Jr., *Social Correlates of Political Activists: The John Birch Society and the ADA* (Ph.D. Thesis, Department of Political Science, University of Pennsylvania, 1968), p. 53.
51. "Catholics and Extremism," *Commonweal*, LXXV (January 19, 1962), 423.
52. S. J. Adamo, "Catholics and the John Birch Society," *Jubilee, A Magazine of the Church and Her People*, XIV (July 1966), 8–11.
53. Robert Welch, *The Neutralizers* (Belmont, Mass.: The John Birch Society, 1963), pp. 22–23.
54. Edgar G. Engleman, *The Changing Appeals of the John Birch Society* (Honors Thesis, Department of Social Relations, Harvard University, 1967), p. 135.
55. See Tables IV, VI, and VII, pp. 89, 91, 92, in *ibid.*
56. *Bulletin* (July 1966), p. 18.
57. Brooks R. Walker, *The Christian Fright Peddlers* (Garden City: Doubleday, 1964), p. 134.
58. *Ibid.*, pp. 135–136.
59. *Ibid.*, p. 137.

60. Revilo P. Oliver, "Marxmanship in Dallas: Part II," *American Opinion,* VII (March 1964), 74.

61. *Bulletin* (November 1965), p. 108. See also *Bulletin* (April 1961) for a detailed argument against anti-Semitism.

62. Welch, *The Neutralizers, op. cit.*

63. *Ibid.,* p. 29.

64. *Ibid.*

65. Westbrook Pegler, "Pegler on Bigotry," *American Opinion,* VI (November 1963), 18.

66. *New York Times,* August 16, 1966, p. 9, as reported in Engleman, *op. cit.,* p. 107.

67. Benjamin R. Epstein and Arnold Forster, *Report on the John Birch Society 1966* (New York, Vintage, 1966), pp. 31–37.

68. Welch, *The Neutralizers, op. cit.,* p. 15.

69. Grupp, *op. cit.,* p. 5.

70. *Bulletin* (February 1966), pp. 19–21.

71. John Rousselot, "Civil Rights," *American Opinion,* VII (February 1964), 11.

72. Book Review of Clarence Manion, *The American Conservative,* in *American Opinion,* VII (September 1964), 49.

73. *Bulletin* (May 1964), p. 17; see also "What's Wrong With Civil Rights," *Bulletin* (November 1965), pp. 45–48; and Rousselot, "Civil Rights," *op. cit.,* 1–11. For comments on the Black Panthers, see *Bulletin* (March 1970), p. 13.

74. Earl Lively, Jr., "Phase Out: Disarmament by Depreciation," *American Opinion,* VII (May 1964), 23.

75. A. G. Heinsohn, "Free Lunch and Boobus Americanus," *American Opinion,* VII (June 1966), 85.

76. Montgomery, *op. cit.,* p. 57.

77. Epstein and Forster, *op. cit.,* p. 12.

78. Gustavus Myers, *History of Bigotry in the United States* (New York: Capricorn, 1960), p. 107.

79. See especially *National Review,* XVII (October 19, 1965), 914–928.

80. "Get Us Out," *National Review,* XVII (October 19, 1965), 92.

81. Letter, *National Review,* XVII (October 19, 1965), 929.

82. Epstein and Forster, *op. cit.,* p. 88.

83. Frederick W. Grupp, Jr., "Political Activists: The John Birch Society and the A.D.A.," paper presented at the 1966 meetings of the American Political Science Association, p. 2.

84. Epstein and Forster, *op. cit.,* p. 193.

85. *Ibid.,* pp. 91–92.

86. Grupp, *op. cit.,* pp. 8–10.

87. Engleman, *op. cit.,* p. 105.

88. Frances Murray Dahlberg, *We Look for Communists Everywhere of Course* (M.A. Thesis, Department of Sociology, Cornell University, 1966), pp. 99, 41.

89. *Ibid.,* p. 54.

90. *Ibid.,* p. 55.

91. *Ibid.,* pp. 57–58.

92. *Ibid.,* Figure 26, p. 98.

93. Engleman, *op. cit.*, pp. 65–66.
94. *Ibid.*, p. 66.
95. *Ibid.*, Table V, p. 90.
96. "Welch Links War to More Controls," *New York Times*, December 10, 1966, p. 25; *Bulletin* (March 1969), pp. 5–6; Robert Welch, *The Truth about Vietnam* (Belmont: American Opinion, 1968).
97. Engleman, *op. cit.*, p. 67.
98. For an analysis of the activities of the Crusade, see John Harold Redekop, *Billy James Hargis: A Case Study of the American Far Right* (Ph.D. Thesis, Department of Political Science, University of Washington, 1965).
99. *Ibid.*, pp. 49–51.
100. *Ibid.*, pp. 97–99, 67.
101. *Ibid.*, pp. 65–66.
102. Billy James Hargis, *The Real Extremists—The Far Left* (Tulsa: Christian Crusade Publications, 1964), p. 16.
103. Redekop, *op. cit.*, pp. 46–47.
104. "Rev. Billy James Hargis: The Christian Crusade," *Facts*, XIV (April 1962), 232.
105. Walker, *op. cit.*, p. 98.
106. *Ibid.*, p. 99.
107. *Ibid.*, pp. 96–97.
108. Lester DeKoster, *The Christian and the John Birch Society* (Grand Rapids: William E. Erdmans, 1966), p. 26. The pamphlet is a *Reformed Journal* monograph. The *Reformed Journal* presents a "Calvinist point of view."
109. David Mark Chalmers, *Hooded Americanism* (Garden City: Doubleday, 1965), pp. 323–324.
110. *Ibid.*, pp. 349–350.
111. See "Rightist Extremism Ku Klux Klan," *American Jewish Year Book, 1966* (Philadelphia: Jewish Publications Society, 1967), pp. 151–153.
112. James W. Vander Zanden, *The Southern White Resistance Movement to Integration* (Ph.D. Thesis: Department of Sociology, University of North Carolina, 1958), p. 311.
113. Milton Ellerin, "Rightist Extremism," *American Jewish Year Book, 1965* (Philadelphia: Jewish Publications Society, 1966), p. 199.
114. Vander Zanden, *op. cit.*, p. 313.
115. *Ibid.*, p. 320.
116. *Ibid.*, p. 321.
117. *Councilor*, May 29, 1964, p. 1.
118. *Ibid.*, July 16, 1964, p. 1.
119. *Ibid.*, June 30, 1964, pp. 1, 4.
120. *Ibid.*, November 19, 1964, p. 4. This theme continues long after Senator Kennedy's death. See advertisement "Senator Kennedy and a Mystery: Strange Death of Marilyn Monroe," *Ibid.*, February 12, 1970, p. 3.
121. *Ibid.*, December 31, 1964, p. 3.
122. See "Resolution to Return Control of U.S. Money to Congress," *Councilor*, January 16, 1965, p. 3.
123. See "California Doctor Warns that Mental Health Program Can Be Used for Political Imprisonment," *Councilor*, March 22, 1965, p. 3.
124. "Know-Nothing Society," *Councilor*, July 15, 1965, p. 4.

125. "Role of Secret Society in Forming History Hinted in 78-year-old Confession by Spitz," *Councilor*, April 9, 1965, p. 1.

126. *Ibid.*; see also "Shrines of History Wantonly Burned in an Orgy of Hate," *ibid.*, February 12, 1970, p. 4 for more on the assassination of Lincoln by the "Bavarian nihilists" and the role of the Rothschilds.

127. "Ancient Conspiracy Linked to Jacobins and Bolshevists," *Councilor*, February 1, 1965, p. 2; see later issues of the *Councilor, The Fiery Cross*, and the *Illuminator* for more of the same. For example, the argument that Benjamin, Slidell and the Rothschilds provoked the Civil War, Reconstruction outrages, and that others in the plot have more recently created the Internal Revenue Service and the civil rights movement may be found in "The Fantastic Story of Big Daddy [Benjamin] and Candlestick Johnny [Slidell]," the *Councilor*, February 12, 1970, pp. 1, 3.

128. "The Black Mass," *Councilor*, September 15, 1965, p. 4.

129. See Rodger A. Remington, *The Function of the "Conspiracy Theory" in American Intellectual History* (Ph.D. Thesis, Department of History, St. Louis University, 1965), pp. 83–118.

130. Toronto: National Federation of Christian Laymen, 1956.

131. Toronto: National Federation of Christian Laymen, 1957.

132. See William C. Baum, *The Conspiracy Theory of Politics of the Radical Right in the United States* (Ph.D. Thesis, Department of Political Science, State University of Iowa, 1960), pp. 10–13.

133. Nesta H. Webster, *World Revolution* (London: Constable, 1921), and *Secret Societies and Subversive Movements* (New York: Dutton, 1924). She was an active early Fascist.

134. Remington, *op. cit.*, p. 84. See Robert Benewick, *Political Violence and Public Order* (London: Allen Lane, The Penguin Press, 1969), pp. 29, 32–33.

135. William G. Carr, *The International Conspiracy* (undated pamphlet), p. 4, cited in Baum, *op. cit.*, p. 12.

136. Cited in *ibid.*, p. 13.

137. *Ibid.*, pp. 32 ff.

138. William Roy McPherson, *Parallels in Extremist Ideology* (Ph.D. Thesis, Department of Social Relations, Harvard University, 1967), p. 49.

139. Solicitation letter from Gerald L. K. Smith, November 7, 1958, reported in Burton Levy, *Profile of the American Right: A Case Study of Michigan* (Ph.D. Thesis, Department of Political Science, University of Massachusetts, 1965), p. 51.

140. *The Thunderbolt* (February 1960), as cited in *ibid.*, p. 124.

8

The Birch Society and Its Contemporaries:
Social Base

Right-Wing Heterogeneity

The concept of "selective support" has threaded its way through the study of a number of right-wing groups. There was evidence that some of Coughlin's opinion poll supporters may have been doing no more than vaguely giving vent to their preservatist feelings, without particularly adopting Coughlin's program. Indeed, some of them may have found this the most convenient way of just expressing their conviction that something was awry. McCarthy's support was marked by the same kind of ambiguity.

It is not just that social movements attract people for different reasons. As Hans Toch has pointed out, "Social movements in search of a mass following frequently follow a saturation method, and try to present a 'cafeteria' of appeals, catering to a diversity of needs."[1]

But "selective support" connotes different levels of commitment as well. There are several ways in which individuals can relate positively to a social movement. They can join it; they can consistently support it, in voting, in financial contributions, and so on; and they can expressively approve of it when asked. The Joiners obviously do all three; the Supporters approve, but do not join; the Approvers do not join or consistently support. The common usage of the term "social movement" confusingly embraces different combinations of these three levels of commitment at different times. The Joiners clearly are part of a movement. In a political context, the preferential Supporters are properly considered part of a movement, the fellow travelers. But the Approvers are more a

Sympathetic Audience than part of the movement. Blumer defines a social movement as a "collective [enterprise] to establish a new order of life."[2] Smelser defines collective behavior, including social movements, as "mobilization on the basis of a belief which redefines social action."[3] Toch offers this psychological definition: "A social movement represents an effort by a large number of people to solve collectively a problem that they feel they have in common."[4]

A social movement's Supporters, and even its Joiners, may support and join for different kinds of reasons, may treat the program of the movement like a cafeteria; but as long as they remain Joiner and Consistent Supporter, they are engaged in a specific collective effort and enterprise directed toward affecting the socal order, based on some compatible generalized beliefs. The Approvers are not, necessarily, so involved. This typology does not really relate to the motivations of members. There are obviously psychological factors which often distinguish joiners from nonjoiners. The typology relates rather to the nature of social movements and denotes certain levels of effective commitment. The three levels of commitment suggested may roughly correspond to the three stages Toch indicates a person must progressively enter if he is to move "from predisposition to susceptibility." To join a social movement, (1) he must sense a problem, (2) he must feel that something can be done about it, (3) he must want to do something about it himself.[5]

The Approver may only sense a problem; he may expressively "approve of" a movement which is apparently built around the same sense of disaffection; but he may well vote against it on balance, even disapprove of its specific program. The Approvers are not part of a social movement, but insofar as they express approval on the basis of some strong disaffection, insofar as they are a sympathetic if restrained audience, they represent a Tendency in society. Such a Tendency, on the one hand, carries a potential for swelling a Movement under conducive circumstances and gives strength and credibility to Movements. The trick for pollsters and main-stream politicians is to interpret exactly what the Tendency is, what the source of disaffection is, what the Approver is approving and what he is not.

It has been indicated that McCarthyism, of all the phenomena reviewed, was more a Tendency than a Movement. No opportunity for joining was even provided. There was active support on many levels, but it was not reflected in voting patterns. But McCarthy was widely approved; he symbolized, stimulated, and probably overrepresented a Tendency in America. The Birch Society, of course, is highly organized.

The gradation discussed above, however, has horizontal application as well. It has been traditional to distinguish among movements which are "general" (such as the labor movement), those which are "specific" (such as the Prohibition movement), and those which are "expressive" (such as a fashion movement).⁶ But many social movements do not fall easily into any of these categories and are significantly idiosyncratic. The Birch Society, for example, is built on twin foundations: its conservatism, and its conspiratorial, monistic set of beliefs. Those who actually join the Birch Society presumably tend to subscribe to both of these sets of beliefs. But the supporters, and even more the approvers, conceivably are selective in their support and in their approval. The Birch Society itself has comprised, at best, a small actual membership, and its significance has been counted in terms of its fellow travelers and in terms of the Tendency which it has presumably represented. Therefore isolating the factors of selectivity is important for evaluating the nature of that Tendency and perhaps accounts for much of the difficulty in attempting to assess the Society membership by unitary standards.

A clue to the heterogeneous nature of Birch support and approval is provided through a special survey of letter writers made in connection with the preparation of this volume. In the spring of 1963, a national Republican party leader had made a widely publicized speech attacking right-wing extremism as a general phenomenon. About two thousand letters objecting to his speech were written to him in the next two days. Two characteristics of this batch of letters distinguished them: they were "spontaneous" responses, to the extent that they were sent within forty-eight hours and presumably not subject to any carefully modeled campaign. They were not responding to any specific issue such as the United Nations, the welfare state, or Communism. They were responding to a generalized attack on "right-wing extremism," and they reacted in terms of their own definitions of that phenomenon.

At the time these letters were given to us for analysis, an extensive national survey attitudes was being planned as part of the ADL supported series studies of anti-Semitism and right-wing extremism. On a random sample basis, 115 of these letter writers were interviewed, to provide some comparison with our national profile. This study will be referred to as the Special Letter Writing Survey. A random sample of 400 of these letters had initially been examined for content and divided into two categories. One category comprised letters which contained an explicit monistic element: a clear note of conspiracy theory or of racism. These were classified as the "M" letter writers, accounting for about 36 per cent of the total letter writers. The others were classified as "Non-M's." Included in our national interview survey were 59 of the M's and 56 of the Non-M's. The initial problem was the extent to which an analysis of such letters could provide a valid clue to the actual attitudes of the letter writers as revealed in interviews. But the further question was whether these categories provided some rough clue to the existence of disparate strains to be found among a typical body of right-wing letter writers.

It is obvious that many factors affect a letter writer's decision as to whether to bare his racist or conspiracy-oriented thoughts. We hypothesized that letter writers who revealed these particular attitudes explicitly would be those who, *as a group*, felt the salience of these attitudes most strongly and had them "on the top of their heads." In fact, this common-sense tautology was supported by the evidence as indicated in Table 28: the M's as a group were substantially more racist in attitude and more conspiracy-minded. While the cells were often small, the pattern was consistent. Twice as many M's thought that Negroes were lazy, that Jews have too much power, that Jews use shady practices. In some cases, the differentials were smaller, but the M bias was constant. Similarly, on questions that related to conspiracy, the M's were consistently higher, 56 per cent of them believing that "much of our lives is controlled by plots hatched in secret places," as against 34 per cent of the Non-M's.

The suggestion here, even without further refinement, is that there are two kinds of people represented among these letter writers and among Birch supporters. When asked how they felt toward the Birch Society, 73 per cent of the M's and 70 per cent of the Non-M's said that they "strongly approved"; only 2 per cent of the M's and 4 per cent of the Non-M's "disapproved" to any degree. They were also united in their attitudes toward substantive right-wing questions, as indicated in Section V of Table 28. Almost all of them—and as many Non-M's as M's—felt that government is gradually taking away our freedoms and that the country is moving toward socialism. These are "pure" antistatist questions, and these letter writers are all antistatists. Even such undiluted antistatism is not automatically related to monistic tendencies. Other kinds of right-wing questions seem to establish the relationship of conspiracy and bigotry. Of the 81 antistatists who believe that American Communists are a very great danger, 43 per cent believe that Jews have too much power; of the 25 who believe that the Communists are not such a danger, only 16 per cent believe that the Jews have too much power, a figure not much higher than that of the general American population. Of the 77 anti-statists who believe that the Communists are a very great danger *and* who disapprove of the UN, 35 believe the Jews have too much power. None of the 10 antistatists who believe that the Communists are not such a danger *and* who approve the UN believe the Jews have too much power. Because of the numbers, these are hardly conclusive, but the clues pile up consistently. They suggest that there are at least two kinds of issues involved in what is usually considered a right-wing pattern. In Table 29, for example, it is indicated that among the general American population,

Table 28.   VARIATIONS IN ATTITUDES OF MONIST AND NONMONIST RIGHT-WING
LETTER WRITERS AND GENERAL PUBLIC (PER CENT AGREEING)

Attitudes	1964 Sample of U.S. Population	Total Letter Writers	"M" Letter Writers	"Non-M" Letter Writers
Number	(1,973)	(115)	(59)	(56)
		I		
"Negroes are lazy"	36	38	58	27
"White children and Negro children should go to the same school"	63	63	44	73
"Before Negroes are given equal rights, they have to show that they deserve them"	60	58	71	54
		II		
"Jews are more likely than other people to be Communists"	3	27	39	20
"Jews have stirred up a lot of trouble between whites and Negroes"	13	26	42	18
"Jews have too much power in U.S."	11	31	46	23
		III		
"Jews are more willing than others to use shady practices"	42	33	47	25
"Jews are shrewd and tricky"	35	25	34	20
"Jews are warm and friendly"	75	71	59	77
		IV		
"Plots are hatched in secret places"	25	42	56	34
"No special group more likely to be Communists"	64	27	12	36
		V		
"Federal government is taking away our freedoms"	43	96	95	96
"Country moving towards socialism"	43	95	95	95
		VI		
"American Communists a very great danger"	17	70	81	64
"In favor of the United Nations"	86	17	12	20

those who "somewhat approve" the Birch Society are slightly more antistatist than those who "strongly approve." In that regard, both are sharply
distinguished from the rest of the population. But when other extremist
questions are asked, the Somewhat-Approvers begin to resemble the rest
of the population more than they do the Strongly-Approvers.

Obviously the principle of selective support is very much at work with
respect to support of the Birch Society and is often hidden by assumptions

Table 29.   POLITICAL ATTITUDES, BY APPROVAL OF BIRCH SOCIETY,
U.S. POPULATION, 1964 (PER CENT)

Attitudes	Opinion of Birch Society*			
	Strongly Approve	Somewhat Approve	Somewhat Disapprove	Strongly Disapprove
Number	(25)	(186)	(293)	(397)
"Government taking away basic freedoms"	68	70	46	29
"U.S. moving to socialism"	64	70	47	32
"Communists a very great danger"	40	24	14	15
"Approve U.N."	64	81	92	95

* The "Don't Knows" and "Have Not Heard of the Birch Society" are omitted.

of unitary character or by undiscriminating statistics. A more thorough typological analysis will be attempted later in the volume. But even at this point it is apparent that it would be a mistake to give a homogeneous stamp to the supporters of the Birch Society, much less to "right-wing extremists." Nevertheless, the analyses of the social base of the Birch Society, as compared with the other right-wing organizational strains, emphasize the dominant common bias of each of these strains, as well as the differences among them.

The Birch Society Public

The existing surveys of right-wing activists in the late 1950's and 1960's have located the individuals to be studied in different ways. Fred Grupp, of the University of Connecticut, was able to get the Birch Society itself to send out a questionnaire to a random sample of its national membership. The Society did the mailing and secured the returned questionnaires so as to guarantee that no outsider could relate opinions to specific individuals. This method produced 650 returns, or a 35 per cent response, which Grupp then transformed to IBM cards for statistical analysis.[7] A second study dealing with Birch Society members, by Burton Levy, sought to compare persons publicly associated with three right-wing groups in Michigan. Levy secured the names of 91 Birch Society members who had admitted membership in letters to the editors of newspapers or had revealed their membership at meetings of the society. He also located 75 members of the Independent American party, a racist organization, who had run for public office on the party's slate in the 1960 and 1962 elections. As a control group of nonextremist right-wingers, he took the names of 217 members of the more moderate Conservative Federation, taken from lists prepared by the organization or published in its monthly paper. A questionnaire was mailed to the names on these three lists in the first week of November 1963. Forty-one per cent of the questionnaires were completed and returned: 50 per cent from the Conservative Federation, 46 per cent from the Birch Society, and 32 per cent from the Independent American party.[8]

A third study of Birch Society members, conducted by Barbara Stone, differed from the other two methodologically, since it involved interviews with 50 members of the Society in California. The 50 interviewed were selected by officials of the Society, after the "author impressed upon the leadership that it was vital for the respondents to represent as accurate a cross-section of the group as possible."[9]

The special letter-writer sample, which was interviewed for our study, is clearly composed of right-wingers. Their backgrounds also give us some indication of the backgrounds of ultraright activists.

A study which sought to compare extremists with other types of political activists drew its samples from different Oregon populations. Ira Rohter secured the names of "rightists" from newspaper accounts in Portland, Oregon, of members of the Liberty (anti-income tax) Amendment Committee and of the John Birch Society. To this group were added the names of persons who had written letters with rightist themes to newspapers in Eugene and Medford, Oregon, and to a local congressman. The non-extremist control samples were composed of two groups: "negative voters," those who had been involved actively in opposing urban renewal, water fluoridation, school bond issues, and other local government measures in Springfield and Eugene, Oregon, and "positive voters," those who supported urban renewal and fluoridation. These three groups were then interviewed in depth. Over half of the rightists (137) and about three-quarters of the nonrightists (199) took part in the interviews.[10]

Another more limited study based on interviews with Oregon extremists was conducted by Scott McNall, who interviewed members of an anti-Communist fundamentalist politico-religious sect, The Freedom Center of Portland, Oregon. This was a small organization whose views on political issues generally paralleled those of the Birch Society. The Freedom Center, however, placed a great deal of emphasis on fundamentalist Protestant beliefs and was more overtly anti-Negro and racist than the Birch Society. McNall interviewed 57 out of the 125 members. He also interviewed another 53 rightists who did not belong to the organization, but had indicated their politics through writing "rightist" letters to editors of newspapers or had indicated support of the Liberty Amendment or the "Manion Forum." Both of the latter were supported by the Birch Society.[11]

A further approach to specifying the characteristics of radical rightists involved securing information from those who paid tuition and attended a School of Anti-Communism conducted by Dr. Fred Schwarz and his Christian Anti-Communism Crusade in Oakland, California, from January 29 to February 2, 1962. Stanford students operating under faculty direction attended the school and approached potential respondents chosen "to represent" the audience in terms of age, sex, and style of dress. One hundred and eight interviews were completed and 625 questionnaires were distributed, of which 244, or 39 per cent, were returned. "The attitudinal and demographic findings were the same in both groups."[12]

Other studies have been based on protest letters inspired by Birch Society campaigns. The recipients of these letters turned them over to scholars for analysis. While the information available from letters is obviously extremely limited, the data do permit us to specify the geographic location of these "activists" and to make estimates of their relative socioeconomic status.[13] Most of the studies supply information on the relatively affluent radical right, the groups whose tone, ideology, and activities uniquely characterize the radical right of the early 1960's. In addition, two of the studies, those by Levy on the Independent American party in Michigan and by McNall of the Portland Freedom Center members, supply a contrasting picture of the background and issues which appeal to the less privileged elements. The data collected by Levy and Rohter of nonextremists among the right provide interesting contrasts.

The Social Base of the Radical Right: Status Indicators

Despite small and unrepresentative samples and varying ways of defining radical rightists, the various studies of right-wing activists agree in several conclusions. Leaving out the supporters of the more fundamentalist and more avowedly racist groups, it is clear that right-wing activists of the Birch Society type of the 1960's are relatively high in education, income, and occupational status. Grupp's sample of the national membership of the Birch Society, Levy's data on Michigan members, and Stone's on Californians, each find that Birch members are clearly more privileged than a national sample of the population. Our national sample of the population collected by NORC in October 1964 indicated that 50 per cent earned less than $6,000 per year, as compared with 14 per cent of the national Birch sample, 27 per cent of the Michigan group, and none of the California sample. (The latter two only involve 42 and 50 people, respectively, and are less representative, so that differences with the national Birch figures may be a result of the variations between the samples, not of real differences.) Conversely, only 4 per cent of the population as a whole reported incomes of over $15,000 per year, as against 22 per cent of the national Birch members, 20 per cent of the special letter writers, 17 per cent of the Michigan ones, and 40 per cent of the California Birchers. Those attending the Christian Crusade in Oakland also were disproportionately well-to-do as compared with a control sample of San Francisco Bay residents employed in nonmanual occupations. The Oregon rightists interviewed by McNall fall in the same pattern, with 30 per cent earning more than $15,000 a year. As might be expected, the data indicate that these people are in relatively high status occupations. Only 14 per cent of the national membership of the Birch Society, 10 per cent of the California members, and 18 per cent of the special letter writers reported being in manual work. The members of the Michigan section were somewhat lower-status (33 per cent manual), a difference which we cannot explain. Wolfinger reported that only 11 per cent of the Bay Area Christian Crusaders were in manual work, while Rohter found that 25 per cent of the Oregon rightists had jobs which fell in this category. Nationally, close to half the labor force were so employed.

The high-status character of the right-wing extremists of the mid-1960's becomes even clearer when we compare the educational attainments of the rightists with those of control sample. Sixty-three per cent of the national Birch sample, 60 per cent of the special letter writers, 66 per cent of the Michigan Birch group, 74 per cent of the California Birchers, and 78 per cent of the California Crusaders have at least some college education, as compared to 22 per cent of the sample of the national population.

The members of the two more racist groups, the Portland Freedom Center and the Independent American party, are much lower in status than the other ultra-rightists. The Independent American sample is, of course, not one of rank-and-file members, but of candidates for public office. In spite of this fact, as the data in Table 30 indicate, they have a lower income than those involved in the Birch Society, Birch-like activities, or the Fred Schwartz Christian Crusade. They also are less well educated and in lower occupational positions. Almost half of the candidates are manual workers. Income is the only category for which the Freedom Center members can be compared with the others, and it is clear that the former are relatively quite poor. Half of them earned less than $4,500, as contrasted with 20 per cent among McNall's sample of other rightists and the 10 per cent or less earning $4,000 or less among the Birch Society and Christian Crusade groups. The differences between the Freedom Center members and those involved in supporting the "Manion Forum," the Liberty Amendment lobby, and other Birch Society-type activities in Portland also point to the clear difference in the backing of the two types of right wings.

This finding concerning the varying class appeal of different types of radical right movements also holds up in the content studies of right-wing letters. A comparative study of mail attacking critics of Senator Joseph McCarthy and of the Birch Society indicated that the former appealed to a much lower stratum of the population than the latter. The supporters of Senator McCarthy were much less literate, and presumably much less well-to-do, than those writing in defense of the Birch Society. The report states that "only 15 per cent of the McCarthy mail could—charitably, at best—be described as reasonable in tone, substance, or literacy. . . . The . . . Birch mail is much more moderate in tone than McCarthy mail, even though it may be as extremist in objective. It is much better written and better reasoned."[14]

Two other detailed content analyses of letters written in response to Birch Society campaigns suggest that the bulk of the writers were in middle-class positions, although possibly somewhat lower in status and in writing ability than is true of the average run of mail to political figures, as indicated in other studies.[15] Wartenburg and Thielens, however, report that the Birchite letters indicated "a fairly high level of literacy."[16]

Age

The different types of extremists also vary consistently with respect to age. The two lower-status groups appear to have attracted an older membership than the Birch-type activists. The three studies of Birch Society members agree that the organization appeals to a relatively youthful constituency. The average age of the members of the Society and of the Special Letter Writers group was considerably less than the population as a whole. These findings are congruent with the results of other studies of recent groups of left and right extremists in many countries, a point which will be elaborated in our discussion of the social base of the George Wallace movement.

Religion

The varying groups of rightists also differ with respect to their religious affiliations. Catholics, on the whole, are considerably underrepresented among all samples, except for two Birch Society ones and the Michigan Independent American party. About one-quarter of the former, nationally and in Michigan, and 30 per cent of the latter are Catholics, proportions which are slightly less than the Catholic percentage in the larger populations. Only 16 per cent of the California Birchers are Catholics. The very low proportions of Catholics among the Bay Area Christian Crusaders and the Portland Freedom Center members are inherent in the fact that these basically made an evangelical Protestant appeal. Fundamentalists are also

Table 30. INCOME, EDUCATION, AND OCCUPATION OF RADICAL RIGHTISTS
(Per Cent)

	Ultra-Rightists							Hate Rightists		Control Group
	Grupp JBS National	Levy JBS Michigan	Stone JBS California	Wolfinger Christian Crusade	Rohter Rightists	McNall Rightists	Special Letter Writers	McNall Freedom Center	Levy IAP	National Control Sample (NORC)
Income										
Under $4,000	5	10	—	9	(b)	20[c]	25[d]	50	25	30
$4,000 to $5,999	9	17	—	20		11	30	14	16	20
$6,000 to $9,999	33	45	14[a]	22		19	—	23	42	27
$10,000 to $14,999	27	7	38	20		13	18	5	—	14
$15,000 and up	22	17	40	21		30	20	6	12.5	4
DK–NA	5	4	8	8		7	7	2	5	5
Number	(650)	(42)	(50)	(308)	(167)	(53)	(115)	(56)	(24)	(1,914)
Education										
8th grade	4	10	2[e]	3		(b)	7	(g)	8	28
9th to 11th grades	7	5		5	28[e]		9		21	
High school	24	19	24	11	51[f]		24		33	50[h]
Some college	33	33	28	26	21		23		25	12
College graduate	30	33	46	52	—		37		12.5	10
DK–NA	1	—	—	3			—		—	—
Number	(650)	(42)	(50)	(308)	(167)		(115)		(24)	(1,914)

Occupation[1]						(b)		
Professional and technical	25	19	24	31	22	33	12	14
Businessmen, managers, and officials	30	12	10	27	17	21	17	9
Clerical and sales	17	21	8	14	15	22	17	19
Skill, semiskilled, and service	14	33	10	11	25	18	46	49
Other	6	15	42[1]	6	21	6	8	8
DK–NA	9	—	6	11	—	—	—	—
Number	(650)	(38)	(50)	(308)	(112)[1]	(115)	(24)	(1,914)

SOURCES: Frederick William Grupp, Jr., *Social Correlates of Political Activists: The John Birch Society and the ADA* (Ph.D. Thesis, Department of Political Science, University of Pennsylvania, 1968); Burton Levy, *Profile of the American Right: A Case Study of Michigan* (Ph.D. Thesis, Department of Political Science, University of Massachusetts, 1965); Scott Grant McNall, *The Freedom Center: A Case Study of a Politico-Religious Sect* (Ph.D. Thesis, Department of Sociology, University of Oregon, 1965); Ira S. Rohter, *Radical Rightists: An Empirical Study* (Ph.D. Thesis, Department of Political Science, Michigan State University, 1967); Barbara Stone, *The John Birch Society of California* (Ph.D. Thesis, Department of Political Science, University of Southern California, 1968); Raymond E. Wolfinger et al., "America's Radical Right: Politics and Ideology," in David E. Apter, ed., *Ideology and Discontent* (New York: The Free Press, 1964), pp. 262–293; The "Special Letter Writer" sample is our own, as discussed on pp. 290–293.

[a] Combines income categories $8,000–8,999 and $9,000–9,999. There were no respondents with lower incomes.

[b] Information not given in original study.

[c] McNall divided his respondents into the following income categories: less than $4,499, $4,500–6,499, $6,500–10,499, $10,500–14,999, over $15,000.

[d] Our "Special Writer Sample" was divided into the following income categories: less than $4,999, $5,000–9,999, $10,000–14,999, over $15,000.

[e] Combines first two education categories.

[f] Combines second two education categories.

[g] See Table 31.

[h] Combines second and third education categories.

[i] Rohter used a different system of classifying occupations than the others. His highest class is "higher executives of larger concerns, proprietors, and major professionals" (10 per cent); his next class is "business managers, proprietors of medium-sized businesses, and lesser professionals" (12 per cent). Both are combined in the first class in the table above. His next class is composed of "administrative personnel, owners of certain small businesses, and minor professionals (17 per cent)," followed by "clerical and sales workers," technicians, and owners of small businesses (15 per cent). The next three classes are manual workers, while the 21 per cent in the other category for Rohter is composed of retired people. Ira S. Rohter, *op. cit.*, pp. 122–124. McNall does not present occupation and education separately. He combined the two to secure a composite index, with the large majority in the upper strata. Our NORC occupational data are not directly comparable to those of the studies of rightists. The NORC data are for the employed only, and exclude housewives, retired, and so on. Grupp's data on the John Birch Society and Wolfinger's data on the Christian Crusaders give occupation for head of household, while Levy and Stone classify housewives as "Other."

[1] Retired sample members excluded.

Table 31.   COMPARISON OF SOCIAL-CLASS POSITIONS OF FREEDOM CENTER MEMBERS
AND OTHER RIGHTISTS IN PORTLAND

| | Social Class (Occupation and Education) | | | | | | | |
	I (High)	II	III	IV	V	VI	VII (Low)	N
Freedom Center	3 %	9	20	14	23	18	13	(56)
Other Rightists	11 %	25	20	20	17	7	—	(53)

SOURCE: Scott Grant McNall, *The Freedom Center: A Case Study of a Politico-Religious Sect* (Ph.D. Thesis, Department of Sociology, University of Oregon, 1965), p. 347.

underrepresented among the national membership of the John Birch Society (20 per cent), although they are close to a third in the California sample. It has already been pointed out that the Birch Society is not only biased *against* Protestant fundamentalism but has a strong inherent appeal to Catholics. The question, under these circumstances, is why the Birch Society does not attract a larger number of Catholics. Proportionately, its Catholic support is much less than that which had been attracted to Coughlin and McCarthy. One answer to the difference lies, of course, in the Irish Catholic identification of those two leaders.

Another answer might be found in the election of John Kennedy to the Presidency in 1960. Kennedy was able to win back to Democratic ranks most of the Catholics who went over to the Republicans during the preservatist McCarthy and Eisenhower eras.[17] The election for the first time in history of an Irish Catholic to the Presidency returned to the Democratic party its role as the symbolic and actual vehicle for Catholic mobility and status. Attacks on Kennedy for his weakness in fighting Communism clearly placed many Catholic conservatives under cross pressures.

But, finally, the relatively lesser participation of Catholics in the Birch Society, as contrasted with their predominance in the Coughlin and McCarthy movements, must also be related to the programmatic nature of the Birch Society itself. While the Society may have drawn on the new objective nativism that was abroad, it never did make a mass appeal on the symbolic basis of such a nativism. And even if it had done so, it probably could not have succeeded in drawing mass support because it was neither committed to the pocketbook needs of the working class nor even neutral with respect to protecting their substantial welfare gains.

As we have seen, Coughlin and McCarthy, in different ways, emphasized antielitist doctrines which secured heavy lower-class support. The Birch Society espouses a version of economic conservatism which strongly opposes the welfare state and labor unions. Many Catholics are both supporters of the welfare state and hard-line anti-Communists. Given the fact that Catholics as a group are still relatively underprivileged as compared

Table 32. AGE OF MEMBERS AND ACTIVISTS IN VARIOUS RIGHT-WING GROUPS*
(Per Cent)

Age	Ultra-Rightists						Hate Rightists		
	Grupp JBS National	Levy JBS Michigan	Stone JBS California	Wolfinger Christian Crusade	Rohter Rightists	Special Letter Writers	McNall Freedom Center	Levy IAP	NORC Control Group
Under 30	20	17[a]	10		14[c]	24[d]		—[a]	29[e]
30 to 39	29	56	28	52[b]	17	23		37	40
40 to 49	24		26		22	30	27[b]		
50 to 59	13	27	26	45	20		73	63	31
60 to 69	10		10		27	23			
70 and over	4		—						
DK–NA	1	—	—	3	—	—	—	—	—
Number	(650)	(42)	(50)	(308)	(168)	(115)	(56)	(24)	(1,914)

* For sources, see Tables 30 and 31.
[a] Under 30, 30–39, 50 and over.
[b] Under 50, 50 and over.
[c] Under 35, 35–40, 45–50, 55–65, 66 and over.
[d] Under 35, 35–49, 50–64, 65 and over.
[e] Under 35, 35–55, 56 and over.

to white Protestants living in urban areas, this difference in their social position undoubtedly has kept many of them out of the Birch Society.

Among the groups which have been studied, it is clear that the Portland Freedom Center, which, though not affiliated to Hargis' movement, strongly resembles it, is decidedly fundamentalist. The right-wing older activists in Oregon studied by McNall and Rohter also have a heavier fundamentalist component than does the Birch Society.

Rohter reports that his sample of right-wingers were much more likely to subscribe to fundamentalist beliefs than the nonrightists interviewed. Rightists were much more likely to subscribe to fundamentalist tenets and to belong to fundamentalist churches; nearly half the rightists (44 per cent, compared to 17 per cent of the nonrightists) were affiliated with fundamentalist denominations.[18] On the other hand, and more curiously, the study of those who attended Fred Schwarz's Bay Area Christian Anti-Communist Crusade School indicated that less than 15 per cent belonged to fundamentalist denominations.[19]

These findings concerning the variable presence of Protestant fundamentalism in important sections of the radical right suggest, as Grace Pheneger has argued, that there are two distinct movements in the extremist right of this period: one is ostensibly concerned with the breakdown in basic religious teachings, with the way in which America has departed from "the old time religion"; while the other is a secular movement much more overtly and exclusively bothered by the changes in the secular order.[20] Both seek to revive what they conceive of as fundamental aspects of an earlier America, but they differ considerably in their programmatic interests. One upholds the Bible; the other, the Constitution.[21]

The two movements are alienated from the dominant tendencies in contemporary society and express alarm about similar aspects of it. But they appeal to different emotions and social groups. They can unite for action purposes, but it is difficult to build organizations which demand commitment from their supporters which combine both groups in the same room. Thus, though we find considerable overlap in their political ideology, and much cooperation and mutual praise, the differing roots of the two movements keep them apart. It is also apparent that the cultural roots of Protestant fundamentalism are in the ever dimmer past and slowly thinning out.

Community Origins

Descriptive studies of earlier extremist movements, as well as of contemporary ones, have suggested that their memberships are heavily drawn from people who have been personally uprooted from the sources of their childhood values either through having experienced various forms of mobility, geographic and social, or through living in communities whose social structure and values have been radically transformed through rapid growth. Those most subject to discontinuities are most likely to become active. A related hypothesis has suggested that those brought up in rural areas or small towns, whose religion and moral tone is most out of step with basic trends, are presumably more disposed to help foster extreme conservative doctrines.

This set of hypotheses, then, has these objective component variables: (1) either the more susceptible people live in rural areas and small towns; or (2) they live in large cities but were raised in rural areas or smaller cities; (3) wherever they come from, they are newcomers; (4) they live in areas of rapid growth.

The research support is weak as it relates to the first three factors. Grupp's findings, in Table 33, indicate that while the Birch members are considerably underrepresented in the rural areas, they are disproportionately located in medium-sized cities, i.e., those from 10,000 to 250,000, which are, of course, the most rapidly growing category of communities. The respondents, however, were asked to list the size of their communities and it is possible that suburban residents reported the population of their particular suburbs, rather than of the metropolitan region. Given the fact that the membership of the Society is heavily middle-class, it is likely that many of them do live in suburbs which are part of metropolitan areas.

As to the hypothesis that Birch members tend to be newcomers, and newcomers from smaller communities, Havens, who studied Birch groups in Texas, does report that "a very large part of the identifiable members of the radical right consists of newcomers to the communities where they now reside," often from rural areas.[22] The study of the members of the three right-wing groups in Michigan, the Conservative Federation, the Birch Society, and the "hate-right" Independent American party, indicates that the "native-born members of the three organizations all show slightly, but not significantly, more geographical mobility than the native-born citizenry of Michigan."[23] Few of them came from the southern states. The thesis that they grew up in small towns or rural areas also is not borne out for the Birch Society by the Michigan data. Almost half of the Birch members (43 per cent) were "raised" in large cities. Grupp's study of the national membership of the Birch Society indicates that the proportion with small-town or rural origins is less than that reported for the nation as a whole in a 1964 Michigan Survey Research Center sample of the national population.[24] That is true of our Special Letter Writers sample as well. And Rohter in his sample of Oregon radical rightists also does not find a consistent relationship between length of residence in present community and right-wing political activity.[25]

The second Oregon study, that of members of the fundamentalist

Table 33.   COMPARATIVE DISTRIBUTION OF BIRCH MEMBERSHIP AND
1960 U.S. POPULATION BY SIZE OF COMMUNITY OF RESIDENCE
(Per Cent)

Size of Community	Population	
	JBS[a]	U.S.[b]
Under 2,500	11	36
2,500 to 9,999	11	10
10,000 to 24,999	17	10
25,000 to 99,999	23	16
100,000 to 249,999	14	7
250,000 to 999,999	11	12
1,000,000 and over	10	10
Not ascertained	4	
Totals	101[c]	101[c]

SOURCES: [a] Frederick W. Grupp, Jr., *Social Correlates of Political Activists: The John Birch Society and the ADA* (Ph.D. Thesis, Department of Political Science, University of Pennsylvania, 1968), p. 23.
[b] From *Pocket Data Book, USA 1967* (Washington: U.S. Bureau of the Census, 1967), p. 37.
[c] Columns do not total 100 per cent due to rounding error.

lower-status Freedom Center in Portland, suggests that relatively few of them (7 per cent) have migrated to the city in the last ten years. Almost half (45 per cent) of this relatively aged group have lived in the metropolitan area for thirty years or more. On the other hand, 60 per cent reported having lived in a rural area or small town before moving to Portland, and 70 per cent indicated they had been raised in such places. Since almost three-quarters of the Center's members were over fifty years of age, it is doubtful that these data indicate that the Center drew disproportionately from those reared in nonurban areas. Much of the country lived in such communities when they were young.[26] The analysis of the backgrounds of those who attended the San Francisco Bay Area Christian Anti-Communist Crusade does, however, report that, holding occupational level constant, Crusaders were more likely to have grown up in small towns than a sample of the Bay Area white population.[27]

While the available data (outside of Texas) do not bear out the hypothesis that Birch Society members, as distinct from supporters, are much more likely to have been geographically mobile or to come from nonurban backgrounds, it is clear, nevertheless, that the Society's strength is heavily based on communities which have experienced rapid population and economic growth.

Murray Havens reports that the Society's strength in Texas is closely correlated with the rate of growth of the different cities, a finding which closely parallels that for the Klan forty years earlier.[28] The available information on the national membership of the Society indicates similar findings. Grupp says that the "twenty states whose population increased between 1950 and 1960 at a greater rate than the national average of 18.5 per cent contain 60 per cent of the Birch members, compared to 45 per cent of the United States population."[29]

A number of different studies of Birch Society members and activists, as judged from samples of letter writers, all agree that the Society's active support is disproportionately located in California and other rapidly growing states. Grupp reports that 25 per cent of the members of the Society are from California; while three different studies of the location of letter writers who wrote in response to Birch Society directives indicate the proportion coming from California to have been 33 per cent, 30 per cent, and 34 per cent.[30] Other rapidly growing states which have contributed heavily to the ranks of Birch activists are Arizona, Florida, and Texas. Conversely, sections of the country which have been declining in population or have remained stable are underrepresented. New England, Robert Welch's home region, is quite weak. It is interesting to note that while the Birch Society is stronger in the western states than in any other part of the country, it is weak in Oregon, the one major state in that region which has shown little growth. Another indicator of the prominent role played in radical right affairs by the regions of rapid growth may be found in an analysis of the locations of the groups listed in the 1962 edition of the *First National Directory of "Rightist" Groups*. Nineteen per cent of them are located or have their headquarters in California, 8 per cent in New York, 6 per cent in Texas, and 5 per cent each in Florida and Illinois.[31]

In California, it is clear that the bulk of Birch activity is concentrated in the southern part of the state, by far the most rapidly growing section. Broyles, in his study of the Society before 1963, reported that observation of a map in the national headquarters which contained pins for chapters and book stores indicated a concentration "in several cities in Texas and southern California."[32] Most of the California-headquartered or based rightist groups listed in the *Directory* are in southern California.[33] And the one study of letter writers which differentiated by section of California reports that over four-fifths were from the southern half.[34] These findings are paralleled by public opinion poll data which indicates that the California support for the Birch Society among the general population is also concentrated in the south, as is the vote for conservative candidates.[35]

Given the ambiguity of the data about the political effect of the personal strains imposed by mobility, the explanation for the concentration of extremist strength in areas of rapid population growth may lie more in structural attributes of such communities than in the personal strains experienced by individuals. Such communities are much less likely to be dominated by an old family wealthy status group which has developed norms of *noblesse oblige* and community responsibility. A comparison of the differences between San Francisco, in which Birch Society membership and popular support are less than the national average, and Los Angeles, in which they are much higher, may serve to illustrate this point.

San Francisco, which dominates the cultural life of northern California, was the first major city of the West. It had a considerable population in the nineteenth century and has, in fact, not grown over the past three decades. Los Angeles and southern California have emerged as major population centers only since World War I, and their really mass growth occurred since 1940. There are many families in the Bay Area who represent four and five generations of wealth, the descendants of those who made their money in mining, commerce, railroads, or shipping in the first decades after statehood, from 1850 to 1880. The wealthy in Los Angeles, on the other hand, are largely *nouveaux riches,* and the well-to-do there possess the attitudes toward politics and economics characteristic of this stratum. They are more likely to back the rightist groups that oppose the welfare state, the income tax, and trade-unions; and, lacking political and cultural sophistication, they are more prone to accept conspiracy interpretations for the strength behind liberal or welfare measures. The social structure of southern California is much less stabilized or institutionalized than in the north. Thus various leading citizens belong to the Birch Society in southern California; the units function openly as important community groups. In northern California, membership in the Birch Society is sufficient to define a man as an extremist, with attendant social opprobrium.

Status Frustrations as a Source of Radical Right Activism

Many of the analysts of the extremist right have suggested that the assorted movements draw from those groups in the population which are most subject to status frustrations. These may include both groups which feel themselves to be "dispossessed," to be declining in status as a result of the rise of other types of communities, occupations, or ethnic groups, and groups which have recently risen, but find themselves barred from being able to claim the concomitants of success. The term "status discrepancy," as used here, refers to possession of status attributes which may lead a man to feel that he is granted less prestige, income, or power than he feels he deserves. Status discrepancy often has meant in the sociological literature discrepant status attributes, as in the case of the college graduate factory worker, the grammar-school-educated business executive, the wealthy Negro, and the like. However, it may also refer to the president of the family-owned corporation who finds his power in his factory to be less than he believes should be associated with ownership. In general, it refers to the conditions which result in violations of expectations about the varying positions which should be concomitant of a given status.

A discrepancy between the way a society esteems a person and his own sense of worth may lead to active political involvement, as also may a discrepancy between a person's personal aspiration level and his achievement level. It is not the underprivileged who revolt; it is those whose privileges, status, and opportunities do not correspond to their expectations.[36]

In the framework of preservatist politics, such discrepancies may result from shifts in society's basis for granting prestige, income, and power. Those subject to such discrepancies are seemingly more likely to support various forms of "backlash" politics, to seek to create the basis for the higher positions which they feel they deserve, and to see limitations on their position as a result of the planned actions of those who now control the polity or other parts of the "power structure." This limited theory of backlash status groups tries both to explain the specific groups to which the extremist right seems to have disproportionate appeal and to account for the influences which have molded its ideology and style.

The available measurements of *generalized* status consistency or crystallization do not disclose an overwhelming relationship to Birch membership. For example, Grupp finds (see Table 34) a higher rate of over-all discrepancy between occupation and education among Birchers than among the general population. Curiously, this discrepancy is concentrated in high education/low occupation, while Elton Jackson's study of sources of stress

Table 34. COMPARISON OF DISCREPANCIES BETWEEN EDUCATION AND OCCUPATION RANKINGS AMONG THE BIRCH SOCIETY MEMBERSHIP AND A UNITED STATES SAMPLE OF MIDDLE-AGED RESPONDENTS (PER CENT)

	Population Universe	
Status Discrepancy	JBS	United States[a]
None	45 %	63 %
Education higher	36	18
Occupation higher	19	19
Totals	100	100
Number	(578)	(1,673)

SOURCE: Frederick W. Grupp, Jr., *Social Correlates of Political Activists: The John Birch Society and the ADA* (Ph.D. Thesis, Department of Political Science, University of Pennsylvania, 1968), p. 118.
[a] United States figures from Elton F. Jackson, "Status Consistency and Symptoms of Stress," *American Sociological Review*, XXVII (1962), Table 1, p. 473.

indicated that it is the other pattern, high occupation/low education, which is associated with high levels of psychosomatic symptoms.[37]

On the basis of his formal status-congruence analysis, Grupp concludes that

whether in terms of status crystallization, occupational prestige, or other objective indicators of status, only a minority of the Birch membership exhibit characteristics which can be associated logically with status politics. . . . On the contrary, the upper and upper-middle class complexion of the Birch membership makes support for the economic conservatism espoused by the Society more consistent with the assumptions of class, rather than status politics.[38]

Other studies of occupational mobility and Bircher backgrounds, implying status inconsistency, are also ambiguous.

Table 35. GENERATIONAL MOBILITY OF BUSINESSMEN AND PROFESSIONALS AMONG MICHIGAN BIRCHERS, CALIFORNIA CRUSADERS, AND WHITE NORTHERNERS

Father's Occupation	Birchers	Christian Crusaders	White Northerners
Business and professional	40 %	41 %	37 %
Clerical and sales	15	8	6
Blue collar	40	12	38
Farmer	5	16	16
No answer	—	23	3

SOURCE: Burton Levy, *Profile of the American Right: A Case Study of Michigan* (Ph.D. Thesis, Department of Political Science, University of Massachusetts, 1965), p. 215; Crusader data are from the Wolfinger study, while the White Northern data are from a Michigan Survey Research Center National Survey in 1964.

Murray Havens, in his study of Texas Birchers, does report findings which are supportive of the status discrepancy hypothesis. He states that those he interviewed tend to be individuals "who have achieved in recent years quite substantial economic gains through business or a profession and are frustrated because of a failure of their social status, influence, and power to climb at a corresponding rate."[39]

On the other hand, the family class backgrounds of businessmen and professionals among Michigan Birchers, and of those who partook in the Bay Area Christian Anti-Communist Crusade, do not sustain the theory (Table 35). Levy, therefore, comes to the opposite conclusion, "that the 'staus shock' of moving from lower class to upper class in one generation is not a significant factor in explaining citizen support of the Radical Right."[40]

The Rohter study of radical rightists in Oregon did concentrate on testing the thesis that mobility should produce status discrepancies which are associated with radical right activity. While most of the statistical differences which he found between rightist and nonrightist activists do correspond to the underlying hypothesis, the differences are for the most part not very large, and in a number of cases they just are not apparent. His results add some weight to the argument that persons exposed to either upward or downward mobility are somewhat more likely to be radical rightists than those who are stationary between two generations; but even accepting this, we must conclude that these variations do not account for much of the difference between the two groups.[41] Rohter himself states that the "data are far from conclusive" and indicates that his measures of achieved status may have been too imprecise to really test the hypothesis.[42]

But if objective measures of possible status discrepancies as measured by social mobility do not produce any exciting results, there is some slight evidence that a "subjective" sense of status discrepancy may differentiate, a finding comparable to Sokol's results in his study of McCarthyite support, reported earlier. Rightists, as a group, tend to overrate their social class, as judged by the relationship between the class they put themselves in subjectively and the class which the analyst places them in on the basis of occupational and educational attainments.

On objective measures of social status, approximately twice as many Non-Rightists as Rightists are in the upper-status ranks. . . . Yet when asked to evaluate their own social class, twice as many Rightists as Non-Rightists said they were "upper class." . . . It is safe to assume that these Rightists, who see themselves on a higher status plane than they objectively "deserve" according to society, are disturbed by the discrepancy.[43]

Unfortunately, this conclusion is based on only a small group of cases. However, it underscores the necessity to overlay mechanical measurements of status discrepancy with specific situational frameworks and their subjective components. Grupp points out that "the inability of the status crystallization theorists to systematically handle the subjective nature of status deprivation weakens the conclusions which may be drawn from this type of analysis."[44] As Andrzej Malewski has indicated, "If incongruence of status depends on normative expectations which may have been formed in other men, such expectations may not be the same in all cases."[45]

There is a particular framework of frustrated normative expectations which can be drawn from the characteristics of the Birch Society membership and which relates at least to the tone of their backlash politics.

Economic Strata

In his introduction to *The Radical Right*, Daniel Bell argues that "the social group most threatened by structural changes in society is the 'old' middle class," the owners of family-owned businesses and self-employed professionals.[46] This group, more than any other, has felt constrained by progressive social legislation and the rise of labor unions. Measures such as social security, business taxes, and the various governmental regulations all bring home to them their seeming loss of power. In the business community, power and status have moved toward the large corporations. And the latter has come to accept many of the changes which have occurred since the New Deal, including trade-unions and the various social reforms.

Although the data concerning the backgrounds of Birch Society members are not precise enough to permit us to test the assumption that the Society draws more heavily from the "old middle class," some evidence that this group is in a controlling position in the Society and determines its ideology comes from an examination of the backgrounds of the twenty-four members of the National Council as of July 1967. The majority of them have backgrounds comparable to Robert Welch himself. That is, they are presidents or vice-presidents of medium-sized corporations, most often family-owned (Table 36).

Table 36. PRIMARY OCCUPATIONS OF MEMBERS OF
THE NATIONAL COUNCIL OF THE BIRCH SOCIETY, 1967

Presidents of companies[a]	14
Physicians	3
Retired military officers	2
Attorneys	2
Business executive	1
Priest	1
Banker	1
Total	24

SOURCE: John Birch Society *Bulletin* (November 1965), pp. 126–130; *ibid.* (July 1967), pp. 16–18.
[a] One is a vice-president.

As interesting as the fact that the majority are the heads of moderate-sized companies is their geographical location. A listing of the companies and their location is the best way to give the flavor of the leadership of the Society.

1. Thomas J. Anderson, Nashville, Tennessee. Publisher, *Farm and Ranch*.

2. John T. Brown, Racine, Wisconsin. Vice-President, Falk Corporation.

3. F. Gano Chance, Centralia, Missouri. Chairman of the Board, A. B. Chance Company.

4. Stillwell J. Conner, Marshfield, Wisconsin. President, Modern Sleep Company.

5. William J. Grede, Elm Grove, Wisconsin. Chairman, Grede Foundries, Knoxville, Tennessee.

6. A. G. Heinsohn, Jr., President, Cherokee Textile Mills, Sevierville, Tennessee, and Spindale Mills, Spindale, North Carolina.

7. Fred C. Koch, Wichita, Kansas. Chairman, Koch Engineering Company, and President, Rock Island Oil and Refining Company.

8. Robert D. Love, Wichita, Kansas. President, Love Box Company.

9. N. Floyd McGowin, Chapman, Alabama. President, W. T. Smith Lumber Company.

10. William B. McMillan, Clayton, Missouri. President, Hussman Refrigerator Company.

11. Floyd Paxton, Yakima, Washington. President, Kwik-Lok Corporation.

12. Louis Ruthenberg, Evansville, Indiana. Chairman, Servel, Inc.

13. J. Nelson Shepard, Sioux Falls, South Dakota. President, Midwest Beach Company.

14. Robert W. Stoddard, Worcester, Massachusetts. President, Wyman-Gordon Company.

Men such as these are clearly among the privileged of the nation. Many of them earn more than the executives of major corporations. Their biographies indicate that they are active in various business and social organizations in their home communities. They are able to contribute a great deal of money to causes which they favor. Yet, they are among the out-groups in the larger national society. The federal government, the mass media, the major national churches, oppose much of what they believe. Most of them have been involved in efforts to change the direction of American politics, but without success. In a real sense, these are the leaders of the marginal provincial power structures of the nation. And they are willing to go along with, or completely accept the conspiratorial world outlook of the Birch Society. Through the Society, they hope to turn the clock back, to recreate a world in which the tendencies toward bureaucracy and centralization of power are reversed.

The second most numerous occupational group in the Council of the Society was physicians. Obviously, we cannot make much of this fact, since it involves only three men. Yet the suggestion that the Society has a special appeal to this group is affirmed in the analyses of letter writers. McEvoy reports that the largest identifiable occupational group in his sample was physicians (2.13 per cent). This figure "indicates a far greater number of physicians than one would expect. In fact, about twenty-one times as many doctors (M.D.'s and D.O.'s) appear in this sample than there were in the estimated resident civilian population for the year in which the letters were written."[47] The mail written to Senator Kuchel in response to a speech attacking the Birch Society included an even larger proportion of medical personnel among the defenders of the Society. Out of a sample of 600 writers, both pro- and anti-Birch, 20, or 3.3 per cent, were physicians. All of them wrote in support of the Society, while all ten attorneys who wrote were anti-Birch.[48]

These results correspond with journalistic reports, particularly from southern California and the South, concerning the presence of medical doctors in the leadership of the Society. One newspaper account, reprinted in the Birch Society *Bulletin* as an accurate report on the activities of the Society in the South, states that a "number of physicians took leadership roles . . . as a means of fighting Medicare."[49]

The attraction of the radical right to physicians in recent years has been clearly related to the fact that medicine is the one profession which feels itself under direct and successful political attack from the liberals and the left. The specter of socialized medicine hangs over the profession. The emergence of various forms of state medicine in different parts of Europe, particularly Great Britain, and even in some Canadian provinces, has frightened many American doctors. The fight over Medicare has brought the issue directly home. Although the United States is far from having a system of socialized medicine, the medical profession has been forced to change many of its practices, to cooperate with various forms of health insurance, and ultimately to accept the beginning of a government medical system for parts of the population. In the debates over medical care, many politicians and writers have expressed serious misgivings about the profession. Medicine was once the most hallowed profession in America. Studies of occupational status placed it in the first rank of all nonpolitical elite positions. To be attacked, and to be defeated, politically, must clearly be experienced as a major blow to the doctors' sense of self-importance. They have also lost out in the struggle for autonomy. And seemingly a minority among the doctors have turned to the radical right, have accepted its image of the world.

A somewhat different occupational group which is frequently mentioned among those who contribute relatively heavily to the membership and support of the extreme right is the professional military, particularly the retired among them. As we have seen, two of the twenty-four members of the National Council of the Birch Society fall into this category. These are Lieutenant General Charles B. Stone, III, who was Commander of the Fourteenth Air Force in China, and Colonel Laurence E. Bunker, former personal aide-de-camp to General Douglas MacArthur from 1946 to 1952.

A number of other members of the Council served as high-ranking officers in the military and retain connections with it, either in the reserve or as officers of groups like the Marine Corps League. Retired generals and admirals appear regularly on the platforms of the Society and other right-wing groups. *American Opinion,* as we noted earlier, has tended to glorify the military profession in its selection of appropriate people to honor with front-page pictures and profiles as the man of the month.

The Society became involved in a dispute initiated by Senator Fulbright and Secretary of Defense McNamara in 1961 concerning the "right of military officers to make statements critical of the nation's domestic and foreign policies."[50] Ironically, the series of events which led to the involvement of the military in rightist activities and the subsequent Fulbright protest had been precipitated by the Eisenhower administration. In 1958, the National Security Council had issued a directive which stated that it would be government policy "to make use of military personnel and facilities to arouse the public to the menace of Communism."[51] In his memorandum to Secretary of Defense McNamara, Fulbright listed many examples of military activity begun in response to this directive which involved support of the radical right. These included seminars and discussion programs to educate service personnel on the problem of Communism.[52] Fulbright's memorandum listed the use in these seminars of various publications of the radical right, as well as the fact that past and present international difficulties were explained as the consequence of "softness," "sellouts," and "appeasement" and that various welfare state programs were equated with socialism and Communism.[53]

Seminars sponsored by the Navy included leaders of the Birch Society, such as E. Merrill Root of the National Council, and Glenn Green, a field director, Dr. Fred Schwarz of the Christian Anti-Communist Crusade, and Dr. Kenneth D. Wells, president of the Freedoms Foundation.[54] Admiral Goldthwaithe, who set up the seminars for Naval Aviation, recommended as sources from which reliable anti-Communist information could be obtained *American Opinion,* the Catholic extreme rightist Cardinal Mindszenty Foundation, the Christian Crusade of Billy Hargis, and the radical rightist magazine *American Mercury.*[55] The Fulbright memorandum also complained about Project Alert, an effort financed and supported by the Navy League of the United States, which was started by Admiral Schindler. The Project involved bringing together representatives of local community groups, usually business people, with those from the Armed Services, to "alert" the population to the Communist menace. The Alert meetings generally involved the same type of speakers as had been brought in by Admiral Goldthwaithe for naval seminars. "Alert committees were distributed around the country in a typically rightist pattern. With few exceptions they were strung out along the hallelujah highway of the far right, from Southern California through Texas to Florida and the Deep South."[56]

The Project Alert campaign was dominated by Navy personnel. It worked closely with personnel from the rightist Harding College. The films and speakers presented by the project argued that the main danger to the country was not from the outside, but from domestic enemies. Its ideology took the following form:

> The United States was surrounded by communist and half-communist powers, including all the neutrals and most of our allies. Nevertheless, the greatest danger did not come from without, but from within. Gradually, bit by bit, the country would be brought to communism, by socialists and other "subversives" creeping into government, the universities, labor, and the churches. The solution was to adopt a policy of "victory over communism" abroad, "free enterprise," and vigorous exposure of the creeping ones at home. . . . In their literature and recommended sources, after their talks and in private discussion, they agitated for the full rightwing program: withdrawal from the U.N., abolition of public welfare and foreign aid, "states' rights," and so on.[57]

The Army, though less involved in such activities than the Navy, did sponsor Project Alert groups and ran "strategy for survival" conferences. In Atlanta, for example, Lieutenant General Paul Adams, commander of the Third Army, sponsored the Alert Movement in his locality. In Germany, Major General Edwin Walker was involved in circulating radical right propaganda among his troops. (He was subsequently relieved of his command for these actions.) "In almost every area of the country, seminars, schools, and projects, organized by the military or by business groups in cooperation with the military, spread the propaganda of the radical right and gave a broad aura of authority and legitimacy to such propaganda and to such pitchmen of the radical right as the Reverend Dr. Schwarz and the Reverend Billy Hargis."[58]

Much of the overt activity on behalf of Project Alert and radical rightist groups by high-ranking officers in the military was sharply reduced after the Fulbright memorandum. A directive was actually issued by McNamara in June 1961, before the memorandum, which stated, "In public discussion all officers of the Department should confine themselves to defense matters."[59] There is some evidence, however, that officers' wives organizations continued to cooperate with Project Alert and similar activities after the McNamara directive.

The Fulbright memorandum and the McNamara directive were attacked by the extreme right as an effort to muzzle the military. Senator Thurmond of South Carolina, the former candidate for President of the States Rights party of 1948, demanded an investigation "of Defense Department censorship of speeches of officers and of the admonishment of Major General Walker."[60] This proposal was strongly supported by the Birch Society. Robert Welch write in the *Bulletin* of September 1961: *"Support Senator Thurmond's demand for the investigation of the military gag rule.* This is the most IMPORTANT item in this month's agenda."[61] Thurmond's investigation did not succeed in changing Defense Department policy, and since then military officers on active duty have largely abstained from public support of right-wing activities and ideology. But retired officers remain among the most publicized figures taking part in various conferences and seminars.

The evidently considerable support for the Birch Society and radical right by the military has a variety of sources. More than any other occupation, the professional military officers are identified with concepts of nationalism and patriotism. Their position commits them to the belief that military strength is the best way to deter war and to assure that national interests are attained. And insofar as issues concerning reliance on strength occur in the party arena, we should expect them to line up with the forces which oppose internationalism and foster military prowess. Since the liberal left has tended to advocate pacifistic and internationalist roads to peace and welfare (even though the Democrats have been in power at the start of all wars in this century), the military should be biased in a conservative direction. The social origins of the military leadership should also dispose them in this direction. In general, the American officer corps tends to "be heavily recruited from native-born, Anglo-Saxon, and upper social stratum parentage."[62]

With the expansion of the Armed Services since 1940, the base has broadened, but this generalization is still accurate. Secondly, the military tend to be "overwhelmingly of rural and small town origin."[63] As Janowitz points out, "there has been an integral association between military institutions and rural society."

The out-of-doors existence, the concern with nature, sport, and weapons which is part of rural culture, have a direct carry-over to the requirements of the pre-technological military establishment. . . . In rural areas traditions and requirements for a military sense of honor could be expected to flourish. . . . At the same time, a simpler kind of patriotism prevails in rural areas.[64]

If we compare the backgrounds of the 1952 business elite studied by W. L. Warner with that of the military leadership in 1950, there is a striking contrast. Almost 70 per cent of the military are from rural backgrounds, as compared with only 26 per cent of the business leadership.[65] Further, the military leaders are disproportionately from the South, as compared with the business elite. In 1950, about 46 per cent of the Army

leaders and 44 per cent of the Navy had a southern background.[66] Given
the ideology inherent in their occupation, and their social background, it is
not surprising that a survey of the opinions of 576 Army, Navy, and
Air Force officers on staff duty in the Pentagon revealed that only "a handful of officers (5 per cent) . . . identified themselves as liberal on an
anonymous questionnaire. . . ."[67] Over a fifth, 21.6 per cent, described
themselves as conservatives, 45.3 placed themselves as "a little on the
conservative side," while 23.1 per cent said they were "a little on the
liberal side."[68]

Perhaps even more significant is the fact that conservative support increased with rank. The generals and admirals were most likely to state
they were conservatives (39.1 per cent). As Janowitz suggests, "Higher
rank means longer organizational experience, greater commitment to the
organization, and more selecting out of deviant perspectives."[69]

There are various components to military conservatism. Perhaps most
important for our consideration are two:

Military conservatism predicates the indispensability of private property as
the basis of a stable political order. At present, as in the past, the military
professional can conceive of no other arrangement.

[The military] . . . lack . . . understanding and respect for the creative
role of the practical politician. . . . There is, moreover, little sympathy for
the particular qualities required to produce political compromise. There is little
appreciation of the fact that a political democracy requires competing pressures. The endless struggles over the military budget only serve to re-enforce
the conception that party politics and pressure group activities are nefarious.
Military conservatism tends to overlook the advantages and safeguards of consensus arrived at by debating conflicting interests and pressures.[70]

These general qualities of the military have taken on a special character
since World War II. During the large war, the American military reached
their highest point in status, general influence, and power. Since then, they
have been in a losing battle with civilian groups concerning decisions which
they often perceive as military ones. The politicians have not been prepared
to support an all-out reliance on military power in the Korean and Vietnam
wars. The struggle with Communism has been complex, and the political
elite has placed the avoidance of a nuclear war as the highest objective.
It has sought to build international institutions to avoid a nuclear holocaust.
And the very control of the military over their own affairs has been
somewhat restricted with the creation of the Defense Department. The
Eisenhower administration cut military expenditures drastically. The Mc-
Namara administration of the Defense Department sharply curtailed the
strategic planning role of the military. The military intellectuals and the
scientists from the universities and the RAND Corporation have become

increasingly important. In a real sense, the military have been experiencing a decline in status, influence, and power.

Within the Armed Services themselves, the older officers have suffered an even greater loss, because they do not have the technical expertise to handle the new technology of modern warfare. Issues concerning strategy, weapons, and tactics have entered the political arena.[71] The more right-wing civilian forces have advocated the traditional concepts of the older military, from favoring a "victory" strategy to supporting the use of older-type weapons. Such events have increasingly pressed a minority of the military elite toward the extreme right.[72] The pattern which has occurred has been well summed up by Samuel Huntington:

> [T]he rapid changes in strategy and technology, the difficult struggle to keep up in the race for expertise and the visible decline in military power give rise to feelings and attitudes more oriented toward the fundamentalist current in American politics. It is not the "unwarranted" power of the military which is cause for concern, but rather the feelings of resentment and frustration which develop when the military believes that it is unaccountably and unjustifiably losing power. At least some elements of the military profession belong, in Daniel Bell's expressive phrase, to "the dispossessed." They share in the "revolt against modernity and the requirements of planned social change," and in "an anti-intellectualism which is a defensive posture against the complexities of modern problems." . . . Such attitudes can lead a small minority of extremists to full-fledged participation in Radical Right organizations. . . . The primary appeal of the Radical Right, however, has been to the older officers, retired from the military hierarchy and unfamiliar with and hostile to the new expertise.[73]

The one relatively low-status occupation which has been reported as visibly present among Birch members is that of policemen. In this respect, the Birch Society resembles its less privileged predecessors, such as the APA, the Klan of the twenties and the fifties, the Black Legion, and the Coughlinites. In 1964, John Rousselot, then National Director of Public Relations of the Society, stated that a "substantial number" of its members were policemen.[74] In 1965, Rousselot claimed that more than 25 policemen and 15 sheriff's deputies in Los Angeles were members. In Philadelphia, the mayor placed 15 members of the police department on limited duty for membership in the Society. In Santa Ana, California, a Birch Society chapter "composed of 23 police officers" is reported to have dominated the police department.[75]

In New York City, a reporter judged that the majority of the audience at a rally in Town Hall sponsored by the Birch Society's Speakers Bureau wore "Police Benevolent Association badges."[76] The Birch Society "estimates that it has five hundred members in the New York City Police Department."[77] A number of prominent police officers have appeared under Birch Society or allied auspices. The late chief of the Los Angeles Police Department, William H. Parker, took part in the "Manion Forum," the weekly broadcast of Clarence Manion, who is a member of the National Council of the Society.[78] Chief Parker also was portrayed on the front cover of *American Opinion*.[79] The former police chief of Salt Lake City, W. Cleon Skousen, and Sheriff James Clark, of Selma, Alabama, have been featured speakers for the Society's Speakers Bureau. Sheriff Clark, famous for his battles with the civil rights movement and a member of the Society, was elected President of the national organization of sheriffs in 1966.

The particular strength of the radical right among the police in the 1960's undoubtedly is related to elements in their background and experience similar to those raised in our earlier discussion of the reasons why police were found in the southern Klan. As Gunnar Myrdal noted over two decades ago, they tend to be recruited from lower-status and less educated segments of the population.[80] "Working-class background, high-school education or less, average intelligence, cautious personality—these are the typical features of the modern police recruit."[81]

Prejudice against Negroes is greater among persons with such backgrounds, and police work, as Myrdal noted, tends to reinforce and intensify such beliefs, since it brings policemen in contact with the worst elements in the Negro community.

The policeman's role is also particularly subject to creating feelings of resentment against society flowing from status discrepancies. On one hand, he is given considerable authority by society to enforce its laws; on the other, he receives little prestige and a relatively low salary. Such pressures could dispose a group to the left, but aspects of the occupational situation and the varying attitude of politically involved groups result in their discontents taking a rightist form.

The particular strength of the Birch Society among them is probably related to the special efforts which the Society has made to support and glorify their work and to back them up in their campaigns to prevent civilian police review boards. The Society has stressed its campaign to "Support Your Local Police," a slogan similar to one used by the Ku Klux Klan in the 1920's, and also strongly endorsed in an official proclamation by George Wallace while he was governor. The Society played an important role in securing petitions to place an initiative measure on the New York City ballot to eliminate the civilian police review board which had been established by the city.

The larger context of American politics tends to press the police to support the rightist or conservative position. A study of the Oakland, California, police force concluded that "a Goldwater type of conservatism was the dominant political and emotional persuasion of police."[82] Liberals and leftists in American society have tended to be concerned with the rights of the less powerful and underprivileged and with the protection of their civil liberties. The police have been involved in supporting authority's efforts to put down the demonstrations and strikes of trade-unionists, radicals, civil rights advocates, and the like.

The American Civil Liberties Union and other groups have fought hard to defend the legal rights of criminals, among other elements. To the police-man, the liberal side of the political spectrum would appear to be engaged in a constant struggle to make his job more difficult, to increase the physical danger to which he is subject. In recent years, the Supreme Court has increasingly sided with the liberal interpretations of individual rights in decisions concerning police tactics in securing confessions, wire tapping, and similar issues.

In the legal sector the police are solidly aligned against the United States Supreme Court which, they suspect, is slowly but surely dismantling the hallowed foundation of law enforcement. . . . To the police the struggle over the Civilian Review Board and the recent trend of the Supreme Court decisions are proof of the breakdown of respect for law and order and their natural tendency is to close ranks against what appears to be a common enemy.[83]

The radical right, by its support of the police, has probably also appealed to their sense of being a low-status out-group in American society. The study of the Oakland Police reports that when asked to rank the most serious problems which police have, the category most frequently selected was not racial problems, "but some form of public relations: lack of respect for the police, lack of cooperation in enforcement of law, lack of un-derstanding of the requirements of police work. . . . Of the two hundred and eighty-two . . . policemen who rated the prestige police work receives from others, 70 per cent ranked it as only fair or poor."[84] A British study of the police also reported that 58 per cent of those interviewed complained about the public's attitude toward them. Some police reported concealing their occupation from others. Clearly the police appear to be a status-deprived group which feels resentment about public lack of appreciation. And overt hostility and contempt for the police, denunications of them as Cossacks, pigs, and fascists, often come from the liberal and left side of the political spectrum. Insofar as the police find any segment of the body politic showing appreciation to them for their contribution to society and for the risks which they take, it is from conservatives, and particularly from the far right. The Birch Society has established awards for heroic policemen and has created funds for the support of the families of police killed in the line of duty. It is hardly surprising that police are to be found in the ranks of the Society.

More important, perhaps, than the location of different political tendencies on issues which directly affect the interests and status of the police in determining their political predispositions are the factors inherent in their occupational role which also press them to a conservative position. A policeman must be suspicious and cynical about human behavior; "he needs the intuitive ability to sense plots and conspiracies on the basis of embryonic evidence."[85] "If the element of danger in the policeman's role tends to make the policeman suspicious, and therefore emotionally attached to the status quo, a similar consequence may be attributed to the element of authority. The fact that a man is engaged in enforcing a set of rules implies that he also becomes implicated in *affirming* them."[86]

Though in a considerably different position from the professional military elite, discussed earlier, the police resemble them in being in an occupation which predisposes them to be conservative and conventional, if not authoritarian, to prefer simple answers, and to resent deviants. They, too, are professionally identified with the upholding of the basic verities of society. It is likely also that the relative status of the police, as an occupational group, has fallen in the less privileged working-class and distinctly ethnic groups from which they are disproportionately drawn. As the occupational structure has shifted to include greater proportions of nonmanual and technical positions, which require increased levels of education, and fewer relatively unskilled positions, the status of policemen in the total occupational structure, and particularly among the groups with which they associated before taking a job, has declined. But more important than this factor, in giving policemen a sense of being deprived statuswise, is the attitude of outsiders, discussed above. Thus they, like the military elite, may see themselves as among the "dispossessed" of America and therefore identify with the values of the radical right.

The data, unfortunately, do not permit us to specify further among occupational strata in seeking to explain the appeal and ideology of the radical right. A sense of status deprivation, however, does not flow simply or solely from factors which affect the status and power of occupational groups. The growing role of education as a status placement mechanism and as a source of skills which give people power as well as status affects those who feel they have been left out, or are underprivileged in this respect.

Education as a Source of Status Discrepancy

The earlier discussions of the ideology of the radical right indicate that its antielitism has been focused on the intellectual elites, specifically the universities, professors, those who write for the mass media, and experts. Extreme rightist spokesmen have repeatedly attacked the academic establishment as supporters of the Communist conspiracy, as seeking to subvert American values. One possible reason for the popularity of the belief in the Illuminati conspiracy is that basically the Illuminati are perceived as the intellectuals. The educational system, at all levels, is subject to radical right attack. One of the main activities of the Birch Society and other rightist groups on the local level has been surveillance of the school and library systems, attacking teachers, librarians, and books which are thought to be politically or morally subversive.

At the same time that the radical right concentrates on intellectuals and the educational system as the main enemy, it attests in various ways to its belief in the high status and value of education and academic learning. Thus, the biographies of the authors of articles in *American Opinion* frequently stress their academic attainments. A remarkable number of the regular contributors are listed as former or present college professors or as having or working for their Ph.D. The flavor of the Birch Society's desire for academic and intellectual respectability may be seen from the following biographies.

Medford Evans, who writes regularly for *American Opinion* and is editor of the newspaper of the White Citizens Council, is never mentioned in the latter capacity. His *American Opinion* biography states:

> Medford Evans, a former college professor and once Administrative officer on the U.S. atomic energy project (1944–1952) holds his Doctoral degree from Yale University. Dr. Evans' work has appeared in Harper's, Sewanee Review, Human Events, National Review, and elsewhere.[87]

Another regular contributor, E. Merrill Root, is identified as follows:

> E. Merrill Root is the brilliant author of two best-selling books, *Collectivism on the Campus* and *Brainwashing in the High Schools*. Professor Root may also be America's greatest living poet. His work has appeared in Human Events, Christian Economic, Bluebook, National Review, Freeman, New York Times, Literary Digest, New York Herald Tribune and elsewhere.[88]

A member of the National Council of the Society is described in the following terms at the head of articles by him:

> Robert H. Montgomery is a nationally known Boston attorney and Shakespearean scholar. Two of his previous articles for American Opinion on Felix Frankfurter and Arthur Schlesinger, Jr. are still being discussed at the tables of the Harvard Faculty Club. Dr. Montgomery is author of the definitive book, *Sacco-Vanzetti: The Murder and the Myth*.[89]

Another frequent contributor to *American Opinion* is introduced to the readers as a major intellectual:

Dr. Allison Anders is a professor of sociology at a well-known Eastern college, a trained natural scientist, and an internationally known geographer. . . . Articles by Dr. Anders have been published internationally in numerous academic and scientific journals.[90]

The biography of a staff member of the Society also stresses her academic attainments:

Susan L. M. Huck is a graduate of Syracuse University, with advanced degrees from the University of Michigan and Clark University. Dr. Huck has taught as a university professor of both geography and sociology, lectured before academic audiences on four continents, acted as advisor to one of the world's leading encyclopedias, and is Analysis Editor of [the Society's] The Review of the News.[91]

Further evidence of this concern of the Birch Society may be found in the books published by its three publishing houses. Many of them, particularly those by Welch, are elaborately footnoted, often with citations by major reputable scholars. The profusion of books and articles can give the rank-and-file nonintellectual member the sense that he has an entire academic establishment on his side.

The largely middle-class members of the Birch Society are clearly well educated in the sense of having achieved a substantial level of education. Sixty-four per cent of them have at least some college education; almost a third are college graduates.[92] Yet these are levels of attainment which do not necessarily fit them for competition at the top levels of the occupational structure. Grupp, comparing them with a sample of members of the liberal Americans for Democratic Action, reports that 54 per cent of the ADA members have completed some graduate work, as contrasted with but 10 per cent of the Birchers. The latter also differ from the liberals in containing many more with "some college." Fully a third of the Birch members, as compared with 13 per cent of those in ADA broke off their college education without receiving a degree.[93] These data would suggest that the Birchers, though much better educated than the American population as a whole, are not drawn from those in the top-ranking professions or occupations.

Additional evidence that the Birchers may suffer from a sense of educational deficiency comes from Grupp's examination of the kind and quality of education received by Birch members who did attend college or university. He ranked the quality of the institution attended by his respondents and reports that most of the Birchers had studied at schools which fall in the lowest group of American institutions of higher learning in quality.[94] The ADA members, as the data in Table 37 indicate, were much more likely to have attended far better schools.

Table 37. QUALITY OF HIGHER EDUCATION OF MEMBERS
OF THE JBS AND ADA

Quality of Institution	JBS	ADA
Highest level	10 %	40 %
Second level	14	24
Third level	14	8
Lowest level	62	28
Number	(366)	(657)

SOURCE: Frederick W. Grupp, Jr., *Social Correlates of Political Activists: The John Birch Society and the ADA* (Ph.D. Thesis, Department of Political Science, University of Pennsylvania, 1968), p. 80.

Similar results, in part, are reported by Ira Rohter in his study of rightist activists in Oregon. Holding occupational level in the middle class constant, he found that among those with high- and middle-level occupations, rightists had a lower level of education than nonrightists who had been politically active, as indicated by participation in various community campaigns or in writing letters to editors of papers. Among those with high positions (executives, higher professionals, proprietors of middle-sized firms), 77 per cent of the nonrightists had graduated from college, as compared with 59 per cent of the rightists. The former were much more likely to have attended graduate school (64 per cent) than the latter (33 per cent), while the rightists contained more who had broken off their college education (29 per cent) than did the nonrightists (18 per cent). Similar differences occurred among those with lower-level middle-class jobs.[95]

These findings bearing on the lesser collegiate attainments, quality, and status of the education of Birchers and other rightists are congruent with our assumptions that middle-class rightists, though relatively affluent by national population standards, may suffer a sense of status discrepancy. They clearly do not have the educational prerequisites to easily become part of the leading social circles of the communities in which they reside. The fact that so many of the Birchers attended low-prestige colleges suggests that they are upwardly mobile individuals. We have no way, of course, of knowing to what extent they have a sense that their education was inadequate, or for that matter that they suffer in any way from it. Nevertheless, the patterns revealed by the Grupp and Rohter analyses do fit in with the assumption that the radical right draws from segments of the middle classes which have reasons for feeling outside of the main social and power circles in American society.

The members of the Birch Society also differ significantly from liberal activists and the college population generally in the subjects which they studied. They are much less likely to have majored in the liberal arts and the humanities. Havens sums up his findings based on interviews with 173 Birchers in nine Texas cities: "Most are at least high school graduates, and a very large number have college or university degrees. Those degrees are almost always in technical fields, such as engineering, the natural sciences, accounting, medicine and dentistry. The absence of those educated in the social sciences is striking. . . ."[96]

Grupp's analysis of the characteristics of the national membership of the Society produced comparable findings. The liberal arts ranked very low in the list of major fields of Birch members. Their favorite undergraduate subject was commerce, with engineering and education ranking second and third. Among ADA members, on the other hand, the most common undergraduate majors were English, history, and political science.[97] These differences correspond to the findings of the many studies of student and faculty political attitudes and activities. Liberals and leftists are found disproportionately among those in the social sciences and liberal arts, while conservatives are located among students and professors in the technical subjects, business school, and the like.[98]

Conservative students, often coming from conservative family backgrounds, are reported to feel themselves to be a minority in a campus sea of liberalism. A study of the members of campus conservative clubs in the early sixties indicates that these people joined together in self-defense, seeking to create a hospitable environment for the ideas which they had brought from home. Most of the politically active faculty and students, largely social scientists, were much more vocal, opinionated, and informed about political matters; hence the need to create an internal membership group of people who agreed with one another.

Characteristic of the radical rightists is that they are not people whose education or occupation gives them information about politics or, more important, the ability to communicate effectively. They also should have lesser sources of prestige than others in their relative social milieu. While we cannot produce any direct evidence for the proposition that their extremism is a product of status frustration, they do not have the quality and type of educational background which is more and more a prerequisite for occupational success in an increasingly bureaucratized and rationalized society.

Birch Approvers

The analyses of the Birch Society appeal have largely been restricted to a study of its membership, partly because of its limited reach as an organization into the general public. Unlike Coughlin, McCarthy, and the Ku Klux Klan, the Society is only dimly known to many people. A Gallup survey which inquired into attitudes toward the John Birch Society in the beginning of 1962, following a considerable barrage of publicity in the national press, found that over two-thirds of those interviewed had not heard of it or else had no opinion about it.[99] Among those who did express an opinion, negative judgments outnumbered positive ones by five to one: 5 per cent favored the Society, and 26 per cent opposed it (Table 38). Over two

Table 38. OPINION OF TWO NATIONAL SAMPLES ON THE BIRCH SOCIETY: FEBRUARY 1962, OCTOBER 1964

	February 1962	October 1964
Favorable to the Society	5 %	11 %
Unfavorable	26	36
No opinion	27	23
Have not heard of it	42	29
	100 %	99 %
Number	(1,616)	(1,909)

years later, in October 1964, at the height of an election campaign in which the Democrats frequently attacked the Society in an effort to link Senator Goldwater with it, and at a point at which it was close to the maximum membership it has ever secured, the national NORC survey of the population conducted for the purposes of this study indicated that over half of those interviewed still either had not heard of the group or had formed no opinion of it. As compared with 1962, the Society had gained in strength: 11 per cent now favored it. Opposition had also increased during this period to 36 per cent. The proportion who admitted not having heard of the Society declined from 42 to 29 per cent.

Because the bulk of the national sample had no opinion on the Birchers, certain limitations are imposed in drawing conclusions from the data. Comparisons between population subgroups, as presented earlier, must be interpreted with extreme caution, since they may at times be misleading. In analyzing support in terms of our categories, it is necessary to compare such small percentages as 7 per cent pro-Birch among Democrats and 18 per cent among Republicans. Such comparisons are made all the more difficult because the proportion of respondents without opinions varies widely from subgroup to subgroup. Nevertheless, within those constraints, the findings of the 1964 national survey confirm our earlier impressions that the appeal of the Society differs widely from that of other groups which have been defined as radical rightist. The approving group is disproportionately strong among the better educated, the more well-to-do in income terms, and those in higher-status occupations. Relative to their proportion in the population, those involved in business and managerial positions are most likely to approve of the Birch Society. The Society has its greatest appeal in the western states and is weakest in the East. Catholics are somewhat less likely to think well of the Society than Protestants. The data also indicate that adherents to liberal Protestant denominations are more likely to approve of the Society than are fundamentalists. These results, on the whole, correspond to the findings about the membership of the society as reported previously.

Other data in the 1964 survey permit us to locate various differences between Birch supporters and opponents, which are suggestive of possible patterns that are causally related to Birch Society support. When asked to place themselves in a social class, Birch supporters turn out to be much more likely than those with other attitudes toward the Society to place themselves in the middle or upper classes, rather than in the working or lower class. By itself, this finding is not surprising or interesting, since we know that the Birchers are more privileged in objective terms. However, when we compare the class identification of the two different groups, holding income and occupational position constant, we find that within the different strata Birchers are still more prone to place themselves in higher-status categories (Table 39).

The fact that Birch supporters are more likely to see themselves in a higher-status position than those opposed to the Society, or the sample at large, within objective socioeconomic strata, suggests that the Society tends to appeal to those who are status strivers. In a sense, these tables may be viewed as indicators of a felt sense of status discrepancy or of status orientation. Those who want to locate themselves in a higher position in the social structure are more likely to approve the Birch Society than those with lesser aspirations or identifications. It is particularly noteworthy that the differences are greatest among the lower-income and manual groups.

The Social Base of Racist Politics

We know little concerning the attributes of those who are most involved in overtly bigoted and racist organizations, as compared to the other radical right movements. There are even relatively little data available concerning the membership and active support of the "third" Klan. From the start, it has been under vigorous police and FBI surveillance and consequently has been even more secretive than its predecessors. The available evidence, however, suggests that the social background of the membership of the postwar Klan closely resembles that of the Klan of the twenties, particularly

Table 39. RELATIONSHIP BETWEEN BIRCH APPROVAL AND SUBJECTIVE CLASS
PLACEMENT, INCOME AND OCCUPATION HELD CONSTANT, 1964

Family Income and Subjective Social Class	Attitude to Birch Society				
	All Ap-provers	Gold-water Ap-provers[b]	Disap-provers	DK/HH[a]	Total Sample
Income under $7,000					
Upper and upper middle	16 %	24 %	7 %	8 %	8 %
Middle	50	55	48	36	41
Working and lower	35	20	45	57	51
Number	(86)	(49)	(354)	(647)	(1,087)
$7,000 and Over					
Upper and upper middle	26 %	28 %	27 %	11 %	21 %
Middle	55	57	52	58	55
Working and lower	10	16	20	30	24
Number	(116)	(77)	(303)	(274)	(693)
Occupational Class and Subjective Social Class					
Manual					
Upper and upper middle	8 %	12 %	5 %	4 %	6 %
Middle	49	59	36	34	36
Working and lower	44	30	59	62	59
Number	(39)	(17)	(165)	(254)	(458)
Nonmanual					
Upper and upper middle	31 %	31 %	23 %	15 %	22 %
Middle	55	52	56	57	56
Working and lower	15	16	21	28	23
Number	(88)	(63)	(271)	(208)	(567)

[a] Don't know or have not heard of the Society.
[b] Supported Goldwater and approved of JBS.

during its latter stages when it had little or no appeal to the well-to-do
middle class. The Klan of the fifties and sixties has been largely an urban
phenomenon. Most of its members are to be found in southern cities.
Like many in the twenties, however, they tend to be lower-status individuals
who have grown up on the farm or in a small town and moved to the city.
An examination of 153 names listed in charter applications for official
incorporation of Klan units, as well as in police records, indicates that all
of them were in manual or marginal nonmanual positions. Thirty-six per
cent were in unskilled or semiskilled jobs; 33 per cent were employed as
skilled workers; 24 per cent were "marginal white collar workers" (grocery

store clerks, service station attendants, policemen); while the remaining 7 per cent were "marginal small businessmen."[100] The leaders of the klaverns came from the lower middle class; for example, men who ran one-pump filling stations, owners of small general stores, salesmen, and the like. A report by the American Jewish Committee states: "Many news and other sources have reported, during the past year [1964], that the Klan's membership is composed to a great extent, of those at the very bottom of the social ladder. . . ."[101]

Although the strength of the contemporary Klan is largely limited to the South, a student of the ultrarightist paramilitary organization, the Minutemen, suggests that it appeals to the same elements as the Klan outside the South. The Minutemen share with the Klan a belief in the historic conspiracy of the Illuminati as the continuing source of revolutionary activity, a deep-seated concern for the breakdown in the moral order, and enthusiasm for the Presidential candidacy of George Wallace.[102]

Although the Minutemen officially eschew racial and religious prejudice, they cooperate openly and frequently with anti-Semitic and anti-Negro groups. Reports on the activities of the group indicate that "a considerable proportion . . . are anti-Semites and racists."[103]

A non-random, one percent sample of membership (based primarily on newspaper reports) suggests that the modal Minuteman is a male of Western European descent and of Christian faith who is married and in his late thirties or early forties. Roughly half the membership is composed of blue-collar workers, and over a quarter are semi- or unskilled laborers. Professionals and salaried white-collar employees are rare, and proprietors are by far the largest white-collar group. Among the proprietors, owners of gun shops seem to be much over-represented.

These findings indicate that the average socio-economic status of the Minutemen is somewhat lower than that of supporters of . . . the John Birch Society, and the Christian Anti-Communism Crusade. . . . Indeed, my estimate of Minutemen membership characteristics is quite similar to Vander Zanden's profile of Klan membership. . . . To overstate the case, it is as though the Klan were the Minutemen of the Fundamentalist South, and the Minutemen the Klan of the Puritan North.[104]

The broad appeal of the Klan can be further specified through analysis of two national opinion surveys conducted by the Gallup poll in 1946 and 1965 inquiring into attitudes toward the Klan. In spite of the considerable difference in the climate of opinion which occurred in the two decades which intervened between the two surveys, the results are surprisingly similar. They tend to bear out the generalizations which have been made by Vander Zanden and other students of the Klan concerning its support (Table 40).

Table 40. SUPPORT OF THE KLAN, 1946 AND 1965, WHITES ONLY

| | 1946 | | | 1965 | | |
	Nation	South	Non-South	Nation	South	Non-South
Pro	6 %	17 %	5 %	6 %	18 %	3 %
Con	79	59	86	85	65	90
Don't know	15	24	14	9	17	7
Number	(2,365)	(298)	(2,067)	(2,179)	(403)	(1,776)

Table 41. KLAN SUPPORT AND RELIGION, 1965, WHITES ONLY

	Protestants	Catholics	Jews	Others	None
Pro	8 %	2.5 %	0 %	0 %	11 %
Con	82	91.0	100	100	77
Don't know	10	6.0	0	0	11
Number	(1,418)	(605)	(53)	(46)	(53)

The fact that the public support for the Klan has continued to be predominantly southern will hardly be a surprise. Neither is the finding that Protestants are much more likely to support the Klan than Catholics, in spite of the fact that the postwar versions of the organization have repressed their anti-Catholicism and have even made overtures for Catholic backing (Table 41).

Since Klan support is largely derived from white Protestants, the remaining analysis of the social traits associated with opinion toward the Klan has been limited to this group. White non-Protestants and Negroes were eliminated from the analysis. In the white Protestant group, the most significant correlates of pro-Klan opinion have continued to be socioeconomic. High education, good income, and higher occupational status are associated with opposition to the Klan. The Klan draws most heavily from uneducated, lowly skilled, blue-collar workers and finds its greatest opposition among college-educated professionals. In line with reports on the earlier Klans, farmers, as a group, have not been attracted to the Klan in disproportionate numbers (Tables 42, 43, 44).

These data, of course, refer to attitudes toward rather than membership in the Klan. It is possible that many of those responding, particularly the less educated, actually do not know what the Klan is or stands for. Some indication to the contrary, however, may be seen in the fact that those who stated that they approved of the Klan in the 1965 sample were also likely to approve of the John Birch Society and to disapprove of the

National Association for the Advancement of Colored People (NAACP) and the Congress of Racial Equality (CORE). Such differences were confirmed, holding occupational class constant (Table 45).

These findings are not surprising, of course, having value mainly in demonstrating that in asking about attitudes toward the Klan, the survey really tapped underlying political and racial attitudes. However, Table 45

Table 42. KLAN SUPPORT AND EDUCATION, 1946 AND 1965, WHITE PROTESTANTS

| | 1946 | | |
	Grammar School	High School and Business School	College
Pro	12 %	6 %	7 %
Con	65	76	86
Don't know	23	18	7
Number	(422)	(752)	(414)
	1965		
	Grammar School	High School	College
Pro	9 %	10 %	3 %
Con	78	78	92
Don't know	13	11	5
Number	(319)	(775)	(33)

Table 43. KLAN SUPPORT AND INCOME STATUS, 1946 AND 1965, WHITE PROTESTANTS

| | 1946 | | | |
	Government Assistance	Poor	Average	Well to Do
Pro	11 %	10 %	7 %	6 %
Con	59	69	79	85
Don't know	30	21	14	9
Number	(46)	(684)	(614)	(230)
	1965				
	Under $2,500	$2,500– $4,999	$5,000– $6,999	$7,000– $9,999	$10,000+
Pro	11 %	8 %	8 %	7 %	6 %
Con	74	79	84	83	89
Don't know	15	15	8	10	4
Number	(194)	(341)	(253)	(308)	(275)

Table 44. OCCUPATIONAL STATUS AND ATTITUDES TOWARD KLAN, 1946 AND 1965, WHITE PROTESTANTS ONLY

1946

	Unskilled	Service	Semi-skilled	Skilled	White Collar and Sales	Business	Professional	Farm
Pro	16 %	14 %	7 %	10 %	7 %	8 %	3 %	8 %
Con	62	71	67	70	80	76	94	73
Don't know	22	16	25	21	13	16	3	19
Number	(73)	(96)	(215)	(175)	(335)	(131)	(175)	(300)

1965

	Unskilled	Service	(*)	Skilled	White Collar and Sales	Business	Professional	Farm
Pro	12 %	7 %		9 %	11 %	4 %	2 %	4 %
Con	69	80		84	80	92	92	85
Don't know	19	13		7	9	4	6	11
Number	(213)	(55)		(250)	(154)	(179)	(168)	(118)

* Category of "semi-skilled" was not used in the 1965 study.

Table 45.   RELATIONSHIP BETWEEN ATTITUDES TOWARD THE KLAN AND
THE NAACP AND THE JOHN BIRCH SOCIETY WITHIN OCCUPATIONAL
STRATA, 1965, WHITE PROTESTANTS

	Nonmanual			Manual		
	Like Klan	Dislike Klan	Don't Know	Like Klan	Dislike Klan	Don't Know
John Birch Soc.						
Like	63 %	17 %	3 %	43 %	11 %	24 %
Dislike	11	71	23	24	55	12
Don't know	26	12	74	33	34	64
NAACP						
Like	18 %	56 %	23 %	14 %	41 %	25 %
Dislike	82	37	26	80	44	53
Don't know	0	7	52	6	15	22
Number	(27)	(443)	(31)	(49)	(389)	(59)

provides another footnote to patterns already discussed. The Birch Society, which advocates conservative economic doctrines and has a basically middle-class constituency, has a greater appeal to middle-class Klan supporters than to working-class ones. Conversely, among the anti-Klan group, working-class opponents of the Klan are less likely to approve of the NAACP than middle-class opponents, a finding which is generally congruent with our knowledge that ethnic prejudice is much more widespread among the less privileged.

The Future

Although the growing violence in northern cities and the increasing militancy of the sections of the Negro civil rights movement have seemingly helped to strengthen the support for the Ku Klux Klan in recent years, the evidence seems clear that the Klan, as an organization which engages in violence and advocates overt racist doctrines, has little future. It is generally opposed as an embarrassment by other extreme right-wing groups. The Birch Society has made membership in the Klan grounds for expulsion from the organization.

The evidence suggests that the potential of the Birch Society, as a national mass movement, is quite limited. The self-image of the Birch Society is that of a tight organization, with members who are involved in specific organizational activity. This activity is largely organized through special-issue projects and satellite committees. There is, for example MOTOREDE (Movement To Restore Decency) which is geared to fighting sex education in the schools. TACT (Truth About Civil Turmoil) relates to civil rights activity and has opposed what it has called "forced integration" in local public schools. TRAIN (To Restore American Independence Now) has addressed itself to foreign affairs and opposes foreign aid to "questionable" countries. There are also specific campaigns, such as "Support Your Local Police," and "When Guns Are Outlawed, Only Outlaws Will Have Guns." While letters and petitions are stimulated on these kinds of issues for transmission to national officials, the activist burden really reposes in local and regional committees, such as those noted above. There is much evidence that in given communities and in some states, these committee activities have not been without considerable influence. They have, for example, stirred battles on sex education in the schools, activating, on a single-issue basis, larger segments of the community. And, in so doing, they have undoubtedly helped to crystallize a certain climate in many communities which transcends that single issue.

It should be noted that these isolated Birch Society issues—in the fashion in which they are presented—strike the preservatist nerve for those large numbers in the cities who feel their power and status declining, as manifested by the deterioration of their accustomed cultural and moral milieu.

On the other hand, most of the people who are activated on, say, a sex education campaign would not support the basic antistatist, economically ultraconservative thrust of the Birch Society (and have little interest in the elaborate conspiracy theory of the Society). The more massive support which the Birch Society receives on a local level with respect to these single issues is very selective, indeed, and does not extend to the national political arena.

Furthermore, there are indications that while the Birch Society gained in membership and financial support under the impetus of the Goldwater campaign, it did not grow under the impress of the 1968 George Wallace campaign. Wallace was able to appeal to some of the same fears that cherished moral and cultural baggage was slipping away, decisively added a new nativist piece to that baggage, did not encumber himself with economic conservatism, and offered a political movement. Without detracting from the local effects of the Birch Society, the state of the knowledge would strongly indicate that if there is a right-wing extremist wave of the future on a national political level, it is likely to be not in the Birch Society, but in the George Wallace mode.

Notes

1. Hans Toch, *The Social Psychology of Social Movements* (New York: Bobbs-Merrill, 1965), p. 17.
2. Herbert Blumer, "Collective Behavior," in A. M. Lee, ed., *New Outline*

334   THE POLITICS OF UNREASON

of the Principles of Sociology (New York: Barnes and Noble, 1951), p. 199.

3. Neil J. Smelser, The Theory of Collective Behavior (New York: The Free Press, 1963), p. 8.

4. Toch, op. cit., p. 5.

5. Ibid., p. 11.

6. See Blumer, op. cit.

7. Frederick W. Grupp, Jr., Social Correlates of Political Activists: The John Birch Society and the ADA (Ph.D. Thesis, Department of Political Science, University of Pennsylvania, 1968), pp. xxiv–xxviii.

8. Burton Levy, Profile of the American Right: A Case Study of Michigan (Ph.D. Thesis, Department of Political Science, University of Massachusetts, 1965), pp. 21–22, 25.

9. Barbara Stone, The John Birch Society of California (Ph.D. Thesis, Department of Political Science, University of Southern California, 1968), p. 16.

10. Ira Rohter, Radical Rightists: An Empirical Study (Ph.D. Thesis, Department of Political Science, Michigan State University, 1967), pp. 37–43.

11. Scott Grant McNall, The Freedom Center: A Case Study of a Politico-Religious Sect (Ph.D. Thesis, Department of Sociology, University of Oregon, 1965), pp. 34–68.

12. Raymond E. Wolfinger et al., "America's Radical Right: Politics and Ideology," in David E. Apter, ed., Ideology and Discontent (New York: The Free Press, 1964), pp. 264–267.

13. Hannah Wartenburg and Wagner Thielens, Jr., Against the United Nations: A Letter Writing Campaign by the Birch Society (New York: Bureau of Applied Social Research, Columbia University, 1964); and James McEvoy, Letters from the Right: Content-Analysis of a Letter Writing Campaign (Ann Arbor: Center for Research on Utilization of Scientific Knowledge, 1966).

14. Herman Edelsberg, "Birchites Make Polite Pen Pals," A.D.L. Bulletin (April 1962), p. 7.

15. McEvoy, op. cit., pp. 21–25.

16. Wartenburg and Thielens, op. cit., pp. 6–8.

17. See S. M. Lipset, Revolution and Counterrevolution (New York: Basic Books, 1968), pp. 286–288.

18. Rohter, op. cit., pp. 140–144.

19. Wolfinger et al., op. cit., p. 282.

20. Grace A. Pheneger, The Correlation between Religious Fundamentalism and Political Ultra-Conservatism since World War II (M.A. Thesis, Bowling Green State University, 1966).

21. Ibid., p. 104.

22. Murray Havens, "The Radical Right in the Southwest: Community Response to Shifting Social-economic Patterns" (mimeographed paper presented to the American Political Science Association, September 1964, Austin: Department of Government, University of Texas), pp. 3, 12.

23. Levy, op. cit., p. 218.

24. Grupp, op. cit., p. 32.

25. Rohter, op. cit., pp. 136–138.

26. McNall, op. cit., pp. 336–339.

27. Wolfinger *et al.*, *op. cit.*, p. 292.
28. Havens, *op. cit.*, p. 3.
29. Grupp, *op. cit.*, p. 27.
30. *Ibid.*, p. 16; Wartenburg and Thielens, *op. cit.*; McEvoy, *op. cit.*; and Rohter, *op. cit.*, pp. 104–107; see also J. Allen Broyles, *The John Birch Society: Anatomy of a Protest* (Boston: Beacon, 1966).
31. Rohter, *op. cit.*, pp. 103–104.
32. Broyles, *op. cit.*, p. 3.
33. Rohter, *op. cit.*, p. 107.
34. McEvoy, *op. cit.*, p. 16.
35. See Lipset, *op. cit.*, pp. 317–319.
36. Robert E. Lane, *Political Life* (New York: The Free Press, 1965), p. 130.
37. Elton F. Jackson, "Status Consistency and Symptoms of Stress," *American Sociological Review*, XXVII (1962), 469–480.
38. Grupp, *op. cit.*, pp. 142–143.
39. Havens, *op. cit.*, p. 15.
40. Levy, *op. cit.*, p. 216.
41. Rohter, *op. cit.*, pp. 126–133; 158–161.
42. *Ibid.*, pp. 159–161.
43. *Ibid.*, p. 145.
44. Grupp, *op. cit.*, p. 134.
45. Andrzej Malewski, "The Degree of Status Incongruence and Its Effects," in R. Bendix and S. M. Lipset, eds., *Class, Status, and Power* (New York: The Free Press, 1966), p. 304.
46. Daniel Bell, "The Dispossessed (1962)," in Daniel Bell, ed., *The Radical Right* (Garden City: Doubleday-Anchor, 1964), p. 24.
47. McEvoy, *op. cit.*, pp. 22–23.
48. Edelsberg, *op. cit.*, p. 8.
49. *Bulletin* (November 1965), p. 116.
50. As cited in Broyles, *op. cit.*, p. 104.
51. Bell, *op. cit.*, p. 5.
52. Marshall B. Jones, "Military Participation in the Rightist Revival 1960–1964," in *The Radical Right. Proceedings of the Sixth Annual Intergroup Relations Conference* (Houston: Department of Sociology and Anthropology, University of Houston, 1966), pp. 24–25.
53. Broyles, *op. cit.*, p. 105.
54. Jones, *op. cit.*, p. 25.
55. *Ibid.*, p. 26.
56. *Ibid.*, p. 29.
57. *Ibid.*, p. 34.
58. Bell, *op. cit.*, p. 8.
59. Jones, *op. cit.*, p. 43.
60. Broyles, *op. cit.*, p. 105.
61. Page 10 as cited in *ibid.*, p. 105.
62. Morris Janowitz, *The Professional Soldier* (New York: The Free Press, 1960), p. 81.
63. *Ibid.*, p. 86.
64. *Ibid.*, p. 85.
65. *Ibid.*, p. 87.
66. *Ibid.*, pp. 88–89.

67. *Ibid.*, p. 236.
68. *Ibid.*, p. 238.
69. *Ibid.*, p. 239.
70. *Ibid.*, pp. 243, 251.
71. Bell, *op. cit.*, pp. 31–35.
72. *Ibid.*, pp. 39–40; Janowitz, *op. cit.*, pp. 390–391.
73. Samuel P. Huntington, "Power, Expertise and the Military Profession," *Daedalus*, XCII (1963), 803–804.
74. "Conspiracy on the Right," *New Republic*, CLI (November 28, 1964), 3; see also Benjamin R. Epstein and Arnold Forster, *Report on the John Birch Society 1966* (New York: Vintage, 1966), p. 52.
75. *Ibid.*
76. *New York Post*, July 9, 1965, as reported in Benjamin R. Epstein and Arnold Forster, *The Radical Right* (New York: Vintage, 1967), p. 180.
77. Arthur Niederhoffer, *Behind the Shield: The Police in Urban Society* (Garden City: Doubleday, 1967), p. 111.
78. Epstein and Forster, *The Radical Right, op. cit.*, p. 54.
79. *American Opinion*, X (September 1967). For a more recent eulogy to the "great" police, see *Bulletin* (March 1970), pp. 14–20.
80. Gunnar Myrdal, *An American Dilemma: The Negro Problem and Modern Democracy* (New York: Harper, 1944), pp. 538–557.
81. Niederhoffer, *op. cit.*, pp. 5–8, 36–38.
82. Jerome Skolnick, *Justice without Trial, Law Enforcement in Democratic Society* (New York: John Wiley, 1966), p. 61.
83. Niederhoffer, *op. cit.*, pp. 2–3.
84. Skolnick, *op. cit.*, p. 50.
85. *Ibid.*, pp. 42–48.
86. *Ibid.*, p. 59. Emphasis in the original.
87. *American Opinion*, X (March 1967), 81.
88. *Ibid.*, IX (February 1966), 1.
89. *Ibid.*, X (January 1967), 17.
90. *Ibid.*, p. 29.
91. *Ibid.*, X (July–August 1967), 61.
92. Grupp, *op. cit.*, p. 69.
93. *Ibid.*
94. Educational quality was rated according to reports in Bernard Berelson, *Graduate Education in the United States* (New York: McGraw-Hill, 1960), for universities, and James Cass and Max Birnbaum, *Comparative Guide to American Colleges* (New York: Harper & Row, 1965), for colleges; Grupp, *op. cit.*, p. 80.
95. Rohter, *op. cit.*, pp. 134–135.
96. Murray Havens, "The Impact of Right-Wing Groups in Selected Texas Cities" (unpublished paper, Department of Political Science, University of Texas), p. 18.
97. Grupp, *op. cit.*, p. 82.
98. See S. M. Lipset and Philip Altbach, "Student Politics and Higher Education in the United States," in S. M. Lipset, ed., *Student Politics* (New York: Basic Books, 1967), pp. 199–252, for a review of the relevant research literature.
99. For a detailed analysis and statistics bearing on attitudes toward the

Birch Society, see S. M. Lipset, "Three Decades of the Radical Right: Coughlinites, McCarthyites, and Birchers," in Bell, *The Radical Right, op. cit.*, pp. 421–439.

100. James W. Vander Zanden, *Race Relations in Transition* (New York: Random House, 1965), p. 4.

101. *The Ku Klux Klan* (New York: Trends Analyses Division, American Jewish Committee, June 1965, mimeographed), p. 4.

102. For the ideology of the Klan, including frequent references to the conspiratorial activities of the Illuminati, see the monthly magazine, *The Fiery Cross*; its contents are similar to those of the *Councilor* discussed in the previous chapter. The Patriotic Party, the public "legal" front of the Minutemen, is supported by the bimonthly *Illuminator*, which, as its name suggests, devotes a considerable portion of its space to exposés of the nefarious activities of the Illuminati.

103. Richard P. Albares, *Nativist Paramilitarism In the United States: The Minutemen Organization* (Chicago: Center for Social Organization Studies, University of Chicago, April 1968, mimeographed), p. 32. For a good journalistic account, see J. Harry Jones, *The Minutemen* (New York: Doubleday, 1968).

104. Albares, *op. cit.*, pp. 25–26, 28.

CHAPTER

9

George Wallace and the New Nativism

The limited resurgence of the Klan and the development of the Wallace movement are both based on the fact that there is a new rising population group in the nation, the Negro. The social strains emanating from the American black man's emergence from subordination were increasingly reflected in American extremist movements since World War II and exploded in the middle 1960's. The "bill" was finally being presented for three centuries of degradation.

World War I had begun a significant migration of Negroes to northern cities. In the decade preceding World War II, their growing political power visibly emerged as they became part of the new national Democratic party coalition. During that period, when old forms were breaking up, they gained a foothold in such American institutions as the union movement and the Democratic party apparatus.

World War II saw another massive migration to the North and to a man-hungry war industry; the accumulating strength of the Negro population came to a head. A threatened March on Washington in 1941 led by a politically potent Negro labor leader resulted directly in historic Executive Order 8802 by President Roosevelt requiring "fair employment practices" in defense industries and government. As a result of the need as well as the Order, the percentage of Negroes in war industries increased from 3 to 8 per cent between 1942 and 1944. Between 1940 and 1947, Negro males in the skilled trades increased by 25 per cent.[1]

After the war, the pressure persisted. Fair Employment Practices laws were passed in many northern and western states. The proportion of non-white males employed as skilled craftsmen more than doubled between 1940 and 1961, while the proportion of white male workers in that category rose by about 25 per cent.[2] Incursions began to be made in the white-collar classifications. Meanwhile, in the South the Negro's inferior status was being seriously challenged, mainly as a result of federal pressures. The Supreme Court's school desegregation decision in 1954 was, of course, the landmark. Segregated transportation and segregated juries were also ruled illegal.

However, in both North and South, these successes just led to heightened pressures from the Negro community. The civil rights revolution began to change character after little more than a decade. The next stage reflected the shift in emphasis from equal opportunity to equal achievement, from civil rights to the war against poverty, from the civil rights revolution to the black revolution. Equal opportunity is not yet equal achievement, except for those who are really equipped to compete. America had created an enclave population whose cultural and educational "equipment" had been comprehensively stunted for generations. Equal opportunity had been enough for the impoverished and uneducated ethnic immigrants to America because other societies, not America, had depressed them. In their minds, America owed them no more than an opportunity and the gradualist road to parity which all emerging groups have traveled.

But America owed the Negroes more than opportunity. The metaphor of the Negro revolution was not an opportunity, but parity. Toward that end, the demands were not just for equal treatment, but for compensatory treatment, on a kind of reparations basis. So, side by side with the visible advances that were being made—into previously all-white jobs, previously all-white institutions, and even previously all-white neighborhoods and schools—there developed a continuing pattern of direct-action protests and demands for actual jobs, actual homes, actual benefits and privileges. As conditions improved, expectations rose; and as expectations rose, frustrations became deeper, especially among those left behind in ghetto poverty and among the young. To the pressure of growing political power was added the pressure of threatened violence and disruption. The line between social protest and social pathology often became thin. There were the riots. And, always, there was a growing curve of "crime on the streets" as the traditional delinquency-bearing population–youth–grew in sheer numbers.

New federal laws were passed affecting the South; vast federal and local expenditures were made or announced toward reducing Negro poverty; accessions to "Black Power" were publicized; extraordinary measures were taken, or seemed to be taken, to fit Negroes into industry, into colleges, into political positions. Numerically, culturally, politically, the Negroes were "taking over" the large cities of the North, just as the eastern European immigrants had once taken them over. And the pressures continued.

At the same time, the Americans were engaged in the most frustrating foreign war in their history against a backdrop of growing bureaucracy and rising taxes. And when the affluent youth of America—on the college campuses in staggering and unprecedented numbers—were not demonstrating, they seemed to be developing startling new mores: marijuana instead of whisky, overt rather than covert sexuality. In the center of this dazzling spiral of change, however, was the black revolution. And one response to the black revolution, and the whole spiral of change, was the movement headed by George Wallace.

The New Nativism

In comparing the contemporary KKK with the more respectable George Wallace movement, the question may be asked: Is not the Wallace movement a racist movement, such as the KKK, operating in the benign name of general preservatism? However, in the light of what has been learned about the nature of right-wing extremism, it would be more to the mark to ask: Is not the KKK a generally preservatist movement operating in the name of racism? This formulation at least puts the backlash before the bigotry, where, analytically, it belongs.

"Racism," of course, has a number of alternate meanings:

Racism 1. *As Ideology:* A formal, explicit articulated belief in the inherited superiority of one group over another and that group's inherent right to supremacy.

Racism 2. *As Attitude:* Negative affects and images about a population group as a whole, held by any number of individuals.

Racism 3. *As Social Behavior:* Institutional or sociocultural patterns of behavior which keep a population group disadvantaged.

These are, of course, three quite different, if connected, phenomena. Racist attitudes can exist, and usually do, without racist ideology or behavior; racist behavior can take place without racist ideology or attitudes. As a matter of fact, the term "racism" probably came into the language to describe racist ideology exclusively. It would still serve the economy of words best if restricted to that meaning, but common usage is no respecter of such a tight economy. The point is that, on the face of it, the KKK featured a racist ideology, while George Wallace, in his national movement, did not. Wallace proposed an ideology of preservatism—for law and order, against government intervention in social problems, against the acceleration of change—which would serve derivatively and automatically to support Racism 3: the maintenance of institutions that would check the rise of the Negro population.

Several different images of this "Wallacism" would all be descriptively correct: It could certainly be seen as "hidden racism"; and it could be seen as serving the subsurface anti-Negro hostility of bigots; but as an illuminator of the common aspects of right-wing extremism, it can best be seen as a backlash against change in which there is an almost absolute congruence between the backlash against dreaded change and the backlash targetry, that is, the change-bearers. This image may do much to expose not just the nature of right-wing extremism but the nature of bigotry, especially in its political uses. The polar image tends to reify bigotry—to conceive of it as a little mental package tucked away in a corner of the brain, waiting for the proper stimulus to bring it full-blown to life.

There has been much generalized evidence in recent decades pointing to the dominance of situation over attitude in shaping bigotry. The variation in the willingness of a thousand Texas manufacturers to hire Negroes was found not to be significantly related to their differential attitudes toward Negroes.[3] It was observed that white Americans in the Panama Canal Zone tended to behave in a less discriminatory fashion when they crossed to the side of the street which was in Panamanian territory.[4]

Indeed, the evidence indicates that situational changes serve to alter negative images and hostilities, rather than the other way round. Prejudiced behavior typically shapes prejudiced attitudes. Slavery preceded racism. Families who were forced to live in integrated housing situations ended up with more favorable attitudes toward Negroes.[5] So did soldiers in the Army.[6] Sheer proximity is not the explanation. White residents who lived on the edge of an expanding neighborhood had fewer negative stereotypes about Negroes, but more hostility toward them than did white families living three miles away.[7] The social situation controls; prejudiced attitudes wax and wane accordingly.[8]

This understanding does not obviate the fact that there is a wide range of personality differences and thresholds with respect to bigotry. But in a political context, a historical situation which creates mass designs of bigotry tends to wash out the statistical significance of these personality differences. It is possible to say that if there were no historical or cultural reservoir of nativist prejudice, it could never be used as an instrument. But the possibility is just as strong that if such a "reservoir" did not exist, it would have to be invented, as it has been in the past. In this case, the fact that bigotry does not have to be invented relates directly to the fact that the Negro population is just now emerging. But the main point is that, reservoir or no reservoir, racism or nativism becomes a political force only when a backlash situation creates and shapes it as a force. This was as true for the KKK with its "Racism 1" as for the Wallace Movement with its "Racism 3"; the nature of political racism, of nativist bigotry, is more clearly revealed in the latter than in the former.

George Wallace entered state politics in Alabama as an assemblyman and quickly gained a reputation as an economic liberal. He was described by one newspaperman as "the number one do-gooder in the legislature."[9] Robert Sherrill says that "there was a time when some Alabamians considered him a dangerous radical. Indeed some still do."[10] A staff member of the governor's office when Wallace was in the assembly reports: "He was the leading liberal in the legislature, no doubt about that. He was regarded as a dangerous left-winger, a lot of people even looked on him as a downright pink."[11] This reputation was built on his populist stance and the kind of legislation he introduced as an assemblyman: provision for vocational and trade schools; scholarships for needy students; additional social security benefits for city and county employees; new health facilities; expanded old age pensions. This stance seemed a natural one for Wallace, who had grown up in relative poverty and had seen the mortgage on his family's farm foreclosed. His platform was welfare liberalism, help for the common man; and he did not notably deal in racial politics one way or another—until after his first gubernatorial campaign in 1958. During that campaign, against John Patterson, the KKK candidate, Wallace maintained his "neutrality" on racial issues and pointedly refused to speak at KKK rallies. He was beaten badly and was widely quoted as saying, "They out-niggered me that time but they'll never do it again."[12]

He featured a defense of segregation in his next campaign, which he won, and told a group of state senators: "I'm gonna make race the basis of politics in this state. I'm gonna make it the basis of politics in this country."[13] In his inaugural address, he promised "segregation today, segregation tomorrow, segregation forever."

Wallace did not abandon his economically liberal stance. He spent more state money than any other governor in Alabama's history, and much of it on welfare measures. Workmen's compensation was increased, as were old age assistance and the medical aid program. He reduced requirements for getting state pensions. He significantly raised teachers' salaries and the budgets for public schools and higher education. He built more than two dozen junior colleges and trade schools. He instituted a free textbook policy.

On this score, his economic populism bears comparison with that of Huey Long, who has been called America's classic welfare demagogue. Sherrill comments that "in the last analysis, one must judge the degree of populism behind a welfare or public works program according to who pays for it. In Alabama it is the consumer who pays."[14] Wallace came to the assembly as an opponent of the sales tax and killed one sales tax increase by filibuster. But he condoned the sales tax as a major instrument of funding for his programs as governor. The increased tax burden fell disproportionately on the low-income consumer rather than big business and industry. "He piled new taxes and debt on the people and they let him."[15]

Nevertheless, his image remained that of the economic liberal, the poor man's friend. One politician observed: "His economic programs surpassed the fondest dreams of every liberal in the state. He did what all the populists have always dreamed of doing."[16] A man who had once been chairman of the State Democratic party Executive Committee said: "Wallace is the most economically liberal politician I know of. He is more liberal than Johnson, I tell you—more liberal than Folsom and Kennedy ever were."[17] In a discussion of Wallace after the 1968 election campaign, the South's best-known black militant leader, Julian Bond, said: "He [Wallace] confuses me because he's liberal on a great many questions, except race."[18]

After his defeat by Patterson, Wallace presumably decided that "economic liberalism" was not enough. He became the chief defender of institutional racism in the South. In his first year in office as governor, he sent the state troopers to put down the massive Birmingham demonstrations led by Martin Luther King, Jr. In the next year, when a Tuskegee high school was about to be desegregated by court order, he sent state troopers to surround the school and keep it closed. In the same year, he fulfilled his campaign promise to defy "illegal" federal court orders for desegregation by "standing at the schoolhouse door in person." When the University of Alabama was ordered by federal court order to admit two Negro applicants, and while the whole world watched, Wallace personally interposed his body between the federalized National Guard, which had been sent to enforce the court order, and the schoolhouse door.

The results were, of course, something less than successful on the issue level. The savage repression of the Birmingham demonstrations spurred the passage of the Civil Rights Act of 1964. The Tuskegee High School was promptly reopened by further court order. The Negro students walked through the doors of the University of Alabama after Wallace made a little speech to the cameras and stepped aside. There were some who suggested that Wallace was something less than the archchampion of segregation that he claimed to be. One prosegregation newspaper, the *Alabama Journal*, editorialized:

It appears that our governor holds the Southeastern Conference title for the most desegregation in the shortest time. How long will his fire-and-fall-back tactics fool the people. . . . Our melancholy conviction is that they will be fooled for a long time because they want to be fooled. Just as the people in London were soothed by the sound of anti-aircraft guns firing at nothing in the early stages of the blitz—a calculated ruse to convince them that Britain was fighting back, thus to bolster their morale—so does Wallace continue to set off impressively noisy blanks. The people love it, sad to say.[19]

The president of an Alabama college said: "I would term the governor a pseudo-demagogue, because he doesn't really believe what he says about the race question. He uses it only as a technique to get the vote of the non-sophisticated white man."[20] Others have suggested that Wallace was not just posturing, but that he had actually metamorphosed into a racist. One old associate said: "He used to be anything but a racist, but with all his chattering he managed to talk himself into it."[21]

But, emotional racist or not, Wallace became the symbol of backlash heroism in Alabama, throughout the South, and—as he entered the Presidential campaign of 1968—throughout the country. His defeats were triumphs of expressive politics, which Gusfield defines as "political action for the sake of expression rather than for the sake of influencing or controlling the distribution of valued objects. The goal of the action, the object of hostility or love, is not a 'solution' to the problems which have generated the action. Politics, in this usage, is a means to express how the actors feel about their situation."[22] By standing in the school doorway, Wallace was expressing for millions of people a frustrated defiance in the face of the tide of status change which seemed about to wash over them. And the defiance was being addressed not so much to the Negroes as to "the establishment" which was seen as the effective engineer of the change. This was the key to Wallace's "new nativism," to his cafeteria appeal, to his brand of conservative populism.

Wallace did not engage in ideological racism during his Presidential campaign and indeed rarely mentioned Negroes as such. As governor he had attempted to draw for the national audience a line between racism and segregationism: "A racist is one who despises someone because of his color, and an Alabama segregationist is one who conscientiously believes that it is in the best interest of Negro and white to have a separate educational and social order."[23] As Presidential candidate his stress was on the right of a citizenry to decide whether it wanted segregation or not, without federal intervention. Asked during the 1964 Presidential campaign whether there was white backlash in his support, Wallace replied: "I don't think that there is a backlash in this country against people because of color. . . . I think there is a backlash against the theoreticians and bureaucrats in national government who are trying to solve problems that ought to be solved at the local level."[24]

In entering the 1968 campaign, Wallace faced the problem of recruiting a number of disparate groups. On one hand, his campaign organization was based to a considerable degree on those groups active in support of ultra-conservative antistatism. These groups had been particularly concerned with the expansion of the welfare state, the increase in the income tax, and the power of trade-unions. On the whole, they advocated a return to small government. The mass appeal of such groups, however, has been limited. On the other hand, Wallace sought to gain the votes of many relatively underprivileged whites who had benefited from the welfare state, but were upset by pressures toward integration, who were concerned about law and order, who reacted strongly to the changes in moral values as reflected in sexual behavior, use of drugs, the liberalization of the churches, and the like.

He attempted to do this by directing his campaign against a network of "establishment" intrusions and failures: civil rights legislation which imposed integration; weakness which permitted a breakdown in law and order, crime in the streets, and riots; the fear of central government power generally. In this way he produced a significant coalition of the right. While his clear institutional racism appealed to KKK members, many of whom participated in his campaign, his attack on central government appealed to Birch Society members, many of whom played a leading role in his organization. Wallace qualified as a "conservative" in their eyes, but he avoided the Birch Society trap. "Liberals," he said, "used to be people who didn't believe in government regimentation and control, and now it has been switched around. In the last election, Mr. Goldwater was running as a conservative, but he did not have the support and confidence of the working people in our country. For some reason, they feared that he was not in their interest."[25] He freely proclaimed that he was a conservative, but one "who has a record of progress in government and support for the workingman."[26] He disclaimed "ultra-conservatism" because "those ultra-conservatives are conservative about just one thing—money."[27] In the terms of Free and Cantril, he was an ideological rather than an operational conservative. And the specific issues used made it clear that such conservatism, at this point in time, is more accurately described as a general preservatism. Wallace sensed that an all-embracing preservatist thrust might enable him to make the necessary "marriage between classes" that a successful right-wing extremist movement needs.

The extensive support Wallace received from Birch Society quarters indicated that he had struck the nerve of many on the radical right who had supported the Republican Goldwater four years earlier. To put it another way, by the nature of his generalized appeal to the backlash and preservatist impulse, Wallace was able to interest a number of different issue publics. Converse's election studies led him to "the simple conclusion . . . that different controversies excite different people to the point of real opinion formation. One man takes an interest in policies bearing on the Negro and is relatively indifferent to or ignorant about controversies in other areas. His neighbor may have few crystallized opinions on the race issue, but he may find the subject of foreign aid very important."[28]

Wallace's generalized preservatism was equipped to attract many whose most salient concerns had crystallized around the issue of statism; or of national weakness; or of moral breakdown; or of Negro intrusion itself. The pollster Louis Harris suggested that "the common bond that sews together Wallace's unusual assortment of political allies in this election is dominantly race. Seventy-three per cent of all Wallace supporters want progress for Negroes to be halted."[29] But, more likely the common bond that really sewed together this coalition was backlash against change— and in this case change for which the governmental establishment was held responsible, by omission or commission. Those most attracted were those most threatened by the change. And even where ideological or attitudinal racism may *not* have been the central issue of change around which this threat was generated, the Negroes became the corporeal bearers and symbols of the change. In that sense anti-Negro sentiment was a secondary bond, of varying saliency, rather than a primary bond; in that sense, nativist bigotry is exposed as the backside rather than the frontside of backlash politics; in that sense, by design or not, Wallace's strategy of conducting his campaign on a broader base than ideological racism was effective.

In appealing to low-status backlash, Wallace recognized that his program could not fly in the face of associated low-income needs. In his speeches, and in the official platform of the American Independent party, Wallace appealed directly to the self-interests of workers and low-income people. His opposition to federal government interference with local institutions did not prevent him from endorsing federal financial support for programs which would assist the poor. Thus the party platform included the following items:

An enlightened and advancing educational program, assisted but not controlled by the federal government.

Job training and opportunity for all Americans willing and able to seek and hold gainful employment. . . .

We offer the laboring man and woman an opportunity to provide for himself and his family a better and fuller life and a greater democratic freedom in the management of his organizations, free from intrusion by the federal government.

An immediate increase in social security payments with a goal of a 60% increase in benefits.

An increase in the minimum payment to $100, with annual cost of living increases.

Restoration of the 100% income tax deduction for drugs and medical expenses paid out by people 65 and over.

Removal of the earnings limitation on people 65 and over in order that they may earn any amount of additional income. . . .

It is the obligation of a responsible government to help people who are unable to help themselves. . . . Medicare should be improved. . . . Through sound fiscal management we set as a goal the following improvements in Medicare:

1. Relief to persons unable to pay deductible charges under Medicare.

2. Relief to persons unable to have deducted from their Social Security checks the monthly fee for physician service coverage under Medicare.

3. Providing for uninterrupted nursing home care for those with chronic illness who require such care. . . .

In this land of plenty, no one should be denied adequate medical care because of his financial condition. . . .

Through the means of their great trade organizations, these [working] men and women have exerted tremendous influence on the economic and social life of the nation and have attained a standard of living known to no other nation. . . .

The concern of this Party is that the gains which labor struggled so long to obtain not be lost to them either through inaction or subservience to illogical domestic policies of our other national parties.

We propose and pledge:

To guarantee to and protect labor in its right to collective bargaining;

To assert leadership at the federal level toward assuring labor its rightful reward for its contribution to the productivity of America;

To propose and support programs designed to improve living and employment conditions of our working men and women;

To prohibit intrusion by the federal government into the internal affairs of labor organizations, seeking to direct and control actions as to seniority and apprentice lists and other prerogatives; . . .

To support programs and legislation designed to afford an equitable minimum wage, desirable working hours and conditions of employment, and protection in the event of adversity or unemployment;

To add efficiency and dispatch to the actions and activities of the National Labor Relations Board, resulting in more prompt decisions by this Agency;

To pledge and assure that labor will be adequately represented in all deliberations of this Party and its administration of the affairs of government. . . .

In the event that a public works program becomes necessary to provide employment for all employable Americans, we will provide such a program assuring, however, that the programs be needful and productive and that the participants engage in labor beneficial to the nation and its economy rather than becoming wards of the government and the recipients of gratuitous handouts.

For those unemployable by reasons of age, infirmity, disability or otherwise, provision will be made for their adequate care through programs of social services based on the requirements and needs of these persons. We hold that all Americans are deserving of and will have the care, compassion and benefits of the fullness of life.[30]

The planks in the AIP platform presented above are not those of a conservative laissez-faire party. Most of them are clearly far to the left of Barry Goldwater and the *National Review*. And during the campaign, Goldwater, William Buckley, and other writers in the *National Review* and *Human Events* attacked Wallace as a New Deal populist who was closer in his welfare and trade-union planks to liberal Democrats than to themselves.

For example, James Ashbrook, the head of the right-wing American Conservative Union, which was originally established as a conservative equivalent to ADA, stated on October 9: "True conservatism cannot be served by George Wallace. At heart he is a Populist with strong tendencies in the direction of a collectivist welfare state. . . . We find George Wallace's candidacy repugnant to ideals of American conservatism."[31] A poll taken by *Human Events* of over a hundred leading American conservatives reported that the overwhelming majority of them were opposed to Wallace because they felt he was not a conservative and that he knowingly appealed to "racial prejudices."[32] Although Wallace's campaign concentrated on issues like "law and order" and local control, it moved to the "left" as evidence from meetings and the opinion polls indicated that he had great appeal among workers, particularly trade-union members. In speeches in various industrial cities, he claimed that he had strongly supported unions in Alabama and began to include the "eastern money interests" among his targets.

This is not to suggest that Wallace was leaning heavily on a program of liberal economic reform, as had Huey Long and Father Coughlin in the depression-stricken 1930's. He was rather only bent on reassuring his low-income constituents that his antistatism did not include the welfare and protective sectors of governmental action which touched them. This was only one segment of his larger need and capacity to establish a strong rapport with his low-status constituents. Central to this populist appeal was his persistent and natural antielitism. As we have seen, antielitism has always been a seemingly strange ingredient of effective perservatist movements in America. In one sense, this reflects the egalitarian bias that effective political action has always needed in this country and has increasingly needed in all modern countries. Antielitism also provides the shadow of economic radicalism where its substance may be missing. Presumably the operative principle is: "If you're against them, you're with us"; which points up again the symbolic status dimension built into relative poverty.

Of course, there is always an element of ambiguity in antielitism as part of a political movement which also includes the preservatist concerns of an elite. This ambiguity is flattened out when the elite targets are safely generalized or carefully specified. Joseph McCarthy and Robert Welch had both built their practical antielitism on the cleavage between the economic conservatives of the "eastern financial establishment" in the Republican party and its midwestern and western Republican opposition. Wallace followed this populist tradition.

The Republicans now, they're having to meet in banks, tryin' to figger out what they gonna do about us down here. I'm not talking about the good banks of Chilton County or Alabama, I'm talkin about the Chase National and the Wall Street crowd. You know, they used to meet in little bitty banks to talk about us, but this time we've got 'em meetin' in the *biggest bank in the world* talkin' about you'n me and what they gonna do about guvnuh Wallace down here in Alabama. . . .[33]

All the accounts of Wallace's campaign meetings in different sections of the country have stressed his populist antielitist appeal.

He is talking about poor people, "ordinary folks," and if you strip him of the Southern accent and some of the surrounding rhetoric you might mistake him for a New Left advocate of the poverty program, urging the maximum feasible participation of the poor and return of local government to the people, "participatory democracy."[34]

Speaking on national television, he said:

The [Wallace for President] movement is a movement of the people and it doesn't make any difference whether top leading politicians endorse this movement or not. I think that if the politicians get in the way in 1968, a lot of them are gonna get run over by this average man on the street, this man in the textile mill, this man in the steel mill, this barber, this beautician, the policeman on the beat, they're the ones—and the little businessman—I think those are the mass of people that are going to support a change on the domestic scene in this country.[35]

Part of his effort to identify with the common people involved deliberately mispronouncing words and claiming not to understand certain terms used by the elite.

"Being from Alabama, we didn't know what it means when the head recapitulator of Maryland said that they were going to recapitulate the vote. . . . We still don't know what recapitulate means, but I'll tell you this, when anyone says he is going to recapitulate on you, you better watch out, because they're fixing to do something to you."

In Oklahoma, Michigan, Oregon and California this week, the candidate belabored such other words as "Latava" (meaning Latvia), "rapport" (pronounced "report" with a hard "t"), and "chomping" for tromping, as in the case of demonstrators and "anarchists" in the streets. . . .

Wallace aides leave no doubt that all of this is calculated, or at least correctable. . . . Local newsmen . . . frequently ask his staff whether Mr. Wallace doesn't know better. . . .

The response is "What do you think?" It is accompanied with a wink, and the inference is that the candidate, whose slogan is "Nobody is for Wallace but the People," is simply prosecuting his war on "the smart folks."[36]

This antielitism bridged easily into anti-intellectualism. He repeatedly appealed to the presumed resentment of the lesser educated against "the smart folks who look down their noses at you and me." The political instincts of the common man are superior to the editorial writer or professor who found reasons for defending Castro before he came to power.

You are just one man and woman. You are just as good as he is. And in fact, the average cab driver in this country, and the beautician, the steelworker, the rubber worker, the textile worker, knew instinctively when he saw him that Castro was a Communist. So we may be better than they are. . . .

And we are going to show them in November that the average American is sick and tired of all those over-educated ivory-tower folks with pointed heads looking down their noses at us.[37]

And both the antielitism and anti-intellectualism bridged into Wallace's rudimentary approach to a conspiracy theory. "The pseudo-intellectual is one who thinks that he has a superior intellect . . . and therefore he must decide what the man on the street does in his everyday life."[38] He saw the "pseudo-intellectuals" in the form of college professors, the heads of the "tax free" foundations, editors of leading newspapers and magazines, members of the Council on Foreign Relations, and high-ranking bureaucrats in Washington as the source of evil and propagators of false doctrine. (The pseudo intellectuals bear close resemblance to descriptions of the Illuminati in Birch Society literature.) Coming out of a southern populist tradition, he suggested the existence of an elitist conspiracy based on the eastern establishment. Thus, during the campaign he argued that the public opinion polls were being deliberately manipulated against him by the "Eastern money interests." Taking a leaf out of Joseph McCarthy's book, he identified Communism with the well-to-do rather than with the down and out, stating, "I don't believe all this talk about poor folks turning Communist. It's the damn rich who turn Communist. You ever seen a poor Communist?"[39]

However, he did not lean on the Communist conspiracy as McCarthy had. He allowed that "the official Communist Party of the United States is an enthusiastic supporter of the civil rights bill. Well, they might be, for this bill takes a long step toward transferring private property to public domain under a central government. It is this way in Russia. It places in the hands of a few people in central government the power to create a regulatory police arm. . . ."[40]

But it was the *parallel* of the all-powerful central government in Washington to the one in Moscow that he emphasized, not specific subversion of the one by the other. "In the 1964 election," Wallace said, "the Communist *Daily Worker* endorsed President Johnson and many of his policies but I would be the last man to say the President is a Communist. He is not a Communist. He is anti-Communist."[41]

The fact is that Wallace—like Huey Long, the welfare demagogue, and Joseph McCarthy, the treason demagogue—never developed either a well-constructed conspiracy theory or an ideological racism. But his institutional racism effectively provided a nativist targetry that neither of his "flawed" predecessors had. And he laid a basis for groundwork for both a full conspiracy theory and an explicit racism, should his movement continue and metamorphose. The movements of both Long and McCarthy were truncated by personal and political events; if Coughlin's movement had been so aborted, neither his conspiracy theory nor his nativist bigotry would have fully emerged. But, like Long, Wallace was surrounded in the wings by ideological bigots and purveyors of conspiracy theory.

Such people were present in the first reported meeting to plan a Wallace campaign for 1968 which occurred in Montgomery on November 8, 1965. It was attended by Ned Touchstone, the editor of the *Councilor,* a leading dispenser of Illuminati and anti-Semitic conspiratorial dogmas; by then Judge and later Congressman John Rarick, of Louisiana, a man close to the *Councilor* and an avowed anti-Semite; and by Richard Cotton, a right-wing radio commentator, who sees a "Zionist-Jewish" conspiracy behind most of the troubles of the country.[42]

A subsequent Montgomery meeting held on January 16, 1967, to get the campaign under way involved Kent Courtney, perennial advocate of a far-right "third party," and Floyd Kitchen, a Missouri rightist who once presided at a meeting addressed by leaders of the racist, anti-Semitic National States Rights party and who had become by early 1968 one of the national directors of the Wallace campaign.[43] That meeting was organized and invitations issued by Asa E. ("Ace") Carter, an admitted former Klansman, who had founded the openly racist and anti-Semitic North Alabama Citizen Council and had distributed the *Protocols of the Elders of Zion* and other materials acquired from Conde McGinley, one of America's leading disseminators of racist, anti-Semitic, and conspiracy-theory materials. In recent years Carter has been adviser and speech writer for Wallace. In addition to having such ideologues influentially close to him during the campaign, Wallace received the active support of every explicitly racist and conspiracy-soaked organization in the country, from the KKK and the extremist wing of the Citizens Council to Gerald L. K. Smith's Christian Crusade.

Wallace clearly recognized that open identification of his campaign with such organizations would alienate the considerable backing he received from many who had never been involved with such groups and regarded them with distaste. He carefully avoided any recourse himself to overt racism or anti-Semitism. Yet he also refused on a number of occasions to repudiate support from the Ku Klux Klan, the Birch Society, or other groups of the extreme or racist right. In an interview he defended the patriotism of the Klan and its right to take part in electoral politics. "At least a Klansman will fight for his country. He doesn't tear up his draft card. But the Klan, it's just innocuous in size and they're just concerned with segregation, not subversiveness."[44]

On September 20, 1968, he is reported as having said about the Birch Society, "I am glad to have their support. I have no quarrel with the Birch Society."[45] *The Wall Street Journal*, which gave extensive coverage to his campaign, reported that "Mr. Wallace has repeatedly refused to disavow the support of extremists. In Boston, the other day he declared, 'I wouldn't know a Bircher if I saw one. I'm concerned about the Communists and anarchists in our country, not the Birchers.' "[46]

Birch Society participation in the campaign resulted in some splits among Wallace supporters. In Texas, for example, the state chairman of the AIP, Bard Logan, a long-time Birch Society member, dismissed several party officials for protesting Birch Society involvement in the campaign and the distribution of Birch Society literature at campaign headquarters. Although the opponents of Logan and the Birch involvement included many prominent people, the national headquarters of the party in Montgomery backed the Birch majority on the state committee. Tom Turnipseed, Wallace's national troubleshooter, commented on the Texas situation: "We believe in local control, and letting them run their own party. . . . Most of the Birchers I know are pretty level-headed people."[47] Another split occurred in the Texas party in protest against the role played by Vance Beaudreau, the head of the party's campaign in the Rio Grande area and a member of the state party's policy-naming executive committee. Beaudreau had been active in the American Nazi party in Dallas in 1965–1966, had been a bodyguard for George Lincoln Rockwell, Nazi party leader, and had been active in 1965 in a local election campaign in Dallas for an ultraright-wing candidate for the city council who had the endorsement of the Ku Klux Klan and the Nazi party. "Beaudreau's rise in the Wallace American Party hierarchy in Texas has been swift and he has been promoted mainly by Bard Logan, the state chairman. . . ." When Logan was confronted with evidence about Beaudreau's background, he refused to do anything about it. He commented: "I wouldn't want it [Beaudreau's background] blown around too much. But I don't think he's let himself get out of hand here lately."[48]

The American Independent party also suffered a sharp split in California in which charges of extremism were leveled against the faction backed by Wallace. The Montgomery-endorsed group chose as Los Angeles party secretary Opal Tanner White. And the head of the opposing wing pointed out that "Mrs. White . . . is a field representative of Gerald L. K. Smith, head of the Christian Nationalist Crusade and identified as a 'racist anti-Semite.' " William Shearer, chief spokesman of the opposition faction, himself a leader of the White Citizens Council of California, "added that Robert Walters, one of the leaders of the [Wallace supported] group . . . already had brought disgrace on the AIP by his appointment of Leonard Holstein, identified as an American Nazi Party activist, as American Independent Party chairman for Napa County."[49]

In spite of the obvious embarrassment which the involvement of overt racists and extremists caused his candidacy, they also brought dividends. The many accounts of his campaign organization by journalists and groups investigating right-wing activity agree that a considerable portion of his campaign organization in different states was manned by members of such groups. Thus *The Wall Street Journal* reported:

> Charges that John Birch Society members and other right-wing extremists play key roles in the George Wallace Presidential campaign appear to be based on solid evidence . . . findings, which . . . emerge from a . . . survey of the Wallace organization in 22 states and scores of cities across the nation. Reporters interviewed and checked the backgrounds of Wallace campaign organizers, state and local chairmen, Presidential electors and delegates—and found that a sizable majority of these key jobs in the areas checked are held by members of the Birch Society, the segregationist Citizens Councils of America, Inc. or other extremist groups. . . .
>
> Roy Harris, president of the Citizens Councils of America (formerly known as the White Citizens Councils) . . . is chairman of the Wallace for President organization in Georgia. . . . A former Birch vice-president in California, Willard S. Voit, says he has resigned his job with the society to work full-time on the Wallace campaign. Another Wallace activist in California is Mrs. Opal Tanner White, secretary to Gerald L. K. Smith, who heads the anti-Negro and anti-Semitic Christian Nationalist Crusade. . . .
>
> In some states, the top ranks of the Wallace organization would practically be wiped out if members of right-wing organizations withdrew from the cam-

paign. . . . Even more significant than sheer numbers is the apparent effectiveness of right wing activists—Birch Society members, in particular—in getting Mr. Wallace's campaign machinery into operation outside the South. . . .

Few Wallace functionaries around the country, including those who don't belong to any extremist group themselves, have any harsh words for the Birch Society. Many indicate they don't regard it as an extremist group—or even a particularly controversial one. . . .

Most Wallace workers also show little concern about the possible influence of even more radical groups, though in some instances they have made some effort to keep rabid extremists from being too visible. Clifford Franklin, head of the Wallace organization in New York, says the Wallace electors there were carefully screened before being put on the ballot. "We tried to stay away from the neo-Nazi types and other controversial groups, but I'm sure we're infiltrated with them," he says. That possibility doesn't bother him, he adds, "as long as they don't wear hobnailed boots and stomp people."[50]

The comments of *The Wall Street Journal* can be expanded and concretized at length from reports from other newspapers and analyses of the campaign in different areas. Thus one of Wallace's most important southern leaders was Leander Perez, of Louisiana, who had been excommunicated from the Catholic church in 1962 for his anti-Negro behavior and had made frequent anti-Semitic statements, such as declaring that "Zionist Jews" are "the most dangerous people in the country." Perez ran the official Wallace campaign in Louisiana and was used as a substitute speaker for Wallace on occasions when he could not appear. In North Carolina, the state chairman of the Wallace campaign, Reid Stubbs, operated an American Opinion (Birch Society) book store and had spoken openly on occasion at Ku Klux Klan rallies. In Texas, as we have seen, campaign activists were dismissed for being opposed to the Birch Society. The Birch Society chairman of the state AIP contended, in answer to the charge that the Society controlled the Texas party, that only half the party state committee members were Birchers. In California, many active in the party were involved in Birch, Citizens Councils, or anti-Semitic activities. Thus the chairman of the party in San Diego was Dr. Orville J. Davis, who has been active in distributing a variety of anti-Semitic literature. In Indiana and Ohio, old Klan strongholds, Klansmen have been prominently identified in the campaign. When asked about "the Klan connections and known anti-Semitism of some of his Cleveland backers . . . Wallace . . . answered that such 'beliefs' were in the area of 'academic freedom.' "[51]

George Wallace personally avoided explicit racist talk and never endorsed the variety of conspiratorial theories expounded by men high in the ranks of his party. Thus a report on the Wallace campaign by the American Jewish Committee, an organization which devotes considerable resources to locating and fighting religious and racial bigotry, emphasizes the extent to which Wallace succeeded in holding his extremist supporters in line.

Despite the fact that almost every anti-Semitic organization and publication endorsed and supported George Wallace, there was no dissemination of anti-Semitic literature, authorized or unauthorized on a national level. Local and state headquarters were devoid of any material even faintly suggesting an aroma of bigotry. Indeed not only was there no distribution of anti-Semitic material, there was surprisingly no national circulation of anti-Negro material; this despite enthusiastic support given to Wallace by the racist White Citizens Councils and the Klan.[52]

However, there can be little doubt that he was aware that he had brought together a coalition of right-wing extremists. Journalists covering the campaign suggested that a major factor behind his decision not to run local candidates or to hold a national convention which would have given him extensive free national television coverage was the desire to prevent his most extremist activists from identifying their views with his campaign. Local Wallace candidates would have inevitably included many who were ardent anti-Semites or believers in the conspiracy of the Illuminati. A national convention would have brought together for exposure in the light of television many who expounded such doctrines. Hence, the decision to keep the campaign completely oriented around the speeches of Wallace himself.

The participation of extremists in the campaign does not, of course, necessarily make the Wallace movement extremist. Communists and radical rightists in the past have infiltrated both major parties without affecting their basic character. It is important, therefore, to stress also that Wallace laid the basis for the most comprehensive ideology of monism the country has seen since World War II, including the element of majoritarian disruption of the democratic process. "There is one thing more powerful than the Constitution . . . than any constitution. That's the will of the people. What is a Constitution anyway? They're the products of the people, the people are the first source of power, and the people can abolish a Constitution if they want to. . . ."[53] When asked whether he had subverted the democratic process by successfully putting his wife up for reelection as governor because the state Constitution prevented his re-election, he answered: "What are democratic processes but the people? When you go to the people with the matter, how is that subverting the democratic process?"[54]

During the 1968 campaign he proposed a plan suggested by the Populists of the 1890's calling for the direct election of federal judges. The courts must be made responsible to the will of the people; the electorate must be able to repudiate those who defend the rights of criminals. From this advocacy of the popular will as the supreme arbiter of law and order, there flowed quite naturally, as it did with his predecessor Tom Watson, proposals to totally disregard the law.

His speeches were replete with statements that he would eliminate the sources of evil in the society without regard to due process or constitutional rights. For example, he denounced intellectual critics of the Vietnam War as "these long-hairs, [who] ought to be treated as traitors, which they are. . . . The average man doesn't understand this pseudo-intellectual talk." And he was fond of saying he had a simple solution for professors who made speeches preaching treason: "I would tell you that if a professor made that kind of speech in Alabama—IF HE MADE THAT KIND OF SPEECH IN ALABAMA . . . he would be a fired professor."[55]

In his campaign addresses, he referred frequently to the "scum of the earth" and the "trash" who demonstrate around the country. And one of his solutions for the problem was to "let the police run this country for a year or two and there wouldn't be any riots."[56] On one occasion, he explicitly talked of a "police state" to solve the problems of law and order. "If we were President today, you wouldn't get stabbed or raped in the shadow of the White House, even if we had to call out 30,000 troops and equip them with 2-foot long bayonets and station them every few feet apart. . . . That's right, we gonna have a *police* state for folks who burn the cities down. They aren't gonna burn any more cities."[57]

Wallace emphasized his contempt for judicial procedure and due process, arguing that the courts have deprived us of our freedom and are responsible for the growth in crime through their decisions protecting the rights of criminals and dissenters. Thus he would "take every one of those Communists in our defense plants and toss them out on the seat of his pants." If a demonstrator should lie down in front of a Wallace motorcade, he told his impassioned audiences, "it will be the last car he ever lies down in front of." If students continue to support the Viet Cong after he is President, "I would have me an attorney-general that would drag them in by their long hair."[58]

In a precampaign interview, he once openly avowed his deep-seated contempt for the constitutional protections of the rights of criminals and ghetto rioters.

Of course, if I did what I'd like to do I'd pick up something and smash one of these federal judges in the head and then burn the courthouse down. But I'm too genteel. What we need in this country is some Governors that used to work up here at Birmingham in the steel mills with about a tenth-grade education. A Governor like that wouldn't be so genteel. He'd put out his orders and he'd say, "The first man who throws a brick is a dead man. The first man who loots something what doesn't belong to him is a dead man. My orders are to shoot to kill."

That's the way to keep law and order. If you'd killed about three that way at Watts, the other forty wouldn't be dead today.[59]

Toward the end of the campaign, as it became clear to many in the movement that Wallace had no chance for election, he began to suggest ways for his followers to gain their way against a hostile government. As he described the process as it would apply to the issue of school desegregation, opponents of desegregation would hold massive protest demonstrations in the streets which would press the state to refuse to cooperate with federal school policies.

Clearly, the Wallace campaign belongs in the category of extremist movements as defined by the criterion of rejection of the democratic process. On lower levels of collective behavior, repressive behavior can take place without accompanying ideology. Such raw impulses toward repressive action can obviously lie at the roots of political movements, but the movements themselves cannot exist without accompanying ideology. The model of monism, of extremism, poses three prime elements of ideology: moralism, conspiracy theory, and a doctrine of monistic repression. The logic of this model can flow in either direction. A doctrine of monistic repression is, of course, both a necessary and sufficient condition by which to define a movement as monistic. As we have seen, the existence of a conspiracy theory does not by itself define an extremist movement. But, on the one hand, its existence is at the least a high risk factor for the development of a doctrine of repression; and on the other hand, a doctrine of repression becomes politically supportable only to the extent that it develops some variant of a conspiracy theory. Moralism—the belief that good or evil intention is specifically determinative in history—is even less a defining condition of monism in itself, but is a necessary element of both conspiracy theory and repressive doctrine. Nativist bigotry, as we have seen, has been a multipurpose element in the American model of monism. Being a specialized form of political repression, it is itself a sufficient condition by which to define a movement as monistic. But it is perhaps even more politically significant as an adjunct of a generalized doctrine of repression: the illegitimation of political differences and deviance; that is, the rejection of democratic process. Nativist bigotry has served in America to flesh out the conspiracy theory and to legitimate a generalized doctrine of repression.

A loose construction of the Wallace movement—as a conglomerate of all its ingredients—would reveal a shifting pattern of all the monistic elements, including conspiracy theories and explicit bigotry. A strict construction of the Wallace movement—more fairly seen as the official doctrine emanating from Wallace himself—reveals only a rudimentary conspiracy theory. Like McCarthy, Wallace invoked a kind of conspiracy surrogate: traitors vaguely abroad, the intellectual elite at mischief. In that sense, like McCarthyism, the Wallace movement was ideologically—and operationally—deficient as a model of monism; but, on the basis of both nativist and generally repressive impulses, its ultimate credentials as an extremist movement were unquestionable.

Social Base

The nature of Wallace's support was not surprising, either in terms of the history of right-wing extremism or in terms of the nature of his appeal.

Wallace first appeared on the national scene during the 1964 Presidential campaign. He entered the Democratic Presidential primaries in Wisconsin, Indiana, and Maryland, running against "favorite son" local Democratic leaders who stood in for President Johnson. Considering the fact that Wallace was, in effect, running against an incumbent Democratic President in his own party, he did astonishingly well. Wallace secured 33.7 per cent of the Democratic primary vote in Wisconsin, 29.8 per cent in Indiana, and 43.0 per cent in Maryland.[60]

The pattern of support for Wallace in the three states was fairly consistent with the exception that in Wisconsin, many Republicans who had no contest in their own party took advantage of crossing over "in the hope of discrediting the Democratic governor or of demonstrating support for Wallace's conservative position."[61] This gave Wallace numerous votes in the Republican suburbs.[62]

In general, Wallace had considerable support in the more conservative well-to-do areas in the two northern states. He was particularly strong in suburban communities in which there was considerable John Birch Society activity.[63] In Indiana and Maryland, Wallace ran well in nonurban areas, which had "characteristics long associated with the supporters of rightist movements—Fundamentalist, native, and nativist."[64] In addition to winning economic conservative and nativist support, Wallace did extremely well in working-class districts, particularly those inhabited by Catholic and foreign stock populations, in Milwaukee, Gary, and Baltimore.[65] In the latter city, he did best in the white working-class neighborhoods of recent southern migrants, semiskilled and unskilled.[66] In Gary and Baltimore, he had a decisive majority in the white working-class precincts. In Baltimore, "local [Democratic] leaders were in a state of panic as they became torn between their obligations to [Senator] Brewster [the stand-in candidate for Johnson], the state organization, and the national party on the one hand and the counter-pressures from the working-class rank and file of the local party units on the other."[67]

The analyses of Wallace's backing in 1964 are necessarily limited, of course, to his support *within* the ranks of participants in the Democratic primaries in three states. Consequently, they tell us little about his actual or potential backing among the electorate as a whole.

As the 1968 election approached, it was clear that Wallace intended to run. Newspapers, magazines, and television began to provide him with extensive coverage. Many of the organizations on the extreme right, including leaders of the Birch Society, the Minutemen, the Ku Klux Klan, and the White Citizens Councils, strongly advocated his candidacy as a third-party nominee. The Gallup poll reported as early as April 1967 that 13 per cent of the national electorate favored him, when offered a choice among Lyndon Johnson as a Democrat, George Romney as the Republican, and George Wallace as the States Rights candidate. Other polls taken later in the year yielded comparable results.

Yet these findings concerning the possible willingness of people to vote for Wallace as a third-party candidate, considered by themselves, underestimated his popularity. Many who would never consider voting for a third-party candidate, even in the opinion polls, may still look positively on an individual and what he stands for. The massive support recorded for Father Coughlin and Senator Joseph McCarthy in the opinion surveys are examples of the ability of men to win mass followings which were not transferable to third-party politics. Clearly, many voters who agreed with George Wallace on racial and other issues were not prepared to take the third-party route. The best available indicators of Wallace's general popularity in 1967 come from two Gallup surveys which asked samples of the electorate whether they viewed him favorably or unfavorably. In one taken in 1967, the proportion of whites interviewed who had a positive impression of Wallace (43.2 per cent) was almost as large as were negative to him (46.7 per cent). Thus it would appear that George Wallace, as of 1967, had about as much general support among the population as Senator Joseph McCarthy did during his heyday. The pattern of the support among different demographic groups is recorded in Table 46.

Analyzing the interrelationships among the variables did not modify the associations reported in the table. Thus, Catholics were more opposed to Wallace than Protestants, in both the North and the South. The occupational strata and education factors were similar in both parts of the country. The poorer and less educated were more favorable to Wallace than were the better educated and more privileged, in the North as well as the South. Within each occupational class, 1964 Goldwater voters were more likely to be favorable to Wallace than were Johnson backers.

Table 46. WALLACE SUPPORT BY ASSOCIATED SOCIAL CHARACTERISTICS, 1967,
WHITES ONLY*
(Per Cent)

Section	Pro	Con	No Opinion	Number
South	63	27	10	(372)
East Central	46	46	8	(220)
West Central	40	50	10	(167)
Rocky Mountains	42	44	14	(52)
Pacific	26	65	9	(188)
Middle Atlantic	34	54	12	(291)
New England	22	66	13	(87)
Size Community				
Farm	64	27	9	(117)
Open country	48	39	13	(271)
2,500–99,999	42	46	11	(361)
100,000–999,999	40	52	8	(391)
1,000,000 and over	32	57	11	(237)
Religion				
Protestant	49	41	10	(921)
Catholic	32	57	11	(42)
Jewish	10	77	13	(31)
Education				
Grammar	54	32	15	(295)
Vocational	48	38	14	(64)
High school	44	46	10	(702)
University	30	65	6	(313)
Occupation				
Farmer	64	26	11	(110)
Nonmanual	31	60	9	(504)
Professional	25	68	6	(189)
Business	42	54	4	(166)
Clerical	31	62	7	(81)
Sales	23	61	16	(56)
Manual	51	36	13	(459)
Skilled	51	37	12	(237)
Unskilled	48	38	13	(190)
Labor	56	28	16	(32)
Service	44	46	10	(63)
1964 Vote				
Johnson	29	52	9	(634)
Goldwater	46	46	8	(371)
Did not vote or forgot	49	37	14	(348)

* Data analyzed from Gallup Survey 744K taken in April 1967.

The relationship between occupational class and attitude toward Wallace did not change when controlled for party affiliation or 1964 election choice. Farmers (mainly southerners) in both political camps were the most pro-Wallace group. Among the urban strata, manual workers were much more likely than those in the nonmanual middle class to be pro-Wallace. Even among Goldwater supporters, a majority of those in white-collar occupations found Wallace objectionable (Table 47).

The pattern of support for George Wallace before the beginning of the 1968 campaign resembled that of Father Coughlin and Senator Joseph McCarthy, reported earlier. Wallace was strongest among the less educated rural, small-town, and working-class population. As a spokesman of the Protestant South, he secured most of his support in the South and more from Protestants than Catholics. During the election campaign, Wallace gradually gained strength as a third-party candidate. He succeeded in getting on the ballot in all fifty states. His campaign organization stated that they had gathered a total of two and a half million signatures to qualify for the ballot.[68]

Wallace reported that he collected about $10,000,000, which enabled him both to cover the country in campaign tours and to have a number of national television broadcasts. This visibility and effort resulted in an increase in his strength in the opinion polls until, by early October, he hit a high point of 21 per cent in both the Gallup and Harris polls.

By the end of September, Wallace had built up a strong image among the bulk of the electorate. The Harris survey found that the large majority were ready to respond in clear terms when asked whether they agreed or disagreed with a number of statements about him (Table 48). The findings of the Harris survey suggest that close to one-third of the electorate tended to see Wallace and the things he stood for in positive terms. Clearly, the Wallace candidacy reached out to the concerns about law and order, race, and political integrity variously harbored by many Americans.

Table 47.   1964 VOTE CHOICE AND WALLACE ENDORSEMENT BY OCCUPATIONAL CLASS, 1967

Attitude Toward Wallace	Johnson Voters			Goldwater Voters		
	White Collar	Manual	Farm	White Collar	Manual	Farm
Favorable	30 %	46 %	57 %	35 %	51 %	67 %
Negative	65	43	30	59	36	26
No opinion	5	11	14	6	13	7
Number	(240)	(209)	(44)	(164)	(76)	(42)

Table 48.   REACTIONS TO STATEMENTS ABOUT WALLACE IN MID-SEPTEMBER 1968

	Agree	Disagree	Not Sure
Positive			
"Has the courage to say what he really thinks"	86 %	5 %	9 %
"Man of high integrity"	46	24	30
"Would keep law and order"	43	36	21
"Is right to want to leave race relations to the states"	43	35	22
Negative			
"Is an extremist"	51	30	19
"Represents only one section"	51	30	19
"Is a racist"	41	40	19
"Would divide the country as President"	45	32	23

SOURCE: Louis Harris, "Wallace Gains Respectability," *Boston Globe*, September 30, 1968, p. 10.

Wallace's actual support was, of course, disproportionately concentrated in the South, where he led both major party candidates. He drew considerable backing, however, in the North as well. Journalistic accounts and opinion surveys singled out two major groups among the general population as contributing disproportionate backing to him: labor and youth. Each group gave him 25 per cent support in October.

Labor and Preelection Support

Wallace's strength among many union members was particularly surprising. In the militant United Automobile Workers, an official union poll among elected *delegates* and local officials completed at the end of September gave Wallace 10.2 per cent, as compared with 87.8 per cent for Vice-President Humphrey and but 1 per cent for Richard Nixon.[69]

In a preferential poll among the 2,041 delegates to the International Association of Machinists and Aerospace Workers, held in Chicago in early September, "in answer to a question about which candidate would bring justice and order to the cities, 26 per cent named Wallace."[70] One president of an international union affiliated to the AFL-CIO, Albert E. Hutchinson of the Asbestos Workers international union, openly endorsed Wallace for President.[71] A number of locals in major industrial unions were also reported endorsing the third-party candidates. A special national survey of trade-union members conducted by Public Opinion Surveys, an affiliate of the Gallup organization, from September 20 to 25 asked the question: "If the Presidential election were being held today, which candidate would you most like to see win—Richard Nixon, the Republican candidate; Hubert Humphrey, the Democratic candidate, or George Wallace, the American Independent candidate?" The survey reported that 34 per cent were for Humphrey, 32 per cent for Nixon, and 25 per cent for George Wallace.[72]

A number of informally conducted newspaper polls taken during September and October reported widespread backing for Wallace in the unionized large factories of the Midwest. The results of the scientific survey conducted in October of a sample of 257 white males in the industrial community of Gary, Indiana, by Robert T. Riley and Thomas F. Pettigrew, of Harvard University, suggest that the various factory-gate surveys may have been correct. The Gary study reported, "Occupationally, blue collar workers (38.0 per cent) support him [Wallace] more frequently than the white collar (12.6 per cent); union members (38.5 per cent) more frequently than non-union members (16.8 per cent)."[73]

Various observers of the trade-union movement reported during the campaign that their leaders were extremely worried about Wallace's appeal to their members. The *New York Times* labor expert, A. H. Raskin, explained the phenomenon in the following terms:

> The worker, as the most recent arrival at a secure handhold on middle-class status, feels most threatened by crime on the streets, the bite of high taxes, the disintegration of the school system, the climb of the welfare rolls and the suggestion that he and his family should give up some of their prosperity to provide a better break for Negroes and others traditionally excluded from a full share of America's abundance.
>
> Perhaps the biggest gripe of labor's rank and file—and the key to much of the Wallace attraction—was summed up two weeks ago by P. L. Siemiller, president of the million-member International Association of Machinists, in his keynote at the union's convention in Chicago. He said that "union members who have worked so hard to build this country are pretty sick of rioters, looters, peaceniks, beatniks and all the rest of the nuts who are trying to destroy it."[74]

Yet the reports that many workers and other lower middle-class people supported Wallace because of their concern over integration in schools and neighborhoods or the breakdown of law and order clearly do not tell the whole story. Barry Goldwater directed a deliberate appeal on such issues in 1964 and gained much less support from these strata than earlier Republican candidates. He failed miserably in the working-class districts of Gary, Milwaukee, and Baltimore, which had cast large votes for Wallace in the 1964 Democratic Presidential primaries. Clearly, Goldwater with his laissez faire antiwelfare-state program went counter to the desires of the less affluent for social security, trade-unions, economic planning, and the like.

George Wallace, as we have seen, shied away from such positions and sought to identify the pressures for Negro equality and integration with the eastern establishment and the intellectual elite. Not being a Republican also probably helped his image with many workers. They can more easily back a candidate and a party which make a direct appeal to the common man. And Wallace constantly made such an appeal. It may be significant to note that the Harris poll reported that many more Wallace supporters in the North chose the term "radical" to describe his political outlook than identified him as a "conservative."

Two very different analysts of the Wallace electorate, the opinion pollster Samuel Lubell and Clark Kissinger, a staff correspondent for the national new left weekly *The Guardian,* both pointed to a strong element of class-conscious working-class identification with Wallace. Early in the campaign, Lubell noted the strong Wallace backing among union members.

But more than half of those interviewed were loyal union members who were using Wallace's candidacy for a double purpose. They wanted to "untie the police and end those riots," but they also were trying to protect their own economic interests.

Asked why they didn't turn to Nixon for a change in racial policy, the invariable reply came back, "Republicans are no good for workers," or, "All our improvements were given to us by the Democrats."

Similar responses have been voiced by labor union Democrats swinging to Wallace in Buffalo, Detroit, Cleveland, New York, Flint, and Dayton.[75]

And Lubell continued to report in late October:

Pro-Wallace supporters in the northern cities . . . voice strong working-class views which prevent them from voting Republican. . . . Most of these Wallace followers maintain, "Wallace is for the workingman. He couldn't be for anyone else." Some even talk of the Wallace movement as "the start of a new labor party."[76]

Kissinger pointed out that, unlike Eugene McCarthy, who directed his campaign to "the white upper middle class," George Wallace would sometimes make "a comment worthy of any new leftist." As he stated,

Wallace loves to point out how the capitalist press is prejudiced against him. . . . He recently remarked, "Some of these liberal newspaper editors are saying one reason the Wallace philosophy is so popular is he says what the people want to hear. And they're saying it in such a manner that it sounds like what the people want is bad."

And this new left spokesman concluded that Wallace was able "to mobilize the very real force of class consciousness in America."[77]

These analyses, which stressed the "class" appeal of the Wallace move-ment for the more class-conscious or class-aware workers, are congruent with the findings of the Riley-Pettigrew survey in Gary. They located their respondents on a four-point continuum of class identification running from "strong working-class" to "strong middle-class." Wallace did best among the strong working-class identifiers (43.7 per cent), next among weak working-class (33.3 per cent), then among weak middle-class (23.1 per cent), and least well among those with a strong middle-class identification (14.5 per cent).[78] The Gary survey inquired also as to attitudes on various issues and found evidence which suggests that economic concerns may have underlain much of Wallace support. Those who agreed with the statement, "In spite of what some say, the condition of the average man is getting worse, not better," were much more likely (41.5 per cent) to support Wallace than those who disagreed (18.0 per cent). Combining sense of grievance with the "lot of the average man" with class identification sharply increased the "prediction" of the Wallace vote. Thus the majority of strong working-class identifiers (57.1 per cent) who agreed that things were getting worse for the average man were for Wallace, as contrasted with only 7.5 per cent for Wallace among strong middle-class identifiers, who disagreed with the statement. The complete analysis is presented in Table 49.

One relatively low-status occupational group which was frequently re-ported as heavily involved in the ranks of Wallace supporters during the campaign was policemen. In this respect, also, the American Independent party resembled its predecessors on the extreme right, which we analyzed

Table 49. RELATIONSHIP BETWEEN VOTE PREFERENCE, CLASS IDENTIFICATION, AND
BELIEF THAT THE CONDITION OF THE AVERAGE MAN IS GETTING WORSE,
WHITE MALES IN GARY, INDIANA (PER CENT)

Class Identifi-cation	Lot of Average Man Worse	Wallace	Nixon	Humphrey	Number
Strong Working	Agree	57.1	18.4	24.5	(49)
	Disagree	25.0	47.2	27.8	(36)
Weak Working	Agree	36.0	36.0	28.0	(25)
	Disagree	30.0	20.0	50.0	(20)
Weak Middle	Agree	26.7	60.9	13.3	(15)
	Disagree	21.7	56.5	21.7	(23)
Strong Middle	Agree	25.9	44.4	29.6	(27)
	Disagree	7.5	60.0	32.5	(40)

SOURCE: Robert T. Riley and Thomas F. Pettigrew, "Relative Deprivation and Wallace's Northern Support" (paper presented at the meetings of the American Sociological Associa-tion, 1969, San Francisco, California), Table II.

earlier.[79] George Wallace had long gone out of his way to appeal to the police. As governor of Alabama, he placed the Birch Society slogan "Support Your Local Police" on the license plates of automobiles. During the campaign he made repeated references to the problems of the police. He attacked court decisions which protected the rights of defendants. He would invariably "include in his speeches both an exhortatory 'Let's hear it' for the local police—and his crowds always applaud on cue, sometimes with a standing ovation—but also a variety of stories about the Federal courts that are calculated to please the police by touching off a reaction of outrage among Mr. Wallace's listeners."[80]

The evidence that Wallace received extensive police backing is varied. John Harrington, president of the Fraternal Order of Police, the largest police organization in the country with 130,000 members in over 900 communities, publicly endorsed him for President.[81] Various newspaper accounts by journalists covering the campaign agreed that Wallace had become a hero of the police, that many of them vied to cover his meetings. A *New York Times* correspondent commented, "Reporters who have interviewed scores of policemen . . . have failed so far to find one [at Wallace meetings] who was not a committed Wallace supporter."[82] Such impressionistic evidence, of course, may be in error, since clearly the police who volunteered to attend Wallace meetings were undoubtedly pro-Wallace to start. One questionnaire survey of police opinion, however, a poll conducted by a magazine, the *Colorado Policeman*, among law enforcement officers in that state, did report that 31 per cent of the 160 respondents indicated they were for Wallace, as contrasted with 44 per cent for Nixon and 25 per cent for Humphrey.[83] Since Wallace received only a 7 per cent election vote in Colorado, the fact that close to one-third of the law officers preferred him indicates a highly disproportionate support among that occupational group.

The factors underlying the appeal of rightist and bigoted candidates for American police have been discussed earlier in connection with the social base of the John Birch Society.[84] To that analysis should be added that the specific context of the events preceding the 1968 campaign—particularly the ghetto riots, the campus demonstrations against the police, and the confrontation between antiwar demonstrators and the Chicago police—seemingly aggravated the hostility felt toward liberal supporters of civil rights and those who would restrain police discretion through juridical decisions and police review boards. Many newspapers around the country wrote of the "revolt of the police," or the development of a "new right" among them during 1968. In a number of cities, heads of police organizations attacked the limitations placed on them in dealing with demonstrators and threatened to enforce the law regardless of orders. While all three candidates, and Republican Vice-Presidential nominee Spiro Agnew, placed increasing emphasis on the issue of "law and order" as the campaign went on, George Wallace could claim with some justification that the others were responding to the evident success which his stress on such matters had among the electorate. And since a variety of opinion surveys among police forces in different cities had indicated that the vast majority of police were concerned with supposed governmental and judicial weakness in dealing with crime and demonstrations, considerable support for Wallace among the police could be expected. He appealed to the perceived interests of the police and, possibly even more important, to their sense of self-esteem. In a real sense, George Wallace was the candidate of the police.

The findings that Wallace appealed strongly to manual workers and to the police during the 1968 election would have come as no surprise to him. Speaking to a reporter in the winter of 1966–1967, Wallace described his support in terms similar to our own.

We run best in the industrial states. We got our biggest vote in sixty-four from organized labor. They're all concerned about crime and property rights. You take a working man, if he lives in a section where law and order breaks down, he can't just up and move like rich folks can. The police, too. I went out to the Governors' Conference in Los Angeles last summer and the patrolman in charge of the police assigned to the Conference came and got me to speak to the ones that was off-duty. I told them we believed in law and order in Alabama and we prosecuted criminals on Monday morning, not policemen. I told them "I wish you could run this country for about two years. You could straighten it out." When I finished, the patrolman in charge told me, "You're our Presidential candidate."[85]

Youth

Among the strata which disproportionately backed George Wallace, young people have been prevalent. Both the Gallup and Harris polls reported in a number of their preelection surveys that those in the category of twenty-one to twenty-nine years were more favorable to the third-party candidate than those in older age groups. Thus, in early October both polls reported that 25 per cent of the younger voters were for Wallace, as compared with 20 per cent among the older groups. This differentiation according to age occurred in both the southern and the nonsouthern states. Two special surveys of youth opinion also pointed to heavy Wallace support among this group. A poll commissioned by *Fortune* magazine by the Daniel Yankelovich polling organization among 718 young people aged eighteen to twenty-four, in October, revealed that 25 per cent of those who were not in college were for Wallace, as compared to 23 per cent for Humphrey, 31 per cent for Nixon, and 15 per cent without a choice.[86] Among college students, Wallace received 7 per cent of the preference votes.

Thanks to the courtesy of Daniel Yankelovich, the data from this survey were made available to us for the purpose of a more detailed analysis of the sources of Wallace support among youth. In general, they indicate that the same factors which differentiated support among the candidates in the electorate as a whole affected youth. Thus, among those not in school, Wallace received more support among those in manual pursuits (27 per cent). This survey inquired as to occupations for fathers, and manual workers who were the children of those in manual occupations were most likely to opt for Wallace (31 per cent), while nonmanuals whose fathers were on the same side of this dividing line were least likely to prefer him (6 per cent). Educational attainment proved to be the strongest correlate of Wallace support other than region, as the data in Table 50 indicate.

Table 50. EDUCATION AND 1968 VOTE PREFERENCE AMONG YOUTH

	Non-High School Graduates	High School Graduates	Some College	College Graduates	Students
Wallace	39 %	32 %	21 %	8 %	7 %
Humphrey	11	18	13	29	19
Nixon	31	33	39	42	37
None	19	17	28	22	38
Number	(173)	(452)	(261)	(119)	(395)

Studies of the political behavior of college students have pointed to the fact that subject major correlates highly with political views. Those undergraduates in the liberal arts tend to be more liberal or left radical than those who seek to prepare for specific professions. The Yankelovich-*Fortune* survey divided the students in the sample into two groups: one composed of those who defined the purpose of education as "practical," to get a good job and earn "more money," and the other of those who stated that they were not interested in "the practical benefits of college." The first group was more likely to come from blue-collar family backgrounds than the second. As expected, Wallace did somewhat better among the less privileged, more vocationally oriented (9 per cent) than among the others (3 per cent).[87]

The sharp differences in the political values of these groups may also be seen through a comparison of the variations in the Presidential choices of those majoring in different subjects (Table 51). The liberal arts students gave Wallace little backing and showed a large plurality for "no candidate," presumably reflecting the fact that many of those on the liberal left were still opposed in early October to backing Hubert Humphrey. The two con-

Table 51. RELATIONSHIP OF SUBJECT MAJOR TO PRESIDENTIAL CHOICE
OF COLLEGE STUDENTS

	Humanities and Social Science	Physical and Biological Sciences	Engineering	Business
Wallace	5 %	5 %	17 %	8 %
Humphrey	19	22	17	20
Nixon	32	29	41	51
None	44	44	24	21
Number	(231)	(41)	(41)	(76)

servative "fields," in which Richard Nixon was strongest, were business and engineering majors. George Wallace, however, did best among engineering students, a result which jibes with findings from other studies that this field attracts more conservative and upwardly mobile students than almost any other.

Somewhat similar findings were reported in a preelection poll among high-school students conducted by The Purdue Opinion Panel which reported that Wallace was the preferred candidate of 22 per cent of the students. And in line with the findings of the Yankelovich-*Fortune* survey, Wallace supporters among high-school youth were much more likely to come from those who planned to go to work or into the military, as compared with those who indicated they expected to go on to college. The authors conclude: "Students who say they would vote for Mr. Wallace are more likely to have the following characteristics: be boys, have mothers who have a grade school education, be in the low income group, be receiving very low grades in school, say they are going into military service after finishing high school, to come from a rural area in the South."[88]

Wallace's support among the young during the campaign was particularly noticeable in the subgroups which gave him considerable backing such as union members and the police. Samuel Lubell, in a number of his preelection commentaries, noted that older unionists tended to be for Humphrey and to recall the economic gains which they had achieved under previous Democratic administrations. Young ones, however, took trade-unions and prosperity for granted and were more prone to defect either to Nixon or to Wallace on issues of taxes, integration, crime in the streets, and the like. A private national poll of union members conducted before the national conventions found considerable discontent with unions among young workers and a heavy predilection to back Wallace. The same pattern of youth discontent moving in a Wallace direction was reported among the police.

"What we're seeing, I think," said a police lieutenant in Lower Manhattan, "are dissident youth on the police force—like around the universities. They're exploding. They're fighting back against what they consider an intolerable situation." Just as there's a New Left on the campuses, there seems to be a New Right among some younger men in the Police Department.

The lieutenant and several other police officials who were interviewed . . . stated [the New Right] was largely composed of men in their 20's who feel—perhaps more strongly than older men—the frustrations of being a policeman: hostility from some segments of the community, overt attacks in slum neighborhoods, the belief that political leaders are preventing them from enforcing the law forcefully enough, a persistent conviction that the police are abused in the courts while criminals are "coddled."[89]

A journalist's report on the emergence of a militantly right-wing organization of New York police, the Law Enforcement Group (LEG), suggests that it symbolizes "a strong swing to the Right among . . . young policemen in particular." The LEG consists largely of younger policemen (one-third of New York's force is composed of men under thirty), while the "traditionally conservative Patrolmen's Benevolent Association, (PBA) . . . [is] dominated by older men. . . ."

This accent on youth has worked to produce a far different picture of police-leftist frictions and clashes than is generally accepted.

Instead of a confrontation between generations, between young radical demonstrators on the one side and wide-beamed, middle-aged cops on the other, the emerging picture portrays a collision of contemporaries. . . .

In their own way these young officers of the right are as displeased with the current state of the republic as their opposite numbers in the new left.[90]

In the population generally, the pattern of a "shift to the right" among the youth was first detected among young southerners. Most studies of racial attitudes conducted during the 1950's had indicated that racial prejudice as reflected in response to sample surveys was correlated with age. The younger a group, the more likely it had been to have liberal attitudes. Seemingly this pattern changed among southern whites during the early 1960's. Two surveys conducted by the National Opinion Research Center (NORC) found "a singular inversion among the two youngest age groups in the South." As Paul Sheatsley, of NORC, reported and explained the finding:

Unexpectedly, the very youngest Southern adults (aged twenty-one to twenty-four) have lower Pro-Integration Scale scores than the twenty-five to forty-four year old group. . . . We have suggested elsewhere that the current group of young white adults in the South have grown up and received their schooling and formed their attitudes during the stormy years which followed the 1954 Supreme Court decision outlawing segregated schools. It is they who have been most immediately exposed to the crises and dislocations brought to the South by the Negro protest movement. Perhaps the surprise is that these Southern white youths are nonetheless more pro-integrationist than are their parents and grandparents who are over the age of forty-five.[91]

But Wallace had more support among the youngest group of voters in both sections of the country. This phenomenon of disproportionate youth support for an extremist racist candidate has largely been ignored by those who have identified young America with left-wing campus demonstrators and student volunteers for Kennedy and McCarthy. In a real sense, the new right of George Wallace, like the new left, is a direct outgrowth of a process of political polarization which emerged around the efforts to secure desegregation from the late fifties on. The struggles over integration which began in the South resulted in major confrontations which pressed southern white segregationists to the right and liberal civil rights supporters to the left. The tactic of civil disobedience to prevent enforcement of unjust law was initiated by such white segregationist leaders as Ross Barnett, of Mississippi, Lester Maddox, of Georgia, and George Wallace, of Alabama. The student left responded in kind with sit-ins. The identification of the segregationist struggle with defense of local autonomy by many in the white South created a climate of opinion which stressed the legitimacy of the white South's cause and silenced many of the moderate whites. Hence many whites growing up in the South were exposed to opinions which stressed the need to protect the institutions, values, and autonomy of the white South against a threat from outside liberals and the federal government. As the issue of government-enforced integration in the schools and neighborhoods spread to the North, adult white opinion in central city areas, usually inhabited by workers, also took on an increased racist character. In effect, growing numbers of white young people in the South and in many working-class areas of the North have been exposed to repeated discussions of the supposed threats to their schools and communities posed by integration. They have been reared in an atmosphere in which the voicing of anti-Negro sentiments in their homes and neighborhoods has been common, in which members of the older generation discussed their fears concerning the adverse consequences of school or residential integration. Hence, while the upper middle-class scions of liberal parents were being radicalized to the left by the civil rights and Vietnam War issues, southern and northern working-class youth were being radicalized to the right. The consequences of such polarization can be seen in the disparate behavior of the two groups in the 1968 election campaign.

The indications that the Wallace movement drew heavily among youth are congruent with the evidence from various recent studies of youth and student politics that young people are disposed to support the more extreme or idealistic version of the politics dominant in their social group. In Europe, radical movements, both of the left and of the right, have been much more likely to secure the backing of the young than the democratic parties of the center. Being less committed to existing institutions and parties than older people, being less inured to the need to compromise in order to attain objectives, youth are attracted to movements and leaders who promise to resolve basic problems quickly in an absolute fashion.

The Wallace campaign also had disproportionate support among the residents of small towns and rural areas who have little contact with blacks in the north. Many in these areas appear to have been responding directly to the prime source of right-wing blacklash politics in the United States: a concern over the decline in their influence in the society, particularly as reflected in changes in American religious and cultural beliefs. As in the 1920's, there has emerged a visible generation of youth who reject traditional morality with respect to sex, dress, drugs, and general social and political values. If this rejection did not occur in a given community, it was made manifest by television. The religious fundamentalists, concentrated in rural areas and small towns or among migrants from such places to big cities, see their values treated as provincial and anachronistic by those who control the mass media and the cultural life of the nation. Liberalizing cultural tendencies have intensified with the passage of time. To a considerable extent liberal revisionist ideas now dominate the major theological tendencies in both Protestantism and Catholicism. The traditionalist Christians, who are now definitely a minority group, are a principal source of support for a politics of alienation and nostalgia. And George Wallace openly and strongly appealed to such sentiments in his espousal of religious morality, in his condemnation of radical changes in culture, and in his attacks on those who control the media and other major institutions of culture diffusion.

It should be noted, however, that except among the minority of committed extremists, the Wallace movement as such failed to make headway with the bulk of affluent and better educated upper- and middle-class conservatives. A national opinion survey by the *New York Times* in mid-October of the presidents of *all* the companies whose shares are listed in the New York Stock Exchange, conducted by the anonymous questionnaire technique, reported that less than half of one per cent (three men) were for Wallace, while 85 per cent endorsed Nixon and 13 per cent backed Humphrey.[92]

While Wallace had much more support in lower levels of the business and professional community, particularly in the South, it is clear from the polls that this stratum was also disproportionately opposed to him. Most of these people, though economic conservatives, are seemingly not afraid that the country is being taken over by Negroes or other minority groups and are not alienated from the body politic. Insofar as they are politically motivated, they are active in the Republican party. In California they united in 1966 behind Ronald Reagan, who embodies the conservative virtues. On a local and congressional level they could find many candidates with kindred opinions in the GOP in 1968. Richard Nixon, who supported Goldwater in 1964 and in turn was strongly supported by him both before and after the Republican convention in 1968, though not as conservative as some of them would have liked, still was sufficiently close to such views to retain the support of most affluent economic conservatives for the Republican party.

Clearly, the more than one-fifth of American adults who indicated a preference for George Wallace in late September and early October included highly varied segments of the population, who supported him for apparently different reasons. The Wallace ideology, as we have noted, contained elements which could appeal to extreme racists, populists, antielitists, and rigid economic conservatives. The backing given to groups like the Birch Society seemingly went to Wallace. Hence, like the two major parties, Wallace had the support of many who believed in trade-unions and the welfare state and of others who thought the country was going down the road of socialism or Communism because of welfare legislation.

We would guess that much of Wallace's middle-class support, particularly outside of the South, came from adherents of extremist groups which perceived the country as the victim of a radical takeover. This group saw in Wallace, not the populist, but the critic of big government and the welfare state. Wallace provided these various population groups with a common conduit for expressing their preservatist and backlash concerns.

Notes

1. Robert C. Weaver, *Negro Labor: A National Problem* (New York: Harcourt, Brace, and World, 1946), pp. 15–17.
2. U.S. Bureau of the Census, *Statistical Abstract of the United States, 1961* (Washington: U.S. Government Printing Office, 1961), p. 216.
3. H. A. Bullock, "Racial Attitudes and the Employment of Negroes," *American Journal of Sociology*, LVI (1950), 448–457.
4. John Biesanz and Luke M. Smith, "Race Relations of Panama and the Canal Zone," *American Journal of Sociology*, LVII (1951–1952), 7–14.
5. Morton Deutsch and Mary A. Collins, *Interracial Housing: A Psychological Evaluation of a Social Experiment* (Minneapolis: University of Minnesota Press, 1951).
6. Samuel A. Stouffer *et al.*, *The American Soldier* (Princeton: Princeton University Press, 1949), II, pp. 570 ff.

7. B. M. Kramer, *Residential Contact as a Determinant of Attitudes towards Negroes* (Ph.D. Thesis, Department of Social Relations, Harvard University, 1950).
8. See Earl Raab and Seymour M. Lipset, *Prejudice and Society* (New York: Anti-Defamation League of B'nai B'rith, 1959).
9. Marshall Frady, *Wallace* (New York: World, 1968), p. 96.
10. Robert Sherrill, *Gothic Politics in the Deep South* (New York: Grossman, 1968), p. 300.
11. Frady, *op. cit.*, p. 98.
12. Sherrill, *op. cit.*, p. 267.
13. Frady, *op. cit.*, p. 140.
14. Sherrill, *op. cit.*, p. 292.
15. *Ibid.*, p. 293.
16. Frady, *op. cit.*, p. 137.
17. *Ibid.*
18. "A Surprising Talk between a Black Leader and a Top Segregationist," *New York Times Magazine*, April 27, 1969, p. 109.
19. Sherrill, *op. cit.*, p. 283.
20. *Ibid.*
21. Frady, *op. cit.*, p. 141.
22. Joseph R. Gusfield, *Symbolic Crusade, Status Politics and the American Temperance Movement* (Urbana: University of Illinois Press, 1963), p. 19.
23. *U.S. News and World Report*, April 20, 1964, p. 120.
24. John J. Synon, *George Wallace: Profile of a Presidential Candidate* (Kilmarnock, Va.: MS Inc., no date), p. 83.
25. *Ibid.*, p. 82.
26. *Ibid.*, p. 85.
27. Sherrill, *op. cit.*, p. 292.
28. Philip E. Converse, "The Nature of Belief Systems in Mass Publics," in David E. Apter, ed., *Ideology and Discontent* (New York: The Free Press, 1964), p. 246.
29. "The Real Wallace," *Boston Sunday Globe*, September 29, 1968, p. 4-A.
30. "Platform of the American Independent Party," *The Conservative Journal*, I (September–October 1968), 5–11.
31. Cited in Milton Ellerin, "The Wallace Movement—A Post Election Appraisal," *Trend Analysis Division Report* (American Jewish Committee, 1969), p. 8.
32. "Poll of Conservatives on Wallace," *Human Events*, XXVIII (January 27, 1968), 57.
33. Frady, *op. cit.*, p. 20.
34. Ward Just, "Discontent Is the Mood of Wallace Audiences," *Washington Post*, October 12, 1967, p. B-4.
35. Interview, "Meet the Press," NBC–TV, April 21, 1967.
36. "A Voter's Lexicon of 'Wallacisms,' " *New York Times*, August 25, 1968, p. 81.
37. Ben A. Franklin, "Politics: Wallace Finds Attack on Press and TV Is a Successful Campaign Tactic," *New York Times*, September 3, 1968, p. 38.
38. Synon, *op. cit.*, p. 122.
39. Barry Goldwater, "Don't Waste a Vote on Wallace," *National Review*, XX (October 22, 1968), 1060.

40. George C. Wallace, *Hear Me Out* (Anderson, S.C.: Drake House, 1968), pp. 25–26.
41. *Ibid.*, p. 71.
42. Reese Cleghorn, *Radicalism: Southern Style* (Atlanta: Southern Regional Council, 1968), p. 10. This meeting was reported in the *Councilor,* November 15, 1965.
43. "The Extreme Right Invasion of the 1968 Campaign," *Facts,* XVIII (October 1968), 467.
44. Tom Wicker, "George Wallace: A Gross and Simple Heart," *Harper's,* CCXIV (April 1967), 44.
45. Cited in *Who's behind George?* (Washington: Institute for Democracy, 1968), p. 10.
46. "Wallace's Workers Right Wing Extremists Provide Vital Manpower for Third Party Drive," *Wall Street Journal,* October 24, 1968, p. 1.
47. Ellerin, *op. cit.,* p. 5. For various details on the Texas split, see the following articles in the *New York Times:* "American Party Divided in Texas," August 25, 1968, p. 60; Roy Reed, "Texas Party Nominates Wallace at Last of the 'National' Conventions," September 18, 1968, pp. 1, 27; Martin Waldron, "Birchers in Texas Head Wallace Bid," September 22, 1968, p. 46.
48. Nicholas C. Chriss, "Wallace Campaign Aide Was Active in U.S. Nazi Party," *St. Louis Globe-Democrat,* October 9, 1968, p. 10-A.
49. Richard Bergholz, "Feuding Erupts Again in Wallace State Party," *Los Angeles Times,* August 23, 1968, Part I, p. 21.
50. "Wallace's Workers . . . ," *op. cit.,* pp. 1, 16.
51. "The Extreme Right Invasion of the 1968 Campaign," *op. cit.,* pp. 473–474. Many of the statements above are brought together in this article.
52. Ellerin, *op. cit.,* p. 6.
53. Frady, *op. cit.,* p. 227.
54. Synon, *op. cit.,* p. 114.
55. Ward Just, "Discontent Is the Mood of Wallace Audiences," *op. cit.*
56. Kenneth Lamott, " 'It Isn't a Mirage They're Seeing,' Says George Wallace," *New York Times Magazine,* September 22, 1968, p. 33.
57. "Wallace and His Folks," *Newsweek,* September 16, 1968, p. 27.
58. David S. Broder, "Wallace's Campaign Really a Call to Anarchy, Violence," *Los Angeles Times,* August 22, 1968, Part II, p. 5.
59. Wicker, *op. cit.,* p. 46.
60. Richard F. Halverson, *Wallace and the Maryland Democratic Presidential Primary* (M.A. Thesis, Department of Public Law and Government, Columbia University, 1966), pp. 25, 28, 41.
61. *Ibid.,* p. 24.
62. *Ibid.,* p. 25; Michael Rogin, "Wallace and the Middle Class: The White Backlash in Wisconsin," *Public Opinion Quarterly,* XX (Spring 1966), 98–108.
63. Lucy Davidowicz, *The Politics of Prejudice: Wallace in the Presidential Primaries in Wisconsin, Indiana and Maryland* (New York: American Jewish Committee Jewish Information Service, July 1964, mimeographed), pp. 7–8, 16.
64. *Ibid.,* pp. 17, 22–23.

65. *Ibid.*, pp. 8, 16, 24; Halverson, *op. cit.*, pp. 25, 28, 40.
66. Davidowicz, *op. cit.*, pp. 23–24.
67. *Ibid.*, p. 40.
68. Lewis Chester, Godfrey Hodgson, and Bruce Page, *An American Melodrama* (New York: Viking, 1969), pp. 284–285.
69. See Jerry Flint, "Auto Union Poll Won by Wallace," *New York Times,* October 6, 1968, p. 75.
70. Crocker Snow, Jr., "Phenomenon: Labor Votes for Wallace," *Boston Globe,* October 6, 1968, p. 6a.
71. Victor Riesel, "Wallace to Outpoll HHH—Even Win?" *New York Daily Column,* October 3, 1968, p. 1.
72. Peter Millones, "Humphrey Leads Labor Poll, 34–32," *New York Times,* October 9, 1968, p. 1.
73. Robert T. Riley and Thomas F. Pettigrew, "Relative Deprivation and Wallace's Northern Support" (paper presented at the meetings of the American Sociological Association, 1969, San Francisco, California), p. 3.
74. A. H. Raskin, "And the Pro-Humphrey Labor Chiefs Are Worried," *New York Times,* September 15, 1968, p. 20.
75. Samuel Lubell, "Man in the Street Looks to Nixon as the Middle Road Alternative," *Boston Sunday Globe,* September 29, 1968, p. 26.
76. Samuel Lubell, "New Type Voter Created by Our Economic Boom," *Boston Globe,* October 27, 1968, p. 24.
77. Clark Kissinger, "Who Supports George and Gene?" *The Guardian,* September 21, 1968, p. 7. See also C. LaRouche and L. Marcus, "The New Left, Local Control and Fascism," *Campaigner,* I (September 1968), 31, for similar comments by another SDS group.
78. Riley and Pettigrew, *op. cit.*, p. 3.
79. See pp. 317–320.
80. Ben A. Franklin, "Wallace Hailed by Police on Tour," *New York Times,* September 8, 1968, p. 78.
81. A. James Reichley, "The Cool Way to Cool the Police Rebellion," *Fortune,* LXXVIII (December 1968), 113.
82. Franklin, *op. cit.*
83. From Report by Harvey Schecter and Barbara J. Coopersmith, "George Wallace Vote—Mountain States Region" (private report to the Anti-Defamation League, January 3, 1969), p. 2.
84. For a detailed analysis of the politics of the police see S. M. Lipset, "Why Cops Hate Liberals—and Vice Versa," *The Atlantic,* 203 (March 1969), pp. 76–83.
85. Wicker, *op. cit.*, p. 46.
86. "What They Believe," *Fortune,* LXXIX (January 1969), 70.
87. *Ibid.*
88. T. R. Leidy *et al.*, "High School Students Look at the 1968 Presidential Election," *Purdue Opinion Panel,* Report No. 84, XXVIII (November 1968), 3.
89. Sylan Fox, "Many Police in City Leaning to the Right," *New York Times,* September 6, 1968, p. 49.
90. Richard Dougherty, "Confrontation between New Left and New Right Emerges in N.Y.," *Boston Sunday Globe,* September 29, 1968, p. 16.

91. Paul B. Sheatsley, "White Attitudes toward the Negro," *Daedalus*, XCV (Winter 1966), 228; see also Herbert H. Hyman and Paul B. Sheatsley, "Attitudes toward Desegregation," *Scientific American*, CCXI (July 1964), 16–23.
92. Terry Robards, "Poll of Executives Puts Nixon Ahead," *New York Times*, October 27, 1968, pp. 1, 72.

10

George Wallace: The Election and the Electorate

The Election Day results confirmed the basic predictions of the opinion polls: George Wallace secured almost 10,000,000 votes, or about 13.5 per cent of the total voting electorate. He captured five states with forty-five electoral votes. All of them were in the Deep South. With one exception, these were the same states won by Barry Goldwater in 1964. Mississippi, Georgia, Alabama, and Louisiana voted for Goldwater and Wallace. Wallace also carried Arkansas, which went to Lyndon Johnson four years earlier, and lost two states, carried by Goldwater: South Carolina, the home state of Nixon's southern leader, the 1948 Dixiecrat candidate, Strom Thurmond; and Arizona, Goldwater's home state. The breakdown of Wallace strength by region is reported in Table 52.

Since the support for Wallace seemingly declined considerably between early October and Election Day, falling from about 21 per cent to 13 per cent, an analysis of his actual polling strength is obviously important. Fortunately, the Gallup poll conducted a national survey immediately after the election in which it inquired both how respondents voted and whether they had supported another candidate earlier in the campaign. The data of this survey were made available by the Gallup poll for our analysis. They are particularly useful, since it would appear that most voters who had supported Wallace, but shifted to another candidate, did report this fact to Gallup interviewers. Among white respondents, 13 per cent indicated they had voted for Wallace, while another 9 per cent stated that they had been for him at an earlier stage in the campaign. The results are presented in Table 53.

Table 52. 1968 POPULAR VOTE FOR PRESIDENT BY REGIONS

	Republican		Democratic		American Independent		Total
	Num-ber[a]	Per Cent	Num-ber[a]	Per Cent	Num-ber[a]	Per Cent	Num-ber[a]
New England	1,855	(39)	2,755	(57)	202	(4)	4,824
Middle Atlantic[b]	6,520	(44)	6,991	(47)	1,028	(7)	14,799
East North Central[c]	7,214	(46)	6,889	(44)	1,561	(10)	15,701
West North Central[d]	3,178	(49)	2,812	(43)	503	(8)	6,504
South[e]	4,648	(34)	4,222	(31)	4,648	(34)	13,539
Border[f]	2,241	(41)	2,102	(39)	1,060	(20)	5,407
Mountain[g]	1,533	(53)	1,097	(38)	248	(9)	2,890
Pacific[h]	4,594	(47)	4,396	(45)	647	(7)	9,694
Total	31,784	(43)	31,266	(43)	9,899	(13)	73,360

SOURCE: Republican National Committee, *The 1968 Elections* (April 1969, mimeographed).
[a] Figures shown in thousands.
[b] Delaware, New Jersey, New York, Pennsylvania.
[c] Illinois, Indiana, Michigan, Ohio, Wisconsin.
[d] Iowa, Kansas, Minnesota, Missouri, Nebraska, North Dakota, South Dakota.
[e] Alabama, Arkansas, Florida, Georgia, Louisiana, Mississippi, North Carolina, South Carolina, Texas, Virginia.
[f] Kentucky, Maryland, Oklahoma, Tennessee, District of Columbia, West Virginia.
[g] Arizona, Colorado, Idaho, Montana, Nevada, New Mexico, Utah, Wyoming.
[h] Alaska, California, Hawaii, Oregon, Washington.

In general, the postelection survey bears out the findings of the preelection analyses of those who approved of Wallace. If we look first at the national data, which, of course, are heavily influenced by the pattern of support in the South, Wallace's voters were most likely to come from persons who, in 1964, did not vote or backed Goldwater rather than Johnson. The pattern of an extremist party recruiting heavily from the ranks of nonvoters coincides with the evidence from previous extremist movements both in this country and abroad, as presented earlier. Wallace clearly appealed to those in smaller communities. His vote strength was greatest among those with the least education. In income terms, his backers were more likely to come from the poorer strata than the more well to do, although he was slightly weaker among the lowest-income class—under $3,000—than among the next highest. Not surprisingly, his support was greatest among those in the least skilled occupations. He was strongest among those in "service" jobs, a conglomorate which includes police, domestic servants, and the military. Among the regular urban occupational classes, his support was highest among the unskilled, followed by the skilled, white-collar workers, those in business and managerial pursuits, and professionals, in that order. Farmers were relatively low in voting for

Table 53. 1968 PRESIDENTIAL VOTING BY SELECTED DEMOGRAPHIC CHARACTERISTICS
(N = 1,479; nonwhites excluded)
(Per Cent)

	Humphrey	Voted for Nixon	Wallace	Considered[a] Wallace	Total Wallace Sympa- thizers[b]	Wallace Non- defection Ratio[c]	Total Voting	Total Sample
Political Party Identification								
Democratic	75	14	11	9	20	.56	433	567
Republican	5	89	6	7	13	.46	364	431
Independent	30	49	22	11	32	.67	333	449
Congressional Vote in 1968								
Democratic	68	18	15	10	25	.59	514	514
Republican	12	78	10	8	17	.55	542	542
Presidental Vote in 1964								
Democratic	66	26	8	8	16	.49	558	646
Republican	13	82	15	10	25	.61	380	413
Didn't vote	36	41	24	11	35	.68	167	374
Region								
South[d]	21	43	34	9	43	.79	249	373
Non-South	44	50	7	9	15	.43	894	1,106
Northeast[e]	49	44	7	7	14	.49	344	424
Midwest[f]	41	52	8	11	18	.42	368	452
West[g]	41	55	5	8	12	.36	182	230
Occupation								
Nonmanual	37	54	9	9	18	.50	456	536
Professional	36	57	7	5	11	.59	158	179

Business	37	55	9	9	18	.50	155	193
White collar[h]	38	50	12	7	19	.62	143	164
Manual	43	40	17	11	28	.60	400	563
Skilled labor	43	43	15	12	27	.55	208	284
Unskilled	47	35	19	12	31	.60	140	207
Service	33	44	23	6	29	.80	52	72
Farm[i]	22	65	13	13	25	.50	74	94
Union family	54	34	12	15	27	.43	210	274
Nonunion	31	47	22	8	29	.75	190	289

Education

Grade school or less	44	37	19	10	29	.67	191	290
High school or less	39	48	13	10	23	.57	537	715
Some college	38	54	9	6	14	.62	330	377

Income

Under $3,000	37	47	16	6	23	.72	132	189
$3,000 to $6,999	38	43	19	8	27	.70	334	487
$7,000 to $9,999	38	50	12	11	23	.53	257	324
$10,000 to $14,999	42	50	8	9	17	.47	243	276
$15,000 and over	35	59	6	9	14	.39	168	191

Religion

Roman Catholic	53	38	9	9	18	.52	311	381
Jewish	86	14	—	2	2	.00	46	54
Protestant	29	56	15	10	25	.60	749	989
Baptist	22	46	32	11	43	.76	147	213
Methodist	29	57	14	8	22	.63	180	231
Presbyterian	23	70	7	12	19	.38	89	103
Lutheran	43	55	3	6	9	.29	85	101
Episcopal	39	54	7	7	13	.43	46	51
Others	29	55	16	12	27	.58	159	222

	Humphrey	Voted for Nixon	Wallace	Considered[a] Wallace	Total Wallace Sympathizers[b]	Wallace Non-defection Ratio[c]	Total Voting	Total Sample
Size of Place								
Rural	31	50	19	8	27	.63	323	416
2,500 to 49,999	36	49	14	6	20	.63	163	224
50,000 to 499,999	38	51	11	8	19	.56	268	361
500,000 to 999,999	43	47	10	6	15	.62	138	189
1,000,000 and over	50	44	7	8	15	.43	250	288
Age								
21 to 25	49	35	17	6	23	.77	81	137
26 to 29	37	49	15	9	24	.63	73	104
30 to 49	38	49	13	12	25	.52	488	608
50 and over	39	50	11	6	17	.65	491	618
Sex								
Men	39	46	15	11	26	.58	588	723
Women	39	51	10	7	17	.60	555	747

SOURCE: AIPO 771-k, November 7, 1968; rows may sum to more or less than 100 per cent due to rounding error.
[a] Thought about voting for Wallace earlier in the campaign, but eventually switched to another candidate.
[b] Combination of the "considered Wallace" category and the Wallace voter category.
[c] The ratio of the total number of Wallace sympathizers to the actual number of Wallace voters.
[d] Those states making up the old Confederacy plus Kentucky.
[e] New England and the Middle Atlantic states, including West Virginia, Maryland, Delaware, and the District of Columbia.
[f] Ohio, Indiana, Illinois, Michigan, Wisconsin, Minnesota, Missouri, and the Trans-Mississippi states of North and South Dakota, Kansas, Nebraska, Iowa, and Oklahoma.
[g] All states west of the Midwest and South, excluding Alaska and Hawaii.
[h] Clerical and sales.
[i] Both farm proprietors and workers.

Wallace, a phenomenon which is later seen to stem from the differences between farmers in the South and in the rest of the country. Among manual workers Wallace was much weaker among union members than non-unionists.

The vote behavior with respect to other factors also corresponds in general to the earlier analyses. Wallace was backed more heavily by men than by women, a pattern characteristically associated with radical movements, whether of the left or right; young voters were more likely to prefer him than old ones. Religion also served to differentiate. Wallace received a higher proportion of the votes of Protestants than Catholics, a product of his strength in the predominantly Protestant South.

The pattern of support for Wallace viewed nationally is a bit deceiving, since so much of his support was in the South. He carried five southern states and received a substantial vote in all the others, plus the border states. To a considerable extent, his movement in the South took on the character of a preservatist defense of southern institutions against the threat from the federal government. In most southern states, it was a major party candidacy. In the rest of the country, however, the Wallace movement was a small radical third party, organized around various extreme right-wing groups. While clearly it gave expression to racial concerns, it also included the disaffected of a number of varieties. A Louis Harris poll conducted in October reported that the majority of Wallace supporters in the South identified him as a "conservative," while the majority of his nonsouthern backers chose the term "radical" to describe his role. One would expect, therefore, some differences in the types of voters to whom he appealed in the different sections. The variation in his support in the two sections is presented in Tables 54 and 55.

The variations between the sections are apparent along a number of dimensions. Northern Wallace voters were more likely than southern to come from the ranks of identified and committed Republicans. Thus, in the South a much larger proportion of people identified as Democrats (37 per cent) than as Republicans (10 per cent) voted for him. Conversely, in the North a slightly larger segment of the Republicans voted for him than did Democrats. This emphasis is reversed, however, with respect to the 1964 vote. In both sections, larger proportions of Goldwater voters opted for Wallace than did Johnson supporters. Relatively, however, he did better among the southern Goldwater voters. The seeming contradiction may be explained by the fact that Wallace did best among "independents" and that there were proportionately many more independents in the South than in the North. Southern independents presumably are people who earlier had opted out of the Democratic party to the right, many of whom voted for Goldwater in 1964 and Wallace in 1968. His greatest support,

Table 54. 1968 PRESIDENTIAL VOTING IN THE NON-SOUTH BY SELECTED DEMOGRAPHIC CHARACTERISTICS
(Per Cent)
(N = 1,106; nonwhites excluded)

| | Voted for | | | Considered Wallace | Total Wallace Sympathizers | Non-defection Ratio | Voting Number | Total Number |
	Humphrey	Nixon	Wallace					
Political Party Identification								
Democratic	83	13	5	9	14	.36	342	424
Republican	6	89	6	8	14	.40	302	356
Independent	37	52	11	10	21	.53	240	303
Congressional Vote in 1968								
Democratic	78	16	6	9	16	.40	392	392
Republican	13	80	6	8	15	.43	440	440
Presidential Vote in 1964								
Democratic	70	26	5	8	13	.38	469	533
Republican	4	89	7	9	16	.42	275	291
Didn't vote	42	43	14	12	26	.55	123	248
Occupation								
Nonmanual	42	53	5	5	10	.52	350	406
Professional	42	55	3	4	6	.43	117	133
Business	39	55	6	4	10	.66	121	144
White collar	44	50	7	8	14	.47	112	129
Manual	49	42	9	13	22	.42	327	426
Skilled labor	47	46	7	13	21	.35	171	212
Unskilled labor	55	33	13	14	26	.48	119	162

Service workers	41	54	5	5	11	.50	37	52
Farm	21	77	2	16	18	.10	57	70
Union family	57	34	9	16	25	.36	189	234
Nonunion	39	52	9	8	17	.52	138	192
Education								
Grade school or less	53	40	7	10	17	.41	134	188
High school or less	43	49	7	9	17	.43	436	558
Some college	43	52	5	4	9	.56	257	286
Income								
Under $3,000	41	53	5	5	11	.50	93	124
$3,000 to $6,999	46	44	10	9	19	.51	246	338
$7,000 to $9,999	42	52	6	11	17	.37	213	261
$10,000 to $14,999	46	47	6	8	14	.44	201	224
$15,000 and over	39	58	3	7	10	.31	133	150
Religion								
Roman Catholic	53	39	8	9	17	.49	292	355
Jewish	87	13	—	3	3	.00	42	50
Protestant	34	53	6	10	15	.38	527	655
Baptist	33	51	16	10	25	.63	64	82
Methodist	32	65	3	10	13	.21	117	150
Presbyterian	28	68	5	11	15	.30	68	78
Lutheran	43	54	3	6	9	.29	83	98
Episcopal	40	61	—	5	5	.00	38	41
Others	31	59	9	13	22	.43	129	163
Size of Place								
Rural	37	56	7	11	20	.36	221	272
2,500 to 49,999	43	52	5	6	11	.42	115	149
50,000 to 499,999	44	51	6	5	10	.48	196	245

	Voted for			Consid-ered Wallace	Total Wallace Sympa-thizers	Non-defection Ratio	Voting Number	Total Number
	Humphrey	Nixon	Wallace					
Size of Place (Cont.)								
500,000 to 999,999	46	45	9	6	16	.59	112	152
1,000,000 and over	50	44	7	8	15	.43	250	288
Age								
21 to 25	54	34	13	7	20	.64	72	108
26 to 29	35	54	11	6	17	.67	54	79
30 to 49	43	49	8	14	22	.36	393	466
50 and over	43	53	3	5	8	.43	366	443
Sex								
Men	43	48	9	11	20	.44	458	550
Women	45	51	5	6	11	.41	436	556

in both North and South, of course, came from the ranks of those who did not vote in 1964. Almost half of the southern 1964 nonvoters who voted in 1968 chose Wallace.

The effects of the social stratification variables were relatively similar in both parts of the country. In general, the better educated, the more well-to-do, and those in middle-class occupations were less likely to vote for Wallace than voters in the lower echelons. The pattern varies some, particularly in the North, with the indication that those at the very bottom of the income ladder (under $3,000) and of the educational ladder (grammar school) were less pro-Wallace than those in the next higher grouping. The greatest difference in the relative position of different occupational groups, North or South, occurred among farmers. Southern farmers were among the highest group of Wallace voters, while northern farmers were extremely low. In the North, farmers seemingly expressed their conservatism by voting for Nixon. Among manual workers, union membership varied in its relationship to Wallace voting. In the North, the percentage of union members who voted for Wallace was similar to that among nonmembers, while in the South, Wallace did somewhat better among non-unionists.

Although nationally Wallace appeared to secure more support among Protestants than Catholics, a sectional breakdown points up the fact that this was an artifact of the relatively small Catholic population in the South. Outside of the South, Wallace secured more support from Catholics than from Protestants. The pattern appears to reverse in the South, but the number of Catholics in the sample is too small to sustain a reliable estimate. What is perhaps more significant than the Catholic-Protestant variation is the difference among the Protestant denominations. Wallace's greatest backing, North and South, came from Baptists, followed by "other," presumably mainly fundamentalist sects. These denominations are the most traditional of the Protestant groups and have a history of disproportionately backing right-wing groups. They contain the core of the religious resistance to modernism and cosmopolitanism. Their main strength has been in small towns and rural areas and from many who adhere to these denominations in the cities who are migrants from more provincial areas. Methodists differed greatly North and South, with the northern Methodists giving little support to Wallace, while those in the South show up as high among the groups backing him. This difference also may reflect the fact that southern Methodists retain much of the evangelical concerns of the nineteenth-century church, while northern Methodism has become a middle-class variant of Protestantism. Jews, not surprisingly, gave no support to the third-party candidate.

The disproportionate backing which Wallace received from Baptists in

Table 55. 1968 PRESIDENTIAL VOTING IN THE SOUTH BY SELECTED DEMOGRAPHIC CHARACTERISTICS
(Per Cent)

	Voted for			Considered Wallace	Total Wallace Sympathizers	Non-defection Ratio	Voting Number	Total Number
	Humphrey	Nixon	Wallace					
Political Party Identification								
Democratic	46	17	37	3	40	.92	91	143
Republican	—	90	10	10	20	.49	62	75
Independent	12	41	47	13	60	.79	93	146
Congressional Vote in 1968								
Democratic	34	24	42	12	54	.78	122	122
Republican	8	69	24	5	28	.83	102	102
Presidential Vote in 1964								
Democratic	49	29	23	8	31	.73	89	113
Republican	1	62	38	11	48	.78	105	122
Didn't vote	19	33	48	10	57	.83	44	126
Occupation								
Nonmanual	22	57	22	14	28	.76	106	130
Professional	21	62	18	8	26	.70	41	46
Business	27	55	18	27	46	.40	34	49
White collar	17	53	30	7	37	.82	31	35
Manual	14	33	53	6	59	.90	73	137
Skilled labor	20	31	49	6	54	.90	37	72
Unskilled labor	5	45	50	5	55	.91	21	45
Service workers	13	20	67	7	74	.91	15	20

Farm	27	20	53	—	53	1.00	17	24
Union family	30	30	40	5	45	.89	21	40
Nonunion	8	34	58	6	64	.91	52	97
Education								
Grade school or less	23	28	49	8	57	.87	57	102
High school or less	21	42	36	11	48	.77	101	157
Some college	19	60	21	10	31	.68	73	91
Income								
Under $3,000	27	30	43	8	51	.84	39	65
$3,000 to $6,999	18	39	44	5	48	.92	88	149
$7,000 to $9,999	17	42	42	12	54	.77	44	63
$10,000 to $14,999	23	63	15	13	28	.55	42	52
$15,000 and over	24	62	15	15	29	.50	35	41
Religion								
Roman Catholic	47	29	24	6	29	.80	19	26
Jewish	*	*	*	*	*	*	4	4
Protestant	18	46	36	10	46	.78	222	334
Baptist	13	43	45	11	56	.80	83	131
Methodist	22	43	35	5	40	.89	63	81
Presbyterian	10	76	14	14	29	.50	21	25
Lutheran	*	*	*	*	*	*	2	3
Episcopal	*	*	*	*	*	*	8	10
Others	21	25	45	7	52	.87	30	59
Size of Place								
Rural	17	38	45	4	49	.90	102	144
2,500 to 49,999	21	43	36	8	44	.74	48	75
50,000 to 499,999	23	52	25	9	33	.63	72	116

Table 55. 1968 PRESIDENTIAL VOTING IN THE SOUTH BY SELECTED DEMOGRAPHIC CHARACTERISTICS—CONTINUED

	Voted for			Considered Wallace	Total Wallace Sympathizers	Non-defection Ratio	Voting Number	Total Number
	Humphrey	Nixon	Wallace					
Size of Place (Cont.)								
500,000 to 999,999	31	58	12	3	15	.75	26	37
1,000,000 and over	*	*	*	*	*	*	—	—
Age								
21 to 25	*	*	*	*	*	*	9	29
26 to 29	26	37	37	5	42	.88	19	25
30 to 49	14	52	34	8	41	.82	95	142
50 and over	26	41	33	10	43	.77	125	175
Sex								
Men	24	39	37	11	48	.78	130	182
Women	18	51	31	8	39	.80	119	191

* Too few cases.

the North suggests that much of his northern vote may have come from transplanted white southerners. Although the studies available to us for secondary analysis did not contain any questions bearing on migration status, we were able to secure a relevant table from the Survey Research Center of the University of Michigan from their 1968 election study. As shown in Table 56, these data indicate that voters who grew up in the South were much more likely to have opted for Wallace in the election than those who were reared in other sections of the country.

Table 56.   RELATIONSHIP BETWEEN SECTIONAL ORIGINS AND
CURRENT RESIDENCE AND VOTE FOR WALLACE, WHITE VOTERS ONLY

	Current Residence	
Section Where "Grew Up"	Non-South	South
Non-South	7 %	10 %
Number	(652)	(39)
South	14 %	30 %
Number	(35)	(202)

SOURCE: From the 1968 election study of the Survey Research Center of the University of Michigan, kindly made available by Philip Converse.

A further note is warranted on the fact that so much of Wallace's support came directly from southern traditional Protestantism and in the North from the Baptists, which is largely a southern migrant church. Reese Cleghorn comments:

The South, James McBride Dabbs has written, institutionalized revivalism in the late 19th century. Other parts of the country moved on past. But the South stayed with revivalism and its heavy emphasis on emotion, simple doctrine and quick assurance of salvation. . . . Martin Luther had asserted each individual's ability to interpret the Scriptures, but the South made a preposterous anti-intellectual, individualistic fetish of that principle. . . .

The relevance of all this to radical rightist influence in the South is clear. Rightist views in the United States are commonly grounded in narrow anti-intellectual views of the world; in moralistic certitude; in a view that opposing ideas are satanic; in a devotion to old practices and old values with the assumption that these are under attack from evil forces; and in an assertion of individualism which, although rightists often are themselves subject to herding, becomes an official virtue. These threads of rightist radicalism are obviously also the central elements in the Southern church's peculiarity (it's heresy, perhaps, from the viewpoint of mainstream Protestantism).[1]

There are, however, several qualifications to be applied to these observations, or to any assumptions that are made about direct relationships between the ideological content of religious fundamentalism and right-wing extremist politics. In the first place, there is a prior relationship which has been found to exist between education and religious fundamentalism. Glock and Stark have found that increased education leads to an erosion of traditional religious beliefs.[2] The particularism of extremist political beliefs and the particularism of religious fundamentalism are in one sense a unitary phenomenon associated with low educational levels, although shaped, of course, by specific political and cultural situations. From that vantage point, religious fundamentalism is seen more as a concomitant cultural phenomenon, with its own impetus, of course, than as a causative ideological commitment. This is not to deny the independent effects of fundamentalist beliefs, but rather to blunt the edge of religious determinism as it might be applied mechanistically to extremist political movements. Fundamentalist religious belief, seen culturally in America, is also traditional religious belief. Traditional religious belief is the symbolic center of a traditional style of life. It is, among other things, "the cultural baggage" of that way of life. When drastic social change shifts the position of that way of life—and the position of those who bear it—traditional religious belief often becomes also the cultural baggage of the backlash political ideology that develops. As one Protestant historian put it:

> As classical mass evangelism disappeared or turned to more subdued methods, many of the groups which continued to use the language without standing for the context of the message of repentance and conversion have become impassioned champions of the American way of life or the southern way of life. In the present controversies the heirs of the liberal tradition of culture-religion have frequently carried the message of prophetic discontinuity, while avowed "Fundamentalists" justify the *status quo*.[3]

Wallace became the protector of the "southern way of life"—and the status of those who bear it—not only for southerners but for the southern migrants to the North. This, apart from education, is one significance of the disproportionate support of Wallace by northern Baptists.

Sex and age were relatively consistent in both sections of the country. Males were more pro-Wallace than women, while young voters were more likely to opt for him than older ones. Both results, as we have noted, are consistent with findings for other radical and new social movements.

Some of the relationships reported here require further specification. It is possible that a number of them are a result of the interrelationship among different factors. For example, the relationship between income and vote may be a function primarily of education. Level of education and age are highly associated with each other, since younger generations contain larger proportions of the better educated than older ones. The statistics in Table 57 clearly indicate that age and education both

Table 57. EDUCATION, AGE, AND WALLACE VOTE

	21–29	Age Groups 30–49	Over 50
		Grammar School	
Percentage Wallace vote		29 %	15 %
Number		(41)	(137)
		High School	
Percentage Wallace vote	20 %	14 %	9 %
Number	(79)	(236)	(103)
		College	
Percentage Wallace vote	10 %	9 %	8 %
Number	(59)	(156)	(99)

* Too few cases.

are associated with support for Wallace. Within each educational stratum, the younger are more likely to have cast a ballot for Wallace than the older electors. Similarly, within each age group, the more poorly educated were more disposed to choose the Alabamian than those with higher school attainments. Although the numbers involved become quite small, it may be noted that these relationships hold up in both the North and the South.

Since stratification variables, occupation, education, and income are closely related, an examination of their combined and separated effects would seem warranted. Looking closely at Table 58 points up the fact

Table 58. STRATIFICATION VARIABLES AND THE WALLACE VOTE

Manual Percentage Wallace Vote	Number	Education Group	Nonmanual Percentage Wallace Vote	Number
		Grammar School		
23	(74)		12	(17)
		High School		
16	(234)		11	(162)
		College		
11	(54)		8	(211)
		Income Group		
		Under $5,000		
29	(70)		16	(31)
		$5,000–$9,999		
18	(206)		12	(153)
		$10,000 and over		
8	(103)		6	(245)

that Wallace support is highest among the most deprived, as judged by their occupational, income, and educational statuses. In each case, combining these factors produces a higher third-party vote when the two factors reflect lower attainments, and a low level of Wallace support when two indicators of high status are joined together. These variations also hold up in both sections of the country.

A preliminary report of the results of the 1968 election study conducted by the Survey Research Center of the University of Michigan permits a check on the reliability of our findings from the various other surveys. Their conclusions on the whole agree remarkably with these other ones.

[The] Wallace vote was relatively rural and small town, particularly in the South. . . .

The well-publicized appeal of Wallace to the unionized laboring man is clearly reflected in our data: outside the South, the proportion of white union members preferring Wallace over the other major candidates was more than three times as great as it was within households having no unionized members (19% to 6%); even in the South where other appeals were present and the unionization of labor is more limited, the contrast between the preferences of union members and non-union households remains dramatic (52% to 28% . . .). Indeed, in both regions the occupational center of gravity of Wallace popularity was clearly among white skilled workers. Nationwide, only about 10% of the Wallace vote was contributed by the professional and managerial strata. . . .

. . . [A]mong white Southerners there is actually a faint *negative* correlation between age and a Wallace vote. And . . . outside the South voting for Wallace occurred very disproportionately among the young. For example, Wallace captured less than 3% of the vote among people over 70 outside the South, but 13% of those under 30, with a regular gradient connecting these two extremes.

. . . Although privileged young college students angry at Vietnam and the shabby treatment of the Negro saw themselves as sallying forth to do battle against a corrupted and cynical older generation, a more head-on confrontation at the polls, if a less apparent one, was with their own age mates who had gone from high school off to the factory instead of college. . . .[4]

As significant as the data bearing on the Wallace vote are those dealing with the defection from Wallace. There are several "defection factors" which might be reflected by an analysis of those who shifted from pre-election to voting-day preference. Presumably many of those who abandoned Wallace did so because they thought he could not win, not because they would not have liked to see him as President. This is the uneasiness of the "lost vote." There is also the factor of the expressive vote in polls which do not count. Casting a straw vote for Wallace was clearly one method of striking a generalized note of dissatisfaction in certain directions.

But total considerations take over in the voting booth. The nature of the defections becomes one way to measure the current saliency of such dissatisfactions in various quarters. On another level, there is the factor of reinforcing and cross-pressure stimuli which exist and are promulgated and which relate to the ability of a third-party candidate to hold his base of support under attack.

In general, Wallace lost most heavily among groups and areas in which he was weakest to begin with. Individuals in such groups would find less support for their opinions among their acquaintances and also would be more likely to feel that a Wallace vote was wasted. Thus, almost four-fifths of all southerners who ever considered voting for Wallace actually voted for him. In the North, he lost over half of his initial support. Only 43 per cent of his original supporters cast a ballot for him. Similarly, Baptists and the small sect "other" Protestants were more likely to remain in the Wallace camp through the campaign than those belonging to less pro-Wallace religious groups.

There were certain significant differences in the pattern of defections with respect to stratification factors. In the South, middle-class supporters of Wallace were much more likely to move away from him as the campaign progressed. He wound up with 90 per cent of his preelection support among southern manual workers and 61 per cent among those in non-manual occupations. In the North, however, Wallace retained a larger proportion of his middle-class backers (52 per cent) than of his working-class followers (42 per cent). The data from this Gallup survey would suggest that the very extensive campaign of trade-union leaders to reduce Wallace support among their members actually had an effect in the North. Almost two-thirds (64 per cent) of northern trade-union members who had backed Wallace initially *did not* vote for him, while over half of the southern unionist workers (52 per cent) who had been for him earlier voted for him on Election Day. A similar pattern occurred with respect to the two other measures of stratification, education and income. Wallace retained more backing among the better educated and more affluent of his northern supporters, while in the South, these groups were much more likely to have defected by Election Day than the less educated and less privileged.

The variations in the class background of the defectors in the different sections of the country may be a function of varying exposures to reinforcing and cross-pressure stimuli in their respective environments. On the whole we would guess that middle-class Wallace supporters in the North came disproportionately from persons previously committed to extreme rightist ideology and even affiliations. Wallace's support among the northern middle class corresponds in size to that given to the John Birch

Society in opinion polls. If we assume that most people who were pro-Birch were pro-Wallace, presumably Wallace did not break out of this relatively small group. And this group which was heavily involved in a reinforcing environment could have been expected to stick with him. In the South, on the other hand, he began with considerable middle-class support gained from people who had been backers of the effort to create a conservative Republican party in that section. The vast majority of them had backed Barry Goldwater in 1964. This large group of affluent southern Wallacites encompassed many who had not been involved in extremist activities. And it would seem that the efforts of the southern conservative Republicans headed by Strom Thurmond to convince them that a vote for Wallace would help Humphrey had effect. Conversely, among northern manual workers, an inclination to vote for Wallace placed men outside the dominant pattern in their class. And seemingly the barrage of anti-Wallace propaganda which suggested that he was antilabor and opposed to social welfare, or that a vote for Wallace would only help elect Republicans, succeeded in moving many workers who sympathized with him on racial and other issues to shift their vote. In the South, however, Wallace support was overwhelmingly among the less privileged, and counterpropaganda, particularly from the left, was not likely to reach them or have effect.

The direction of defection from Wallace clearly varied according to background. Three-fifths of those who shifted away from Wallace during the campaign ended up voting for Nixon. The differences related to various social and political characteristics are reported in Table 59. Essentially, the data suggest that Wallace backers who decided to vote for one of the major party candidates almost invariably reverted to their traditional party affiliation. The pattern is even clearer when we eliminate southern Democrats. Among the 29 northern Democrats in our sample who defected from Wallace, 90 per cent voted for Hubert Humphrey. Humphrey recruited from among the less educated and poorer Wallace voters, Nixon from the more affluent and better educated. Perhaps the most interesting item in the table is the one reporting on the relationship between union membership and subsequent vote among manual workers. Humphrey secured 69 per cent among the union members who decided to leave Wallace, while Nixon pulled 71 per cent among the nonunionist workers who changed their vote intention.

The pattern of shifting among the Wallace voters points up our assumption that Wallace appealed to two very different groups: economic conservatives concerned with repudiating the welfare state, and less affluent supporters of the welfare state who were affected by issues of racial integration and law and order. Insofar as some individuals in each of these groups felt motivated to change their vote, they opted for the candidate

Table 59. FACTORS ASSOCIATED WITH VOTING CHOICES OF WALLACE DEFECTORS

Social and Political Characteristics	Actual Vote		
	Per Cent Humphrey	Per Cent Nixon	Number
Region			
South	23	77	(22)
North	45	55	(75)
Party Affiliation			
Republican	12	89	(26)
Democratic	79	21	(38)
Independent	18	82	(33)
1964 Vote			
Goldwater	11	89	(36)
Johnson	63	38	(43)
No vote	47	53	(17)
Religion			
Protestant	34	66	(71)
Catholic	60	40	(25)
Age			
Under 29	27	73	(11)[a]
30 to 49	44	54	(57)
50 and over	36	64	(28)
Education			
Grammar school	65	35	(17)
High school	46	54	(50)
College	18	82	(17)
Income			
Under $5,000	50	50	(18)
$5,000 to $9,999	44	56	(43)
$10,000 and over	26	74	(34)
Occupation			
Nonmanual	13	87	(30)
Manual	56	44	(43)
Farm	22	78	(9)[a]
Unionism—Manuals only			
Union members	69	31	(29)
Nonunion	29	71	(14)

[a] Too few cases for a reliable estimate.

who presumably stood closer to their basic concerns. These data also underline the difficulty in building a new movement which encompasses people with highly disparate sentiments and interests.

Attitudes and Political Choice in 1968

After specifying the correlations that exist between gross population groups and voting preference, the most interesting question still remains, especially with respect to deviant and extremist political movements: What creates the differentials in each of these groups? Quite clearly, members of the same heuristic group or class may vary greatly in their perception of the world and will, therefore, differ as to political choice. Since candidates do differ in their ideology and stand on particular issues, we should expect that the values of the electorate should help determine which segments of particular strata end up voting one way or another.

Data collected by two different national survey organizations, the Louis Harris poll and the Opinion Research Corporation, permit us to analyze the connection between political attitudes and voter choice in 1968. The Harris data are derived from a special reanalysis of the results of a number of surveys conducted during the campaign which was prepared by the Harris organization for the American Jewish Committee. Based on 16,915 interviews, it unveils consistent variations. The Opinion Research Corporation data are from a study commissioned by the Columbia Broadcasting Company, which was taken in early October. Both sets of data are from pre-election surveys, so they miss switchers and include many who were still undecided when interviewed.

The primary indicator of varying attitudes among candidate preference group in the Harris surveys was a battery of items which asked respondents, "Which groups are responsible for trouble in the country?" They were provided with choices, from the federal government to Communists, students, professors, Jews, and others. The relevant responses, differentiated according to some social characteristics and candidate preference, are presented in Table 60.

The findings of the Harris organization clearly distinguish the supporters of the different candidates in 1968 and 1964. On most items, the rank order of opinions goes consistently from right to left, from Wallace to Goldwater to Nixon to Johnson to Humphrey. That is, the Wallace supporters show the most right-wing opinions, while the Humphrey ones are most left. As a group, those who voted for Goldwater in 1964 are somewhat more preservatist than the Nixon supporters in 1968. There is, of course, a considerable overlap. Since none of these items bear on attitudes

Table 60. GROUPS RESPONSIBLE FOR THE TROUBLE IN THE COUNTRY
(Per Cent Responsible)

	Federal Government	Communists	Students	Negroes	Ministers and Priests	Jews	Hippies	Police	Professors	KKK
Total (16,905)	49	76	55	56	25	6	53	14	29	34
1968 Vote										
Wallace (2,589)	75	88	57	71	41	10	62	9	36	21
Nixon (6,436)	54	80	58	61	27	5	54	11	33	34
Humphrey (6,476)	34	68	51	46	28	5	49	19	25	41
1964 Vote										
Johnson (8,838)	40	75	55	52	20	5	52	14	25	38
Goldwater (4,716)	64	81	58	64	35	8	57	9	42	30
1968 Vote South										
Wallace (1,321)	79	90	54	73	43	9	67	8	34	16
Nixon (867)	60	84	51	69	36	7	60	12	37	30
Humphrey (1,297)	35	64	51	40	17	8	51	21	22	40
1968 Vote Non-South										
Wallace (1,268)	71	86	61	70	38	12	54	9	37	27
Nixon (5,569)	54	79	59	60	25	4	57	11	32	35
Humphrey (5,179)	34	68	52	48	18	5	53	18	25	41

SOURCE: Table constructed from data presented in a "Memorandum" to the American Jewish Committee from Louis Harris and Associates dealing with a "Survey on groups 'responsible' for 'trouble' in the country." We are extremely grateful to Mrs. Lucy Davidowicz of the American Jewish Committee for permission to use these analyses.
NOTE: Figures in parentheses show total number of respondents.

toward the welfare state, what they attest to is the disdain which rightists feel toward groups identified with social changes they dislike.

The Wallace supporters differ most from the population as a whole with respect to their feelings toward the federal government, Negroes, the Ku Klux Klan, and—most surprisingly—"ministers and priests." Although Wallace himself did not devote much attention to attacking the liberal clergy, his followers seemingly were more bothered by their activities than by those of professors. Although the electorate as a whole were inclined to see "students" as a major source of trouble, Wallace backers hardly differed from the supporters of the two other candidates in their feelings. Insofar as we can make any judgments from these results, they confirm the impression that Wallace appealed strongly to people who identified their distress with changes in race relations, with federal interference, and with changes in religious morality. It is of interest that the Wallace supporters in the South and those in the non-South project about the same pattern. The southern differential is very slight with respect to blaming Negroes, still slight but higher with respect to blaming clergymen, higher yet with respect to blaming the federal government. In keeping with our hypotheses, the preservatist pattern of the South as a region is involved with a greater cultural package than simply the thrust of the blacks.

The ORC–CBS survey was available for secondary analysis and permitted some direct elaborations of the impact of ideological preferences on voter choice. It included a few questions dealing with general political and social attitudes. These questions allowed an analysis of the issue appeal of the three candidates, as well as a rudimentary analysis of some "issue publics" and their electoral behavior. In this case the issue-public configuration was made around two axes: orientation to government welfare activity and orientation to race relations.

The welfare question was: "Would you favor more government programs to help the poor in things like medical care, education, or housing, or would you prefer the government do less of this?"

The question which has been frequently used to uncover white hostility to Negro civil rights demands was: "Do you think that Negroes in this country are making too much progress or not enough progress in getting the things they want?"

The results of the simple cross tabulation of response to these two items to 1968 candidate preference among white voters as of early October are shown in Tables 61 and 62.

The findings in these two tables indicate that Wallace supporters differed from both Humphrey and Nixon supporters on the question of race relations. They were more conservative than the Humphrey supporters on the question of welfare, but more Wallace backers than Nixon voters favored

Table 61.   ATTITUDES TOWARD GOVERNMENT WELFARE ACTIVITY BY 1968 CANDIDATE
PREFERENCE, WHITES ONLY

	Humphrey	Nixon	Wallace	Total Per Cent	Number
Need more programs	67 %	40 %	46 %	49	(904)
Maintain existing ones	16	18	19	18	(325)
Need fewer programs	13	37	32	29	(527)
No opinion	5	5	4	5	(82)
Total	30	50	20		(1,838)
Number	(553)	(916)	(369)		

NOTE: Columns may not add up to 100 per cent due to rounding.
We are grateful to the Columbia Broadcasting Company and the Opinion Research
Corporation for permission to analyze these data.

Table 62.   ATTITUDES TOWARD NEGROES AS A POLITICAL GROUP
BY 1968 CANDIDATE PREFERENCE

	Humphrey	Nixon	Wallace	Total Per Cent	Number
Negro progress not fast enough	35 %	34 %	15 %	30	(607)
About right	30	32	29	31	(618)
Too fast	24	22	44	27	(536)
No opinion	12	12	11	12	(233)
Total	30	50	20		(1,994)
Number	(590)	(999)	(405)		

NOTE: Columns may not add up to 100 per cent due to rounding.

government welfare measures. The relationship between candidate preference and attitudes toward welfare was not as strong as might have been
expected. More supporters of each candidate supported more welfare programs than thought we needed fewer ones. Humphrey, as the candidate of
the New Deal–Fair Deal–Great Society party, was obviously identified with
the welfare state. Richard Nixon, however, sought very deliberately to avoid
Goldwater's mistake of being perceived as an opponent of welfare and indicated his acceptance and endorsement of many of these programs. We
have previously noted George Wallace's emphasis on the retention and extension of many welfare measures. Hence, the lack of larger differences
among supporters of the three candidates on this issue is not surprising.
Nor is it surprising that the Wallace electorate differed sharply from those
of Nixon and Humphrey with respect to race relations. It is much more
curious that over half of the Wallace supporters were *not* willing to say

that Negro progress was "too fast." Presumably, many who are disturbed by integration may still feel that as a group Negroes are underprivileged and favor their moving ahead.

What is suggested again is the desimplification of race relations as a standard concern of the Wallacite backlash: for most, it was not dislike of the Negro which moved them, not the progress of the Negro which bothered them, as much as what was happening to *them* in the course of that progress. The distinction is, as always, critical to an understanding of the nature of nativist bigotry.

The tables above, of course, are given for the nation as a whole. The way in which supporters of the three candidates varied when such factors as region, education, and class are controlled is presented in Tables 63 and 64.

The data presented in Table 63 indicate that the South as a whole is more conservative with respect to the extension of the welfare state than the rest of the country. Southern supporters of Nixon and of Humphrey are clearly less favorable to government welfare than northern backers of the same candidates. In general, the differences with respect to this issue for Wallace supporters are less linked to regionalism. It is interesting to note that the most privileged of Wallace supporters, and of Nixon voters in the

Table 63. PROPORTION WITH FAVORABLE ATTITUDES TOWARD GOVERNMENT WELFARE ACTIVITY BY 1968 CANDIDATE PREFERENCE WITH CONTROLS FOR REGION, OCCUPATION, EDUCATION, AND POLITICAL PARTY*

	Humphrey		Nixon		Wallace	
	Per Cent	Number	Per Cent	Number	Per Cent	Number
Non-South nonmanual	68	(269)	35	(449)	43	(68)
Non-South manual	68	(173)	48	(267)	50	(111)
South nonmanual	51	(37)	29	(75)	37	(60)
South manual	56	(18)	41	(39)	51	(75)
Non-South college[a]	71	(116)	33	(294)	37	(33)
Non-South high school[b]	68	(375)	45	(221)	48	(175)
South college	52	(21)	19	(36)	14	(28)
South high school	50	(38)	43	(91)	53	(130)
Democratic	68	(444)	51	(146)	48	(181)
Independent	64	(80)	46	(200)	45	(113)
Republican	63	(19)	33	(542)	39	(54)

* The figures in each cell represent the percentage of respondents in each category to agree that more government welfare programs were needed; the numbers in parentheses represent the total number of cases from which the percentages shown were calculated.
  [a] "College" indicates respondents with at least some college experience.
  [b] "High school" indicates respondents with educational attainments up to and including a high-school diploma.

Table 64.   PROPORTION WITH FAVORABLE ATTITUDES TOWARD NEGROES AS A POLITICAL
GROUP BY 1968 CANDIDATE PREFERENCE WITH CONTROLS FOR REGION,
OCCUPATION, EDUCATION, AND POLITICAL PARTY*

	Humphrey		Nixon		Wallace	
	Per Cent	Num- ber	Per Cent	Num- ber	Per Cent	Num- ber
Non-South nonmanual	42	(291)	37	(504)	25	(72)
Non-South manual	34	(183)	33	(286)	17	(128)
South nonmanual	28	(39)	29	(79)	9	(67)
South manual	15	(20)	17	(42)	9	(79)
Non-South college	64	(126)	47	(332)	38	(34)
Non-South high school	28	(398)	29	(527)	17	(198)
South college	38	(24)	27	(37)	16	(32)
South high school	15	(39)	21	(97)	7	(138)
Democratic	33	(423)	30	(158)	14	(202)
Independent	47	(86)	40	(222)	17	(120)
Republican	50	(20)	32	(587)	17	(59)

* The figures in each cell represent the percentage of respondents in each category to feel that the progress experienced recently by the Negro people ought to be speeded up; the numbers in parentheses represent the total number of cases from which the percentages shown were calculated.

South, are by far the least enthusiastic for welfare. Seemingly "upper-class" southern conservatives are much more consistent ideologically than their compeers in the rest of the country.

Race-connected attitudes, of course are, much more associated with regional differences than are welfare ones. In each case, southern supporters of the three candidates are less favorable to Negro progress than those elsewhere, controlling for occupational class and education. In both regions, the manual workers and the less educated are less favorable to Negro progress than the nonmanuals and those who attended college. The range is quite great. Only 7 per cent of Wallace's southern backers who did not go to college favored more rapid progress for blacks, as contrasted to 64 per cent among Humphrey voters in the North who attended college.

Because of the ambiguities in the single race relations question used so far, patterns of response were further checked with three items from the interview schedule which seemed to test the respondent's feeling toward Negroes as fit partners for social intercourse of varying degrees of intimacy. From the vantage point that has been developed, these responses might be seen as measuring the cultural shock involved in this aspect of change. Those interviewed were asked to reply whether or not they "personally approved" of (1) a Negro family moving next door; (2) busing Negro school children from crowded, big-city schools to schools in outlying neighborhoods, towns, or suburbs; (3) being in a club or organization that admits Negroes. These items were found to be scalable by Guttman procedures yielding a scale of "Negrophobia" on which 88 per cent of the voter sample could be placed. Table 65 reports the relationship between Negrophobia and 1968 Presidential voting.

Anti-Negro responses were positively related to preference for the Alabamian, and, as before, the relationship held true for all occupational, educational, regional, and partisan groups. The new piece of evidence uncovered by Table 65 is the fact that to some degree Nixon voters also proved to be more Negrophobic than Humphrey enthusiasts. This recalls a similar pattern manifested by some sample subgroups reported on Table 64, where upper-status Nixonites—especially the college-educated of both regions—appeared a good deal less likely to propose a quickening of the pace of Negro progress than similarly situated Humphreyites. It would appear that the members of upper-status groups laboring under racial tensions were more likely to cast a Republican ballot while racially upset workingmen were more disposed to vote for George Wallace.

Finally, there is some evidence that Wallacite sympathies are associated with opposition toward "protest demonstrations."
The exact wording of the question was as follows: "How do you feel about marches or demonstration by various groups to call public attention to their cause or complaints? On the whole, do you approve or disapprove of such demonstrations?"

It is difficult, of course, to estimate what kind of demonstration respondents had in mind when answering this question. The question itself seemingly inquires about legal demonstrations, which do not involve disruptive illegal activities. Since southerners were more likely to think of such demonstrations in the context of black civil rights protest, the data in Table 66 are presented for nonsoutherners only. The large majority of respondents, North as well as South, stated that they disapproved of protest marches or

Table 65.   NEGROPHOBIA SCALE BY 1968 CANDIDATE PREFERENCE
(Per Cent)

	Humphrey	Nixon	Wallace	Total	Number
High I	10	10	35	15	(209)
II	12	18	23	17	(232)
III	37	43	26	38	(510)
Low IV	41	30	16	30	(401)
Total	31	53	16		(1,352)
Number	(393)	(675)	(284)		

NOTE: Columns may not add up to 100 per cent due to rounding.

Table 66.   NEGATIVE ATTITUDES TOWARD PROTEST DEMONSTRATIONS BY 1968
CANDIDATE PREFERENCE WITH A CONTROL FOR EDUCATION
(SOUTHERN RESPONDENTS EXCLUDED)*

	Humphrey		Nixon		Wallace	
	Per Cent	Num-ber	Per Cent	Num-ber	Per Cent	Num-ber
With some college	43	(126)	66	(332)	79	(34)
High school or less	79	(398)	83	(527)	91	(198)

* The figures in each cell represent the percentage of respondents in each category who said they tended to disapprove of protest demonstrations; the numbers in parentheses represent the total number of cases from which the percentages were calculated.

demonstrations. As most previous studies of attitudes toward civil liberties have shown, the better educated a person, the more likely he is to support civil liberties for unpopular minorities, or in this specific case, marches or demonstrations. Within each educational stratum, however, Wallace voters were more likely to oppose such activities, while Humphrey backers were most liberal.

Another way of undertaking to investigate the social and political attitudes which may underlie voting in any particular election is to locate voters who are particularly concerned with a certain political issue and then determine for whom they tended to cast their ballots. The schedule used by ORC in the survey permitted the isolation of such "special interest publics." The interviewer handed each respondent a deck of twenty-six cards, each stamped with a different political issue, such as "rising cost of living," "stricter gun control," "better housing for Negroes." The issues represented ran the full gamut of contemporary American political and social controversy. Then each respondent was instructed to take the four or five cards which represented the four or five problems he most wanted to see on the next President's order of priorities. In this way each respondent chose membership in four or five different issue publics. Table 67 shows the association of membership in different issue publics and 1968 Presidential vote.

The degree of involvement of the three candidate preference groups is shown for eighteen of the original twenty-five domestic issues. Both "operational" and statistical significance were used as a criteria for selection. The involvement levels of the candidate preference groups were considered differentiated in an "operationally" significant way if the involvement level of one voter group for a particular issue was at least 5 per cent greater or less than that of either of the other two groups. Using the Chi Square Test, statistical significance was considered achieved if the involvement pattern for an issue had less than a .05 probability of chance occurrence. The issue concerns on Table 69 have been sorted roughly into three types:

those which distinguished Wallace's supporters from both Humphrey and Nixon leaners; those which distinguished Humphrey voters from Wallacites and Nixonites; and those which distinguished Nixon voters from Wallace and Humphrey supporters.

The results are very clear and corroborate the previous data. Wallace sympathizers were singular in their inordinate concern over issues which had clear racial components. Many more tended to give priority to the question of riot control and abuse of federal welfare programs and to withhold interest from the question of improving housing for Negroes or ending racial discrimination in hiring. The issue concerns which Wallacites and Nixonites tended to have in approximately equal proportions were more generally preservatist, involving the theme of declining social order (for example, crime and violence or laxity in law enforcement), or were antistatist, involving a concern about federal spending. Thus those with preferences for the American Independent candidate showed themselves both more anti-Negro and fiscally conservative. So far, it might be concluded

Table 67. MEMBERSHIP IN ISSUE PUBLICS AND 1968 CANDIDATE PREFERENCE*

	Humphrey	Nixon	Wallace	Total
Riots[a]	29 %	28 %	38 %	30 %
Stricter gun control	15	9	5	10
Equal job opportunities for Negroes	15	8	4	9
Abuse of government welfare programs	18	21	28	21
Better housing for Negroes	7	5	2	5
Rising living cost	27	34	35	32
Dissatisfactions of youth	12	7	6	8
Help for the aged	23	12	13	16
Educational opportunities	20	15	14	16
Crime and violence	35	43	46	42
Federal government spending	14	32	30	26
High taxes	25	30	32	29
Concentration of power in Washington	3	10	13	8
Laxity in law enforcement	12	18	19	16
Help for the poor	22	8	13	13
Power of labor unions	5	9	4	7
Gold drain and devaluation of the dollar	6	13	6	10
Unemployment	11	6	9	9
Total	30	50	20	
Number	(583)	(988)	(397)	(1,968)

* The figures in each cell represent the percentages of Humphreyites, Nixonites, Wallacites, or the total sample which listed a particular issue as a Presidential priority.
[a] Exact wording.

that the Alabamian drew most of his strength from the authoritarian right and traditional ultraright groups. However, on some issues of social welfare *policy* (as opposed to *spending*) Wallace voters seemed to resemble the involvement of Humphrey balloters, though always to a lesser degree. The Wallace bloc was *more* concerned about the needs of the poor and the unemployed and *less* concerned about the power of labor unions than Nixonites.

Nixon voters were also concerned about race, but to a lesser degree, and were more consistently conservative regarding socioeconomic and fiscal issues. Humphrey voters, in every case, revealed the most liberal postures on both civil rights and economic questions.

The 1968 election study conducted by the Survey Research Center of the University of Michigan, referred to earlier, explored the relationship between issue positions and candidate choice in depth. Significantly, they report that as contrasted to the two major party candidates, the Wallace candidacy was much more "reacted to by the public as an issue candidacy."

For example, about half of the reasons volunteered by our respondents for favorable feelings toward Wallace had to do with the positions he was taking on current issues; only a little more than a quarter of the reactions supporting either of the two conventional candidates were cast in this mode. . . . Among the *whites* who voted for one of the two major candidates, only 10% favored continued segregation rather than desegregation or "something in between"; among Wallace voters, all of whom were white, almost 40% wanted segregation. . . . Or again, 36% of white voters for the conventional parties felt that we should "take a stronger stand (in Vietnam) even if it means invading North Vietnam. Among Wallace voters, the figure was 67%. . . ."

. . . One measure of ideological location which we use involves the respondent in rating the terms "liberal" and "conservative". . . . [I]n both political regions of the country Wallace voters were more favorable to the "liberal" label than Nixon voters! . . .

. . . [I]n the area of social welfare measures such as medicare and full employment guarantees . . . Wallace voters were significantly more "liberal" than Nixon voters, and almott matched the liberalism of Humphrey voters.[5]

One further attempt was made using the ORC–CBS data to clarify the heterogeneity of the electorate along the axes that have emerged. Four "issue" publics were posed, foreshadowing the more elaborate exploration of typologies to be developed in the next chapter. The axis of race relations, using the question about Negro progress, was for this purpose taken as measurement of "tolerance-intolerance." The ambiguity of the term "tolerance" fits the ambiguity of the question itself; but whatever its full meaning, the race relations question has been clearly revealed to be of a different dimension than that of partiality to government welfare programs. The axis of concern with government welfare was taken as a meaure of "liberalism-conservatism," the liberal being the welfare statist, the conservative being the antistatist. Four issue publics then became possible, on the basis of the two key questions: Tolerant Liberals, Intolerant Liberals, Tolerant Conservatives, and Intolerant Conservatives. The relationship between the ideology paradigm and the 1968 Presidential preference is presented in Table 68. Actually, a ninefold table was produced, and the four extreme boxes were those used to provide the clues to the relationship between these four issue publics and electoral behavior.

Table 68.   BIDIMENSIONAL IDEOLOGY BY 1968 CANDIDATE PREFERENCE

| | | Federal Welfare Programs | | |
		Need More	Keep as Now	Need Fewer
Tolerant Liberals	*Negro Progress* Should Be Faster	H[a]:48 N[b]:44 W[c]: 8	H:21 N:61 W:18	H:16 N:75 W: 9 } Tolerant Conservatives
	Number	(314)	(62)	(152)
	Keep Same Rate	H:39 N:41 W:20	H:30 N:52 W:18	H:11 N:69 W:19
	Number	(226)	(143)	(175)
Intolerant Liberals	Should Be Slower	H:33 N:35 W:32	H:31 N:41 W:28	H:12 N:52 W:35 } Intolerant Conservatives
	Number	(254)	(88)	(147)

[a] Per cent in cell for Humphrey.
[b] Per cent in cell for Nixon.
[c] Per cent in cell for Wallace.

As expected, Humphrey did best among the Tolerant Liberals, only fairly well among the Intolerant Liberals, and very poorly with the Tolerant Conservatives and Intolerant Conservatives. Nixon took three-quarters of the Tolerant Conservatives and won the support of over half of the Intolerant Conservatives. The Republican candidate lured a fair proportion of the sample's Tolerant Liberals and, although he did poorest among them, even managed to pick up a third of the Intolerant Liberals. George Wallace scored highest among the Intolerants, both Liberal and Conservative, but failed substantially among groups not agitated over the race issue. Looking at the manner from a slightly different angle, 32 per cent of Humphrey's support came from the Tolerant Liberals, 18 per cent from the Intolerant Liberals, and only 4 per cent and 5 per cent from Conservatives, Intolerant and Tolerant. These percentages do not sum to 100 per cent because here we are giving mention to the four polar types only. Nixon's voter coalition is more evenly distributed among Liberals, Tolerant (18 per cent) and Intolerant (11 per cent), and Conservatives, Tolerant (10 per cent) and Intolerant (13 per cent). Wallace achieved a marriage between the Intolerant Liberals (26 per cent) and Intolerant Conservatives (17 per cent) with the former predominating; but his following contained only a smattering of Tolerant Liberals (8 per cent) and Conservatives (4 per cent). In other words, though Nixon attracted over half of the Intolerants, only Wallace's following was built almost entirely on their support. And though the Intolerant Liberals split evenly three ways, only Wallace depended on them as the cornerstone of his support.

Of course, if the ideological paradigm explained all the variation in the 1968 Presidential vote, logic would have Humphrey, the pro-civil rights, pro-welfare candidate, receiving 100 per cent of the Tolerant Liberal vote; Nixon, the closest to a pro-civil rights, anti-welfare candidate, taking 100 per cent of the Tolerant Conservative vote; Wallace the Intolerant Liberal, corraling all of that sentiment, with the vote of the unrepresented ultra-right Intolerant Conservative sector split evenly between Wallace and Nixon. Many other modifying factors were at work on the American electorate besides its ideological distribution; we will discuss two which appeared particularly capable of causing individual voters to deviate from their basic political orientations: social status and party identification.[6]

Tables 69 and 70 show the effects on ideology's connection with the 1968 vote when controls for region, occupational group, and party identification are introduced. These tables use education and occupational class as indicators of status. Since the number of cases available for analysis is reduced to very few when four items are being analyzed, looking at both indicators of status provides a bit more leeway in finding boxes with enough cases for analysis. Although the numbers, in any case, are frequently much too small for reliable estimates, the differences which correspond to the expected result are often so large as to lend weight to the hypothesis that these four issue publics did strongly affect candidate choice.

The salience of ideology in the 1968 election seems to have been a genuine independent factor, and not the product of the distributions of the different social groups in the ideological categories. Both attitudes related to welfare and race contributed to Wallace's support, North and South, and among lower- and higher-status groups. Although at the time of the ORC survey, Wallace had the support of only 7 per cent outside the South, he was backed by 40 per cent of the manual workers who were Tolerant Conservatives in that part of the country; his southern strength in the survey was 34 per cent, but 73 per cent of the southern Intolerant Conservative

Table 69. BIDIMENSIONAL IDEOLOGY BY 1968 CANDIDATE PREFERENCE WITH CONTROLS FOR EDUCATION AND REGION

Non-South

	College			High School or Less		
Tolerant Liberals (119) / (171)	H:50	N:46	W: 4	H:47	N:43	W: 9
Intolerant Liberals (20) / (172)	H:30	N:55	W:15	H:39	N:38	W:23
Tolerant Conservatives (67) / (70)	H:10	N:82	W: 8	H:21	N:67	W:11
Intolerant Conservatives (27) / (79)	H:—	N:89	W:11	H:17	N:51	W:33

South

	College			High School		
Tolerant Liberals (9) / (18)	H:*	N:*	W:*	H:22	N:56	W:22
Intolerant Liberals (8) / (59)	H:13	N:19	W:69	H:17	N:22	W:61
Tolerant Conservatives (7) / (10)	H:*	N:*	W:*	H:*	N:*	W:*
Intolerant Conservatives (16) / (26)	H:13	N:19	W:69	H:12	N:35	W:54

NOTE: Figures in parentheses show total number of respondents.
* Too few cases.

Table 70. BIDIMENSIONAL IDEOLOGY BY 1968 CANDIDATE PREFERENCE WITH CONTROLS FOR OCCUPATION AND REGION

	Non-South		South	
	Nonmanual	Manual	Nonmanual	Manual
Tolerant Liberals	H:53 N:42 W: 5 (161)	H:45 N:44 W:10 (108)	H:35 N:47 W:18 (17)	H:* N:* W:* (8)
Tolerant Conservatives	H:17 N:78 W: 6 (85)	H:18 N:71 W:11 (38)	H:17 N:83 W:— (12)	H:* N:* W:* (4)
Intolerant Liberals	H:47 N:41 W:12 (78)	H:30 N:37 W:33 (91)	H:35 N:30 W:45 (20)	H:17 N:22 W:61 (36)
Intolerant Conservatives	H:13 N:74 W:13 (53)	H:13 N:48 W:40 (40)	H:18 N:32 W:50 (22)	H: 7 N:20 W:73 (15)

NOTE: Figures in parentheses show total number of respondents.
* Too few cases.

manual workers were for him. Conversely, his backing among middle-class northern Tolerant Liberals was 5 per cent, while he took 18 per cent of the vote among nonmanuals in that ideological category in the South. In general, Richard Nixon was able to secure the bulk of the conservative vote in all upper-status categories, with the exception of the southern Intolerants. Privileged southerners who were Intolerant Conservatives voted for Wallace, although their northern ideological compeers opted for Nixon. Wallace seemingly cost Nixon many votes among the lower-strata Intolerant Conservatives in both sections of the country.

The evidence of the relationship of ideological groupings to Wallace support suggests that Wallace's major failing in winning the fidelity of groups who agreed with him was among northern middle-class voters. The Intolerants among them stayed with Richard Nixon and the Republican party. Presumably as a relatively aware group politically, they may have been sensitive to the argument that Wallace had no chance to be elected, that a vote for him in the North would help Hubert Humphrey. Wallace, of course, also had untapped strength among lower-strata voters in the North, even though a considerable minority of the Intolerants among them were disposed to vote for him in October.

These data point up the dilemma facing a racist third-party candidate in becoming a viable alternative to the two major parties. The intolerant tend to be concentrated among the underprivileged and the undereducated, but these groups are also disproportionately favorable to welfare measures. To appeal to them on such issues means antagonizing the Conservative Intolerants, who are relatively stronger among the middle class than in the working class. Hence an appeal to the large group of the economically liberal working-class Intolerants may lose the middle-class conservative ones. This is, in effect, what did happen in 1968.

It may also be argued that the effort of Wallace's opponents to identify him as a "racist" seriously hurt him, even among voters who themselves had negative feelings about Negroes. Gunnar Myrdal suggested in the early forties that most Americans preferred to believe that they believe in the American creed of equality, regardless of their actual practices with respect to blacks. He argued that the cause of Negro equality could be furthered by sensitizing whites to the discrepancies between their valuations and actions.[7] In this election, it may be that a reverse pattern of bringing valuations and beliefs into line occurred. That is, as the charges that Wallace is racist hit home, many who agreed with him on specific issues may have turned against him, perceiving him as a racist. Such a possibility is indicated by the results of a Harris survey presented earlier which found that 41 per cent of a national sample agreed in mid-September with the statement that Wallace is a racist, while 40 per cent disagreed and 19 per cent said they were not sure. Among the 60 per cent who indicated they agreed with the statement or were not sure, Wallace secured only 4 per cent of the vote. Conversely, however, he was the preferred candidate of 44 per cent of those who denied that he was a racist.[8] Subsequent surveys reported that the proportion who regarded Wallace as a "racist" increased, a phenomenon which may help to explain his inability to expand or retain his following.

The Future of the Wallace Movement

As this book goes to press, it is still too early to anticipate the future role of the American Independent party. As we have noted, the party brought together almost every right-wing extreme group in the country and undoubtedly also recruited many new activists for the extreme right. Many of the state parties now have a formal legal status as a recognized political party who may nominate candidates for local and state office. Many have set up regular party structures and have announced that they intend to nominate candidates during the next few years in an effort to build the party. George Wallace himself has sent out a clear signal that he has plans for the future. He began publishing the *George Wallace Newsletter* as a monthly publication. The old mailing address for Wallace activities had been Box 1968, Montgomery, Alabama. It is now Box 1972. The *Newsletter* was sent initially to a mailing list of over one million names which had been assembled during the election.

The effort to maintain and build the party, however, faces the perennial problem of ideological extremist movements, splits among its supporters. During the 1968 campaign, sharp public divisions occurred in a number of states, often revolving around the fact that complete control over the finances and conduct of the party's work was kept in the hands of coordinators directly appointed by Wallace and responsible to the national headquarters in Montgomery. In a number of states, two separate organizations existed, both of which endorsed the Wallace candidacy while attacking each other. Since the 1968 election, two competing national organizations have been created.

Both groups denounce each other as extremist. The group which is directly linked to Wallace has had two national conventions, the first in Dallas in early February 1969, which was attended by 250 delegates from forty-four states and initially set up a group known as The Association of George C. Wallace Voters. The Dallas meeting was attended by a number of top Wallace aids, including Robert Walters, who represents Wallace in California; Tom Turnipseed, a major figure in the Wallace presidential effort since it started; Dan Smoot, a right-wing radio commentator; and

Kent Courtney, the editor of *The Conservative Journal*.[9] This same group met again on May 3 and 4 in Cincinnati and formally established a new national party to be called the American party. T. Coleman Andrews, of Virginia, long active on the ultra-conservative front, was chosen as chairman of the party. Wallace gave his personal blessing to the new party and its officers. One of his Montgomery aids, James Taylor Hardin, who maintains a national office with twenty employees in Montgomery, indicated that the party would have a considerable degree of "central control."[10]

This Wallace-controlled movement continues his antielitist emphasis. A description of its Dallas conference in one of the party's major organs mentions as a primary concern of the delegates "the monopolistic control of chain newspapers." They favored government action to break up chains, and common ownership of newspapers, radio, and television stations. Such action was advocated as a logical extension of antitrust laws which are designed to eliminate big-business empires.[11]

The competing national group met in Louisville on February 22, 1969, and established a new national conservative party to be made up of largely autonomous state parties. As if to emphasize the extent to which it fostered local control, this organization called itself "The National Committee of the Autonomous State Parties, known as the American Independent Party, American Party, Independent Party, Conservative Party, Constitutional Party."[12] This group or constellation of groups was united in its opposition to domination by Wallace and his Montgomery aides. Although the former candidate received compliments at the convention, the delegates were much more concerned with building a movement that was not limited to his supporters in 1968. The national chairman of the group, William K. Shearer, of California, editor of the *California Statesman*, had already broken with Wallace during the campaign on the issue of autonomy. At the Louisville convention he said:

> Governor Wallace has not shown any interest in a national party apart from a personal party. A candidate properly springs from the party and not the party from the candidate. The party should not be candidate-directed. While we have great respect for Mr. Wallace, we do not think there should be a candidate-directed situation. We want our party to survive regardless of what Mr. Wallace does.[13]

The Shearer group also appears to be more conservative on economic issues than the Wallace-dominated one. During their convention, Wallace was criticized for being "too liberal" for his advocacy during the campaign of extended social security and farm parity prices. By the beginning of 1970, Shearer was publishing articles exposing the efforts of Wallace's representatives to control all local campaigns during 1968, to eliminate conservatives from influence in the state organizations, and to force a "Socialist Platform" on the party. The Andrews'-chaired party is denounced as a deliberate effort to lead "true Conservatives . . . down the primrose path into supporting a Socialist deceit."[14]

The leaders of each faction denounce the other as containing extremists. Thus Robert Walters attacked Shearer's group as composed of "radicals and opportunists"[15] and as having "a pretty high nut content." Shearer, on the other hand, has referred to the fact that he finds many in the Wallace-dominated party not "too savory."[16]

The first issue of a monthly national organ of the (Andrews) American party, *Eagle*, published in November 1969, dedicated its lead editorial to the fight against extremism among the Wallace supporters.

There is no place for extremism in the leadership of the American Party. It is our desire to ferret out the peddlers of this extremism and expose them. . . . Extremists are often sick or emotionally disturbed. . . . They never represent the majority of constructive new party movements.[17]

The publications of the competing groups indicate that each is supported by viable segments of the 1968 party. The Shearer National Committee, however, is clearly much weaker financially, since the Wallace national campaign retained a considerable sum from the 1968 campaign for future activities. The competition for support, however, does give each group an immediate function, and the state organizations affiliated to each appear to have been busy holding state and local conventions designed to win over those who were involved in the Presidential campaign.

It is difficult to tell how much support the American party retains. Early in 1969, the party ran a candidate in a special election for Congress in Tennessee's Eighth District. Wallace ran first in this district in the Presidential race, but the AIP congressional candidate, William Davis, was a bad second to the victorious Democrat. The AIP secured 16,319 votes (25 per cent) in the congressional race, as contrasted to 32,666 for the Democrat and 15,604 for the Republican. Wallace himself took an active part in the campaign, making speeches for Davis, but he was clearly unable to transfer his Presidential support to his follower.[18] While Davis' showing in Tennessee was fairly respectable, another AIP by-election candidate, Victor Cherven, who ran for the state senate in Contra Costa County in California in late March, secured only 329 votes out of 146,409 votes cast. Cherven even ran behind two other minority party nominees.[19] In mid-June, in a by-election for a seat in the California assembly from Monterey, an AIP candidate, Alton F. Osborn, also secured an insignificant vote, 188 out of 46,602.[20] The first effort to contest a congressional seat outside the South failed abysmally, when an American party candidate in a Montana by-election secured half of one per cent of the vote, 509 out of 88,867 ballots on June 25.[21]

Election Day, November 4, 1969, produced the best evidence of the inability of the Wallace followers to develop viable local parties. In Virginia, a state in which Wallace received 322,203 votes or 23.6 per cent in 1968, both rightist parties ran candidates for Governor. Dr. William Pennington, the gubernatorial nominee of the Wallace–Andrews American Independent party, obtained 7,059 votes, or .8 per cent of the total. Beverly McDowell, who ran on the Conservative Party ticket of the Shearer segment of the movement, did slightly better, with 9,821 votes, or 1.1 per cent of the electorate.[22] Pennington's and McDowell's combined total in 1969 only equaled 5 per cent of Wallace's vote in Virginia, a year earlier.

But if Wallace's strength cannot be transferred to local and state candidates, most of it still remained with him on the level of national politics during 1969. The Gallup poll which chronicled his rise in popularity through 1967 and 1968, continued to examine his possible strength in a future Presidential contest. In three national surveys in April, June, and September, samples of the electorate were asked how they would vote in a contest among Richard Nixon as the Republican, Edward Kennedy as the Democrat, and George Wallace as a third party candidate. Nixon gained from both parties, as compared with the 43 per cent which he received in the 1968 election. His support remained consistently high, 52 per cent in April, 52 in July, and 53 in September. Kennedy's backing fluctuated more—33, 36, and 31, as contrasted with the 43 per cent which Hubert Humphrey had secured. Wallace also dropped, securing 10, 9, and 10 per cent in the same three polls. Early in 1970, in February, Gallup analyzed the strength of four different potential Democratic nominees, Humphrey, Muskie, Kennedy, and McCarthy against Nixon and Wallace. Wallace secured from 11 to 13 per cent, while Nixon obtained around 50 per cent. Each Democrat had about one-third, except for Senator McCarthy who trailed badly with 24 per cent. Wallace running against Nixon and Humphrey won "30 per cent . . . in the South and 7 per cent outside the South." Wallace's social base remained comparable to that which backed him in the election. "The pattern of support for Wallace in today's experimental test election compares closely with his election profile. The core of the ex-Alabama governor's appeal is with the working man and with persons who have had relatively little formal education."[23]

The fears expressed by many that Wallace would seek to convert his following into an extraparliamentary opposition, which sought to influence the government and terrorize opponents by taking to the streets—fears based on statements which Wallace himself made during the campaign—have thus far proved to be unwarranted. Wallace seems largely concerned with maintaining his electoral base for a possible new Presidential campaign in 1972. The effort to continue control of the party from Montgomery is seemingly dedicated to this end.

The existence of local electoral parties, even those willing to follow Wallace's lead completely, poses another problem for him. His electoral following is clearly much greater than can be mobilized behind the local unknown candidates of the American party. To maintain the party organizations, they must nominate men for various offices. Yet should such people secure tiny votes, as is likely in most parts of the country, Wallace may find his image as a mass leader severely injured. He seemingly recognizes this, and though concerned with keeping control over the party organization, he has also stressed the difference between the "movement" and the "party," describing the two as "separate entities" which agree on "purposes and aims." His emphasis is clear: "The *movement* will be here in 1972. The *movement* is solvent and it will be active."[24]

The disastrous results of the by-elections may have reinforced Wallace's propensity to avoid supporting efforts to turn his "movement" into a minor third party. Speaking at the Virginia convention of the American party in mid-July of 1969, he said "A new party ought to go very slow. It ought to crawl before it walks. It ought to nominate a candidate only if he has a chance to be elected."[25] In Tulsa, he again warned his followers to move slowly, if at all, in nominating congressional and local candidates. He argued that if he were elected President in the future he "wouldn't have any trouble getting support from Congress, because most of its [major party] members were for the things he's for."[26]

One aspect of the nonparty "movement" may be the reported expansion of the Citizens Councils of America, whose national headquarters is in Jackson, Mississippi. Its administrator, William J. Simmons, helped direct Wallace's Presidential campaign in Mississippi, where he received 65 per cent of the vote. In June 1969 Simmons said: "There has been no erosion in Wallace strength. Wallace articulates the hopes and views of over 99 per cent of our members. This state is not enchanted with Nixon, and Wallace sentiment is very strong indeed." Simmons reported that the Council, mainly interested in the maintenance of segregation in the schools, had expanded "as a result of backlash generated by campus riots and better grassroots organizational work."[27] The impetus of the Wallace campaign had obviously helped. The Citizens Councils remained one reservoir of future organizational strength for Wallace.

Wallace has attempted to maintain his ties to other groups who backed him in 1968. The principal campaign of the Birch Society during 1969 has been against sex education and pornography. Wallace has also devoted a considerable part of his talks during the year to the subject.[28] He "also embraced publicly, for the first time, the ultraconservative Christian Crusade" of Billy James Hargis by attending its annual convention.[29]

In his speeches and printed literature Wallace has retained the same combination of preservatist moralism and populist economic issues which characterized his Presidential campaign. On one hand, he continued to emphasize the issues of "law and order," "campus radicalism," "military failures in Vietnam," and "the need for local control of schools." On the other hand, speaking in Tulsa, one of the principal centers of the oil industry, he called for tax reform which would benefit the little man, while saying that "the 27½ per cent oil depletion allowance ought to be looked into."[30] He argued that we must "shift the burden to the upper-class millionaires, billionaires, and tax-exempt foundations."[31]

But some indication of the problem which Wallace faces from supporters who seek to build an extremist movement, rather than an electoral organization for one man's candidacy, can be seen in the activities of an autonomous youth organization, the National Youth Alliance, formed by those active in Youth for Wallace. As of May 1969, the NYA claimed 3,000 dues-paying members recruited from the 15,000-person mailing list of the Youth for Wallace student organizations.[32] This group takes on a more absolutist and militant character than the adult party. It is much more unashamedly racist than any adult pro-Wallace organization. Members wear an "inequality button," which contains the mathematical symbol of inequality. Among other things, the Alliance advocates "white studies" curriculums in colleges and universities. According to national organizer Louis T. Byers, "The purpose of these will be to demonstrate the nature of mankind. The equality myth will be exploded forever."[33] An article describing its objectives by a national vice-president states that it "is an organization with the determination to liquidate the enemies of the American people on the campus and in the community."[34]

The tone of this pro-Wallace youth group sounds closer to that of classic fascism than any statements previously made by Wallace's associates.

The National Youth Alliance is an organization that intends to bury the red front once and for all. . . . The NYA is made up of dedicated self-sacrificing young people who are ready to fight, and die if necessary, for the sacred cause. . . . Now is the time for the Right Front terror to descend on the wretched liberals. In short, the terror of the Left will be met with the greater terror of the Right. . . .

Tar and feathers will be our answer to the pot pusher and these animals will no longer be allowed to prowl and hunt for the minds of American students. . . . A bright future full of conquest lies ahead of us. . . . Soon the NYA will become a household word and the Left will be forced to cower in the sewers underground as they hear the marching steps of the NYA above them.[35]

Louis Byers boasts that the NYA intends to guarantee that its members can crush campus leftists by training them in the "Martial Arts." These include "karate, judo, wrestling, and boxing."[36]

The racism of NYA leaders seemingly includes approval, if not advocacy, of virulent anti-Semitism. Its national headquarters in Washington distributes literature by Francis Parker Yockey, including his book *Imperium,* which defines Jews, Negroes, Indians, and other minorities as "parasites" in the Western world. The five members of its adult advisory board have all been involved in anti-Semitic activities. Two of them, Revilo P. Oliver and Richard B. Cotten, were forced out of the Birch Society because of their overt racist and anti-Semitic views. A third, retired Navy Rear Admiral John Crommelein, ran for President on the anti-Semitic National States Rights party ticket in 1960; while a fourth, retired Marine Lieutenant General Pedro A. Del Valle, is an officer of the Christian Educational Association, which publishes the overtly anti-Semitic paper, *Common Sense.* The fifth member of the board, Austin J. App, former English professor at LaSalle College, is a contributing editor to the anti-Semitic magazine *American Mercury.*

Perhaps most interesting of all is the advocacy by the national chairman of the American party, T. Coleman Andrews, of the Birch Society's version of the international conspiracy, the historic plot of the Illuminati. In a newspaper interview following the establishment of the party in May, he declared openly: "I believe in the conspiratorial theory of History. . . . [The Birch Society has been] responsible, respectable. . . . Recently, the Birch Society has begun to prosper. People are beginning to see that its original theories were right. . . . There is an international conspiracy."[37]

Thus, though George Wallace himself has never publicly stated a belief in the conspiracy of the Illuminati and prefers to talk about the role of Communists, pseudo-intellectuals, and the Council on Foreign Relations, the formal organization of his personally controlled national party is headed by a man who has no such hesitation. On May 26, 1969, "Mr. Wallace formally sanctioned the American party as the political arm of The Movement and said that if he ran for President again it would be under the American party's banners."[38]

However, while the pulls toward conspiracy theory and ideological racism are evident in the background and the logic of the Wallacite movement, its future as a mass movement obviously lies on other foundations. S. M. Miller points out that many had been shocked by "the attraction of George Wallace as a presidential candidate to a large number of union members. . . . Racism appeared to be rampant in the working class."[39] When the vote came, "racism, to the extent that it existed, seemed to have receded before economic concerns."[40] But their disaffection remains. "About half of American families are above the poverty line but below the adequacy level. This group, neither poor nor affluent, composed not only of blue-collar workers but also of many white-collar workers, is hurting and neglected."[41] It is on the members of this group that the Wallacite movement must grow, if it is to grow, not out of their ideological racism as much as out of their general sense of neglected decline.

In seeking viable issues for the early 1970's, Wallace appears preparing to capitalize on reactions to an American "defeat" in Vietnam. As 1969 drew to a close, he devoted increased attention to the war issue, and visited Vietnam and Southeast Asia for three weeks. Before leaving on that trip, he predicted that Vietnam would be a "major issue in the 1972 Presidential elections whether the war was settled or not." He stated: "If South Vietnam were turned over to the Communists, either in effect or in substance, that indeed would be an issue in the 1972 election."[42] On his return from Vietnam, Wallace reported that the Vietnamese and American leaders he met in that country thought "the war is winable." He went on to condemn President Nixon's plan to gradually reduce America's troop commitment and Vietnamize the war. He argued that "there's no way to withdraw combat forces until the enemy is crushed," that "it would take less casualties to win the war than withdraw."[43]

At the same time that Wallace is setting up for a campaign which will argue that the only reason we did not win the war is a civilian stab in the back by the Nixon administration, he has also put himself on record as desiring to withdraw American troops immediately if the administration is not willing to fight to win. In his *Newsletter*, he stated, "should it be that Washington has committed itself to a policy of American withdrawal irrespective of reciprocal action on the part of the enemy, in effect acknowledging defeat for our forces, which is inconceivable, we feel that such withdrawal should be swiftly accomplished so that casualty losses may be held to a minimum."[44]

Whether the George Wallace movement itself will have returned to full or fuller electoral vigor by 1972 depends on a number of factors which have already emerged from an examination of America's right-wing extremist past. Determinative—not just for the Wallace movement but for any extremist movement—will be the larger historical circumstances. Vietnam may provide him with an issue, but even if it does not, the continued disaffection of the white working class and lower middle class may be enough to sustain another campaign. If that disaffection grows, and *at the same time* the pressures of an increasingly disaffected black population grow, the soil will be fertile, of course, for a George Wallace kind of movement. It is the pressure of the emergent black population which provides an essentially *preservatist* thrust to the social and economic strains of the vulnerable whites. Whether the major political parties can absorb these concomitant pressures in some pragmatic fashion, as they have in the past, is another conditional factor, which is also partly dependent on historical development. As far as the particular George Wallace movement is concerned, it is subject to the traditional organizational hazards of such a movement, notably fragmentation and the ascendancy of overt extremist tendencies which will alienate the more respectable leadership and support. Since the Presidential election, Wallace has performed as though he understood these hazards well. He has avoided expressions of overt extremism. He has attempted to keep his organization formally separated from the fringe groups and more rabid extremists, even those who were in open support of him. In a letter sent to key Wallace lieutenants around the country, asking about the local leadership that might be involved in the next Wallace campaign, James Taylor Hardin, administrative assistant to Wallace, carefully emphasized that "perhaps of greatest importance, we would like your opinion as to those who demonstrated neither ability nor capability to work with others and who were, in fact, a detriment to the campaign. . . ."[45]

Another factor, of course, will be the extent to which Wallacism may be further coopted by one of the major political parties. Much attention has been paid by political commentators to the seeming use by the Nixon administration of the so-called "Southern strategy" as outlined by Kevin Phillips, Special Assistant to John Mitchell, both in his former capacity as Nixon's 1968 Campaign Manager, and as Attorney-General of the United States.[46] Mitchell is reputedly still in charge of future campaign plans. Phillips attempts to document the thesis that a new realignment is underway in American politics in which all sections of the Establishment, including the summits of the major conglomerate corporations whose headquarters are centered in New York City, have become liberal and are moving to the Democratic party. He points to the fact that not only did they abandon Barry Goldwater in 1964, but that in 1968, New York's upper-class "silk-stocking" congressional district supported Humphrey, elected a Democrat to Congress, and sent two "young liberal Democratic scions of prominent families" to the state legislature.[47] Conversely, he sees the bulk of the rest of the country, including the South, turning away in revolt against the liberal northeast, in a conservative anti-Establishment protest. The task of the Republican party, therefore, is "to fashion a majority among the 57 per cent of the American electorate which voted to eject the Democratic Party from national power."[48] And he argues that the "great political upheaval of the Nineteen-Sixties is not that of Senator Eugene McCarthy's relatively small group of upper-middle-class and intellectual supporters, but a *populist revolt* of the American masses who have been elevated by prosperity to middle-class status and conservatism. *Their* revolt is against the caste, policies and taxation of the mandarins of Establishment liberalism."[49]

Since Wallace's strength lies predominantly in the South, and among those concerned with changes in racial and morally relevant practices, the Phillips–Mitchell plan involves sending forth a series of messages to these groups offering them a home in the Republican party. Thus, the Nixon administration asked the Supreme Court to defer the due date for desegregation in certain southern school systems, which the Court refused to do. President Nixon subsequently refused to back away from his candidate for the Supreme Court, southern Judge Clement Haynsworth, even after it was clear that the Senate was not going to confirm the appointment. His subsequent nomination of Judge G. Harrold Carswell, a man with an open record of support for segregation, is clear testimony of the lengths he is going to win the Wallace Southern vote for the GOP. These three cases represented defeats for the President, but his popularity in the South increased considerably. Vice-President Spiro Agnew has consistently presented many of his colorful anti-eastern Establishment speeches before southern audiences. This is deliberate as Agnew, himself, made clear in an interview:

He . . . said that because the Administration had taken steps "which the South understands and appreciates," the political appeal of George C. Wallace has been reduced, and he argued that "Wallace can't get off the ground now." . . .

"In 1968, they felt they had no place to go but Wallace. But that's no longer true."[50]

It was not just a "Southern strategy" that was involved, but an appeal to a nation-wide vein of thought with which Wallace had become identified. Agnew characterized those who encouraged the massive nationwide demonstrations for withdrawal from Vietnam as "an effete corps of impudent snobs who characterize themselves as intellectuals and blamed campus violence on "well-born" elitists.[51] These were as compact expressions of antielitism as any that Joseph McCarthy or George Wallace had been able to fashion. The Vice-President has repeatedly attacked the mass media which he suggests are controlled from New York.[52]

Perhaps the most interesting election result demonstrating the efficacy of the Agnew–Mitchell strategy occurred in the 1969 New Jersey gubernatorial race. The Republican candidate, William Cahill, swept to victory, running far ahead of Nixon's vote a year earlier by absorbing the large (9 per cent) Wallace vote. A study of this election reported: "By and large the GOP gained most where Wallace had been strongest. . . ."[53] A national Gallup survey taken late in 1969 asked Wallace voters how they would vote for Congress in 1970. In the North, the Republicans led "by the ratio of about 2–1," but they were also ahead by a smaller margin, 49 to 42 per cent in the South.[54]

In a detailed end-of-the-year (1969) survey, a *New York Times* article concluded that the Republican strategy for building a new majority coalition out of the Nixon and Wallace 1968 vote was working, thanks largely to Mr. Agnew's role.

It is evident that if President Nixon is pursuing . . . an effort, officially discounted, to build a winning constituency out of the South, the Midwest and the West while ignoring the northeastern urban states—he is making headway.

Republican officials throughout the South consider Mr. Agnew the leader in the drive to expand Republic strength in the South. . . .

For Mr. Wallace the Agnew threat is awesome. The Vice-President is cutting seriously into Mr. Wallace's base of strength in the South. Many observers believe that Mr. Agnew's Southern popularity may have surpassed Mr. Wallace's. . . .

Mr. Agnew's soaring popularity in the South can be traced directly to his recent speeches denouncing antiwar demonstrators, the television networks and the press.[55]

George Wallace is, of course, aware that he is being pursued by the party in power. Speaking to American reporters during his trip to southeast Asia, he called Mr. Agnew, ". . . a copy-cat. I said everything he's saying first." On his return, he told a national television audience: "I wish I had copy-righted or patented my speeches. I would be drawing immense royalties from Mr. Nixon and especially Mr. Agnew."[56] Wallace has tried to undercut Agnew's appeal by a renewed Populist attack:

Agnew is appealing to "Chamber of Commerce folks who are already Republican" and "the elite group of moneyed interests who are out of touch with the mass of the people."

"He may please the president of a bank with a $200,000 home, but he's not pleasing the little fellow, the taxi driver or the steelworker." . . .

"Mr. Mitchell's a Wall Street lawyer," he said, "Folks are tired of Wall Street running everything."

Instead of vetoing the tax bill because it's inflationary, Wallace said Nixon ought to raise the personal exemption from $600 to $1200 a year and accept a 15 per cent increase in Social Security benefits.[57]

A pattern in American political life seemed about to be repeated, at least up to a point. A major extremist movement may have lost, but in losing had affected the course of a major political party. In adopting some of the rhetorical and programmatic direction of the extremist movement, the Republican party might cause the substantial demise of that movement, at least for a while. But there are presumably limits beyond which a mainstream national party cannot go. The critical votes in defeating the Haynsworth and Carswell appointments to the Supreme Court were, after all, those of Republican Senators.

Whether Wallace can succeed in avoiding the organizational and competitive hazards of which he seems aware, and whether historical circumstances will be favorable, are, of course, problematical. His weak showing in the 1970 Alabama gubernatorial primaries may have eliminated him as a national figure. Significantly, when Alabama turned against him, it produced the same pattern as the nation. He was defeated in the May primary by "the country club set and the Negro wards voting together for Brewer in about the same proportions," while his support came from white workers and poorer farmers.[58] But whether his particular movement survives or not, George Wallace has put together and further revealed the nature of those basic elements which must comprise an effective right-wing extremist movement in America. The question which is next ripe for detailed inquiry is whether—even if all the technical elements were present and all the historical circumstances propitious—more than 10 or even 20 per cent of the modern American population could become seriously engaged in such a movement. What, in short, is the state of countervailing commitment?

Notes

1. Reese Cleghorn, *Radicalism: Southern Style* (Atlanta: Southern Regional Council, 1968), pp. 28–29.
2. Charles Y. Glock and Rodney Stark, *Religion and Society in Tension* (Chicago: Rand-McNally, 1965), Chapter 14.
3. Franklin Hamlin Littell, *From State Church to Pluralism* (Garden City: Doubleday-Anchor, 1962), p. 133. Emphasis in the original.
4. Philip E. Converse, Warren E. Miller, Jerrold G. Rusk, and Arthur C. Wolfe, "Continuity and Change in American Politics: Parties and Issues in the 1968 Election." *American Political Science Review*, LXIII (December 1969), pp. 1101–1104.
5. *Ibid.*, pp. 1097, 1100–1101.
6. Among the more important ones not discussed here are variations in the perception of a candidate's ideological position among different individuals and social groups (for example, in 1964 Republican Presidential candidate Barry Goldwater, according to his speeches and writing, was basically a very strong-spoken economic conservative and at least a moderate when it came to civil rights; yet he probably tended to appear as a prototype ultra-rightist to the ultra-right and appears to have been taken as

a populist by large numbers of southerners). Another is what may be called variations in "saliency." Many citizens may be quite easily fitted to an ideological scale, but due to basic lack of interest in politics or one of the scale's dimensional components (such as great concern over race, but little interest in government welfare policy) may fail to make the proper connection between his position on it and his logical vote. Of course, in our own case, a special source of deviation may be the fact that we are not working from scales or indices at all, but with two simple questionnaire items which may not be wholly capable of carrying the weight of ideological differentiation by themselves.

7. Gunnar Myrdal, *An American Dilemma: The Negro Problem and Democracy* (New York: Harper, 1944), pp. xliii–xlvi, 1027–1031.

8. Louis Harris, "Wallace Gains Respectability," *Boston Globe*, September 30, 1968, p. 10.

9. See " '68 Wallace Backers Urge a Conservative Party," *New York Times*, February 23, 1969, p. 57; John C. Waugh, "Third Party Revival Planned," *Christian Science Monitor*, December 21, 1968, p. 5.

10. "Organization Waits, Ready if Wallace Decides to Run," *Boston Evening Globe*, May 6, 1969, p. 20.

11. "Association of Wallace Voters Meet," *Conservative Journal*, II (February 1969), 16.

12. See " '68 Wallace Backers . . .," *op. cit.*; E. W. Kensworthy, "Wallace Backers Form a Party and are on Way to Saving U.S.," *New York Times*, February 24, 1969, pp. 28; "Now, NCASPAIPAPIPCPCP," *Time*, March 7, 1969, p. 22.

13. " '68 Wallace Backers . . .," *op. cit.*

14. *Time, loc. cit.* "Washington's Independent Party Issues Statement on Disruption During Campaign," the *California Statesman*, January 1970, pp. 6–7.

15. Waugh, *op. cit.*, p. 5.

16. *Ibid.*, " '68 Wallace Backers . . .," *op. cit.*

17. "New Party Hits 'Extremism,' " *Washington Post*, December 1, 1969, p. B-2.

18. William B. Street, "Wallace Steps into Limelight," *Memphis Commercial Appeal*, March 19, 1968, p. 1; Gregory Jaynes, "Visiting Campaigner Keeps His Options Open," *Memphis Commercial Appeal*, March 19, 1969, p. 7; Martin Waldron, "Wallace Man Defeated in Tennessee," *New York Times*, March 27, 1969, p. 23.

19. "Election Gives G.O.P. Control of California Senate First Time in 15 Years," *New York Times*, March 27, 1969, p. 26.

20. Lawrence E. Davies, "Calif. G.O.P. Wins Third Election of 1969," *New York Times*, June 19, 1969, p. 37.

21. "Democrats Win Race in Montana," *New York Times*, June 26, 1969, p. 19.

22. "Statewide Virginia Returns," *Washington Post*, November 6, 1969, p. B-4. A third "Independent" candidate for Governor, George R. Walker, had also backed Wallace in 1968. He secured 1,117 votes, or .12 per cent.

23. "Poll Shows Nixon Ahead of Ted, 5–3, Wallace Has 10%," *Boston Sunday Globe*, May 4, 1969, p. 18; "Ted Still Has 3–1 Margin of Favor," *Boston Sunday Globe*, August 3, 1969, p. 23; "Muskie Tops Poll of '72 Democrats," *New York Times*, Sept. 28, 1969, p. 38; "No Democrat Yet Emerg-

ing as Clear Top Vote-Getter for '72 Contest," *Gallup Poll Release*, February 22, 1970.

24. Don F. Wasson, "Wallacites Vow Action in '72," Montgomery *Advertiser*, May 27, 1969, p. 1. Emphases ours.

25. "Convention Fare: An AIP Ticket?" *Richmond Times-Dispatch*, July 19, 1969, p. B-1; see also Helen Dewar, "Wallace Cautions Va. Backers," *Washington Post*, July 19, 1969, p. F-1.

26. Lee Slater, "Wallace May Make 2nd Try for President," *Tulsa Daily World*, August 2, 1969, p. A-4.

27. Homer Bigart, *New York Times*, June 12, 1969, p. 29.

28. See "Pornography in the Guise of Sex Education Sure Way to Destroy Minds, Morals of Youth," *George Wallace Newsletter*, I (July 1969), 2, 6; "Huge Crowds Hear Wallace at Decency Rallies," the *George Wallace Newsletter*, I (May 1969), 2.

29. Donald Janson, "Wallace Speaks at Christian Crusade's Convention," *New York Times*, August 3, 1969, p. 48; Slater, *op. cit.*, p. 1.

30. *Ibid.*

31. Roy Bode, "100 Fervent Followers Hear Wallace Retrace His Theme," *Tulsa Daily World*, August 3, 1969, p. A-4.

32. Paul W. Valentine, "The Student Right: Racist, Martial, Insular," *Washington Post*, May 25, 1969, p. A-9.

33. *Ibid.*

34. Dennis C. McMahon, "The National Youth Alliance," *American Mercury*, CV (Spring 1969), 61; see also issues of N.Y.A.'s paper, *Attack*.

35. *Ibid.*, pp. 61–63.

36. Valentine, *op. cit.*

37. Shelley Rolfe, "Andrews Has Party Plans," *Richmond Times-Dispatch*, May 8, 1969, as reprinted in *Conservative Journal*, II (May–June 1969), 1–2.

38. Homer Bigart, "Wallace Has No 'Political Plans,' but his Staff in Alabama is Larger than That of the National Democrats," *New York Times*, June 22, 1969, p. 34.

39. S. M. Miller, "Sharing the Burden of Change," *New Generation*, LI (Spring 1969), 2.

40. *Ibid.*

41. *Ibid.*, p. 3.

42. "Wallace Expects War to Be Issue," *New York Times*, October 28, 1969, p. 11.

43. See "Nixon Plan Prolongs War, Wallace Says," *Washington Post*, December 1, 1969, pp. 1, A-16; "Wallace Warns Nixon on Vietnam," *New York Times*, December 1, 1969, p. 11; "Wallace Urges Win," *Boston Globe*, December 1, 1969, pp. 1, 21.

44. George C. Wallace, "What is the Answer To Vietnam," *The George C. Wallace Newsletter*, I (September 1969), p. 1.

45. Cited in *Boston Globe*, July 10, 1969, p. 2.

46. Kevin P. Phillips, *The Emerging Republican Majority* (New Rochelle: Arlington House, 1969).

47. *Ibid.*, p. 92.

48. *Ibid.*, p. 461.

49. *Ibid.*, p. 470. First emphasis ours.

50. "Agnew Defends 'Punchy Language,'" *New York Times*, October 27, 1969, p. 4.
51. *Ibid.*; "Agnew Excoriates 'Elitists'," *Washington Post*, May 5, 1970, p. A3.
52. "Agnew Lashes Eastern Establishment Press," *Human Events*, XXIX (November 29, 1969), p. 5.
53. "Cahill Victory Points the Way," *Human Events*, XXX (January 24, 1970), p. 3.
54. "Agnew Aiding Republican Strategy in South," *The Gallup Opinion Index*, December 1969, p. 17.
55. Roy Reed, "G.O.P., Aided by Agnew, Surges in South," *New York Times*, December 7, 1969, pp. 1, 60.
56. "Wallace Urges Win," *op. cit.*, p. 21.
57. Robert C. Boyd, "Wallace: Spiro After 'My' Folks," *Miami Herald*, December 13, 1969, p. 13-A.
58. "Wallace Setback Laid to Blacks and Affluent Whites," *New York Times*, May 7, 1970, p. 32.

CHAPTER
11

Extremists and Extremism

The history of political extremism in America has consisted of three different kinds of meshed conditions: conditions of ideology, conditions of history, and conditions of popular attitude.

The basic ideology of extremism is contained in the model of monism. Extremism describes the violation, through action or advocacy, of the democratic political process. The democratic political process refers fundamentally to democratic political pluralism: an "open democratic market place" for ideas, speech, and consonant political action. Monism amounts to the closing down of the democratic market place, whether by a massive majority or by a preemptive minority. The monistic impulse, however, in the context of the American political metaphor, must be legitimated by rendering illegitimate those who are to be ruled out of the market place. Enter the imputation of deliberate evil, rather than lack of wisdom; enter the elements of absolutism, moralism, and conspiracy; and enter, of course, the conspiracy target.

Historically, extremist movements are movements of disaffection. Occurring in periods of incipient change, they are addressed to groups who feel that they have just been, or are about to be, deprived of something important, or to groups whose rising aspirations lead them to feel that they have always been deprived of something important they now want. Such deprivation is accompanied by political dislocation. The traditional political party structure with which these groups have been associated no longer seems to be serving their needs. They are politically volatile segments of population, with broken loyalties. Party alignments are shifting, and there is much political displacement. Preservatist (right-wing) movements have typically had as a requisite for success in America some "marriage" of interest, some symbiosis, between members of the upper and of the lower economic strata. They are guarding different kinds of self-interest together. The common grounds they find are some symbolic and effective aspects of the changing times: a disappearing way of life, a vanishing power, a diminishing group prestige, a heart-sinking change of social scenery, a lost sense of comfort and belongingness. This is status deterioration which is seen in political terms as a general social deterioration. The changing cultural impedimenta—modernism in dress, speech, religion, sexual relations—are the terms in which this deterioration is described. The emerging groups, who are bearing this modernism with them to power, are the common targets. In America these emerging groups have typically had an ethnic or racial identification. This is one of the obvious points at which the conditions of history and the conditions of ideology can coincide.

There is a natural compatibility between such historically disaffected portions of the population and the ideology of extremism. But what attitudinal qualities in the population permit that compatibility to become a reality? Is there a section of the population which holds undemocratic, antimodernist, and bigoted attitudes to begin with and is therefore susceptible to extremist movements during periods of disaffection? Or do people who hold democratic attitudes abandon them during periods of disaffection? What are the nature and extent of the common democratic commitment among the American public?

There is much evidence to suggest that an important distinction can be drawn between such a "common democratic commitment" (the pervasive popular attachment to democratic pluralism, which is essentially affective in nature) and an "ideological democratic commitment" (a more uncommon attachment to democratic pluralism which is cognitive as well as affective in nature).

The common democratic commitment exists more as a loyalty to institutions, groups, and systems which support democratic procedure than as an internalized conceptual commitment. When that loyalty is shaken, so is the democratic commitment.

Philip Converse has suggested that comprehensive integrated political belief systems in general are probably restricted to the "talented tenth" of the American population and disappear rapidly as we move down the educational ladder. He defines a belief system as "a configuration of ideas and attitudes in which the elements are bound together by some form of constraint or functional interdependence."[1]

There are two kinds of information with respect to the relationship of ideas in such a configuration: the knowledge of what goes with what; and the knowledge of why. The latter is the heart of the abstract, "contextual" belief system that we think of as "ideology." Studying the 1956 American electorate, Converse concludes that

the contextual grasp of "standard" political belief systems fades out very rapidly, almost before one has passed beyond the 10 per cent of the American population that in the 1950's had completed standard college training. Increasingly, simpler forms of information about "what goes with what" . . . turn up missing. . . . Instead of a few wide-range belief systems that organize large amounts of specific information, one would expect to find a proliferation of clusters of ideas among which little constraint is felt, even, quite often, in instances of sheer logical constraint.

At the same time, moving from top to bottom of this information dimension, the character of the objects that are central in a belief system undergoes systematic change. These objects shift from the remote, generic and abstract to the increasingly simple, concrete or "close to home." Where potential political objects are concerned, this progression tends to be from abstract, "ideological" principles to the more obviously recognizable social groupings or charismatic leaders and finally to such objects of immediate experience as family, job, and immediate associates.[2]

Converse further points out that "the changes in belief systems of which we speak are not a pathology limited to a thin and disoriented bottom layer of the *lumpenproletariat*; they are immediately relevant in understanding the bulk of mass political behavior."[3]

This image helps us to understand the principle of "selective support" by which so many people could apparently embrace one element of Coughlin's ideology without accepting others; support Coughlin's anti-Semitic platform without themselves being anti-Semitic. As more information is transmitted to them, they might learn better "what goes with what" and learn to associate anti-Semitism with the "package," but even then it is not necessarily a central object for them. They do not have to be—and for the most part are not—ideologues of extremism. The question is: What has happened to their democratic commitment—a commitment which would presumably countervail to make them recoil from an extremist program which contained undemocratic elements? The suggestion is that such a firm and comprehensive commitment does not exist in the large American public, or in any other public.

To say that the large public does not consist of ideologues is not to say that it is feckless. The American public demonstrably has a strong sense of its own basic democratic rights and has no reluctance to assert itself with respect to those rights. This is the strong popular spine in the body of our republic, which serves us well in most situations. But the application of abstract and ideological democratic principles to the matter of balancing these rights under stress calls for conceptual skills, historical perspective, and wide-based integrated belief systems which for the most part do not exist. Thus, the bulk of the data indicates that massive numbers of Americans who presumably have a ritual attachment to the concept of free speech and would reject any gross attempts to subvert it do not understand or have a commitment to the fine points of that concept when hardcore dissenters intrude upon their sensibilities. The American people would reject any gross attempt to subvert religious freedom, but almost half of them say that if a man does not believe in God, he should not be allowed to run for public office. And a majority of them, while jealous of due process, would throw away the book and resort to the whip when dealing with sex criminals.

In short, what is suggested is that abstract and complex democratic institutions and practices have stood and flourished in America because some people understood them and most of the rest were loyal to them. This loyalty was based on an inertia of investment in the country, the system, and the traditional political structure. When mass dislocations of loyalty have occurred, the common democratic commitment has been subject to undemocratic subversion.

There is much evidence that this declining ideological commitment to democracy correlates strongly with declining socioeconomic status. A number of different reasons have been adduced for this. The lower socioeconomic segments of the population are more isolated, less informed, less educated, culturally less oriented to the abstract.[4]

There is the theory, of course, that the lower socioeconomic segment of the population is also psychologically susceptible to authoritarianism and extremism because of childhoods culturally marked by lack of love, by punishment and hostility. This theory may have some substance, but it remains largely hypothetical. Some studies indicate that the development of the authoritarian personality as a psychological type is more clearly seen among the higher socioeconomic class, perhaps extremist ideologues, than among those in the lower classes who have undemocratic attitudes. This suggests that the lower socioeconomic groups score lower in "democratic tolerance," not because of a perverse quality which they have, but because of a redeeming quality which they do *not* have: a countervailing "ideological commitment to democratic principle." Of course, there is a concomitant quality which they do not have, even in periods that are without historical stress; their countervailing stake in and loyalty to the traditional structure is at a lower pitch, which depresses the common democratic commitment at lower socioeconomic levels.

That quality which is missing as democratic commitment diminishes is a quality of restraint. If all political behavior can be seen as an amalgam of impulse and restraint, impulse represents salient economic and symbolic objectives; restraint represents the curbs that are placed on the pursuit of those objectives.

In those terms, democratic commitment can be seen essentially as a matter of restraint. That is, after all, the nature of the democratic process itself; the Bill of Rights is couched in the language of restraint: Congress "shall make no law" which abridges the basic freedoms, the right to bear arms "shall not be infringed," the security of the home "shall not be violated," and so forth. The democratic process is political superego. In this sense, low socioeconomic and educational status correlates with absence of democratic restraint, of either an ideological or a situational nature.

In other words, low socioeconomic and educational status correlates with "illiberalism" as far as democratic restraints are concerned. But the impulse of the lower socioeconomic and educational groups is "liberal" as far as economic issues are concerned. This apparent dilemma is only partly a matter of semantic and historical confusion. The doctrines of liberalism developed in the eighteenth and nineteenth centuries as antistatist doctrines on two levels. The chief motivation came from the middle class which wanted government's heavy hand out of business life and the economy. Its companion ideology was antistatist in terms of keeping government's heavy hand generally out of the private lives of the citizenry. If liberalism is to be thought of generically as the movement toward egalitarian change, economic antistatist liberalism became transferred into conservatism perhaps as early as the middle of the nineteenth century, when business interests began to be fearful about the effect of extended suffrage on sensitive governments. Their fears were borne out. A new economic liberalism began to develop in the twentieth century, as Theodore Roosevelt and Woodrow Wilson began to recognize the need for government to intervene in economic affairs on the side of the underprivileged. This liberalism, so called because of its interest in egalitarian change, is now statist and has to do with the involvement of government in matters of welfare, protection of collective bargaining, and so forth. The other liberalism, so called because of its interest in the maintenance of individual rights, has remained unchanged—antistatist in nature. This confusion is reflected by the two different elements which are usually defined into "democratic life" and not always distinguished: the democratic impulse, which has to do with egalitarian achievement on both economic and symbolic levels; and democratic restraint, which has to do with the nonviolation of individual and group integrity and freedom in political life. These two elements obviously touch at many points; but in modern history they have often been placed in antagonistic design.

It is democratic restraint which is identified with that aspect of freedom generally called the democratic process, pluralism, civil liberties. Extremism (monism) is identified with the elimination of that restraint, although it might well be executed on behalf of another aspect of freedom, the "democratic impulse" toward egalitarian change. This is what Talmon had reference to in talking about "the paradox of freedom": "Is human freedom compatible with an exclusive pattern of social existence even if this pattern aims at the maximum of social justice and security? The paradox in totalitarian democracy is in its insistence that they are compatible."[5] There is a clear problem for right-wing extremist groups in the fact that the lower socioeconomic segment of the population tends to be "liberal" in democratic impulse, but "illiberal" in democratic restraint.

Since right-wing extremist groups typically seek to win support for "illiberal" positions with respect to both democratic impulse—for example, economic egalitarianism—and democratic restraint, they face a dilemma. The bases of support for these two positions are largely different segments of the population. If intolerance of difference—racial, religious, and cultural—can be taken as an index of lack of democratic restraint, the distinction between those who tend to be economically conservative and those who tend to be intolerant is pertinent to the dilemma. The distinction between these two population bases is certainly pertinent to the history and nature of right-wing extremist movements in America. A summary of some of the evidence in the field, combined with some elaboration from the national interview data collected by NORC for the Berkeley Survey Research Center's 1964 study, serves to point up the distinction between the intolerant and the economically conservative. (That study was designed, in part, for use in this analysis of right-wing extremism.)

Racial Prejudice

The most comprehensive efforts to sum up the knowledge concerning attitudes toward racial segregation and Negroes generally indicate that education and other indicators of socioeconomic status are strong correlates. The lower the education, income, and occupational status of persons interviewed in diverse studies, the more likely they are to oppose integration and to harbor prejudices of various sorts against Negroes. Southerners, of course, are much more prejudiced than northerners, but the interclass differences hold up North and South.[6] Farmers, as a group, show a high level of prejudice.

Other differences which seem relevant are religion and age. Jews are the most liberal group of the three major categories, followed by Catholics, with white Protestants revealing the least support for integration North and South. Age variations differ somewhat in the two broad sections of the country. The younger a group, the more favorable it is to integration generally as our data indicate. In the South, however, recent data discussed in the previous chapter indicate that those under twenty-five are slightly *less* favorable to integration than those in the category twenty-five to forty-four. Paul Sheatsley suggests that the youngest group of "white adults in the South have grown up and received their schooling and formed their attitudes during the stormy years which followed the 1954 Supreme Court decision outlawing segregated schools. It is they who have been most immediately exposed to the crises and dislocations brought to the South by the Negro protest movement."[7] This finding is comparable to that reported earlier for youth support for George Wallace, indicating that this may be a persistent phenomenon.

The finding that Protestants as a group are somewhat more anti-integration than Catholics is ambiguous, since the category of Protestants includes a wide diversity of groupings. A detailed study of southern white attitudes toward integration reveals that fundamentalist Protestants, particularly those adhering to the southern Baptists and other sects, are more likely to support segregation than other denominations, even when class and educational factors are held constant.[8]

The data from our national sample in 1964 essentially tend to re-affirm the findings of the previous studies. The main factors associated with Negro prejudice as measured by various attitude items in this survey are reported in Table 71. As can be seen from this table, the anti-Negro prejudice factor is linked to low education, low income, manual occupation. Those harboring these feelings are also more likely to be fundamentalists and to adhere strongly to traditional religious beliefs.[9] They are more likely to have been born and to live in southern and border states and to come from rural and small-town origins. The factors which are related to anti-Negro feeling locate the individuals characterized by them as outside the main stream of power, influence, status, and cultural sophistication in American society. In effect, they indicate that the deprived and the provincial are more likely to possess strong anti-Negro attitudes.

Religious affiliation and commitment to strong traditional religious beliefs, and education, would appear to be among the two strongest correlates of anti-Negro feelings, outside of regional background. The relative relationship among these factors is presented in Table 72. It is clear from the table that religious affiliation and belief and education each play an important independent role in affecting prejudice against Negroes. Among the college-educated, fundamentalist affiliation and strong religious commitment are still linked to prejudice. The most prejudiced of all are the fundamentalists and those with strong religious commitment who have not

Table 71.   CORRELATES OF ANTI-NEGRO PREJUDICE FACTOR AMONG WHITE CHRISTIANS
(Per Cent in Two Highest Categories of a Five-Category Scale)*

	Whole Country		South and Border		Rest of Country	
	Per Cent	Number	Per Cent	Number	Per Cent	Number
Education						
8th grade	60	(435)	84	(139)	47	(296)
High school	50	(836)	75	(190)	43	(646)
Some college	32	(204)	54	(56)	24	(148)
College graduate	27	(179)	53	(45)	18	(134)
Income						
Under $5,000	53	(603)	79	(199)	40	(404)
$5,000 to $9,999	44	(649)	64	(123)	39	(526)
$10,000 to $14,999	44	(259)	67	(72)	35	(187)
$15,000 and over	40	(71)	56	(11)	37	(60)
Subjective Class						
Lower	52	(625)	79	(156)	43	(469)
Middle	44	(823)	69	(201)	36	(622)
Upper	39	(234)	66	(61)	30	(173)
Occupation						
Farm	66	(101)	92	(38)	51	(63)
Worker and Service	49	(510)	81	(109)	40	(401)
Clerical and Sales	45	(249)	68	(68)	36	(181)
Business and Professional	35	(288)	65	(69)	36	(219)
Retired	54	(221)	89	(71)	43	(150)
Religion						
Liberal Protestant	46	(583)	66	(128)	40	(455)
Fundamentalist Protestant	53	(410)	80	(226)	42	(184)
Catholic	39	(486)	50	(42)	38	(444)
Religious Commitment						
Low	38	(88)	†	(5)	37	(83)
Middle	38	(604)	60	(118)	33	(486)
High	62	(479)	80	(209)	48	(270)
Age						
Under 35	44	(471)	66	(128)	36	(343)
35 to 54	45	(657)	70	(152)	38	(505)
54 and over	55	(528)	81	(150)	44	(378)

* For a description of the sample and the interview schedule, see the report in Gertrude J. Selznick and Stephen Steinberg, *The Tenacity of Prejudice* (New York: Harper and Row, 1969), pp. xv–xx; Appendix A: "Interview Schedule," pp. 1–32.
† Too few cases.

Table 71. CORRELATES OF ANTI-NEGRO PREJUDICE FACTOR AMONG WHITE CHRISTIANS
—CONTINUED
(Per Cent in Two Highest Categories of a Five-Category Scale)*

	Whole Country		South and Border		Rest of Country	
	Per Cent	Num-ber	Per Cent	Num-ber	Per Cent	Num-ber
Sex						
Male	46	(826)	76	(208)	36	(618)
Female	47	(891)	70	(222)	40	(669)
Generation in America						
First	41	(126)	†	(6)	41	(120)
Second	43	(399)	72	(39)	40	(360)
Third	38	(371)	62	(52)	36	(319)
Fourth or more	56	(758)	75	(333)	41	(425)
Childhood Region						
Northeast-Middle Atlantic	36	(396)	56	(29)	34	(367)
Midwest	43	(547)	58	(60)	42	(487)
South-Border	73	(429)	75	(327)	62	(102)
Mountain-Pacific	28	(145)	†	(4)	28	(141)
Present Region						
Northeast-Middle Atlantic	36	(496)				
Midwest	45	(513)				
South-Border	73	(430)				
Mountain-Pacific	30	(278)				
Where Raised						
Farm	58	(556)	80	(216)	44	(340)
Small town	46	(440)	74	(88)	34	(352)
Small city	37	(138)	54	(24)	33	(114)
Middle city	39	(203)	61	(41)	36	(162)
Big city	40	(316)	67	(46)	37	(270)
Suburb	33	(63)	†	(15)	31	(48)
Present City Size						
Under 5,000	58	(473)	81	(57)	47	(316)
5,000 to 20,000	42	(392)	53	(79)	37	(313)
20,000 to 100,000	43	(355)	73	(88)	33	(267)
100,000 to 500,000	53	(241)	76	(86)	40	(155)
Over 500,000	32	(95)	45	(20)	28	(75)

* For a description of the sample and the interview schedule, see the report in Gertrude J. Selznick and Stephen Steinberg, *The Tenacity of Prejudice* (New York: Harper & Row, 1969), pp. xv–xx; Appendix A: "Interview Schedule," pp. 1–32.
† Too few cases.

Table 71. CORRELATES OF ANTI-NEGRO PREJUDICE FACTOR AMONG WHITE CHRISTIANS
—CONTINUED
(Per Cent in Two Highest Categories of a Five-Category Scale)*

	Whole Country		South and Border		Rest of Country	
	Per Cent	Num- ber	Per Cent	Num- ber	Per Cent	Num- ber
Party Identification						
Republican	47	(606)	70	(133)	41	(473)
Democrat	45	(951)	73	(253)	35	(698)
Independent	48	(121)	72	(32)	39	(89)
1964 Vote Preference						
Johnson	41	(972)	67	(193)	34	(779)
Goldwater	56	(469)	80	(166)	43	(303)
DK–NA	54	(119)	73	(33)	47	(86)
Media Exposure						
Low	58	(377)	84	(129)	44	(248)
Middle	48	(748)	70	(185)	31	(563)
High	45	(357)	62	(73)	40	(284)
High Culture Knowledge						
Low	69	(313)	87	(112)	59	(201)
Middle	48	(762)	74	(188)	39	(574)
High	37	(568)	59	(125)	31	(443)
Years in Town						
Less than 5	42	(462)	68	(128)	32	(334)
6 to 20	44	(516)	69	(131)	36	(385)
20 and over	51	(738)	79	(171)	43	(567)
Geographically Mobile						
Static	49	(1,255)	76	(343)	39	(912)
Mobile	47	(262)	61	(77)	41	(185)

* For a description of the sample and the interview schedule, see the report in Gertrude J. Selznick and Stephen Steinberg, *The Tenacity of Prejudice* (New York: Harper & Row, 1969), pp. xv–xx; Appendix A: "Interview Schedule," pp. 1–32.
† Too few cases.

been educated beyond the eighth grade. However, a poorly educated Catholic or liberal Protestant will be more anti-Negro than a fundamentalist who went to college.

Bigotry against Religious Groups

The history of right-wing extremism in the United States has been a record of association with religious-group bigotry. Although, since World War II,

Table 72.   RELATIONSHIP BETWEEN RELIGION AND EDUCATION AND
ANTI-NEGRO PREJUDICE*

Education	Liberal Protestants		Fundamentalist Protestants		Catholics	
	Per Cent	Number	Per Cent	Number	Per Cent	Number
8th grade or less	24	(130)	42	(223)	27	(128)
9 to 12 grades	23	(315)	25	(274)	16	(283)
13 to 15 grades	15	(94)	22	(50)	4	(51)
16 grades or more	5	(92)	13	(30)	6	(47)

Education	*Religious Commitment Index*					
	Low		Middle		High	
	Per Cent	Number	Per Cent	Number	Per Cent	Number
8th grade or less	43	(14)	53	(98)	68	(183)
9 to 12 grades	49	(37)	42	(323)	61	(230)
13 grades or more	24	(37)	25	(183)	37	(66)

* All tables report on white Christians only.

most right-wing extremist groups have so far either played down or
formally opposed overt expressions of such sentiments, the fact remains that
their political tendencies attract many bigots. Robert Welch has frequently
discussed the problem he faces from Birch Society members who attempt to
press that organization in an anti-Semitic direction. The various Jewish defense organizations have reported many incidents involving the presence of
well-known anti-Semites at meetings of rightist groups which themselves are
not anti-Semitic. The 1960 election campaign bore eloquent witness to the
continuation of anti-Catholic prejudice. Any effort to evaluate the potential
for various forms of extremist politics in the United States must take into
account the continued existence of bigotry against these religious groups.

The NORC national survey conducted for our research in 1964 inquired in depth concerning the extent of anti-Semitic attitudes among
American Christians. The survey indicated that many Americans hold
anti-Semitic beliefs. The various items in the study dealing with attitudes to Jews were subjected to factor analysis, producing an Anti-
Semitism Scale independent of the many other attitude items dealt with in
the survey. Respondents were then ranked on this scale as being high or
low on anti-Semitism. The correlates of high anti-Semitism are reported in
Table 73.[10] It is clear from the findings presented in the table that our data
reinforce the results of earlier studies which reported with "virtual unanimity

Table 73. CORRELATES OF THE ANTI-SEMITISM FACTOR
(Percentage High)

	Per Cent	Number		Per Cent	Number
Education			*Generation in America*		
8th grade	51	(435)	First	49	(126)
High school	32	(836)	Second	35	(399)
Some college	26	(204)	Third	33	(371)
College graduate	16	(179)	Fourth or more	33	(758)
Income			*Childhood Region*		
Under $5,000	42	(603)	Northeast-		
$5,000 to $9,999	31	(649)	Middle Atlantic	24	(396)
$10,000 to $14,999	29	(259)	Midwest	38	(547)
$15,000 and over	32	(71)	South-Border	37	(429)
			Mountain-Pacific	33	(145)
Subjective Class			*Present Region*		
Lower	39	(625)	Northeast-		
Middle	31	(823)	Middle Atlantic	27	(496)
Upper	30	(234)	Midwest	38	(513)
			South-Border	37	(430)
Occupation			Mountain-Pacific	33	(278)
Farm	52	(101)			
Worker and service	53	(510)	*Where Raised*		
Clerical and sales	30	(249)	Farm	45	(556)
Business and professional	26	(288)	Small town	32	(440)
Retired	39	(221)	Small city	30	(138)
			Middle city	35	(203)
Religion			Big city	22	(316)
Liberal Protestant	37	(583)	Suburb	30	(63)
Fundamentalist					
Protestant	37	(410)	*Present City Size*		
Catholic	32	(486)	Under 5,000	41	(473)
			5,000 to 20,000	31	(392)
Religious Commitment			20,000 to 100,000	32	(355)
Low	15	(88)	100,000 to 500,000	35	(241)
Middle	32	(604)	500,000 and over	30	(95)
High	46	(479)			
			Party Identification		
Age			Republican	35	(606)
Under 34	25	(471)	Democrat	33	(951)
34 to 54	31	(657)	Independent	31	(121)
54 and over	48	(528)			
			1964 Vote Preference		
Sex			Johnson	34	(1,055)
Male	39	(826)	Goldwater	35	(533)
Female	29	(891)	DK–NA	29	(119)

Table 73.   CORRELATES OF THE ANTI-SEMITISM FACTOR—CONTINUED
(Percentage High)

	Per Cent	Num-ber		Per Cent	Num-ber
Media Exposure			*Years in Town*		
Low	41	(377)	Under 5	27	(462)
Middle	34	(748)	6 to 20	29	(516)
High	31	(357)	20 and over	41	(738)
High Culture Knowledge					
Low	50	(313)	*Geomobile*		
Middle	36	(762)	Static	35	(1,255)
High	25	(568)	Mobile	27	(262)

that anti-Semitism is most widespread and virulent among the uneducated, unenlightened, and poorer members of American society."[11] Education appears to be the principal factor related to this set of beliefs. Low income and occupational status are also correlated with this factor. Manual workers and farmers are much more likely to be high on anti-Semitism than those in white-collar, business, and professional pursuits.

The findings concerning the relationship of religious affiliation to anti-Semitism indicate no difference between the fundamentalists and the liberal Protestants in ranking on the anti-Semitism factor, although Catholics seem slightly less prejudiced. This finding is somewhat surprising, since fundamentalists ranked higher on other dimensions of prejudice and are a less educated and lower-status group on the average than those adhering to liberal Protestant denominations.

Using other categories in an analysis of the same data, Selznick and Steinberg found that 17 per cent of "conservative Protestants," 14 per cent of Catholics, and 5 per cent of "liberal Protestants" who attended church at least once a month ranked as "extreme" anti-Semites.[12] An additional 21 per cent, 18 per cent, and 18 per cent, respectively, ranked as "high" anti-Semites. There is the suggestion in such figures that the larger categories hide various statistically potent subgroups.

In assessing the effect of education, Selznick and Steinberg found that the percentage of white churchgoers qualifying as anti-Semitic was about the same for Catholics and liberal Protestants at all educational levels, and about the same for those who had attended college in all three religious categories. There was a spread of ten to fifteen percentage points in the extent to which conservative Protestants below the college level measured higher in anti-Semitism than the other two groups. But, as the authors pointed out, "Within each group education is strongly related to anti-

Semitism. Among those in conservative Protestant denominations, there is a 52-percentage-point spread between grade schoolers and college graduates, almost exactly as occurs in the sample as a whole."[13]

In any case, sheer adherence to a given type of Protestant denomination may not be a good indicator of fundamentalist orientation. In most denominations, there are liberal and fundamentalist groupings, so that a more direct measure of religious beliefs is undoubtedly a better indicator of religious orientation. To test out this possibility, we have constructed a scale of religious commitment derived from three scales used by Glock and Stark in an earlier publication, using items which were also in the national survey data. These scales deal with religious dogmatism (acceptance of literal biblical truths), religious particularism (belief in the supremacy of one's own church), and religious libertarianism (degree of tolerance for those with differing religious beliefs). The resultant index of religious commitment correlates strongly with anti-Semitism, thus confirming the assumptions of those who hypothesize that strong commitment to fundamental Christian beliefs is linked somehow to prejudice against Jews. Since strength of religious commitment is itself linked to level of education, it is important to see how much of the relationship survives when we hold education constant (Table 74).

Table 74. ANTI-SEMITISM AND RELIGIOUS COMMITMENT WITHIN EDUCATIONAL GROUPS
(Percentage High on Anti-Semitism)

Score on Religous Commitment Index	8th Grade		High School		College	
	Per Cent	Num-ber	Per Cent	Num-ber	Per Cent	Num-ber
Low	29	(14)	22	(37)	3	(37)
Middle	52	(98)	31	(323)	22	(183)
High	60	(183)	39	(230)	29	(66)

The Glock-Stark study of the relationship of religious belief to anti-Semitism, largely based on a northern California sample, reported that religious belief is a much more important correlate of anti-Semitism than educational level or other indicators of social position. This study varied from ours not only in the source of its data but in its index of religious orientation. Glock and Stark constructed an index of religious "bigotry" which included the items contained in our measure of religious commitment, plus two questions concerning religious attitudes toward Jews. These dealt with whether the respondents viewed the Jews as a people who had historically crucified Jesus and also saw the Jews as a people who are still being punished by God. Position on the index of religious bigotry was highly predictive of secular anti-Semitism among the respondents who belonged to northern California denominations. However, when Glock and Stark replicated their analysis on the national survey data, the same data we are using here, they found that within each level of religious bigotry the lowly educated were much more likely to report secular prejudices against Jews than those who went to college (Table 75). Thus their findings do not challenge the conclusion that educational level remains an important predictor of anti-Semitic feelings, independently of religious prejudice or orientation.

Age, another factor associated with anti-Semitic prejudice, is also closely correlated with education. The evidence indicates that better educated and younger people are less prejudiced than others. Since the educational attainments of the American population have gone up year by year, the younger are also better educated as a group than their elders. Table 76 indicates how these two factors relate to anti-Semitism. It points out clearly that education and age both contribute separately to anti-Semitism. Within each age category, the less educated, the greater the proportion high on the anti-Semitism factor. But within each education group, the older are more anti-Semitic.

Anti-Catholicism

Anti-Catholicism remains an important, although relatively underground, prejudice in the United States. During the 1960 election, it cost John F. Kennedy many votes. Although most of the active radical rightists have dropped any overt reference to such sentiments, some continue to voice them. We have seen that Carl McIntire continues to combine anti-Communism and anti-Catholicism. Some of the smaller Ku Klux Klan organizations also retain their opposition to the Catholic church. While there is little likelihood of the revival of a massive anti-Catholic campaign by the organized right, the persistence of these sentiments does affect the ability of the radical right to unite in one camp. To the extent that any of these groups link their politics to religious beliefs, it is to Protestant fundamentalism. By so doing, they effectively reject Catholic support, whether consciously or not.

Social scientists in recent years have paid little attention to the social roots of anti-Catholicism. Seemingly, it is not a problem like anti-Negro feeling or anti-Semitism. The Berkeley 1964 national survey focused on anti-Semitism. It also included a number of questions concerning attitudes toward Negroes, as we have seen. Unfortunately, the interview schedule

Table 75. RELATIONSHIP BETWEEN RELIGIOUS BIGOTRY (HIGHLY PARTICULARISTIC RELIGIOUS BELIEFS AND BELIEF IN LITERAL ASSUMPTIONS ABOUT THE JEWS AS BEING RESPONSIBLE FOR THE DEATH OF CHRIST) AND SCORING HIGH ON INDEX OF SECULAR ANTI-SEMITISM, BY EDUCATION GROUPS

Education	Religious Bigotry Index											
	0		1		2		3		4		5	
	Per Cent	Number	Per Cent	Number	Per Cent	Number	Per Cent	Number	Per Cent	Number	Per Cent	Number
Less than high-school graduate	14	(14)	48	(62)	42	(142)	54	(136)	57	(103)	66	(62)
High-school graduate	14	(73)	16	(198)	32	(321)	36	(157)	45	(100)	53	(73)
Some college or more	2	(57)	11	(104)	15	(137)	11	(48)	38	(26)	40	(22)

Source: Charles Y. Glock and Rodney Stark, *Christian Beliefs and Anti-Semitism* (New York: Harper & Row, 1966), p. 204.

Table 76.   RELATIONSHIP OF EDUCATION AND AGE TO ANTI-SEMITISM
(Percentage High on Anti-Semitism)

		Age Groupings			
Under 35		35–54		Over 54	
Per Cent	Number	Per Cent	Number	Per Cent	Number
		8th grade or less			
44	(39)	48	(111)	54	(285)
		9th–12th grade			
27	(276)	31	(401)	47	(159)
		13 plus			
17	(155)	21	(145)	31	(83)

contained only one item bearing on Catholics, a question which asked respondents whether they thought Catholics had too much power in the United States. The answers to this one question, however, do permit us to make some estimates as to the location of anti-Catholic sentiments. The correlates of the answers to this question are presented in Table 77.

It is evident from the data presented that the factors associated with anti-Catholic feeling are quite similar to those correlated with anti-Semitism. Among white Protestants, those who think Catholics have too much power tend to be less educated and underprivileged economically. They tend to be found in smaller communities and in the South. They are much more likely to be fundamentalist than liberal Protestants and to be high on the religious commitment scale. Significantly, although the high anti-Catholics are relatively underprivileged as a group, more of them are to be found among Republican voters than among Democratic voters. Possibly the image of the Democratic party as containing many Catholics in its leadership pressed the anti-Catholics away from it, even when a southern Protestant headed the Democratic ticket. Efforts to control the factors related to anti-Catholicism produced results comparable to those found for anti-Semitism.

Racial and Religious Prejudice

Our examination of the social correlates of prejudice against Negroes, Jews, and Catholics suggest that these forms of bigotry are rooted among similar strata. Essentially, the more fundamentalist, provincial, education- and status-deprived elements in the country are most prone to harbor such feelings. There are, of course, some differences in the correlates of these three types of prejudice. Anti-Negro sentiment is strongest in the southern

Table 77.   CORRELATES OF ANTI-CATHOLICISM, WHITE PROTESTANTS ONLY
(Per Cent)

	Per Cent	Number		Per Cent	Number
Education			*Generation in America*		
8th grade	45	(311)	First	33	(66)
High school	21	(560)	Second	27	(192)
Some College	17	(158)	Third	22	(234)
College graduate	13	(134)	Fourth or more	27	(671)
Income			*Childhood Region*		
			Northeast-		
Under $5,000	36	(459)	Middle Atlantic	12	(394)
$5,000 to $9,999	21	(428)	Midwest	19	(546)
$10,000 to $14,999	17	(182)	South-Border	31	(427)
$15,000 and over	16	(45)	Mountain-Pacific	15	(145)
Subjective Class			*Present Region*		
Lower	32	(422)	Northeast-		
Middle	24	(592)	Middle Atlantic	23	(269)
Upper	16	(184)	Midwest	24	(361)
			South-Border	32	(386)
Occupation			Mountain-Pacific	21	(209)
Farm	32	(88)			
Worker and service	30	(346)	*Where Raised*		
Clerical and sales	23	(174)	Farm	33	(479)
Business and professional	17	(215)	Small town	22	(300)
Retired	40	(178)	Small city	27	(95)
			Middle city	13	(133)
Religion			Big city	23	(170)
Liberal Protestant	21	(581)	Suburb	21	(47)
Fundamentalist					
Protestant	35	(407)	*Present City Size*		
			Under 5,000	33	(400)
Religious Commitment			5,000 to 20,000	24	(269)
Low	12	(69)	20,000 to 100,000	20	(234)
Middle	21	(381)	100,000 to 500,000	26	(167)
High	40	(389)	500,000 and over	12	(50)
Age			*Party Identification*		
Under 34	18	(314)	Republican	29	(506)
34 to 54	21	(432)	Democrat	23	(603)
54 and over	37	(418)	Independent	25	(88)
Sex			*1964 Vote Preference*		
			Johnson	21	(620)
Male	25	(603)	Goldwater	33	(400)
Female	26	(622)	DK–NA	28	(88)

Table 77.   CORRELATES OF ANTI-CATHOLICISM, WHITE PROTESTANTS ONLY—CONTINUED
(Per Cent)

	Per Cent	Number		Per Cent	Number
Media Exposure			*Years in Town*		
Low	37	(263)	Under 5	24	(341)
Middle	22	(514)	6 to 20	23	(374)
High	24	(255)	20 and over	30	(510)
High Culture Knowledge					
Low	46	(226)	*Geomobile*		
Middle	28	(532)	Static	27	(892)
High	13	(398)	Mobile	21	(196)

and border states. This is not true of anti-Semitism. Anti-Catholic sentiments are stronger in the South than in other parts of the country, but
the difference is much less than with respect to anti-Negro feelings. A
second variation concerns the length of family residence in the United
States. Those high on anti-Negro feelings are more likely to be of old
family background (four generations or more in the country), while anti-
Semitic and anti-Catholic feelings are strongest among first-generation
citizens. This variation is linked to the fact that many of the anti-Negro
respondents are in the South, an area which has not had much immigration.

More striking than the differences in the backgrounds of those most
prejudiced on each of these attitudes are the similarities among them. And
this fact points up the problem of uniting the various bigoted groups in
one movement. The most intolerant Catholics, those who supported
Coughlin, who were pro-McCarthy, and who today are strongly anti-Negro,
are lower in status and education and strongly committed to their church,
much like the strong anti-Catholics among the Protestant community. The
Protestant bigots will find it difficult to follow a Catholic; many Catholics
will not want to back a man who preaches fundamentalism or who, like
George Wallace, refuses to repudiate support from the Ku Klux Klan and
other anti-Catholic elements.

Most significantly, at this stage of analysis, there are initially identified
the characteristics of the population which, despite subcultural variations,
shares some striking weakness in the "democratic restraint" which is essential to democratic pluralism.

Intolerance of Difference

Another index of this lack of democratic restraint is the more generic
intolerance of differences in values and ideas. Right-wing extremist groups

have typically exhibited this intolerance. They assume the existence of basic American religious or secular verities which are being undermined by conspirators seeking to change the society for the worse. Change and opposing belief systems are not the natural outcome of endemic social processes or the working of a democratic society, but rather reflect the triumph, or the existence, of evil. Given the either/or assumption of truth versus error, God versus Satan, the American system versus Communism, they are intolerant of opposing belief systems and groups.

The factor analysis of the items in the national survey pointed to the existence of a complex of attitudes which may be labeled intolerance of difference, or antimodernism.

A look at the findings presented in Table 78 indicates that most of the factors correlated with the cultural intolerance or antimodernism factor are similar to those related to racial and religious bigotry. The cultural intolerants are also the lowly in education and occupational status, the

Table 78. CORRELATES OF THE CULTURAL INTOLERANCE FACTOR
(Percentage High)

	Per Cent	Number		Per Cent	Number
Education			*Religion*		
8th grade	52	(435)	Liberal Protestant	35	(583)
High school	39	(836)	Fundamentalist		
Some college	28	(204)	Protestant	45	(410)
College graduate	12	(179)	Catholic	40	(486)
Income			*Religious Commitment*		
Under $5,000	47	(603)	Low	6	(88)
$5,000 to $9,999	35	(649)	Middle	29	(604)
$10,000 to $14,999	29	(259)	High	62	(479)
$15,000 and over	27	(71)			
			Age		
			Under 34	23	(471)
Subjective Class			34 to 54	36	(657)
Lower	43	(625)	54 and over	56	(528)
Middle	37	(823)			
Upper	27	(234)	*Sex*		
			Male	34	(826)
			Female	41	(891)
Occupation					
Farm	47	(101)	*Generation in America*		
Worker and service	39	(389)	First	47	(126)
Clerical and sales	41	(370)	Second	39	(399)
Business and professional	24	(288)	Third	36	(371)
Retired	53	(221)	Fourth or more	38	(758)

Table 78. CORRELATES OF THE CULTURAL INTOLERANCE FACTOR—CONTINUED
(Percentage High)

	Per Cent	Number		Per Cent	Number
Childhood Region			*Party Identification*		
Northeast-			Republican	39	(606)
Middle Atlantic	42	(396)	Democrat	38	(951)
Midwest	37	(547)	Independent	28	(121)
South-Border	41	(429)			
Mountain-Pacific	17	(145)	*1964 Vote Preference*		
			Johnson	39	(972)
Present Region			Goldwater	36	(469)
Northeast-			DK–NA	34	(119)
Middle Atlantic	40	(496)			
Midwest	38	(513)	*Media Exposure*		
South-Border	42	(430)	Low	42	(377)
Mountain-Pacific	26	(278)	Middle	38	(748)
			High	38	(357)
Where Raised					
Farm	47	(556)	*High Culture Knowledge*		
Small town	37	(440)	Low	54	(313)
Small city	32	(138)	Middle	42	(762)
Middle city	29	(203)	High	26	(568)
Big city	32	(316)			
Suburb	25	(63)	*Years in Town*		
			Under 5	29	(462)
Present City Size			6 to 20	33	(516)
Under 5,000	44	(473)	20 and over	46	(738)
5,000 to 20,000	37	(392)			
20,000 to 100,000	34	(355)	*Geomobile*		
100,000 to 500,000	41	(241)	Static	39	(1,225)
500,000 and over	26	(95)	Mobile	34	(262)

provincials from small towns and rural areas, the older and retired people, and those who rank high on the index of religious commitment. The one major difference between them and the religious-racial bigots relates to religious affiliation and areas of the country in which they are to be found. Catholics who are relatively low in racial and religious bigotry are higher than liberal Protestants in cultural intolerance. And the eastern part of the country, which also showed up on the low side with respect to the other prejudices, ranks about the same as the South and Midwest on the anti-modernism scale. Only the western states show up as lower on this factor.

The finding that Catholics seem to be more culturally intolerant than bigoted suggests that the same factors which press Protestants toward rejecting those who are different operate among them as well. What may reduce their giving voice to religious and ethnic bigotry is their specific subcultural history. The differences, however, between them and the liberal

Protestants are to a large extent a function of variations in educational attainment. When we control for education, we find that fundamentalists remain more antimodern than others with the same level of education, but that there is little or no difference between the Catholics and the liberal Protestants (Table 79). In short, the cultural intolerance scale helps further to cut through subcultural variations and identify segments of the population, who, through their explicit lack of democratic restraint on several fronts, exhibit monistic tendencies.

Table 79.   RELATIONSHIP BETWEEN EDUCATION, RELIGIOUS ADHERENCE,
AND CULTURAL INTOLERANCE
(Percentage High in Cultural Intolerance)

Education	Liberal Protestant		Fundamentalist Protestant		Catholic	
	Per Cent	Number	Per Cent	Number	Per Cent	Number
8th grade or less	53	(130)	65	(223)	52	(128)
9 to 12 grades	39	(315)	45	(274)	42	(283)
13 to 15 grades	30	(94)	32	(50)	31	(51)
16 grades or more	11	(92)	27	(30)	11	(47)

Sociopolitical Beliefs

Thus far we have noted that intolerance of ethnic and racial minorities, of cultural diversity, of people and tendencies which are different and modern are associated with low status, education, provincialism, and commitment to traditional religious beliefs. But running through most right-wing extremist groups is a conservative set of economic and political beliefs. They tend to oppose the welfare state, to view the growth of state power as evil, to see socialism and Communism as underlying all the political and economic reforms which involve any type of collective action to improve the situation of the more deprived parts of the population. Presumably such a set of doctrines would appeal to the relatively privileged, rather than the underprivileged. The national survey items produced a factor bearing on this set of attitudes which we call economic conservatism—anti-Communism (Table 80).

It is clear from examining this table that the variables associated with economic conservatism–anti-Communism factor are quite different from those correlating with the intolerance factors discussed earlier. Those who rate high on the conservatism factor tend to come from the ranks of the better educated and more privileged strata. They are also more disposed to be found among those of old American stock. In spite of these major

Table 80.   CORRELATES OF THE ECONOMIC CONSERVATISM FACTOR
(Percentage High)

	Per Cent	Number		Per Cent	Number
Education			*Generation In America*		
8th grade	34	(435)	First	25	(126)
High school	36	(836)	Second	33	(399)
Some college	44	(204)	Third	35	(371)
College graduate	51	(179)	Fourth or more	44	(758)
Income			*Childhood Region*		
Under $5,000	36	(603)	Northeast-		
$5,000 to $9,999	36	(649)	Middle Atlantic	29	(396)
$10,000 to $14,999	42	(259)	Midwest	35	(547)
$15,000 and over	52	(71)	South-Border	44	(429)
			Mountain-Pacific	34	(145)
Subjective Class			*Present Region*		
Lower	32	(625)	Northeast-		
Middle	37	(823)	Middle Atlantic	30	(496)
Upper	48	(234)	Midwest	32	(513)
			South-Border	50	(430)
Occupation			Mountain-Pacific	37	(278)
Farm	49	(101)			
Worker and service	31	(389)	*Where Raised*		
Clerical and sales	39	(370)	Farm	41	(556)
Business and professional	44	(288)	Small town	33	(440)
Retired	40	(221)	Small city	35	(138)
			Medium city	38	(203)
Religion			Big city	34	(316)
Liberal Protestant	40	(583)	Suburb	37	(63)
Fundamentalist					
Protestant	49	(410)	*Present City Size*		
Catholic	24	(486)	Under 5,000	38	(473)
			5,000 to 20,000	37	(392)
Religious Commitment			20,000 to 100,000	41	(355)
Low	39	(88)	100,000 to 500,000	37	(241)
Middle	38	(604)	500,000 and over	28	(95)
High	43	(479)			
			Party Identification		
Age			Republican	54	(606)
Under 34	36	(471)	Democrat	25	(951)
35 to 54	37	(657)	Independent	45	(121)
54 and over	40	(528)			
			1964 Vote Preference		
Sex			Johnson	16	(972)
Male	41	(826)	Goldwater	74	(469)
Female	33	(891)	DK–NA	39	(119)

Table 80. CORRELATES OF THE ECONOMIC CONSERVATISM FACTOR—CONTINUED
(Percentage High)

	Per Cent	Number		Per Cent	Number
Media Exposure			*Years in Town*		
Low	34	(377)	Under 5	38	(462)
Middle	37	(748)	6 to 20	37	(516)
High	43	(357)	20 and over	36	(738)
High Culture Knowledge					
Low	35	(313)	*Geomobile*		
Middle	38	(762)	Static	38	(1,255)
High	40	(568)	Mobile	44	(262)

differences which associate conservatism with privilege and status, there are a number of similarities with the intolerants on other variables. Thus the economic conservatives are more likely to be found among those living in southern and border states, among those reared on farms, and among those still working as farmers today. They also tend to be more prevalent among fundamentalists and those high in religious commitment, even though the latter groups are predominantly lowly in socioeconomic backgrounds. Conservatives are also older on the average. It should also be noted that the western states, which are the lowest region on the intolerance items generally, constitute the second highest one on economic conservatism. One sharp difference between the pattern for the economic conservatives and the intolerants is their political affiliation. There were relatively small differences in party affiliation and 1964 vote which were related to the different measures of intolerance. There is, as might be expected, a major variation with respect to the conservative Republicans and Goldwater supporters who are much more likely to be extreme conservatives than Democrats and 1964 Johnson voters.

The high correlations between party orientation and position on the conservatism scale suggest the possibility that the relationships are primarily a function of the varying composition of the two parties; that is, Republicans are more well-to-do and better educated. Major partisan differences occur, however, even after education and income are controlled (Tables 81 and 82).

The differences between the various religious groupings indicate that fundamentalists are slightly more conservative than liberal Protestants, while Catholics are the least supportive of the complex of economic conservative attitudes. It is possible that these differences, particularly those between Catholics and Protestants, are a result of variations in educational

Table 81.   ECONOMIC CONSERVATISM FACTOR AND PARTY IDENTIFICATION,
BY EDUCATION
(Per Cent High on Factor)

	Republican		Democrat		Independent	
Education	Per Cent	Number	Per Cent	Number	Per Cent	Number
8th grade	55	(129)	25	(255)	55	(31)
High school	51	(282)	29	(477)	44	(63)
College	67	(190)	29	(165)	52	(23)

Table 82.   ECONOMIC CONSERVATISM FACTOR AND PARTY IDENTIFICATION,
BY INCOME
(Per Cent High on Factor)

	Republican		Democrat		Independent	
Income	Per Cent	Number	Per Cent	Number	Per Cent	Number
$5,000	55	(210)	26	(328)	54	(43)
$5,000 to $9,999	55	(215)	28	(377)	40	(45)
$10,000 and over	63	(152)	31	(156)	57	(21)

and economic attainments. The evidence, however (Table 83), suggests that religion acts as an independent factor. Differentiating according to education even increases the significance of the differences between fundamentalist and liberal Protestants. Within each group, the fundamentalists turn out to be higher on this factor than the liberal Protestants. Since income and education are both correlated with this factor and, as we know, with each other, it is conceivable that the factor is largely a product of the conservatism of the more well-to-do, rather than being independently related to education.

The data (Table 84) suggest that income level is a more consistent determinant of extreme conservatism than education. That is, in this case, economic conservatism–anti-Communism would appear to be linked with greater income. The correlation in the sample as a whole with education is a product of the fact that higher education is associated with earning more, more than with elements inherent in education itself.

The Issue Publics and the Radical Right

The information discussed so far clearly indicates important differences with respect to the opinions which have contributed at various times to

Table 83.   ECONOMIC CONSERVATISM FACTOR AS RELATED TO RELIGION AND EDUCATION
THE ECONOMIC CONSERVATISM FACTOR

Education	Liberal Protestant		Fundamentalist Protestant		Catholic	
	Per Cent	Number	Per Cent	Number	Per Cent	Number
8th grade	32	(130)	37	(223)	16	(128)
High school	36	(315)	38	(274)	22	(283)
Some college	40	(94)	52	(50)	33	(51)
College graduate	51	(92)	53	(30)	47	(47)

Table 84.   RELATIONSHIP BETWEEN INCOME AND EDUCATION AND
THE ECONOMIC CONSERVATISM FACTOR
(Per Cent High on Factor)

Education	Income Class					
	Under $5,000		$5,000– $9,999		$10,000 and over	
	Per Cent	Number	Per Cent	Number	Per Cent	Number
8th grade or less	33	(359)	36	(115)		*
9 to 12 grades	31	(323)	31	(437)	46	(156)
13 grades or more	27	(96)	47	(149)	51	(159)

* Too few cases.

the support of right-wing extremist groups. Essentially, it has been apparent that racial and religious prejudice and intolerance for people and ideas which are different are associated with less education, lower status, isolation from the main sphere of cultural influence as reflected in living in rural regions and small towns, and fundamentalist religious beliefs. The conservative factor, however—that which contains attitudes relating to the welfare state, the role of government, and fear of socialism—tends to be related to a different set of social characteristics. In particular, the conservative antistatist tends to be drawn from the wealthier and better educated sections of the public. This finding clearly points up the difficulty facing movements, like that of Wallace, which seek to embrace both populations.

Similar findings have been reported in a study of the political behavior of southerners. This study, which involved the analysis of the interviews of a sample of 694 whites living in the South, concentrated on analyzing the effect of adherence to different denominations on attitudes toward integration, philosophical conservatism (attitudes toward change), and the welfare state. The author, Donald Freeman, reported adherents to the more fundamentalist groups, low education, low occupational status, rural residency, and having been brought up in a rural area as significantly correlated with anti-Negro sentiment. These factors retain their significance even after they are controlled for each other, as the data in Table 85 from Freeman's work indicate.[14]

The same pattern is reported with respect to philosophical conservatism; that is, resistance to change and modernism. This factor of Freeman's seems to deal with similar reactions to the one which we have been calling antimodernism. Freeman's philosophical conservatism factor is associated with sectarian affiliation, low income, low education, and rural residency.[15] Thus, as in our national survey data, opposition to integration and to modernism are associated with those factors which keep people outside the main currents of sophistication and privilege.

When Freeman turned to a consideration of attitudes toward the welfare state, he found an exact inversion, much as we do. Those groups which are most philosophically conservative and anti-Negro are the most liberal on welfare state items.

The Sects and Baptist groups, which were most conservative philosophically (in attitude toward change . . .) [and prosegregationist] are the most liberal Protestant groups on domestic policy issues; the Presbyterian and Episcopal Congregationalist-Christian groups, which were most liberal philosophically, are the most opposed to the Welfare State, as measured by a negative posture toward Welfare State type domestic policy questions.[16]

The picture of the high status-pair [Presbyterians and Episcopal-Congregational Christians] is thus complete: they have high socio-economic status, they are more cosmopolitan, more knowledgeable of the political world, have a high sense of political efficacy, are comparatively active in civic and political affairs, give the Republican party its strongest support in the South, were less affected by anti-Catholic feeling in the 1960 election, are more liberal on the race question . . . are liberal in political philosophy, and *are conservative on domestic policy*. The sectarians and Baptists are exact opposites to the high-status pair.[17]

It is obvious that there are two ideological sources of extremism which are associated with different structural variables. In order to specify the potential sources of support and opposition for the extreme right, we have created a number of issue publics, based on their location on two scales. The first was a new scale of intolerance which combined factors dealing with attitudes toward Negroes and those involving cultural intolerance. This was designed to place people on a monism-pluralism axis. The

Table 85. ATTITUDES OF SOUTHERN RELIGIOUS AND DENOMINATIONAL GROUPS TOWARD SEGREGATION WITH SELECTED CONTROLS

Religion or Denomination	Per Cent of Group Favoring Segregation by Control Block							
	Blue Collar	White Collar	Working Class	Middle Class	Low Education	Medium Education	High Education	Entire Group
Jewish	0.0[a]	0.0[a]	0.0[a]	0.0[a]	0.0[a]	0.0[a]	0.0[a]	0.0[a]
Catholic	42.1	18.8[a]	36.8	25.0	42.9[a]	41.7	22.2[a]	31.6
Episcopal-Congregational-Christians	50.0[a]	46.4	55.6	44.0	75.0[a]	50.0	41.7	47.5
Presbyterian	84.6	40.6	68.4	40.0	62.5	60.0	43.8	50.0
No preference	55.6	50.0[a]	77.8	33.3[a]	75.0[a]	57.1	40.0	52.4
Methodist	71.4	47.1	66.2	45.9	80.0	59.6	40.7	55.6
Other Protestants	50.0	35.3	76.9	33.3	88.2	41.2	38.5	56.3
Baptist	84.2	58.4	78.0	74.2	84.7	80.0	58.8	76.5
Sects	85.7	70.6	82.6	77.4	86.1	78.6	60.0	78.5
ALL GROUPS	75.3	48.4	73.0	54.3	81.5	67.2	46.0	63.8

[a] Based on less than 0.5 per cent of the sample.
SOURCE: Donald Freeman, *Religion and Southern Politics: The Political Behavior of Southern White Protestants* (Ph.D. Thesis, Department of Political Science, University of North Carolina, 1964), Table 5.2, p. 184.

economic conservatism scale was used to place people on a liberal-conservative axis. Four categories resulted: conservative monists, liberal monists, conservative pluralists, and liberal pluralists. To make these categories more easily distinguishable, they have been further designated by names which tend to identify them in terms of common usage. Thus, the conservative monists are called the Radical Right; the liberal monists are called Rednecks; the conservative pluralists are called the Old Guard; and the liberal pluralists are called Consistent Liberals.

The resultant typology enabled us to place over half of our respondents in one of four categories (Table 86). The remaining group were left in

Table 86.   DISTRIBUTION OF RADICAL RIGHT TYPOLOGY
(Percentage)

Rednecks (Liberal Monists)	19
Radical Rightists (Conservative Monists)	15
Consistent Liberals (Liberal Pluralists)	11
Old Guard (Conservative Pluralists)	8
Others (Miscellaneous Category)	47
Number	(1,975)

a miscellaneous category, composed of those who were not high on these dimensions. The typology is, of course, scale-created; it is useful for purposes of analysis and is not an attempt to describe the total population quantitatively.

There are, to begin with, two distinguishable axes among these groups, underlying the dimensions of bigotry and "conservatism": an educational axis and a "Quondam" axis.

Educational Differences

In the Educational Pattern (Table 87), a sharp difference is apparent between the more highly educated pluralists (Liberals and Old Guard) and the monists (Rednecks and Right Radicals). This is scarcely surprising, given the strong correlation between educational level and bigotry. This difference may be further specified through the analysis of a "sophistication" index developed by Selznick and Steinberg, based on an accurate identification of four authors (Robert Frost, Herman Melville, William Faulkner, and Mark Twain). Education held constant, this turns out to be a powerful factor in identifying bigots. There is a sharp difference between the monists and pluralists on this index, even holding education constant (Table 88). Another index was developed by these authors based on whether respondents knew that Congress did not have the right to prohibit

Table 87. CORRELATIONS OF TYPOLOGY PERCENTAGED BY ATTITUDE GROUP (DOWN)

	Rednecks	Right Radicals	Consistent Liberals	Old Guard	Others
Education					
8th grade	36	38	12	10	24
High school	56	47	41	39	44
Some college	6	9	18	21	14
College graduate	3	6	30	30	8
Number	(348)	(285)	(168)	(145)	(708)
Income					
Under $5,000	47	51	22	20	37
$5,000 to $9,999	39	34	47	48	42
$10,000 to $14,999	12	12	24	23	17
$15,000 and over	2	3	7	9	5
Number	(324)	(271)	(166)	(141)	(680)
Subjective Class					
Lower	46	38	22	25	38
Middle	45	50	56	49	49
Upper	8	13	22	26	13
Number	(345)	(283)	(172)	(143)	(739)
Occupation					
Farm	11	17	5	8	6
Worker and service	55	44	26	33	47
Clerical and sales	23	16	19	20	24
Business and professional	11	23	50	38	23
Retired*	15	21	6	5	12
Number	(208)	(203)	(129)	(99)	(509)
Religion					
Liberal Protestant	32	41	45	47	40
Fundamentalist Protestant	28	46	11	24	25
Catholic	40	13	43	29	36
Number	(321)	(248)	(141)	(127)	(642)
Religious Commitment					
Low	3	1	18	17	8
Middle	40	31	70	73	58
High	57	67	12	11	34
Number	(235)	(224)	(115)	(103)	(494)

* "Retired" not included in base from which the occupations in the labor force are computed.

Table 87. CORRELATIONS OF TYPOLOGY PERCENTAGED BY ATTITUDE GROUP (DOWN)
—CONTINUED

	Rednecks	Right Radicals	Consistent Liberals	Old Guard	Others
Age					
Under 34	20	18	38	42	32
35 to 54	41	34	46	41	39
54 and over	39	48	16	17	29
Number	(348)	(285)	(169)	(145)	(709)
Sex					
Male	38	50	50	56	50
Female	62	50	50	44	50
Number	(350)	(288)	(179)	(146)	(754)
Generation in America					
First	8	5	8	3	9
Second	26	18	24	22	26
Third	21	17	30	32	22
Fourth or more	44	60	38	43	44
Number	(347)	(285)	(169)	(145)	(708)
Childhood Region					
Northeast-Middle Atlantic	29	18	28	26	28
Midwest	36	28	38	43	38
Border	12	19	3	4	8
South	18	31	13	7	17
Mountain-Pacific	5	4	19	20	10
Number	(315)	(268)	(152)	(138)	(644)
Present Region					
Northeast-Middle Atlantic	31	21	34	23	31
Midwest	32	22	30	33	32
Border	12	15	4	3	6
South	14	34	9	12	14
Mountain-Pacific	10	8	23	30	18
Number	(350)	(288)	(179)	(145)	(754)
Where Raised					
Farm	36	50	19	19	30
Small town	28	20	30	24	26
Small city	7	6	11	10	9
Middle city	10	7	13	15	14
Big city	17	14	21	24	19
Suburb	3	3	6	8	3
Number	(350)	(288)	(178)	(146)	(754)

Table 87. CORRELATIONS OF TYPOLOGY PERCENTAGED BY ATTITUDE GROUP (DOWN)
—CONTINUED

	Rednecks	Right Radicals	Consistent Liberals	Old Guard	Others
Present City Size					
Under 5,000	34	40	20	22	29
5,000 to 20,000	26	19	33	30	25
20,000 to 100,000	19	21	24	28	24
100,000 to 500,000	16	17	10	16	16
500,000 and over	5	3	14	5	6
Number	(327)	(274)	(160)	(132)	(663)
Party Identification					
Republican	25	48	21	57	36
Democrat	69	44	71	33	57
Independent	6	8	7	10	7
Number	(338)	(281)	(178)	(144)	(737)
1964 Vote Preference					
Johnson	79	35	89	36	63
Goldwater	15	58	6	58	30
DK–NA	6	7	5	6	8
Number	(348)	(286)	(179)	(143)	(751)
Media Exposure					
Low	31	27	17	24	24
Middle	50	49	47	47	53
High	19	24	36	30	23
Number	(319)	(259)	(144)	(122)	(638)
High Culture Knowledge					
Low	29	28	4	6	17
Middle	50	51	36	40	46
High	21	21	60	54	37
Number	(345)	(283)	(167)	(144)	(704)
Years in Town					
Under 5	22	24	37	34	27
6 to 20	27	26	33	32	32
20 and over	52	51	30	34	41
Number	(349)	(288)	(179)	(146)	(754)
Geomobile					
Static	86	82	80	79	83
Mobile	14	18	20	21	17
Number	(315)	(268)	(152)	(138)	(644)

speech to dissenters and did not have a right to pass a law preventing an atheist from becoming President. Again, a sharp difference exists between monists and pluralists on this dimension, even if formal education is held constant (Table 89). In all cases of similar formal educational level the Rednecks and Right Radicals on the one hand show remarkably identical patterns, as do the Old Guard and the Liberals on the other hand. What are the differentiating factors between the two monist groupings, the Rednecks and the Right Radicals?

The Quondam Complex

The examination of those who are somehow out of joint with their society has usually been drawn from several slightly different conceptual viewpoints: alienation, anomie, status frustration, social disorganization, mass man. As these concepts of social disharmony apply to right-wing extremism, they might well be, for the moment, banded together for purposes of demystification as a kind of Quondam Complex. This simply describes the condition of those who have more of a stake in the past than in the present. The attachment to the past may be to some corporate identity

Table 88.   SOPHISTICATION BY TYPOLOGY AND EDUCATION*
(Per Cent)

Degree of Sophistication	Rednecks	Right Radicals	Consistent Liberals	Old Guard
8th Grade				
Unsophisticated (0 to 1)	57	68	55	29
Sophisticated (3 to 4)	14	12	15	42
Number	(126)	(108)	(20)	(14)
High School				
Unsophisticated	27	15	4	7
Sophisticated	41	44	68	61
Number	(194)	(133)	(68)	(57)
College				
Unsophisticated	11	9	0	0
Sophisticated	61	73	95	89
Number	(28)	(44)	(80)	(74)
Total				
Unsophisticated	37	33	8	6
Sophisticated	33	37	76	74
Number	(348)	(285)	(168)	(145)

* The middle group with sophistication scores of 2 is not reported in the table.

Table 89.   CONSTITUTIONAL KNOWLEDGE BY TYPOLOGY AND EDUCATION*
(Per Cent)

Extent of Knowledge	Rednecks	Right Radicals	Consistent Liberals	Old Guard
8th Grade				
Knowledgeable	11	14	65	57
Ignorant	53	43	0	7
Number	(126)	(108)	(20)	(14)
High School				
Knowledgeable	23	16	72	70
Ignorant	38	37	4	4
Number	(194)	(133)	(68)	(57)
College				
Knowledgeable	21	25	86	78
Ignorant	50	32	3	3
Number	(28)	(44)	(80)	(74)
Total				
Knowledgeable	18	17	79	73
Ignorant	45	39	3	3
Number	(348)	(285)	(168)	(145)

* The middle group is not reported.

which is anachronistic: an age group, an economic group, a regional group, an ethnic or religious group, an identifiable style-of-life group. The weak attachment to the present may be compounded by an absence of attachment to any group, the disorientation of the "mass man."

Kornhauser writes: "People are available for mass behavior when they lack attachments to proximate objects. When people are divorced from their community and work, they are free to reunite in new ways. Furthermore, those who do not possess a variety of relations with their fellows are disposed to seek new and often remote sources of attachment and allegiance."[18] One of the conditions of this "available nonelite" is the breakdown of old group allegiances because the old groupings have either lost significance in general, or have lost significance for the individual, or both.

This is the distinction between corporate status preservatism and anomic status preservatism. In the former case, the group has lost its former status and the individual clings to his group identification, striving to restore its former status. In the second case, the individual has lost his identification with former groups, but is seeking new forms of attachment and allegiance which are somehow redolent of the status that was once drawn from these former groups. In either case, the Quondam Complex describes a preponderance of symbolic investment in the past, related to some past group identity which has declined in symbolic significance. The Quondam Complex is politically actionable in these terms.

A number of observers have pointed out that the symbolic meaning in political action is often more salient than the economic, especially for the lower class. Morris Rosenberg warns that "we must not ignore the fact that political involvement may supply the individual with . . . the practical gratification of satisfying some material need. But psychologically speaking, the less obvious 'meanings' of politics to people are probably more influential in determining their political behavior."[19] And Robert Lane observes, on the basis of an election study:

> There are . . . reasons for believing that lower income groups, instead of relating their economic well-being to political decisions more closely than others, in fact are less likely to perceive this relationship. . . . And for a very good reason. Businessmen receive more individualized benefits from government: contracts, tariffs, tax abatements, etc. For them, therefore, there is an opportunity to relate personal gain to individual effort. Others, and especially workers, receive benefits only as members of larger groups and therefore see the rewards of effort as more tenuous and less probable.[20]

Murray Edelman also comments on the special pertinence of symbolic politics to the available nonelite:

> The political realm, unlike work and church, is always available for evocative use as masses need to use it. There is no tie to a manifestly trivial and mechanical function as in unskilled work, but rather the assurance that each voter's part is significant. Nor is there a setting calling for a competitive display of clothes, conformity and sentimentality as in many churches, but rather a sense of belonging to something real and decisive. Politics can therefore become a residual supplier of the symbols that men require. A number of students influenced by Freud have observed that an increase in demand for political acts that gratify sensuality accompanies widespread alienation or loss of faith in the rationality of social processes. One way to fight anomie is to fall back upon the excitement of the senses.[21]

Parsons suggests that "an increase in anomie may be a consequence of almost any change in the social situation which upsets previously established definitions of the situation, or routines of life, or symbolic associations."[22]

These various approaches to the effects of social disorganization, of noncohesion in society, are all related to the disintegration of meaningful group attachments fixed in the past. "In a pluralist society . . . the inner cohesion of local groups and cultures provides a firmer basis for self-relatedness, and the diversity of groups and cultures permits the individual to form a distinctive self-image."[23] This self-image is related, of course, to the concept of status, which is finally a self-perception, however much based on "objectively" accorded deference. Whenever that status seems to be in a state of decline, the Quondam Complex is likely to be operative; it is associated with a declining sense of social comfort, as many observers have noted, a declining sense of social and political efficacy.

A strong stake in the present—occupationally, for example—will apparently diminish the effect of the Quondam Syndrome. And a high level of education seems to act as an independent countervailing factor.

There are a number of objective indices which hypothetically bear on the development of Quondam tendencies. Initially, questions of age, region, size of community, where raised, and generational history all carry on their face, other things being equal, some assumption of relative stake in the past.

Age

The age difference, with its built-in educational disparity, sharply divides the monists from the pluralists (Table 87). These age differences generally hold up when education is kept constant (Table 90). However, a further analysis of the relative effect of age and education on producing the various types (Table 91) suggests a difference between the Rednecks and right-wing Radicals. High age is more associated with Right Radicals at low educational levels. This is not the case for the Rednecks.

Region

It can be hypothesized that the South in its subjectively embattled state would reflect more intense Quondam impulses than the North. And it can be expected that both categories of monists will have a disproportionately heavy representation from the South and border states, as they do, because of the built-in measure of bigotry. But, of course, the educational factor is also built into the bigotry syndrome. An analysis of the relative role of region and education (Table 92) again suggests a special Quondam factor among Right Radicals. Proportionately as many eighth-graders from the North as from the South are likely to end up in the Redneck columns. The same is true for high-school and college graduates. However, at each educational level, there are more southerners among the Right Radicals than northerners. Being a southerner has a special meaning for the Right Radical category that it does not have for the Rednecks.

Table 90. AGE, BY TYPOLOGY AND EDUCATION
(Per Cent)

Age Group	Rednecks	Right Radicals	Consistent Liberals	Old Guard
		8th Grade		
Young (under 35)	10	5	10	7
Old (over 54)	64	77	30	71
Number	(126)	(108)	(20)	(14)
		High School		
Young	27	25	40	39
Old	22	29	13	7
Number	(194)	(133)	(68)	(57)
		College		
Young	25	30	43	51
Old	43	34	15	14
Number	(28)	(44)	(80)	(74)

Where Raised

It is no longer axiomatic that those who were raised on a farm are more likely to be nostalgic for the past than those who were raised in the big city. Too much has happened in the city itself. It is still true that farm origins are more heavily represented among the monists than among the pluralists (Table 87), but when educational factors are analyzed, this disproportion largely slips away as an analytical factor (Table 93). However, even here the one exception is the indication that while 26 per cent of the farm-raised college graduates are Right Radicals, only 8 per cent of the college graduates raised in big cities are in this group, in somewhat inverse proportion to the Rednecks. Here again is the suggestion of a special Quondam impulse among Right Radicals.

Generation

Generational history—being of old stock—seems to have some special relationship to Right Radicals that it does not have to Rednecks (Table 87). And, again, subjected to analysis by education, it is revealed that for the Right Radicals this generational factor has a meaning that is not washed out by education (Table 94). Since Old Americans are more likely to live in the South and to be engaged in relatively lower-income work in rural areas and small towns, income and region were held constant to see if this generational difference held up for the ideological types. It did.

Table 91.   TYPOLOGY, BY EDUCATION AND AGE
(Per Cent)

Education	Old (over 54)		Young (under 35)	
	Per Cent	Number	Per Cent	Number
Rednecks				
8th grade	28[a]	(285)	31	(40)
High school	27	(159)	19	(276)
College	14	(83)	5	(155)
Right Radicals				
8th grade	29	(285)	13	(40)
High school	24	(159)	12	(276)
College	18	(83)	8	(155)
Consistent Liberals				
8th grade	8	(285)	5	(40)
High school	6	(159)	10	(276)
College	14	(83)	22	(155)
Old Guard				
8th grade	3	(285)	3	(40)
High school	3	(159)	8	(276)
College	12	(83)	25	(155)

[a] Twenty-eight per cent of those who have eighth-grade education or less and are over fifty-four are Rednecks.

Occupation

Occupational status lies astride both axes under discussion. There is, of course, a fundamental correlation between occupation and education. But there is also a correlation between occupation and income and status, both of which bear some Quondam implications. The pluralist categories naturally have a generally higher occupational status level than the monists (Table 87). The Right Radicals reflect a special emphasis among farmers and business professional people, the Rednecks among manual workers. The Right Radicals tend to have a higher occupational status than the Rednecks (Table 95) among those who did not go to college.

This leads to another path. An analysis of the relationship of income to occupation reveals that the Right Radicals have lower income than do the Old Guard for the same occupational levels (Table 96). Indeed, an analysis of relationship between age and income shows that the older Right Radicals receive considerably less income than the older members of the Old Guard (Table 97). Here, perhaps, in the specific form of

Table 92. TYPOLOGY BY REGION AND EDUCATION
(Per Cent)

Education	Southern and Border States		Rest of Country	
	Per Cent	Number	Per Cent	Number
Rednecks				
8th grade	27[a]	(139)	30	(296)
High school	25	(190)	23	(646)
College	7	(101)	8	(282)
Right Radicals				
8th grade	42	(139)	17	(296)
High school	29	(190)	12	(646)
College	27	(101)	6	(282)
Consistent Liberals				
8th grade	2	(139)	6	(296)
High school	4	(190)	9	(646)
College	12	(101)	24	(282)
Old Guard				
8th grade	0	(139)	5	(296)
High school	3	(190)	8	(646)
College	15	(101)	21	(282)

[a] Percentage of those with eighth-grade education or less and living in southern and border states who are Rednecks.

status disparity, is another suggestion of the special Quondam potential among the Right Radicals, as distinct from the Old Guard.

Subjective Indices

In the schedule of questions used in our national sample, the one that seems, on its face, most reflective of a Quondam stance asked respondents about the state of morals in this country. Of the population that proffered an opinion, 47 per cent said that morals were "bad and getting worse." Education did not make a difference for this question. At both the eighth-grade level and the high-school level, 48 per cent gave this answer, and 41 per cent did so at the college level (Table 98). This is a bigotry-pure question, unrelated to education, yet reflecting a generalized attitude that people's behavior was better in the past and is still deteriorating. This "moral" dimension, we have seen, has always been at the explicit center of Quondam-based ideology.

Reversing the education and bigotry pattern, 64 per cent of the Right Radicals and 63 per cent of the Old Guard held this view, as against 34

Table 93. TYPOLOGY BY WHERE RAISED AND EDUCATION
(Per Cent)

Education	Farm		Big City	
	Per Cent	Number	Per Cent	Number
Rednecks				
8th grade	25[a]	(246)	23	(43)
High school	24	(234)	25	(165)
College	9	(76)	13	(72)
Right Radicals				
8th grade	29	(246)	26	(246)
High school	16	(234)	13	(234)
College	26	(76)	8	(76)
Consistent Liberals				
8th grade	4	(246)	7	(246)
High school	5	(234)	8	(234)
College	16	(76)	32	(76)
Old Guard				
8th grade	2	(246)	9	(246)
High school	5	(234)	8	(234)
College	17	(76)	24	(76)

[a] Percentage of those with eighth-grade education or less and raised on farm who are Rednecks.

Table 94. TYPOLOGY BY GENERATION AND EDUCATION

Education	Per Cent 4th Generation or More		Per Cent 3rd Generation or Less	
	Per Cent	Number	Per Cent	Number
Rednecks				
8th grade	27[a]	(175)	27	(248)
College	6	(199)	9	(141)
Right Radicals				
8th grade	34	(175)	15	(248)
College	15	(199)	8	(141)
Consistent Liberals				
8th grade	3	(175)	6	(248)
College	19	(199)	23	(141)
Old Guard				
8th grade	2	(175)	4	(248)
College	16	(199)	23	(141)

[a] Percentage of those with eighth-grade education or less, of fourth generation or more, who are Rednecks.

Table 95. TYPOLOGY, BY EDUCATION AND OCCUPATION
(Per Cent)

Occupation	Rednecks	Right Radicals	Consistent Liberals	Old Guard
		8th Grade		
Farmer	19	31	13	22
Worker and service	63	52	63	56
Business and professional	5	13	19	0
Clerical and sales	13	4	6	22
Number	(79)	(82)	(16)	(9)
		High School		
Farmer	8	8	7	15
Worker and service	60	51	41	54
Business and professional	6	21	30	5
Clerical and sales	27	20	22	27
Number	(107)	(85)	(46)	(41)
		College		
Farmer	0	6	3	0
Worker and service	5	9	3	13
Business and professional	55	52	71	73
Clerical and sales	40	33	23	15
Number	(20)	(33)	(61)	(48)

per cent of Rednecks and 30 per cent of Liberals. This pattern holds up at all educational levels.

The same kind of pattern developed in response to a series of questions relating to the loss of United States power, another question with clear Quondam implications. This also turns out to be bigotry-pure, largely unrelated to education. While 61 per cent of the Old Guard and 50 per cent of the Right Radicals believed that the United States is losing power, 16 per cent of the Liberals and 7 per cent of the Rednecks held this belief, and there was no essential variation in this pattern at the different educational levels (Table 99).

Religious Commitment

Religious commitment—that is, particularistic and orthodox views about religion—again seems to divide the monists sharply from the pluralists (Table 100). This division remains constant at the various educational levels. But an analysis of the relative effect of education and of religious commitment indicates that both seem to have an independent effect (Table 101). This squares with our earlier analyses of the effects of

Table 96.   TYPOLOGY, BY OCCUPATION AND INCOME
(Per Cent)

Income	Rednecks	Right Radicals	Consistent Liberals	Old Guard
		Farmers		
Under $5,000	61	70	*	*
$5,000 to $9,999	13	15	—	—
$10,000 and over	26	15	—	—
Number	(23)	(33)	(6)	(8)
		Worker and Service		
Under $5,000	50	60	31	36
$5,000 to $9,999	44	33	59	55
$10,000 and over	6	7	9	10
Number	(110)	(85)	(32)	(31)
		Clerical and Sales		
Under $5,000	41	21	21	15
$5,000 to $9,999	30	52	50	70
$10,000 and over	28	28	25	15
Number	(46)	(29)	(24)	(20)
		Business and Professional		
Under $5,000	39	39	8	6
$5,000 to $9,999	28	34	43	44
$10,000 and over	33	27	48	50
Number	(18)	(44)	(60)	(36)

* Too few cases.

education and religious commitment on prejudice. Finding an "independent" effect for religious commitment does not yet pin down causal relationships. Glock and Stark, in reporting similar independent effects for religious commitment and education in producing anti-Semitism, suggest that "the way in which education affects anti-Semitism, is through a changing of religious views of the world. Education is accompanied by religious changes, the more educated taking up a less traditional religious outlook, and, consequently, tending to lose a religious basis for anti-Semitism."[24] However, the authors agree that the time order postulated is a matter of inference:

It might be argued that we have postulated this developmental sequence backwards, that while our correlations cannot be denied, they can be interpreted in a way that removes all causal burden from religion. Thus, it might be claimed that secular anti-Semitism comes first and that persons then embrace religion to provide an additional justification for their anti-Semitism. A definitive solution to this question of time order cannot be provided by a survey of

Table 97. TYPOLOGY, BY AGE AND INCOME
(Per Cent)

Age	Rednecks		Right Radicals		Consistent Liberals		Old Guard	
	Per Cent	Num- ber	Per Cent	Num- ber	Per Cent	Num- ber	Per Cent	Num- ber
Low Income (under $5,000)								
Under 35	41	(66)	35	(49)	27	(63)	27	(60)
Over 54	73	(125)	74	(129)	33	(27)	29	(24)
High Income (over $10,000)								
Under 35	15	(66)	10	(49)	13	(63)	17	(60)
Over 54	6	(125)	5	(129)	30	(27)	13	(24)

Table 98. TYPOLOGY, BY OPINION THAT "MORALS ARE BAD AND
GETTING WORSE" AND EDUCATION
(Per Cent)

Education	Rednecks		Right Radicals		Consistent Liberals		Old Guard	
	Per Cent	Num- ber	Per Cent	Num- ber	Per Cent	Num- ber	Per Cent	Num- ber
8th grade	33	(104)	70	(102)	21	(19)	86	(14)
High school	34	(187)	60	(126)	37	(59)	71	(55)
College	30	(27)	59	(44)	27	(66)	52	(65)
Total	34	(319)	64	(275)	30	(152)	63	(135)

Table 99. TYPOLOGY, BY OPINION THAT "U.S. IS LOSING POWER" AND EDUCATION
(Per Cent)

Education	Rednecks		Right Radicals		Consistent Liberals		Old Guard	
	Per Cent	Num- ber	Per Cent	Num- ber	Per Cent	Num- ber	Per Cent	Num- ber
8th grade	8	(116)	46	(99)	16	(19)	77	(13)
High school	7	(188)	53	(129)	5	(64)	51	(55)
College	0	(26)	51	(43)	23	(78)	65	(72)
Total	7	(332)	50	(273)	16	(171)	61	(141)

Table 100. TYPOLOGY, BY RELIGIOUS COMMITMENT AND EDUCATION
(Per Cent High in Religious Commitment)

Education	Rednecks		Right Radicals		Consistent Liberals		Old Guard	
	Per Cent	Number	Per Cent	Number	Per Cent	Number	Per Cent	Number
8th grade	67	(82)	78	(86)	25	(12)	10	(10)
High school	51	(133)	64	(103)	13	(48)	13	(39)
College	55	(20)	51	(35)	9	(55)	9	(54)
Total	57	(235)	67	(224)	12	(115)	11	(103)

Table 101. TYPOLOGY, BY RELIGIOUS COMMITMENT AND EDUCATION
(Per Cent)

Religious Commitment	8th Grade		High School		College	
	Per Cent	Number	Per Cent	Number	Per Cent	Number
	Rednecks					
High	30[a]	(183)	30	(227)	17	(66)
Low	14	(14)	8	(37)	3	(37)
	Right Radicals					
High	37	(183)	26	(227)	27	(66)
Low	7	(14)	5	(37)	0	(37)
	Consistent Liberals					
High	2	(183)	3	(227)	8	(66)
Low	14	(14)	10	(37)	42	(37)
	Old Guard					
High (1)	1	(183)	2	(227)	8	(66)
Low	14	(14)	16	(37)	24	(37)

[a] Percentage of those who have an eighth-grade education or less and have a high religious commitment who are Rednecks.

persons taken only at one point in time. Conclusive proof could only be obtained through a longitudinal or panel study in which changes in individuals' religious outlooks and in their anti-Semitism could be examined to see which occur first. But the absence of conclusive proof does not mean the question must be left entirely open; some evidence can be adduced. First of all, there seems no persuasive theoretical reason to expect anti-Semitism to produce religious commitment. It seems reasonable to expect an anti-Semite to be attracted to hate groups, but why should we expect him to turn to abiding faith in God because of his bigotry? Furthermore there seems to be strong inferential evidence that religious beliefs and traditions are typically learned earlier than are attitudes towards Jews.[25]

The question, however *does* have to be left open, in terms other than those used by the authors. First of all, if active bigotry is partly a function of historical backlash to begin with, the interpretation is turned somewhat if religious commitment is seen as often having more of a cultural quality than an ideological quality. The cause and effect then become blurred. Religious commitment then may, indeed, under certain circumstances, be intensified by a backlash which is associated with nativist bigotry. At least, within our political context, there is some indication that religious commitment is often a secondary characteristic of some other condition which directly affects the activation of bigotry.

The Radical Rightists show a tendency at both the lower and higher educational levels to be more responsive to the factor of religious commitments than do the Rednecks. For example, while the proportion of high religious commitment among college Rednecks is about the same as the proportion of low religious commitment among eighth-grade Rednecks (17 per cent and 14 per cent), the proportion of high religious commitment among college Right Radicals is markedly higher than the proportion of low religious commitment among eighth-grade Right Radicals (27 per cent and 7 per cent). It is suggested that religious commitment is "cultural baggage" for many who are involved with the Quondam Complex; and this pattern again underlines a significant difference between Right Radicals and Rednecks.

In brief, the variance among these "types" emerges in the designs laid out in Table 102. There are a number of implications in these analyses of population characteristics which corroborate and suggest refinements for generalizations made about right-wing extremist movements on the basis of historical study. There are at least three different kinds of right-wing strains:

1. *The economic conservatism and preservatism represented by the Old Guard with its relatively high economic position.* This is a position which is also laced with connected high-status considerations; that is, the Old Guard exhibits a prima facie Quondam dimension as compared to the relatively high-income Consistent Liberals, with respect to such matters as Protestantism, age, and generational vintage. The Old Guard is also less likely to live in large cities (Table 87). The analytical tables lean in the direction of this Quondam differential, although they do not show up as sharply as that between the Radical Right and the Rednecks.

2. *The status preservatism represented by the Radical Rightists with*

Table 102.   VARIATIONS BETWEEN THE DIFFERENT ANALYTIC TYPES

Differences between Monists and Pluralists

Monists	Pluralists
(Radical Right and Rednecks)	(Old Guard and Consistent Liberals)
Less educated	More educated
Higher socioeconomic status	Lower socioeconomic status
More Religious Commitment	Less Religious Commitment

Differences between Radical Right Monists and Redneck Monists

Radical Right	Rednecks
More middle-class	More working-class
More fundamentalist Protestant	More Catholic
More from Southern and Border states	More from Eastern and Midwestern states
More from rural areas and small towns	Less from rural areas and small towns
Older stock	Newer stock
Republicans	Democrats

Differences between the Old Guard and Consistent Liberals

Old Guard	Consistent Liberals
More Protestant	More Catholic (and Jewish)
More from the West	More from the East
Older	Younger
Older stock	Newer Stock
Less exposed to mass media	More exposed to mass media
Republicans	Democrats

their strong Quondam position. This is a position which is also laced by a measure of economic conservatism. An initial comparison of occupational proportions provides an on-the-surface clue to that conservatism, if farmers and white-collar workers are considered most likely to hold economically conservative views, as distinct from manual workers. About 46 per cent of the Old Guard and 39 per cent of the Radical Right fall into that joint category, as against 22 per cent of the Rednecks. But, unlike the Old Guard, a substantial portion of these putative conservatives among the Right Radicals are farmers, with their own (Quondam-connected) qualities; and it has already been shown that, within occupational divisions, the income of the Old Guard is higher, indicating that a more refined occupational analysis would reveal higher occupational investment among the Old Guard. And, in fact, the income status of the Radical Right closely resembles that of the Rednecks, not that of the Old Guard (Table 87). The two "conservative" categories of the Right Wing seem to be partly distinguished by different *kinds* of conservatism, referred to by Freeman as "economic" and "philosophical." Philosophical conservatism is, in fact, status preservatism, and that is the thrust of the Radical Right strain.

3. *The common democratic commitment, marked by low democratic restraint, represented by the Rednecks, with their low educational position.* It is true that the Right Radicals share this common democratic commitment with the Rednecks, as they share with the Rednecks a relatively low economic status. But the Quondam Complex dominates the normal political stance of the Radical Rightists, as distinct from the Rednecks.

This scarcely means that the Rednecks are not subject to status concerns, along with everyone else. However, it does mean, in terms of this gross typological construct, that their political thrust is anchored in their economic position; just as that of the Old Guard is anchored in *its* economic position, with Quondam overtones; just as that of the Radical Right is anchored in its Quondam position. However, the Rednecks, as history has suggested, are quite susceptible to status preservatism, whenever it becomes or is made salient *and* when it jibes with their economic position, or at least does not interfere with it. On that status level, the backlash targetry is typically ethnic or racial in nature, to which, because of their relatively low level of democratic restraint, the Rednecks are also susceptible; and, of course, as seen on the longer historical canvas, the "Rednecks" of today can cross that mythical line and become the normative "Radical Right" of tomorrow, given persistent changes in their historical circumstances.

The practical political implications are many. It is relatively easy to "marry" the Old Guard and the Radical Right around a generally preservatist position. Table 103 indicates a strong measure of support for the Birch Society among the Radical Right and the Old Guard, as compared to the Rednecks. The economic conservatism of the Birch Society would be more unacceptable to the Rednecks. The one group, however, which produced a large segment strongly disapproving of the Birch Society was the Consistent Liberals. The Rednecks were much more likely to fall

Table 103.   ATTITUDES TOWARD BIRCH SOCIETY, BY TYPOLOGY
(Per Cent)

Attitude to Birch Society	Rednecks	Right Radicals	Consistent Liberals	Old Guard	Others
Strongly approve	1	2	1	2	1
Mildly approve	5	14	4	19	12
DK	32	34	19	36	30
Mildly disapprove	11	16	22	23	17
Strongly disapprove	13	10	48	17	24
Have not heard of it	38	23	6	4	17
Number	(350)	(288)	(179)	(145)	(753)

into the category of mild disapprovers. Similarly, in the 1964 election, when Goldwater dramatically represented a generally preservatist line including economic preservatism, he drew the equal support of the Radical Right and the Old Guard as sharply distinct from the Rednecks (Table 104). The lines in that case notably exceeded the differences in party lines between the Radical Right and Rednecks, which normative difference is itself another index to the point being made.

An analysis of the relationship between party identification, issue publics, and 1964 vote shows how Goldwater appealed to and alienated these groups differently (Table 104). It tells us that Johnson gained among Republicans from the Consistent Liberals and the Rednecks. Seemingly about half of the latter group were negatively affected by Goldwater's extreme economic conservatism. Conversely, he retained the support of almost everyone who fell in the category of Radical Rightists or Old Guard.

On the other hand, Wallace had a more substantial appeal than Goldwater to the Rednecks and less of an appeal to the Old Guard. In Table 105 is reproduced Table 87 of the last chapter, substituting the typology for the terms used in the former table. It should be evident that the different terms are not operationally the same, since the items used to construct them are different, but the analytic logic is similar. Wallace was presumably more attractive than Goldwater to the Rednecks because he combined a status preservatism appropriate to the social strains of the day with a relatively nonthreatening economic stance. The Old Guard, having Nixon, were resistant to Wallace's apparent lack of democratic restraint.

This typological analysis underlines the kind of difficulty which a radical

Table 104. TYPOLOGY, PARTY IDENTIFICATION, AND THE 1964 VOTE
(Per Cent)

1964 Vote	Rednecks	Right Radicals	Consistent Liberals	Old Guard	Others
			Republicans		
Goldwater	42	85	20	86	61
Johnson	49	12	63	9	28
DK–NA	9	4	17	5	11
Number	(79)	(113)	(35)	(64)	(248)
			Democrats		
Goldwater	4	38	1	29	10
Johnson	92	51	98	69	87
DK–NA	4	11	2	3	4
Number	(223)	(97)	(121)	(35)	(408)

Table 105.   TYPOLOGY, BY 1968 VOTE, WHITES ONLY*

	Humphrey	Nixon	Wallace	Number
"Consistent Liberals"				
(Tolerant Economic Liberals)	48 %	44 %	8 %	(319)
"Rednecks"				
(Intolerant Liberals)	33	35	32	(254)
"Old Guard"				
(Tolerant Conservatives)	16	75	9	(152)
"Radical Right"				
(Intolerant Conservatives)	12	52	35	(147)

* Data from 1968 Gallup postelection survey.

right movement has in putting together a program that will bridge the preservatism of the upper class and the preservatism of the lower class without violating the pocketbook interests of the latter. But it also indicates the kinds of terms in which it can be done.

Free and Cantril make a distinction between the Operational Liberal and the Philosophical Liberal, which provides further support for this conceptual analysis from a slightly different angle.[26] Respondents to a 1967 survey were classified as Operational Liberals if they tended to favor government intervention in specific welfare matters: Medicare, federal housing, urban renewal, federal funds for education, reduction of unemployment, and so forth. Respondents were classified as Ideological Liberals if they tended to favor government intervention in the abstract; that is, if they disagreed with the following kinds of statements: "The federal government is interfering too much in state and local matters"; "The government has gone too far in regulating business and interfering with the free enterprise system"; "We should rely more on individual initiative and ability, and not so much on governmental welfare programs."

On these measures, about 65 per cent of the American people showed up as Operational Liberals (statist on economic issues); only about 16 per cent showed up as Ideological Liberals (statist conceptually). One of the main reasons for this discrepancy was that so many of the lower socioeconomic and educational groups were operationally liberal and ideologically conservative. This demonstrates again low levels of ideology, of integrated belief systems. But something else may be involved that is significant for extremist movements of the right. This blue-collar, lower-educated group that registered as operationally statist and conceptually antistatist tended to be white. Poor Negroes were consistently "liberal." There was also a disproportionate number of southerners among them. What is suggested in the ideologically conservative vote is not a conceptual vote at all, but a vote against some of the concrete actions government was taking in areas of symbolic interests (such as civil rights), just as the operationally liberal vote was a vote for concrete actions the government was taking or should take with respect to certain of their economic interests. This sector of "ideological conservatism," then, would mean something different for the upper socioeconomic groups than it does for the lower ones who vote for it, but it becomes a kind of common sector in which the two groups can engage in common political activity. The delineation of such a common symbolic sector is necessary, as we have seen, for the effective establishment of a right-wing preservatist extremist movement.

In other terms, this common sector emphasizes the kind of symbolic status-connected questions which distinguish the lower-class members of the Radical Right public from those of the Redneck public. After all, almost half of the Radical Right public is from the working class. This indication meshes with the fact that the Radical Right public, compared to the Redneck, is heavily Protestant, rural, old American, and southern.

The typological analysis also throws further emphasis to the nature and extent of the Common Democratic Commitment and the vulnerability of the populace to extremism. The monists are not distinguished from the pluralists by conservatism and liberalism, but by the connected factors of socioeconomic status, education, and religious commitment. If we look at the "others" in the typology tables, we can see that these characteristics much more closely resemble those of the Rednecks and the Radicals of the Right than those of the Old Guard and of the Consistent Liberals.

The Factor of Democratic Restraint

There is other corroborative evidence that the absence of democratic restraint which characterizes the monists is also present in the bulk of the population.

For example, among the right-wing letter writers described in the chapters on the Birch Society, one item which attracted attention was that which asked the respondents whether they thought that the Jews have too much power, perhaps the most basic staple in the propaganda of political anti-Semitism. Almost half of those whose letters had evinced some overt evidence of monism subscribed to this belief, as against less than a quarter of the other letter writers. This is a much wider margin of difference than had appeared on items of folk anti-Semitism. The "Too Much Power" items similarly distinguished the letter writers from the national population. About a third of the total group of letter writers held this view, as against only 11 per cent of the population, again a much more significant gap than developed between letter writers and the national population on items of folk anti-Semitism. It was also discovered that almost none (5 per cent) of the letter writers who said the Jews have too much power disagreed with both of two items: the Whip Sexers item and the Hatched Plots item.[27] These are two of the items usually used in the Authoritarianism (F) Scale, presumably to measure the "authoritarian personality."

The authoritarian (F) scale itself as applied to the typology reveals a predictably high ranking among the monists, especially the Radical Right, at lower educational levels, and very little spread among the three "right-wing" groupings at the college level (Table 106). The literature has indicated that this scale is most pertinent to personality analysis at the higher educational levels and may be indicative of other factors at lower levels. In the case of the right-wing letter writers, the two items in question seemed to behave in independent fashion. The number of cases in the cells became too small at many points to be conclusive, but the results were so consistent and interesting that they are cited as illustrative of some of the points that have been made and as clues to further research.

The entire letter-writing sample was divided into four categories: M1 includes those who agreed on both the Whip Sexers and Hatched Plots; M2, those who agreed on Whip Sexers but not Hatched Plots; M3, those who agreed on Hatched Plots but not on Whip Sexers; and M4, those who disagreed on both.

Table 107 indicates the sharp drop-off with respect to political anti-Semitism, from 76 per cent to 7 per cent, as we move from M1 to M4. It also dramatizes the fact that this differential occurs among a group which is constant in its right-wing political sentiments, which we could, of course, have assumed from the nature of the letter writers.

The first distinction between the two items, Whip Sexers and Hatched Plots, is suggested by the fact (Table 108) that the Whip Sexers item is about the same for the letter writers, the national population, and the Goldwater voters. However, almost twice the proportion of letter writers affirm Hatched Plots in comparison with the other two groups. The propor-

Table 106. AUTHORITARIANISM (F SCALE)
(Per Cent High on Factor)

Education	Rednecks		Right Radicals		Consistent Liberals		Old Guard	
	Per Cent	Num-ber	Per Cent	Num-ber	Per Cent	Num-ber	Per Cent	Num-ber
8th grade	62	(130)	64	(100)	*		*	(10)
High school	47	(188)	62	(125)	13	(67)	31	(52)
College	23	(26)	28	(47)	3	(77)	20	(66)

* Too few cases for an estimate.

Table 107.   RELATIONSHIP OF WHIP SEXERS AND HATCHED PLOT ITEMS TO
OTHER ATTITUDES (RIGHT-WING LETTER WRITERS)

	M1	M2	M3	M4
Per cent agree that				
"Jews have too much power"	76	29	7	7
Per cent agree with *both* items:				
"In the past 25 years, this country has moved dangerously close to socialism"				
and	97	100	93	93
"The federal government is gradually taking away our basic freedoms"				
Number	(36)	(25)	(15)	(28)

Table 108.   PER CENT WHO AGREE WITH WHIP SEXERS AND HATCHED PLOT ITEMS
BY POPULATION GROUPS

Attitude Items	Letter Writers	National Population	Goldwater Voters
Whip Sexers	56	57	56
Hatched Plots	45	25	27
Number	(115)	(1,914)	(474)

tion who affirm both is about the same for the letter writers, but Hatched Plots drops off sharply for both the national population and the Goldwater voters.

A second item of differential note: If we break down the letter writers by education, we find (Table 109) that the Hatched Plots factor stays about the same through all the educational levels, but that the Whip Sexers item drops off sharply from 90 per cent to 33 per cent, from grade level to college.

A third differential item of note: In Table 110 we can see that if we lump high anti-Semitism and very high anti-Semitism, the Whip Sexers factor makes a tremendous difference, but Hatched Plots makes no significant difference. On the other hand, Hatched Plot is the factor which pushes into the very high anti-Semitism columns, which, according to other indices, suggests a tendency toward political anti-Semitism.

If we reexamine Table 107, we will similarly see that a belief in Hatched Plots, by itself, does not end up in a belief in too much power; but if there is a belief in Whip Sexers, belief in Hatched Plot pushes a preponderance of people into the category of believing that the Jews have too much power.

The indication is that the Whip Sexers item represents in some way lack of democratic restraint, while the Hatched Plot item represents an

Table 109. RELATIONSHIP OF WHIP SEXERS, HATCHED PLOTS, AND TOO-MUCH-POWER
ITEMS TO EDUCATION (LETTER WRITERS)
(Per Cent Agree with Item)

Education	Whip-Sexers	Hatched Plots	Jews Have Too Much Power	Number
0 to 8th grade	90 %	60 %	50 %	(10)
9th to 11th grades	83	75	54	(13)
High school graduate	56	48	36	(23)
Some college	64	40	46	(28)
College graduate	39	62	11	(18)
Postgraduate	33	66	24	(22)

Table 110. RELATIONSHIP OF WHIP SEXERS AND HATCHED PLOT ITEMS
TO ANTI-SEMITISM (LETTER WRITERS)

Anti-Semitism Scale	M1	M2	M3	M4
High	20 %	25 %	12 %	11 %
Very High	48	25	0	0
Total High	68	50	12	11
Number	(35)	(25)	(15)	(28)

ideological or paraideological cast; that is, a politicalization. Of course,
the population of letter writers tends to be politicalized by definition. The
Whip Sexers item falls steadily as the educational ladder rises; not so the
Hatched Plot item. It is the lack-of-restraint item which controls the
expression of political anti-Semitism; that is, without it, there is no political
anti-Semitism. But it is the addition of the politicalization item which
creates the greatest bulge of political anti-Semitism, which stands in for
this purpose as a measure of monism. Now, if we go back to the fact that
the national population is as high as this letter-writing population in
registering lack of restraint, as measured by our indicial item, but is very
much lower in registering a state of politicalization, we can thus detect not
just another sign of the potential for monism in the broad population,
which is more soundly substantiated elsewhere, but also a kind of explanatory model for that potential.

How does the typology compare on these key items (Table 111)? The
Rednecks are well above the national population in the Whip Sexers item
(70 per cent to 57 per cent), but just match the national population
on the Hatched Plots item (28 per cent to 27 per cent). The Right
Radicals are somewhat further above the national average in Whip Sexers

Table 111. RELATIONSHIP OF WHIP SEXERS AND HATCHED PLOTS TO TYPOLOGY

	Whip Sexers	Hatched Plots	Number
Rednecks	70 %	28 %	(273)
Right Radicals	76	45	(241)
Old Guard	41	31	(129)
Consistent Liberals	24	5	(150)
Other	55	25	(587)
Total Population	57	27	(1,380)

(76 per cent), but are also considerably above both the Rednecks and the national population in Hatched Plots (45 per cent). The Old Guard is significantly below the national average and further below the Rednecks and Radicals on Whip Sexers, but is even a little higher than the Rednecks on Hatched Plots. This pattern intensifies the suggestion that the Rednecks and Right Radicals are relatively characterized by lack of democratic restraint, and the Right Radicals are further characterized by a relatively high level of politicalization.

This leads to the simple fact that at least one factor in the success of extremist movements has always been their ability to organize and to communicate to the vulnerable segment of the population; that is, to politicalize a following so that it would at least have some idea of "what goes with what," in Converse's terms, even if it does not know "why." Herbert Blumer writes that

the gaining of sympathetic support and the recruitment of followers for a movement involve much more than the psychological conditions of individuals on one hand and, on the other, a set of "appeals" which are supposed to fit the psychological conditions. . . . Instead the prospective sympathizer or member has to be aroused, nurtured, and directed, and the so-called appeal has to be developed and adapted. . . . Thus, realistically, it is not the mere appeal that counts; instead it is a *process of agitation* that is important.[28]

Politicalization, then, means beginning to effectively transmit some generalized belief to a particular segment of the population, relating to the particular strains being suffered by that population. Smelser defines a generalized belief as one "which identifies the source of strain, attributes certain characteristics to the source, and specifies certain responses to the strain as possible or appropriate."[29] Such generalized beliefs "create a 'common culture' within which leadership, mobilization and concerted action can take place."[30] Politicalization describes the spectrum of stages which leads from the transmission of a generalized belief to mobilization in a movement which relates to and is promulgating that belief. The politicalization, in any given case, is of a "politically available" population.

With respect to right-wing extremism, the available populations are those which exhibit some appropriate combination of these characteristics: (1) Common Democratic Commitment (low democratic restraint); (2) Quondam Complex; (3) Economic Conservatism. The circumstances of their availability, the mechanics of their politicalization, and the possibilities for social control must be seen in the framework of the total historical and psychosocial examination of right-wing extremism.

Notes

1. Philip E. Converse, "The Nature of Belief Systems in Mass Publics," in David E. Apter, ed., *Ideology and Discontent* (New York: The Free Press, 1964), p. 207.
2. *Ibid.*, p. 213.
3. *Ibid.*
4. See S. M. Lipset, *Political Man* (New York: Doubleday, 1960), Chapter IV, "Working Class Authoritarianism," pp. 115–130.
5. J. L. Talmon, *The Origins of Totalitarian Democracy* (New York: Frederick A. Praeger, 1960), p. 2.
6. For a detailed analysis of differences, see Mildred A. Schwartz, *Trends in White Attitudes towards Negroes* (Chicago: National Opinion Research Center, University of Chicago, 1967), pp. 113–134; and Paul B. Sheatsley, "White Attitudes toward the Negro," *Daedalus*, XCV (Winter 1966), 226.
7. *Ibid.*, p. 228.
8. Donald Freeman, *Religion and Southern Politics: The Political Behavior of Southern White Protestants* (Ph.D. Thesis, Department of Political Science, University of North Carolina, 1964), pp. 184–185.
9. A more thorough analysis of the relative significance of religious affiliation and religious commitment is contained in the next section on anti-Semitism.
10. A thorough analysis of the American pattern of anti-Semitism, as revealed by this survey, has been made by Gertrude J. Selznick and Stephen Steinberg, *The Tenacity of Prejudice* (New York: Harper & Row, 1969).
11. Charles Y. Glock and Rodney Stark, *Christian Beliefs and Anti-Semitism* (New York: Harper & Row, 1966), p. 173.
12. Selznick and Steinberg, *op. cit.*, p. 109. Liberal Protestants included Unitarians, Congregationalists, and Episcopalians. Conservative Protestants included Presbyterians, Methodists, Baptists, Lutherans, Evangelical and Reform, Disciples of Christ, and sects.
13. *Ibid.*, p. 111.
14. Freeman, *op. cit.*, pp. 184–186.
15. *Ibid.*, pp. 246–250.
16. *Ibid.*, p. 252.
17. *Ibid.*, p. 269. Emphasis ours.
18. William Kornhauser, *The Politics of Mass Society* (New York: The Free Press, 1959), p. 60.
19. Morris Rosenberg, "The Meaning of Politics in Mass Society," *Public Opinion Quarterly*, XV (1951), 8.
20. Robert Lane, *Political Life* (New York: Free Press, 1959), p. 104.

21. Murray Edelman, *The Symbolic Uses of Politics* (Urbana: University of Illinois Press, 1967), p. 184.
22. Talcott Parsons, *Politics and Social Structure* (New York: The Free Press, 1969), p. 85.
23. Kornhauser, *op. cit.*, pp. 109–110.
24. Glock and Stark, *op. cit.*, p. 176.
25. *Ibid.*, pp. 185, 186.
26. Lloyd A. Free and Hadley Cantril, *The Political Beliefs of Americans* (New Brunswick: Rutgers University Press, 1967).
27. "Sex crimes, such as rape and attacks on children deserve more than mere imprisonment; such criminals ought to be publicly whipped, or worse." "Much of our lives are controlled by plots hatched in secret places."
28. Herbert Blumer, "Collective Behavior," in J. B. Gitler, ed., *Review of Sociology* (New York: John Wiley, 1957), p. 148.
29. Neil J. Smelser, *The Theory of Collective Behavior* (New York: The Free Press, 1963), p. 16.
30. *Ibid.*, p. 82.

12

Political Extremism: Past and Future

One of the broad confirmations resulting from an examination of right-wing extremism in America is that it is not itself subject to interpretation through diabolism. Extremist movements are not primarily the product of extremists. The critical ranks in extremist movements are not composed of evil-structured types called "extremists," but rather of ordinary people caught in certain kinds of stress. Some of the more dramatically diabolic aspects of extremism, such as bigotry and conspiracy theory, are not so much the source of extremism as its baggage. In looking for the points at which countermeasures might be applied by society, the constant design of right-wing extremism in America might be mapped in this way:

Historical Dynamics
　Social Change
　Population Displacement
　Political Disorganization
Population Dynamics
　Quondam Complex
　Status Preservatism
　Low-Status Backlash
　Low Democratic Restraint
Political Dynamics
　Cultural Baggage
　　Moralism
　　Fundamentalism

> *Political Baggage*
> Political Moralism
> Nativist Bigotry
> Conspiracy Theory
> *Politicalization*

Historical Change, Displacement, and Political Disorganization

Right-wing extremist movements in America have all risen against the background of economic and social changes which have resulted in the displacement of some population groups from former positions of dominance. After the American Revolution, it was the growth of farmer power, as the frontier expanded, beginning to be felt by the mercantile interests of the eastern seaboard. The elite of the East and the disestablished clergy were caught up in this displacement. Behind the Know-Nothings were the technological advances which began to corrode the hegemony of the skilled craftsmen in the cities with unskilled labor, at the same time that it foreshadowed the movement back to the cities. After the Civil War, as the APA movement developed, the processes of urbanization and industrialization came into full flow. Economic power had shifted to the cities. The farmers were in increasing trouble. The workers in the city began to feel the pressure of immigrant workers. At the upper level, the old elite was feeling the pressure of the new wealthy. And in all cases, the displaced tended to be Protestants; those displacing, non-Protestant immigrants. This came to a head in the 1920's as the KKK developed: urban power had clearly become dominant; everything outside the city was becoming the backwater. The "backwater" population was streaming to the city; and on another level, labor power was beginning to challenge the economic power monopoly of the industrialists. In the 1930's of Coughlin, that challenge became thunderous for the economic elite; and the lower non-Protestant middle class became concerned for their newly won position, at the same time that they desired some change. In the 1950's of McCarthy, the displacement was on a national scale as America's corporate position in the world seemed to slip badly. And the Birch Society, perhaps the last backlash gasp of economic royalism, began to reflect a new displacement, that of white dominance. George Wallace flourished on that displacement.

In addition to identifiable group displacement, there was something more precise taking place in each of these periods: formal political alignments were shifting, and the conservative political party was usually in trouble.

The early anti-Illuminati flurry of the late 1790's coincided with the

decline of Federalism. The Anti-Masons arose with the defeat of the conservative John Quincy Adams and the rise of the Jacksonian party. The
emergence of the Know-Nothings as a mass movement occurred after the
breakup of the conservative Whig party following its defeat in the election
of 1852. Party lines had begun to crumble during this period as a result
of the slavery issue. The Republicans suffered their greatest defeat since
their formation in the congressional elections of 1890, and the Democrats
won the Presidency in 1892 with their first decisive plurality since before
the Civil War. The 1890's saw the dramatic rise of the APA. The Republican party was not in trouble in the 1920's as it shifted back into power,
along with the postwar rise of the KKK, but it had just emerged from the
first shock of government interventionism. And there was a new alignment
developing in the country: the first southern Democratic–northern Republican issues coalition against northern urban Democrats. In Coughlin's 1930's,
of course, the Republican party collapsed. In the 1950's, McCarthy came to
prominence after victory had been snatched away from a desperate Republican party at the last moment in 1948. The Birch Society came to prominence as the desperate ultraconservatives found that Republican victory
no longer meant a return to Harding. George Wallace became politically
potent at a time when the creaking Democratic party coalition seemed
to be seriously breaking up.

The political disorganization of these periods was marked not only by
dislocations of the great party coalitions but also by the process which
has become known as "polarization." This term generally describes the
condition whereby significant sections of the population are thrown out
to both the left and the right; that is, to both ends of the preservatist-
innovative axis. The early Anti-Masons were accompanied by the Jacksonian radicals and the urban-based workingmen's parties; the nativists of
the 1840's and 1850's by the Abolitionists; the APA by the Populists; the
Klan of the twenties by the Farmer-Labor Progressive movement; Coughlin
by the active radical left movements of the 1930's; George Wallace by the
"New Left" and the "Black Revolution." The history of modern European
politics reveals the same recurrent phenomenon.

One meaning of the polarization process is that it poses two forces in
the political arena which react not only to the issue but to each other.
And as they begin to react more to each other—or to their perceptions
of each other—than to the issues, the condition of ideological polarization
approaches the condition of extremism or monism. The issue market place
is replaced by the Armageddon of good and evil forces.

From another vantage point this means that the legitimacy of the political
system is at least partially breaking down. The legitimacy of the American
system exists to the extent that consensus about the rules of conflict prevail.

But, as we have seen, the common commitment to the democratic rules of conflict is not internalized, but is rather more often related to a sense of loyalty to the legitimacy of the general social system. On each occasion when a major extremist movement was on the rise, the condition of political disorganization and volatility was matched and related to a condition of social disorganization and volatility. Segments of the population were feeling the press of displacement and dislocation. The traditional loyalties to social and political institutions were loosened. The low democratic restraint most prevalent among the less privileged was exposed. In the case of right-wing political movements, the natural economic interests of the concerned elite and of the disaffected lower strata were conflicting, and the political appeal had to be made on other than a class basis. It is at this point that the phenomenon of low-status backlash becomes critical to the development of extremist movements.

This construct of the genesis of political extremism is not tied to any of the technical definitions of status deprivation. The variety of the states of disaffection which have attended right-wing extremist movements in America defies the monopoly of any particularistic definition. The Quondam Complex is meant to describe the common strand of those disaffections as they affect right-wing movements. The dislocation, corporate or anomic, is related to the past, real or imagined.

Cultural Baggage

The working substance of the Quondam Complex consists not so much of an abstract attachment to the reference groups of the past, but to the cultural baggage associated with those groups. This is a necessity in an egalitarian society where ascribed status must be justified by some kind of achieved rather than inherited superiority. Linton points out that in all nativist movements

certain currents or remembered elements of culture are selected for emphasis and given symbolic value. The more distinctive such elements are with respect to other cultures with which the society is in contact, the *greater their potential value as symbols of the society's unique character.*[1]

Linton's description of such societies applies to those encapsulated in a society who are bearing the Quondam Complex. He writes:

Rational nativist movements are almost without exception associated with frustrating situations and are primarily attempts to compensate for the frustrations of the society's members. The elements revived become symbols of the period when a society was free or in retrospect happy or great. . . . By keeping the past in mind, such elements help to re-establish and maintain the self-respect of the group's members in the face of adverse conditions.[2]

With this perspective, customs, mores, sexual habits, religious habits, styles of life, are seen as the specific symbolic content of lost-group status. Thus religious fundamentalism and fanaticism is seen primarily as the specific symbolic content of lost-group status, of the Quondam Complex, rather than as a kind of intellectual mind-set which is the direct source of right-wing extremism. Since the defense of ascribed group status must also be made on a moralistic basis, the use of moral and religious dimensions as the "remembered elements of culture" is particularly appropriate.

Political Baggage

The basic elements of the monistic model—*political moralism, nativist bigotry,* and *conspiracy theory*—which make a snug fit of one's own reference group through its cultural paraphernalia, are already there. But nativism—defined along Linton's broad terms as a strong attachment to a reference group to which one has, so to speak, "been born"—requires an out-group. As one early observer of nursery-school children reported: "The existence of an outsider is in the beginning an essential condition of any warmth or togetherness within the group."[3] But these are all only steps on the road to nativist bigotry. The Quondam Complex is more than nostalgia; it describes a condition whereby the *primary* symbolic investment, the *primary* status investment, is in the past and is related to some reference in-group whose symbolic and status significance has dwindled. Status preservatism describes the political activation of the Quondam Complex: the impulse to reverse or stem the direction of change which seems to be related to that status reduction. But *backlash* describes the displacement of hostility toward the designated source of that change.

Smelser has described these stages in the development of generalized beliefs: a condition of ambiguity arising from social strain; anxiety resulting from that ambiguity; the attachment of this anxiety to some agent; and the exaggeration of the threatening character of this agent. This results in the preoccupation with evil and the agents of evil; the belief that society's normative regulations are failing and perhaps that its values are threatened; the "short circuit" to blaming this failure and threat on the agent and the specific norms which relate to the control of that agent; and the necessary reconstitution of those norms or the regeneration of the threatened values.[4] In Smelser's terms, the strain in this case is bound up with the Quondam Complex. Before action can be taken to reconstitute the situation, it must be made meaningful by some generalized belief which identifies the source of strain (politicalization). That generalized belief would include the "cultural baggage" of the change that has taken place. But the real "short-circuiting" that takes place to identify the specific source of the change fixes on some identifiable group which has apparently engineered that change. The strain, the change, the bearer of status warfare, is thus corporealized. This corporealization serves the purpose of the short circuit; of the collective impulse to move toward the most proximate, the most concrete and least abstract; and of the reinforcement of the threatened in-group status. Ethnically identifiable population groups have for the most part served that purpose well in America. For over a century, immigrants—especially Catholic immigrants—fitted the role perfectly because they were corporeally in fact displacing rural, skilled Protestants. Their new cultural baggage was out there for everyone to see. "Nativism" during that period bore its narrowest meaning: antagonism toward immigrants.

In the 1930's, American nativist bigotry took a definitive turn. It was not just a turn away from anti-Catholicism; it was a turn from more particular to more generalized, from more concrete to more abstract, forms of nativist bigotry. There were, during that period, no emerging ethnic groups. Real Catholic and real Jewish immigrants were diminishing as specific status threats. But concomitantly, and more significantly, perhaps, the nature of the Quondam Complex became more generalized. There was a movement from corporate status preservatism to anomic status preservatism. There was a tendency for the retrospective cultural baggage to change from the more concrete to the more general; for example, from Protestantism to Christianity, from a special quality of ethnicity to a special quality of nationalism. The 1930's, of course, were a period of transition for American nativist bigotry and were fragmented in character. There were still old-fashioned Protestant-nativist tendencies; there were the preservatist tendencies of the Catholic community which was on the way to "making it"; there were the generalized anomic tendencies of those who had lost their explicit group attachments. But in their different ways their concern with status reduction was related to a former or threatened group status. And, in their different ways, they sought an out-group which would serve their nativist needs. The Jews emerged as the prime nativist target during this period for a number of reasons, all of them related to the suitability of the Jew as an "abstract" population target.

In the 1950's, McCarthy's attempt to develop an even more abstract target for short-circuitry—shadowy Communists and some selected Ivy League intellectuals—failed. These were not really corporeal entities. The Birch Society, with its limited ideological appeal to ultraconservatives, did not succeed in corporealizing an enemy for the broad population, either.

Under these circumstances, the distinction between status backlash and nativist bigotry disappears. They are functionally the same. Reservoirs of prejudice and discrimination may exist continuously; but nativist bigotry—

bigotry as a political force—has become operative in right-wing movements in America only as status backlash. And for right-wing movements, the status backlash has not so much emerged from the reservoirs of prejudice as the latter have emerged from, been activated by, been replenished by status backlash whose antecedent is the Quondam Complex.

Associated with this proposition is the fact that *conspiracy theory* has always developed concomitantly with nativist bigotry in American right-wing extremist movements. Backlash is a phenomenon of political desperation. Status has diminished or is diminishing in the regular processes of society. Those processes must therefore be short-circuited. But if those processes involve the democratic "open market place" of ideas, politics, and cultures, that market place must be closed down. The only way that market place can be closed down within the American ethos is by closing it down to an "illegitimate" actor. The only illegitimate actor is one who is not just wrong but whose motives are evil and whose operations are themselves not out in the open. The conspirators, to serve the purpose, must be largely distant, hidden, faceless, cabalistic. But, most minds being geared to the concrete, it usually becomes necessary to connect these abstractions to some visible body of people. Thus, when nativist bigotry is attached to conspiracy theory, the model is complete. There were the actual Catholic immigrants— and the Vatican. There were the actual Jews—and the *Protocols of the Elders of Zion*. McCarthy's failure to corporealize left him with an empty conspiracy theory. The conspiracy theory fleshes out nativist bigotry; and nativist bigotry fleshes out the conspiracy theory. Conspiracy theory is the constant companion of right-wing extremist movements, not because it creates them, but because it is the piece of political baggage which opens the way to monistic repression of status change.

In short, nativist bigotry of some stripe has continually proved to be a critical element in the structure of right-wing extremism, but not the source element that it is often supposed to be. Preservatist status backlash triggered by social change "invents" nativist bigotry, politicalized by conspiracy theory, as its primary instrument.

This phenomenon of invention is most starkly revealed by a historical examination of various forms of nativism. Ruth Benedict sums up such an examination and reinforces Linton's broad definition of "nativism" in this way:

Persecution was an old, old story before [modern] racism was thought of. Social change is inevitable, and it is always fought by those whose ties are to the old order. . . . Those who have these ties will consciously or unconsciously ferret out reasons for believing that their group is supremely valuable and that the new claimants threaten the achievements of civilization. They will raise a cry of rights of inheritance or divine right of kings or religious orthodoxy or racial purity or manifest destiny. These cries reflect the temporary conditions of the moment. . . .[5]

Once a nativist bigotry—regional, national, religious, or racial—is invented, it can, of course, develop a stubborn cultural continuity. Even color bigotry needs to be transmitted from generation to generation. Allport quotes one little boy's response to his mother's warning that he should never play with "niggers": "No, Mother, I never play with niggers, I only play with white and black children."[6] Negative effect toward black skin itself develops only to the extent that the institutions and behavior patterns of society develop them, as in segregated schools, segregated water fountains, inferior patterns of employment and education. The rationalizations for prejudice follow the effective transmission of prejudiced feelings and images.

The cultural transmission of such negative feelings and images can continue, of course, automatically for many generations after their "invention." These feelings and images can comprise a backlog or reservoir of nativist bigotry, part of a common cultural heritage. But in order to maintain an indefinite vitality, these patterns of prejudice need to be periodically refreshed or reinvented. More to the point, such reservoirs have typically been revitalized by and used by political developments, rather than being the genesis of them. Thus, in America, racism against Negroes was reinvented after the hardware invention of the cotton gin. Before that, anti-Negro racism had been on the decline in America. A Virginia court had ruled that Negroes could hold other Negroes in slavery. For a while the abolitionist movement was at least as strong in the South as it was in the North. Again, after Reconstruction, racism was reinvented in a preservatist backlash that classically coalesced both upper and lower classes.

The point is that right-wing extremist movements have not sprung up out of nativist bigotry; they have sprung up out of a backlash against change which invented or reinvented nativist bigotry. But while such bigotry has not been the wellspring of right-wing extremism, it has been a critical element. Right-wing extremism—that is, preservatist extremism—has always had to find a symbolic base to justify that preservatism and to justify a coalition between upper and lower class. That symbolic base has typically been made nonabstract by nativist bigotry.

A question for the future, then, is whether nativist bigotry has become so outmoded in America that it can no longer serve as a critical instrument for right-wing extremism.

George Wallace's "new nativism" indicates otherwise. So do certain recurrent seams of anti-Semitism. As a matter of fact, an examination of political anti-Semitism as it relates to this analysis of nativist bigotry would reinforce an understanding of both phenomena.

Political Anti-Semitism

Political anti-Semitism refers, of course, to the attempt to establish the corporate Jew as a generalized public menace, the implication being that some official public remedy is called for. Similar distinctions have been made as between "objective" and "subjective" anti-Semitism, "concrete" and "abstract" anti-Semitism, and the "real Jew" and the "mythical Jew" as target.

So perceived, political anti-Semitism did not become significant in America until the 1920's. As so-called anti-Catholicism was the anti-Semitism of the nineteenth century in America, so did anti-Semitism seem to become the anti-Catholicism of the twentieth century. As we have seen, Henry Ford became a major purveyor of political anti-Semitism; the KKK took it up in earnest; Father Coughlin had a regular audience of millions; and well over a hundred organizations in the 1930's were in the primary business of promoting political anti-Semitism. A few short years later, America appeared to emerge from the war against Hitler as a nation in which anti-Semitism was miraculously dead. Political anti-Semitism seemed stripped of any respectability. The belief developed in some quarters that the American people had become too sophisticated for political anti-Semitism. But such a notion miscalculates the nature of political anti-Semitism and its satellite relationship to monism.

Perhaps a cameo case study in which one of the authors was involved will serve to illustrate the point. Early in the 1960's it was revealed that a Jewish couple in San Francisco had been terrorized for over a year by a juvenile gang. This event was described across the country as a shocking case of anti-Semitism. There were insulting phone calls every night between midnight and dawn. The couple ran their business from their home and could not have an unlisted number. Anti-Semitic slogans and swastikas were painted on their home. Garbage was left at their door. The torments were constant and cruel, and the middle-aged couple lived a year of hysterical fear. Finally the police caught a handful of teenage ringleaders. The investigation of these young men, their history, family, psychology, was thorough. In sum, no particular "anti-Semitic" background was discovered. The families were bewildered and provided no clues. There were no anti-Semitic organizations, insignia, pamphlets, or cartoons found hidden in the woodpile. The history of the teenage group exhibited no particular anti-Semitic proclivities.

The history of their year-long sport was further revealing. It had started casually. with anonymous phone calls being made rather widely and at random. The prank proved to be most fun with this couple because they responded with lively anger and fear. The game became increasingly intense. But for many months, these teenagers did not invest their tricks with any evidence of anti-Semitism. Only well into the year did they discover that anti-Jewish comments added new life to the sport, drawing even more heated and fearful responses. It was then that they began to concentrate on anti-Semitic references.

In short, the evidence indicates that these young men did not engage in tormenting activity because they possessed some quality called anti-Semitism. Rather, they committed anti-Semitic acts because they were engaged in tormenting activity. They were not cruel out of anti-Semitism, but anti-Semitic out of cruelty. During the 1930's anti-Semitism was generally understood to be a tool of repressive politics, but it was also thought that the use of this tool was possible only because a large mass of people were anti-Semitic in the first place, held unusually negative attitudes toward Jews, and had become ideologically committed to these attitudes. But the behavior of this juvenile gang gives us a different analytical perspective: willing to engage in a certain type of behavior, they did not reject anti-Semitism as an instrument.

It is possible, of course, to say that if there were no historical or cultural reservoir of differential feelings and images about Jews, anti-Semitism could never be used as an instrument. But that is begging the question.

First of all, it is not very likely that one of the most stubborn cultural conventions of Western civilization for well over a thousand years will erode very quickly—in less than a number of generations—even if a process of erosion has started. The French Revolution did not succeed in obliterating the cultural continuum of anti-Semitism, but only invested it with new secular forms. The Russian Revolution did not succeed. And neither did a dramatic fresh start in a New World. This generationally transmitted reservoir of cultural anti-Semitism is, again, not best conceived as a mass of little dark corners in people's minds, but rather as a kind of collective subconscious, a *common* reservoir, built almost ineradicably into our literature, into our language, into our most general cultural myths. We all have some taproots into that common reservoir. It is further sustained by real-world conditions which will not disappear swiftly: Jews as marginal, minority, visible, alien—in the Diaspora, and perhaps even in the Middle East.

But what about the reported drop in level of this reservoir of cultural anti-Semitism, "Folk Anti-Semitism," comprising a familiar body of negative stereotypes? Charles Stember has suggested an apparently spectacular decline in the holding of such stereotypes between the 1930's and the 1960's, as evidenced by the poll data. But, as Stember himself points out, these findings require some independent evaluation as to meaning: "our findings . . . do not always tell us whether anti-Semitism has changed in prevalence or only in overtness."[7] The reservoir may, indeed, have dropped somewhat, but how much of this reflects the fact that such stereotypes may be less fashionable or less salient to express at this time?

After all, these attitude changes as reported by Stember did not take place over a thirty-year period. They dropped rather suddenly, after the war, not during it. He reports that the American people were asked by one poll or another in every year since 1937 whether they thought anti-Jewish feeling was increasing in the country. About a quarter of the people thought so in 1937. The figure rose steadily until 1946, when over half of the people thought anti-Semitism was increasing. In 1950, a poll recorded that only 16 per cent of the people thought so. The American people certainly did not seem to undergo any ideological revulsion against anti-Semitism because of their war against Hitler. Asked what groups are a menace to America, 17 per cent named the Jews in 1940; the figure had risen to 22 per cent by 1946, then dropped to 5 per cent by 1950. Stember suggests that the Jews have been in these recent years less in the consciousness of America, either unfavorably or favorably. To stretch the imagery, this may speak of a quiescent rather than an emptying reservoir.

And Selznick and Steinberg, in their definitive study of the 1964 national survey of anti-Semitic attitudes, find that, contrary to Stember, the reservoir of conventional anti-Semitism has not appreciably receded.

Political anti-Semitism . . . has declined radically in recent decades . . . [but] "conventional" anti-Semitism [has] . . . not declined radically. . . . In 1952 and again in 1966 national samples were asked: "Do you think the Jews stick together too much, or not?" In 1952, 47 per cent, in 1966, 39 per cent said Jews stick together too much, a decline of only 8 percentage points over the 14-year period. The same conclusion applies to other questions whose anti-Semitism content is less open to doubt. . . . The conclusion seems justified that conventional anti-Semitism not only continues at fairly high levels, but has hardly declined since 1952.[8]

The authors suggest that the discrepancy between Stember's conclusions and theirs is largely to be explained by their use of direct questions, as distinct from many of the surveys which Stember depended on, which used open-ended questions. But in any case, one of the difficulties in measuring any total level of such feeling at any given time may be the change in its forms of expression. One investigator found that postwar college graduates had apparently divested themselves to a considerable degree of the traditional and unsophisticated Shylock image of the Jew. But these college graduates were just as likely as others to believe that Jews were "clannish" and "aggressive."

Stember concludes at one point that "the belief that Jewish businessmen are dishonest has become markedly less current during the past 20 or 25 years. It has largely been replaced by the notion that they are merely shrewd or tricky." He goes on to say: "Even this less extreme image is less widespread than the belief in Jewish dishonesty once was, though only a minority of the population reject it outright."[9] The last clause is perhaps all that counts for any reappraisal of the potential of political anti-Semitism. Whether the reservoir of folk anti-Semitism has dropped in fact or only in appearance, it is still immense. Whether it's a matter of Jewish aggressiveness, Jewish clannishness, Jewish shrewdness, or whatever, the great majority of Americans still hold *some* pattern of differentiating and of negative stereotypes about Jews. On a scale of eleven anti-Semitic beliefs, Selznick and Steinberg found that 16 per cent of the population were "extreme anti-Semites" (8 to 11) and another 21 per cent were "high"-scoring anti-Semites (5 to 7).

And there is scarcely an American who does not know what these stereotypes are, even if he does not profess to hold them. The instrument is there, readily available in our culture. The juvenile gang in San Francisco had no difficulty plucking it out when they had use for it, although their previous acquaintanceship with it had been no greater than that of other Americans. The level of their folk anti-Semitism was not the key to their anti-Semitic activity; the key was their inclination toward cruelty and their willingness to use anti-Semitism to further that cruelty.

The parallel is found in political anti-Semitism. Father Coughlin's movement, after a certain point, was explicitly and overtly anti-Semitic. Yet, as we have seen, surveys found little difference in anti-Semitic beliefs between his Union party followers and the rest of the American population. However, it is not just that there is not an automatic correspondence between folk anti-Semitism and political anti-Semitism. The point is greater than that: given our common cultural background, there is not necessarily much of a relationship between anti-Semitism of any kind and support of an anti-Semitic movement. Only 20 per cent of Union party supporters said they would back a campaign against Jews; but the other 80 per cent were *in fact* openly backing a campaign against Jews in their support of Coughlin. It was apparently not a salient part of their reasons for supporting Coughlin, but they were willing to support him for other reasons, and his anti-Semitism did not bother them. Similarly, many observers of the German scene before 1933 reported that the Nazis were supported by large numbers who were not anti-Semitic. In this way is it possible to be anti-Semitic without being an anti-Semite—at least any more of a conventional anti-Semite than anyone else.

Thus, as far as the "vulnerability" of the population is concerned, the key is not the level of anti-Semitic beliefs, but the level of resistance to political anti-Semitism. The question is not whether people dislike Jews more or less, but whether they are committed *against* the violation of democratic rights for Jews—or anyone else; the level of their "democratic restraint." Asked in a recent poll whether they would support or oppose a congressional candidate who was running on an anti-Jewish platform, one-third of a national sample said that they would neither support nor oppose him for that reason; his anti-Jewish program would be a matter of indifference for them.

Here we return to the common democratic commitment, the lack of democratic restraint, which is key to real understanding of the nature of nativist bigotry. Selznick and Steinberg conclude from their study,

> If there is any danger of political anti-Semitism in this country, it stems not from virulent anti-Semitic prejudice, but from widespread indifference. Because of this indifference, only 60 per cent of the national sample indicated they would vote against an anti-Semitic political candidate. Even this figure probably over-estimates the extent to which Americans are prepared to oppose political anti-Semitism. Some opposition to the candidate came from people who hold many anti-Semitic beliefs. How firm their opposition would be under the pressure of an actual anti-Semitic campaign is open to question. Some opposition came from people who are opinionless and do not reject anti-Semitism on principled grounds. The danger is that in a period of heightened anti-Semitic propaganda they would take on beliefs they do not now hold, or might be appealed to on grounds other than anti-Semitic prejudice. Though few Americans now openly advocate political anti-Semitism, their ranks might easily be swelled by the already prejudiced anti-Semites and by those who, while not intolerant of Jews, are tolerant of anti-Semitism.[10]

As long as there exists this prevalent lack of democratic restraint which characterizes the common democratic commitment, political anti-Semitism can become or be made a convenient form of nativist targetry during a period of social upheaval. Political anti-Semitism is more a function of monism than of conventional anti-Semitism.

Politicalization

The three potential elements in a model of right-wing extremism—low democratic restraint, Quondam Complex, and economic conservatism— fuse together in some form and in some combination when the various populations subject to these elements are politicalized and mobilized under a unifying banner of preservatism. But it is a banner of status preservatism, not of economic preservatism, which must be flown if the mass low-income population is to be included. The social strain for such a population is some sense of status loss, felt as a corporate or anomic loss or absence of power, prestige, or way of life. This sense of loss is best expressed in terms of pertinent cultural baggage: moral and "fundamental" values lost.

Indeed, this might be seen as the first stage in politicalization: the development of a primary symbolic and status investment in the past, or imagined past. A further stage is the development of a self-conscious sense of status preservatism: the sense that the loss is actionable. The heart of the politicalization process is, then, the transmission of a generalized belief consisting of some form of the political baggage: nativist bigotry and the conspiracy theory. This generalized belief serves to "identify" the presumed common source of the social strain for the affected populations and points the way to remedy. Such a generalized belief, by nature, is monistic. The final stage of politicalization is some mobilization into a related movement.

There are, as we have seen, many disparate kinds of population that need to be knitted together for such a movement. The economic conservatives often have a strong self-interest in such a movement, but have a relative resistance to its monistic implications. Those that do not have such a resistance probably become the most virulent of the type that we have called the Radical Right. But the bulk of the Radical Right comprises those low-income elements of the population who have a low level of democratic restraint and are already politicalized in the Quondam sense; their primary status investment is in the past. Then there is the critical mass of the population, those we have typed as Rednecks, who have a low level of democratic restraint, are low-income, but still have a primary investment in their current status. That status can be threatened by certain kinds of preservatism, which portend a return to a past which holds little attraction for the Rednecks. But that status can also be threatened by innovative tendencies. If they are to be unified under the banner of status preservatism, an appropriate accommodation must be found.

This construct is, needless to say, highly artificial, hiding many important differences of concern and circumstances; but it is no more artificial in that sense than many of the right-wing extremist movements themselves. As has been pointed out, these movements have typically had a "cafeteria" kind of quality. The selective support which they have attracted has been selective on two connected levels: issue and intensity of affiliation. There are many ways in which the quality of an individual's attachment to a political movement can be, and has been, described. For our purposes, these individuals might be differentiated as "Joiners, Consistent Supporters, and Expressive Approvers." Some right-wing movements have been essentially organizational in nature, built around Joiners. The Birch Society is an example. Such an organization is designed to do specific educational and agitational work. Some right-wing "movements" have been essentially nonorganizational, built primarily around Expressive Approvers. McCarthyism was a prime example. It might be described more aptly as a "right-wing Tendency" than as a movement, just as the Birch Society might be most aptly called a "right-wing Organization."

The right-wing Organization is composed of actors, with a comprehensive loyalty to program, whose strength is formally measured by membership. The right-wing Tendency is composed of an audience, with a single-issue loyalty to "program," whose strength is formally measured by public opinion polls. As distinct from these phenomena, a right-wing Movement may have both Joiners and Expressive Approvers, but depends most heavily on Consistent Supporters.

The effectiveness of a right-wing Movement is formally measured by electoral votes. The most recent attempt to build a full-fledged right-wing Movement was that of George Wallace. Obviously he overestimated, as had Father Coughlin before him, the extent to which his followers were Consistent Supporters and the extent to which they were only Expressive Approvers.

There are two possible measures of ultimate success for any political thrust: to actually take over political power, or to affect public policy. Most right-wing extremist movements have attempted to do the first—and have succeeded only in doing the second. In fact, their failure to take political power can largely be ascribed to their ability to affect public policy in some way; that is, to affect the currents of the major political parties.

The Process of Decline in Right-Wing Extremist Movements

Smelser makes a distinction between norm-oriented and value-oriented movements which is pertinent to the decline of right-wing extremist movements. The purpose of a norm-oriented movement is to change the regulations which control. It is not so much that normative changes are not contemplated by value-oriented movements (immigration laws, school segregation laws), but rather that these normative changes are seen as part of a "fundamental reallocation of values." Adherents see a new world, not merely an improvement of individuals or a reform of institutions—even though the latter are an aspect of regeneration. The potential for regeneration may rest in a personal savior, in impersonal values such as liberty or Communism, in national destiny, or in a combination of these. In any case, the value-oriented belief involves a preoccupation with the highest moral bases of social life.[11] In this sense, with considerable variation, right-wing extremist movements in America have tended to be value-oriented movements.

Value-oriented political movements, by their nature, tend to be primarily interested in taking political power, rather than merely changing public policy. The "evil intent" of those causing or collaborating in the social strain is built into the value-oriented generalized belief. Therefore, real regenerative change will take place only if the evil agents are removed.

Right-wing extremist movements in America have typically been value-oriented movements which ended up, at best, in creating normative change. Their ability to create normative change has been a major reason for their demise as value-oriented movements. Smelser writes:

> Value-oriented beliefs . . . arise when alternative means for reconstituting the social situation are perceived as unavailable. . . . [T]his unavailability has three main aspects: a) The aggrieved group in question does not possess facilities whereby they may reconstitute the social situation; such a group ranks low on wealth, power, prestige, or access to means of communication. b) The aggrieved group is prevented from expressing hostility that will punish some person or group considered responsible for the disturbing state of affairs. c) The aggrieved group cannot modify the normative structure, or cannot influence those who have the power to do so.[12]

Because of the coalition and cafeteria nature of the two-party system in America, it has had the flexibility to respond to extremist movements and tendencies when they appeared substantial. These movements and tendencies have had the ability to influence those parties which have the power to modify the normative structure. Restrictive immigration laws, for example, and repressive measures in general have been embraced and enacted by main-stream parties, undercutting the support of right-wing extremist movements. Of course, the same phenomenon has taken place on the left in America. This conduciveness of the American political system to absorb new directions has been the source of much complaint by right-wing and left-wing extremist leaders. They call this process "cooption" and ascribe it, in their fashion, to the evil designs of the main-stream political leaders, who wish to maintain the basic value system. But whether the word is "cooption" or "responsiveness," this conduciveness of the major parties has always helped to draw the bulk of Consistent Supporters back into their ranks. In terms of right-wing politics, it has also sometimes helped the preservatist major party to move back into power.

More specifically, the propensity of the American political system to produce extraparty movements rather than third or fourth parties is directly related to the nature of our electoral system. From the courthouse to the White House, ours is a plurality system; that is, constituencies elect a single representative. The point of comparison is the proportional representative systems common in western Europe in which groups elect representatives in strength proportional to the size of these groups. In plurality systems a minority group can achieve maximum power only in coalition with other groups. Minority representation is, of course, much more direct in a proportional system.

It is clear that electoral systems based on proportional representation encourage new movements and interest groups to go into party politics. Conversely, electoral systems based on plurality representation discourage such a course of action. In plurality systems, the larger the size of the constituency, the less likely it is for minority movements to compete successfully as parties. Thus, when we look at examples of relatively successful third-party efforts in American history we find evidence of considerable success at the local levels in electing mayors and congressmen and more moderate success at the state level. However, such parties have invariably met with disaster when they went national and attempted to elect a President.

The role of America's Presidential system in discouraging and frustrating "third" party politics is highlighted in comparison with the greater prominence of such efforts in the parliamentary systems with single-member (plurality) districts in which voters do not choose a central executive, but rather cast their ballot for a local representative. In such a system new parties with geographically distinct sources of strength (that is, in occupations such as mining, or in ethnic, religious, or regional groupings) can focus their efforts on electing members to parliament in the areas in which they are strong, though they are not in a position to receive a significant national vote. Thus we find that in Canada, which has such a parliamentary system, ecologically isolated minorities such as wheat farmers and French Canadians are in a position to elect minority party M.P.s without having to face the challenge to go national.

Another factor contributing to the difficulty of creating "third" parties in America is the decentralized structure of our political parties. At the constituency level this is manifested by the prominence of primary elections which give minority interests an opportunity to express themselves within the party and thus, ironically, serve to legitimize their relative lack of control of the party. A perhaps more important manifestation at the national level is the looseness of party discipline in the Congress which allows for cross-party alignments on particular issues. Thus, congressmen who represent minority ideologies in one party do not have to join or form another party in order to please their constituents. This factor has enabled southern conservatives to maintain their position in the Democratic party for as long as they have. The importance of this factor is evident when we look at the Canadian case.

Canadian political parties are run with tight discipline. Whenever a

Canadian region, class, ethnic group, or province comes into serious conflict with its party of traditional allegiance, it must either change over to the other party, with which it may be in even greater disagreement on other issues, or form a new "third" party. The result of combining social diversity with a rigid constitutional structure has been the regular rise and fall of relatively powerful "third" parties.[13]

Another variable factor in the decline of right-wing extremist movements has been the diminution of the source of social strain. In this case, the conduciveness of the American society to upward mobility has served to both generate and alleviate much pertinent social strain. The pressure of new immigrant groups has been assuaged by the movement of older immigrant groups into higher-status positions. Often this has been marked off, in terms of political saliency, by dramatic changes in historical circumstances, such as the ending of an economic depression.

The sheer practicalities of American coalition politics have often militated against the acceptance of all-out monistic politics by "respectable" national political leaders, or the "respectable" practice of national politics. At the same time, it would be a mistake to underestimate the extent to which the monistic excesses of some extremist movements have offended the personal value system of many Americans and their political leaders. Time and again, the more educated and established segments of the American public and leadership have pulled away from right-wing movements when they became explicitly monistic. The symbiosis between more and less educated preservatist groups was, at the least, often uneasy. This situation was often aggravated by the classic instability of the smaller extremist movements. Many of these were, by their nature, charismatic movements, and as Weber pointed out: "By its very nature, the existence of charismatic authority is specifically unstable. The holder may forego his charisma; he may feel 'forsaken by his God,' as Jesus did on the cross; he may prove to his followers that 'virtue is gone out of him.' It is then that his mission is extinguished, and hope waits and searches for a new holder of charisma."[14] Many of the movements have demonstrated at a certain point that the "virtue" has gone out of them. The various scandals of the KKK provided an example. But, more often than not, such exposure served to accelerate a decline which had already been destined by other circumstances.

Control

The basic circumstances under which political extremism germinates and flourishes have to do with some fairly constant human conditions and some highly variable historical conditions, none of which are subject to social control in the usual sense.

As far as we know, the human personality is universally subject to status needs, to needs of self-esteem in the social setting. These needs obviously run a wide range of individual differences; but under precipitating historical circumstances the range quickly leaves the pathological and embraces the normal personality. Creating optimal historical circumstances would, by definition, mitigate political extremism, but no one is sure what these optimal conditions might be, much less how to obtain them. We have seen that peacetime does not rule out right-wing extremism, nor does economic prosperity, nor does the creation of socialist systems, nor does any increment of egalitarianism insofar as we have been able to conceive it.

Of course, one can guess about changes in historical conditions which might alter the nature of right-wing extremism. The continual waves of population displacement in a spectacularly heterogeneous America during the nineteenth and early twentieth centuries provided an explicit matrix for the classic style of American right-wing extremism. As immigration was brought to a virtual halt, as the face of white Christian America began to blur, as the big cities began to grind past loyalties into present anonymity, the style changed. The character of the status preservatism, of the nativist bigotry, of the conspiracy theory moved from the concrete to the abstract, from the corporate to the anomic. But the substance was still there; the basic model of monism did not change. As a "final" wave of immigration hit America, that of the black population moving in from the backwaters, right-wing extremism began to return to its classic style, barely veiled. In some ways, the statistical progress of the Negro population in the 1960's resembled that of the early ethnic immigrants to America, during their first stage of integration, in their pattern of economic penetration and educational advancement. If substantial integration does take place—if America does become pervasively homogeneous—the classic style of right-wing extremism will presumably recede again; but, as American and European history have indicated, this development might only affect the specific style of extremism. If interracial life does not become integrated, but instead settles down into some kind of separate but fairly equal entities, a new variant style in American right-wing—and left-wing—nativism may ensue.

But there is no reason to believe that any historical circumstance which we can now envision will alter the human condition or eliminate the emergence of social strains, which are the soil of political extremism. Any working remedial concern might more sensibly be attached, not to "primary prevention," but to "secondary prevention"; that is, to reduce the high-risk conditions which can turn human strain and conflict into political extremism. These high-risk conditions, as we have isolated them for right-wing extremism, are (1) the relative conduciveness of the political structure, (2) the Quondam Complex, and (3) low democratic restraint.

The Political Structure

The chief practical bulwark against the development of effective value-oriented right-wing extremist movements in America has probably been the existence of the two-party system as it has already been described. These parties have not been ideological agents, but coalition parties, compromise parties, designed pragmatically for electoral victories. In describing basic elements of the Jeffersonian strategy of majority rule, James MacGregor Burns writes:

> Majority rule in a big, diverse nation must be moderate. No majority party can cater to the demands of any extremist group because to do so would antagonize the great "middle groups" that hold the political balance of power and hence could rob the governing party of its majority at the next election. A democratic people embodies its own safeguards in the form of social checks and balances—the great variety of sections and groups and classes and opinions stitched into the fabric of society and thus into the majority's coalition. . . . Moreover, the majority party—and the opposition that hopes to supplant it—must be competitive; if either one forsakes victory in order to stick to principle, as the Federalists did after the turn of the century, it threatens the whole mechanism of majority rule. Majoritarian strategy assumes that in the end politicians will rise above principle in order to win an election.[15]

There are a number of pertinent implications. While no party can afford to cater to an "extremist" group (Burns uses the term in its generic sense), it must also be responsive to any swell of expression or aspiration which deviant political movements feed or feed on. In being so responsive, the two major parties vitiate the popular appeal of the deviant movements. This may be cooption, but it is also responsiveness to needs. At best—and in order to prevail pragmatically in the long run—this pragmatic responsiveness must take place within the value constraints of egalitarianism. When social strain results from the pressure of one population group or another, there are the alternatives of suppression for one or situational improvement for the other. In the past, a continuing process of upward mobility for population groups in America has finally relieved that pressure. The future demands no less.

The coalition aspect of the two parties has another pertinent dimension: the existence of cross pressures within each party. The Republican party, for example, typically embraces cosmopolitan big businessmen from the East, with their sophisticated interest and self-interest in foreign and urban affairs; midwestern farmers with their rural and isolationist interests; new Texas millionaires; and small businessmen. They all have certain political interests in common, generally antistatist, and for various reasons a common stake in Republican party victories. This condition poses a problem of political immobility on the one hand; but, on the other, it helps to maintain the stability and level of democratic restraint in each party.

It is not, of course, just the fragmentation of political parties which would increase the risk of political extremism. To the extent that the entire political system and its institutions are conducive to normative change—and to the orderly discussion, dissent, and conflict which are attendant on normative change—value-oriented extremist movements will have less room in which to grow. This is, of course, just a restatement of what has been said so many times in so many ways: the best defense against the development of monism is the insistent maintenance of pluralism.

It should also be axiomatic that the definition of pluralism includes the concept of constitutionalism: the operation of the "open market place" in the framework of common rules which cannot be violated. Thus, Smelser, in his discussion of the containment of value-oriented movements, talks not only about the firm and unhesitant "ruling-out [of the] uninstitutionalized expression of hostility" but also of "ruling out direct challenges to legitimacy. This involves drawing a definite circle around those governmental activities which are constitutionally inviolable."[16]

The Quondam Complex

The Quondam Complex is not meant to be another analytic concept, but rather a large descriptive category. Most broadly, it describes those who have a greater symbolic investment in the past than in the present. This "past" may be real or imagined, corporate or anomic. MacIver describes the anomic as living "on a thin line of sensation between no future and no past."[17] But even for the anomic man, the Quondam Complex becomes operative when he seizes upon some aspect of the past with which to identify and express his dissatisfaction with the changing present. And in either case, there are variably involved his power, his prestige, his self-esteem, his accorded esteem, his sense of connectedness, his sense of privilege, his sense of social comfort: in brief, and in general, his status.

In a radical sense, these status problems have their genesis in global historical conditions. In an ameliorative sense, however, they may be affected by the immediate "openness" of the political and social structure. Scott G. McNall discusses the concept of "availability" in examining why people joined a particular deviant right-wing organization. He cites a study of peyote use among Navajo Indians, which indicated that a community named Towaoc had the earliest history of peyote use and that the use of peyote in the other Navajo communities could best be accounted for by distance from Towaoc.

The concept of availability can also account for membership in other organizations. Availability means more than how close a person is to the source of a phenomenon. It also has to do with the number of intervening opportunities which present themselves. In the case of peyote users they were few, for example, other religious organizations, fraternal organizations, and so forth. Availability therefore involves at least two major variables—distance from the phenomenon and/or the number of alternatives available to an individual for involving himself in some other group.[18]

This concept of availability may partly explain why certain right-wing extremist "organizations" have concentrations of membership in one place rather than another. But it may also have other implications. Attempts to provide "intervening opportunities" for those seeking status satisfactions have largely been restricted to social work agencies with little outreach and, finally, little to offer. There have been few attempts to invent such opportunities on a large scale in the political context. Actually, this may have been the basic purport of the community action components of the vaunted War on Poverty launched by President Johnson. The "maximum feasible participation" in community action by impoverished ghetto residents was the keynote. The program may not have reached very deeply among these residents; but, on the other hand, mechanisms of participation were made available, and more were invented in the wake of the program, with which many residents could and did identify. Similar inventions are obviously needed in the working-class and white middle-class neighborhoods of the cities, where there is a mounting and palpable sense of having been cut off from political participation.

Low Democratic Restraint

The most directly accessible, if difficult, social means of building a countervailing factor to political extremism has to do with rising levels of democratic restraint. There can be no illusion that increasing education is a panacea for low levels of democratic restraint. Thresholds of restraint are conditioned by the stability of social and political loyalties; this is one of the dimensions of the common democratic commitment.

But education is itself an independent factor in modifying the common democratic commitment. Selznick and Steinberg, finding an empirical syndrome of relationships between a "primitive cognitive style" and low democratic restraint as measured by prejudice, intolerance of cultural diversity, and ignorance of democratic norms, suggest the following:

The uneducated are cognitively and morally unenlightened because they have never been indoctrinated into the enlightened values of the larger society and in this sense are alienated from it. For analytic purposes, we can distinguish in the United States between the official, or ideal culture and the unofficial, or common culture. The official culture contains the ideal norms that characterize our society in its public and secular spheres. These norms are derived from scientific and democratic values and represent the cognitive and moral commitments of a society whose political order is a democracy and whose economy is based on technology. . . . Alongside the official culture is an unofficial or common culture which not only differs from the ideal culture but is at odds with it. Historically more archaic, the common culture is not only pre-scientific and pre-democratic but anti-scientific and anti-democratic.[19]

As we have seen, the *kind* of educational experience is also, itself, a powerful factor. For example, Table 112, drawn from our 1964 study of the

Table 112. RELATIONSHIP BETWEEN EDUCATION AND
SOPHISTICATION AND AGREEMENT WITH THE
"WHIP SEX OFFENDERS" QUESTION
(Per Cent in Agreement)

Degree of Sophistication	Education	
	Per Cent	Number
8th Grade		
Unsophisticated	81	(164)
Sophisticated	64	(64)
High School		
Unsophisticated	72	(109)
Sophisticated	51	(377)
College		
Unsophisticated	61	(13)
Sophisticated	36	(293)
Total		
Unsophisticated	77	(286)
Sophisticated	46	(734)

national population, indicates that both levels of education and levels of educational sophistication affect the "Whip Sexers" item which is related to democratic restraint.[20] As many unsophisticated college graduates are as likely to accept this item as sophisticated grade-school graduates. The evidence mounts on this score, at the same time that many "progressive" educators seem willing to abandon those aspects of "middle class" sophisticated education which seems so closely tied to an ideological democratic commitment as offensive to the self-esteem of those reared in brutalizing poverty.

A close examination would probably reveal that in the long run, prevailing "levels of democratic restraint" in America have been on the rise, at least within the last fifty years, paralleling the general rise in educational product. There have been increasing cadres of opposition to undemocratic excess. The difference between the relatively small band who opposed the excesses after World War I and those who opposed McCarthyism after World War II is highly instructive on this score.

This does not mean, of course, that high education and high democratic restraint are necessarily related in any given individual. As a matter of fact, it is rather clear that the most dangerous and persistent monists are those who are highly educated, who *have* an integrated system of belief which deliberately rejects pluralism. However, it is also clear that so far as the general population is concerned, the overwhelming weight of education has been in a democratizing direction.

At the same time, while the proportion of democratic ideologies has importantly increased, it has been shown that by educational level, by attitudinal level, by every index of low democratic restraint, the majority of the American people remain highly susceptible to monistic political appeal. At a point when historical circumstances shake loose their traditional group commitments and loyalties and produce serious social strains, there is no reason to believe that substantial numbers of Americans will not be subject to the blandishments of extremist movements. So far, the easing of such historical circumstances, and the stability of the two-party system, have prevented such extremist movements from growing past a certain point.

Deviant left-wing movements in America have declined for roughly the same reasons as have those of the right wing. They have been coopted; the two-party system has been open to them; the normative changes have been adopted which prevented them from becoming effective value-oriented movements, especially in a nation where the relative absence of rigid forms of status stratification has blocked the development of pervasive class consciousness in the first place. One of the basic questions in America today is whether normative changes can be made deeply enough and swiftly enough to forestall the development of effective value-oriented black movements. But insofar as such movements develop on the left, the dangers of monism are no less than on the right. The model of monism applies, including the promulgation of conspiracy theory and nativism—probably more of the abstract and anomic rather than the concrete and corporate variety. As George Lichtheim, among others, has pointed out: "The phenomenon of socialist anti-Semitism was in its origins the poisoned root of a tree planted—alongside the more familiar tree of liberty—in the decades following the French Revolution. The anticapitalist and the anti-Jewish theme were intertwined. . . ."[21]

Two of the three points of possible social control at the "secondary" level—relative political conduciveness and low democratic restraint—apply for left-wing political extremism as well. It is the Quondam Complex which specifically distinguishes the right wing in that respect, although status considerations are not absent from the dynamics of left-wing movements, however laced they may be with direct economic concerns. The symbolic nature of contemporary black movements is evidence of that.

Conclusion

In sum, the evidence indicates that the American population is still highly vulnerable to political extremism; the American political system is less vulnerable, but scarcely fail-safe. The evidence suggests what should not be surprising: there is no prophylaxis against political extremism. Bigotry and conspiracy theory are more consequence than cause. Education is a necessary but probably not a sufficient deterrent. The nature of American coalition politics has so far managed to retard the growth of political disorganization, but does not guarantee such stability.

The construction of party coalitions and the development of party ideologies and rhetoric appropriate to keeping such coalitions together are clearly a rather delicate task. Once the task has been completed, the forces pushing for stabilization of party constituent groups, ideology, and rhetoric are quite strong. However, similar stabilizing forces are not in operation for the society as a whole. America is a highly dynamic society. Few groups in it stand still for very long and the demands which they make upon the political system—the issues which concern them, the answers which appeal to them—move with them. Under these circumstances, groups in America often find themselves out of step with their party of traditional allegiance on specific issues, but also out of step with the alternative party on other issues. These issues may be more or less "legitimate" (ranging from demands for equal rights for women to demands for the exclusion of immigrants), but they are invariably real and often preoccupying to the participants themselves. Meanwhile, the parties, particularly at the national level, are resistant to changes in their basic orientation, as are most organizations of a similar structure. Such shifts take place when changes in the society at large becomes so pervasive—hit so many groups—that the coalitions on which the parties are based become patently untenable. In short, party change comes through crisis.

The current state of the Democratic party would seem to be illustrative of this phenomenon. Since the days of Franklin Roosevelt the party's strength has been based on a majority coalition composed, among others, of the urban white minority ethnic groups, trade-unionists, and urban Negroes. The Democratic program and orientation through the New Deal and most of the postwar years was satisfactory for these groups. Pledges of equal rights under the law for Negroes did not particularly impinge upon the interests of white ethnic groups or union members. Promises of higher minimum wages and various social welfare legislation were seen in a positive light by each group. But times have changed, and so have these groups.

While the objective position of Negro Americans has improved considerably, their expectation level has increased even more sharply, and consequently so has their sense of relative deprivation. Those who have risen economically are embittered because their advance on other fronts has not been correspondingly great. For those who have not advanced economically, the relative progress of their fellow Negroes provides additional basis for alienation, above and beyond their generally deprived situation vis-à-vis the white community. This kind of "crisis of rising expectations" has been, of course, the seeding ground for many protest and revolutionary movements throughout history.

There is, in addition, the special dimension which has been referred to earlier. The Negro population is the only group—besides the American Indians—who have been depressed *by* the American society rather than by the countries of their origin. This not only adds a special edge of bitterness but also leads to demands for immediacy of remedy—and reparations rather than just progress.

Meanwhile, the white workers participate in the generally affluent economy only to find many of their hard-earned dollars going for taxes for programs to aid the Negroes, and to see their long-sought-for position of affluence and comfort threatened by urban riots. The reasons for the greater participation in the Wallace movement by white trade-union members as compared with members of the middle class are inherent in the fact that the former are more likely to live inside the central cities relatively close to black ghettos. Hence, they are also more likely to be directly and personally concerned with the consequences of efforts to integrate schools and residential neighborhoods.

But beyond that, Pete Hamill has drawn a poignant picture of the strains on the white workingman in New York City in 1969:

> The working-class white man is actually in revolt against taxes, joyless work, the double standards and short memories of professional politicians, hypocrisy and what he considers the debasement of the American dream. . . . Any politician who leaves that white man out of the political equation does so at very large risk. The next round of race riots might not be between people and property, but between people and people. And that could be the end of us.[22]

A congressman from one of New York's white working-class districts is quoted as saying:

The average working stiff is not asking for very much. He wants a decent apartment, he wants a few beers on the weekend, he wants his kids to have decent clothes, he wants to go to a ball game once in a while, and he would like to put a little money away so that his kids can have the education that he could never afford. That's not asking a hell of a lot. But he's not getting that. He thinks society has failed him and, in a way, if he is white, he is often more alienated than the black man. At least the black man has his own organizations, and can submerge himself in the struggle for justice and equality, or elevate himself, whatever the case may be. The black man has hope, because no matter what some of the militants say, his life is slowly getting better in a number of ways. The white man who makes $7000 a year, who is 40, knows that he is never going to earn much more than that for the rest of his life, and he sees things getting worse, more hopeless.[23]

This disaffection of members of the white lower middle-class and working class is inevitably set against what they feel is not just the rise of the Negro population but a rise which is taking place at their inordinate expense. Hamill says that "a large reason for the growing alienation of the white working class is their belief that they are not respected."[24]

The nativist bigotry of such whites finds its genesis not so much in hatred of Negroes, but in the felt diminution of their own status. This is the crucial nature of backlash which feeds rather than is fed by racism. And here is revealed what might be called the New American Dilemma: how to square America's promise with the reality of life for Negro Americans without at the same time seeming to withdraw that promise from other relatively disadvantaged sections of the population. Discussing this dilemma from the point of view of the white working-class youth, a group of sociologists have pointed out that the weight of the "establishment" seems to be against these youth:

Part of the problem has been the failure of the society's cultural middle men, its intellectuals, even to begin to recognize this population. . . . These anti-establishment intellectuals may be hard to distinguish from the establishment itself. . . . For working-class populations, particularly the young, these anti-establishment groups have become the establishment, at least to the degree that they set the tone for the surface imagery of our times. . . . For example, much is said of the crisis of the colleges and the ghetto schools, both apparently requiring growing investments of society's resources. Does anyone for a moment think that the quality of education in the working-class schools in this country—both public and parochial—is any better? That the slaughter of human potential and sensibility is any less severe? Or that a crisis of identity equal in magnitude to that of the children of the affluent middle class or those of the ghetto is not going on among the youth of the working class? . . . For him [the working-class youth] racial integration (and the disruption of community life that he feels, not without justification, must follow) is part of an organized effort within which agents of government, the mass media and even the church are co-conspirators. Thus he too becomes anti-establishment, but for him it is a liberal establishment, and before it he feels increasingly powerless. . . .[25]

A Pennsylvania steel-town clergyman noted that prejudice had always existed in "seed form" among the workingmen, but something else had been added to bring that prejudice into full bloom: ". . . *alienation*—as severe, disorienting and thingifying as that felt by the black, the young and the poor."[26]

"They" is a familiar word in the lexicon of a steel valley worker. It comes into play in a variety of settings, "They" are the company which is to blame when the mill is shut down for lack of orders, or when a new piece of automated equipment is introduced that eliminates old jobs, or when an explosion occurs and kills a man in furnace 6. But "they" can also be the union when a strike drags on interminably, or when things appear to be decided by "the clique" who regularly attend the meetings at local 1473. There are times when "they" are the government—national, state, local—that presides over one's destiny in the matter of meat prices, gun ownership and downtown parking space. And "they" can be the big hospital where one is merely "the ulcer in 306." "They" can even be the church where the priest "runs things as he pleases" and the minister thinks of you as a name on a file card. . . .

To be human includes the power of self-determination and the opportunity to participate in relationships of care. From these comes the capacity to love. But the worker is overcome by a sense of powerlessness, and by an awareness that the fabric of personal community has been shredded. . . .

In the mind of the blue collar worker, the black citizen had "gotten to" the effective centers of cultural change. In fact, as far as he could see from changes in his own existence, "they" were in cahoots with the blacks. As he saw it, strings were pulled that took Negroes off sweeper jobs, and put them on the line next to him or, miracle of miracles, in foreman and executive jobs above him. He even heard rumors of preferential hiring which, according to bar room talk, would put him out on the street in favor of the black man. And when he came home from the frustrations of work what did he find? "They" were pushing black faces at him through the TV screen which was supposed to be his escape hatch from the harsh realities of daily life. Furthermore "they" were rearranging his neighborhood so that these "outsiders" could move in, and "they" were conducting social experiments with his kids, moving things around in the schools so that the blacks could "take over" there too. In all these cultural shifts, it seemed clear to the white worker, "they" were at it again. And, of all things, "they" were giving the Negro the decision-making power and personal recognition he so desperately craved.[27]

In 1969, four municipal elections took place in New York, Detroit, Minneapolis, and Los Angeles, which seemed to embody the revolt of the white working-class majority caught in this "New American Dilemma." In these cases, those seen as the more "law and order" candidates pointedly won a majority of the votes against those seen as "liberal" candidates.

Even in Cleveland, where a black mayor, Carl Stokes, won re-election, 80 per cent of the whites voted for his white opponent. In Minneapolis it was a policeman who won against both Democratic and Republican candidates. Commenting on this aspect of the "revolt," Gus Tyler wrote:

> To ask people to be fearless when they have every reason to be afraid is to ask normal folk to act abnormally. They couldn't do it even if they wanted to. They will seek safety—no matter what political ribbon is wrapped around the prized package of survival. Castigating these people as stupid (some are) or racist (others are) does not solve the problem. They will in the end simply conclude that the lofty lecturer who thus looks down on them is himself either stupid or a racist, or both.[28]

Finally, there are reorientation periods during which the parties themselves are in movement seeking new and relevant coalitions of support and ideologies of appeal. If they are successful, a new stable period follows.

The question, of course, is whether we have reached a pass, as we did once before in our history, where the depth of the crisis will disrupt the "normal" cycle. For example, the Democratic party currently finds itself hard pressed to formulate a program—at whatever level of generality —that appeals to both of these traditionally Democratic groups, the Negro population and the white working class. It should not come as a surprise that many Negroes are finding action on the street a more satisfying form of political behavior than voting Democratic at the ballot box, or that many white workers appeared to be strongly sympathetic to the Wallace third-party effort. The Democratic coalition is in the midst of a crisis, an event made manifest in the formation of movements operating outside the normal rules of the game of two-party electoral politics.

Michael Rogin has properly pointed out that the mechanics of our coalition political system will not necessarily suffice in the face of deeply divisive crises; and he suggests that the current crisis is possibly a breaking point.

> [T]he race issue is not like traditional American ethnic and economic political controversies. Because Negro-white relations involve serious conflict and deep feelings, Madisonian politics has not been successful in dealing with race. It has succeeded neither in preventing violence nor in incorporating the Negroes into the Madisonian system. And it has failed because it is not a system which saves us from ideological extremism, but one that works in its absence. The Wallace vote should serve as a reminder both of racist emotion in America and the consequent failure of a pragmatic politics of race.[29]

However, the critical question, as we have seen, is not whether something called "racism" can be expunged from the minds of men or beaten back in open assault, but whether our system can deal with both dimensions of the New American Dilemma. And with all its special edges, which may indeed finally make the tragic difference, the New American Dilemma is really just the old pre-Myrdal American Dilemma: can we provide new rewards and new status for the displaced as well as for the displacing segments of our population? The game is clearly not yet lost. The prevailing aspirations of the Negro population and of the white working-class population are not yet incompatible—if they are both given room in which to move.

Still, even while America is wrestling with this substantive crisis, another development with disturbing if incalculable portent for political extremism is taking place, in a generational as well as a racial context. We have already discussed the left-right polarization of American youth and the similarities between the growing extremism on both poles.[30] The national new left weekly the *Guardian*, in reporting on a meeting of the National Youth Alliance, the offshoot of "Youth for Wallace," discussed in Chapter 10, noted the similarities between the extreme left and right in this fashion:

Contemporary commentators often lump the extremes of right and left together. Indeed, despite obvious differences there were striking similarities exhibited at the Taft [Hotel] Meeting:

Leaders hit hard at the establishment, the liberals and their elders for botching up the country. "We are more anti-establishment than anyone" [Vice President] McMahon said.

The alliance had harsh words for the nation's involvement in Vietnam. "For 50 years our parents and grandparents have allowed themselves to be tricked into fighting wars for others," read a policy statement. The alliance attacked the "criminal politico-economic system of maintaining full employment and buying votes by intervention in alien wars." It charged that "in the past 20 years alone, 60,000 of America's finest young men have been murdered to forward the ambitions of vote-hungry politicians. We shall fight the involvement of America in further wars overseas with every means at our command."

The alliance warns rightists of the consolidation of corporate concerns. In its publication, *Statecraft*, the editors report on a liberal plot to secure mass censorship; and go on to reveal a Presidential committee recommendation that all competing international communications carriers be merged into one private company under government control. . . .

The NYA resembles the New Left also in seeing its primary constituency as young workers and college students. It "vowed" to forge a "revolutionary" alliance of students and young workers to crush the left, stem the "liberal tide" and save a dying republic. . . . The alliance seeks to carry the banner of "the forgotten American"—the exploited young American worker. "We are going to wage our fight in the factories and the campus. . . ."[31]

These rightist youth, unlike many of their elders in the Wallace movement, but like the new left, openly proclaim their opposition to conservative economic principles and "bourgeois values."

We do not concern ourselves with the intricacies of economic conservation. We shall never deny what is needed to those who need it. . . . Those who seek to put bourgeois values over the hopes and aspirations of the people are enemies of the Right Front.

The NYA hopes to unite all American youth in a movement for peace, progress, and the restoration of the rights of the American people.[32]

The Alliance even makes some of the same complaints about American higher education that new leftist students have uttered. "You are no longer the individual you thought you were; but are now a mere number in a file. . . . Your English professor hardly shows up for class."[33]

However, it is not just in the matter of anti-establishment alienation that these two youth segments resemble each other, if antagonistically, but also in their common propensity for monistic politics. Some sections of the new left have even pointed to strong similarities between segments of their movement and the original Fascist party of Italy. Thus an editorial in the *Campaigner,* published by the New York and Philadelphia Regional SDS Labor Committees, stated, "There is a near identity between the arguments of anarchists (around the Columbia strike movement, e.g.) and Mussolini's polemics for action against theory, against program. . . ."[34] An article in the same issue argues:

It is an irony of history that certain New Leftists today would be quite at home with Mussolini's radical polemics. . . . We must look to historical precedent in order to reveal the dangers inherent in certain New Left rhetoric today. . . . [Mussolini] fought for the idea that the revolution would be decided in the streets. . . . Similarly, fascism celebrated youth as a class. "Giovenezza" was the official Italian hymn to youth; similar examples are found in Nazi propaganda. The image of youth was extended to attack on the "older" capitalist nations, the "old," effete parliamentary bureaucrats.

The authors of this article go on to point to other similarities, including the evolution of the ideas of Georges Sorel, the French syndicalist theoretician, "the spiritual leader of those Italian syndicalists who produced the fascist movement. 'Purgative violence,' so recently repopularized by the writings of Franz Fanon, played a central role in the revised [fascist] syndicalist theory."[35]

Unveiled, once again, is the age-old perversion of the inherent tension between social egalitarianism—the democratic impulse—and political liberty —democratic restraint. Much of the thrust of the new left and black revolution ideologues is essentially egalitarian in nature, cutting through their concerns with the system, bureaucracy, hypocrisy, relevant education, the individual. They are interested in a broader sharing of power, a diminution of hierarchy, a shifting of status deference. Much of the thrust of the right-wing youth ideologues, reminiscent of the fascist mode, also relates to a broader sharing of power, a diminution of hierarchy, a shifting of status deference—but in a preservatist framework. In a practical sense, social egalitarianism denotes the impulse to broaden bases of economy, power, status, and is a direction, a constant state-of-becoming. It relates to welfare orientation; to economic liberalism; to our typological Rednecks, among others. Political liberty, the exercise of democratic restraint, is relatively a state-of-being.

Social egalitarianism and political liberty are scarcely incompatible, but there is a constant tension between the two, and they are discrete values of what we now call democracy. But it is important to remind ourselves finally that it is political liberty—the exercise of democratic restraint, pluralism—which is *the* subject and *the* victim of political extremism, of monism. The growth of monistic ideology among youth—as an instrumental approach to the achievement of either egalitarian or preservatist goals, or a combination of both—may yet prove to be the most important and destructive aspect of the decline in political civility in the 1960's.

A low level of democratic restraint which prevails through default in ideology is one kind of hazard. The deliberative denial of democratic restraint through a commitment to extremist ideology is quite another. This is to apotheosize political moralism, that deadly *élan* of extremism which must wither any human society.

Prince Guiseppe di Lampedusa, contemplating Italy's metamorphosis from autocracy to liberal democracy, was depressed: "All this shouldn't last; but it will, always; the human 'always,' of course, a century, two centuries . . . and after that it will be different but worse. We were the Leopards, the Lions, those who'll take our place will be little jackals, hyenas; and the whole lot of us, Leopards, jackals and sheep, we'll all go on thinking *ourselves* the salt of the earth."[36]

Notes

1. Ralph Linton, "Nativistic Movements," in R. H. Turner and L. M. Killian, eds., *Collective Behavior* (Englewood Cliffs, N.J.: Prentice-Hall, 1957), p. 388. Emphasis ours.
2. *Ibid.*, p. 390.
3. Susan Isaacs, *Social Development in Young Children* (New York: Harcourt, Brace, 1933), p. 250.
4. Neil J. Smelser, *The Theory of Collective Behavior* (New York: The Free Press, 1963), pp. 111–122.
5. Ruth Benedict, *Race, Science and Politics* (New York: Modern Age Books, 1940), pp. 230–231.
6. Gordon W. Allport, *The Nature of Prejudice* (Cambridge: Addison-Wesley, 1954), p. 305.
7. Charles Herbert Stember, *Jews in the Mind of America* (New York: Basic Books, 1966), p. 44.
8. Gertrude J. Selznick and Stephen Steinberg, *The Tenacity of Prejudice* (New York: Harper & Row, 1969), pp. 16, 18.
9. Stember, *op. cit.*, p. 71.

10. Selznick and Steinberg, *op. cit.*, p. 65.
11. Smelser, *op. cit.*, p. 122.
12. *Ibid.*, p. 325.
13. For fuller discussion, see Seymour Martin Lipset, *The First Nation* (New York: Basic Books, 1963), pp. 286–317.
14. *From Max Weber: Essays in Sociology*, H. H. Gerth and C. Wright Mills, trans. (New York: Oxford University Press, 1946), p. 248.
15. James MacGregor Burns, *The Deadlock of Democracy* (Englewood Cliffs, N.J.: Prentice-Hall, 1963), pp. 40–41.
16. Smelser, *op. cit.*, p. 364.
17. R. M. MacIver, *The Ramparts We Guard* (New York, Macmillan, 1950), p. 84.
18. Scott G. McNall, "Social Disorganization and Availability: Accounting for Radical Rightism," Robert Schoenberger, ed., *The American Right Wing* (New York: Holt, Rinehart and Winston, 1969), p. 136.
19. Selznick and Steinberg, *op. cit.*, p. 157.
20. See pp. 478–481, which describe the significance of the item.
21. George Lichtheim, "Socialism and the Jews," *Dissent*, XV (July–August 1968), 316. See also, S. M. Lipset, "Socialism of Fools," *Encounter*, XXIII (December 1969), 24–35.
22. Pete Hamill, "The Revolt of the White Lower Middle Class," *New York*, II (April 14, 1969), 30.
23. Congressman Hugh Carey, quoted in *ibid.*, p. 28.
24. *Ibid.*
25. William Simon, John H. Gagnon, and Donald Carns, "Working Class Youth: Alienation without an Image," *New Generation*, LI (Spring 1969), 16–17.
26. Gabriel Fackre, "The Blue Collar White and the Far Right," *Christian Century*, May 7, 1969, p. 645. Emphasis in the original.
27. *Ibid.*, p. 646. Emphasis in the original.
28. Gus Tyler, "A Tale of Three Cities: 1969," *New Leader*, July 7, 1969, p. 9, in New York City, John Lindsay, the Liberal candidate was re-elected, but his two more conservative "law and order" rivals took 58 per cent of the vote. In both Minneapolis and Los Angeles, the final election was a "run-off" between the two leading candidates in the primaries. A similar system in New York would presumably have resulted in Lindsay's defeat.
29. Michael Rogin, "Politics, Emotion and the Wallace Vote," *British Journal of Sociology*, XX (March 1969), 45.
30. Pp. 366–372.
31. "Rightists Launch Offensive," *Guardian*, XXI (February 8, 1969), 8.
32. Dennis C. McMahon, "The National Youth Alliance," *American Mercury*, CV (Spring 1969), 63.
33. National Youth Alliance leaflet headed "Lost and Alone."
34. *Campaigner*, I (September 1968), 9.
35. See C. LaRouche and L. Marcus, "The New Left, Local Control and Fascism," *Campaigner*, I (September 1968), 10–33 *passim*.
36. Giuseppe di Lampedusa, *The Leopard* (New York: Signet, 1961), pp. 190–191. Emphasis ours.

13

Epilogue: The 1970's

The 1970's have seen a withdrawal from extremism. The characteristic relationship between political extremism and the American political system has held firm.

Most notably, the major political parties have continued to demonstrate their capacity to absorb radical tendencies and to deter the formation of major extremist movements. The Democratic party, fulfilling its traditional role with respect to containing extremist impulses of left-wing origin, moved away from a coalition base to a more factional one in 1972; much as the Republican Party, more open to right-wing extremist impulses (nativist, preservatist, backlash), had done in 1964. In both instances, the parties suffered stunning defeats.

The Republican party had become a coalition party again by 1968, although extremists of the right complained that Richard Nixon had laced his "eastern establishment" moderateness with enough backlash temper to draw off the strength of George Wallace. By 1976, the Democratic party was also again a coalition party and the object of similar complaints by the right wing for having brought culturally conservative Democrats back into the fold. Ironically, Jimmy Carter was able to secure the backing of militant blacks and Wallace supporters.

Conspiracy Theories

The political events of the later 1960's and the 1970's merely led the radical right wing to deepen its conspiracy theory and ascribe it to both

517

major political parties, in the manner of the extreme left wing. "How is it," asked one of the leading theorists of the John Birch Society in the summer of 1977, "that this great nation with so small and unimportant a Communist Party could be so often on the side of the Communists? . . . The answer is a vast Conspiracy which has very little to do with Gus Hall and the misfits of the Communist Party, U.S. . . . The Carter cabinet was the straw which broke the back of those who maintained it was inconceivable that a single Establishment Conspiracy controlled the Executive branch of our country under both Democrats and Republicans."[1]

Thus the extreme right wing continued to de-emphasize the conspiratorial role of the Communist parties of Russia, China, and the United States. This de-emphasis always fit the Birch Society's theoretical construct of a comprehensive conspiracy which predated and created the Communists. The Society continues to constantly refer to the Illuminati or Insiders as having created the Communist party for their own purposes. These Insiders are still identified with "such fronts of conspiracy as the Council on Foreign Relations, the Trilateral Commission, and the Bilderbergers. . . . Does this mean that the billionaire elitists who sponsor the Council on Foreign Relations and the Trilateral Commission are Communists? Certainly not. They know very well what an unproductive system Marxism is. . . . They see Marxism as a useful foil, to prod the West towards world Government under their control."[2]

Articles in *American Opinion,* the principal Birch Society organ, point out that Jimmy Carter, no less than Ford, Nixon, and their predecessors, is under the control of these "billionaire elitist fronts." Carter's appointments to the posts of National Security Advisor, Secretary of State, Secretary of Defense, and Secretary of Treasury—those offices which control the country's foreign policy, national defense and money —are all traced in some way to these three Illuminati "fronts." And the link to all these fronts, for Democratic and Republican Presidents alike, is Nelson Rockefeller, the master billionaire elitist. This constant reference to Rockefeller as the master conspirator is matched only by the left-wing publications of the U.S. Labor party.

The Birch Society conspiracy theory, however, continued to lack the ingredient needed to become the basis of a mass movement. As we commented earlier:

A political conspiracy theory, after all, is a matter of personifying the causes of some social strain. Apparently this personification cannot remain very abstract and be persuasive. It is not usually enough to corporealize a plot theory by identifying a vague group of elite intellectuals as the prime manipulators. . . . The plot theory is most cogent when the social strain can itself be personified through that theory. . . . So it is that through most of America's history, ethnic groups have served as a key [target] link between extremist groups, the social strains they have addressed themselves to, and the plot theories with which they have explained these strains.[3]

The Absence of an Organized Backlash

Such social strains have usually been associated with some sense of status displacement by a mass of Americans, occurring most dramatically during the emergence of some new ethnic or other population group. The result has been "backlash," the fodder for extremist movements and their conspiracy theories.

During the 1960's, the American condition seemed ripe for such backlash in connection with the dramatic rise of the black population. The twin objective indices to the sense of displacement have usually been occupational and political power. In the five-year heart of the civil rights drive, between the mid-sixties and 1971, the nonwhite rate of new entry into the white-collar occupations was 127 per cent, while the increase for whites was 14 per cent. In that short span, the ratio of nonwhites to whites in these more visible, higher-status, higher-paying occupations jumped from 29 to 58 per cent.[4] The median income of nonwhite families moved from one-half to two-thirds that of white families. In the same period, the number of blacks in state or federal legislatures jumped from less than 50 to over 200, and there was a corresponding increase in blacks elected to city and county offices, including the mayoralties of several large cities.[5]

These figures demonstrate, if nothing else, the extent to which the white dominance in occupational and political life could appear to be threatened. Accompanying this objective displacement were the hallmarks of a traditional displacement in other symbolic status patterns. There was no longer any comfortable way to keep blacks spatially "in their place." Federal and state laws, by the end of the sixties, prohibited discrimination in all places of public accommodation and in most housing. With increased income, some blacks were, in fact, "moving elsewhere." Southern schools had given up the overt fight against de jure segregation; and Northern schools were under a flood of court orders to take extraordinary measures to correct de facto segregation. The number of black students in college doubled during the sixties—but more to the point, at the beginning of that decade about two-thirds of all black students were attending exclusively or predominantly black colleges, but by the end of the decade two-thirds of them were attending mixed colleges.[6] Of course there was still much covert discrimination, especially effective in the case of housing, but that is exactly the symbolic point: such exclusivity now was illicit in the society and had been driven underground. Such a situation is bound to dent any sense of dominance, and create, instead, a sense of impending displacement.

The massive backlash which might have been anticipated—and which might have been expected to feed a major right-wing extremist movement, as in the past—did not eventuate. Why? The ability of the major political parties to adjust to and absorb extremist tendencies needs further explanation. The fact is that the backlash, as connected with ethnic targets, remained limited, even at the height of the black "emergence."

Some indices suggested that the "happy ending" prophesied by some sociologists was taking place: changed circumstances were changing basic attitudes. Thus in 1964 over 60 per cent of American whites told interviewers from the University of Michigan's Survey Research Center (SRC) that they objected to the speed of racial integration; by 1973 that figure was down to 53 per cent, and by 1976 down to 39 per cent. In 1944, 42 per cent of white Americans queried by the National Opinion Research Center (NORC) of the University of Chicago had said that they supported equal job opportunity; by 1972, 96 per cent reported that they supported equal job opportunity. Asked by NORC whether they favored school integration, 30 per cent answered affirmatively in 1942, 48 per cent in 1956, and 85 per cent in 1977. In 1976, according to SRC, only 8 per cent of white Americans thought they had a right to keep black people out of white neighborhoods, although the figure had been 24 per cent only a dozen years before.

According to the "happy ending" scenario, resistance to integration diminishes after the first skirmishes, when proximity reduces fears and blunts stereotypes. There was a wealth of evidence in the 1950's and 1960's to support that thesis. Stark prejudice dimmed when whites worked with blacks in equal status, or lived in the same neighborhoods, or went to the same schools.

But there was also evidence which suggested that, under other circumstances, proximity increases hostility. Integration becomes more rather than less threatening under a variety of circumstances involving more massive changes, more severe cultural shock, more direct economic hazard. And as the civil rights drive gathered momentum in the late 1960's, these more threatening factors were perceived everywhere.

In 1963, NORC reported that about one-third of white Americans thought that Negroes were "asking too much"; by 1968, about two-thirds of white Americans said that Negroes were "asking too much." In part, the difference in response might only mean that the black population was not asking enough in 1963. But in any case it is clear that at the high tide of the civil rights movement, most white Americans were quite upset about both the demands and the results. In 1971, the majority of white Americans agreed with the proposition that blacks were "too pushy." In 1970, about half of white Americans freely admitted that they preferred a separate black society, and this was not the way they perceived things to be going. At the same time, the "cultural baggage" which signals the traditional way of life was under the most explicit attack since the 1920's. Language taboos, sexual mores, and clothing standards were spectacularly flouted, while rates of crime, welfare, and drug use soared.

The Wallace Constituency

Why was there not a backlash reaction? The fact is that there *was*. In 1972 and 1976, George Wallace continued to represent a backlash vote in the Presidential primaries and opinion polls. In 1972, Wallace did well in a number of Democratic primaries. He carried Florida in March with 42 per cent, running ahead of Senators Humphrey (18 per cent) and Jackson (13 per cent). In April, he captured 51 per cent of the votes in the Michigan primary. A Yankelovich survey of primary voters in that state, published in the *New York Times* on May 17, indicated that Wallace supporters backed him because of his opposition to busing, welfare, and high taxes. At the time that he was shot, newspaper tabulations of delegate strength gave him 317 delegates, compared to McGovern's 503, Humphrey's 305, and Muskie's 106.

As the 1976 race began to receive attention from the pollsters, the evidence accumulated that Wallace still had appeal. Late in 1974, Pat Caddell for Cambridge Survey Research reported that one-fifth of those interviewed stated that they would vote for Wallace as an independent candidate if the major party nominees were Gerald Ford and Henry Jackson. Fully 35 per cent reported that they would consider voting for Wallace. And in line with our findings on support for extremist parties in earlier elections, Caddell noted "that it is the half of the population who are non-voters who are most likely to opt for a candidate such as George Wallace."[7] In the spring of 1975, when Wallace was pitted in three separate hypothetical elections against Ford and McGovern, against Jackson, and against Teddy Kennedy, he was supported respectively by 23 per cent, 21 per cent, and 18 per cent of all those interviewed. At the end of 1975, the Gallup poll reported that 28 per cent said they would vote for him against Ford and Humphrey. A Harris survey taken about the same time indicated that 21 per cent would vote for Wallace as a third party candidate. As the Presidential race was heating up in the spring of 1976, a Caddell poll pitted him against Gerald Ford and Jimmy Carter, and Wallace's backing fell to 14 per cent. Apparently Jimmy Carter, a fellow Southerner with a populist anti-Washington establishment image, undercut the Wallace appeal. As *Cambridge Report* noted, "Jimmy Carter is the Democratic candidate with the major appeal to the Wallace constituency."[8] In January 1976, when the Harris Survey presented respondents with a list of 24 possible Democratic party candidates (which included Hubert Humphrey and Jimmy Carter) Wallace came out second only to Senator Edward Kennedy (17 to 25 per cent). When Kennedy was removed from the list, Wallace still came out second to Hubert Humphrey (19 to 25 per cent). These patterns describe the fact that Wallace had a hard core of supporters going into the 1976 election year, even though an overwhelming majority would always vote against him in favor of almost any other candidate.

There was, as always, a disparity between the numbers of those who preferred Wallace in the opinion polls and of those who chose him in the voting booths. When one 1976 poll asked why they preferred Wallace in the abstract but would not vote for him, many respondents said that they were afraid of his "extremism." This might be taken as a measure of built-in democratic restraint on the part of American people, at least under certain qualified conditions.

"By 1972," wrote one observer, "politicians of both major parties began to adopt Wallace's stand on many of the issues."[9] After the 1972 election, Wallace said that Nixon's victory occurred partly because he adopted "many of the positions that I took."[10] In 1976, Wallace complained in Wisconsin that "The candidates are stealing all my stuff after Florida."[11] Wallace, however, continued to be the lightning rod for more extreme political alienation. In 1976, close to half of the Democrats voting in the primary states told NBC interviewers that "Wallace expresses many of my feelings about what is wrong with the country," even though many fewer than half of these actually voted for Wallace in the primaries.[12]

In the 1970's, analyses of Wallace's speeches suggest that he concentrated less on specific issues, more on the general rhetoric of protest. Typically, he struck this note: "We're getting fed up with the courts, and we're getting fed up with bureaucrats, and we're getting fed up with militants, and we're getting fed up with law violators, and when enough of us get fed up about it . . . we're gonna get some relief."[13]

Our analysis of the Wallace vote in 1964 and 1968, reported in chapter 10, suggested that there were several issue strains to be disproportionately found among Wallace supporters: racial backlash, opposition to cultural change in general, and antistatism. Various opinion polls indicated that these characteristics marked the Wallace supporters in the 1970's as well.

Throughout the various elections, Wallace's constituency remained roughly the same. An inventory by Stephen Winn of 22 surveys taken from 1964 on found that "the principal sources of support for George Wallace from 1964 to 1972 were manual workers, the less educated, males, political independents, economic conservatives, and segregationists."[14]

Wallace supporters in the 1970's continued to be disproportionately blue-collar workers, both in the South and in the rest of the country, as measured in polls pitting him as a prospective third party candidate against Democrats and Republicans (Table 113). Concomitantly, the educational level of Wallace supporters remained low (Table 114).

Table 113.   OCCUPATION AND PERCENTAGE OF WALLACE VOTE, 1972 AND 1976
(GALLUP)

Occupation	Nation		South		Non-South	
	Total	Wallace	Total	Wallace	Total	Wallace
				1972		
Number	(1080)	(181)	(241)	(73)	(839)	(108)
White Collar	46	31	43	38	47	23
Blue Collar	47	61	46	52	47	70
Farm	7	8	11	10	6	7
				1976		
Number	(1798)	(523)	(453)	(186)	(1345)	(337)
White Collar	46	31	47	30	45	31
Blue Collar	52	67	50	67	53	67
Farm	2	2	3	3	2	2

SOURCE: Calculated from original data of two Gallup surveys, AIPO 847 and AIPO 944. Data analyses obtained from the Roper Center, The University of Connecticut, Storrs, Connecticut.

A February 1976 Gallup survey which asked respondents how much "trust and confidence" they had in various political leaders also found that those who reported a "great deal" in Wallace were disproportionately Protestant, male, less educated, less skilled, and of lower income than those with high confidence in other Democratic and Republican contenders (Table 115).

A number of surveys taken in 1976 indicated that Wallacites were a very distinctive group. They were, by and large, more racist, more

Table 114. AGE AND EDUCATION, PERCENTAGE OF WALLACE VOTE, 1972 AND 1976
(GALLUP)

	21 to 29	30 to 49	50 and over
		1972	
Grammar School	*	30 (10)	19 (30)
High School	28 (35)	21 (56)	12 (30)
College	10 (12)	7 (11)	13 (14)
		1976	
Grammar School	*	46 (37)	39 (94)
High School	44 (88)	35 (145)	25 (133)
College	16 (39)	20 (50)	16 (35)

* Too few cases.
Figures in parentheses indicate numbers of individuals in the cell.
SOURCE: Same as Table 113.

Table 115.   OCCUPATIONAL AND EDUCATIONAL BACKGROUND OF THOSE EXPRESSING
"GREAT DEAL OF TRUST AND CONFIDENCE" IN VARIOUS CANDIDATES
(GALLUP, PER CENT, FEBRUARY 1976)

Candidates	Occupations					
	Prof./ Mgr.	Clerk/ Sales	Skilled	Unskilled and Service	Farm	No.
Wallace	14.5	13	20	48	5	(193)
Reagan	30	9	26.5	32	2	(185)
Ford	39	18	20	19	3	(231)
Carter	34	16.5	23	22	5	(109)
Humphrey	40	17	16	20	8	(144)

	Education			
	College	High School Grad	< 12 Grades	No.
Wallace	13	37.5	50	(269)
Reagan	23	45	29	(240)
Ford	31	44	25	(314)
Carter	34	36	31	(140)
Humphrey	28	37	35	(195)

SOURCE: Calculated from Gallup Survey AIPO 946, as analyzed by the Roper
Center.

opposed to cultural change, more antistatist, and less trusting of government than supporters of any other major figure inquired about in
the polls. They were, however, not more conservative. Those who
endorsed Reagan or Ford were generally much more conservative
than Wallace supporters on issues involving economic or welfare
policy.

The issues which most differentiated the Wallacites were linked to race. Thus in the 1976 election survey of the Center for Political Studies (CPS) of the University of Michigan, 73 per cent of Wallace supporters (those who scored 85 or above on a 100 point scale question) agreed that civil rights leaders were pushing too fast, as contrasted to only 42 per cent of all whites interviewed and 51 per cent of Reagan enthusiasts. On questions inquiring whether the government should ensure school integration or give aid to minorities, Wallace backers opposed these measures by 79 and 57 per cent respectively. Of all other whites surveyed, only 43 per cent opposed the government taking a role in school integration and 39 per cent rejected government aid to minorities.

A Knight-Ridder survey taken early in 1976 reported that 40 per cent of Wallace supporters said that "civil rights is progressing too fast," as compared to 24 per cent among others interviewed. Samples of those voting in the various 1976 Presidential primaries were asked by NBC interviewers to identify those issues which most affected their vote. The problem which received the highest mention from Wallace supporters was busing, an issue which did not appear among the top six issues of any of the other candidates (Table 116).

In the Democratic primaries outside of the South, Wallace had his greatest success in carrying the city of Boston, then bitterly polarized on the issue of court ordered school integration through busing. In the Wisconsin primary, where he obtained 12.7 per cent of the Democratic primary vote, the *New York Times*/CBS survey taken on primary day indicated that the "one issue position that most separated Wallace voters from other candidate factions was the issue of government attention to blacks and other minorities. . . . And according to the *Milwaukee Journal* poll, 56% of Wallace's supporters were *strongly* opposed to court ordered busing, while 42% of the whole sample were strongly opposed and 39% of the Democrats in the sample were strongly opposed."[15]

The various opinion polls also pointed to the fact that, as in the 1960's, Wallace support was disproportionately founded not only in racial backlash, but also in opposition to change in general. Attitudes toward changing morals continued to be associated with support of the backlash candidate. For example, the Knight-Ridder January 1976 survey found that Wallace supporters were more likely than others to think that punishment for criminal offenses should be made more severe, while they were less disposed to believe that marijuana should be made a minor offense like a traffic violator. The Center for Political

Table 116. RANKING OF ISSUES AFFECTING VOTES, BY CANDIDATES, PRIMARY STATES, 1976

Issues	Democrats						Republicans	
	Wallace	Carter	Jackson	Humphrey	Harris	Udall	Ford	Reagan
Inflation	2 (40)	3 (45)	2 (44)	1 (66)	3 (46)	2 (49)	1 (54)	3 (44)
Unemployment	3 (39)	1 (49)	1 (51)	2 (56)	1 (62)	1 (63)	3 (36)	(33)
Busing	1 (52)	(23)	(22)	(19)	(16)	(26)	(18)	(34)
Environment	(13)	(17)	(17)	(21)	4 (38)	4 (37)	(13)	(10)
Watergate	(16)	(20)	(17)	(23)	6 (23)	(25)	(10)	(13)
Russia	(27)	(17)	4 (29)	(23)	(18)	(20)	(19)	1 (45)
Defense Spending	(29)	6 (25)	6 (25)	5 (33)	5 (25)	5 (36)	5 (25)	6 (37)
Trust in Government	5 (37)	2 (48)	3 (34)	3 (50)	2 (51)	3 (48)	2 (46)	4 (41)
Federal Power	6 (32)	5 (28)	(15)	(12)	(20)	(16)	4 (26)	2 (44)
Welfare	4 (39)	(22)	(19)	6 (27)	(22)	6 (27)	(16)	5 (40)
Social Security	(29)	4 (28)	5 (29)	4 (42)	—	(26)	6 (22)	(26)

Figures in parentheses indicate percentage of candidate's voters choosing that issue as having affected their vote.

SOURCE: NBC News/Elections, *Decision 76: Election Day Results*, multilith, June 3, 1976, pp. 6, 37–40.

Studies election survey of that year supported this finding. In that poll 75 per cent of Wallace supporters favored penalizing use of marijuana more severely than it is now, compared to 49 per cent of all whites surveyed. An earlier study in North Carolina indicated that traditionalism and racial concerns were independent factors in Wallace support (Table 117).

Table 117. RELATIONSHIP BETWEEN TRADITIONALISM AND RACISM AND WALLACE SUPPORT (NORTH CAROLINA 1971)

Characteristics	Percentage	Number
Low Racism	18	(221)
Low Traditionalism and		
Low Traditionalism and		
High Racism	51	(108)
High Traditionalism and		
Low Racism	54	(100)
High Traditionalism and		
High Racism	67	(225)

SOURCE: Harold S. Grasmick, "Rural Culture and the Wallace Movement in the South," *Rural Sociology,* XXXIX (Winter 1974), p. 462.

Antistatism continued to be part of the syndrome which distinguished Wallacites. Seventy-nine per cent of them told Center for Political Studies interviewers that the Federal Government is getting too powerful, compared to 58 per cent of all whites interviewed. On this issue, Reagan supporters resembled the Wallacites with 78 per cent agreeing.

In the Knight-Ridder poll, a higher percentage of Wallace backers than others believed that the federal government "interferes too much in matters that should be left to state and local governments." And concern with federal power was an important issue for more Wallace primary supporters in 1976, according to NBC, than for the supporters for any candidate other than Reagan (see Table 116).

The attitudes of Wallacites toward race, cultural changes, law enforcement, and the role of government generally, clearly placed them on the conservative side of the political spectrum. And the evidence clearly indicates that most people who were enthusiastically for Wallace in 1976 saw themselves on the right or conservative side. Thus when the Center for Political Studies asked respondents in 1976 to locate themselves "on a scale ranging from extremely liberal to extremely conservative," a majority of Wallace people put themselves on the conservative side, although by a slightly smaller percentage than did the Reagan and Ford enthusiasts (Table 118).

Table 118. IDEOLOGY SCALE
(CENTER FOR POLITICAL STUDIES, 1976; WHITES ONLY)
(PER CENT)

	Liberal	Moderate	Conservative	Number
Wallace	17	34	53	(152)
Reagan	9	31	60	(355)
Ford	8	38	54	(405)
Carter	28	51	21	(443)
Kennedy	34	47.5	18.5	(104)
McGovern	56	30	14	(104)

Liberals were those who placed themselves as one, two, or three on a seven point scale which ran from extremely liberal (1) to extremely conservative (7). Moderates were in position four, while conservatives located themselves at five, six, or seven.

In spite of identifying themselves as conservatives, the populism or economic liberalism associated with the Wallace syndrome came out strikingly in the responses to a series of CPS questions dealing with specific proposals for government action to benefit the ordinary citizen or "little person." On issues such as a government-guaranteed job and living standard, state-provided medical care, and governmental regulation of job safety standards, Wallace supporters were much more likely to favor state intervention than Reagan or Ford backers, although they were generally somewhat less liberal than enthusiasts for Democratic leaders (Table 119).

Wallace enthusiasts proved to be the most alienated of all political constituencies from the body politic and social. They scored lowest on measures of trust and of belief in their own efficacy in both the political and the personal arenas. According to the CPS 1976 data, they had the lowest sense of trust in government and of being politically efficacious of supporters of six major political figures. They were also the least disposed to believe that people are fair.

A striking indication of mass frustration with the political process is the response to a question posed by Gallup in February 1976: "Some people think what this country needs is some really strong leadership that would try to solve problems directly without worrying how Congress and the Supreme Court might feel. Others think that such strong leadership might be dangerous. What do you think?" A

Table 119.   ATTITUDES TOWARD STATE INTERVENTION
(CPS, 1976) (PER CENT)

	Wallace	Reagan	Ford	Carter	Kennedy	McGovern
Government should guarantee a job and good standard of living	27	18	18	38	41	51
Each person should get ahead on his own	43	63.5	59	39	34	31
	(178)	(404)	(444)	(556)	(444)	(121)
Government should cover all medical and hospital expenses	43	28	32	51	58	63
Individual and Blue Cross should pay	43	55	54	32	28	16.5
	(178)	(408)	(467)	(552)	(463)	(122)
Government should regulate job safety standards of local business	72.5	59	68	78	81	84
Opposed	27	41	32	21	19	16
	(179)	(377)	(448)	(527)	(419)	(119)

Figures in parentheses indicate numbers of respondents.

Table 120.   TRUST AND SENSE OF EFFICACY: POLITICAL AND PERSONAL
(CPS, 1976) (PER CENT)

	Wallace	Reagan	Ford	Carter	Kennedy	McGovern
No trust in government	69	60	50	63	66	68
	(212)	(475)	(553)	(562)	(392)	(119)
Government officials are crooked	54	43	33.5	42	42	40
	(211)	(475)	(547)	(559)	(390)	(117)
Respondent does not feel well represented	45	35	23	33	35	39
	(204)	(465)	(536)	(552)	(389)	(118)
Government does not pay attention to people like respondent	45	33	28	33	34	38
	(211)	(476)	(545)	(558)	(390)	(118)
People like respondent do not have a say in government	51	36	36	43	46	42
	(209)	(475)	(540)	(548)	(386)	(113)
People cannot be trusted	59	41	39	46	49.5	42
	(208)	(471)	(545)	(552)	(382)	(117)
People are not fair	48	30	30	35	38	28
	(202)	(460)	(537)	(548)	(382)	(114)

Figures in parentheses indicate numbers of respondents.

plurality, 49 per cent, preferred the populist "strong leadership" willing to override Congress and the Court, while 44 per cent thought such leadership might be dangerous. Not surprisingly, Wallace backers were much more likely to favor strong leadership, 64 per cent doing so. This anti-Constitutional reaction had less but still considerable strength among supporters of 11 other political leaders. The only demographic groups to reject the need for such leadership were people in professional and managerial occupations, those earning over $20,000, the college educated, and the Jews.

In 1976, two candidates for the Presidency were described as "right-wing," George Wallace and Ronald Reagan. Wallace, of course, ran as a populist Democrat, while Reagan presented himself as a conservative or libertarian Republican. The survey data indicate that, independently of party, the two men appealed to sharply diverse constituencies, much as Goldwater and Wallace did in the 1960's.

Wallacites generally ranked higher than all others in racism, opposition to cultural change, and antistatism. They were also fairly cynical about the federal government and tended to feel a lack of political efficacy. They were, however, much less conservative than Reagan and Ford supporters with respect to economic questions, although they were less liberal than supporters of other Democrats.

Reaganites, by contrast, were the most conservative group as far as economic issues were concerned. They ranked relatively high in racism, opposition to cultural change, and antistatism. They did not, however, score as high as Wallacites and actually were quite similar to Ford supporters on these issues. Finally, Reaganites were not cynical about society and polity. They scored very high on measures of their sense of personal and political efficacy, and were the most likely to believe that people in general can be trusted. In short, Reagan enthusiasts were conservative Republicans who were not turned off by the political process.

Wallace basically remained the "general-duty" protest figure in American politics in 1972 and 1976, attracting a composite of the most severely alienated with respect to racial, cultural, and antistatist backlash. Analyzing the changes in Wallace supporters as revealed in the polls over the twelve years that Wallace participated in Presidential elections, David Bronston notes that he "has progressively attracted the support of those parts of the society which are most isolated, politically frustrated and least economically well off. His best support comes from those groups having the least faith in political institutions and the lowest feeling of political efficacy—in short, among the least politically socialized."[16]

Nixon and the Backlash

Although the various surveys taken prior to the Presidential nominations in 1972 and 1976 clearly indicate that George Wallace retained a large constituency—that about a quarter of white Americans identified with him and his views—the fact remains that Wallace was not on the Presidential ballot in November. In 1972, Richard Nixon was able to swing the bulk of the Wallace supporters behind his candidacy, while in 1976, Jimmy Carter, a Southern antiestablishment candidate, seemingly attracted many Wallacites.

In 1972 Nixon's overwhelming victory, over 60 per cent of the vote, was produced not only by the fact that he appeared to some as more moderate than the Democratic nominee, George McGovern, who was identified with the counterculture and the various left-wing and antiwar protests of the 1960's, but also because of his perceived resistance to what were seen as runaway civil rights advances. The latter reaction was particularly stimulated by the quota issue, an outgrowth of affirmative action, which had begun to raise direct images of displacement concerning the two most objective criteria of displacement, occupation and political power. In the late 1960's, pressure developed to apply numerical goals or quotas for minorities and women, not only in such matters as professional schools admissions, but also in the hiring and upgrading of employees, and even as an alternative criterion to seniority in firing. There was also increasing pressure to apply mandatory quotas to political appointments. This movement reached a crescendo in public attention in the Democratic political convention of 1972, when "proportional representation" was dramatically invoked to ensure certain numerical proportions of blacks and other racial and ethnic groups, as well as women and youth, among the delegates. There was much open controversy about the displacement through that process of some of the traditional elements of the Democratic party. A resultant alienation was expressed by more culturally conservative segments within the party, particularly the labor movement and the white ethnic groups. Nixon and Agnew spoke up in strong terms in favor of maintenance of the competitive or meritocratic principle, and against quotas in general. Thus Nixon seemed to serve the backlash sentiment without generally being branded as an extremist.

Watergate: Extremism in the White House

But if Nixon was perceived in 1968 and 1972 as an opponent of extremism on the left as well as the right, it is ironic that the Watergate-related events raised the spectre of extremism and conspiratorial thinking operating within the White House itself. The behavior associated with the Watergate events could fit the classic definition of "extremism": attempted illegal repression and violation of civil liberties in a political cause. This sordid episode in American history, however, was a particular demonstration not only of the continuing principles by which extremism operates, but also of those by which it is deterred in American political life. The key to this particular occurrence is that the Nixon administration brought into the White House many of the classic characteristics of an extremist temper, but could only exercise that temper within the constraints which it had necessarily imposed upon itself in order to enter the White House.

While Nixon stood against and resisted blatant backlash extremism, and while he repudiated comprehensive conspiracy theories such as were held by the KKK and the Birch Society, he developed a markedly adversary relationship to those elements which have always formed the central core of conspiracy theories: the intellectual community, the journalists, the Ivy League elite, the liberals. Furthermore, Nixon explicitly put these elements together into a network which he contended was hostile toward him and traditional American values. It was ironic that this man, one of whose conscious political purposes was to contain the excesses of right-wing extremism which he saw as inimical to the Republican party and to his Presidency, should have carried the atmosphere and the logic of that very extremism right into the White House and into the heart of the Republican establishment. Once in the White House, however, it became easy for the logic of extremism to unfold, especially given the circumstances which the Nixon people found in Washington in 1969.

The Washington they entered was still a Democratic town. Democrats not only held a majority in Congress, they also clearly retained the sympathies of the potent civil service, including its upper echelons, and of the press corps, particularly those representing the most influential papers and the national TV news programs. The bulk of expert consultants were heavily liberal, as were the largely government-financed think tanks, from Brookings to Rand. (Brookings was to be the target of a planned break-in, and Henry Rowen, then the president of Rand, appeared on the enemies list.) Then the evidence began to pile up, in the form of leaks and pilfered documents, that persons in high places in government were in collusion with this elite to expose and frustrate the new administration. As John Ehrlichman described the way the administration people saw their situation: "There were a number of holdovers in the executive branch who actively opposed the President's policies. . . . These people conducted a kind of internal guerrilla warfare against the President during his first term, trying to frustrate his goals by unauthorized leaks of part of the facts of a story, or of military and other secrets, or by just plain falsehood. The object was to create hostility in the Congress and abroad and to affect public opinion."[17]

Meanwhile, outside government there was the antiwar movement. Even though the New Left was obviously exhausted, and the campuses had begun to quiet down by the fall of 1969 in response to troop withdrawals and the disappearing draft, many in the White House, finding confirmation in the May 1970 demonstrations on Cambodia, persisted in believing that the same "extra-parliamentary" forces which had destroyed Lyndon Johnson would, if left unchecked, destroy Richard Nixon too.

It was also believed in the White House that the disruptive forces were being supported by foreign funds. When the FBI and the CIA reported that they could unearth no evidence of significant foreign involvement in the domestic New Left or in the antiwar movement, the White House staffers concluded that a new intelligence operation, controlled by the White House itself, was needed. Arguing for such an operation, to include proposals he himself described as "clearly illegal," a young White House aide, Tom Huston, wrote in a September 1970 memo to Haldeman:

> The biggest risk we could take, in my opinion, is to continue to regard violence on the campus and in the cities as a temporary phenomenon. . . . I believe we are talking about the future of this country, for surely domestic violence and disorder threaten the very fabric of our society. For eighteen months we have watched people in this government ignore the President's orders, take actions to embarrass him, promote themselves at his expense, and generally make his job more difficult.[18]

The original plans, though initially approved by the President, were killed by the opposition of J. Edgar Hoover, who apparently saw the scheme as reflecting a negative evaluation of the FBI by the White House; in this he was correct.

In placing blame on the FBI or other investigative agencies for failing to uncover the terrorists, however, the White House ignored the nature of the protests of the 1960's. Unlike the Communist party of earlier decades, or the Arab terrorists of today, both of which have centralized leadership, the recent American movement was composed of literally hundreds, if not thousands, of separate, independent cells, many bitterly hostile to one another on ideological grounds. There were a few national organizations (the SDS, the Young Socialist Alliance, the Progressive Labor party, the Spartacus League), but most of these did not take part in terrorism, either for ideological or practical reasons. The bombings, the arson, the raids on government offices, were largely conducted by small local groups often comprising a handful of people. It was quite impossible for the FBI or even the local police to penetrate these cells; most of them evidently were clever enough not to let anyone in the aboveground antiwar organizations know who they were.

There was, then, no single large leftist conspiracy, there were hundreds of small ones. Few of these were in a position to secure foreign funds or help, although some probably did. Alien subversive forces would have had as little luck in locating the American terrorists as did the FBI; and Robert Mardian and Egil Krogh were later equally unsuccessful in finding them. Hence both the CIA and the FBI were undoubtedly correct in reporting to the White House that foreign-supported conspiracies did not explain the continuation and spread of terrorism.

But such reports did no good, for conspiracy-theory logic had enveloped the Nixon White House. Much as extremists, both of the Left and of the Right, found it impossible to accept the fact that Lee Harvey Oswald was a loner linked neither to the CIA nor to Castro, so the White House could not accept a nonconspiratorial interpretation of Daniel Ellsberg, former supporter of the Vietnam war, who turned confidential government material over to the media in his latter-day opposition to that war.

Faced with the "betrayal" of a once-trusted supporter of the Vietnam war, they refused to see Ellsberg as a man who has always shown a need for passionate commitment; as one who, in the words of the CIA psychological profile which they rejected, had always been "either strongly for something or strongly against," and who had now reached a time of life when many men, especially very ambitious ones, "come to doubt their earlier commitments, and are impelled to strike out in new directions." The CIA profile asserted that "There is no suggestion that [Ellsberg] thought anything treasonous in his act. Rather, he seemed to be responding to what he deemed a higher order of patriotism."[19] But in the White House view Ellsberg had to be part of a broader conspiracy, and anyone who doubted this—even the CIA or so reliable an ally as J. Edgar Hoover—must have been either misled or somehow corrupted.

In short, the behavior summed up in the name of Watergate was typical, at least in form, of American backlash extremism. But this still leaves two important questions to be answered. First, how did the extremist syndrome get seated so directly in the White House and in the Republican establishment? There have been other backlash administrations in Washington but such administrations have usually taken care to separate themselves from extremist behavior while sympathizing with or tolerating it in others. Even after World War I, when the U.S. Attorney General's office was directly involved in Watergate-type behavior, it was responding to activist-extremist centers like the KKK or the American Defense League, which were outside the government exerting pressure. In Watergate the activist-extremist center was in the White House itself, and it was evidently self-starting. And second, why should Watergate have been so pale and tepid an expression of extremist action, emanating as it did from the highest places?

The answer to both of these questions lies in Richard Nixon. Nixon remarkably personified the basic division in the country: for some people he stood for the backlash, while for others he stood for the resistance to factional extremism. In that way, he managed to reach the White House and helped to prevent the formation of a classic extremist movement. He certainly defused George Wallace, who expressed annoyance about it many times. As noted earlier, Wallace had complained: "I wish I had copyrighted or patented my speeches. I would be drawing immense royalties from Mr. Nixon and especially Mr. Agnew." In order to defuse the backlash however, Nixon absorbed some of its basic elements in his own appeal, and it was this that brought the extremist syndrome right into the White House. At the same time, the cosmopolitan climate in which the backlash now had to operate blunted it and made it relatively ineffectual. After World War I, Attorney General A. Mitchell Palmer set up an extralegal intelligence agency and promptly swept many thousands of people into jail. Nixon's first attempt to set up an extralegal intelligence agency was shot down by a cross word from J. Edgar Hoover, and he fell back to a "plumbers" operation which was neither massive nor very efficient. The plumbers found nothing in the office of Ellsberg's psychiatrist, and indeed managed only to guarantee Ellsberg's acquittal. Enemies lists were prepared, but for the most part they ended up in John Dean's files without being acted on. The proposal to deny government research grants to MIT because of the objections of its president, Jerome Wiesner, to administration, military, and foreign policies, was never carried through, apparently because of opposition from the Pentagon and other government agencies. In order to harass people through examination of their income tax, White House staff had to resort to sending anonymous "citizen's" letters to the IRS, with scarcely impressive results. They bugged the wrong phones. They tried to "get something" on Daniel Schorr of CBS, but succeeded only in alerting him. Nor did they have a "chilling" effect on anyone, in the way that Joseph McCarthy so often did with an essentially one-man operation.

This is not to minimize the seriousness of these activities, nor to dismiss them as merely inept. Presumably, with more practice the Watergate group could have improved its skills. In any case, a botched burglary is still a burglary, an unsuccessful assault on constitutional liberties is still an assault. But the point is that whereas in the 1920's, the illegal activities of the government were carried out in the open, and apparently with the overwhelming approval of the American people, the Watergate horrors were perpetrated covertly. In the Nixon administration the most elaborate operation was the cover-up, which itself is a measure of the restraining power of American political institutions and of prevailing antiextremist sentiment.

Social Strains and Personal Satisfaction

These "closet extremists," as distinct from mass extremist movements, failed miserably. The American people later confirmed Nixon's perception of their hesitancy about extremism by overwhelmingly expressing their disdain and lack of support for his extremist misadventures. Again, it was demonstrated that the backlash sentiment which existed was not ready to be linked to political extremism as we have defined it. Of course, the resistance of the American people to extremist or modern nativist movements must also be related to the lesser intensity of the social strain and therefore of the backlash. While there was demonstrable backlash sentiment with respect to the spectacular rise of the black population, there were objective factors which limited the intensity of the response. The increase in real income (constant dollar median income) for white Americans between 1947 and 1970 was only two-thirds of that for black American families, but it was still a healthy 86 per cent increase. And during the height of the black revolution, the white unemployment rate dropped along with that of the blacks.[20] The inflation and recession of the early 1970's also did not get desperately out of hand for the large majority of Americans. While the real income of white Americans did not increase between 1970 and 1975, neither did that of the black families, and in neither case did it significantly decrease. While the number of unemployed between 1970 and 1976 grew by about 2 million, the number of employed increased by about 7 million. A catastrophic economic crunch for white America just did not eventuate.

At the same time, the social strain was limited by an apparent deceleration of the civil rights movement. By 1970, the Harris Survey reported that almost two-thirds of American blacks thought that "things were getting better," while only 13 per cent said they "were getting worse." After Nixon took office expectations for progress dropped. Over 70 per cent of American blacks told Harris interviewers that President Johnson could be "greatly counted on" for support; only about 3 per cent had the same conviction about Nixon.

There is no way to accurately assess the countervailing role of sheer democratic restraint as a factor in the American people's resistance to extremist temptation. As noted earlier in the book, our analyses constantly find a relationship between this restraint factor and educational attainment. Between 1960 and 1975, the percentage of American whites 25 years of age or older who had at least a high school education reached a majority, increasing from about 42 per cent to about 65 per cent. The proportion of whites of that age with some college education went from about 17 per cent to about 27 per cent. Those figures had approximately doubled since 1950.[21]

Certain gross indices of bigotry seem to have declined, possibly in response to this rise in educational attainment. For example, perceptions of inherent racial inferiority have altered greatly. In 1939, about 22 per cent of the white American population thought that blacks were as intelligent as whites; by 1956, about 80 per cent of white Americans agreed that blacks were as intelligent as whites. Certain traditional anti-Semitic stereotypes seemed also to decline in acceptance. The percentage of Americans who believed that Jewish businessmen were "less honest" than other businessmen declined from 42 and 49 per cent in polls taken in 1938 and 1939 to 28 per cent in a 1964 poll and 19 per cent in a 1974 poll. In general, there was a modest drop in the prevalence of conventional stereotypes. In 1964, about 34 per cent of the population accepted some anti-Semitic stereotypes; the figure was down to 29 per cent by 1974.[22]

Earlier we pointed out that the falling away of more blatant stereotypes of bigotry may only signify their lack of fashion and the possible substitution of more sophisticated forms of affective prejudice. We also noted that overt mass bigotry is more often the baggage of backlash extremism than its source. Given the reservoir of prejudice which continues to exist, there is always the possibility that it can be activated by extremist politics. Finally, it may be reiterated that the burden of democratic restraint—and perhaps the major effect of educational attainment—is not so much to reduce bigotry, as to put value limitations on the acting out of bigotry. This would seem to characterize the softness of political bigotry in the 1970's. The backlash sentiment of this period certainly has not been without racial and ethnic content. Almost half of the white population told pollsters in 1970 that they would prefer to have a separate white society in all respects, but that sentiment did not translate into expressed opposition to civil rights laws on accommodations, housing, or employment. Nor did it translate into accepting politically extremist platforms which would have rescinded such laws. The laws were accepted, by and large, even where the backlash sentiment prevailed. This is an illustration of democratic restraint.

It is especially notable that the extremist movements had such little impact during a period when there seemed to be a decline in the American population's confidence about their institutions. One of the factors presumed to operate in democratic restraint is the general acceptance of the legitimacy of government. Yet the American people expressed a sharp loss of "great confidence" in the people running their institutions in the decade between the mid-1960's and the mid-1970's. In 1966, 41 per cent of the people expressed "great confidence" in the executive branch of the Federal government, compared to a low of 11 per cent by 1976. The comparable figures for the Supreme Court were 50 per cent in 1966 and 22 per cent in 1976, and for Congress 42 per cent and 9 per cent. This loss of confidence affected other areas of life: confidence in medicine dropped from 73 per cent to 42 per cent; in higher education from 61 to 31 per cent; and in major companies from 55 to 16 per cent.[23]

Many Americans also felt upset by the cultural changes which the country had undergone. In the summer of 1975, interviewers for Cambridge Survey Research asked for reactions to this comment: "Some people say that there is a breakdown of morality in America. Other people say that behavior has always been going on and is just more public now. Still others say that behavior has actually gotten better— that people were harmed by restrictions in the past." A large minority, 40 per cent, replied that there had been a breakdown in morality; the plurality, 47 per cent, thought behavior had only become more public; and only 7 per cent believed that behavior had improved. When asked about a number of specific changes, majorities, usually large ones, reacted negatively to increased use of drugs (85 per cent against the use of marijuana), cohabitation of unmarried men and women, coed dorms in colleges, greater availability of pornographic materials, and increased use of abortion. It may be noted, however, that most respondents approved of males with long hair, or less emphasis on formal clothing, and of increased use of birth control (79 per cent approving of the last). In addition to its association with increased age, disapproval of the changes correlated highly with lower economic status, lesser education, and conservative political views.[24] This 1975 poll clearly indicated that a large minority of Americans, whose social characteristics paralleled those of the Wallace constituency, were offended by the changes in cultural styles which had occurred during the previous decade.

Dramatic indicators of widespread alienation in the mid-seventies were also reported by Cambridge Survey Research. In four surveys taken from fall 1974 to the end of 1976, they found half or more of those interviewed disagreeing with the statement, "Despite what some people say, this country is run for the good of the average person," as compared to about two-fifths approving. Over two-thirds felt that "over the last ten years this country's leaders have consistently lied to the American people." More striking was the finding that over two-fifths (44 per cent in fall 1974 and 41 per cent in winter and summer 1975) agreed with the fairly extreme statement that "the true American way of life is disappearing so fast that we may have to use force to save it," while less than half (47 per cent in fall 1974, 45 per cent in winter 1975, and 49 per cent in summer 1975) disagreed. As Cambridge Survey Research notes, these data give "us some idea of the amount of anger that runs beneath the relatively calm surface of the American scene."[25] In spring 1975, major groups against whom it was considered that force might have to be used were politicians and political leaders (mentioned by 22 per cent), the government (by 11 per cent), Communists and radicals (by 11 per cent), criminals, crime, "hippy young people," "outside agitators," and big business (each by 4 per cent). The frustration conveyed by the responses to this question was, however, not solely or primarily an expression of right-wing backlash. In Cambridge Survey Research's summer 1975 poll, persons calling themselves liberals were almost as disposed (41 per cent) to endorse use of force as self-identified conservatives (44 per cent). Blacks were much more favorable to force (53 per cent) than whites (39 per cent). Approval of violent tactics, however, correlated most strongly with low income and education, much like sentiment favorable to Wallace. Age correlated in reverse of the Wallace pattern: the older respondents, presumably more disturbed by social challenges, were more disposed to verbally approve of the use of force (Table 121).

The responses to the various surveys attest to the presence of considerable frustration about American society and institutions among

Table 121. ATTITUDES TOWARD USE OF FORCE
(CAMBRIDGE SURVEY RESEARCH, 1975) (PER CENT)

"The true American way of life is disappearing so fast that we may have to use force to save it."

	Agree	Don't know	Disagree
Overall	41	10	49
Total household income			
$0–3,999	58	16	27
4–6,999	56	9	35
7–9,999	48	12	40
10–12,999	38	10	52
13–14,999	35	8	57
15–19,999	36	9	54
20–24,999	28	8	64
Over 25,000	31	6	63
Age			
18–25	39	9	52
26–35	38	11	50
36–45	34	9	57
46–55	43	9	48
56–65	50	8	42
Over 65	52	12	36
Sex			
Male	41	8	51
Female	42	12	46
Race			
White	39	9	52
Black	53	14	33
Head of household			
Yes	44	9	46
No	38	11	51
Education			
Some grade school	59	16	25
Some high school	57	13	30
High school grad.	45	9	47
Tech/voc.	41	10	49
Some college	35	7	57
College grad.	17	10	72
Grad. school	16	8	76
Religion			
Protestant	45	8	47
Catholic	39	11	50
Jewish	33	11	56
Other	34	25	41
None	28	11	61
Political ideology			
Liberal	41	8	51
Moderate	38	13	49

Table 121—*continued*

	Agree	Don't know	Disagree
Conservative	44	7	49
Don't know	41	27	32
Urban/rural			
Urban	42	10	48
Suburban	39	9	51
Rural	43	10	47
Areas			
Northeast	37	11	51
Industrial	45	7	48
Midlands	36	9	55
South	49	11	40
Central	44	10	46
Pacific	28	14	59

SOURCE: *The Cambridge Report,* No. 4. (Summer 1975), p. 93.

the less privileged. This anger, however, did not take a radical form. Many more of the alienated expressed concern about the social issues, criminals, hippies, communists, and radicals, than gave economically radical answers.

Generalizing from the results of the myriad of opinion polls in the seventies which showed high levels of alienation, survey analyst Daniel Yankelovich commented:

What we are witnessing today is, then, a new chapter in the history of American populism. The essential point about populism, especially in its current version, is that despite an antibusiness emphasis, such as we normally associate with the political Left, it has a profoundly conservative thrust. It seeks to restore, not change. It is fueled by a sense of public morality outraged. It is accompanied by a harsh punitive attitude toward criminals, "welfare bums," pornographers. It is an anguished outburst of resentment by those who feel they have worked hard and sacrificed, only to reap exploitation in return. This social resentment is probably the most potent political force in America today.[26]

Clearly, during the mid-seventies, as earlier, a mass constituency existed with feelings close to those being voiced by George Wallace and other, less well-known spokespersons of the radical right. Why then did the United States not experience a mass outburst comparable to those of previous decades? The answer, in part, lies in the fact that alienation was concentrated among the poorer and less educated segments of the population, groups that normally are less prone to participate in any form of political activity including voting. More probably, the low level of protest activity reflects the curious fact that the seeming growth in disgust with the political and social system was not accompanied by any increase in frustration about personal situations. On the whole, the opinion polls indicated that the overwhelming majority of people were satisfied with their jobs, their neighborhoods, their family situation, the education of their children, and other aspects of their personal lives.

As Albert Cantril and Charles Roll, Jr. noted in reporting on an elaborate survey taken in 1971, *Hopes and Fears of the American People,* the national mood was "one of seeming paradox: grave apprehension about the state of the nation juxtaposed against a tempered sense of personal achievement and optimism."[27] Three years later, William Watts and Lloyd A. Free detected this same tension in a heightened form. About eighty per cent of the populace expressed satisfaction with the work that they did, and more than seventy per cent with their standard of living and housing situation. Forty-five per cent stated that "in terms of . . . personal happiness and satisfaction" they were better off than a year earlier, while only 14 per cent felt they were worse off. Most citizens thought not only that they were better off at present than they had been in the past, but also that in the future their personal circumstances would be better still.[28]

In 1976, Francis Rourke, Lloyd Free, and William Watts, repeating the same questions in a national survey, "found that Americans continued to be well satisfied with the state of their personal lives, although they took much less comfort in the general state of the nation."[29]

Cambridge Survey Research has compared personal expectations with attitudes toward the future of the country using the same question first asked in 1959 by Cantril, Watts, and Free. They report that in ten surveys taken between 1959 and the summer of 1977 (eight taken from fall 1975 on) Americans were more optimistic about their personal situation and future than they were about their country's. The gap between the two was small in 1959, but has been large in all the surveys conducted in the 1970's. Expectations for self and for country were both on the upswing in polls taken from the winter of 1975 to the spring of 1977. Cambridge's summer 1977 survey, however, revealed a drop-off in both from the spring peak, although optimism was still higher than in 1975.[30] And it may be noted that as of the summer of 1977, according to the Gallup poll, "two-thirds of Americans . . . express satisfaction with the future facing themselves and their families . . . a sharp increase since 1973 when the comparable figure was 53 per cent."[31] As might be expected, Cambridge Survey Research found that the more well-to-do and the better educated people were, the more optimistic they were about their personal futures. Curiously, however, these and other demographic factors did not appear to be associated with expectations about the nation. In the summer of 1977, opinions on this subject correlated most to political outlook: liberals had more faith in the future of the country than moderates or conservatives, a finding which may be related to the fact that the Democrats controlled the government.

The measures of alienation cited above do not permit an estimate of intensity, of the extent of the bitterness. It is likely that the polls accurately picked up the growth of disgust derivative from the Vietnam War experience, Watergate, revelations about other political scandals in the CIA, Congress, and the like, plus the resentments by many against the changing forms of social behavior encompassed in feminism and the civil rights movement, and against the "new morality" expressed by changes in sexual behavior, use of drugs, the growth in pornography, legalized abortion, and so on. But these events and changes, while leading many to form an increasingly negative estimate of American institutions, did not motivate them to look for an extreme outlet for their frustrations.

The Mild Backlash of the Seventies

It should be noted that a mild type of political backlash occurred within the normal confines of the electoral system. In many municipalities the more conservative law-and-order candidates won mayoral elections. Many liberal Democrats, including a number coming out of the New Politics of the 1960's and early 1970's, sought to identify themselves as conservatives. The conservative reaction expressed itself in issues such as homosexual rights, the Equal Rights Amendment, the Panama Canal, the death penalty, and abortion. Major party candidates from Richard Nixon to Jimmy Carter won support by presenting themselves as opponents to the growth of government and as supporters of traditional morality and American patriotism. In a real sense the political system had worked, responding to the complaints of the discontented on the right, much as it did in the late sixties and early seventies, when the candidacies of Eugene McCarthy, Robert Kennedy, and George McGovern coopted left-wing resentment into the Democratic party. In 1976, Ronald Reagan and Jimmy Carter, in very different ways, helped to keep right-wing and traditionalist protest within the two party system.

Whatever the strength of the various deterring ingredients—democratic restraint, limited social strain, the continuing incorporative function of the American coalition political system—the kind of virulent backlash that would have married mass discontent with a right-wing extremist movement just did not develop.

Extremist Groups

In the early 1970's there was a certain amount of apparent activity by the fringe vehicles of bigotry, which sensed the backlash sentiment abroad in the country but made no headway against the general resistance to extremism. Various spokesmen of American Nazi and Ku Klux Klan groups gained some mass media notoriety. In 1977, a Nazi march scheduled for a suburb of Chicago was halted by court injunction; a Nazi bookstore was trashed in San Francisco by Holocaust survivors; a Nazi ran for mayor in Milwaukee. All these events received widespread attention, but the national membership of these various Nazi groups was to be measured in the hundreds.

David Duke, a new national director of a wing of the factionalized Ku Klux Klan, appeared on the media scene in the 1970's. He attempted to fashion a "sanitized version of the KKK." Duke received one-third of the votes cast in a race for the Louisiana State Senate, running in opposition to gun control and busing, while muting explicit racism. The *New York Times* reported his tactics as "all part of the new cleaned-up image he is trying to impart to the Klan—college educated, media oriented, the man in the gray flannel bedsheet."[32]

In midsummer 1977, the Anti-Defamation League, which keeps close watch on the activities of anti-Semitic groups, estimated total Klan membership at 8,000 to 10,000, an increase from an estimate in 1975 of 6,500. The ADL also judged the Klan to have about 40,000 sympathizers, mainly in the South. The larger extremist groups which did not specialize in direct bigotry notably failed to grow. The Birch Society, whose annual budget in 1975 was about 8 million dollars, was reported to have "declined in membership."[33] The Liberty Lobby, which flirted with anti-Semitism of an "anti-Zionist" nature, had about 25,000 members nationally; but it was not so much a political organization as a mass media organization, with a widely distributed newspaper and programs on about a hundred radio stations. Such groups had some political successes in the 1970's, mainly in areas of cultural backlash.

The Cultural Backlash

A number of issues in the 1970's apparently have struck a chord in the large segment of the population which tends to be economically liberal and culturally conservative. As has been pointed out, this segment of the population typically serves as the mass base for right-wing extremism. There have been two kinds of issues involved: one relating to morality and family values, the other to antistatism. Both represent a potential backlash against emerging populations and the antitraditional values they carry with them. And both sets of issues have become the major agenda for right-wing extremist groups.

Prominent in the first set of issues has been reaction to the developing "gay rights" revolution. In 1977, national attention was focused around an attempt to repeal a local ordinance in Miami, Florida, which outlawed discrimination against homosexuals. National forces, pro and con, concentrated their strength on Miami. The antigay effort, whose public standard-bearer was a show business personality, Anita Bryant, won by a two to one margin. Right-wing groups exulted. *The Spotlight,* a periodical of the Liberty Lobby, headlined: "Support for Anita Bryant's morality crusade grows . . . galvanizing American sentiments."[34] An article on the same page was headed: "Deviates, Democrats have long courtship." Medford Evans of the Birch Society had been calling for a "return to normal sexuality" since the inception of the gay rights movement.[35] Phyllis Schlafly published a report on International Women's Year, calling it "a Front for Radicals and Lesbians."[36]

The issue obviously has struck a nerve. The Gallup poll reported in July 1977 that the American people were equally divided on the question of whether homosexual relations between consenting adults should be legal, 43 per cent saying yes and 43 per cent saying no. Two other traditional morality and family issues which have divided the nation are abortion and the discriminalization of marijuana. Opposition to the Equal Rights Amendment for women has also been thrown in as part of the traditionalist agenda. According to the Birch Society, "Betty Ford is an apologist for marijuana and an advocate of ERA and abortion."[37]

Antistatist sentiment has flourished around the issues of Laetrile and gun control. Successful efforts have been mounted in many states to remove the ban on Laetrile, a homeopathic drug which most medical authorities have labeled as ineffective as a cure for cancer. The center for these campaigns has been a national "Committee for Freedom of Choice in Cancer Therapy, Inc." This is an offshoot of the Birch Society, and its foremost legislative spokesman is Congressman Larry McDonald of Georgia, erstwhile member of the National Council of the Birch Society, and leading opponent of legislation prohibiting discrimination against homosexuals. The attempt to regulate the private sale of guns to citizens is typically referred to by the Birch Society as an "attack on the American dream."[38]

Antistatist issues are categorized in each edition of the Liberty Lobby's organ, *The Spotlight,* in a column called "Vanishing Liberties." Medford Evans of the Birch Society struck the nostalgic note epitomizing all the issues of cultural displacement in extolling the Victorian age: "The Victorian age[s] is [are] the last great epoch of human achievement, since which we have declined in every cultural and intellectual field. . . ."[39]

One unhappy liberal observer, Andrew Kopkind, used the term "New Right" to describe the network of forces and sentiments in this cultural backlash; and maintained that this New Right is politically ascendant.[40] He cited a number of legislative victories the New Right network has won on the state and national level, on the issues of Laetrile, homosexuality, and abortion.

But the fact is that the popular base of this cultural backlash has not become part of any mass political extremist movement. The reasons again relate to the standard dynamics of political extremism in America. The major political parties have obviously continued to absorb the backlash sentiment. As one Washington observer said:

> There's no question that the right is getting increasingly successful on Capitol Hill. The *anti* people are winning bigger and bigger majorities. . . . In the House, the new freshmen of '76 were supposed to make up the most liberal Congress in history. But they've made it one of the most conservative. Their mail is running . . . a hundred to one against . . . abortion, gay rights. They believe that life-style issues will re-elect them or defeat them, and they're voting with the antis.[41]

Although the right-wing may be winning on cultural backlash issues, these issues have not built a right-wing extremist movement, in part because the major parties have been so responsive. But, of course, the parties have not reacted to the extent that the extremist groups would like them to, nor can they. Nor indeed has there been any indication that the populace wants them to take extremist stances on these issues. On the homosexual issue, for example, while less than a majority of Americans (43 per cent) approve of legalizing homosexual relations, 56 per cent believe that homosexuals should be allowed equal job rights in positions which do not involve dealing with children.[42]

The Decline of Alienation

As the 1970's wind down, with the disasters of Vietnam and Watergate fading into memory, and with politicians seeking to identify with a more conservative and patriotic mood, the pollsters' indicators of alienation have begun to decline. The Harris Survey's annual analysis of confidence in American institutions reported in 1977 that "confidence in leadership of the nation's major institutions . . . had begun to rise."[43] The National Opinion Research Center of the University of Chicago, which used the same question as Harris, reported comparable results. Thus, those expressing a "great deal of confidence" in banks increased from 31 per cent in 1975 to 42 per cent in 1977; for organized religion, the improvement was from 24 per cent to 40 per cent; for education, the change was from 31 per cent to 41 per cent.

It is too soon to know whether the changes reported by Harris and NORC reflect the beginning of a long-term improvement in confidence in American institutions. There is some indication in these and other reports that the steady decline in positive feelings about American society which seemingly began in 1965 with the escalation of protest against the Vietnam War and the growth of militant groups, bottomed out by 1975, after the Nixon resignation. Even before the resignation, an increase in the confidence ratings had followed the end of the Vietnam War and the reemergence of social peace, but this change was stopped and reversed by the Watergate exposes. Apparently many Americans would like to regain a positive sense about their society if only their leaders and events would give them a chance to do so.

It is obvious that specific events and the personalities of the nation's leaders affect the trends reported by the pollsters. At all times, most people voiced "some confidence" in most institutions. Clearly, even when American morale was at its lowest in the late 1960's and early 1970's, most people retained some general belief in the viability and legitimacy of the system, though they had lost confidence in those who were running it.

At the beginning of the third century of the United States' existence as an independent nation, there is no indication that a social base exists for mass extremist or revolutionary movements, either on the right or the left. The political institutions of the country have survived threats to their stability posed by a massive antiwar movement, a major scandal in the White House which deposed a President, sharp changes in conceptions of sexual morality, and major improvements in the social, political, and economic status of minorities and women, without provoking any major backlash movements, other than the electoral constituency mobilized behind George Wallace. And that constituency vanished almost without a trace and could not be transferred to other right-wing groups or candidates. The politics of unreason is at a low ebb at the start of America's third century. But as we noted at the end of the first edition of this book, "In sum, the evidence indicates that the American population is still highly vulnerable to political extremism; the American political system is less vulnerable, but scarcely fail-safe." Any country in which 40 per cent of the citizens approve of the statement that "we may have to use force" to save "the true American way of life" or 49 per cent agree that "what this country needs is some really strong leadership that would try to solve problems directly without worrying how Congress or the Supreme Court might feel," cannot be regarded as safe from the threat of extremism. The ultimate test of democratic restraint and prophylactic American political institutions may still await more dire and comprehensive circumstances. The history of the 1970's gives us good cause for satisfaction about the viability of the American polity, but no reason to feel that we can let down our vigilance.

Notes

1. Gary Allen, "America, 1977," *American Opinion,* XX (July–August 1977), p. 1.
2. *Ibid.,* pp. 2, 20.
3. P. 38, this book.
4. U. S. Bureau of the Census, *The Statistical Abstract of the United States, 1971* (Washington, D.C.: Government Printing Office, 1971), p. 223.
5. *Ibid.,* p. 466.
6. Fred E. Crossland, *Minority Access to College* (New York: Schocken Books, 1971), p. 33.
7. *The Cambridge Report,* No. 2 (Winter 1975), p. ix.
8. *The Cambridge Report,* No. 6 (First Quarter 1976), p. 161.
9. Becky S. Drury, *A Rhetorical Analysis and Comparison of the Speaking of William Jennings Bryan and George Corley Wallace within a Political Framework of Populism* (Ph.D. Thesis, Department of Communications, Purdue University, 1976), p. 122.
10. *Meet the Press,* November 26, 1972, quoted in Drury, p. 123.
11. David E. Bronston, *Protest Politics in Wisconsin: The Social Bases of the Wallace Vote 1964–1976* (Honors Thesis, Department of Government, Harvard University, 1976), p. 58.
12. NBC News/Elections, *Decision 76: Election Day Poll Results* (New York: NBC News, June 1976, multilith), p. 50.
13. "The Wallace Stand." Recorded excerpts of George Wallace speeches and news conferences during the 1972 campaign, quoted in Howard S. Erlich, *An Investigation of George Wallace's 1972 Campaign Rhetoric: Was It Populist?* (Ph.D. Thesis, Department of Speech, University of Massachusetts, Amherst, 1975), p. 111.
14. Stephen Winn, *An Analysis of Empirical Research Concerning Electoral Support for George Wallace from 1964 to 1972* (Ph.D. Thesis, Department of Sociology, Washington State University, 1976), p. 72.
15. Bronston, *op. cit.,* pp. 63–64.

16. *Ibid.*, p. 81.
17. "Excerpts from Ehrlichman's Testimony Before Senate Committee on Watergate," *New York Times*, July 25, 1973, p. 27.
18. See S. M. Lipset and Earl Raab, "An Appointment with Watergate," *Commentary* (September 1973), p. 41; "Texts of Documents Relating to Domestic Intelligence-Gathering Plan in 1970," *New York Times*, June 7, 1973, p. 36.
19. "Text of Study on Ellsberg," *New York Times*, August 3, 1973, p. 10.
20. U.S. Bureau of the Census, *The Statistical Abstract of the United States, 1972* (Washington, D.C.: Government Printing Office, 1972), p. 322, and *idem, The Statistical Abstract of the United States, 1976* (Washington, D.C.: Government Printing Office, 1976), p. 356.
21. *The Statistical Abstract of the United States, 1976*, p. 123.
22. S. M. Lipset and William Schneider, *Israel and Jews in American Public Opinion* (forthcoming).
23. Louis Harris, "Confidence Climbing," *The Harris Survey*, March 14, 1977.
24. *The Cambridge Report*, No. 4 (Summer 1975), pp. 289–310.
25. *The Cambridge Report*, No. 3 (Spring 1975), p. 118.
26. Daniel Yankelovich, "A Crisis of Moral Legitimacy?" *Dissent*, XXI (Fall 1974), pp. 531–532.
27. Albert H. Cantril and Charles W. Roll, Jr., *Hopes and Fears of the American People* (Washington, D.C.: Potomac Associates, 1971), p. 5.
28. William Watts and Lloyd A. Free, *State of the Nation 1974* (Washington, D.C.: Potomac Associates, 1974), p. 8.
29. Francis E. Rourke, Lloyd A. Free, and William Watts, *Trust and Confidence in the American System* (Washington, D.C.: Potomac Associates, 1976), p. 29.
30. *The Cambridge Report*, No. 11 (Second Quarter 1977), pp. 10–16.
31. The Gallup poll, August 11, 1977.
32. Wayne King, "Klan Radio Ads Seek Public Support," *New York Times*, November 24, 1975, p. 37.
33. Oscar Cohen, "Politics and Intergroup Relations," *American Jewish Yearbook 1977* (New York: American Jewish Committee, 1976), p. 43.
34. *The Spotlight*, August 1, 1977, p. 12.
35. Medford Evans, "Review of Sexual Guide," *American Opinion*, XVIII (April 1975), p. 63.
36. Andrew Kopkind, "America's New Right," *New Times*, IX (September 30, 1977), p. 21.
37. Alan Stang, "The 1976 Republican Convention," *American Opinion*, XIX (October 1976), p. 42.
38. Gary Allen, "Attack on the American Dream," *American Opinion*, XVIII (July–August 1975), p. 1.
39. Medford Evans, "The Victorians: A World Built to Last," *American Opinion*, XIX (January 1976), p. 57.
40. Kopkind, *op. cit.*
41. *Ibid.*, p. 30.
42. George Gallup, "Majority Support Equal Rights in Principle in Hiring of Homosexuals," *The Gallup Poll*, July 17, 1977.
43. Harris, *op. cit.*, p. 1.

Methodological Appendix to Chapter 11

The analysis of the various issue publics or typologies presented in Chapter 11 was first formulated on an a priori *ad hoc* basis. That is, we assumed from our knowledge of public opinion research and political behavior that there were two very distinct sets of attitudes or ideologies which are supported by very different types of people among the general public, although they often are found together in the program of various ultra-rightist groups. These are economic conservatism, opposition to the welfare and socialist state on one hand, and cultural conservatism, including support for traditional religious values and customs, opposition to people and ideas which are different, on the other. In general, as we have pointed out in various places in the book, economic conservatism correlates with socioeconomic status, the more well-to-do tend to be most conservative. Cultural conservatism tends to be associated inversely with education, the better educated are the most liberal. Since the better educated, on the average, are much more affluent than those with lesser schooling, this means, as we have seen, that the more well-to-do tend to be more liberal on cultural issues, as defined here. Many of the extreme right-wing groups, however, are ideologically conservative on both dimensions. They tend to favor laissez faire, to be opposed to welfare state measures economically, and also to be opposed to efforts to gain equal rights for minority groups or to defend the civil liberties of Communists, atheists, and other dissident minorities. This analysis of the opinion public situation within which the ultra-right has been operating led us to assume from the start that an analysis of the propensity of different groups in the population to back such groups would require a differentiation of the electorate into groups who were economically conservative or liberal, and culturally conservative or liberal, thus ultimately producing four attitude groups or issue publics, those conservative on both, liberal on both, and the two which were liberal on one and conservative on the other. Working with the data from the over 150 questions in the national sample survey gathered by N.O.R.C. for the purposes of this study, we first developed a descriptive typology. That is, we classified questions into the "cultural" or "economic" conservatism-liberal groups, and on the basis of their responses to these questions placed the respondents in one of four issue-publics, corresponding to those discussed in Chapter 11.

The analyses of the correlates and political behavior of these four groups "made sense," that is corresponded to our assumptions. Discussions with more statistically sophisticated colleagues, however, raised some serious methodological issues about our procedures. Arbitrarily constructed scales such as we developed by selecting those items which fit our preconceptions and showed high differentiating power could exaggerate considerably the "real" state of opinion. We might, in effect, be forcing four separate issue groupings to appear by selecting from a very large number of questions, when in fact other attitude dimensions might be more significant. There was never any compelling logical basis for choosing among questions and assigning them to a particular cluster of attitudes. We, therefore, asked Irvin Bupp and Peter Natchez, then graduate students in the Harvard Department of Government, who had training in methods of scale construction through different statistical data reduction procedures to analyze the survey materials so as to locate the factors which existed in the patterns of responses to the various questions. Their technical report of what they did, how they produced the factors used for analysis in Chapter 11 follows:

The general goal of factor analysis is simply the reduction of a set of m variables on which measurements have been taken across a set of n units to a *smaller* set of new *unobserved* or "latent" variables which are defined solely in terms of the original "m-dimensional variable space." Descriptions of the mathematics of factor analysis are widely available at levels which are understandable to most social scientists.[1] Hence the following discussion is meant only to highlight some of the more important characteristics of the technique.

As originally proposed by Spearman the "classical factor model" *postulated* that each of the "manifest" variables could meaningfully be described as a *linear, additive* combination of k common factors plus a "*unique factor*," where k was very much smaller than m. This is the first point which needs to be stressed about factor analysis. Spearman had theoretically respectable reasons for postulating the relevance of such a model to the explanation of measured performance on various verbal and written "intelligence" tests. Whether this model is also applicable in other research contexts.is *always* an important theoretical consideration which each researcher must address for himself. Our own position is a strong suspicion that in general "factors" do not exist, i.e., that Spearman's theory is not easily transferable to other contexts. The rather limited type of "causal model" ordinarily assumed of factor analysis does not seem appropriate for the explanation of most empirical reality. Suppose, as Hubert Blalock has suggested,[2] that the manifest variables of a research design are the typical demographic variables—education, income, occupation, etc. In accounting for their joint covariance, it seems eminently more sensible simply to postulate education as a direct cause of income rather than try to account for their intercorrelation by some mythical "latent factor" for which one needs to be a poet even to name.

Thus, as Douglas Price points out, factor analysis can produce the "shadows" of a variety of variables, but it is rarely helpful to suppose that the shadows create the variables.[3] Moreover, *even* if there were some underlying (latent) variables which in fact explain the behavior of a large number of manifest variables, there is a considerable chance that factor analysis would not find them.[4]

The basic reason for these problems is straight forward enough to justify the introduction of some formal notation:

For m measured variables, n units (e.g., people) and k underlying factors ($k \leqq m$) the factor model is:

$$Z_{1j} = a_{11}F_{1j} + a_{12}F_{2j} + \cdots + a_{1k}F_{kj} + U_{1j}$$
$$Z_{mj} = a_{m1}F_{1j} + a_{m2}F_{2j} + \cdots + a_{mk}F_{kj} + U_{mj}$$

More compactly: $Z_{ij} = \sum\limits_{i=1}^{k} a_{ik}F_{kj} + U_{ij}$

for: $i = 1$ to m (the variable number)
$j = 1$ to n (the unit number)
$k = 1$ to k (the "factor" number)

Or, in the even more convenient matrix notation:

$Z = A \, F + U$; where Z is an M $\times$ N matrix, A is an M $\times$ K matrix, F is a K $\times$ N matrix, and U is an M $\times$ N matrix.

The factor model postulates each manifest variable (the Z's) to be some linear additive combination of K underlying factors plus a "specific" factor or error term. As is obvious, the model is in this form strikingly similar to the standard multiple regression model; but there is an equally striking difference. The factor model is grossly "underdetermined." All that is known are the Z's; *both* the a's (normally called the "loadings") and the F's must somehow be estimated. Obviously some very drastic additional assumptions need to be made in order to get a unique calculation of the a's and the F's. In regression analysis the independent variables are observable. In factor analysis they are hypothetical constructs which must be estimated, *along with* their coefficients or "loadings" from the manifest data.

A very large number of methods have been proposed for solving the estimation problem.[5] The most popular of these are based on the objective of extracting the maximum variance from the observed variables. The idea is to find the smallest number of linear combinations of the original variables which account for most of the observed variance and thereby achieve a measure of theoretical "parsimony." It is important to recognize that this objective is quite distinct from that of Spearman's classical factor model, the point of which was "to maximally reproduce the (observed) correlations."[6]

The principal difference between Spearman's model and the solutions which attempt to extract maximum variance is that the latter describe each of the m manifest variables simply as a linear combination of m *new* uncorrelated variables:

$$Z_j = a_{j1}F_1 + a_{j2}F_2 + \cdots + a_{jm}Fm \ (j = 1 \ to \ m)$$

Note that the absence of the U term implies that the "content" of each observed variable is *totally* explainable by the new factor. Obviously this is a very questionable "causal" assumption. Moreover, since the number of "factors" is now equal to the number of variables (m). The principal components model in a sense throws parsimony to the winds. In practice, however, only a few "components" are extracted, each having, in turn, made a maximum contribution to the total variance of the m variables. The point to be emphasized is that in order to reproduce completely the initial correlations, all of the m "components" are necessary. The practical research problem is to account for as much variance as possible while attaining some reasonable amount of parsimony, i.e., accounting for as much of the variance as possible with the fewest number of factors.

In geometric terms the essence of the procedure can be seen as the construction of a new "space" which is maximally representative of the space defined by the original variables, but utilizes a minimum number of linearly independent dimensions. The (orthogonal) reference axes of the new "factor space" correspond to the extracted "principal components." The cosine of the angle θ between any one of the original variables and a given reference axis is the correlation or "loading" of the variable with the "factor" or "component" defined by the reference axis. The sum of the squared loadings for any factor is known as the "eigenvalue" of the factor. The magnitude of a particular eigenvalue measures the amount of variation explained by that factor.[7]

It is quite common that the nature of the factors which result from a principal components solution is unclear. In fact this should be anticipated since the factor loading pattern simply reflects the characteristics of the extraction process. The eigenvalues of each successive column of loadings have been maximized until, typically, the iteration procedure reaches some prespecified minimum eigenvalue. The columns of loadings which result may or may not be substantively interpretable. Usually they are not.

The orientation of the factor axes, however, is arbitrary. There are a variety of *mathematically equivalent* ways of expressing the relationships between factors and original variables. The process of defining new reference axes according to some specified criterion is known as "rotation." One of the most popular "rotation" techniques—called "simple structure"—is based on the principle of maximizing the variances of all the columns of loadings simultaneously rather than successively. The idea is that this is likely to simplify— make more readily interpretable—the resulting factor pattern as much as possible in keeping with the constraint of orthogonality of loading rectors.

It was the latter possibility which initially suggested to us the potential utility of factor analysis in connection with the Lipset–Raab research. In general we would agree that "factors" do not exist, that at best factor analysis can perhaps produce only the "shadows" of variables. However, if these "shadows" do in fact overlap to a substantial degree with conceptually distinct sub-sets of the original variables, the technique may be a very handy one for creating, by deliberate intent, a composite index of such *prespecified* sub-sets. The criterion for prespecification is of course the substantive theory of the individual researcher which suggests which variables somehow "belong together"—i.e., "tap" a common dimension.

Johann Galtung's very thorough discussion of the problem of index formation focuses on the distinction between "intensive" and "extensive" methods.[8] Factor analysis can conveniently be used as an "extensive" solution to the index formation problem. The technique will create indices on the basis of the empirical distribution of the units on the variables rather than on the basis of the supposed "meaning" of the variables. As Galtung notes, the problem of index formation is, in this context, a direct analogue to the problem of parameter construction: to reduce variety without losing information.

With these considerations in mind we selected 181 items from the interview schedule which were clearly related to Lipset's and Raab's concerns. We eliminated those questions which were at first glance less clear in their intent. The principle components factor analysis and subsequent Varimax rotation of these 181 questions produced five factors which were readily interpretable. These five factors seemed related to anti-Negro prejudice, economic conservatism, anti-Semitism, cultural intolerance or anti-civil libertarian attitudes, and psychological instability. We experimented with rotating three and four of the principle components and found that this procedure did not provide readily interpretable factors. Further, we attempted a solution which extracted six principle components and found that this also provided a less substantial interpretation. We then tried similar factor analogies of all items which seemed related in any way to right-wing prejudice. This brought the total number of variables in the matrix to 181. The results indicated again that a five factor solution was the most stable. In the case of 181 variables, however, less of the total variance was accounted for by these five factors, than among the smaller group. Finally we removed from consideration questions and indices which appeared to be redundant, leaving us with 143 attitudinal questions as the basis of our analysis. The five dimensions previously reported defined the components of right-wing opinion for this study. A copy of the complete results of the analysis are available at the Data Center of the Government Department of Harvard University.

The ready emergence of these dimensions promised considerable help in organizing the unwieldly number of single-item questions and "intensively derived" indices coded in the original data.[9]

Again, we want to stress that we were not interested in arguing that the results of the factor analysis and rotations in any sense "proved" the existence of five underlying "causes" of radical opinion. Our objective was simply to develop ordinal representations of complicated sets of attitudinal dimensions, good evidence for the "reality" of which *already* existed.[10] The next step in the basis of the reported loadings was to obtain factor scores for each of the 1,975 respondents to the Berkeley survey. As potential index numbers these scores— i.e., the position of a given respondent on a particular factor axis have some very desirable properties.

For us, the characteristic that was most important was that they represent standardized scores. This means that individual (unit) scores are indirectly comparable across dimensions and between people. That is, a particular individual's score on the economic conservativism dimension can be directly compared to his score on the dimension of cultural intolerance, a score of 1.9 on the first dimension and a similar score in the second are equivalent since they both are expressed in standard deviation units.

To take advantage of these properties it was necessary first to "merge" the factor scores for all respondents on each of the five factors back into the original data, in effect to *create* five new variables. These new variables then provided the data basic for the description of right-wing opinions. Briefly, Lipset and Raab proposed to organize radical opinion by crossing two dimensions— Economic Conservatism and Intolerance. The factor analysis, it will be recalled, had given us three potential components for an ordinal representation of the latter, and one for the former. Consequently, we assigned respondents to one of five positions (categories) on an index of general intolerance as a function of their position on the anti-Negro, anti-Semite, and cultural intolerance factors *as measured by factor scores*. An index of Economic Conservatism was similarly derived using the single factor so named.

This typology isolated four distinct groups of people: Radical Rightists, those who had high scores on *both* the intolerance and economic conservative dimensions; Rednecks, those highly intolerant but *not* economic conservatives; the Old Guard, economic conservatives but otherwise *un*prejudiced; and the Consistent Liberals, those who had very low scores on *both* the dimensions. This typology, which corresponded to the initial theoretical differentiation of issue publics suggested by Lipset and Raab *before* our factor analysis became the base for their analysis in Chapter 11.

Notes

1. See especially, R. J. Rummel "Understanding Analysis," *Journal of Conflict Resolution*, IX (December, 1967), pp. 444–480; Hayward R. Alker, "Statistics and Politics," in S. M. Lipset, ed., *Politics and the Social Sciences* (New York: Oxford University Press, 1969), pp. 244–313; and H. H. Harmon, *Modern Factor Analysis* (Chicago: University of Chicago Press, 1960). This is the most comprehensive and rigorous discussion of factor analytic techniques.
2. H. M. Blalock, *Causal Inferences in Nonexperimental Research* (Chapel Hill: University of North Carolina Press, 1964), p. 169.
3. Private communication.
4. As an amusing illustration of this point, Price cites J. S. Armstrong, "Tom Swift and His Electric Factor Analysis Machine," *American Statistician*, XII (1967), pp. 17–21.
5. See Harmon, *op. cit.*, Parts II and III.
6. *Ibid.*, p. 15.
7. "An eigenvalue is the root of the characteristic equation $[R - \lambda I] = O$, where R is the correlation matrix, λ is an eigenvalue, I is an identity matrix, and the brackets mean that the determinant is being computed." Rummel, *op. cit.*, p. 466 n.
8. Johann Galtung, *Theory and Methods of Social Research* (New York: Columbia University Press, 1969), Part II, Chapter 3. We highly recommend this chapter as a supplement to this discussion.
9. The latter, it should be noted, had been prepared by investigators chiefly concerned with studying anti-Semitism.
10. We do not, as we have said, believe factor analytic techniques capable,

by themselves, of proving that anti-Semitism, for example, exists. That a factor emerges which with little difficulty can be *named* "anti-Semitism" is at best only a very weak test of a theory. Had such a factor *not* emerged, it is more likely that the interview schedule and/or factor analysis, not the theory, would have been suspect.

General Index

Index of Proper Names

See also GENERAL INDEX

Aaron, Daniel, 203 *n*. 5
Acheson, Dean, 219
ADA World, 17–18
Adamo, S. J., 284 *n*. 52
Adams, Brooks, 94
Adams, Henry, 94
Adams, John, 37
Adams, John Quincy, 44, 45, 486
Adams, Paul, 314
Adler, Les K., 246 *n*. 33
Adler, Selig, 145 *n*. 6
Agnew, Spiro, 366–67, 422–23, 531
Alabama Journal, 343–44
Albares, Richard P., 337 *n*. 103 and 104
Alexander, Charles C., 120, 145 *n*. 13 and
   14; 116; 121; 146 *n*. 25; 147 *n*. 55, 66,
   70 and 77
Allen, Frederick Lewis, 133; 145 *n*. 2, 3, 5;
   147 *n*. 82; 149 *n*. 131; 198; 207 *n*. 142
   and 144
Allen, Gary, 260
Allen, Henry J., 127
Allport, Gordon W., 491
Altbach, Philip, 336 *n*. 98
America, 261
American Alliance, 77
American Civil Liberties Union, 111, 319
American Conservative Union, 348
American Council of Christian Churches,
   275
American Defense Society, 140
American Jewish Committee, 137, 277, 328,
   354–55, 398
American Jewish Yearbook, The, 149 *n*.
   117, 118 and 119; 286 *n*. 111
American Labor Bureau, 86
American Mercury, The, 275, 313, 419

American Nazi party, 532, 353, 544
American Opinion, 7, 18, 251, 252, 256,
   260, 263, 264, 265, 266, 272–73, 313,
   318, 321, 518
American Opinion Speakers Bureau, 267,
   268
American Party (California), 83
American Patriotic League, 82
American Progress, 190; 206 *n*. 116
Americans for Democratic Action, 17–18,
   217, 322–24
Ander, Fritief, 105 *n*. 40, 43 and 46; 106
   n. 61
Anders, Dr. Allison, 322
Anderson, Jack, 245 *n*. 21
Anderson, Thomas J., 310
Andrews, T. Coleman, 414, 419
Anti-Defamation League (ADL), 265, 544
App, Austin, J., 419
Apter, David E., 374 *n*. 28
Argyle, Michael, 145 *n*. 9
Aryan Order of St. George, 82
Asbestos Workers, 362
Ashbrook, James, 348
Association Against the Prohibition Amend-
   ment (AAPA), 200
Association of George C. Wallace Voters,
   413–15
Association of Georgia Klans, 276
Atlantic Monthly, 142
Avin, Benjamin H., 149 *n*. 124, 126, 127
   and 128

Baltzell, E. Digby, 107 *n*. 91 and 92
Barker, Earlene T., 147 *n*. 83; 149 *n*. 125
   and 128
Barnes, Gilbert, 71 *n*. 117

571